D1566461

Louisiana Reconstructed,
1863–1877

LOUISIANA RECONSTRUCTED

1863-1877

Joe Gray Taylor

LOUISIANA STATE UNIVERSITY PRESS

Baton Rouge

ISBN 0–8071–0084–6
Library of Congress Catalog Card Number 74–77327
Copyright © 1974 by Louisiana State University Press
Manufactured in the United States of America

Designed by Dwight Agner. Set in 11/13 Linotype Caledonia, designed by W. A. Dwiggins. Composed and printed by Heritage Printers, Inc., Charlotte, North Carolina.

To the memory of
FRANCIS BUTLER SIMKINS

Contents

Illustrations

Acknowledgments

I MUST FIRST express my gratitude to McNeese State University, which by means of a leave with pay and a grant greatly aided this study. Equal appreciation must be expressed to the American Association for State and Local History, which made a generous grant without which some of my research travel would have been impossible. The late James W. Patton and his staff at the Southern Historical Collection of the University of North Carolina were most helpful, as were the late Virgil Bedsole and his staff at the Department of Archives of Louisiana State University. Connie Griffith of the Tulane University Library and A. Otis Hebert of the Louisiana State Archives and Records Department spared no effort to aid my research. Thanks must go also to Elaine Tieman, Denise des Aimes, and Joanne Durand of the Frazer Memorial Library of McNeese State University, and to Mrs. A. V. McCutchen of the Calcasieu Parish Public Library, for their ever-cheerful help in obtaining research materials.

Walter M. Lowrey of Centenary College not only wrote two most useful articles which are frequently cited; he also called my attention to a number of valuable manuscripts in the Centenary College Library. President William E. Highsmith of Asheville-Biltmore College, Asheville, North Carolina, supplied me with what may be the only existing copy of his doctoral dissertation on Louisiana during Reconstruction. Raleigh A. Suarez, now vice president for academic affairs at McNeese State University, was kind enough to read and criticize the earlier chapters. Margie Wright, Marjorie T. Turko, and Harriette Taylor assisted in the typing of the manuscript. I wish to thank Richard Wentworth, former director of the Louisiana State University Press, and Charles East, present director, for encouraging this study in the first place, and then for being patient when health problems delayed my completing the assignment. Finally, I must acknowledge the continuous support of my beloved wife Helen Taylor, without whom I could have accomplished nothing.

Obviously, I take full personal responsibility for my interpretations and for errors which may exist in this work.

Joe Gray Taylor

Louisiana Reconstructed,
1863-1877

I   *Introduction*

ON JANUARY 7, 1861, approximately twenty thousand adult white male Louisianians voted in an election for delegates to a state convention. The convention met on January 23 and three days later adopted an ordinance of secession. Some disagreement exists as to whether a majority of the voters of Louisiana favored secession. This controversy may never be fully resolved, although recent research does throw new light on the subject.[1] Two facts are beyond dispute. First, a large majority of the white people of the state supported the Confederacy once the Civil War had begun. Secondly, however, a small but significant minority of white Louisianians remained loyal to the Union throughout the war. Unionists were to be found both in the country parishes and in New Orleans.[2]

1 Charles B. Dew, "The Long Lost Returns: The Candidates and Their Totals in Louisiana's Secession Election," *Louisiana History*, X (Fall, 1969), 353–69.
2 Ethel Taylor, "Discontent in Confederate Louisiana," *Louisiana History*, II (Fall, 1961), 410–28; Walter McGehee Lowrey, "The Political Career of James Madison Wells," *Louisiana Historical Quarterly*, XXXI (October, 1948), 1,007; William E. Highsmith, "Social and Economic Conditions in Rapides Parish During Reconstruction" (M.A. thesis, Louisiana State University, 1947), 20; Gerald M. Capers, *Occupied City: New Orleans Under the Federals, 1862–1865* (Lexington, Ky., 1965), 20; Willie M. Caskey, *Secession and Restoration of Louisiana* (Baton Rouge, 1938), 55–56.

Louisiana was not fated to remain a united state for long after secession. While Louisiana troops were fighting at Shiloh and in Virginia, a northern fleet was preparing to seize New Orleans. After a six-day bombardment of the two forts between the city and the Gulf of Mexico, Admiral Farragut ran his fleet past the forts in the early morning darkness of April 24, 1862. Once the gunboats had passed the forts, New Orleans was defenseless. The city officials and much of the population put on a great show of defiance, but Farragut, his guns floating above the city, could afford to refrain from bombardment. On May 1 transports arrived carrying troops under the command of Major General Benjamin F. Butler.[3]

New Orleans was suffering economically before Butler's men landed. The city had a population of 149,063 whites, 14,484 slaves, and 10,939 free Negroes according to the census of 1860, and directly or indirectly all of these people depended upon trade for a livelihood. Trade had been reduced to a fraction of its prewar proportions, and an orgy of destruction preceded the arrival of the Federal forces. Some fifteen thousand bales of cotton, many steamboats, and even warehouses containing foodstuffs were put to the torch. The specie in the banks, worth about six million dollars, was hurried out of the city by rail. The public and private property destroyed has been estimated at ten million dollars, and this was done at a time when thousands of people in New Orleans were, if not starving, definitely hungry.[4]

While awaiting the arrival of Butler's troops, Farragut raised the Stars and Stripes over the United States Mint. As prayers were in progress aboard the ships, a man named William Mumford, reported to be a professional gambler, tore down the flag, dragged it along the ground, then ripped it to shreds. Butler was informed of this event before his arrival, and he announced that Mumford would be hanged.[5]

3 For the best account of the fall of New Orleans, see Charles L. Dufour, *The Night the War Was Lost* (Garden City, N.Y., 1960), *passim*; see also Capers, *Occupied City*, 60–61.

4 Harold D. Woodman, *King Cotton and His Retainers: Financing and Marketing the Cotton Crop of the South, 1800–1925* (Lexington, Ky., 1968), 209; William E. Highsmith, "Louisiana During Reconstruction" (Ph.D. dissertation, Louisiana State University, 1953), 50–51; Capers, *Occupied City*, 44–45; Thomas Ewing Dabney, "The Butler Regime in Louisiana," *Louisiana Historical Quarterly*, XXVII (April, 1944), 493.

5 Robert S. Holzman, *Stormy Ben Butler* (New York, 1954), 69–70; Hans L. Trefousse, *Ben Butler: The South Called Him Beast* (New York, 1957), 105.

Butler did not make this threat idly. Mumford and six Confederate soldiers who had violated parole were arrested and brought before a court martial. All were sentenced to death. Butler finally gave the soldiers their lives, but Mumford was publicly hanged before the mint where his insult to the flag had been perpetrated. This was one of many deeds for which Butler was hated in New Orleans, but Mumford's execution made it clear to the population that the general meant what he said, which was what Butler had hoped to accomplish. He was as severe with his own men: when a group of them forged orders and used them to burglarize homes, four men were arrested, tried, sentenced, and hanged in little more than twenty-four hours. It is interesting that the people of New Orleans made few complaints against Butler's men; their hate was directed toward the occupation commander himself.[6]

City officials and former United States senator Pierre Soule attempted passive resistance to the occupation, maintaining that since there were no military authorities, the city could not be surrendered. But this type of resistance was to be of short duration. Merchants who refused to sell to the occupation forces had their entire stocks confiscated. When the New Orleans *True Delta* refused to print Butler's first proclamation, the paper was seized and held until the proprietor apologized. John T. Monroe, who had drifted penniless into New Orleans and worked his way up from stevedore to mayor, was imprisoned with a number of lesser city officials. General George F. Shepley, as military commandant of New Orleans, took over Monroe's duties. Pierre Soule was sent north under arrest. Butler made it clear that he alone ruled: "New Orleans is a conquered city. . . . Would you or would you not expel us if you could? New Orleans has been conquered by the forces of the United States, and by the law of nations lies subject to the will of the conqueror."[7]

Nothing was passive about the conduct of the women of New

6 Trefousse, *Ben Butler,* 107–17; Holzman, *Stormy Ben Butler,* 66–67; Capers, *Occupied City,* 55–56, 60–61; Louis Taylor Merrill, "General Benjamin F. Butler and the Widow Mumford," *Louisiana Historical Quarterly,* XXIX (April, 1946), 341–54.

7 Quoted in Capers, *Occupied City,* 63 (see also 65–66); Trefousse, *Ben Butler,* 113–14; John Smith Kendall, *History of New Orleans* (Chicago, 1922), I, 277–82; Dabney, "Butler Regime in Louisiana," 498.

Orleans. At best, they disdainfully turned their backs upon the conquerors. At worst, they cursed and spat upon Union officers and men. Butler tried at first to ignore these incidents, but the women, presumably lower-class women in the main, became bolder as their defiance went unchallenged. This brought about the issuance of Butler's famous (or infamous, depending upon one's sectional point of view) General Order Number 28, better known as the "Woman Order." It was simple and to the point: "When any female shall, by word, gesture, or movement, insult or show contempt for any officer or soldier of the United States, she shall be . . . held liable to be treated as a woman of the town plying her vocation."[8] This order raised a storm of controversy, abroad as well as in the South. Butler was not disturbed. He wrote to a friend: "On the 24th day of February last, my officers were insulted by she-rebels in Baltimore. On the 24th day of May last, they were not insulted in New Orleans by he or she."[9]

Under General Shepley, a bureau of finance and a bureau of streets and landings were established to administer New Orleans. These bureaus were headed, respectively, by Edward H. Durell, of whom more will be heard later, and Julian Neville.[10] For the administration of justice, Butler established a provost court which was to function throughout the occupation. High crimes and misdemeanors were to be tried by a military commission of five officers. The state court system had collapsed with the beginning of the occupation, but in time three district courts were reestablished with jurisdiction limited to civil cases. Finally, President Abraham Lincoln established in New Orleans the very powerful Provisional Court for Louisiana, which was granted both civil and criminal jurisdiction, including law, admiralty, equity, and revenue cases. Basically, this was the government of occupied Louisiana until the functioning of state government began under the constitution of 1864. By the end of 1863, occupied Louisiana consisted of New Orleans, the banks of the Mississippi as far north

---

8 Quoted in Holzman, *Stormy Ben Butler,* 85.
9 Benjamin F. Butler to O. C. Gardner, June 10, 1862, quoted in Howard Palmer Johnson, "New Orleans Under General Butler," *Louisiana Historical Quarterly,* XXIV (April, 1941), 496; see also Capers, *Occupied City,* 67–68; Trefousse, *Ben Butler,* 110–11, 117.
10 Kendall, *History of New Orleans,* I, 282–83.

as Baton Rouge, and the lands along and between Bayou Lafourche and Bayou Teche.[11]

New Orleans newspapers were a potential source of trouble to Butler. The hostile *Crescent* and *Bulletin* soon disappeared. The *Daily Delta* and *True Delta* became, for all practical purposes, Union papers. The *Bee* and the *Daily Picayune* were suspended for a time, then allowed to resume independent publication, but this independence existed only so long as it was not exercised in any manner displeasing to the commanding general. Five years later Butler wrote to Henry Clay Warmoth that once after the editor of the *Picayune* had been brought before him and corrected for some misconduct, a pool of liquid had been discovered where the editor had stood. Perhaps this memory compensated Butler for the widespread story that the women of New Orleans put his picture in the bottom of their chamber pots.[12]

The Protestant ministers of New Orleans posed as great a problem as the newspapers. One of Butler's early orders forbade the observance of days of fasting and prayer proclaimed by Jefferson Davis. Apparently the first pastors to come into direct conflict with the Union commander were Episcopalians, who refused to offer prayers for the president of the United States. The disposition of the general was not improved when the funeral procession of a Union officer who had been shot down by a sniper was jeered by crowds in the streets and the curate of Christ Church failed to appear to conduct the funeral. In October, 1862, Christ Church was taken over completely by Union forces. A Union chaplain became the rector, and a vestry of local Unionists and Union officers was appointed. Disciplinary measures were not confined to Episcopalian churches. Soon only five Presbyterian ministers remained in New Orleans out of the twenty-four who had been there before the war. Most of the Methodist churches in the city were closed by Butler's order or because no ministers were available. In all, before the end of hostilities, at least forty Protestant churches had closed their doors. There is no record of Catholic churches having been closed. Presumably they were saved, first, by

11 *Ibid.*, 282–84, 292–93; Caskey, *Secession and Restoration*, 153–56.
12 Holzman, *Stormy Ben Butler*, 78–79; Capers, *Occupied City*, 178; Benjamin F. Butler to Henry Clay Warmoth, March 11, 1867, in Henry Clay Warmoth Papers, Southern Historical Collection, University of North Carolina.

the fact that the sermon played a small part in the service, and, secondly, because eighteen centuries of experience had taught the Catholic hierarchy how to behave in the presence of a conqueror.[13]

Butler did not hesitate to offer relief to the impoverished; he later reported that he spent fifty thousand dollars a month feeding hungry whites. To resident paupers, black and white, were added perhaps ten thousand Negroes who fled from plantations and flocked to New Orleans. The opening, in May, 1862, of the New Orleans, Opelousas, and Great Western Railroad to what is today Morgan City brought in some additional foodstuffs, but the road was frequently cut by Confederate raids, and the railroad also transported more hungry mouths. Furthermore, the food brought into New Orleans had to be paid for.[14]

Butler employed as much labor as possible to clean up New Orleans. The Crescent City had never been a pleasant place to live. From May to October business was slack, and everyone who could afford to go somewhere else did so. Few strangers dared to come to town, because this was the yellow-fever season. In 1853 this pestilence had killed one fourth of the city's population. In fact, when Federal occupation began, many southern sympathizers expected the fever to conquer Butler even as it had conquered General LeClerc in Santo Domingo. These hopes did not allow for Yankee energy, or for the fact that General Butler had to find work for the unemployed laboring class. He had found the filthiest city in the United States. Garbage, the contents of chamber pots and slop jars, dead animals, and other filth mixed with the mud of the mostly unpaved streets. There was no police force worthy of the name, and certain areas of the city were left to the mercies of the criminal element. Even though law enforcement was

---

13 Capers, *Occupied City*, 92; Caskey, *Secession and Restoration*, 51; Hodding Carter and Betty Werlein Carter, *So Great a Good: A History of the Episcopal Church in Louisiana and of Christ Church Cathedral, 1805–1955* (Sewanee, Tenn., 1955), 132–36; Penrose St. Amant, *A History of the Presbyterian Church in Louisiana* (New Orleans, 1961), 115; William W. Sweet, "Methodist Church Influence in Southern Politics," *Mississippi Valley Historical Review*, I (March, 1915), 546–47.

14 Trefousse, *Ben Butler*, 109–10; Capers, *Occupied City*, 5–6; Howard Ashley White, *The Freedmen's Bureau in Louisiana* (Baton Rouge, 1970), 64; John Cornelius Engelsmen, "The Freedmen's Bureau in Louisiana," *Louisiana Historical Quarterly*, XXXII (January, 1949), 164–65.

lax, half the inmates of the state penitentiary had been sentenced for crimes committed in New Orleans.[15]

Butler put the unemployed, runaway Negroes and his own troops to work. New Orleans was soon cleaner than ever before in its history, and probably than it was to be again before the twentieth century. The purpose of all this labor was served. No epidemic of yellow fever or of any other serious disease struck New Orleans during the Civil War. One historian, not at all friendly to Butler or to the Union cause, says that Butler deserved no credit for the prevention of fever, that the blockade was responsible because it kept out ships from the tropics.[16] One is inclined to doubt this conclusion, however. In 1867, when New Orleans had restored its customary filthiness, yellow fever came back.[17]

Care of the people of New Orleans was expensive. In August and September of 1862 assessments were levied upon wealthier citizens. Especially singled out were factors who had advised upriver planters not to ship their cotton to New Orleans. Also, everyone who had bought city bonds issued in 1862 was assessed 25 percent of the amount he had invested. Since these Confederate Louisiana bonds were never to be redeemed, investors lost 125 percent. This assessment applied to banks as well as to individuals. In the areas he controlled outside the city, Butler levied a tax of three dollars a year on black laborers, one third to be paid by the worker, two thirds by the planter who employed him.[18]

The general attempted to restore financial stability. Obviously, Confederate currency must be outlawed, but he allowed it to circulate until late May because no other currency was available. When the time came to halt this circulation, the commander saw to it that the banks bore the main loss. Deposits which had been made in Confederate currency had to be redeemed in United States currency or

---

15 Capers, *Occupied City,* 11–12; Trefousse, *Ben Butler,* 95; Holzman, *Stormy Ben Butler,* 120–21.
16 Caskey, *Secession and Restoration,* 48.
17 Kendall, *History of New Orleans,* I, 286; New Orleans *Daily Picayune,* 1867.
18 Kendall, *History of New Orleans,* I, 286–87; Johnson, "New Orleans Under Butler," 476–77; White, *Freedmen's Bureau in Louisiana,* 64; Stephen A. Caldwell, *A Banking History of Louisiana* (Baton Rouge, 1935), 96.

its equivalent. When the banks attempted to conceal the little specie they had left, Butler's network of spies, mostly Negroes, kept him informed, and he confiscated hidden gold and silver. This policy reduced the hardships which might otherwise have afflicted the poorer people of the city, but it damaged the financial health of Louisiana banks. By February, 1863, seven of the thirteen banks previously operating in New Orleans had to close their doors. Inadequate banking facilities were to be a handicap to Louisiana's economy for many years after the Civil War had ended.[19]

To reestablish the general prosperity of New Orleans, Butler needed to restore the shipments of sugar and cotton which had been the foundation of prewar business activity. The sugar trade could not be revived because the sugar plantations were, with few exceptions, producing little or no sugar. Some cotton was being grown, and the price of cotton was very high, but even as Butler lifted the Federal blockade on trade with the interior, in May, 1862, the Confederate government placed an embargo on all trade with New Orleans. Some goods filtered through the lines, but too much of the profit of this trade went to unscrupulous officers and speculators, too little to legitimate business.[20]

As soon as the reality of Federal control was apparent, country blacks began to make their way to New Orleans. The occupation of Baton Rouge and the 1862 expedition down Bayou Lafourche gave thousands of slaves an opportunity to escape the plantations where they had been held. One writer stated that the march of a Union column into the sugar parishes had the same effect as thrusting a stick into an anthill, so numerous were the blacks who swarmed about the blue-clad troops. Thousands of them, even though Federal officers urged them to remain in their homes, walked to the Crescent City. Other thousands made their way to Grant's army opposite Vicksburg.[21]

19 Caldwell, *Banking History of Louisiana*, 91, 93, 96; Trefousse, *Ben Butler*, 116, 119–20; Holzman, *Stormy Ben Butler*, 71; Kendall, *History of New Orleans*, I, 276.
20 Charles P. Roland, *Louisiana Sugar Plantations During the American Civil War* (Leyden, Netherlands, 1957), *passim*; Capers, *Occupied City*, 82–91; Caldwell, *Banking History of Louisiana*, 96.
21 James Parton, *General Butler in New Orleans* (New York, 1864), 489; E. Franklin Frazier, *The Negro in the United States* (New York, 1957), 193, 202–203; Charles H. Wesley, *Negro Labor in the United States, 1850–1925: A Study in American*

Not all the blacks who came to New Orleans were inspired by the sight of Union troops or by their own desire for freedom. By mid-1862, field hands were becoming more and more reluctant to work under plantation discipline, and their masters were becoming more and more reluctant to feed them. Partly to rid themselves of a burden, partly to embarrass the Federal commander, a substantial number of masters deliberately sent their slaves within the Union lines. Butler decided to consider this an act of emancipation, and well before Lincoln's Emancipation Proclamation went into effect he was treating Negroes, many of whom came from the parishes exempted by Lincoln's edict, as free men.[22]

Earlier, in Virginia, Butler had begun the practice of retaining blacks who came within his lines rather than returning them to their masters. He did this on the ground that they were "contraband of war."[23] He was determined to do something useful with the "contrabands" who came to him in New Orleans. The greatest obstacle he encountered was race prejudice on the part of his own officers and men. Some of his troops held strong abolitionist sentiments and believed that black men, given the opportunity, could equal other men in intelligence, industry, and morality. Others, though opposed to slavery, wanted no personal contact with Negroes. Finally, a sizable proportion of Union troops were just as anti-Negro as many lower-class southerners. These prejudices might slow Butler down, but they would not divert him from his course. He himself was a far cry from an abolitionist. He had supported John C. Breckinridge, the Southern Rights candidate, in the 1860 presidential campaign, but when war began he took whatever measures he believed would hasten victory for the Union.[24]

Economic History (New York, 1926), 88–89; George R. Bentley, *A History of the Freedmen's Bureau* (Philadelphia, 1955), 16; Joe Gray Taylor, "Slavery in Louisiana During the Civil War," *Louisiana History,* VIII (Winter, 1967), 27–34.

22 Roland, *Louisiana Sugar Plantations, passim*; Taylor, "Slavery in Louisiana During the Civil War," 27–34; Highsmith, "Louisiana During Reconstruction," 53; W. E. Burghardt DuBois, *Black Reconstruction in America* (New York, 1962), 68.

23 Allan Nevins, *The War for the Union: The Improvised War, 1861–1862* (New York, 1959), 397–98.

24 Gerald M. Capers, Jr., "Confederates and Yankees in Occupied New Orleans, 1862–1865," *Journal of Southern History,* XXX (November, 1964), 425; Highsmith, "Louisiana During Reconstruction," 83; Caskey, *Secession and Restoration,*

Public-works projects could not absorb all the able-bodied blacks who entered the Union lines. Thought was given to colonizing Negroes in Africa or the West Indies, but this was impractical. Also it was proposed that the "contrabands" be scattered over the United States, but some people in the North, especially of the working class, were strongly opposed to this idea. Some blacks, as will be seen, could be returned to plantation labor, but the simplest solution was to enlist able-bodied young men in the Union army. Before the end of 1862 Butler had decided that Negro troops should be used in the Union army; by 1864 such Confederate leaders as Henry Watkins Allen of Louisiana and General Robert E. Lee were advocating the mobilization of blacks for Confederate service.[25]

Butler had a good precedent for enlisting Louisiana Negroes. Thousands of blacks had served in the armies of the American Revolution. Closer to hand, however, there already existed in Louisiana units of militia made up of free Negroes from New Orleans. A half-century earlier they had participated valiantly in the Battle of New Orleans. These Native Guards had offered their services to the Confederacy at the beginning of the Civil War, but the southern authorities had declined to use them. Butler himself was hesitant for a time. When General John W. Phelps began enlisting Negroes, he was ordered to desist and to put the black volunteers to work cutting timber. Phelps resigned in protest, and Butler was severely criticized by the Radical press of the North.[26]

Whether motivated by this criticism or by something else, the occupation commander decided he should use black troops. In August of 1862 he ordered the enlistment of "free Negroes." He reported to the secretary of war that he would soon have a regiment of a thousand men, the darkest of about the same complexion as Daniel Webster. The one regiment was soon expanded to three; a number of local black leaders, including P. B. S. Pinchback, were set to work raising

---

54; Vernon Lane Wharton, *The Negro in Mississippi, 1865–1900* (New York, 1965), 25–26.

25 Wharton, *The Negro in Mississippi,* 24–25; Bentley, *The Freedmen's Bureau,* 17–18; DuBois, *Black Reconstruction,* 96–97, 117.

26 Roland C. McConnell, *Negro Troops of Antebellum Louisiana: A History of the Battalion of Free Men of Color* (Baton Rouge, 1968), *passim;* Trefousse, *Ben Butler,* 131; DuBois, *Black Reconstruction,* 115.

troops. Butler, having begun with the Native Guards, made up largely of cultured, well-educated men, favored the use of Negro officers. There was, however, much objection to the commissioning of Negroes. Butler granted commissions to a dozen or more, but his successor, General Nathaniel P. Banks, halted this practice in Louisiana. A few northern states later issued commissions to Negroes, but only about seventy-five black men attained officers' rank during the war.[27]

The enlistment of Negroes continued in Louisiana and elsewhere until the end of the war, by which time some 200,000 had worn the blue uniform of the Union. Most of these were refugees. Perhaps such recruits were motivated by a desire to put an end to slavery, but a great many of those who enlisted were confused fugitives who had just arrived in the Union lines. Blacks who were able to resist the first persuasion often succumbed later to the bounties offered by recruiting officers from the northern states. Because free Negroes and refugees in south Louisiana and refugees at Vicksburg offered one of the best pools of potential enlistees, a goodly proportion of the blacks in northern uniform were from Louisiana.[28]

Contrabands who could not be put to work in New Orleans or enlisted in the Union army were, whenever possible, set to work on plantations. It should be borne in mind that upriver, downriver, and westward from New Orleans was one of the major plantation regions in the South. Under Butler private employment of blacks was handled in a rather haphazard manner. The provost marshal was in charge; he had the authority to punish those who refused to work, but it is questionable whether this authority was ever used. One unfortunate result of this compulsory plantation-labor system was that Louisiana planters as well as northerners who leased plantations in occupied Louisiana too often defrauded the freedmen of their wages.[29]

This, then, was the condition of Louisiana when, under pressure from Washington, Butler took the initial steps toward the restoration of the state to the Union. For more than a dozen years Louisiana was

---

27 DuBois, *Black Reconstruction,* 99–100, 113; Holzman, *Stormy Ben Butler,* 100–101; Trefousse, *Ben Butler,* 131–32; Caskey, *Secession and Restoration,* 54.

28 Caskey, *Secession and Restoration,* 53; Wharton, *The Negro in Mississippi,* 31.

29 White, *Freedmen's Bureau in Louisiana,* 102; Engelsmen, "Freedmen's Bureau in Louisiana," 175–76; Samuel S. Cox, *Three Decades of Federal Legislation, 1855–1885* (Providence, R.I., 1888), 425.

to be in one phase or another of this process. It was a traumatic break with the state's past, and it was to have tremendous effects on her future. The tale has never been told as a whole, and the incomplete accounts which exist express the prejudices of an earlier generation and lack the increased knowledge and understanding made possible by the great amount of research done on Reconstruction and by the new interpretations set forth during the last third of a century. The study that follows is an attempt to remedy this situation.

II *The Beginnings of Reconstruction in Louisiana*

GENERAL BUTLER was under constant pressure from President Lincoln to begin the establishment of a state government in Louisiana. But before this could be done, there had to be a criterion to determine who was and who was not a loyal citizen. Opponents of secession in New Orleans and, to a lesser degree, in the surrounding parishes had been fairly numerous, but practically all of these "Unionists," once secession was an accomplished fact, had worked for the success of the Confederacy. Christian Roselius and John A. Rozier were examples of these accommodating Unionists. The few men who openly opposed the Confederacy, such as Dr. A. P. Dostie and Benjamin F. Flanders, were driven into exile, jailed, or frightened into silence.[1] There is no way of accurately estimating the number of persons in New Orleans who had been Unionists at heart after secession. Undoubtedly a great many of them resembled the baker whose sign, before the war, read *United States Bakery.* After secession he converted it to *Confederate States Bakery.* After the occupation began he painted out the word *Confederate*, leaving *States Bakery* preceded by a blank space so that he might be ready for whatever turned up.[2]

1 Capers, *Occupied City*, 123–24; Holzman, *Stormy Ben Butler*, 73–74.
2 New Orleans *Delta*, May 4, 1862, quoted in Johnson, "New Orleans Under Butler," 506.

Certainly many of the people of the Crescent City and surrounding areas, when they discovered that the occupation was likely to be permanent, found that deep in their hearts they had always been loyal to the Union. Butler took advantage of these sentiments and devised an oath for various classes, including former Confederate soldiers and aliens who had lived in the United States for at least five years. Interestingly enough, all but three hundred of the several thousand former Confederate troops in the city swore to their loyalty. On August 6, 1862, Provost Marshall James H. French reported that a total of 11,723 persons had sworn that they were loyal to the United States. This was enough for a beginning of political reconstruction.[3]

In July, 1862, Congress passed an act providing for the confiscation of the property of disloyal persons but allowed sixty days for these persons to return to their proper loyalty to the United States. Even before the sixty days had elapsed, Butler seized the property of John Slidell, General David E. Twiggs, and other presumably irredeemable Confederates. In September, after sixty days, Butler ordered all persons who refused to take a loyalty oath to be registered as enemies and to provide a list of their property. Some four thousand people registered as enemies, compared with more than sixty-one thousand who swore their loyalty. John Rose Ficklen quotes Butler as saying that $800,000 worth of money and property was seized. It should be pointed out that under Article III, Section 3 of the United States Constitution, confiscated property of Confederates could be held only during the lifetime of the disloyal person. Therefore, although the federal government could use confiscated property, it could not permanently alienate it. The heirs of the owner could eventually get it back. In practice, most of those who lost property in New Orleans were pardoned by President Andrew Johnson soon after the end of the war and therefore regained possession quickly.[4]

---

3 Lowrey, "James Madison Wells," 1,010; Capers, *Occupied City*, 123–24; John Frederick Nau, *The German People of New Orleans, 1850–1900* (Leyden, Netherlands, 1958), 42–43; Caskey, *Secession and Restoration*, 58–60; John Hope Franklin, *Reconstruction After the Civil War* (Chicago, 1961), 15–16; William A. Russ, Jr., "Disfranchisement in Louisiana (1862–1870)," *Louisiana Historical Quarterly*, XVIII (July, 1935), 555–80; for an example see Oath Certificate, September 20, 1862, in André Family Papers, Department of Archives, Louisiana State University.

4 Russ, "Disfranchisement in Louisiana," 560–61; John Rose Ficklen, *History of Reconstruction in Louisiana (Through 1868)* (Gloucester, Mass., 1966), 38–39.

By mid-1862 the Radical Republicans in Congress were beginning to develop their arguments against admitting senators and representatives from the Confederate states to Congress. Butler attracted favorable attention from these men because of his harsh treatment of rebels and because he began to enlist Negro troops. Seemingly the Radicals began to look upon Louisiana as a laboratory where their ideas of Reconstruction might be tested. Lincoln had no intention of permitting any such experimentation; he was determined that Louisiana should be restored under executive direction and according to his ideas. Butler had no choice but to follow the president's instructions, but he would nonetheless leave his own imprint upon the Reconstruction process in Louisiana.[5]

Butler's first Reconstruction task was to bring about the election to the United States House of Representatives of men from the two Louisiana congressional districts he controlled. Louisiana Unionists believed, or professed to believe, that a state which sent representatives to Congress before January 1, 1863, would not be considered in a state of rebellion and would therefore be exempted from the provisions of the Emancipation Proclamation.[6] As a first step, Butler encouraged the formation of a Union Association with the avowed object of restoring the Constitution and laws of the United States to Louisiana. United States citizens, aliens who declared their intention of becoming citizens, citizens of Louisiana, and others who subscribed to the association's principles and took an oath of loyalty to the United States were eligible for membership. Butler permitted, and perhaps encouraged, the formation of a number of Unionist clubs made up of Negroes, "all of which," according to a southern chronicler, "naturally became inflated with a growing sense of their own importance."[7] Among those who gave strong support to the Unionist movement were John E. Bouligny, a Louisianian who had refused to resign his seat in Congress when Louisiana seceded, and Dr. A. P. Dostie, a true

5 Albert Mordell (comp.), *Selected Essays by Gideon Welles: Lincoln's Administration* (New York, 1960), 77; Trefousse, *Ben Butler*, 130–31; Fred Harvey Harrington, *Fighting Politician: Major General N. P. Banks* (Philadelphia, 1948), 101–102; T. Harry Williams, *Lincoln and the Radicals* (Madison, Wis., 1941), 220–21.
6 Mordell (comp.), *Selected Essays by Gideon Welles*, 75, 95; Caskey, *Secession and Restoration*, 63.
7 Caskey, *Secession and Restoration*, 54.

Radical, who was to die for his convictions in the New Orleans riot of 1866.[8]

These Unionists of 1862 expressed the conviction that secession had been illegal and that Louisiana was an inseparable part of the Union. They advocated "unconditional" subjection to Federal authority, but also the forgiving of erring rebels. Since Louisiana was still officially a part of the Union, they said, the people of the state should elect United States representatives and establish a loyal state government as soon as possible. It is interesting that at the end of 1862 the views of most Louisiana Unionists were close to those eventually to be advocated with such passion by President Johnson.[9]

Butler ordered that the election of two representatives to the national House of Representatives should take place in December of 1862. Apparently all otherwise qualified electors who had taken a loyalty oath could vote. The election demonstrated that this early there was a division among Unionists. Both factions were primarily concerned with saving the Union, but one desired to restore the Union with slavery; the other was hopeful that somehow the Negro could be eliminated from Louisiana, making the state into "white man's country." This second faction had no specific plan for deportation or colonization, but it expressed the inchoate anti-Negro feeling of working-class Louisianians. Obviously, neither faction had any intention of granting political rights to the Negro.[10]

Butler was an experienced politician. Before the election he saw to it that a Unionist organization was established, extending downward from a central committee (which he supported with patronage) to women's auxiliaries. This "machine" nominated Edward H. Durell as its candidate from the First Congressional District and Bavarian-born Michael Hahn from the Second District. The existence of factionalism and of Unionist resentment of Butler was demonstrated when an opposition candidate, Benjamin F. Flanders, defeated Durell. The two victors proceeded to Washington, where the House of Representatives debated their status at great length. It was brought

8 *Ibid.*, 54–56; Francis Byers Harris, "Henry Clay Warmoth, Reconstruction Governor of Louisiana," *Louisiana Historical Quarterly*, XXX (April, 1947), 523.
9 Caskey, *Secession and Restoration*, 57.
10 *Ibid.*, 63–66.

out that the 7,147 votes cast in the two districts amounted to more than a majority of the votes cast in the same two districts in 1859. Before the adjournment of Congress, both men were seated for the term coming to an end, but they were to be the last recognized Louisiana representatives until 1868.[11]

By the time of the election, Butler's days in New Orleans were numbered. Although there is no evidence that he actually purloined any spoons, as Confederates charged, an odor of corruption began to arise about his headquarters. Quite possibly Butler himself was not personally implicated in any illegal trading in cotton with the Confederate enemy, but his brother and a number of officers on his staff almost certainly were. Reverdy Johnson, sent to New Orleans to investigate charges that had been made, returned to Washington with a distinctly unfavorable report. It was even suggested that the lives of Federal soldiers had been risked to bring about favorable trading opportunities.[12]

Charges of corruption were not the only factor, and probably not the most important one, in bringing about Butler's relief from command. The general was no diplomat, and he was soon at odds with foreign consuls in the Crescent City. These consuls played an important role because the population included such a large number of aliens. France felt an especial attachment to the city and people of New Orleans, and the British had been strongly opposed to Butler ever since his "Woman Order." More important, practically all the consuls were Confederate sympathizers who made no effort to cooperate with the Federal commander. When Butler sought to prevent the deposit of specie belonging to Confederates with foreign consulates and when he required loyalty oaths of certain aliens resident in New Orleans, strong protests found their way to Washington. In late 1862 and early 1863 the federal government could not afford to antagonize foreign powers. To reduce Butler's direct control over New Orleans, General George F. Shepley was made military governor of Louisiana, leaving Butler in command of the Department of the Gulf.

---

11 *Ibid.*, 64–65; Capers, *Occupied City*, 128–29; John W. Burgess, *Reconstruction and the Constitution* (New York, 1902), 14; Mordell (comp.), *Selected Essays by Gideon Welles*, 95–96.
12 Highsmith, "Louisiana During Reconstruction," 80–82; Trefousse, *Ben Butler*, 122–24.

This was only a temporary solution, however, and in early 1863 Butler was relieved and replaced by General Banks.[13]

Hatred of Benjamin F. Butler has been assiduously cultivated in New Orleans since his departure. Years later George Washington Cable wrote: "I wonder to this day which of the two, Jeff Davis or Ben Butler, tried harder to make the United States Government hateful to the people of [Louisiana]."[14] This judgment seems overly harsh. By modern standards, Butler's rule seems more humane than severe. The notorious "Woman Order" can be considered the least harmful— and a wryly humorous— means of dealing with an intolerable situation. It is highly significant that there were few complaints against the behavior of Butler's troops, and that is perhaps the best test of an occupation commander. It cannot be said that his policy should have been milder. Banks attempted to treat the people of occupied Louisiana kindly, but the main result was the reemergence of open support for the Confederacy. Putting aside sectionalism, and taking full advantage of the privilege of hindsight, one can conclude that Butler provided just the kind of government that was needed for the military occupation of a hostile city inhabited by a kindred people.[15]

2

General Banks was appointed to succeed Butler because there was some ground for believing that he could conciliate the uncooperative "Unionists" of occupied Louisiana. The Confiscation Act had already gone into effect. The Emancipation Proclamation, distasteful though it might be to Louisiana Unionists, was an established fact, but it exempted those portions of Louisiana occupied by the Union army. Louisiana was, at least nominally, represented in Congress. When Banks arrived in New Orleans he publicly declared that since Louisiana was represented in Congress, it could not be considered in a state of rebellion. The first shot at Fort Sumter, he said, had announced the end of slavery, but he would not encourage laborers to leave the plantations. He even hinted that loyal Louisianians might receive com-

---

13 Capers, *Occupied City*, 103; Holzman, *Stormy Ben Butler*, 79; Trefousse, *Ben Butler*, 125–26.
14 George Washington Cable, *The Negro Question: A Selection of Writings on Civil Rights in the South*, ed. Arlin Turner (Garden City, N.Y., 1958), 3.
15 Capers, *Occupied City*, 94; Capers, "Occupied New Orleans," 422.

pensation from the United States for losses inflicted by Federal forces, including the loss of slave property. As might be expected, Banks at first was almost popular compared with his hated predecessor.[16]

In addition to a general relaxation of the rigors of occupation, Banks reopened most of the churches that had been closed. He hoped to use them as a means of educating New Orleanians in the principles of true Unionism, and he encouraged his chaplains to preach in the city's churches. The War Department aided his policy by giving Bishop E. A. Ames control of Methodist churches in the South which had been abandoned by their pastors. As might have been expected, neither northern ministers nor southerners who announced that they prayed for the president of the United States only to keep the churches open made many converts to the cause of the Union.[17]

Banks's efforts at conciliation were no more successful with the press, which attacked him front and rear. The then-Radical, pro-Butler New Orleans *Times* was a thorn in his side, and he eventually suppressed the *Daily Delta* because of its attacks upon his conciliation policy. At the other extreme was the *Daily Picayune*, which took as strong an anti-Republican stand as its editor dared. The only paper which consistently supported Banks was the New Orleans *Era*, which he subsidized with official printing.[18]

In truth, Banks was attempting the impossible. No course of action open to him could have made real Unionists out of a majority of the Louisiana whites who were under Union control. New Orleanians might take an oath of loyalty to the Union, but they welcomed news of Confederate victories. Even after mid-1863, when most men of the city realized that the Confederacy was losing the war, support of the Union was grudging. In the countryside, the general's policies were even less successful than they had been in the city. Louisiana's yeoman farmers had many disagreements with the planters, and not a few of them had opposed secession. But opposition to secession in 1861 did not mean that northern armies would be welcomed in 1863

16 Caskey, *Secession and Restoration*, 70–71; Harrington, *Fighting Politician*, 92–93; Capers, *Occupied City*, 105–106; Ficklen, *History of Reconstruction in Louisiana*, 37–41.
17 Harrington, *Fighting Politician*, 96–97.
18 *Ibid.*, 96; Fayette Copeland, "The New Orleans Press and Reconstruction," *Louisiana Historical Quarterly*, XXX (January, 1947), 149–75.

and 1864. Even if the yeoman farmers had been inclined toward Unionism, which they were not, the occupied area was for the most part plantation country. Also, outside New Orleans, much of the occupied territory was subject to Confederate raids, and the rebels might take savage vengeance upon a real supporter of the Union. Finally, Louisianians seem to have realized that when the war ended they would once more have to live with those who had supported the Confederacy to the bitter end. A record of Unionism not only would confer no prestige, it might make life intolerable. Even when Banks's edicts concerning Negro labor and his refusal to grant military commissions to Negroes coincided with the views of white Louisianians, he received little credit from them. As the commander of an army of occupation, he should have expected none.[19]

Because of his leniency, Banks found himself fighting some of Butler's battles over again. Until the fall of Vicksburg, New Orleans bankers refused to accept greenbacks. Children in school learned to sing *Dixie* and the *Marseillaise*, but Union songs were ignored. Most galling of all, women of all classes resumed the practice of insulting Federal officers and men. The outstanding incident was the February, 1863, "Battle of the Handkerchiefs," when a crowd of several thousand, almost all women, gathered at the levee to cheer captive Confederate officers departing to be exchanged. The crowd became so hostile, cheering for the Confederacy, waving handkerchiefs, and screaming insults at Union troops, that reinforcements were called to break up the demonstration.[20]

Banks did not follow Butler's example and issue another "Woman Order," but he did reluctantly conclude that conciliation was a failure. On May 1, 1863, he ordered all registered enemies of the United States to leave his lines within fifteen days. Furthermore, these registered enemies were forbidden to transfer property, so when they departed

19 Capers, *Occupied City*, 107; Harrington, *Fighting Politician*, 98–99; Agnes Smith Grosz, "The Political Career of Pinckney Benton Stewart Pinchback," *Louisiana Historical Quarterly*, XXVII (April, 1944), 529–30; Eric L. McKitrick, *Andrew Johnson and Reconstruction* (Chicago, 1960), 37.
20 Capers, *Occupied City*, 108–109; Elizabeth Joan Doyle, "Nurseries of Treason: Schools in Occupied New Orleans," *Journal of Southern History*, XXVI (May, 1960), 161–79; Harrington, *Fighting Politician*, 94–95.

their property came under the terms of the Confiscation Act. From this time on, Banks held a much tighter rein on the area he controlled. Pro-Confederate manifestations came to be dangerous recreation, and penalties were not reserved for drunks and women of lower classes. A year later Henry Clay Warmoth, then judge of the provost court, recorded with satisfaction that he had sent two "respectable ladies" to women's prison for sixty days because they cheered for Jeff Davis.[21]

3

It will be recalled that under Butler a Unionist political organization had been created to contest the congressional elections of 1862. Under Banks, this organization came to be known as the Free-State party. It had not been unified under Butler, and the dissident Benjamin F. Flanders had defeated the official organization candidate. After Butler's departure the more moderate faction, encouraged by Banks and headed by Michael Hahn, and an opposition pro-Butler faction were in evidence. Since Banks gave his rather extensive patronage to the Hahn faction, the Radical group tended to oppose it. Banks was wise enough to transfer most officers who remained loyal to Butler away from the Department of the Gulf, but as one result the Butler faction, having nothing to gain by moderation and compromise, grew steadily more Radical. The Radical group might not have survived, but the Treasury Department gave its leaders jobs collecting revenue and carrying out other tasks. In a sense the "Custom-House Ring" had come into being as early as 1863.[22]

In addition to the moderate and Radical factions of the Free-State party, there existed in Louisiana a third group, aptly referred to as Conservative Unionists. These men agreed that secession was illegal and that therefore the state constitution of 1861 was illegal. It was their contention, however, that as soon as Union forces occupied any portion of Louisiana, the Louisiana constitution of 1852 was restored.

21 Henry Clay Warmoth Diary (Warmoth Papers), August 27, 1864; Caskey, *Secession and Restoration*, 71–72.
22 Harrington, *Fighting Politician*, 100–102; Roger W. Shugg, *Origins of Class Struggle in Louisiana: A Social History of White Farmers and Laborers During Slavery and After, 1840–1875* (Baton Rouge, 1939, 1968), 198–99; Capers, *Occupied City*, 112, 126–27; Ficklen, *History of Reconstruction in Louisiana*, 45–47.

This party was undoubtedly sincere in its loyalty to the Union, perhaps more so than many of the one-time secessionists who had become adherents of the Free-State party, but it sought the impossible, a return to the status quo, including Negro slavery, which had existed before secession. This attitude received some encouragement when Lincoln's Emancipation Proclamation exempted the occupied portions of Louisiana, but it is now obvious that this faction had no chance of success. But what is obvious today was not so obvious in early 1863, and these Conservative Unionists would do what they could to prevent the reorganization of the state on any basis other than a return to prewar conditions. They were to be a fairly serious obstacle to Lincoln's and Banks's plans to restore Louisiana to the Union as quickly as possible.[23]

As noted previously, Michael Hahn and Benjamin F. Flanders had been elected to Congress in 1862, but they had been elected to the Congress then sitting, not to the new Congress which would convene in 1863. Thus, although they were seated, they were members for only a short time.[24] The Conservative Unionist sought to take advantage of this situation and to elect members of their faction to represent Louisiana in the Thirty-eighth Congress. They called for an election for November 2, 1863, but the unprepared Free-State party refused to participate, and when General Banks made it clear that he was opposed, the election was called off.[25]

Either the order to halt the election did not reach some of the polling places outside the city, or some of the Conservative Unionists decided to carry on despite the order. Only a few hundred votes were cast, but A. P. Field and Thomas Cottman claimed election. They went to Washington and were allowed to take seats pending a decision as to their claims. Thus they took part in the organization of Congress, but soon after Field's claim was rejected. Cottman then resigned. It should be noted that the Free-State party filed a protest with Schuyler Col-

23 James Amédée Gaudet Papers, 1863–64, Southern Historical Collection, University of North Carolina; New Orleans *Daily Picayune*, June, 1863–January, 1864; Ficklen, *History of Reconstruction in Louisiana*, 46–49; Caskey, *Secession and Restoration*, 74–76, 86–87; Kendall, *History of New Orleans*, I, 289; Cox, *Three Decades of Federal Legislation*, 426; Capers, *Occupied City*, 125, 130–31; F. B. Harris, "Henry Clay Warmoth," 524.
24 Ficklen, *History of Reconstruction in Louisiana*, 42.
25 Caskey, *Secession and Restoration*, 82–84.

fax, Speaker of the House, when it appeared that Field and Cottman might be seated.[26]

Shortly after this abortive election, President Lincoln issued a proclamation setting forth what is usually referred to as Lincoln's Plan of Reconstruction. This document took note of the Emancipation Proclamation, but it otherwise granted full pardon and restoration of property rights to citizens of the rebellious states who would take a prescribed oath of loyalty to the United States. There were exceptions, primarily persons who had left the service of the United States to aid the Confederacy and higher-ranking officers of the Confederate army, navy, and government. The proclamation went on to say that whenever a number of persons, not less than one tenth of those who had voted in the presidential election of 1860, should take the prescribed oath and then in an election reestablish a loyal state government, the government thus created, so long as it should be republican in form, would be recognized by the president as the lawful government of the state. The president would also accept whatever provision the new state government should make for freed Negroes, so long as their permanent freedom was recognized and provision made for their education. Finally, Lincoln gave a word of caution, reminding all that, although new state governments under his proclamation could elect United States senators and representatives, only the houses of Congress could determine whether such senators and representatives should be seated.[27]

Radicals in Congress, and the very few Radicals to be found in Louisiana at this time, were no doubt disappointed that Lincoln had not done something to encourage the granting of suffrage to Negroes. Apparently, however, the president did not even consider such action. He was seeking to coax still-rebellious states back into the Union, and a suggestion of Negro suffrage would have negated any attraction the proclamation might otherwise have had. Gideon Welles later wrote that in drawing up the proclamation there had been some disagreements in the cabinet, but that no one had even suggested that the

26 *Ibid.*, 80–85; Ficklen, *History of Reconstruction in Louisiana*, 49–50; Russ, "Disfranchisement in Louisiana," 562–63.
27 James D. Richardson (ed.), *A Compilation of the Messages and Papers of the Presidents* (Washington, D.C., 1903), VI, 310–14.

president or Congress could give the vote to Negroes who were not qualified to vote under the laws of the state concerned.[28]

Lincoln was eager to get state governments organized under his direction because he was well aware that Congress could set its own conditions. After his pocket veto of the Wade-Davis Bill, a congressional plan of Reconstruction more severe than his own, he pointed out that there could be no true state government under the Constitution without representation in Congress. Therefore, when Congress admitted senators and representatives from a state, that state would be conclusively restored to the Union; however, if its representatives should be rejected by Congress, the very existence of the state would be denied, and the president would have no choice but to submit to this congressional decision.[29] One might suppose that the southern states, and Louisiana in particular, would have taken heed of the president's warning, but they did not, even when the warnings became more specific.

Naturally, President Lincoln wished to put his plan into effect in Louisiana because the state afforded such an excellent opportunity. This was one of Banks's primary missions. Lincoln wrote him a letter regarding the formation of a state government soon after the issuance of the Reconstruction Proclamation. On August 5, 1863, he wrote again, urging Banks to "go to work, and give me a tangible nucleus which the remainder of the state may rally around as fast as it can, and which I can at once recognize and sustain. . . . Time is important."[30] Banks certainly wished to comply with the president's command, but much of his time was taken up with his military duties as departmental commander. Also, at this time he was attempting to get idle blacks back to work. More important, powerful men in Washington were opposed to the organization of a loyal state government in Louisiana lest it should prove a conservative precedent for the other Confederate states. Divisions in Washington were reflected in Louisiana, where moderate Unionists desired a state government, and Radicals—and by this time the name was appropriate—worked against

28 Mordell (comp.), *Selected Essays by Gideon Welles*, 117; Caskey, *Secession and Restoration*, 96–97; Franklin, *Reconstruction After the Civil War*, 18.
29 Mordell (comp.), *Selected Essays by Gideon Welles*, 171–73.
30 Abraham Lincoln to N. P. Banks, August 5, 1863, in John G. Nicolay and John Hay (eds.), *Complete Works of Abraham Lincoln* (New York, 1894), II, 466.

such action. Shepley, who favored the Radicals, was able in his position as military governor to put many obstacles in Banks's way, and he did not hesitate to do so.[31]

The slowness of nineteenth-century communications, despite the telegraph, and the preoccupation of both Banks and Lincoln with the purely military aspects of the war, delayed any final action for several months. Banks, to break the impasse, suggested that General Shepley, Thomas J. Durant, who had been unofficially registering "loyal" voters, and other Radicals be relieved of Reconstruction duties and that he, Banks, be allowed to take complete charge. Lincoln replied on Christmas Eve, 1863, that he had always intended for Banks to be in full charge of organizing a loyal government in Louisiana. "I now tell you that in every dispute . . . you are master. . . . I wish you to take the case as you find it, and give us a free State reorganization of Louisiana in the shortest possible time."[32] This left Banks free to proceed. He and Lincoln were both moderates, and they could be expected to agree. The Radicals would no doubt be dissatisfied, but a constitutional convention, *after* a state government was in operation, would give them a chance to express themselves. Whether Banks noted it or not, a Republican party was formed in Louisiana in late 1863. It was composed of twenty-six men, six of whom were free Negroes. But at the time this was a small cloud on the moderate horizon.[33]

While Banks was consolidating his authority, the Radical wing of the Free-State party, led by Flanders and Durant, was continuing its efforts to register enough voters to call a constitutional convention. In New Orleans the Union Associations met frequently and, in mid-December, 1863, combined to hold a convention of "Friends of Freedom of the State of Louisiana." It was apparently the intention of the Louisiana Radicals to petition Governor Shepley, whom they expected to be complaisant, to call an election of delegates to a constitutional convention for January 25, 1864. Lincoln's grant of plenary

31 Mordell (comp.), *Selected Essays by Gideon Welles*, 71; Caskey, *Secession and Restoration*, 93; Capers, *Occupied City*, 133–34.
32 Lincoln to Banks, December 24, 1863, in Nicolay and Hay (eds.), *Works of Lincoln*, II, 466; Harrington, *Fighting Politician*, 143; Capers, *Occupied City*, 133.
33 DuBois, *Black Reconstruction*, 462; Charles Barthelemy Rousseve, *The Negro in Louisiana: Aspects of His History and His Literature* (New Orleans, 1937), 100–101.

powers to Banks may well have prevented such a call; moreover Lincoln probably would have frowned upon any group containing persons known to favor Negro suffrage.[34]

Banks ignored Radical plans and himself issued a call, not for a constitutional convention, but for the election in February of a governor and six other state officials. To legalize this action, he declared the Louisiana constitution of 1852 in effect except insofar as it recognized slavery. His proclamation sought to give something to all factions. He assured Conservative Unionists that his exception of slavery laws under the constitution of 1852 was no obstacle to any claims they might make for compensation for lost slaves. The moderate members of the Free-State party could take satisfaction in the expectation of winning the election. A sop was thrown to the Radicals by an announcement that a constitutional convention would be called for the first Monday in April, 1864.[35]

Banks followed Lincoln's plan, including the oath the president had prescribed. Although certain persons were disfranchised by Lincoln's proclamation, the oath dealt with future conduct, not with what had been done in the past. Thus, not only could former sympathizers with the Confederacy take the oath, but also returned Confederate soldiers. Some loyalists objected to taking the same oath prescribed for former rebels, but this was a small obstacle. Banks needed all the votes he could get in order to be sure of mustering the 10 percent called for in Lincoln's proclamation. Therefore he called upon all potential voters to take the oath; indifference he called criminal, and factionalism treason. He saw to it that all white Louisiana soldiers in the Union army in the Department of the Gulf cast ballots. It was even suggested that there were more soldier votes than there were Louisiana soldiers.[36]

Banks chose to ignore the ten thousand free people of color in New

34 Ficklen, *History of Reconstruction in Louisiana*, 50–52, 55; New Orleans *Daily Picayune*, November, 1863–January, 1864; Capers, *Occupied City*, 133–34; Lowrey, "James Madison Wells," 1,011–12.

35 New Orleans *Daily Picayune*, February 2, 1864; Caskey, *Secession and Restoration*, 94, 96–98; Kendall, *History of New Orleans*, I, 290; Cox, *Three Decades of Federal Legislation*, 427.

36 Caskey, *Secession and Restoration*, 106–107; Harrington, *Fighting Politician*, 144; Russ, "Disfranchisement in Louisiana," 563–64; Ficklen, *History of Reconstruction in Louisiana*, 53–57.

Orleans. Many of them were well educated, and they owned property valued at more than fifteen million dollars. Perhaps an equal number of former slaves in New Orleans had a degree of sophistication matched by few other Negroes in the South. So far as can be judged after the passage of a century, the blacks of New Orleans, as a whole, were probably as well-qualified to vote intelligently as were the white voters of the normal hill parish in Louisiana.[37] In November a group of free men of color presented a petition to Governor Shepley, asking that they be permitted to vote. They received no reply. By January, 1864, these men were organized into the Union Radical Association, and they sent a committee to Shepley to repeat their request. Shepley referred them to Banks; Banks's reply was evasive, but it was obvious that he did not intend to grant the petition. Eventually the association sent one of its members, P. M. Tourné, to Washington to present its case to President Lincoln. Perhaps Tourné's arguments influenced Lincoln's attitude a few months later when he recommended that well-qualified blacks be permitted to vote, but this is uncertain. What is certain is that an opportunity for Louisiana whites to checkmate the most radical congressional Republicans had been missed. There would be other opportunities, but race prejudice, northern as well as southern, would see them all passed by.[38]

It was generally assumed that the electoral contest in February, 1864, would be between the Conservative Unionists, who favored insofar as possible a return to the state of affairs which had existed before secession, and the moderate Free-State party, which was expected to have the support of Banks and the national administration. What was not fully recognized was the extent of the schism between the more radical members of the Free-State party, led by Durant and Flanders, and the moderate faction, led by Hahn. When the Free-State Convention met on February 1, 1864, it was at first unable to conduct business. Eventually the radical faction withdrew, claiming a majority of delegates. The moderates who remained proceeded to

37 Franklin, *Reconstruction After the Civil War*, 22; Caskey, *Secession and Restoration*, 89–90.
38 Ficklen, *History of Reconstruction in Louisiana*, 58–59; Cox, *Three Decades of Federal Legislation*, 426–27; E. Merton Coulter, *The South During Reconstruction, 1865–1877* (Baton Rouge, 1947), 61–62; Mordell (comp.), *Selected Essays by Gideon Welles*, 127.

nominate Hahn as their candidate for governor, James Madison Wells for lieutenant-governor, and a full slate of candidates for the other offices to be filled. Wells was a native-born planter of Rapides Parish, educated largely in the North, who had been an uncompromising Unionist since 1861.[39]

The Radical faction chose as their candidate for governor Benjamin F. Flanders, a native of New York who had lived in the South for twenty-five years. His Unionism had made his departure necessary in 1861, but he had returned as an agent for the Treasury Department after the fall of New Orleans. This attachment to the Treasury Department was in itself enough to align Flanders against Banks. As their candidate for lieutenant-governor, the Radicals also turned to Wells.[40]

The Conservative Unionists could not accept either of the Free-State candidates, and a nominating convention of this persuasion tendered the gubernatorial nomination to the renowned jurist, Christian Roselius. When Roselius refused it, J. Q. A. Fellows was named to head the ticket. The Conservative Unionists might have made a better showing had not all voters been required to take Lincoln's oath of allegiance. Men like Roselius, who had proved their loyalty by their actions and sworn to it once, felt insulted that they should be asked to swear their loyalty again. Also, they hesitated to swear to support all the acts that Congress had passed and might pass in the future, as the Lincoln oath required.[41]

By early 1864, New Orleans "was once more alive with economic and social bustle, even though some members of the cast had changed."[42] Men could pay less attention to the problem of survival and more to politics. The February campaign was a short but active

39 Caskey, *Secession and Restoration*, 80, 92, 98–101; Ficklen, *History of Reconstruction in Louisiana*, 57; F. B. Harris, "Henry Clay Warmoth," 525; Lowrey, "James Madison Wells," 1,008–1,009, 1,018.

40 Caskey, *Secession and Restoration*, 100–102, 104, 108; Whitelaw Reid, *After the War: A Southern Tour* (Cincinnati, 1866), 268–69; Ficklen, *History of Reconstruction in Louisiana*, 57–58, 60; Philip D. Uzee, "Republican Politics in Louisiana, 1877–1900" (Ph.D. dissertation, Louisiana State University, 1950), 5; New Orleans *Daily Picayune*, February, 1864.

41 New Orleans *Daily Picayune*, February 3, 5, 1864; Lowrey, "James Madison Wells," 1,014; DuBois, *Black Reconstruction*, 142; Caskey, *Secession and Restoration*, 79–80, 105–106; F. B. Harris, "Henry Clay Warmoth," 526.

42 Capers, "Occupied New Orleans," 426.

one. Hahn had the active support of General Banks, and it was known that President Lincoln also looked with favor upon Hahn's candidacy. The Louisiana Radicals probably had no chance for presidential support under any circumstances, but any chance they might have had was forfeited when their mouthpiece, the *Times*, severely criticized the president's lenient amnesty program. The Conservative Unionists, denounced as a "copperhead party," had too many ties with secession to be a serious threat.[43]

The status of the Negro was the major topic of campaign oratory. Hahn took a safe middle ground. He was absolutely opposed to slavery, thus separating himself from the Conservative Unionists. On the other hand, he was unalterably opposed to any form of equality, including political equality, for the Negroes. He, and others speaking in his behalf, succeeded in identifying the Flanders ticket with demands for Negro suffrage. The Radicals fought back as well as they could by pointing out that Hahn had held the office of notary public under the Confederacy, but when it became evident that the Flanders cause was hopeless, many Radicals went over to Hahn.[44]

Another important characteristic of the campaign of February, 1864, must be noted. The old ruling class of Louisiana was either discredited, absent in Confederate service, or both. Banks, himself an experienced politician, hoped to construct a new political organization based upon the laboring class of New Orleans and the yeoman farmers of the countryside. This was not a new idea. Labor had risen to political power in the city before the Civil War; the last two prewar mayors had been, respectively, a printer and a stevedore. Hahn, the Banks candidate, appealed to the labor vote with his attacks on the Conservative Unionists and by his opposition to political rights for Negroes. The labor orientation of the new politics was to be further demonstrated at the constitutional convention of 1864.[45]

The February election met Lincoln's 10 percent standard easily.

43 Caskey, *Secession and Restoration*, 102; Ficklen, *History of Reconstruction in Louisiana*, 59–60.

44 New Orleans *Daily Picayune*, February 17, 1864; Capers, *Occupied City*, 228–29; Ficklen, *History of Reconstruction in Louisiana*, 58; Caskey, *Secession and Restoration*, 99–100; Lowrey, "James Madison Wells," 1,015.

45 Shugg, *Origins of Class Struggle in Louisiana*, 199; Harrington, *Fighting Politician*, 97–98; Capers, *Occupied City*, 127.

Some 11,355 votes were cast, more than 20 percent of the number cast in Louisiana in 1860. Hahn was elected with 6,171 votes, a firm majority. It was of significance, however, that Fellows, the Conservative Unionist, received considerably more votes than the Radical Flanders. Wells was elected lieutenant-governor.[46]

Although Wells was the only native Louisianian elected in February, 1864, the others were not in any sense of the word "carpetbaggers." The Bavarian-born Hahn had been in New Orleans for many years. His secretary of state, Stanislas Wrotnowski, was a Polish scholar who had come to Louisiana in 1849. Bartholomew L. Lynch, the attorney general, was Irish-born but had been in Louisiana since 1851. The treasurer was Dr. James G. Belden, a nephew of Noah Webster, who had been practicing medicine in Louisiana for seventeen years. John McNair, superintendent of education, had been a teacher in New Orleans since 1845, but had come originally from New York. Auditor A. P. Dostie, a dentist, was also a native of New York, but he had been in New Orleans since the 1840s except for a brief period of exile under the Confederacy. These were capable enough men, and they were valid Louisiana residents, but it was of ominous significance that they were not native-born.[47]

A valid objection to the election was the fact that the larger part of the area and population of Louisiana was not under Federal control. Banks agreed that this was true, but he pointed out that it was equally true that a majority of the population was not under the control of the Confederate government. Most of Louisiana was a no-man's-land.[48] Probably the greatest weakness of Hahn's government, however, considering the constitutional quibbling to which southerners were addicted, was its uncertain legal status. To the Conservative Unionists, the government was valid only as it existed under the constitution of 1852. The Radicals, on the other hand, maintained that secession had put an end to Louisiana as a political entity and that the

46 Perry H. Howard, *Political Tendencies in Louisiana* (Rev. ed.; Baton Rouge, 1970), 117; Caskey, *Secession and Restoration,* 107.
47 Caskey, *Secession and Restoration,* 107–108; Capers, "Occupied New Orleans," 412; Capers, *Occupied City,* 135–36; Lowrey, "James Madison Wells," 1,016.
48 Nathaniel P. Banks, *The Reconstruction of States: Letter of Major General Banks to Senator Lane* (New York, 1865), 12; Shugg, *Origins of Class Struggle in Louisiana,* 198–99; Ficklen, *History of Reconstruction in Louisiana,* 62.

state must be reconstituted before it could have anything other than a military government. Thomas J. Durant, a brilliant lawyer, gradually became the most notable Louisiana spokesman for the Radical faction. But Banks was not disturbed. He had already ordered the election of delegates to a constitutional convention, and he expected to bring most of the rest of Louisiana under his control by his planned expedition up the Red River. Had his military abilities been equal to his political skills, he might actually have brought about the restoration of Louisiana to the Union.[49]

Hahn and his officials were inaugurated on March 4, 1864. Perhaps much is revealed by the fact that Banks was the main speaker. No effort was spared to make the occasion an impressive one; the expense came to almost ten thousand dollars. This included $613.71 for six barrels of spirits and $250 for fifty musicians. A crowd reported to number thirty thousand persons was on hand.[50] Henry Clay Warmoth wrote in his diary that the inauguration was "the most brilliant thing I have ever seen. Artillery and musketry firing continuously—Brass bands, 6,000 children singing . . . speeches by Governor Hahn and General Banks."[51]

Thus a semblance of civilian government was restored to occupied Louisiana. President Lincoln recognized Hahn as governor under the constitution of 1852, but he also named him military governor to replace General Shepley. In truth, Hahn's authority rested on Federal bayonets. The Confederate state government of Louisiana continued to function in the Red River Valley, and it would do so until the surrender of the Confederate armies.[52] But Hahn had opponents enough in the area controlled by the Union. There were secessionists opposed

49 Uzee, "Republican Politics in Louisiana," 5; Ficklen, *History of Reconstruction in Louisiana*, 62–63; Cox, *Three Decades of Federal Legislation*, 426; David Donald, *Lincoln Reconsidered* (New York, 1956), 139; Avery Craven, *Reconstruction: The Ending of the Civil War* (New York, 1969), 76.

50 Capers, *Occupied City*, 137; Caskey, *Secession and Restoration*, 109–10, 114–15; New Orleans *Daily Picayune*, March 5, 1864.

51 Warmoth Diary, March 4, 1864.

52 *Acts Passed by the Twenty-Seventh Legislature of the State of Louisiana in Extra Session at Opelousas in January, 1863* (Natchitoches, 1864), *passim*; Thomas O. Moore, *Annual Message of Governor Thomas O. Moore to the Twenty-Eighth General Assembly of the State of Louisiana, January, 1864* (Shreveport, 1864), *passim*; Vincent H. Cassidy and Amos E. Simpson, *Henry Watkins Allen of Louisiana* (Baton Rouge, 1964), 102–33.

to his government, and their opposition was little stronger than that of the Conservative Unionists. At the other extreme were the Radicals. In numbers they were not threatening, but they reflected a growing segment of northern public opinion. More important, the Treasury Department did all that it discreetly could to aid the Radicals. Thus their leaders were kept nourished, and their ideas were kept alive until circumstances should make it possible for their influence to be felt.[53]

4

In the midst of all this political activity, and while he was also preparing for the Red River expedition, Banks had to give attention to the problem of the Negroes in his department. With few exceptions, the blacks who had been free during slavery days were perfectly capable of supporting themselves. So, to a lesser degree, were those "contrabands" who had been domestic servants or artisans under slavery. But it was the most numerous class of all, the field hands, who were least able to make their own way under the new dispensation. And it was the field hands who were most likely to flee into the Union lines. Many of them had no desire to do any kind of work. Large numbers of idle blacks gathered at Vicksburg, many of them from Louisiana, and many more at New Orleans. Whenever northern armies penetrated Confederate territory, the number of Negroes under Federal protection increased.[54]

One of the most remarkable facts concerning the American Civil War is that there was no significant uprising of slaves against their masters anywhere in the South during the fighting. This was not because blacks were incapable of revolt; there had been two dangerous uprisings in the history of prewar Louisiana. Certainly it was not because slaves were contented; their running away to Union army camps

---

53 Lowrey, "James Madison Wells," 1,017; Caskey, *Secession and Restoration*, 111; Capers, *Occupied City*, 112; Harrington, *Fighting Politician*, 166; Shugg, *Origins of Class Struggle in Louisiana*, 102–103.
54 Taylor, "Slavery in Louisiana During the Civil War," 27–34; John Eaton, *Grant, Lincoln and the Freedmen: Reminiscences of the Civil War with Special Reference to the Work for the Contrabands and Freedmen of the Mississippi Valley* (New York, 1907), 132–33, 135; Roussève, *The Negro in Louisiana*, 99–100, 118–20; DuBois, *Black Reconstruction*, 6; Nathaniel Prentiss Banks, *Emancipated Labor in Louisiana* (N.p., 1864?), 6–7; Wesley, *Negro Labor in the United States*, 140.

is evidence enough of discontent. John Rose Ficklen, pioneer historian of Louisiana Reconstruction, believed that the absence of revolt was due "to the unconscious appeal which unprotected women and children made to a simple race made conservative by the long discipline of slavery."[55] A British traveler suggested just after the war that slavery had so destroyed the manhood of Negro men "as to make them passive instruments of their masters' will."[56] Probably of far more significance, however, was the fact that southern Negroes were well aware that the troops in blue, though perhaps opposed to slavery, were just as prejudiced against black people as were southern slave owners. In fact, the attitude of most northerners seems to have resembled that of the strongly anti-Negro southern yeoman farmer. Thus a revolt by slaves would almost surely have been put down by northern troops.[57]

The legal status of Louisiana Negroes was confused throughout 1863 and 1864. Lincoln's Emancipation Proclamation did not apply to the thirteen parishes controlled by the Union army. It did apply, apparently, to runaways from other parishes who made their way into occupied territory. In actual practice, the blacks within the Union lines seem to have been free in fact if not in law well before the end of 1863. Moreover, the distinction between free Negroes and freedmen quickly became blurred. Banks solved the problem in all areas controlled by his bayonets in January, 1864, when he, in effect, declared slavery ended in all of Louisiana. The slaves were free, but just what freedom meant when applied to a black man was very uncertain.[58]

Obviously the black was not free in the same sense that a white man was free. Streetcars in New Orleans had been segregated before the Civil War, so-called "star cars" being set aside for blacks. This continued throughout the war and did not end until 1867. In May, 1864, a Negro was brought into court for having had sexual relations with a white woman. The *Picayune* carried an editorial opposing

55 Ficklen, *History of Reconstruction in Louisiana*, 127.
56 David McRae, *The Americans at Home* (New York, 1952), 319–20.
57 Taylor, "Slavery in Louisiana During the Civil War," 33–34; New Orleans *Daily Picayune*, March 6, 1864; C. Vann Woodward, "The Anti-Slavery Myth," *American Scholar*, XXXI (Spring, 1962), 312–38.
58 Ficklen, *History of Reconstruction in Louisiana*, 124–25; Harrington, *Fighting Politician*, 113; Roussève, *The Negro in Louisiana*, 99.

slavery in February, 1864, but at the same time described as absurd the idea of any kind of equality between blacks and whites. Six weeks later the same paper carried an account of a reported revival of cannibalism in Haiti. No doubt most readers got the point of this story.[59]

The Negro was not completely without white friends. Some former abolitionists believed in his capacity for self-support and full citizenship. Other whites, for humanitarian reasons, sought to alleviate suffering among the blacks. In all fairness, it must also be remembered that planters generally cared for those Negroes who remained on the plantations, even though work in the fields became ever more slipshod and unreliable.

As early as March, 1863, Dr. Samuel Gridley Howe, Colonel James McKaye, and Robert Dale Owen, under the auspices of the American Freedmen's Inquiry Commission, visited Canada, the Sea Islands, and New Orleans to see at first hand what was needed to help the freedmen. Later in the same year James Yeatman, president of the Western Sanitary Commission visited the freedmen in occupied areas along the Mississippi River. These investigators found misery, disease, and death in the contraband camps. Colonel McKaye, after looking over the situation in New Orleans, concluded that the federal government must actively support the freedmen or some other form of slavery would be devised. Before the end of the war societies to aid the freedmen, materially or spiritually, were springing up all over the North. Indeed, there were so many that they interfered with one another.[60]

During 1863 and 1864 the recruitment of freedmen for the Union army increased. In practice, this often went beyond recruitment and was more nearly impressment. The removal of able-bodied men from plantations in northeastern Louisiana was a constant embarrassment to northern lessees in that area. In south Louisiana, Banks halted, for a time, the enlistment of men found at work on plantations. He was

59 Germaine A. Memelo, "The Development of State Laws Concerning the Negro in Louisiana (1864–1900)" (M.A. thesis, Louisiana State University, 1956), 40, 180–81; New Orleans *Picayune*, February 21, April 3, May 3, 1864.
60 Wesley, *Negro Labor in the United States*, 116–19; J. Carlyle Sitterson, "The Transition from Slave to Free Economy on the William J. Minor Plantation," *Agricultural History*, XVII (October, 1943), 219; John G. Sproat, "Blueprint for Radical Reconstruction," *Journal of Southern History*, XXIII (February, 1957), 336–40; DuBois, *Black Reconstruction*, 79; Banks, *Emancipated Labor*, 5–6;

unable, however, to keep his ruling completely in effect because President Lincoln ordered that full advantage be taken of the freedmen as a source of manpower. The president sent Brigadier General Daniel Ullman to New Orleans with authority to organize a black brigade. Banks, an expert at political and bureaucratic infighting, proceeded to enlist so many Negroes—about ten thousand—that Ullman became merely one brigade commander among many.[61]

The freedmen in contraband camps at Vicksburg and in the adjacent Louisiana parishes did not come under the Department of the Gulf. They came under General Ulysses S. Grant's overall command, but General Lorenzo Thomas actually administered their affairs insofar as the army was concerned. Some of the Negroes who gathered in this area found employment in the little towns, others with the army, either as enlistees or servants. A great many were employed as woodcutters to provide fuel for the Union navy and for the civilian steamboats which plied the Mississippi after the fall of Vicksburg and Port Hudson. Children, the elderly, and the sick were unemployable and were cared for at the expense of the federal government with some help from northern charitable organizations. There were many able-bodied men and women, however, who fell into none of these categories. Efforts were made to return them to plantation labor, the work they knew best.[62]

Land was available. Many, if not most, of the larger planters along the Louisiana side of the Mississippi had abandoned their lands and fled westward as the Union army advanced. Before the end of 1862, freedmen were paid twelve and a half cents per pound for picking and ginning cotton found in the fields. Citizens who had remained on their lands could get their cotton picked and ginned on the same terms. The returns from abandoned cotton were credited to the federal government, presumably in recompense for the expense of caring for the freedmen and their families.[63] In 1863 this system was aban-

Richard Bryant Drake, "The American Missionary Association and the Southern Negro, 1861–1868" (Ph.D. dissertation, Emory University, 1959), 14.

61 Bell I. Wiley, "Vicissitudes of Early Reconstruction Farming in the Lower Mississippi Valley," *Journal of Southern History,* III (November, 1937), 445; New Orleans *Daily Picayune,* February 4, 1864; Harrington, *Fighting Politician,* 112–13.

62 Eaton, *Grant, Lincoln and the Freedmen,* 132–33.

63 Dorothy Lois Ellis, "The Transition from Slave Labor to Free Labor with Special Reference to Louisiana" (M.A. thesis, Louisiana State University, 1932), 9–10.

doned and the freedmen on plantations were expected to make arrangements with owners or lessees.

Abandoned plantations were offered for lease, and northerners hurried southward to take advantage of what they expected to be a quick bonanza. A few Negroes were allowed to cultivate land on their own account, but these were usually small tracts. Some thrifty blacks leased land cooperatively in Carroll Parish in 1863, but there is no record of whether they did well or poorly. Others, who leased land near Helena, Arkansas, made substantial profits. Most of the plantations, however, were let to northern speculators.[64]

General Thomas' plan certainly afforded lessees a good opportunity to make money. The only rent required was two dollars per bale for cotton produced. Any equipment found on the plantation was to be used, and the lessees, insofar as possible, were to be provided with work stock from confiscated horses and mules. They were obligated to feed and provide shelter for the Negroes assigned to them, but the wages set were very low, from $2.50 to $5.00 per month. From this pittance the cost of clothing was to be deducted, and the hands were to be docked for any time missed from work.[65] This plan did not produce happy working conditions. The lessees did not hesitate to take advantage of their laborers. One observer wrote: "The majority . . . were unprincipled men. They had as little regard for the rights of the Negro as the most brutal slaveholder. . . . Some . . . made open boasts of having swindled the Negroes out of their summer's wages."[66]

This system of leasing was severely criticized. Therefore, in the winter of 1863–1864, control of plantation leasing passed, at least nominally, from the War Department to the Treasury Department. The army did not gracefully surrender control of the plantations along the Mississippi River. Corruption which already existed was not corrected, and there is some evidence that it grew worse. The wage scale set by the Treasury was unrealistically high, which encouraged cheating. One northerner reported that a Negro still could not "gain redress for wrongs committed by the lessees. . . . The provost marshals and

64 *Ibid.*, 17.
65 Wharton, *The Negro in Mississippi*, 32–33; DuBois, *Black Reconstruction*, 75–76; Ellis, "The Transition from Slave Labor to Free Labor," 22.
66 Thomas W. Knox, *Camp Fire and Cotton Field* (New York, 1865), 316, quoted in Wiley, "Vicissitudes of Early Reconstruction Farming," 442.

lessees are linked together in a scheme to defraud the Negro."[67] In fact, although it is difficult to sympathize with the speculators who leased the plantations, both they and the blacks were victims of bureaucratic infighting between the War and Treasury Departments.[68]

After the passage of a century it is difficult to say whether plantations which the army could not protect were leased, or whether the army had little interest in protecting plantations leased by the Treasury.[69] But there can be no doubt of the results. In the fall of 1863 a certain James Douglas, claiming to be the agent of the plantation owners, gathered all the cotton in the neighborhood of Lake St. Joseph. Many lessees left, and those who remained were in danger of life and limb. A Mr. Allen of Illinois "was stripped naked and chased through a field grown up with cockle burrs, after which . . . he was shot by guerrillas and buried by Negroes."[70] Some blacks were carried away, others chased into the swamps, and still others butchered. One of the more fortunate lessees was captured and taken to Brownsville, Texas, where he was released to make his way home as best he could.[71] Overall, the experience gained in north Louisiana may have been useful in some respects, but it brought little profit to the lessees, little credit to the federal government, and a great deal of suffering to freedmen victimized by men and circumstances.

In the Department of the Gulf the number of blacks gathered at and about New Orleans was so great that even though many of them were employed, the cost of feeding the indigent rose to sixty thousand dollars per month.[72] At the same time, most plantations in the occupied zone had an inadequate labor force. A letter to Banks in August, 1863, stated: "Our slaves have been rendered valueless. . . . They must be clothed and fed. . . . They should be made to earn their own livelihood."[73] Relatively few planters about New Orleans had abandoned

---

67 Quoted in Wiley, "Vicissitudes of Early Reconstruction Farming," 444.
68 Wharton, *The Negro in Mississippi*, 36–38.
69 *Ibid.*, 37; Eaton, *Grant, Lincoln and the Freedmen*, 147–48.
70 Alexander Winchell to Zachariah Chandler, May 2, 1864, in Martha M. Bigelow (ed.), "Plantation Lessee Problems in 1864," *Journal of Southern History*, XXVII (August, 1961), 363–64.
71 *Ibid.*, 359; Ellis, "The Transition from Slave Labor to Free Labor," 15–16.
72 Bentley, *The Freedmen's Bureau*, 23–24.
73 Jacob Barker to N. P. Banks, August 3, 1863, in "Investigator," *The Rebellion: Its Consequences and the Congressional Committee Denominated the Reconstruction Committee with Their Action* (New Orleans, 1866), 179.

their lands, but with inadequate labor, they could produce but little. Near New Iberia guards were placed at the Weeks and McCarty plantations in the spring of 1863: "Much alarm and confusion in the neighborhood from Yankie straglers [*sic*] and marauding Negroes."[74] Planters were eager to employ hands if they could get them. Banks was eager to get plantations back into production and Negroes back to work. Later Banks was to say that the only way really to supplant slavery and prepare states for permanent restoration was to give land to the freedmen, but in early 1863 he had to deal with a condition rather than a theory. As a first step he sent a group of well-educated free men of color into the countryside to see what the freedmen wanted.[75]

The desires expressed by the plantation Negroes reveal a great deal about the life they had lived under slavery. According to Banks, their first request was that families should not be separated, "second, that they should not be flogged; third that their children should be educated; fourth that they should not be compelled to labor where they had been abused; and fifth that they should be paid reasonable wages for their work. Not one of them ever suggested that he did not expect to work."[76] Subsequent developments revealed that the general was somewhat overoptimistic about the attitude of some of the blacks.

On January 29, 1864, Banks issued his General Order Number 23 which deserves attention as an attempt to solve the labor problem created by the end of slavery. It declared that "labor is a public duty, and idleness and vagrancy a crime." Planters and laborers were instructed to make contracts, and when such a contract had been made, continuous service, discipline, "and perfect subordination shall be enforced on the part of the Negroes, by the officers of the government." In return the blacks were to receive "just treatment, healthy rations, comfortable clothing, quarters, fuel, medical attention, and wages." The rate of wages for various categories of laborers was set; it was far more generous then the original scale set by the army

---

74 Bayside Plantation Records, 1860–1866, Vol. II, May 1, 1863, Southern Historical Collection, University of North Carolina; see also E. W. Burbank to A. Roselius, October 3, 1863 in André Family Papers.

75 Banks, *Emancipated Labor*, 6–7, 18; Ficklen, *History of Reconstruction in Louisiana*, 130–31; Wesley, *Negro Labor in the United States*, 97.

76 Banks, *Emancipated Labor*, 7.

in northeastern Louisiana. Freedmen could decide for whom they wished to work, but once an agreement was reached, they were bound for the remainder of the year. For the benefit of the blacks, the order required that they be allowed to cultivate foodstuffs on small private plots and that schools should be provided for their children under twelve years of age. Some other provisions of the order might have been taken from the prewar slave code. Hands could move from one plantation to another only under regulations set by the provost marshal, and all persons were forbidden to purchase goods from plantation hands or to sell intoxicants to them.[77]

Included in Banks's order were instructions to the quartermaster of the department to put unemployed blacks to work on abandoned plantations. Presumably this was the genesis of the "home colonies," of which more will be said later. Banks also established the Free Labor Bank in New Orleans, which was the first bank established for Negroes only. Negro soldiers and plantation laborers were encouraged to make deposits.[78]

Obviously, Banks's labor regulations were a continuation of the efforts begun by Butler. Also, they were a precedent for the notorious Black Codes later enacted by the legislatures of Louisiana and several other southern states. The "Bureau of Free Labor" served as the foundation upon which the Freedmen's Bureau was erected in Louisiana. General Banks, who appointed the Reverend Thomas M. Conway to head the bureau, was proud of his handiwork which, he believed, demonstrated that southern agriculture could once more be productive, but without slavery.[79]

Apparently Banks was one of the few persons in the nation who was pleased with his labor regulations. Planters preferred General Order Number 23 to outright confiscation, but in early 1864 they still hoped

77 New Orleans *Daily Picayune*, February 4, 1864; see also Williams, *Lincoln and the Radicals*, 274–76; Alice Douglas Daspit, "The Governors' Messages of Louisiana, 1860–1900" (M.A. thesis, Louisiana State University, 1932), 53; Harrington, *Fighting Politician*, 105–106.

78 Williams, *Lincoln and the Radicals*, 275–76; Walter L. Fleming, *The Freedmen's Savings Bank: A Chapter in the Economic History of the Negro Race* (Chapel Hill, 1927), 20.

79 Engelsmen, "Freedmen's Bureau in Louisiana," 157–58; White, *Freedmen's Bureau in Louisiana*, 103–104; Banks, *Emancipated Labor*, 8; Roland Paul Constantin, "The Louisiana 'Black Code' Legislation of 1865" (M.A. thesis, Louisiana State University, 1956), 20–22.

to preserve slavery, and they resented the necessity for paying wages. The Negroes preferred the new arrangement to slavery, but they objected to being compelled to remain on a single plantation for a whole year. In truth, they found too little difference between this new freedom and slavery. Although they received wages for their plantation work, they were well aware that wages in New Orleans were higher. The former free people of color, who were coming to realize more and more that their own future was tied to that of the freedmen, came to be strongly opposed to Banks's labor regulations. They advocated confiscation of the plantations and the division of land in small plots among the freedmen.[80]

As military commander of an occupied area, Banks did not have to pay too much attention to local opposition. But he did have to take notice when opposition to his plan for Negro labor became strong in the North. This was brought about in part by Louisiana Radicals who denounced Banks to their northern correspondents, but Treasury agents, often indistinguishable from the Radicals, were mainly responsible. They were opposed to Banks and, to a considerable degree, to Lincoln. It seemed to many northerners, hearing but one side of the story, that Banks was for all practical purposes restoring slavery. Secretary of the Treasury Salmon P. Chase sought to put his own set of labor regulations into effect in Louisiana, but this Banks ignored, and his provost marshals continued to control plantation labor in the Department of the Gulf. Even so, opposition was strong enough that Banks prepared and published a defense of his actions which he entitled *Emancipated Labor in Louisiana*. This was merely one episode in a long battle between Banks and the Radicals.[81]

At the end of 1863, Banks was becoming more and more receptive to the idea of limited Negro suffrage. Whether he came to his conclusion on his own or was pushed into it by Lincoln is difficult to say. As noted earlier, the free men of color of New Orleans had petitioned Governor Shepley for the vote and, after the failure of an appeal to Banks, had sent a delegation to call upon Lincoln. Probably these cul-

---

80 DuBois, *Black Reconstruction*, 105–106; New Orleans *Tribune*, September 24, 1864; Harrington, *Fighting Politician*, 105–106; Banks, *Emancipated Labor*, 7–8.
81 Bentley, *The Freedmen's Bureau*, 27, 43; Constantin, "Louisiana Black Code," 20–22; Banks, *Emancipated Labor, passim*; Carl Sandburg, *Abraham Lincoln: The War Years* (New York, 1939), III, 16–17.

tured men, white to all appearance, made an impression on the president, despite the fact that he advocated colonization as a solution to the race problem in America. At any rate, Banks toyed with the idea of permitting some Negroes (by Louisiana definition) to vote in the election of February 22, 1864, by classifying as white any person who had more white than Negro blood. This idea was not carried through. Southerners—and many northerners—were opposed to giving the vote to any Negroes at all. Only ultra-Radicals as early as 1864 were thinking of giving the vote to blacks on the same basis as whites. In New Orleans, the educated Negroes objected to dividing the population into white, "whitewashed," and black categories. W. E. B. Du-Bois suggests that if the first attempt at Reconstruction had taken place anywhere other than in Louisiana, "It is possible that the whole question of Negro suffrage would not have been raised then or perhaps for many years after."[82] But in Louisiana there existed a sizable group of free Negroes as qualified by intelligence, property holding, and service to the Union to vote as any other men in the country. Thus Negro suffrage would become a Radical policy, and Lincoln would recommend limited black suffrage to Governor Hahn. From these hesitant beginnings to the Fifteenth Amendment, the path is fairly clear.[83]

5

Once Banks had seen to the establishment of a state administration for Louisiana, he turned militarily to preparations for his ill-fated Red River campaign, politically to the election of delegates to a constitutional convention which, it was hoped, would make possible Louisiana's complete restoration to the Union. In the meantime the white people of New Orleans and occupied Louisiana were attempting to live as normally as possible under abnormal circumstances.

The columns of New Orleans newspapers published during 1863 and 1864 demonstrate that there was a revival of economic activity

82 DuBois, *Black Reconstruction*, 153.
83 *Ibid.*, 154; New Orleans *Times*, November 6, 1863, cited in Caskey, *Secession and Restoration*, 90; Harrington, *Fighting Politician*, 114–16; Franklin, *Reconstruction After the Civil War*, 23; F. B. Harris, "Henry Clay Warmoth," 525; Ficklen, *History of Reconstruction in Louisiana*, 64; Uzee, "Republican Politics in Louisiana," 13; Frazier, *The Negro in the United States*, 123.

and, seemingly, of popular morale. The pay of Union troops no doubt contributed to the city's economy, as did the inflation which accompanied the war. During 1863 it was necessary for the authorities to fix the price of bread according to the price of flour; but the advertising columns of newspapers offered cigars, liquors, restaurant fare, coffee, groceries, and haberdashery. One might conclude from a careful perusal of these advertisements that tobacconists and money-changers provided the chief forms of business activity until mid-1864. Regularly scheduled travel north was possible up the Mississippi and Ohio rivers and then to Chicago by way of the Illinois Central Railroad by the spring of 1864, and regular steamboat service to the Lafourche region was offered in February of that year.[84]

By twentieth-century standards, the occupation was a remarkably mild one. The theater in New Orleans had its regular seasons. Stores offered for sale a biography of Stonewall Jackson, official reports of the Confederate government, and Pollard's *Southern History of the War.* One item which apparently sold well was a portrait of New Orleans' own hero, General Pierre Gustave Toutant Beauregard. Mardi Gras may have been less exuberant in 1864 than in prewar years, but it was a gay occasion nonetheless. And in March of 1864 convivial hearts were gladdened by the arrival from Boston of a cargo of 812 tons of ice, the first shipment of the year.[85]

6

On March 11, 1864, Banks called for the election of delegates to a convention, to meet on March 28, to amend and revise the constitution of Louisiana. Thus he continued the fiction that the constitution of 1852 was still in effect. All adult white male citizens who had been in Louisiana one year, in the parish of residence for six months, and who had taken the amnesty oath prescribed by President Lincoln were eligible to vote. A total of 150 delegates was to be elected, assuming that elections would be held in each of the forty-eight parishes. It was, of course, unrealistic to assume that all the parishes

---

84 Caldwell, *Banking History of Louisiana,* New Orleans *Daily Picayune,* July–October, 1863; January 17, February 3, May 1, 1864.
85 New Orleans *Daily Picayune,* January–March, 1864.

would participate, but Banks was launching his Red River campaign with high hopes of bringing many additional parishes under Union control, and he expected these to then elect delegates.[86]

In one respect the election of March, 1864, completely ignored the constitution of 1852. That document had provided that legislative representation should be on the basis of total population, giving the plantation parishes influence out of all proportion to their white population. New Orleans, under this arrangement, had less power than it would have had on a voting population basis. Banks ordered that representation in the convention be based upon white population only, as counted in the census of 1860. Each parish was to elect one delegate for approximately two thousand white inhabitants.[87]

The election of delegates to the convention seems to have aroused only moderate interest. When seats were contested moderate "Free-State" men on the Hahn model were opposed by men of more Radical views or by Conservative Unionists. The Conservative Unionists, with representation based upon white population and many of the plantation parishes unrepresented, could elect some delegates, but they had no chance of controlling the convention. Radicals had even less chance, because they really had no voting constituency. The Conservative Unionist John A. Rozier was highly critical because the constitution of 1852 was not being followed to the letter; the Radical Thomas J. Durant condemned the convention because Banks clung to the fiction that he was observing the constitution of 1852. One man of Radical sympathies wrote in his diary on election day: "The way things are going is quite disheartening to the true Union people. . . . Oh, for the days of 'beast' Butler, when a man had to present good certificates of loyalty."[88]

The number of votes cast was far less than had been cast for state

86 *Ibid.*, March 12, 27, 1864; Ficklen, *History of Reconstruction in Louisiana*, 67–68; Caskey, *Secession and Restoration*, 116; Cox, *Three Decades of Federal Legislation*, 428.

87 New Orleans *Daily Picayune*, March 12, 1864; Ficklen, *History of Reconstruction in Louisiana*, 67.

88 Kenneth E. Shrewmaker and Andrew K. Prinz (eds.), "A Yankee in Louisiana: Selections from the Diary and Correspondence of Henry R. Gardner, 1862–1866," *Louisiana History*, V (Summer, 1964), 291; Caskey, *Secession and Restoration*, 116–17.

officials in February. A completely accurate count was never made, but the total was more than 6,000 and less than 6,500, which must have been a disappointment to Banks. Had he not been so preoccupied with his Red River campaign, he might have seen to it that more votes were cast. The small turnout and the trend of the vote cast makes it obvious that a goodly number of Conservative Unionists and Radicals did not vote. Of the nineteen parishes electing delegates, all except Concordia, Madison, and Avoyelles were in the area long controlled by Federal arms. It was reported that delegates were elected also in Natchitoches, St. Landry, Winn, and Catahoula parishes, but these did not participate. The vast majority of those present, sixty-three, were from New Orleans, with thirty-five from other parishes. The convention came together on April 6, 1864, and in a few days it was to hear of Banks's defeat at Mansfield.[89]

The delegates to this convention were not well-known men. Only a few names stand out, whether as a result of previous or subsequent actions. From the Fourth District of Orleans Parish came R. King Cutler and Judge Edward H. Durell, Durell being elected president of the convention. From Orleans' Fifth District came Edmund Abell, the convention voice of antebellum Louisiana. Best known of all the delegates was Christian Roselius, the most noted attorney in Louisiana, who represented Jefferson Parish until his resignation from the convention.[90]

The constitution adopted by these delegates demonstrates that the delegates knew what they wanted and that, unless pressured by the military, they knew how to put their ideas into fundamental law. They did not represent the dominant class of Louisiana, the merchant-planter oligarchy; they did represent working-class whites and, to a lesser degree, yeoman farmers. They were inexperienced in parliamentary procedures; they were, in many cases, boorish when ex-

---

89 Ficklen, *History of Reconstruction in Louisiana*, 67–68; New Orleans *Daily Picayune*, April 7, 1864; Cox, *Three Decades of Federal Legislation*, 428; Caskey, *Secession and Restoration*, 117–18; Banks, *The Reconstruction of States*, 12–13, 18–23; F. B. Harris, "Henry Clay Warmoth," 526–27.

90 *Journal of the Convention for the Revision and Amendment of the Constitution of Louisiana* (New Orleans, 1864), *passim*; Lowrey, "James Madison Wells," 1,018; Kendall, *History of New Orleans*, I, 291.

amined from aristocratic elevations; and they were greedy for the pay and perquisites which went with their role as delegates. They were antislavery, but they were so because they were anti-Negro and antiplanter.

Naturally they were despised by the conservatives of the state, but the conservatives were not alone. A Radical wrote in his diary: "If I am not mistaken the time will come . . . when the acts of this assembly will be declared illegal and a new one will be called to do something else than drink and carouse."[91] On the other hand, Lieutenant Colonel Henry Clay Warmoth noted: "I was invited to meet the president and members of the Constitutional Convention at General Banks' House. . . . Very agreeable company and some of them are very sensible men."[92]

The delegates were very much aware that great areas of the state were unrepresented in their deliberations. For this reason they adopted a rule that seventy-six members, a majority of the total representation originally planned, should constitute a quorum. Since only ninety-eight delegates actually appeared, this meant that twenty-three malcontents could prevent the carrying on of business. In practice, a dozen men could usually halt proceedings simply by failing to attend. The situation was made worse in the early days of the convention when, objecting to a decision which required delegates to take a loyalty oath even if they had done so earlier, Christian Roselius and R. S. Abbott resigned. They were followed in time by three other delegates. Most, if not all, of these empty chairs were eventually filled, but while they were empty it was that much more difficult to obtain a quorum.[93]

In the spring and early summer of 1864, the Civil War was far from over. Grant's offensive in the east was to meet with bloody repulses; no one yet knew how successful Sherman's Georgia campaign would

91 Shrewmaker and Prinz (eds.), "A Yankee in Louisiana," 291–92.
92 Warmoth Diary, May 31, 1864, see also New Orleans *Daily Picayune*, April 7, 10, 30, 1864; Shugg, *Origins of Class Struggle in Louisiana*, 203, 206–207; Caskey, *Secession and Restoration*, 120–21; Highsmith, "Louisiana During Reconstruction," 98–100; Harrington, *Fighting Politician*, 147–48.
93 New Orleans *Daily Picayune*, April 10, 30, 1864; Caskey, *Secession and Restoration*, 120; *Journal of the Convention, 1864, passim.*

be; and Banks had been soundly defeated on the Red River. Therefore it was not nearly so unrealistic as it might seem at first glance for some members of the convention of 1864 to seek compensation, if not for all emancipated slaves, at least for those owned by loyal Unionists. Edmund Abell was the chief spokesman for all those opposing uncompensated emancipation. He resorted to all the old proslavery arguments in his pleas, asserting that emancipation would be detrimental to the Negro, making him prey to death, disease, and dissipation, with cruel exploiters substituted for humane masters. Abell then went on to tell the delegates that complete emancipation would either leave 300,000 blacks to compete with the white labor of Louisiana or bring on a system of peonage. Probably most delegates had no idea how accurate his prophecy of peonage was, but Negrophobia struck a sympathetic chord in the convention. Even though reminded that Negro troops were at that moment defending the gathering, one delegate hoped that all blacks could be expelled from American soil. Another would have been satisfied with sending all of them to Massachusetts, the home of the abolitionists. A more reasonable suggestion was that loyal slaveholders be compensated by the seizure of the property of rebels. In the final analysis, the convention voted to declare slavery illegal without any provision for compensation, but to memorialize Congress to compensate loyal owners.[94]

While the convention sat, a case in court brought the status of former slaves to the fore. A Negro brought suit before Judge D. W. Hamlin of the Third District Court of Appeals, and Judge Hamlin rejected the suit on the grounds that the plaintiff, who was among those excepted by the Emancipation Proclamation, was still a slave and therefore could not sue. The convention responded with a resolution that any judicial decision recognizing slavery was contrary to the fundamental law of Louisiana. Hahn, acting as military governor, removed Hamlin, whereupon Judge Rufus K. Howell resigned in protest. The legal question was soon rendered academic when the convention abolished slavery in the state, but since both Howell and

94 *Journal of the Convention, 1864, passim*; Caskey, *Secession and Restoration*, 124–25, 131; Ficklen, *History of Reconstruction in Louisiana*, 70–71, 75; *House Reports*, 39th Cong., 1st Sess., No. 30, p. 134; New Orleans *Daily Picayune*, April 28, May 10, 1864; Shugg, *Origins of Class Struggle in Louisiana*, 205–206.

Hamlin were strong loyalists, this incident demonstrated the extent of proslavery sentiment among Unionists.[95]

The members of the constitutional convention of 1864 had no intention of giving the vote to any Negro. This was one matter on which conservatives, moderate Unionists, and at this time the Radicals could agree. Louisiana Radicals felt that the time was not ripe for Negro suffrage, and they probably doubted that it ever would be. The moderates represented the laboring class which was the most anti-Negro part of the population. The conservatives were probably not so racist as the moderates, but they were well aware that, despite the propertied free Negro class in New Orleans, most Negro voters would be poor voters. The conservatives were as opposed to more votes for the poor as they were to enfranchisement of "inferior" Negroes. By this time the free men of color of the city, despairing of obtaining the suffrage for themselves alone, had come out boldly for equal voting for all blacks. Also, as previously noted, they had reached President Lincoln with their arguments. But the convention, on May 19, adopted a resolution offered by Abell which prohibited the legislature under the new constitution from ever granting suffrage to any free Negroes whatsoever.[96]

Banks reacted to this. Even before the election, Lincoln had written a carefully worded letter to Hahn. Had the advice in this letter, which suggested that very intelligent Negroes and veterans of the Union army be granted the franchise, been followed, it is very possible that so-called "Black Reconstruction" could have been avoided. Lincoln was well aware that the exclusion from the franchise of all Louisiana Negroes would strengthen the Radical faction in his party. All the pressure Banks applied, however, could not persuade the convention to enfranchise Negroes. Grudgingly it did provide that the

95 Caskey, *Secession and Restoration*, 134; Ficklen, *History of Reconstruction in Louisiana*, 73–74.
96 DuBois, *Black Reconstruction*, 223; Caskey, *Secession and Restoration*, 128–30; New Orleans *Daily Picayune*, May 11, 1864; T. Harry Williams, *Romance and Realism in Southern Politics* (Baton Rouge, 1966), 23; Donald E. Everett, "Demands of the New Orleans Free Colored Population for Political Equality, 1862–1865," *Louisiana Historical Quarterly*, XXVII (January, 1944), 43–64; Shugg, *Origins of Class Struggle in Louisiana*, 206–207; Ficklen, *History of Reconstruction in Louisiana*, 71–72.

legislature could enlarge the franchise in the future, but it was a safe assumption that a legislature elected by white Louisianians would never do so.[97]

Education for Negroes was another topic which aroused fierce debate in the convention of 1864. The delegates obviously did not favor any action at all to provide schools for black children. A resolution of Abell's that Banks's appointment of a board of education was unconstitutional was adopted by a vote of seventy-two to nine. This too brought a reaction from Banks; the convention under pressure from the general approved a dual system of public schools, those for whites financed by taxes on whites, those for blacks by taxes on blacks. Probably prodded by Banks once more, the delegates finally adopted a requirement that public schools, supported by general taxation, be made available for all children. It was assumed by all, Banks included, that black and white children would attend separate schools.[98]

The convention wasted a great deal of time. Often a quorum was not on hand, and when it was, many hours were devoted to minor matters, such as criticizing the expense involved in Governor Hahn's inauguration. The delegates also spent much time discussing the repeal of Louisiana's ordinance of secession. Since this was something that obviously had to be done, it is difficult to understand the reason for so much discussion, unless the delegates were prolonging their per diem. It was not until the closing days that secession was declared null and void. Another incident occurred when the editor of the New Orleans *Times*, Thomas P. May, wrote that members had accused Judge Durell of being drunk and called him a damned fool. May was called before the convention, where R. King Cutler urged that he be sent to jail: "Let him know that he lives in a land of liberty!"[99] May was ordered to prison for ten days, but Banks set him free. In reading the debates of the convention, one is struck by the fact that much

---

97 Lincoln to Michael Hahn, March 13, 1864, in Walter L. Fleming (ed.), *Documentary History of Reconstruction, Political, Social, Religious, Educational and Industrial, 1865 to the Present Time* (Gloucester, Mass., 1960), I, 112; Coulter, *The South During Reconstruction*, 62; Kenneth M. Stampp, *The Era of Reconstruction 1865–1877* (New York, 1967), 47.

98 *Debates in the Convention for the Revision and Amendment of the Constitution of the State of Louisiana* (New Orleans, 1864), *passim*; Ficklen, *History of Reconstruction in Louisiana*, 74–76; Caskey, *Secession and Restoration*, 126–27.

99 Quoted in Ficklen, *History of Reconstruction in Louisiana*, 78.

oratory was expended on the organization of the state's courts, more on establishment of maximum hours and minimum wages. The last two subjects received as much attention as slavery, suffrage, or education.[100]

A reading of the debates and the newspaper accounts of the convention of 1864 can lead to the impression that the delegates were really not eager to establish a state government. After the Federal defeat and retreat from Mansfield and Pleasant Hill, some of them could not return home. Probably all of them were aware that they did not represent a majority of the people of the state. Their sense of frustration crops out in the debates. One delegate complained: "When there is anything to do you adjourn; when there is nothing to do, you stay." Another said, "Even now what little protection we have is due to the Federal armies." A third averred: "The time has not come to restore civil government . . . for if you do the streets of this city will run red with blood. . . . I don't believe we could sit here two hours and a half if the military were withdrawn." A fourth delegate had almost reached a frenzy when he announced that it was his program for "the copperheads, rattlesnakes, and rebels" to "go down to hell together."[101]

It is significant that the extravagance and corruption for which Louisiana Reconstruction is noted did not begin in 1868 with Radical Reconstruction. The convention of 1864 may not quite have been "a disgrace to the government which fostered it,"[102] but it was not too different from conventions and legislatures which came later. The members voted themselves ten dollars per diem, a large sum in 1864, and this, plus the salaries of the clerks, came to more than $150,000. Total expenses were $346,000, including $156,000 for printing the journals and debates, for which the historian can be grateful, and $9,400 for liquor and cigars, for which the delegates were no doubt grateful. Critical comments were not limited to pro-Confederate Louisianians. A northerner stated that at adjournment Durell was too drunk to preside. "Common state productions were not good enough

---

100 *Debates in the Convention, 1864*, passim; Ficklen, *History of Reconstruction in Louisiana*, 77–79; Caskey, *Secession and Restoration*, 126–27.
101 *Debates in the Convention, 1864*, 359, 414, 600; New Orleans *Daily Picayune*, April–July, 1864.
102 Lowrey, "James Madison Wells," 1,019.

for this 'assembly of notables.' They must have the best of imported wines, liquors, and cigars. . . . They adjourned when there was nothing more to steal."[103] This criticism was overly severe, but it does help make it clear that corruption in Louisiana government did not begin in 1868.[104] For that matter, it was an old, old story by 1864.

The constitution drawn up by the convention of 1864 was to last only four years. It was never really accepted as legitimate. For more than a year after its adoption, Louisiana was under strict military rule and state government was but a pretense. Later the constitution was called invalid by conservatives who wanted to restore the constitution of 1852. Finally the document was discarded by the Radicals after the Reconstruction Acts of 1867 had restored military rule. Yet it was a landmark in Louisiana constitutional history and deserves some detailed examination.

In the first place, it definitely repudiated the constitution of 1852. That organic law had been a Whig instrument. In 1852, as Roger Shugg says, "The delegates were simply voting themselves favors. Among the members were to be found directors and large stockholders of . . . railways, who were seeking state aid. . . . It was a speculator's convention. They knew what they wanted and by changing the constitution they were able to get it from the legislature."[105]

In comparing the instruments of 1852 and 1864, it should first be noted that the latter abolished slavery in Louisiana. This was a result of war more than of will, but it was a radical change. The powers of the governor remained largely the same, as did the organization of the judicial system. However, under the constitution of 1852, judges were elected and could be removed only by impeachment or by address of three-fourths of the members of the legislature. Under the instrument of 1864, judges were appointed by the governor and could be removed by him on address of a majority of the elected members of the legislature.[106]

103 Shrewmaker and Prinz (eds.), "Yankee in Louisiana," 291–92.
104 Highsmith, "Louisiana During Reconstruction," 104; DuBois, *Black Reconstruction,* 158; Franklin, *Reconstruction After the Civil War,* 47–48; Caskey, *Secession and Restoration,* 136–37.
105 Roger Wallace Shugg, "Suffrage and Representation in Ante-Bellum Louisiana," *Louisiana Historical Quarterly,* XIX (April, 1936), 401.
106 Francis Newton Thorpe (ed.), *The Federal and State Constitutions: Colonial Charters and Other Organic Laws of the States, Territories, and Colonies Now or*

In 1852, as noted earlier, representation in the legislature was based upon total population. In addition there was a provision, designed to limit the power of New Orleans, that one parish could not have more than five out of thirty-two senators. In 1864, representation was based upon qualified electors, and one parish could have as many as nine out of thirty-six senators. Under both constitutions, representatives were elected to two-year terms, senators to staggered four-year terms. Another provision of 1864 which encouraged working-class representation in the legislature was the increase of legislative per diem from four to eight dollars per day.[107]

Among other notable provisions of the constitution of 1864 were such items as the requirement that all voters be registered, a provision for a graduated income tax, and the clause which permitted the legislature to extend suffrage to freedmen. This last provision, although most unwillingly adopted, possibly could have served as a means for the gradual enfranchisement of Louisiana Negroes, though this is improbable. Also of importance was the provision for the education at state expense of both white and Negro children.[108]

Thus the constitution of 1864 was certainly more than "a revised and amended copy of the Constitution of 1852,"[109] as it was called by John Rose Ficklen. Roger Shugg, author of the classic *Origins of Class Struggle in Louisiana*, called it "an extraordinary document which . . . remedied the chief grievances of which farmers and laborers complained before secession."[110] The most radical step, considering the era, was the establishment of minimum wages and maximum hours for artisans. This was in response to a petition signed by almost fifteen hundred laborers, which said in part: "The past recurs to our vivid memory, when the capitalist could demand and exact from us ten to twelve hours a day devoted to toil . . . [and that] they frequently reserved for the white that [work] which was detrimental to the black."[111] Thus the constitution of 1864 was definitely a reform con-

---

Heretofore Forming the United States of America (Washington, D.C., 1909), III, 1,415–21, 1,436–40.
107 *Ibid.*, 1,412–15, 1,430–35.
108 *Ibid.*, 1,429–45.
109 Ficklen, *History of Reconstruction in Louisiana*, 79.
110 Shugg, *Origins of Class Struggle in Louisiana*, 203.
111 Quoted *ibid.*, 207–208.

stitution. Sadly, the reforms it made were ones which a majority of white Louisianians would not willingly retain once the Civil War was over, and it neglected one reform, Negro suffrage, which a victorious North was going to demand.

Before adjourning, the convention adopted a resolution making it possible for the body's president to call it back into session. "It shall also in that case call upon the proper officers of the state to cause elections to be held to fill any vacancies that may exist in parishes where the same may be practicable." [112] Apparently this resolution was intended to permit reconvening the delegates in case the voters refused to ratify the constitution, but its vagueness was to lead to tragic consequences two years later.

The convention of 1864 adjourned on July 23, 1864. An election to ratify the constitution and to elect a legislature was set for September 5, 1864. In the meantime, President Lincoln had pocket-vetoed the Wade-Davis Bill, so the completion of the restoration of Louisiana was more urgent than before. Once more Banks used all his authority and prestige to get out the vote, encouraging even those who opposed the constitution to cast ballots, thus increasing the total vote cast. Twenty parishes voted, and only Pointe Coupee, Plaquemines, and St. Bernard voted against ratification. Overall, the vote was 6,836 for, 1,566 against, far more than 10 percent of the fifty thousand votes cast in the presidential election of 1860. Insofar as the people of occupied Louisiana and General Banks could effect it, Louisiana was back in the Union. In reality, restoration was far from accomplished. [113]

112 Quoted in Caskey, *Secession and Restoration,* 138.
113 Capers, *Occupied City,* 139–40; Mordell (comp.), *Selected Essays by Gideon Welles,* 170; Stampp, *The Era of Reconstruction,* 31–32; New Orleans *Daily Picayune,* July 24, September 9, 1864; Harrington, *Fighting Politician,* 149; Ficklen, *History of Reconstruction in Louisiana,* 80–81; Caskey, *Secession and Restoration,* 139–40; Howard, *Political Tendencies in Louisiana,* 119.

III   *Louisiana Under the Constitution of 1864*

AT THE SAME TIME they ratified the constitution of 1864, the voters of occupied Louisiana elected members of the state legislature and representatives to the lower house of the United States Congress. The only overt opposition came from the Negro-edited New Orleans *Tribune*, which referred to "the vain and fruitless effort now being made to hoist the new constitution upon the unwilling people of Louisiana, while martial law is the fundamental law of the state."[1] Despite the *Tribune*, the moderate Free-State faction was to carry the day. Henry Clay Warmoth urged loyalist unity upon J. Q. A. Fellows and in this cause dined with conservative Christian Roselius; the evening was such a pleasant experience that Warmoth recorded in his diary: "Returned . . . at eleven o'clock and all tight but me and I not very sober, not tight though."[2]

In the congressional elections there were only two contests. In the First District M. F. Bonzano was opposed by the very conservative Edmund Abell, and in the Second District the Radical Dr. A. P. Dostie opposed A. P. Field. The conservatives, who were to rejoice when Dostie was murdered two years later, praised him during this cam-

1 New Orleans *Tribune*, September 3, 1864.
2 Warmoth Diary, August 14, 17, 1864.

paign because they hated Field more. However, Field was elected, as was Bonzano. Three other Free-Staters elected to Congress were W. D. Mann in the Third District, T. M. Wells in the Fourth, and R. M. Taliaferro in the Fifth. None of these gentlemen, of course, was to ever sit in Congress. The state legislature elected at this time was composed of eighty-six representatives, forty-four of whom were from Orleans Parish, and a senate of twenty-nine men. Nine of the senators represented Orleans Parish, but two of them were shared by St. Bernard and Plaquemines parishes.[3]

The new legislature met on October 3, 1864. On October 5, it elected R. King Cutler and Charles Smith as United States senators to replace John Slidell and Judah P. Benjamin, respectively. Smith's term would run only until March, 1865, and when the legislature reconvened in January, 1865, Michael Hahn was elected to the full term. None of these men would ever be a United States senator, but Hahn's election made James Madison Wells governor of Louisiana. In the meantime, the presidential election of 1864 was held. The new legislature decided to name electors for Lincoln without a popular election. Since Lincoln had a majority without these votes, they were not counted. Perhaps if they had been needed they would have been used.[4]

The authority of the new state government was not great. Military courts continued to function, even in New Orleans, and outside the city the military provided almost all the government that existed. In New Orleans the police seem to have been as much racketeers as enforcers of the law. As for Baton Rouge, a resident wrote in February of 1865: "A few of the old citizens have got back but our Town is nothing more now than a Negro Village. . . . A great portion of the town that is left is thrown out in the commons as the fences are all burnt up, they even pull up the plank crossings of the corners of the streets and if one plank or paling starts all is gone."[5] In much of Loui-

---

3 New Orleans *Daily Picayune*, September 3, 15, 1864; New Orleans *Tribune*, August 18, 1864; Lowrey, "James Madison Wells," 1,020; Caskey, *Secession and Restoration*, 145, 156; James A. Payne to Kate E. Sterrett, September 18, 1864, in John D. Barnhart (ed.), "Reconstruction on the Lower Mississippi," *Mississippi Valley Historical Review*, XXI (December, 1934), 389.

4 New Orleans *Daily Picayune*, October 2, 1864, January 10, 1865; Caskey, *Secession and Restoration*, 149–50, 157–59; Lowrey, "James Madison Wells," 1,022–23.

5 Payne to Mrs. Sterrett, February 18, 1865, in Barnhart (ed.), "Reconstruction on

siana legal and effective local government was to be almost nonexistent for the next twelve years.

In the meantime Louisiana's United States senators and representatives–elect were attempting to take their seats in Congress. President Lincoln favored seating them, hoping to set a precedent under which the remainder of the Confederacy could be rapidly restored to the Union when fighting ended. A majority in each house of Congress was determined not to move so fast. One factor was that the end of slavery had outmoded the three-fifths clause of the United States Constitution, and therefore, under the president's plan, the southern states would be rewarded for rebellion with increased representation in Congress. Probably more important, however, was a feeling among many northern members of Congress that the southern people should publicly repent of the sin of rebellion and in some way atone for the devastation of war before being restored to fellowship in the Union. Louisiana's position as a petitioner was not improved when A. P. Field drew a knife and slightly wounded Pennsylvania representative William D. Kelley in a Washington restaurant.[6]

With help from the *Tribune* and such Louisiana Radicals as Durant and Warmoth, the Radicals in Congress set out to prevent the seating of Louisiana's representatives. The opponents of seating were not all Radicals. Included were men who opposed presidential reconstruction on constitutional grounds and others who did not believe that enough votes had been cast in Louisiana for the applicants to be truly representative. The Radicals, however, took the lead in opposition. It was Senator Charles Sumner who described the constitution of 1864 as "a mere seven-months abortion, begotten by the bayonet in criminal conjunction with the spirit of caste, and born before its time, rickety, unformed, unfinished—whose continued existence will be a burden, a reproach, and a wrong."[7] All the applicants were rejected, but the

the Lower Mississippi," 390–91; see also Cox, *Three Decades of Federal Legislation,* 428–29; Kendall, *History of New Orleans,* I, 298–99; New Orleans *Daily Picayune,* August–December, 1864, January–June, 1865.

6 New Orleans *Tribune,* February 3, 1865; Fawn M. Brodie, *Thaddeus Stevens: Scourge of the South* (New York, 1959), 210; Jay A. Sigler, "The Rise and Fall of the Three-Fifths Clause," *Mid-America,* XLVI (October, 1966), 275–77.

7 Quoted in Ficklen, *History of Reconstruction in Louisiana,* 92.

House of Representatives did pay the Washington expenses of Field and Bonzano.[8]

The legislature elected in 1864, which met in special session in October and then in regular session in January, 1865, was not a distinguished body. Among its positive actions, probably the most important was the ratification of the Thirteenth Amendment to the United States Constitution, which abolished slavery. There was some objection on the ground that "Congress and the President had no right to deprive citizens of . . . valuable property, especially without remuneration,"[9] and while ratification was being debated there was difficulty in maintaining a quorum for carrying on business. Almost certainly pressure from Governor Hahn and the military played a large part in obtaining prompt and affirmative action, completed on February 14, 1865. Louisiana's approval, like that of the other former Confederate states, was counted toward ratification, but the amendment had the support of enough northern states to be ratified without the South.[10]

This legislature continued a practice of the Confederate state government by granting an extension of the time for paying 1861–1863 state taxes to March 31, 1865. Another precedent was set when a group of entrepreneurs was granted authority to dig a canal from Vermilion Bay to the Sabine River, in return for which they were to be granted certain state-owned lands. The canal was never begun, and the promoters received no land, but the event was noteworthy as the first of scores of internal improvements acts passed by Louisiana legislators during Reconstruction.[11]

In October Governor Hahn recommended legislation to define the status of emancipated Negroes. A member of the lower house objected on the grounds that if the freedmen were free, they came under the

8 John G. Clark, "Radicals and Moderates on the Joint Committee on Reconstruction," *Mid-America*, XLV (April, 1963), 79–98; Williams, *Lincoln and the Radicals*, 324–25, 357–58; Cox, *Three Decades of Federal Legislation*, 342–43; Caskey, *Secession and Restoration*, 156–57.

9 Quoted in Caskey, *Secession and Restoration*, 148.

10 *Ibid.; Debates in the Senate of the State of Louisiana, Session of 1864–[1865]* (New Orleans, 1865), 155–57; New Orleans *Daily Picayune*, February 15, 1865; Burgess, *Reconstruction and the Constitution*, 55.

11 New Orleans *Daily Picayune*, December 2, 1864; *Acts Passed by the First General Assembly of Louisiana at Its First and Second Sessions, Held and Begun at the City of New Orleans on the 4th of October, 1864* (New Orleans, 1865), 136–40.

same laws as other free men. As a result, no action was taken at this time. On the other hand, a bill to abolish the slave code of 1855, although passed by the lower house, was not acted upon by the senate. A bill to legalize marriage between whites and blacks was decisively rejected. Not only was a bill to make elementary education compulsory defeated, but the debate revealed strong opposition to any publicly supported education. The legislature was so firmly opposed to Negro suffrage that when a petition was received asking that black veterans of the Union army be allowed to vote, it was not accepted and not even permitted to be read. One legislator expressed the sentiment of the majority on this matter when he said it would be time enough to consider Negro suffrage when it had been adopted by the free states of the North. "I am," he continued, "a native of Louisiana and when this state extends to Negroes the right of suffrage, I shall leave it forthwith and go to China."[12] At a more practical level, a bill to grant suffrage to persons of mixed blood who had served in the Union army, or who paid taxes of thirty dollars or more a year, or who were intellectually fitted for suffrage, was rejected in the senate by a decisive fifteen-to-five vote.[13]

Complaints against this legislature were numerous. One sin complained of was extravagance, since $35,000 was appropriated for the expense of the legislature, not including printing. The state auditor reported in 1865 that total receipts had amounted to $875,658 as compared to total expenditures of $1,162,623. In justice it must be noted that this was a small deficit as compared to some that came later. The legislature was also damned for its lack of decorum. The men elected in 1864 were not of the relatively polished ruling class which had led Louisiana to secession and ruin. The city's music-halls ridiculed the members frequently, and on one occasion a legislator moved that the Academy of Music on St. Charles Street be closed for this offense. The motion was tabled, whereupon another member moved that all who had voted against tabling be declared to be jackasses. The *Tri-*

---

12 Quoted in Caskey, *Secession and Restoration*, 147–48.
13 New Orleans *Daily Picayune*, October 8, November 16, December 20, 1864; *Debates in the House of Representatives of the State of Louisiana, Sessions of 1864–65* (New Orleans, 1865), 139, 190–94, 271, 358–59, 385–94; Caskey, *Secession and Restoration*, 150–51; New Orleans *Tribune*, November 15, 1864; Ficklen, *History of Reconstruction in Louisiana*, 88–89.

bune regarded the legislature as a humbug and a sham, but the
Picayune had perhaps the most damning comment. When the legislature finally adjourned, the paper recalled the chaplain of an Illinois
assembly who, as the members were about to return to their homes,
"prayed the good Lord to keep them there."[14]

Both the radical *Tribune* and the conservative *Picayune* were un-
necessarily severe. In fact, the debates were equal in most respects to
congressional debates of the period, and they were equal to much of
what is now heard in state legislative chambers.[15]

2

James Madison Wells was inaugurated as governor on March 4, 1865.
The Civil War was near its end, but this was not so evident in March
as it would be in April. Long lists of names of draftees still appeared
in the papers, and Messrs. Andrews and McBeth advertised their services for those seeking exemptions. Wells's first need was to consolidate his position. He named as mayor of New Orleans Dr. Hugh
Kennedy, who had held that office before the war. This appointment,
Wells hoped, would bring him conservative support in the city. His
ultimate object was to remove his administration from General Banks's
control. The rapidly shifting orientation of Louisiana politics is demonstrated by the fact that Banks, criticized as too conservative a few
months earlier, was now too radical for Louisiana tastes. In preparation for a showdown, Wells ordered an investigation of voter registration and came to the conclusion that some five thousand men had
been illegally registered under Banks. This information he held in reserve until it could be profitably used.[16]

In April and May the Civil War finally sputtered to an end. Wells
was astute enough to realize that the return of the Confederates, the
natural leaders of Louisiana, would make a significant difference. In
April and May he tried to steer a middle course between moderate

14 New Orleans *Daily Picayune*, April 6, March 17, 1865; "Report of State Auditor,"
  in Appendix, *Legislative Documents, Louisiana, 1864–65* (N.p., n.d.), 122; *Debates in the House of Representatives of the State of Louisiana, 1864–65*, 282;
  Caskey, *Secession and Restoration*, 151–52; New Orleans *Tribune*, June 6, 1865.
15 *Debates of the Senate of Louisiana, 1864–[1865], passim*; *Debates in the House
  of Representatives of the State of Louisiana, 1864–65*, 1–244.
16 New Orleans *Daily Picayune*, March 5, 18, 22, 1865; Lowrey, "James Madison
  Wells," 1,025–26, 1,029–30.

Unionists and Confederates resigned to defeat. He made no concessions to the numerically insignificant white Radicals. Returning rebels were pleasantly surprised to find themselves treated with consideration. The conservative *Picayune* praised the governor highly. Wells now felt secure enough to declare the New Orleans registration books prepared under Banks void and to order a new registration. This was a shrewd move, because a new group of men would almost certainly dominate New Orleans anyway, and Wells hoped for their support.[17]

In the meantime the governor was making appointments. He named a state supreme court to be headed by Christian Roselius, with associate justices of respectable legal reputation. Roselius, however, refused to serve, on the grounds that final power still lay with the military rather than with civil government. Banks proved Roselius right by ousting Kennedy and naming Colonel Samuel M. Quincy as mayor of New Orleans. Later Kennedy was restored to office. But even as this took place, Wells was in the East where he conferred with Andrew Johnson and was assured of the new president's support. Wells also appointed parish officials, including those in parishes so recently under Confederate control. His appointments seem to have given satisfaction; at least they received the approval of the few parish newspapers in existence, which suggests that they were not obnoxious to Confederate sympathizers.[18]

The Radicals attempted to strike back. There was a long-standing charge that Wells, as tax collector of Rapides Parish in 1840, had failed to turn over to the state a considerable sum of money which he had collected. These charges may or may not have been true. State auditor Dostie, a Radical leader, requested Judge Charles Leaumont to begin proceedings to remove the governor under a law which stated that a defaulter could never again hold state office. The judge refused, and Wells declared that Dostie had not posted sufficient bond, that he feared the auditor might embezzle state funds, and that therefore Dostie was dismissed from office. The auditor had to be physically carried out of his office, but his protests were of no avail because Wells

17 Lowrey, "James Madison Wells," 1,030, 1,035, 1,038–39; Brodie, *Thaddeus Stevens*, 274; New Orleans, *Daily Picayune*, March 25, May 5, 1865.
18 New Orleans *Daily Picayune*, March 15, 17, 22, June 1, 30, July 18, 1865; New Orleans *Tribune*, May 4, 1865; Highsmith, "Louisiana During Reconstruction," 121; Lowrey, "James Madison Wells," 1,026, 1,031–34, 1,037.

had the backing of General Edward R. S. Canby, the new military commander in Louisiana. The *Picayune* once more praised Wells for "doing so much to cement a union of all the whole, entire, great people of Louisiana and bring them back into the common fold."[19]

Unionists could not control Louisiana without the help of the military. This became more and more obvious as Confederate veterans returned home. The Louisiana legislature had taken no steps toward disfranchising the disloyal, so only those persons named in President Johnson's Reconstruction Proclamation, mainly higher civil and military officers of the Confederacy and persons owning property worth twenty thousand dollars or more, were prevented from taking an active part in government. Most of these Confederates easily secured a presidential pardon. The one-time Confederates who could vote, and those who sympathized with them, made up an overwhelming majority of the electorate. Unionists had good reason to fear being overthrown by returning rebels. The *Tribune* noted on June 1 that at that time Unionists could not carry a single parish in Louisiana. Three days later the same paper ruefully noted: "It must be acknowledged that the rebels have . . . accomplished their long-boasted exploit and taken New Orleans . . . in a political point of view."[20]

During the first weeks of his governorship, Wells seems to have made an effort to satisfy both Unionists and rebel sympathizers. But after receiving promises of support from President Johnson, he leaned so far toward the rebels that the Radicals began numbering him among their opponents. Warmoth, admittedly not an impartial observer, said that the speech Wells made after returning from Washington in June, 1865, was "just such as a rebel would make."[21]

Wells cemented his former rebel support by repeated statements of his opposition to Negro suffrage and by the appointment of former Confederates and Confederate sympathizers to office. When the Central Committee of the Friends of Universal Suffrage petitioned the state to grant the vote to all loyal citizens, Wells replied that he con-

19 New Orleans *Daily Picayune*, June 18, 1865; see also New Orleans *Tribune*, June 15, 1865; Lowrey, "James Madison Wells," 1,031, 1,034.
20 New Orleans *Tribune*, May 18, June 1, 4, 1865.
21 Warmoth Diary, June 17, 1865; Lowrey, "James Madison Wells," 1,024–25; Shugg, *Origins of Class Struggle in Louisiana*, 211–12.

sidered it dangerous even to discuss the subject and that he strongly opposed granting suffrage to people who had so much to learn. In addition, he expressed opposition to public education outside of New Orleans; to be sure of putting an end to public education for Negroes, he suggested that only taxes collected from blacks be used to finance schools for their children. His positions brought him support from most of the state's conservative newspapers. In the country parishes he used the military to oust Unionists, some of whom he had himself appointed, and to put returnees from the Confederate army in their places. Leading former Confederates were consulted frequently and openly. The police chief of New Orleans was instructed to fill vacancies with Confederate veterans who had recommendations from their officers or one or more well-known citizens. The chief testified later that he had warned the governor that the police were plotting against Louisiana Unionists, but to no avail. Carl Schurz noted that in Louisiana, "Men who . . . aided the rebellion . . . are crowding into places of trust and power." Schurz also was wise enough to see that southern Unionists "were not in communion with leading social and political circles; and that their existence in the South was of a rather precarious nature."[22] The situation of Unionists was perhaps best described by a correspondent of the Shreveport *Sentinel,* who wrote that Union men at Shreveport were far more willing to forget the past than were the secessionists: "Jealousy is manifested even if a union man receives the same favor which is freely accorded to all."[23]

Naturally, Louisiana Unionists were discouraged and angered by Wells's actions. As early as May 17 a Unionist meeting denounced him for appointing enemies of the United States to office. In July Unionists complained again of the appointments given Confederates and suggested, in a petition to President Johnson, the restoration of military rule. In August, at a meeting in Lafayette Square, Radicals resolved that Wells had proved false to the trust placed in him. In September

22 *Senate Executive Documents,* 39th Cong., 1st Sess., No. 2, pp. 1, 11.
23 Quoted in New Orleans *Daily Picayune,* June 25, 1865; see also New Orleans *Tribune,* October 7, 1865; E. R. S. Canby to Carl Schurz, September 8, 1865, in *Senate Executive Documents,* 39th Cong., 1st Sess., No. 2, pp. 56–57; Lowrey, "James Madison Wells," 1,037, 1,040–45, 1,067; Capers, *Occupied City,* 144; Ficklen, *History of Reconstruction in Louisiana,* 104–105.

Warmoth had a long talk with Wells and confided to his diary that the governor was very much opposed to Warmoth's views. What particularly infuriated Warmoth and other Radicals was that they could see that Wells was following exactly the right course to secure his election as governor in the autumn of 1865.[24]

3

Louisianians serving in Lee's and Johnston's armies in the East surrendered and were paroled, but Kirby Smith's troops in northern Louisiana and Texas generally ignored the formalities of surrender. They simply went home to resume their interrupted lives as best they could. Being defeated and subject to the will of an armed conqueror was an unfamiliar role, and the course of events was slow. The *St. Martin Democrat* of May 13, 1865, carried news of the dissolution of the Confederacy, but the same issue carried a number of official notices from the Confederate state government. Not until June was all of Louisiana declared under Federal occupation, doing away with the requirement for passports between Union and Confederate Louisiana.[25]

The actual occupation proceeded even more slowly than the proclamations. Union Major General Francis J. Herron, from Baton Rouge, wrote to the Confederate colonel Alcibiades DeBlanc at Natchitoches June 5, 1865, asking DeBlanc to use the reserve troops under his command to keep order until Union soldiers could take over the task. DeBlanc, later reputed to be the leader of the Knights of the White Camellia and certainly the leader of one armed insurrection against the government of William Pitt Kellogg, was delighted to comply with Herron's request. He issued General Order Number 2, Headquarters Louisiana Reserves, which required all Negroes and other persons of color to remain in their usual places of employment; promised jayhawkers that they would be arrested and turned over to the United States authorities; and divided the area under his command into beats to be patrolled by the citizenry. This was largely, of course, a revival of prewar slave controls. At about the same time the *Courier*

24 New Orleans *Daily Picayune*, May 18, 1865; Lowrey, "James Madison Wells," 1,039, 1,045; Warmoth Diary, September 3, 1865.
25 *St. Martin Democrat* (St. Martinville, La.), May 13, 1865; Craven, *Reconstruction*, 96; Stampp, *The Era of Reconstruction*, 9–10.

of the Teche carried a letter from DeBlanc justifying secession at in-terminable length.[26]

Not everyone was resigned to defeat. One Louisianian wrote on April 23, 1865, that in "the midst of great and sad disasters . . . one piece of cheering news reached us . . . the death of the tyrant 'Old Abe'."[27] But Louisiana soldiers were aware that they had been de-feated. They, and most politicians, in the spring and summer of 1865, were prepared to do whatever their conquerors told them to do. If the federal government had had a firm set of conditions to impose upon the South, even if the conditions had been those imposed later by the Reconstruction Acts, there would have been little or no resistance in mid-1865. The Red River Presbytery spoke for many when it acknowl-edged "the hand of God . . . in the . . . establishment of the authority of the United States . . . and [bowed] . . . in humble submissiveness to the Providence of the Most High."[28] In retrospect, it seems a pity that the pervasive race question prevented a firm northern policy, be-cause the quarrel between President Johnson and Congress was to encourage hopes in the South which were unrealistic for a defeated people.[29]

At war's end, Louisiana outside of New Orleans and the adjacent parishes was almost without local government. A resident of Baton Rouge reported the streets unsafe after dark. When forced to go out, he walked in the middle of the street with an open knife in his hand. When the Confederate army dissolved, there was no force to keep order in the area it had occupied. Even after Union troops took over, they were too few in number to control events at any distance from their posts. Bands of jayhawkers raided at will. Planters walked in fear of their Negroes, and there were enough cases of murder and assault to justify this fear. Men who had remained loyal to the Union

26 *St. Martin Democrat* (St. Martinville, La.), June 17, 1865; New Orleans *Tribune*, July 21, 1865.
27 L. D. Bringier to [?], April 23, 1865, in Bringier Family Papers, Department of Archives, Louisiana State University.
28 Minutes of the Red River Presbytery, Vol. II (1863–1881), in the Presbyterian Historical Foundation, Montreat, N.C. (microfilm provided by Austin Presby-terian Theological Seminary, Austin, Tex.).
29 Craven, *Reconstruction*, 96–97, 113; W. R. Brock, *An American Crisis: Congress and Reconstruction, 1865–1867* (London, 1963), 150; McKitrick, *Andrew Johnson and Reconstruction*, 35.

during the war might be fawned upon one day, murdered the next. But the Negroes were the chief victims of anarchy. Reports of atrocities against blacks in 1865 and 1866 must be evaluated with care, because the Radical press was eager to report such incidents for political effect. But even if the accounts of violence directed at Negroes are discounted by one half, which is probably too great a discount, it is still evident that a reign of terror existed in some parts of Louisiana immediately after the war. When the racial attitudes of Louisianians are taken into account, then combined with a tendency toward violence which preceded the war, with some assertions of independence on the part of some Negroes, with the frustrations of defeat, and with the knowledge that no white man was likely to be convicted for a crime against a black, atrocities were inevitable. The southerner could not prevent the end of slavery via northern bayonets, but he could be revenged upon the Negro.[30]

The Confederate veterans who returned from the war, and their neighbors who had remained at home, faced a future in which the only certainty was hardship. A few joined Governor Henry Watkins Allen, Judah P. Benjamin, Pierre Soule, and John Slidell in taking refuge abroad, but most came back to Louisiana. New Orleans in late 1865 was reported full of officers and men still in uniform because they had nothing else to wear. William Stone, brother of Kate Stone of Brokenburn, had sent his slaves to Texas to prevent their falling into Union hands. In November, 1865, he kept the promise he had made them and brought them back to the family plantation in Tensas Parish. C. J. Barrow came home to Pointe Coupee and found the family plantation ruined. He first tried finding work in New Orleans, taught school for a time in West Baton Rouge Parish, then borrowed two mules and planted twenty acres of cotton with his own hands. A break in the levee ruined this attempt. When the waters receded, he managed to plant a few more acres, but these fell victim to the army

---

30 Payne to Mrs. Sterrett, February 18, 1865, in Barnhart (ed.), "Reconstruction on the Lower Mississippi," 390; *Senate Executive Documents*, 39th Cong., 1st Sess., No. 2, pp. 3–4, 13–14; *House Reports*, 39th Cong., 1st Sess., No. 30, p. 54; New Orleans *Tribune*, July 26, 28, August 2, 1865; Shreveport *Southwestern*, June 28, 1865, cited in New Orleans *Daily Picayune*, July 9, 1865; *Courier of the Teche* (St. Martinville, La.), June 10, 1865; *Nation*, II (March 1, 1866), 270; Henry Clay Warmoth, *War, Politics and Reconstruction: Stormy Days in Louisiana* (New York, 1936), 42.

worm. Town dwellers had their problems, too. Attorneys could not practice in the federal courts without taking the "ironclad" oath, and many could not stretch their consciences to the extent of expressing repentance for their Confederate service. Merchants and would-be merchants could not purchase stock. Cows, swine, and poultry, then normally kept by town dwellers, fell victim to hungry whites and freedmen. In Baton Rouge heads of families which badly needed wild game to supplement their diet found it difficult to obtain permits to buy ammunition. Very few of these returning Confederates were concerned with politics in 1865 or even early 1866. The problem of survival came first.[31]

The ordinary Confederate soldier had no difficulty in recovering the civil and political rights he had lost by participation in rebellion. Under President Johnson's proclamation of pardon and amnesty he was required to do no more than take an oath of allegiance to the United States. Those higher officials and property owners who were excluded from amnesty found it fairly easy to get pardons. The pardoning process, in fact, was so rapid, and rebel leaders found it so easy to recover their property and political rights, that many people in the North became concerned lest southerners should once more dominate the national government.[32]

4

In general the Louisianian accepted defeat, and he accepted the emancipation of the slaves. On the other hand, he did not repent of secession, and he would not accept the Negro as an equal politically, socially, or otherwise. A northern correspondent reported in 1865 that the feeling of the South toward the North was similar to that of Poland toward Russia. He said that prosouthern and antinorthern

31 *Senate Executive Documents*, 39th Cong., 1st Sess., No. 2, pp. 3–4; Sarah L. Wadley Diary, November 4, 1865 (Southern Historical Collection, University of North Carolina); Warmoth Diary, May 14, 1865; New Orleans *Daily Picayune*, August 18, 1865; C. J. Barrow to "Aunt Emma," July 21, 1866, in Barrow Family Papers, Department of Archives, Louisiana State University; Coulter, *The South During Reconstruction*, 189; Ficklen, *History of Reconstruction in Louisiana*, 97; Baton Rouge *Weekly Advocate*, 1866.
32 Franklin, *Reconstruction After the Civil War*, 34; Hodding Carter, *The Angry Scar: The Story of Reconstruction* (Garden City, N.Y., 1959), 70; J. T. Dorris, "Pardoning the Leaders of the Confederacy," *Mississippi Valley Historical Review*, XV (June, 1928), 3–21; *Nation*, I (July 6, 1865), 4.

sentiments were stronger among the young, and that women and preachers asserted them most strongly of all. Any criticism of the South in northern publications was resented. The Baton Rouge *Weekly Advocate* asserted flatly, despite the record of Andersonville, that no northern prisoners had ever been mistreated during the war. Politically, Whigs, Douglas Democrats, Breckinridge Democrats, and the few native Republicans were not yet united into the "Solid South," but insofar as possible they were united in their intention for the post-war South to have the same values as the antebellum South. They did not believe that the loss of a war made it necessary for them to give up an old and beloved culture. In this respect Louisiana did not differ from the rest of the South, and the area of the state long occupied by Union troops did not differ from the regions occupied after the close of hostilities. Indeed, the attitude of some Louisianians could best be described as arrogant. The majority report of the Joint Committee on Reconstruction was correct when it stated that southern newspapers abounded in abuse of northern people and institutions. The editor of the *Courier of the Teche* railed against the occupation until it became necessary to put him under arrest. As early as July of 1865 the New Orleans *Daily Picayune* truculently maintained that state questions of a political nature should be decided only by the electors of the state. A few months later this same paper announced that in surrendering, the people of the South did not give up the right to call Yankees hard names.[33]

The South, of course, could have been expected to behave as it did. In part it was due to the southern tendency toward overstatement, but, as Wade Hampton pointed out, the southern people could not be expected to express boundless love for a Union from which they had desperately fought to escape for four years. On the other hand, the people of Louisiana would have been wiser to have played better the role of the conquered. Northerners were infuriated by the seeming

---

33 *Nation*, I (October 26, 1865), 523; New Orleans *Daily Picayune*, July 4, August 17, September 30, 1865, January 24, 1866; Baton Rouge *Weekly Advocate*, March 31, 1866; *House Reports*, 39th Cong., 1st Sess., No. 30, xvi–xvii; Georges Clemenceau, *American Reconstruction of 1865–1870 and the Impeachment of President Johnson* (New York, 1928), 85–86; Paul Lewinson, *Race, Class, and Party: A History of Negro Suffrage and White Politics in the South* (New York, 1963), 25.

arrogance of the defeated and by the treatment northerners received in the South. There can be little doubt that this resentment contributed to the growth of radicalism.[34]

In general, relations between men who had fought in the war, whatever the army, were good. The shared experience of battle, even on opposing sides, gave them a respect for one another which to some extent overcame political differences. The Confederate soldier knew that he had been defeated, but the Union trooper knew that the rebel had fought with great valor. It was Louisianians who had avoided combat who were most prone to insult northerners, in uniform or out, and the malice of women overshadowed all else. One observer testified: "Over southern society . . . woman reigns supreme, and they are more embittered against those whom they deem the authors of all their calamities than are their brothers, sons, and husbands."[35]

One factor contributing to bad feeling was the fact that during 1865 and 1866 many of the Union troops in Louisiana as well as in neighboring states were Negroes. These, in southern eyes, demanded no respect at all, and the officers who commanded them deserved no more. Also, suits were brought against officers of the occupation in state courts. This certainly inhibited them in carrying out their functions, because it seemed quite possible at the time that the existing state governments were valid, in which case damages assessed by a judge in some rural Louisiana parish might have to be paid.[36]

In view of existing conditions, it is remarkable that so few outrages were charged to the occupation forces in Louisiana. In part this was because so few troops were used. Even so, perusal of hundreds of contemporary sources, newspapers, letters, diaries, and memoirs, has not brought to light a single case of rape, more than one or two mur-

34 *Nation*, II (April 5, 1866), 43; Reid, *After the War*, 237–38; Stampp, *The Era of Reconstruction*, 76; U. S. Grant to Andrew Johnson, December 18, 1865, in *Senate Executive Documents*, 39th Cong., 1st Sess., No. 2, p. 98.

35 Quoted in Fleming (ed.), *Documentary History of Reconstruction*, I, 44–45; see also Daniel Thompson to Cyrus Woodman, April 11, 1866, in C. J. Marquette (ed.), "Letters of a Yankee Sugar Planter," *Journal of Southern History*, VI (November, 1940), 523–24; James E. Sefton, *The United States Army and Reconstruction, 1865–1877* (Baton Rouge, 1967), 54–55; McKitrick, *Andrew Johnson and Reconstruction*, 39–40.

36 Sefton, *United States Army and Reconstruction*, 52; Harold M. Hyman, "Johnson, Stanton and Grant: A Reconsideration of the Army's Role in the Events Leading to Impeachment," *American Historical Review*, LXVI (October, 1960), 88.

ders, or more than a dozen assaults upon civilians by Union troops in Louisiana during 1865 and 1866. Apparently the same high standards of discipline and conduct prevailed all over the South. The main complaint against occupation troops was pilfering, which presumably has been a characteristic of all armies at all times.[37]

It could not be expected that soldiers of the occupation forces would be loved by the people of Louisiana. The treatment of officers was particularly bad because Louisianians made no distinction between those officers on strictly military duty and those acting as agents of the hated Freedmen's Bureau. Even so, there was little violence; most hatred and dislike was expressed verbally and in social snubs. Officers and their wives were sometimes refused service in New Orleans restaurants and turned away from the better hotels. A Colonel Biddle and his lady aboard the steamer *General Quitman*, sailing upstream from New Orleans, were completely ostracized the first day. That night, however, a southern lady aboard became seriously ill and was unable to nurse her infant. The baby refused a bottle, so Mrs. Biddle, who had an infant of her own, fed the hungry child at her breast. The next day she was treated much more courteously.[38] A witness before a congressional committee said that Louisianians divided the people from the North into two classes. Those who had not served in the army were "damned Yankee sons of bitches." Those who had worn or did wear the United States uniform were "damned blue-bellied Yankee sons of bitches."[39] This was probably an overstatement, but these phrases were still in use in Louisiana in the mid-twentieth century.

With the end of the war many northern men settled in Louisiana. A few were already seeking opportunities for political advancement, but the vast majority of them hoped to improve their economic position. These northerners brought in much-needed capital, but in

---

37 *Senate Executive Documents*, 39th Cong., 2nd Sess., No. 6, p. 68; Myrta Lockett Avary, *Dixie After the War: An Exposition of Social Conditions Existing in the South During the Twelve Years Succeeding the Fall of Richmond* (New York, 1906), 118; Highsmith, "Social and Economic Conditions in Rapides Parish," 12.
38 *Senate Executive Documents*, 39th Cong., 2nd Sess., No. 6, p. 68; Howard K. Beale, *The Critical Year: A Study of Andrew Johnson and Reconstruction* (New York, 1930), 163; Ellen McGowan Biddle, *Reminiscences of a Soldier's Wife* (Philadelphia, 1907), 24–25.
39 *House Reports*, 39th Cong., 1st Sess., No. 30, p. 126.

general they were received grudgingly. A defender of the South before a congressional committee stated that northern men in the South could expect to be treated with contempt for a while, but that if they would refrain "from political discussion and conduct themselves with ordinary discretion" they would eventually be accepted. He admitted, however, that there were "localities in many of the Southern states where it would be dangerous for a northern man to live."[40] New Orleans, where northerners were most active politically in 1865 and 1866, was apparently more tolerant than the country parishes.[41]

There were other reasons for the dislike of northerners besides the recently ended war. Men from the North had not been popular in the South, generally, since the beginning of the abolitionist controversy. The sight of northerners buying up plantations which Louisianians had owned must have been galling to a proud people. The functioning of the Freedmen's Bureau, even though it afforded relief to many hungry whites, angered southerners. The activities of Treasury agents, who seized much cotton claimed by private individuals on the grounds that it had belonged to the Confederate government, fostered antagonism. Not least important were the activities of the northern Methodist and Presbyterian churches, which seem to have assumed at the end of the war that even as the states had been forcibly returned to the Union, the southern branches of these churches should be reunited with the northern branches. Finally, political activity directed toward the achievement of Negro suffrage caused more and more fear and dislike of northerners as 1865 came to an end and 1866 began.[42]

It is difficult to evaluate the degree of discrimination against north-

40 Quoted in Fleming (ed.), *Documentary History of Reconstruction*, I, 44–45.
41 William W. Chenault and Robert C. Reinders, "The Northern-Born Community of New Orleans in the 1850's," *Journal of American History*, LI (September, 1964), 232–47.
42 New Orleans *Daily Picayune*, July 2, 1865; Ficklen, *History of Reconstruction in Louisiana*, 108; *House Reports*, 39th Cong., 1st Sess., No. 30, quoted in Fleming (ed.), *Documentary History of Reconstruction*, I, 30–31; Shrewmaker and Prinz (eds.), "A Yankee in Louisiana," 392; Report of Sherrard Clemens to President Andrew Johnson, 1865, quoted in Fleming (ed.), *Documentary History of Reconstruction*, I, 28; Ralph E. Morrow, "Northern Methodism in the South During Reconstruction," *Mississippi Valley Historical Review*, XLI (September, 1954), 214–15, 217–18; "Pastoral Address of the Southern Methodist Bishops," New Orleans *Daily Picayune*, August 30, 1865.

ern civilians in Louisiana in 1865 and 1866. Northerners who left records were definitely fearful of violence outside of New Orleans, but actual instances were not numerous. Most discrimination was more subtle. One tactic was to enforce the letter of the law against northerners, but not against southerners. There was some economic discrimination. During the occupation of New Orleans, the northern-born members of the Pilots' Association had taken the oath demanded by Butler, but most of the southern-born pilots had registered as enemies of the United States. After the war all those who had not registered as enemies of the Union were expelled from the association. But most of the pressure against northerners was social. One newspaper asserted that those men from the North who gave up and left Louisiana were chagrined because they were not socially acceptable to Louisianians. Social ostracism could, of course, be very effective, especially against those northerners who, rather than exploiting the defeated South, hoped to make homes for themselves and their families.[43]

5

Practically all observers agreed that opposition to the Republican party, which in the minds of many northerners was the same as opposition to the Union, grew stronger with every passing month after mid-1865. Undoubtedly this was encouraged by President Johnson's liberal amnesty-and-pardon policy and by his more and more apparent devotion to states' rights principles. As it became apparent that the national administration would not take repressive measures in Louisiana, the Democrats, admittedly the party of secession, came more and more to the fore. When it became evident that Governor Wells would call an election in which the whole state could participate, the Democrats began to organize for the contest.[44]

43 W. B. Stickney to Thomas W. Conway, August 26, 1865, in *Senate Executive Documents*, 39th Cong., 1st Sess., No. 2, p. 91; *Nation*, II (March 1, 1866), 270, (March 22, 1866), 365; J. P. Newsham to Warmoth, April 5, 1866, in Warmoth Papers; *House Reports*, 39th Cong., 1st Sess., No. 30, p. 133; New Orleans *Daily Picayune*, May 13, 1866; Clemenceau, *American Reconstruction*, 82–83.

44 New Orleans *Daily Picayune*, August, 1865; Whitelaw Reid, *After the War: A Southern Tour* (Cincinnati, 1866), 235–37, 578; *Senate Executive Documents*, 39th Cong., 1st Sess., No. 2, p. 5; *House Reports*, 39th Cong., 1st Sess., No. 30, pp. 55, 57; Caskey, *Secession and Restoration*, 149, 161–62; Lowrey, "James Madison Wells," 1,051.

Until Reconstruction was near its end, the revived Louisiana Democrats preferred to be called Conservatives. Most of the old Democratic leaders were gone, and the newer version of the party had to bring former Whigs and Know-Nothings into its ranks if it was to win elections. Little research has been done on the survival of Whig politicians and Whig principles in Louisiana but, unless Louisiana differed from other southern states, Whiggery died very slowly. Some Whigs became Republicans, at least for a time, but the vast majority of them, apparently, held their noses and joined with the Democrats under the Conservative label. In fact, there is a strong probability that former Whigs became important Conservative leaders. It would seem that the Know-Nothings, who were strong in Louisiana before the Civil War, went over to the Conservatives almost unanimously. The sizable German population of New Orleans was Unionist, but divided between moderate and Radical factions as the war ended. Race prejudice rather quickly drove them into the Conservative fold.[45]

On September 21, 1865, Governor Wells called for an election of state officials to be held November 6. By this time Wells himself was identified fairly closely with the Democratic faction in Louisiana. It was generally agreed that the Democrats would win the election, but a split in that party's ranks gave the Conservative Unionists some hope. The Radicals knew that they had no chance in a statewide election in which only whites could vote. Therefore, as will be seen, they boycotted the election called by Wells and held one of their own.[46]

Three parties entered the field: the National Democratic party, the Conservative Democratic party, and the National Conservative Unionist party, the last-named being the moderate Republicans of the Banks era. The National Democratic party met in convention

---

45 Thomas B. Alexander, "Persistent Whiggery in the Confederate South, 1860–1877," *Journal of Southern History*, XXVII (August, 1961), 305–29; Thomas B. Alexander, "Persistent Whiggery in Mississippi: The Hinds County *Gazette*," *Journal of Mississippi History*, XXIII (April, 1961), 71–93; Thomas B. Alexander, "Whiggery and Reconstruction in Tennessee," *Journal of Southern History*, XVI (August, 1950), 291–305; C. Vann Woodward, *Origins of the New South, 1877–1913* (Rev. ed.; Baton Rouge, 1971), 1–2, 26–27; Robert T. Clark, Jr., "The New Orleans German Colony in the Civil War," *Louisiana Historical Quarterly*, XX (October, 1937), 1,011–12; Lowrey, "James Madison Wells," 1,067.

46 New Orleans *Daily Picayune*, September–October, 1865; New Orleans *Tribune*, September–October, 1865; Reid, *After the War*, 262, 408.

October 2, 1865. The first draft of its platform asserted the right of secession, but the majority was cool-headed enough to vote this down. However, one Dr. Riddle, a delegate to the convention, was censured and required to apologize when he stated that secession was a crime and a blunder. These National Democrats were strenuously opposed to Negro suffrage: "We hold this to be a government of white people, made and to be perpetuated for the exclusive benefit of the white race."[47] The platform maintained that Negroes could never constitutionally be citizens of the United States and that there could never be any sort of equality between the races. The Louisiana constitution of 1864 was condemned as a fraud, but it was accepted *de facto* until a legitimate basic law could be drawn up. After declaring itself in favor of President Johnson's Reconstruction policy, the National Democratic party proceeded to nominate Wells as its candidate for governor, mainly because he had been recognized by President Johnson. Some Democrats could not stomach Wells. They formed the Conservative Democratic party, declared the constitution of 1852 to be still in effect, and nominated Henry Watkins Allen, the last Confederate governor and an exile in Mexico, as their candidate. Finally, the Conservative Unionists entered the contest. They also opposed Negro suffrage and supported the president's Reconstruction policy. However, they upheld the validity of the constitution of 1864 which was, after all, largely their creation. They then proceeded to join the National Democrats in naming Wells as their candidate. Wells gratefully accepted both nominations.[48]

Since all three parties participating in the election of November, 1865, repudiated Negro suffrage, it would seem on the surface that this issue was removed from the election, which would have left the validity of the constitution of 1864 as the only issue. However, the existence of the Radical Republican party, which contained men who did advocate Negro suffrage, kept this issue alive even though the Radicals did not take part in the election. In Houma the Democratic

47 Quoted in Lowrey, "James Madison Wells," 1,056.
48 Warmoth Diary, October 2, 1865; New Orleans *Daily Picayune*, August 20, September 12, October 1–31, 1865; Lowrey, "James Madison Wells," 1,055–58; Cox, *Three Decades of Federal Legislation*, 429; Ficklen, *History of Reconstruction in Louisiana*, 109–11; "Investigator," *The Rebellion*, 26.

convention denied the vote to any delegate who approved of Negro suffrage. Democrats opposed education for blacks at public expense, and many favored forcing those who had gone to town from the plantations to return to the soil. The Conservative Democrats were even stronger in their Negrophobia, and the Conservative Unionists agreed.[49]

The result of the election was never really in doubt. Wells was swept into office with a substantial majority everywhere except in his native Rapides Parish where, presumably, he was best known. There Allen had a majority. Elected with Wells were Albert P. Voorhies as lieutenant-governor, Robert M. Lusher as superintendent of education, and four other state officials, two of whom were pardoned former Confederates. The National Democrats also swept the legislative contest, gaining almost 100 percent of the membership. A large number of the newly elected legislators were former Confederates; having served in the rebel army was already a distinct advantage in Louisiana politics.[50]

6

In the meantime the Radical Republican faction in New Orleans was growing. As early as May, 1864, Republican delegates from a number of the occupied parishes had met and endorsed Lincoln's administration. In January, 1865, a group of "colored people" met to elect delegates to a state convention of the Equal Rights League, following an example already set in some northern states. Delegates from New Orleans and at least five other parishes attended. By April this movement for Negro rights had merged with the Radical Republicans. On the night of May 24, 1865, a meeting of men favoring universal suffrage was held at the old Carrollton Depot. The *Tribune* commented: "It was . . . a new spectacle to see the community of feeling and sentiment

49 New Orleans *Daily Picayune*, September–October, 1865; Lowrey, "James Madison Wells," 1,059–60; New Orleans *Tribune*, September 17, 1865.
50 New Orleans *Daily Picayune*, November 1865; Lowrey, "James Madison Wells," 1,061–62; Franklin, *Reconstruction After the Civil War*, 44; Constantin, "Louisiana Black Code," 42; Ficklen, *History of Reconstruction in Louisiana*, 11–12. The other elected officials were J. H. Hardy, secretary of state, Adam Giffen, treasurer, J. H. Peralta, auditor, and A. S. Herron, attorney general.

between men of all races and all shades."[51] A Republican mass meeting was called for the evening of Saturday, April 15, and some blacks were among the seventy-eight whose names were appended to the published call. The *Picayune* published an account of the meeting and the many speeches made and noted particularly that one of the white speakers had called for Negro suffrage.[52]

The only organ of Radical Republican opinion in Louisiana during the years 1864–1867 was the bilingual New Orleans *Tribune*, published first as a biweekly, then daily except Mondays. The publishers were Dr. Louis Charles Roudanez and his brother, Joseph B. Roudanez, and for part of the period Paul Trevigne was editor. All were Negroes. Warmoth implies in his memoirs that these men were from Santo Domingo and that they planned to "Africanize" Louisiana. In reality, the Roudanez brothers were native Louisianians; Trevigne was probably native-born also. The *Tribune* did advocate giving blacks, who made up half the population of Louisiana, a voice in government proportionate to their numbers, but only to this extent did it favor "Africanization." The paper was not a financial success, partly because it never fully trusted or was fully trusted by white Radicals like Warmoth. It was forced to suspend publication in 1868. Its columns are important, because they reflect the aspirations of the upper-class blacks of Louisiana.[53]

As hostilities ended, the organization of Radical Republicans gathered speed. A meeting in New Orleans on May 17 set the tone for other meetings. Dostie and Warmoth, among others, attacked Wells and Mayor Kennedy of New Orleans, advocated Negro suffrage, and urged that all "traitors" be disfranchised. The *Picayune* published a mildly neutral account of this gathering, but after receiving much adverse mail, published an editorial denouncing the resolutions which had been adopted and declaring war on the Radicals. By July most of the members of the old Friends of Universal Suffrage were listed as Republicans. The organization was largely confined to New Orleans,

---

51 New Orleans *Tribune*, May 25, 1865.
52 New Orleans *Daily Picayune*, May 18, 1864, April 15–16, 1865; New Orleans *Tribune*, July 23, 1864, January–April, 1865.
53 Warmoth, *War, Politics and Reconstruction*, 32; Roussève, *The Negro in Louisiana*, 118–20; A. E. Perkins, "James Henri Burch and Oscar James Dunn in Louisiana," *Journal of Negro History*, XXII (July, 1937), 326.

but emissaries went out and held meetings in such places as Thibo-
deaux, Donaldsonville, and Baton Rouge. At all of these meetings
blacks were encouraged to participate.[54]

It is obvious that Radical Republicanism was not introduced into
Louisiana entirely by "carpetbaggers" from north of the Mason-Dixon
Line. Nor were all the resident Radicals black. Thomas J. Durant, one
of the leaders in the formation of the Friends of Universal Suffrage,
had been admitted to the Louisiana bar many years before the war
and had served as United States attorney for Louisiana under President James K. Polk. He also had been attorney general of Louisiana.
A Douglas Democrat, he had opposed secession and had freed his
slaves soon after the beginning of the occupation. Of the seventy-two
men who called the Union meeting of April 15, 1865, at least forty-
two were Louisiana residents before the war. Of the seventeen officers
of the Republican Club mentioned in the *Picayune* in July, 1865,
eleven are known to have been Louisiana residents before the war.
On the other hand, the prominence of Henry Clay Warmoth in the
Louisiana Republican organization demonstrates that northerners already had an important voice in Louisiana Radicalism.[55]

Obviously, not all Unionists were Radicals. During his tour of the
South, Whitelaw Reid attended a dinner at which Durant, Judge J. T.
Whitaker, and Christian Roselius were present. Roselius was conservative and just as much a strict constructionist of the United States
Constitution as any Confederate statesman. Durant, on the other
hand, was an out-and-out Radical. Judge Whitaker "was always a
Union man, but he took pains not to make himself personally offensive
to the Rebels. . . . Now that the Union cause has triumphed, he would
move very slowly. Negro suffrage may become necessary, but . . . if
there were any possible way of avoiding it he would avoid it."[56] Men
like Roselius could never become Radicals. The Whitakers, on the
other hand, might go either way. Some, probably most, were so op-

54 Warmoth Diary, May 16, June 24, 1865; New Orleans *Daily Picayune*, May–
   September, 1865; New Orleans *Tribune*, May–October, 1865; Ficklen, *History of
   Reconstruction in Louisiana*, 111–12.
55 Uzee, "Republican Politics in Louisiana," 5, 13; New Orleans *Daily Picayune*,
   April 15, July 6, 1865; Shugg, *Origins of Class Struggle in Louisiana*, 215–16;
   Gardner's New Orleans Directory for the Year 1859 (New Orleans, 1858), *passim*;
   Gardner's New Orleans Directory for 1860 (New Orleans, 1859), *passim*.
56 Reid, *After the War*, 232–33.

posed to Negro suffrage and came under so much pressure from their neighbors, that they left the Republican party and sooner or later became Democrats. Some, however, remained staunch. In February of 1866 one such Unionist wrote to Warmoth: "I want you to understand that . . . nothing will ever cause me to join the Democratic Party. . . . If the people of the United States . . . [decide] the universal right of all men to suffrage this will be law to me. I think it would [be] better . . . to continue the privilege of voting as now exercised."[57]

In response to Governor Wells's call for an election, the Friends of Universal Suffrage issued a call for a convention to meet in New Orleans in late August, 1865. This convention, as expected, drew up resolutions demanding universal suffrage and equal rights for all men. It did, however, startle Conservatives by deciding to enter no candidates in the election. Instead the convention accepted the contention of Warmoth, who had recently conferred in Washington with Republican leaders, that Louisiana had ceased to be a state and had reverted to territorial status by the act of secession. After it had been ascertained that Durant would not accept a nomination, Warmoth was nominated as a candidate for territorial delegate to the United States Congress. The convention planned a separate election for the same day as the one called by Governor Wells in which voting by Negroes would not only be permitted but would be encouraged.[58]

Despite a quarrel with General Ulysses S. Grant after the Vicksburg campaign, Warmoth had risen to the rank of lieutenant colonel in the Union army. Warmoth was fully vindicated in this dispute, but there is reason to believe that some rancor persisted on the part of both men. In the spring of 1864 Warmoth was assigned to the Department of the Gulf, and General Banks made him judge of the New Orleans Provost Court. The records indicate that he was a satisfactory judge, even though he was only twenty-two years old when appointed. In this office he came to know the leading Union men of New Orleans, including Durant and Roselius; he dined in the latter's home several

57 S. Belden to Warmoth, February 20, 1866, in Warmoth Papers; see also Williams, *Romance and Realism in Southern Politics*, 28–29; Franklin, *Reconstruction After the Civil War*, 195–96; David H. Donald, "The Scalawag in Mississippi Reconstruction," *Journal of Southern History*, X (November, 1944), 447–60.
58 New Orleans *Tribune*, September–October, 1865; Warmoth, *War, Politics and Reconstruction*, 45; Ficklen, *History of Reconstruction in Louisiana*, 112–13.

times. If one may judge by the diary Warmoth kept and the letters he wrote during this time of his life, he was rather naïve, somewhat puritanical, but a very charming young man. On the other hand, although he had no known family resources, he was able in August, 1864, to withdraw fifteen thousand dollars from a New Orleans bank. He was tall and handsome; somewhat later a friend wrote to him, saying: "I think that little affair of yours with the young creole lady on Canal Street will be a more difficult problem to solve than the territory of Louisiana."[59]

Warmoth's military career ended in late 1864 when his regiment was consolidated with several others. In early 1865 he returned to New Orleans and opened a reasonably successful law practice. By the spring of 1865 he was definitely interested in politics, and he apparently realized that the Unionist cause in Louisiana could not prosper without Negro suffrage. On a trip to the North he conferred with "my friend," John Hay, and then he met Chief Justice Salmon P. Chase. "I found that he is in favor of Negro suffrage. . . . He is an honest and patriotic old gentleman." Also he "got well acquainted with Vice President Andrew Johnson and Ex-Senator King. Good men both." On fateful April 14, 1865, Warmoth "saw and spoke with General Grant. He remembered me perfectly."[60]

On his return to New Orleans, Warmoth began to play an active role in politics. On May 17 he spoke to a meeting of the Friends of Universal Suffrage and was delighted at the accounts of his remarks in the New Orleans newspapers. In June a preliminary meeting for the purpose of organizing a Union club was held in Warmoth's office, and this led to the formal organization of a Republican club on July 5. By early summer, if not before, Warmoth had gained enough political power to have a voice in the naming of men to places in the Custom House. During that spring and summer he was reading a biography of Robespierre. In September, as already noted, he was nominated by the Radical convention as its candidate for delegate to Congress from "the Territory of Louisiana."[61]

59 Alfred Shaw to Warmoth, March 22, 1866, in Warmoth Papers; Warmoth Diary, June–August, 1864; Warmoth, *War, Politics and Reconstruction,* 16–24.
60 Warmoth Diary, March 6, 14, April 6, 14, 1865.
61 *Ibid.,* May 16–28, June 14, 24, 1865; New Orleans *Daily Picayune,* October, 1865; Ficklen, *History of Reconstruction in Louisiana,* 112–13.

The audacity of the Radicals in holding a separate election on November 6, 1865, left the Democrats almost sputtering in their indignation. Warmoth gleefully pointed out to them that they regarded the constitution of 1864 as invalid, but that nonetheless they were participating in an election under that constitution. The Radicals, he said, agreed with them that the constitution of 1864 was null and void, but they were consistent and kept their election separate from the one called by the pretender who sat at the governor's desk. Warmoth campaigned actively, and agents in the parishes worked to get freedmen to the polls. They stressed that the object of the Radicals was to obtain for the black man all the rights enjoyed by white men.[62]

In parts of the state the special election met with active opposition. In Terrebonne Parish two Radical organizers were indicted by the grand jury and imprisoned on a charge of inciting to riot. Bail was set at $2,500, but when this was raised, the charge was changed to treason and bail set at $5,000. Then the prisoners were transferred to New Orleans for safekeeping because the parish did not have a jail secure enough for such dangerous men. Eventually they were released, but too late to do any effective Radical organizing in Terrebonne Parish. In Assumption Parish the military authorities and the local sheriff combined forces to smash the special ballot boxes and scatter the contents. At Covington the special election was simply not permitted, and commissioners from St. John the Baptist Parish were arrested as they attempted to carry the returns to New Orleans. Despite these incidents, the *Tribune* was able to report that both elections were quiet.[63]

Warmoth claimed to have received 21,400 votes in the special election, of which 2,300 had been cast by white men. There is no way to check the accuracy of his claim, but it is obvious that the black people voted enthusiastically. Perhaps the most important thing about this election was the practice it gave Negro voters. Wells accused Warmoth of collecting money from each voter to pay his expenses in

62 New Orleans *Tribune*, September 27–November 6, 1865; New Orleans *Daily Picayune*, October, 1865; Ficklen, *History of Reconstruction in Louisiana*, 112–13.
63 Henry Clay Warmoth, *Letter of H. C. Warmoth, Claimant of a Seat in the House of Representatives as Delegate from the Territory of Louisiana, Addressed to Senator Williams, Chairman of the Sub-Committee on Reconstruction for Louisiana* (Washington, D.C., 1866), 8–9, 15–17; New Orleans *Tribune*, October–November 10, 1865.

Washington. Certainly some of the voters made contributions, but it cannot be determined whether or not regular assessments were levied. On November 13 a mass meeting was held in the Orleans Theater to draw up resolutions for Warmoth to take to Washington. After Benjamin F. Flanders had advised Negroes to seek full equality before the law and Rufus Waples had proved at length that Louisiana was a territory and not a state, Warmoth thanked all those who had voted for him and told them that they were the Louisianians who really loved the Union. Soon afterward he set out for the nation's capital.[64]

Probably Warmoth never expected to be formally seated in the House of Representatives. Nonetheless he made his appearance as an applicant, along with Randall Hunt and Henry Boyce, who had been elected to the United States Senate by the new legislature. Mainly, Warmoth concentrated on his opportunities to make himself known to Radical leaders in Washington. Thaddeus Stevens was the first man he called on. When he visited Chief Justice Chase, he took Whitelaw Reid along to entertain the ladies of the Chase household so he and the justice could concentrate on politics. Among many others, he conferred with Benjamin F. Butler, now a Radical Republican politician. Significantly, his diary for this trip made no complimentary reference to Andrew Johnson. Warmoth's political influence was growing to the extent that he was instrumental in getting Dostie appointed a surveyor of customs at the port of New Orleans.[65] Probably much of the Radical strategy for Louisiana in the months to come was planned during this visit to Washington.

7

From the time of the special election of 1865, the attitude of the conservative Louisiana press toward the Radical Republicans hardened.

64 New Orleans *Daily Picayune*, November 10, 1865; New Orleans *Tribune*, November 10, 1865; Ficklen, *History of Reconstruction in Louisiana*, 113–14; Lowrey, "James Madison Wells," 1,063; Cox, *Three Decades of Federal Legislation*, 429; New Orleans *Times*, November 14, 1865, quoted in Caskey, *Secession and Restoration*, 181–82.

65 Warmoth Diary, December, 1865, February 4, 1866; Ficklen, *History of Reconstruction in Louisiana*, 115; James G. Blaine, *Twenty Years of Congress: From Lincoln to Garfield, with a Review of the Events That Led to the Political Revolution of 1860* (Norwich, Conn., 1893), I, 224; New Orleans *Daily Picayune*, December 27, 1865.

Wells's organ, the New Orleans *Southern Star*, said of a Republican meeting: "The Negro people, black and white, held a meeting last night. Some of the speakers will be taken in hand by the Grand Jury. . . . We do not report the proceedings; no decent paper would."[66] The *Times* said of the same meeting: "The highest judicial power in the government has pronounced upon the Negro status. . . . Therefore it is treason against our entire population to attempt to deceive the Negro by a solemn electoral farce."[67] When Warmoth returned to Louisiana in March, 1866, a Baton Rouge weekly reported: "A fellow named Warmoth, a Yankee nigger worshipper who has recently 'squatted' in New Orleans, has just returned from a visit to Washington, bringing with him orders . . . as to how Louisiana shall be 'reconstructed'."[68]

In the meantime the state government continued to function under the constitution of 1864. The Unionist local officials whom Wells had appointed at the end of hostilities did not meet the approval of the "rebel" legislature elected in 1865. Wells had promised that he would call a special session of the legislature elected in November, 1865, as soon as the returns were in; this special session began at Mechanics' Institute on November 23. While this overwhelmingly Democratic body was in the process of organizing, a Confederate veteran who had lost both arms put on his uniform and applied for the position of doorkeeper. The Federal provost guards arrested him, but turned him over to the custody of the legislature. The legislators named him doorkeeper and ordered him to continue to wear his Confederate uniform. A new election was held in December, 1866, but the Democratic majority remained as strong as ever.[69]

One of Wells's purposes in calling the November, 1865, extra session was to elect two United States senators. The state already had two unseated senators-elect, but Wells hoped that senators elected by

66 Quoted in Caskey, *Secession and Restoration*, 182.
67 Quoted *ibid.*, 183.
68 Baton Rouge *Weekly Advocate*, March 31, 1866.
69 New Orleans *Daily Picayune*, June 11, November–December, 1865, March 3, June 5, 1866; *Acts Passed by the General Assembly of the State of Louisiana at the First Session of the Second Legislature, Begun and Held in the City of New Orleans on the 22d of January, 1866* (New Orleans, 1866), 40–41 (contains some acts of the special session of 1865); Ficklen, *History of Reconstruction in Louisiana*, 115–16; Lowrey, "James Madison Wells," 1,064–65, 1,084–85.

a legislature representing the whole state would have a better chance of being accepted in Washington than those elected while so much of Louisiana was under Confederate control. Henry Boyce was elected to the short term, Randall Hunt to the long, but they had achieved an empty honor. They went to Washington just as the United States representatives elected in November were returning home in despair. Louisiana was not to be represented in Congress for three more years.[70]

Wells did not remain on good terms with the Democrats who had elected him governor. He vetoed a bill which would have paid the salary of a district judge from the beginning of the occupation until his removal for disloyalty some months later and another which, in effect, granted immunity from state taxes for the years 1861 through 1864 to those persons who had been in Confederate-occupied Louisiana. The legislature retaliated by awarding state printing to the *Picayune* rather than to Wells's *Southern Star*. The final break came when the legislature passed a bill calling for municipal elections in New Orleans. This meant the ouster of Kennedy and other Wells appointees, so the governor vetoed the bill, but it was passed over his veto. The ensuing election brought back into office Mayor John F. Monroe, who had refused to take an oath of allegiance to the Union after the occupation began and who was among those proscribed by President Johnson's Reconstruction Proclamation. General Edward R. S. Canby, the Federal military commander, forbade Monroe to take office, but a pardon from the president cleared the way. Later the legislature ordered new elections in all of the country parishes. In these elections practically all local Unionist officeholders were replaced by Confederate sympathizers.[71]

The election of Monroe did not improve the corrupt and inefficient government of New Orleans. In August, 1865, a grand jury had concluded, while Kennedy was still mayor, that persons sentenced to jail terms could obtain release at any time by making payments to the

---

70 New Orleans *Daily Picayune*, December 6–8, 1865; Lowrey, "James Madison Wells," 1,069; Ficklen, *History of Reconstruction in Louisiana*, 116.
71 New Orleans *Daily Picayune*, May 9, 1865, February–May, 1866; Lowrey, "James Madison Wells," 1,070–71, 1,073–74; *Acts of Louisiana, 1866*, 108; Highsmith, "Louisiana During Reconstruction," 129; Ficklen, *History of Reconstruction in Louisiana*, 147; Cox, *Three Decades of Federal Legislation*, 430.

right persons. Also, said the grand jury, the city police force was notoriously corrupt. The new Monroe administration created a 550-man police force which did, apparently, bring about a reduction in the robbery and burglary from which no section of the city had been safe. Nonetheless corruption continued. An out-of-town newspaper was indignant when it learned that city tax collectors were collecting taxes in greenbacks, buying depreciated state notes at a discount, then using them at face value to pay what they owed the state. The citizens of New Orleans apparently accepted this as normal practice.[72]

Relations between Wells and the Democrats were openly hostile by March, 1866, but since the legislature was not then in session, no action could be taken against the governor. But when the newly elected legislature met in early 1867, the majority was determined to oust Wells from office. In the meantime the governor had gone over to the Radicals; his appointments after August of 1866 had been native or imported Republicans. In July he had cooperated with the Republican majority on the congressional committee investigating the New Orleans Riot of July, 1866. When the legislature convened, the house charged Wells with defaulting while tax collector of Rapides Parish, with responsibility for the deaths in the New Orleans Riot, and with usurping the authority of the state by proclaiming that voting qualifications must be in conformity with the Reconstruction Acts of Congress. Probably an impeachment trial would have been held and Wells ousted had it not been for the restoration of military rule. As it was, Wells's term was to be cut short when he was removed by General Philip Sheridan.[73]

The merchants and planters who dominated the legislature in late 1865, 1866, and early 1867 were not content with the constitution of 1864. They contended that the convention of 1864 was illegal, and the public arguments against the constitution were legalistic. The *Picayune* said in December, 1865: "It is undoubtedly a great hardship ... that our legislature should not be able to legislate upon ... the levees, the militia ... and the regulation of labor. But these great needs of our state ... do not supply any arguments in favor of an

72 New Orleans *Daily Picayune*, August 20, 22, 1865, March 14, April 10, 14, 1866; Baton Rouge *Weekly Advocate*, June 23, 1866.
73 New Orleans *Daily Picayune*, January–March, 1866, January–March, 1867; Lowrey, "James Madison Wells," 1,084–88.

illegal and invalid constitution."[74] Louisianians, like other southerners of the time, were great sticklers for legalistic niceties, but objections to the labor clauses, the education provisions, and above all, the possibility that some future legislature might grant Negro suffrage were the major causes of hostility to the constitution of 1864. Nor did legalism prevent the regulation of labor by the Black Codes.[75]

By 1866 the demands for a new constitutional convention were becoming strong. Congress, it was argued, had declared the constitution of 1864 invalid by refusing to seat representatives from Louisiana. The lower house of the legislature called for the election of delegates to a new convention, but the senate never enacted this bill into law. President Johnson used his influence to prevent a new convention. He had recognized the constitution of 1864, and his position vis-à-vis the Radicals in Congress would be further weakened if the Louisiana Democrats repudiated it. In early 1867, after Johnson himself had been repudiated by northern voters, the question of a constitutional convention again came to the fore in the Louisiana legislature. Partly this was bravado, partly a maneuver to help bring about the impeachment of Wells, who was adamantly opposed. On February 27, 1867, an act was passed providing for an election to call a convention for the purpose of drawing up a new constitution and at the same time electing delegates to that convention. Less than a week later, the first Reconstruction Act passed Congress establishing military rule in the South. As the Louisiana legislative session drew to a close, the act of February 27 was quietly repealed.[76]

Obviously, the leaders of Louisiana were feeling less and less that they were a conquered people; more and more, slavery aside, they were prepared to continue in the political arena the struggle lost on the battlefield. They did not have the advantage of a century of history to demonstrate what fundamental changes the war had wrought, but it is nonetheless amazing that so many of them believed that the

74 New Orleans *Daily Picayune*, December 1, 1865.

75 *Ibid.*, January 25, 1865, January 26, 1866; Ficklen, *History of Reconstruction in Louisiana*, 108; Warmoth, *War, Politics and Reconstruction*, 40.

76 New Orleans *Daily Picayune*, February 2, March 9–10, 22, 1866, February, 1867; *Acts Passed by the General Assembly of the State of Louisiana at the Second Session of the Second Legislature, Begun and Held in the City of New Orleans on the 28th of January, 1867* (New Orleans, 1867), 45–47, 277; Ficklen, *History of Reconstruction in Louisiana*, 148–49.

situation existing before secession, except that the Negro would be a peon rather than a slave, had been restored. This was not universal. An Opelousas newspaper suggested that a return to territorial status might be preferable to the antics of the legislature elected in 1865, and the private papers of many prominent families show little concern with or knowledge of political developments. Even so, encouraged by President Johnson's support, Louisiana's conservative politicians seemed to look for ways to assert their southernism. Had they set out to antagonize the people of the North they could hardly have done better than to reject the gift of an American flag made by Negro women of New Orleans, or to invite a group of Confederate generals, less than two years after Lee's surrender, to take seats inside the bar of each house of the legislature. It should be noted also that the opening prayer for legislative sessions was frequently offered by Benjamin F. Palmer, the Presbyterian divine who was sometimes credited with preaching Louisiana into secession.[77]

Insofar as taxes were concerned, the legislatures of 1865–1866 and 1867 were definitely more concerned with the welfare of the landowner than with the financial stability of the state. Taxes collected from October 1, 1864, to January 1, 1866, amounted to $875,658, of which Orleans Parish paid $666,000. In 1866 the legislature suspended all taxes due for the years 1860–1864 until January 1, 1868. Since the people in formerly occupied territory had already paid these taxes, this was an obvious concession to property owners in formerly Confederate-occupied Louisiana. The 1867 legislature extended this concession to January 1, 1870.[78]

The legislature of 1866 appropriated a total of $980,557 in the

77 New Orleans *Daily Picayune*, November, 1865–March, 1866, January–March, 1867; Opelousas *Sentinel*, December 16, 1865, quoted in New Orleans *Daily Picayune*, December 24, 1865; *Nation*, II (April 5, 1866), 431, (April 12, 1866), 461; *De Bow's Review*, After the War Series, I (February, 1866), 132–46; Reid, *After the War*, 266; McKitrick, *Andrew Johnson and Reconstruction*, 236. For examples of lack of concern see Margaret Butler Correspondence, Butler Family Papers; Joseph Vidal Papers, Department of Archives, Louisiana State University; Gaudet Papers, Gibson-Humphrey Papers, and Shaffer Papers, all in the Southern Historical Collection, University of North Carolina.
78 New Orleans *Daily Picayune*, January 27–28, February 10, 25, 27, 1866; *Acts of Louisiana, 1866*, 44–46, 112; *Acts of Louisiana, 1867*, 79–81, 197, 209, 285–87, 295–97; Highsmith, "Louisiana During Reconstruction," 407–408.

general appropriations bill. Of this total, $262,000 went to salaries, $199,000 to interest on outstanding bonds, and $250,000 for public education. Concerning the money for education, however, a qualifying clause provided that no more should be spent than should be collected from certain specified taxes, so that the actual amount hardly exceeded $100,000. In addition to appropriations, the legislature of 1866 authorized the issuance of $1,500,000 in state bonds to pay certain state debts, and also the issuance of $2,000,000 in certificates of indebtedness (state treasury notes) to pay current expenses. These certificates, when discounted, did serve one useful purpose. They, along with the certificates of the city of New Orleans, provided the main circulating medium in Louisiana for a number of years. The general appropriation for 1867 was $1,802,674, almost a million dollars more than in 1866. Salaries and contingent expenses had increased by almost $100,000, and interest on bonds had increased about the same amount. The bill for printing, with Democrats completely in control of the legislature, was $225,000.[79]

These appropriations were obviously far greater than any revenues which could be anticipated, but the legislatures of 1866–1867 were not satisfied with large appropriations. In 1865 the issuance of $1,000,000 in bonds for levee repairs had been authorized, but only $300,000 worth of the bonds had been sold. This act was repealed in 1867, and the state treasurer was instructed to issue $4,000,000 in levee bonds at 6 percent interest. The state auditor was to determine what tax was necessary to pay the interest and $100,000 a year principal on these bonds, and this tax was then to be levied. An additional $3,000,000 in bonds was authorized to "relieve" the state treasury. Last, but not least, the city of New Orleans was given the "privilege" of issuing $2,500,000 in city notes and lending these notes to the state without interest. Few Louisiana historians have paid attention to the statement of Benjamin F. Flanders before a congressional committee that the legislatures of 1866 and 1867 were largely responsible for Louisiana's state debt of the 1870s. A careful student of this subject has

---

79 *Acts of Louisiana, 1866*, 8–12, 26–28, 224–32; *Acts of Louisiana, 1867*, 223–25; Governor's message of January 28, 1867, in *Legislative Documents, Louisiana (1867)* (New Orleans, 1867), pages unnumbered.

concluded that the state debt was $26,000,000 at the end of the war. Repudiation of the Confederate debt reduced this to $11,000,000. By the end of 1867 the state debt had increased to $17,000,000. This burden was incurred before any Radical Republican, unless Wells be so designated, had been elected governor of Louisiana. To emphasize this point, well over one half of the actual debt of Louisiana at the height of Reconstruction had been incurred by Democratic legislatures before Radical Reconstruction began.[80]

The frantic struggle for internal improvements which was to characterize the early years of Radical Republican rule in Louisiana also had its beginning under the Democrats. Before the Civil War the owners of land liable to flooding had been required to maintain the levees protecting their property. After the end of the war, planters, without slaves and largely without capital, were unable to restore levees ruined by four years of neglect. Thus the state was forced into the business of levee maintenance and construction. Little or nothing was accomplished. Floods did much damage in 1866, far more in 1867. The levee board created to oversee flood control may or may not have been corrupt, but it was certainly inefficient.[81]

Other promotional measures were not so expensive, but they set an example which was to be costly in the future. In 1865 the legislature authorized an abortive scheme to build a railroad from Avery Island to New Iberia, and also to dig a waterway between the two points. In February of 1866, the New Canal in New Orleans, which had reverted to state ownership, was ordered leased. Former Confederate general Richard Taylor leased the canal for fifteen years, agreeing to pay a gradually increasing rental—$36,000 the first year, $85,000 the last. Taylor operated the canal from March, 1866, to August, 1873, and paid not one cent of rental for the entire period. Also in 1866 the state agreed to buy stock in the Baton Rouge, Grosse Tete, and Opelousas Railroad with state bonds at the rate of $6,000 per additional mile constructed, payable whenever five miles had been prepared for the

80 New Orleans *Daily Picayune*, March 1, 1867; *Acts of Louisiana, 1867*, 131–35, 137–39, 169, 171–73, 213–19; *House Miscellaneous Documents*, 42nd Cong., 2nd Sess., No. 211, p. 521; Highsmith, "Louisiana During Reconstruction," 407–408.
81 *Acts of Louisiana, 1866*, 56; New Orleans *Daily Picayune*, March 15–31, 1867; Lowrey, "James Madison Wells," 1,088.

laying of track. Before adjourning, the legislature authorized a corporation to make Bayou Plaquemine navigable for the entire year from the Mississippi to Grand Lake. Fortunately, the state did not subsidize this quixotic scheme; the entrepreneurs were to receive their reward from tolls charged for the use of the channel.[82]

The legislature which met in 1867 was even more inclined than its predecessor toward internal improvements. Among its grants was a free right-of-way to the Southern Telegraph Company, headed by generals Kirby Smith and Simon Bolivar Buckner. The New Orleans Lightering and Wrecking Company was given a fourteen-year monopoly of lightering ships over the bars at the mouth of the Mississippi, provided that it had its India-rubber devices for lifting ships in operation within a year. The New Iberia and Orange Railroad was granted a 150-foot right-of-way provided the track was completed between the two points within five years. The right to expropriate a right-of-way was given to the New Orleans and Selma Railroad, with the proviso that work must commence within one year and be completed within five. None of these schemes succeeded, and the only cost to the state was the time of the legislature. But the liberal attitude toward internal improvements was clearly demonstrated.[83]

Another development during this period was the creation of a board of immigration. This, it was hoped, would encourage white farmers and laborers to move to Louisiana. Still another legislative act required a license of ten thousand dollars for vendors of lottery tickets. In effect, this act confirmed the monopoly already granted to the Louisiana Lottery Company. Another act went further and provided that no license for selling lottery tickets should be issued until a twenty-five thousand-dollar bond had been posted by the vendor.[84]

An act was passed in 1866 which authorized planters and farmers to sell supplies to their tenants without purchasing a retail merchant's license. An act of 1867 amended the Civil Code so as to give debts owed for supplies furnished to a plantation, or cash advanced to the

82 *Acts of Louisiana, 1866,* 20–22, 280, 284, 288–90; Jackson Beauregard Davis, "The Life of Richard Taylor," *Louisiana Historical Quarterly,* XXIV (January, 1941), 116.

83 *Acts of Louisiana, 1867,* 81, 189–91, 203–205, 241, 243–45, 349–51.

84 *Acts of Louisiana, 1866,* 38–42, 68–70, 198–202, 242–52.

planter, priority over debts owed by the planter to laborers or artisans on the plantation. These acts had much influence on the future because they strengthened the crop lien as a means of financing agriculture.[85]

8

During 1865 and 1866 a sizable number of southerners in general and Louisianians in particular believed that the abolition of slavery had been a mistake. Such men and women, and the poorer whites who felt economically threatened by Negroes, obviously resented the sudden change in the status of the black man. Negro troops were especially obnoxious, but so were the freedmen who tested their freedom by descending upon the towns. Some of the freedmen were guilty of indecorous conduct, some of petty thievery, some of major crimes. But it is difficult to see how they could have won the approval of the white population except by continuing to behave exactly as they had behaved as slaves. Even those Louisianians who approved, in the abstract, of the end of slavery resented any effort on the part of the blacks to assert their freedom.[86]

Some men did consider themselves friends of the Negro and desired to help him, but their attitude was paternal, not fraternal. If there were white men in Louisiana who did not believe in the racial inferiority of the black man they were few in number and spoke in a low voice. This was not a debatable question, and for a century no Louisianian could publicly question the dogma of white superiority without ostracism. It should be noted, however, that the belief in Negro inferiority was not confined to the South. Northern Republi-

---

85 *Ibid.*, 236; *Acts of Louisiana, 1867*, 351–53.
86 *De Bow's Review*, After the War Series, I (June, 1866), 595–609, II (July, 1866), 91–94; Reid, *After the War*, 264–65; New Orleans *Daily Picayune*, December 14, 29, 1865; "A Pastoral Letter from the General Assembly to the Churches Under Their Care (1865)," in *The Distinctive Principles of the Presbyterian Church in the United States, Commonly Called the Southern Presbyterian Church. . . .* (Richmond, Va., n.d.), 66–67 (microfilm provided by Austin Presbyterian Theological Seminary, Austin, Texas); Shreveport *Southwestern*, August 30, 1865, quoted in New Orleans *Daily Picayune*, September 5, 1865; Franklin *Planters' Banner*, September 23, 1865, quoted in New Orleans *Daily Picayune*, September 29, 1865; *Nation*, II (March 15, 1866), 335, (April 19, 1866), 492; Cable, *The Negro Question*, 148; Avary, *Dixie After the War*, 203; Frazier, *The Negro in the United States*, 127–28; Franklin, *Reconstruction After the Civil War*, 5–6.

cans proclaimed white superiority when they sought office. Northern laborers were especially bitter toward the Negro, as had been demonstrated in the New York riots of 1863. The Louisianian did not feel that his belief in white superiority put him in a minority position; he found it hard to believe that any group of rational men would promote any sort of racial equality, political or otherwise.[87]

Emancipation apparently did nothing to quiet the Louisianians' old fear of a Negro insurrection. There had been slave revolts in Louisiana history, but these relatively minor uprisings had been attempts to achieve freedom. Yet now that freedom had come, whites were seemingly more fearful than before of a black *jacquerie*. This apprehension was sometimes shared by northern troops stationed in the South. The white Louisianian apparently felt that the best preventive measure was a restoration of regulations as much as possible like those which had existed under slavery. Obviously, this fear of insurrection contributed to bad feeling between the races.[88]

The Joint Committee on Reconstruction reported in 1866: "The feeling in many portions of the country toward emancipated slaves, especially among the uneducated and ignorant, is one of vindictive and malicious hatred."[89] This report was absolutely correct, and it is necessary to make a distinction between the apparently universal belief of white Louisianians in white supremacy and the truly vicious hatred which characterized much of the population. It was perfectly possible for a man who believed unquestioningly in Negro inferiority to nonetheless treat freedmen fairly, help them adjust to the new order, and maintain amicable, and even affectionate, personal relationships. Many Louisianians fell into this category, but they were few in number as compared to those whose dislike of the black man

87 Williams, *Romance and Realism in Southern Politics*, 19–20; Stampp, *The Era of Reconstruction*, 87; Cable, *The Negro Question*, 137; John Hope Franklin, "Jim Crow Goes to School: The Genesis of Segregation in the South," in Charles E. Wynes (ed.), *The Negro in the South Since 1865: Selected Essays in American Negro History* (University, Ala., 1965), 137–38; *Nation*, I (August 24, 1865), 229, (October 2, 1865), 523–24; New Orleans *Daily Picayune*, August 26, 1865; Woodward, "The Anti-Slavery Myth," 312–38; Williston H. Lofton, "Northern Labor and the Negro During the Civil War," *Journal of Negro History*, XXXIV (July, 1949), 251–73.
88 *Senate Executive Documents*, 39th Cong., 1st Sess., No. 2, p. 32; New Orleans *Daily Picayune*, August, 1865–December, 1866.
89 *House Reports*, 39th Cong., 1st Sess., No. 30, p. xvii.

ranged from avoidance of contact whenever possible to a rage that could be slaked only by Negro blood. In all fairness, however, it must be stated once more that this attitude, or range of attitudes, was not confined to the South. It existed in the North as well.[90]

Expressions of this hatred are not so abundantly recorded as are the results of it, but they are enough. *De Bow's Review* resurrected Dr. Josiah Nott, who had maintained before the war that Negroes and whites were of different species. Nott wrote in 1866: "Not a single full-blooded Negro has ever made a name worthy of being remembered, and . . . the best educated are the most vicious. The colored preachers . . . are the worst citizens we have."[91] A New Orleans newspaper stated: "It is our . . . belief, fixed and unalterable, that this country was discovered by white men, peopled by white men, defended by white men, and it is our settled purpose that none but white men shall participate in its government."[92]

The labor situation in Louisiana will be discussed in detail later, but it must be noted briefly here that it was a source of considerable irritation. The southerner did not know how to work free labor, nor did the ordinary freedman know how to work as a free man. The black was prone to test his freedom by coming and going as he pleased. Thus he was an exasperating employee. The planter who wrote in his diary, "I am perfectly disgusted with free negroes,"[93] expressed a thought held by thousands. The Negro whose former master attempted to keep him in bondage did not keep a diary, but there were such instances.[94] We do read that in Baton Rouge, "Mrs. Nelson . . . and Mrs. Knox have great trouble with their servants. They want to treat the Negroes as of old and . . . [the servants] won't put up with it."[95]

Planters and farmers were desperate to put in crops as soon as pos-

90 Coulter, *The South During Reconstruction*, 163; Frédéric Gaillardit, *L'Aristocratie en Amerique* (Paris, 1883), 67; White, *Freedmen's Bureau in Louisiana*, 170–71.
91 *De Bow's Review*, After the War Series, I (March, 1866), 271.
92 New Orleans *Crescent*, January 11, 1867, quoted in Copeland, "The New Orleans Press and Reconstruction," 152.
93 H. Capell Diary, December, 1866, in S. H. Capell Papers, Department of Archives, Louisiana State University.
94 Engelsmen, "Freedmen's Bureau in Louisiana," 184.
95 Payne to Mrs. Sterrett, June 10, 1866, in Barnhart (ed.), "Reconstruction on the Lower Mississippi," 93.

sible, and the scarcity and unreliability of black labor infuriated them. They were especially indignant that so many freedmen crowded into the towns, large and small. Even the Union army sought to halt this trend, but to little avail. The majority of white Louisianians simply did not believe that the Negro would work except under compulsion, and in 1865 and 1866 this was true often enough to strengthen the belief.[96]

In discussing violence as a factor in Reconstruction during 1865 and 1866, two circumstances must be borne in mind. First, the South, including Louisiana, was a section where violence was a common and generally respected method of settling disputes long before the Civil War and long after Reconstruction was over. Secondly, a war of tremendous violence had just come to an end. Not only had this war brought violence on the battlefield, but in remote areas of both north and south Louisiana bands of semiguerrillas, semioutlaws known as jayhawkers, had terrorized the population. Thus violence was not new. What had changed was the greatly increased incidence of violence directed against Negroes. This was true because the Negro was no longer protected from murder and mayhem by his value as a slave.

In all fairness, it must be pointed out that whites were not the only violent people in Louisiana. Crimes by blacks against blacks were very common. No reliable statistics are available, but a careful study of the entire Reconstruction period in Louisiana can lead to the opinion that, if the major massacres such as New Orleans and Colfax are discounted, more black men were killed or wounded by black men than by whites during all the years from 1865 through 1878. This was probably not true, however, in 1865 and 1866.

There were also blacks who indulged themselves in violence against whites. Accounts of such must be taken with care. Louisiana news-

96 N. P. Banks to T. M. Poore and others, August 17, 1864, in New Orleans *Tribune,* August 18, 1864; New Orleans *Daily Picayune,* September 28, December 28, 1865; *De Bow's Review,* After the War Series, II (November, 1866), 488; New Orleans *Crescent,* September 5, 1866, quoted in White, *Freedmen's Bureau in Louisiana,* 208; Shreveport *Southwestern,* June 4, 1865, quoted in New Orleans *Daily Picayune,* June 23, 1865; Highsmith, "Social and Economic Conditions in Rapides Parish," 13, 82; James W. Garner (ed.), *Studies in Southern History and Politics Inscribed to William A. Dunning . . . by His Former Pupils, the Authors* (Port Washington, N.Y., 1914), 137–38; Stampp, *The Era of Reconstruction,* 75–76, 121–22.

papers delighted in tales of Negro insolence and criminality. For three days in December of 1865 the *Picayune* was full of stories concerning two separate Negro riots in New Orleans. One was an attempt by longshoremen to halt the unloading of a ship by other blacks working at reduced wages; this was settled by negotiation. The other was supposed to have taken place on Christmas Day, and on December 29 the *Picayune* noted that after all the blood-and-thunder reports, it had been determined that nobody had been killed, which was quite a comedown from original reports of twenty or more dead.[97]

On the other hand, it must have alarmed citizens of Iberia Parish when a group of Negro troops, probably drunk, fired a dozen or more poorly aimed shots at citizens. An "insurrection," which would probably be called a strike today, occurred on a Natchitoches Parish plantation in December, 1865. The freedmen resisted the authorities, but the only man killed was black. Another group of Negro soldiers got out of hand in Algiers in March, 1866, but there was damage only to property. In Baton Rouge in May, 1866, it was reported to be dangerous for white persons to go on the streets at night. Two white men were reported murdered by Negroes in Caddo Parish in November of 1866, and in Tensas Parish a peddler was shot and killed by a black robber the next month. During a parade in New Orleans in early 1867 in which blacks carried a United States flag, a woman on the sidewalk jeered: "Look at the d——n niggers; go way with that Yankee dishrag!" The man carrying the flag stabbed her with the flagstaff, but the wound was not serious.[98] Kate Stone was terrified by a black mob which threatened to kill her brother and "brandished pistols and guns." This had been provoked, however, when her brother shot and killed a black man.[99]

Scores of pages could be written giving details of violence by whites against blacks. Agents of the Freedmen's Bureau made matter-of-fact reports which cannot be disregarded. Contrary to the impression given in some writings on Reconstruction, these men were not former abolitionists who went into the countryside to complete the revolu-

97 New Orleans *Daily Picayune*, June–December, 1865.
98 *Ibid.*, March 23, 1867; see also *ibid.*, August 31, 1865, January 11, March 2, November 29, December 12, 1866; Baton Rouge *Weekly Advocate*, May 26, 1866.
99 Kate Stone, *Brokenburn: The Journal of Kate Stone, 1861–1868*, ed. John Q. Anderson (Rev. ed.; Baton Rouge, 1972), 368.

tion they had begun. Most were former officers of the Union army who shared the usual American prejudice against blacks and who were as often as not on the planter's side in labor disputes. It is possible that by 1866 a few of them were prescient enough to sense future opportunities as "carpetbaggers" and therefore might feel that it was in their interest to play up atrocities, but it was in 1865 rather than 1866 that the worst atrocities were reported from the countryside. Carl Schurz repeats one Louisiana agent's report as follows:

The threat of shooting the laborers, so frequently made by the planters . . . usually has the effect of causing a general stampede from the plantation. . . . The fact that the body of a Negro was seen hanging from a tree in Texas near the Louisiana line; or of the murder in cold blood, in the northern part of the Parish of Caddo, of Mary, a colored woman, by John Johnson, the son of the proprietor of the plantation . . . and that instances have repeatedly occurred similar to the case presented at my office, where an old man had received a blow over his head with a shillalah one inch in diameter, which was so severe as to snap the stick asunder; and also the fracturing of the skull and the breaking of the arm of the helpless, inoffensive colored woman by a . . . planter in the Parish of Natchitoches.[100]

The report of the Joint Committee on Reconstruction abounds in incidents of violence, such as the case of eight freedmen arrested for murdering a planter in Caldwell Parish who, on their way to jail, were intercepted by a disguised mob. Two of them were shot on the spot; four others were never seen again. In Franklin Parish a "Black Horse Cavalry" was said to devote itself to terrorizing freedmen with whippings and worse if necessary to prevent their leaving the parish. General Joseph A. Mower reported 70 murders of freedmen by whites which had come to his attention, plus 210 cases of whipping, beating, and stabbing which did not result in death. He added that these were only the cases reported to him, and that the real total may have been twice as great.[101] A Shreveport newspaper reported in December, 1865: "Scarcely a day has passed from the latter end of last week, but

100 Stickney to Conway, August 1, 1865, in *Senate Executive Documents*, 39th Cong., 1st Sess., No. 2, pp. 87–90.
101 *House Reports*, 39th Cong., 1st Sess., No. 30, *passim; Senate Executive Documents*, 39th Cong., 2nd Sess., No. 6, pp. 86–87; John A. Carpenter, "Atrocities in the Reconstruction Period," *Journal of Negro History*, XLVII (October, 1962), 235; Bentley, *The Freedmen's Bureau*, 110; William Archibald Dunning, *Reconstruction, Political and Economic, 1865–1877* (New York, 1962), 45.

some negro had been drowned or killed. This is disgraceful, and should receive investigation of the authorities. A negro in our employ . . . was brickbatted the other morning without having given any provocation."[102]

Unfortunately, it was not possible to prevent these atrocities. The rapid demobilization of the Union army made effective military occupation of rural areas and small towns impossible. Freedmen's Bureau courts ordinarily dealt only with employer-employee disputes. Crimes of violence against freedmen were taken to the state courts, and in these courts it was almost impossible to convict a white man of a crime against a black. Not even the schools established for freedmen by northern missionary societies and the Freedmen's Bureau were safe from harm. According to the Freedmen's Bureau, not a single white man was punished for a crime against a Negro in Louisiana from the end of the war up to March 9, 1867. At Shreveport two white men who were convicted of murdering a freedman rose and walked out of court after the verdict was announced, and no effort was made to stop them.[103]

9

As has been often noted, if the former Confederate states had been willing to grant suffrage to some Negroes, those who owned property, for example, when the first postwar state constitutions were drawn up, Radical Reconstruction might have been avoided. This was cautiously advocated by Lincoln, and even by Andrew Johnson. Among the blacks best qualified to vote were the upper-class members of the former free Negro community of New Orleans. In education and property interest they were as well qualified as any white men in the nation. Thousands of Louisiana blacks had fought in the Union army, and it was difficult to argue that they should remain without suffrage while it was exercised by former Confederates who had done their

102 Shreveport *News*, December 12, 1865, quoted in Warmoth, *Letter of H. C. Warmoth*.
103 John Hope Franklin, "The Negro and Reconstruction," in Harold M. Hyman (ed.), *New Frontiers of the American Reconstruction* (Urbana, Ill., 1966), 69; New Orleans *Daily Picayune*, August 15, 17, 1866; Franklin, *Reconstruction After the Civil War*, 152; Thomas J. Durant to Warmoth, January 12, 1866, in Warmoth Papers; *Nation*, II (March 8, 1866), 304, (March 22, 1866), 368; *House Reports*, 39th Cong., 1st Sess., No. 30, pp. 79–80; White, *Freedmen's Bureau in Louisiana*, 144–45.

best to tear the Union apart. Many former slaves had learned to read and write in defiance of the law, and many had learned skills which would make them economically independent as free men. Thus there were thousands of black men in Louisiana at least as well qualified to vote as the average white voter.[104]

Yet only the very few Radicals in the South strongly advocated universal male suffrage. Some of these men were certainly sincere. On the other hand, many of them were as anti-Negro as their conservative neighbors, but they saw that only through Negro suffrage did they have a chance of gaining power. A few planters were willing to let the Negro vote because they believed that they could control him, but there were not many of these in Louisiana. Most Bourbons who did not object to Negro voting on racial grounds did object on economic grounds, believing that the Negro would favor expensive governmental programs and thus add to the tax burden. To the vast majority of white southerners, the idea of Negro suffrage under any condition, and to any extent, was unacceptable. Political equality, they believed, was a first step toward social equality, to which death was preferable. These southerners could not believe that northerners, most of whom did not permit the few blacks living in their states to vote, would force the South, where Negroes in many districts were in an overwhelming majority, to submit to such degradation.[105]

104 Coulter, *The South During Reconstruction,* 62; Franklin, "The Negro and Reconstruction," 65–68; Craven, *Reconstruction,* 228; New Orleans *Daily Picayune,* June 25, 1865; Carl Schurz, *The Reminiscences of Carl Schurz, Volume III, 1863–1869. With a Sketch of His Life and Public Services from 1869 to 1906 by Frederic Bancroft and William A. Dunning* (New York, 1909), 204–205; Leslie H. Fishel, Jr., "Northern Prejudice and Negro Suffrage, 1865–70," *Journal of Negro History,* XXXIX (January, 1954), 18; Lawanda and John H. Cox, *Politics, Principle and Prejudice, 1865–1866* (New York, 1963), *passim;* McKitrick, *Andrew Johnson and Reconstruction,* 58–59, 308; Brock, *An American Crisis,* 11, 19, 47; *Senate Executive Documents,* 39th Cong., 1st Sess., No. 43, quoted in Fleming (ed.), *Documentary History of Reconstruction,* I, 98; DuBois, *Black Reconstruction,* 200; Beale, *The Critical Year,* 178–79; Dunning, *Reconstruction, Political and Economic,* 125.

105 New Orleans *Daily Picayune,* May 20, August 8, October 6, 1865, October 12, 1873; Baton Rouge *Weekly Advocate,* March 17, October 6, 1866; Franklin *Planters' Banner,* November 25, 1865, cited in New Orleans *Daily Picayune,* December 1, 1865; Reid, *After the War,* 218–19; *De Bow's Review,* After the War Series, V (January, 1868), 41; Giulio Adamoli, "Letter from America, 1867," *Louisiana Historical Quarterly,* VI (April, 1923), 275; *Debates in the Senate of Louisiana, 1864,* 50; Lewinson, *Race, Class, and Party,* 37; T. Harry Williams, "An Analysis of Some Reconstruction Attitudes," *Journal of Southern History,* XII (November, 1946), 477.

Louisianians were almost correct in their belief that the North would not impose Negro suffrage. In 1865 many northern states rejected constitutional amendments which would have permitted their Negro residents to vote. On the other hand, a majority of the northern people were strongly opposed to permitting secessionists to regain the power in the national government that they had exercised before the war, and they were reluctant to see secessionists gain power in southern state governments. One powerful argument for Negro suffrage was the belief that freedmen were more loyal to the Union than southern whites. Another concern in the minds of politically aware northerners was the status of the freedmen. Few northerners thought of the Negro as an equal, but they had fought a bloody war to end slavery, and they were not willing that the black man should be returned to a servile status. The black might be protected in his freedom by an army of occupation, but it would be much simpler if protection was afforded by giving him a ballot with which to protect himself. Thus whenever an atrocity against freedmen was reported in northern newspapers, more and more men of the North began to feel that the granting of suffrage was essential. By early 1866 black-suffrage sentiment in the North was still in the minority, but it was growing. The people of the southern states in general, and of Louisiana in particular, were doing just those things that needed to be done to encourage the growth of this attitude. First came atrocities; then came the Black Codes, which were widely interpreted as attempts to restore the blacks to semislavery. Southern objections to the Freedmen's Bureau seemed to confirm this interpretation. Then came the Memphis Riot and the New Orleans Riot, which demonstrated conclusively that freedmen and white advocates of Negro suffrage were not safe in the South.[106]

The role of the Bureau of Refugees, Freedmen, and Abandoned Lands, commonly known as the Freedmen's Bureau, must be noted in

---

106 William A. Russ, Jr., "The Negro and White Disfranchisement During Radical Reconstruction," *Journal of Negro History*, XIX (April, 1934), 171–72; Franklin, *Reconstruction After the Civil War*, 13; *Senate Executive Documents*, 39th Cong., 1st Sess., No. 2, pp. 42–44; DuBois, *Black Reconstruction*, 155; McKitrick, *Andrew Johnson and Reconstruction*, 56–57; Clemenceau, *American Reconstruction*, 114; Blaine, *Twenty Years of Congress*, I, 24; *Nation*, I (July 6, 1865), 4.

considering political developments in Louisiana in 1865 and 1866. The Bureau was established by Congress on March 3, 1865, as an agency in the War Department. It was intended primarily as a means of providing relief for freedmen, although in practice it fed many destitute whites. Despite this, the bureau very quickly became unpopular in the South and remained so. One reason was that the bureau became an issue in the struggle between President Johnson and Congress; the southern Conservatives sided with the president and therefore had to oppose the bureau. But more important, the bureau, by its existence, forced planters to observe some degree of due process in their dealings with former slaves. The planters usually were able to do as they wished with the blacks on their land, but they were not able to do so quite as arbitrarily as would have been the case without the bureau. The fact that the bureau was in charge of lands confiscated because they had been abandoned by their Confederate owners also made it unpopular, even though almost all of these lands were soon returned to their former owners by President Johnson. Frequently, also, Freedmen's Bureau agents were the only persons qualified to act as election officials under the Reconstruction Acts of 1867. Here is the probable source of the incorrect belief that practically all Freedmen's Bureau officials were chiefly occupied with Radical Republican political activity. In fact, a great many, if not most, of the local officials discouraged political activity because it interfered with the freedmen's work.

Obviously the bureau agents, who were from the North, would be unpopular in the South because they represented the victorious Union. Whatever their real function, Louisianians saw them as occupation authorities. But most important of all, the bureau officials, however paternalistically, dealt with the newly emancipated blacks as free men and women and, insofar as lay within their power, they required the whites of Louisiana to do the same. This, in southern eyes, was the unforgivable sin.[107] A Virginia lady later noted of this

107 New Orleans *Tribune*, August 25, 1865; Baton Rouge *Weekly Advocate*, January 13, 1866; New Orleans *Daily Picayune*, October 10, December 1, 21, 1865, June 30, 1866, March 15, 1867; *De Bow's Review*, After the War Series, I (January, 1866), 109; Reid, *After the War*, 577; *House Reports*, 39th Cong., 1st Sess., No. 30, p. 82; *Senate Executive Documents*, 39th Cong., 2nd Sess., No. 6, pp. 85–86;

era: "Many good people came down to do good to us and to the Negroes; we were not always so nice to them as we should have been. But very good people can try other very good people sorely sometimes."[108]

When the war ended there were few Louisianians who would publicly aver that slavery should be restored as before the war, but the object, conscious or unconscious, of most Louisiana whites was to establish for the black man a status as near as possible to what had existed before the war. Slavery was impossible, but a state of serfdom, or peonage, might be brought about. The individual Negro would no longer be the property of one owner. Negroes in general might, however, be made into the servants of whites in general. Attempts to accomplish this were to play into the hands of the Radicals.

In Louisiana the towns of Opelousas in St. Landry Parish and Franklin in St. Mary Parish led the way. These municipalities adopted ordinances which, for all practical purposes, were reenactments of the municipal regulations in force for slaves in 1860. For example, Negroes were forbidden to come into town without permission of their employers; freedmen on the streets after 10:00 P.M. were to be fined five dollars or five days labor. In Opelousas no black was to be in town after 3:00 P.M. on Sundays. No Negro could live in town unless he was the servant of a white resident, nor could any Negro own firearms, sell or barter goods, or preach without a license. Farther to the north, in Bossier Parish, the prewar patrol was established once more to arrest all persons found on the roads without proper employment. To many whites such enactments seemed necessary in order to preserve order in the towns and to keep labor on the plantations. But when news of these ordinances spread over the nation, and the Radical press saw to its wide dissemination, it seemed to the people of the North that the South was attempting to reverse the decision of the war and to restore slavery. Thus these measures contributed to the eventual enactment of the Military Reconstruction Acts.[109]

Bentley, *The Freedmen's Bureau*, 57–58, 80, 159–61, 167–68; Floyd M. Clay, "Economic Survival of the Plantation System within the Feliciana Parishes, 1865–1880" (M.A. thesis, Louisiana State University, 1962), 22; White, *Freedmen's Bureau in Louisiana*, 17–40; Stampp, *The Era of Reconstruction*, 134–35.
108 Avary, *Dixie After the War*, 311.
109 New Orleans *Tribune*, July 15, 1865; *Senate Executive Documents*, 39th Cong.,

What these communities and others began in alienating northern public opinion, the legislature elected in 1865 continued by joining other southern states in enacting the notorious Black Codes. One motive for passage of the Louisiana Black Code was to define legally the rights and status of the freedmen. Chattel slavery was ended, but Louisianians simply could not imagine that their former slaves should now be considered free men. Ignorant of northern sentiment on the subject of the freedmen and placing undeserved confidence in the ability of President Johnson to have his way over the opposition in Congress, leaders in the legislature sought by law to create for the freedman a place in society legally equivalent to that of free Negroes before the Civil War. The legislators could say, and probably believe, that they were improving the status of the black man, because the station established by the Black Code was an improvement over chattel slavery. But their real purpose was to put the Negro, by statute, in a subordinate position conformable to Louisiana opinion as to his intellect, education, culture, and generally inferior nature.[110]

Probably a more compelling motive, at least in Louisiana, was the firmly held belief that the Negro would not work without compulsion. This had been generally true under slavery; a system of rewards and, especially, punishment had been necessary to keep most slaves at work. Since a bondsman had little or nothing to gain by working, his reluctance is not surprising. With the dislocations brought on by war, the quality and quantity of work had suffered. The end of the war and the end of slavery had brought further deterioration. It has been said that the blacks thought that freedom meant freedom from work, which was probably true to some extent. But probably more characteristic was a necessity to test freedom, to go to a neighboring plantation or to the nearest hamlet without a pass, or to gather at night for a frolic which did not leave the participants in the best of condition for work

---

1st Sess., No. 2, p. 23; "Ordinance Relative to the Police of Negroes or Colored Persons within the Corporate Limits of the Town of Franklin," in Warmoth, *War, Politics and Reconstruction*, 275–77; Warmoth, *War, Politics and Reconstruction*, 42–43; Schurz, *Reminiscences*, III, 188; Highsmith, "Louisiana During Reconstruction," 116; White, *Freedmen's Bureau in Louisiana*, 20–21, 136–37.

110 Constantin, "Louisiana Black Code," *passim*; Theodore Brantner Wilson, *The Black Codes of the South* (University, Ala., 1965), *passim*; Garner (ed.), *Studies in Southern History and Politics*, 139–40; Cox and Cox, *Politics, Principle and Prejudice*, 170–71.

the next day. Large numbers migrated to town permanently, beginning a trend which has continued for more than a century. Finally, toward the end of 1865, a rumor spread that freedmen were going to be given forty acres and a mule. How widespread this belief was among the freedmen it is difficult to say; it has probably been exaggerated by historians with conservative points of view; but to the extent that the belief existed it interfered with work in late 1865 and made blacks reluctant to sign labor contracts for 1866.[111]

The labor problem was, of course, one of those entrusted to the Freedmen's Bureau. Perhaps, if the bureau had been given a chance, it might have brought about some solution. But the bureau existed to protect the interests of the freedmen as well as those of the planters, and this situation was not satisfactory to the dominant class in Louisiana. Newspapers during the summer of 1865 began calling for some sort of compulsory labor system. As early as September an address to the people from the National Conservative Men of Louisiana advocated laws to regulate labor and to make the monstrous Freedmen's Bureau unnecessary. The special session of the new legislature which met in the fall of 1865 needed little persuasion and set to work almost immediately to draft laws to define the freedmen's permanent place in society and to make it possible to force them to labor.[112]

From these deliberations a number of statutes emerged. One act forbade Negroes to carry firearms and provided fines and/or imprisonment for violations. Another provided that any trespasser upon a plantation should be similarly punished. Yet another provided a fine of five hundred dollars for any person convicted of tampering with employees under contract. This last act was probably intended to prevent the fraudulent activities of labor agents who imported Negroes, placed them upon plantations in return for a fee from the planter,

111 Joe Gray Taylor, *Negro Slavery in Louisiana* (Baton Rouge, 1963), 59–92, 194–205; Taylor, "Slavery in Louisiana During the Civil War," 27–34; New Orleans *Daily Picayune*, August 22, 1865; Ella Lonn, *Reconstruction in Louisiana After 1868* (New York, 1918), 13.
112 New Orleans *Daily Picayune*, August 22, September 3, 17, 1865; Constantin, "Louisiana Black Code," 20–22, 40–52, 86–87; Ficklen, *History of Reconstruction in Louisiana*, 137–38; Engelsmen, "Freedmen's Bureau in Louisiana," 183; Lonn, *Reconstruction in Louisiana*, 13; *Senate Executive Documents*, 39th Cong., 1st Sess., No. 2, p. 40; Stampp, *The Era of Reconstruction*, 79–80.

and then persuaded them to run away so they could be placed again.[113]

Louisiana's legislators had some warning of the reaction to be expected from the North because the legislatures of Mississippi and several other states had completed their action before Louisiana. The northern reaction to these codes was indeed hostile. Therefore the Louisiana code did not go quite so far toward restoring slavery, and it was more carefully drafted than the codes of most of the other former Confederate states. The legislators did approve a bill requiring every adult freedman or freedwoman to provide himself or herself with a comfortable house and a means of making a living within twenty days; upon failure to do so, one was subject to arrest and the sale of his or her labor to the highest bidder for one year. Governor Wells had the good judgment to veto this bill, and the veto was sustained.[114]

The new vagrancy act was the one expected to return freedmen to the cotton and sugar fields. It anticipated laws passed after Reconstruction in that such words as *Negro, freedman,* or other synonyms for nonwhite did not appear in it. On the surface this act, modeled in large part after the Vagrancy Act of Massachusetts, was applied equally to people of all races. It provided that any vagrant could be arrested, and that upon conviction of vagrancy by a justice of the peace, he could be hired out to a private employer for a year or put at public work for the same length of time. Defenders of the statute made much of the fact that it closely resembled laws already in force in the North. This defense was hypocritical. It was understood when the act was passed that it was to be used against blacks but not against whites. In this respect it resembled the literacy requirements of the suffrage acts of the southern states in the 1890s and early 1900s.[115]

---

113 *Acts Passed by the General Assembly of the State of Louisiana at the Extra Session of the Second Legislature, 1865* (New Orleans, 1866), 14–26; Wilson, *Black Codes,* 79; Highsmith, "Louisiana During Reconstruction," 136; Constantin, "Louisiana Black Code," 74; New Orleans *Daily Picayune,* December 17, 1865.
114 Highsmith, "Louisiana During Reconstruction," 126; Constantin, "Louisiana Black Code," 86–87, 95.
115 New Orleans *Tribune,* November 12, 1864, November 28, 1865; New Orleans *Daily Picayune,* November 28, December 17, 1865; *Acts of Louisiana, Extra Session, 1865,* 14–17, 24–26; Ficklen, *History of Reconstruction in Louisiana,* 138–45; Memelo, "The Development of State Laws Concerning the Negro in Louisiana," 24; Germaine A. Reed, "Race Legislation in Louisiana, 1877–1898," *Louisiana*

The majority of the politically aware people in the North saw the Black Codes in simple terms. They were attempts by the South to evade the decision of arms and to restore a form of slavery. So far as the vagrancy provision of the Louisiana code was concerned, this was true. It is obvious that had the codes remained on the books and been enforced, justices of the peace all over Louisiana would have spent most of their time assigning "vagrant" laborers to planters needing labor or, more likely, blacks would have been constrained to accept whatever terms planters chose to offer in order to avoid being seized as vagrants.

The New Orleans *Tribune* did much to call national attention to the Black Codes. The Radical press of the North quickly took up the cry. The people of the North expected the southern states to adopt measures which could prepare the freedmen for full citizenship, and many felt that if the states did not do so, then this would be the duty of the federal government. It is difficult to comprehend the reasoning of Louisiana's legislators. The hostile northern and congressional reaction to the codes developed by other southern states was already evident before final action was taken in Louisiana. Governor Wells counseled caution. Even the conservative *Picayune* warned against hasty action. The *Tribune* rejoiced, prophesying that the legislature would enact the code and that these excesses would be the final blow to President Johnson's policies.[116] The Chicago *Tribune* was speaking directly to the legislature of Mississippi, but Louisianians should have paid attention when it said: "We tell the white men of Mississippi that the men of the North will convert the state into a frog pond before they will allow such laws to disgrace one foot of soil in which the bones of our soldiers sleep and over which the flag of freedom waves."[117]

History, VII (Fall, 1965), 380; Highsmith, "Louisiana During Reconstruction," 126; Wilson, *Black Codes*, 79.

116 New Orleans *Tribune*, November 28, December 13–14, 1865; New Orleans *Daily Picayune*, November 28, 1865; *Nation*, II (May 31, 1866), 89; Craven, *Reconstruction*, 121–22; Memelo, "The Development of State Laws Concerning the Negro in Louisiana," 19; Ficklen, *History of Reconstruction in Louisiana*, 142–43; Constantin, "Louisiana Black Code," 66–67, 97; Garner (ed.), *Studies in Southern History and Politics*, 142; DuBois, *Black Reconstruction*, 280.

117 Chicago *Tribune*, December 1, 1865, quoted in McKitrick, *Andrew Johnson and Reconstruction*, 178.

During late 1865 and early 1866 the news of the Black Codes reverberated across the North. The codes strengthened the impression of southern intransigence already formed by reports of atrocities, the election of former Confederates to high office, and such relatively minor matters as the Opelousas and Franklin ordinances in Louisiana. In Washington, President Johnson was unintentionally doing what was necessary to strengthen Radical sentiment, which was strong enough in February to pass the Civil Rights Bill of 1866 over his veto. Whether his ineptness could have succeeded, alone, in bringing about passage of the Military Reconstruction Acts is doubtful. He needed cooperation from southerners. Louisiana contributed much more than her share toward the complete alienation of northern opinion in July, 1866, when the New Orleans Riot took place.

10

As already noted, Governor Wells and the Unionists who agreed with him had by early 1866 come to a parting of the ways with the Democratic majority in the legislature. Wells had hitherto opposed Negro suffrage, first on simple racial grounds, then, in a reply to the Radical Friends of Universal Suffrage, because "I am persuaded, from my knowledge of the negro character, that nine out of ten . . . would support their former masters."[118] But this was before the New Orleans election which made Monroe mayor and before Wells's record of uncompromising Unionism during the Civil War had become a liability rather than an asset in dealing with the legislature. By early 1866 it was obvious that former Confederates were in control in Louisiana, that they had the support of President Johnson, and that they represented the vast majority of the white citizens of the state. Unionists such as Wells had no chance of retaining influence in government under the existing suffrage laws. And, although the constitution of 1864 empowered the legislature to grant suffrage to Negroes, there was no prospect of the Democratic legislature's taking any such action.[119]

It took no political genius to conclude that the only hope for the survival of a Unionist party in Louisiana lay in Negro suffrage. Thus

118 New Orleans *Daily Picayune*, July 12, 1865.
119 Lowrey, "James Madison Wells," 1,071–77; Ficklen, *History of Reconstruction in Louisiana*, 146–47.

the Negrophobe Unionists of 1864, or at least those who had not already gone over to the Democrats, found themselves forced into an alliance with the Radicals. When his political survival depended upon it, Wells discovered that black suffrage was not nearly so distasteful as he had once thought. The estimate of these Unionists should not be too cynical. They had remained loyal to the Union when such loyalty meant great danger to life, liberty, and property. Even though they had serious misgivings about Negro suffrage, they certainly looked upon it as a lesser evil than control of the state by men who, only a few months earlier, had been fighting to destroy the Union.

In late March, 1866, Warmoth recorded in his diary that Wells had said in a private conversation that, "By the Eternal, he intended to beat the rebels and keep them from power if in so doing he destroyed the state government and produced anarchy for twenty years. That he had fought them and [would] continue to fight them forever. He also said that he was in favor of calling the Convention of 1864 and disfranchising the rebels and admitting the Negroes to vote."[120] Thus the old-line Louisiana Unionists were pushed into an alliance with the Radicals who had been advocating Negro suffrage for more or less the same reasons. This alliance did not go without notice. The Baton Rouge *Weekly Advocate* reported in late June that Wells had "sold himself out to the Cutler-Hahn nigger suffrage party."[121]

The plan to call the convention of 1864 back into session had the virtue of simplicity. Before adjourning, that body had adopted a resolution giving its president the power to call it back. The intent of the resolution was almost certainly to permit recall if the voters refused to ratify the constitution, but no time limit was set. Thus, although two years had elapsed, a case could be made for the legality of recalling the delegates. It would be necessary to elect additional delegates from the parishes not represented in 1864, but since seventy-six was a quorum, those strong Unionists who were already members could convene the convention and pass upon the credentials of those who might be elected. Therefore, on June 23, 1866, an invitation signed by the secretary and purporting to represent the executive and

120 Warmoth Diary, March 28, 1866, see also *Nation*, III (August 16, 1866), 121;
    Franklin, *Reconstruction After the Civil War*, 97–98.
121 Baton Rouge *Weekly Advocate*, June 30, 1866.

several members, was sent to the members of the convention asking them to meet at Mechanics' Institute on July 26, 1866. A storm of protest arose, but the meeting was held nonetheless. However, only about forty men appeared; the remainder had stayed away, most of them because they feared violence, and the president, Judge E. H. Durell, was among the absentees.[122]

Judge Durell's absence was an inconvenience, but it was not enough to prevent the carrying out of Unionist plans. R. King Cutler called the meeting to order, and Rufus K. Howell, associate justice of the state supreme court, was elected president pro-tem. A delegation called on Durell, but he refused to attend, saying that Governor Wells was responsible for the convention's being called, and that Wells would betray it a second time as he had already betrayed it once. It was decided to go ahead. On June 27 Wells issued a proclamation taking note of the fact that Howell, as president pro-tem, had called the convention to meet in New Orleans on July 30. Wells also called for the election of delegates to fill vacancies, but this election was not to be held until September 3, 1866. Thus the Unionist delegates left over from 1864 would have ample time to take firm control of the convention.[123]

Without doubt, Louisiana Unionists had some assurance of support from Radical members of Congress. In fact, Wells probably waited until he was promised such support before he gave official sanction to the convention's recall. Howell had conferred with Radical leaders in Washington during July. When District Judge Edmund Abell of New Orleans charged a grand jury that any person attempting to subvert the government of Louisiana by participating in the convention was guilty of a crime, the judge was arrested by military authorities on a charge of treason. The charge was not pressed, but Louisiana Democrats, who had become more and more sure of their dominance and more and more contemptuous of Radicals at home and in the North, now realized that the convention of 1864 would reconvene. The bet-

---

122 New Orleans *Daily Picayune*, June, 1866; Ficklen, *History of Reconstruction in Louisiana*, 80, 156–58; Lowrey, "James Madison Wells," 1,079–80.
123 New Orleans *Daily Picayune*, June, 1866; New Orleans *Tribune*, June, 1866; Lowrey, "James Madison Wells," 1,080; Warmoth Diary, June 30, 1866; Ficklen, *History of Reconstruction in Louisiana*, 159–60; Cox, *Three Decades of Federal Legislation*, 431.

ter informed and better educated among them were inclined to ignore it, believing that its actions would be declared illegal by the courts, but the ordinary whites of Louisiana in general and New Orleans in particular became more and more restless as July 30 drew near.[124]

The New Orleans Riot cannot be considered in isolation. Largely in response to the Black Codes, Congress had passed the Civil Rights Act of 1866 over President Johnson's veto. This act forbade discrimination against Negroes on grounds of race and empowered blacks who believed that they could not obtain justice in state courts to seek relief in federal courts. To many Louisianians it seemed that all legal methods of local control of the black population were being destroyed. The constitutionality of the Civil Rights Act was questionable, and its major provisions were therefore included in the proposed Fourteenth Amendment to the Constitution, but this was little comfort to Louisianians.

Nor must it be forgotten that violence directed at freedmen, not so extensive as pictured in the Radical press, but nonetheless very real and very deadly to its victims, had been a constant feature of life in Louisiana since the end of the war. Finally, in May, 1866, a dozen or so newly demobilized black soldiers had been massacred by the Memphis police. There were no repercussions against the police, and it would seem reasonable to conclude that the Memphis example was duly noted by white Democrats, and by the police in particular, in New Orleans. The actions of the Radicals in Congress left many southern whites feeling that almost any course of action was justified. "Some of the speeches made in our Congress would disgrace an assembly of New Zealanders, convened to determine the fate of their miserable captives—whether they should be eaten raw or cooked."[125]

Mayor Monroe was determined that the convention should not meet. He approached General Absalom Baird, who was commanding the United States forces in New Orleans while General Philip Sheridan was absent in Texas, and informed Baird that the proposed conven-

124 Lowrey, "James Madison Wells," 1,080; Ficklen, *History of Reconstruction in Louisiana*, 155–56; Caskey, *Secession and Restoration*, 222; Donald E. Reynolds, "The New Orleans Riot of 1866, Reconsidered," *Louisiana History*, V (Winter, 1964), 5–27.

125 New Orleans *Daily Picayune*, May 16, 1866; *ibid.*, May–July, 1866; Baton Rouge *Weekly Advocate*, January–June, 1866; *Nation*, II (May 14, 1866), 616; Reynolds, "The New Orleans Riot Reconsidered," 5–10.

tion was a violation of municipal ordinances and that it would be dispersed unless supported by the military. Baird forbade dispersal, noting that if the convention were legal, it should be permitted to meet; if it were not, it should be ignored. Three days later the mayor and the Democratic lieutenant-governor, Voorhies, tried again. They informed Baird that it was their intention to have the members of the convention indicted by the Orleans Parish grand jury. Baird forbade this also, saying that if the sheriff arrested any delegates, the military would release them and arrest the sheriff.

Now both parties telegraphed Washington. Voorhies sent his wire to President Johnson, who replied that the military would be expected to sustain the proceedings of the courts. General Baird asked Secretary of War Stanton for instructions, and Stanton did not reply. Since Stanton at this time was cooperating with the Radicals in their vendetta with President Johnson, his action has been interpreted to mean that the Radicals deliberately decided to incite a riot in New Orleans, knowing that this would improve their chances in the congressional elections of 1866. This is a most improbable theory. There was no way Stanton could be sure a riot would break out, and the Radicals probably had more to gain if the convention should meet and Louisiana should "voluntarily" adopt Negro suffrage. But even if Stanton was more Machiavellian and farsighted than Machiavelli, nothing forced the whites of New Orleans to cooperate with the Radicals by staging a riot to demonstrate rebel intransigence.[126]

With tempers already at a dangerous pitch, Republican meetings during the last few days of July seem to have made things worse. Henry Clay Warmoth described one such meeting in his diary: "The Republicans held a large meeting at the Mechanics' Institute . . . to endorse Congress and the call of the convention. The governor had issued his proclamation . . . and everybody friendly to it is in good spirits. The press and the Democracy are mad against it. It is hoped that it will pass off without trouble whichever way it may terminate."[127]

126 This account of the New Orleans Riot, unless otherwise noted, is derived from *House Reports*, 39th Cong., 2nd Sess., No. 16, *passim*. See also Ficklen, *History of Reconstruction in Louisiana*, 163–65; Reynolds, "The New Orleans Riot Reconsidered," 5–27.
127 Warmoth Diary, July 29, 1866.

At this or another meeting the Radical Dr. A. P. Dostie made a speech widely regarded as incendiary. In it he was reported to have pointed out that the black men and Unionists in Louisiana outnumbered the rebels, and to have asserted that if any affair like that at Memphis was attempted, the Republicans, white and black, would fight back and that the streets of New Orleans would run with blood. He was said to have urged the many Negroes present at the meeting to be on hand when the convention met on Monday, July 30.[128] This speech, if delivered as reported, could hardly have been considered incitement to riot unless the Democrats were planning to break up the convention. However, Dr. Dostie's speech attracted little attention when delivered. The supposed quotations from his address were published in the New Orleans *Times* on August 3, 1866, three days after Dostie's death in the riot. By this time the conservative press of New Orleans had begun picturing the riot as the result of a deliberate Radical conspiracy, and it is possible that the account of Dostie's speech is an invention.[129]

The convention was scheduled to meet at noon. An opposition force composed of police and citizens—many of the latter were probably firemen—was formed the evening before. Warmoth, who witnessed much of the riot, wrote in later years, when he was seeking to gain the good opinion of the Louisiana planters among whom he lived, that the police were in uniform and that the participating citizens were identifiable by the fact that they were in shirt sleeves and had white handkerchiefs tied about their necks.[130] Certainly there were planned preparations; it is impossible otherwise to account for the fact that so many armed white men were on hand. This does not preclude the possibility, of course, that when the excitement began many bystanders joined in the fun.

The members of the convention held a preliminary meeting at

---

128 *Appleton's Annual Encyclopedia, 1866*, 451, 454, quoted in Fleming (ed.), *Documentary History of Reconstruction*, I, 232; Ficklen, *History of Reconstruction in Louisiana*, 161–62.

129 New Orleans *Times*, August 3, 1866, quoted in Ficklen, *History of Reconstruction in Louisiana*, 161–62; New Orleans *Daily Picayune*, July 20–August 10, 1866; Francis P. Burns, "White Supremacy in the South: The Battle for Constitutional Government in New Orleans, July 30, 1866," *Louisiana Historical Quarterly*, XVIII (July, 1935), 606.

130 Warmoth, *War, Politics and Reconstruction*, 48–49.

10:00 A.M., the purpose of which, apparently, was to arrange for the posting of bond in case the delegates were arrested. The *Picayune*, in its evening edition for the day, carried the following statement: "Between the freedmen . . . and our regular and permanent citizens there exists now . . . a feeling of the most kindly and friendly character. Indeed . . . the freedmen are treated with an indulgence, a sympathy, a kindly good will which are rarely exhibited in any country by a superior to an inferior race."[131]

The convention gathered formally at noon without difficulty. A quorum was not present, however, and after a prayer by Dr. Horton, a Radical minister, the meeting adjourned for one hour. In the meantime, General Baird had somehow gained the impression that the meeting would open at 6:00 P.M. and had made his plans to have troops on hand at Mechanics' Institute at that time. At an hour after noon, however, he had no troops on hand or instantly available.

At about noon a procession of Negroes carrying a United States flag and led either by a band or a single drum, depending upon which testimony is believed, crossed Canal Street moving toward the Mechanics' Institute. Probably there was some jostling; at any rate, a white man fired a revolver at one of the Negroes. No one was hit, and the procession passed on to the institute. By 12:30 P.M. there were some thirty white men inside the building and a crowd of three to four hundred Negroes outside. At about 1:00 P.M. fighting broke out, supposedly over an attempt by the police to arrest a Negro newsboy. The police and the men joined with them seem to have opened fire at once, and very few of the assembled blacks were armed.

The Negroes ran into the Mechanics' Institute building seeking shelter. Warmoth, who had just arrived at 150 Canal Street from the meeting hall, wrote in his diary that he "saw policemen and citizens deploying across the end of Dryades and firing briskly. The fire was kept up for two hours and a half."[132] The few armed men in the hall fired back from the windows, but their fire was weak and ineffective. Those inside did their best to hold the doors against the now blood-maddened police. They could not hold out for long against such superior fire power, but several times they did beat back the attackers

131 New Orleans *Daily Picayune*, July 30, 1866.
132 Warmoth Diary, July 30, 1866.

with chairs. Dr. Horton waved an improvised white flag and sought to surrender; he was shot dead on the spot. Dr. Dostie was a special target; he was shot through the spine and stabbed through the abdomen with a sword. John Henderson, a member of the convention, was also killed within the hall, as were more than a few Negroes.

When it became evident that the police and their helpers would show no mercy, those inside the hall began leaping out the windows in an attempt to save themselves. Former General Richard Taylor of the Confederate army had forgotten about the convention and arrived downtown at the height of the riot. He wrote that he "saw a crowd of roughs . . . and negroes running across Canal Street. . . . A negro came flying past, pursued by a white boy, certainly not above fifteen years of age, with a pistol in his hand. . . . Many poor negroes had been killed most wantonly."[133] Warmoth "saw policemen shoot two negroes dead, who had been knocked down by rocks. I saw a policeman followed by hundreds of infuriated men and boys . . . beat a poor old negro over the head and shoulders until he fell and was then pitched upon by the rabble and kicked and stamped until they themselves were ashamed."[134] Former Governor Hahn was wounded, but he and several other members of the convention were protected from the mob and escorted to prison. At 2:40 P.M. General Baird's troops finally arrived on the scene, and the riot was over.

The best estimate of casualties was that 3 white and 34 black Unionists had been killed, 17 white and 119 black Unionists wounded. Ten policeman had been injured, but the only fatality among those attacking the Mechanics' Institute was a young man who had been shot in the back of the head. The next day the *Picayune* reported: "It was certainly a trying day for the police, but under the circumstances they performed their duty well. . . . Some few, as it is rumored, may have exceeded their duties, but under the circumstances . . . they did even better than expected."[135] After returning to the city, however, Sheridan wired General Grant: "The more information I obtain . . . the more revolting it becomes. It was no riot, it was an absolute massacre by the police which was not excelled in murderous cruelty by

133 Richard Taylor, *Destruction and Reconstruction: Personal Experiences of the Late War,* ed. Charles P. Roland (Waltham, Mass., 1968), 249.
134 Warmoth Diary, July 30, 1866.
135 New Orleans *Daily Picayune,* July 31, 1866.

that at Fort Pillow. It was a murder which the mayor and police of the city perpetrated without the shadow of a necessity. Furthermore, I believe it was premeditated."[136]

It is safe to say that, contrary to what came to be believed by many Louisianians, the 1866 riot was not brought about by a Radical conspiracy in Washington. The Radicals were, of course, happy to take advantage of the event after it happened; it did demonstrate rather clearly that the lives of freedmen in the South were not protected by state authority. There is circumstantial evidence that Mayor Monroe and his followers in New Orleans did plan the attack on the convention, but this evidence is far from conclusive. The most recent study of the riot concludes that it did not result from a Radical conspiracy, but that it probably was not the handiwork, at least directly, of white public officials. Rather, "Behind . . . the explosion of blind rage lay a fundamental inability of the whites to accept . . . emancipation . . . and its revolutionary implications." The Black Codes had shown white "determination to keep the Negro as nearly in his old status as possible. Negro suffrage would have defeated that determination. . . . Not only did the whites reject this prospect, but many of them regarded even the serious discussion of such proposals as odious." As a result, in "the charged atmosphere of July 30 . . . many white citizens and policemen could not resist the compulsion to vent their rage upon the Negroes and white Radicals. Given their racial views, the reaction was perhaps inevitable."[137]

The Louisiana press preferred, if possible, to play down the riot, even though it led to what amounted to martial law in New Orleans. As late as August 8 the *Picayune* sneered at *Harper's Weekly* for publishing a "fancy sketch of a negro riot."[138] The national repercussions could not be ignored, however, and two days later this paper announced that the whole affair had been planned in Washington for the benefit of the Radical Republican party.[139] A Baton Rouge paper

---

136 Sheridan to Grant, August 2, 1866, quoted in Beale, *The Critical Year*, 352n.
137 Reynolds, "The New Orleans Riot Reconsidered," 26–27. This is the best short account of the riot. Another balanced account can be found in Ficklen, *History of Reconstruction in Louisiana*, 146–79. Kendall's description in his *History of New Orleans*, I, 307–11, is biased, and Burns, "White Supremacy in the South," is both biased and inaccurate.
138 New Orleans *Daily Picayune*, August 8, 1866.
139 *Ibid.*, August 10, 1866.

stated on August 4 that Mayor Monroe should be censured for getting the people of Louisiana in trouble.[140] A week later, however, the editor had learned the party line: "We are in a queer condition. Our social and civil laws are outraged and if we had not resisted there is no telling the extent to which dirt would have been crammed down our throats. We chose another course and our civil authorities arrest, after a riotous resistance, the offenders, and lo! the *innocent* blacks, armed to the teeth, and the cowardly throng of white men who marshalled them are the sufferers from every conceivable outrage from the hands of insolent rebels and traitors."[141]

This came to be the accepted version of the riot insofar as Louisianians were concerned for the next seventy years and more. A few months later, during the holiday season, an editorial in a prominent newspaper in New Orleans read: "Louisianians are gentle and confiding. . . . Louisianians are a plain old-fashioned people. . . . Louisianians are gay, polite, and sociable. . . . The people of Louisiana have lived under too many governments to be restless, turbulent, or given to excitement of any kind."[142]

In the real world of 1866, the riot was received in an entirely different way. There had been many more Negroes killed before July 30 than were murdered on that date, but the previous killings had been scattered over time and space. The concentration of so much bloodshed in one hot afternoon aroused northern public opinion far more than the events that had gone before. This could not be dismissed as Radical propaganda. Louisiana Radicals, many of them going into exile for personal safety, were on hand in the North to tell what had happened and probably to embellish their accounts with a few added details of blood and slaughter. It was evident that some method had to be found to protect the Negro from resurgent rebels. Humanitarianism had a large part in this sentiment. Hatred of the South left over from the war was also a factor. Partisan politics certainly played a major role. Also involved to some extent was fear that if life was not made safe for the Negro in the South, he might decide to migrate to the North.[143]

140 Baton Rouge *Weekly Advocate*, August 4, 1866.
141 *Ibid.*, August 11, 1866.
142 New Orleans *Daily Picayune*, December 28, 1866.
143 G. J. Holt to Warmoth, August 1, 1866, in Warmoth Papers; New Orleans *Tribune*,

Congress sent a committee to investigate the riot. The Republican majority concluded that the fault lay with the local Democrats, particularly those in public office. It recommended that Louisiana be provided with a provisional government upheld by military power until a state government loyal to the United States could be established. The Democratic minority held that the disturbance was purely local but, paradoxically, Radical conspirators in Washington had helped bring it about. The committee heard 117 witnesses, and its report constitutes excellent source material. The conclusions of the majority and the minority, however, were completely partisan and could have been reached without the hearings and without any testimony. This report was not published until February of 1867. By that time the people of the North had expressed their opinions in the congressional elections of 1866, giving the Radicals an overwhelming majority in both houses. Louisiana had contributed her share and more to bringing about military Reconstruction.[144]

September 27, October 17, 1866; *Nation,* III (August 9, 1866), 101, (August 30, 1866), 161; *Harper's Weekly,* XI (March 2, 1867), 130; Craven, *Reconstruction,* 187–88; Burgess, *Reconstruction and the Constitution,* 98; Brock, *An American Crisis,* 159; DuBois, *Black Reconstruction,* 314, 465–66; Beale, *The Critical Year,* 343; Rembert W. Patrick, *The Reconstruction of the Nation* (New York, 1967), 84; C. Van Woodward, "Seeds of Failure in Radical Race Policy," *Proceedings of the American Philosophical Society,* CX (February, 1966), 3; Blaine, *Twenty Years of Congress,* 236.
144 *House Reports,* 39th Cong. 2nd Sess., No. 16, *passim.*

IV   *Military Reconstruction in Louisiana*

A T THE END of the Civil War, the South was utterly defeated militarily; there was no significant desire to continue the struggle or to prepare for another in the future. There were a few irreconcilables, and women tended to maintain love of the "lost cause" and hatred of the North more intensely than men, but the people of the South were conquered, and they were well aware of that fact. In April of 1865 President Johnson could have imposed practically any conditions he chose. He did force the former Confederate states to abolish slavery and to ratify the Thirteenth Amendment to the Constitution. He could have forced Louisiana and the other states of the South to grant full civil rights to Negroes; he certainly could have required, as indeed he did suggest, that the right to vote be granted to black veterans of the Union army, to educated blacks, and to black men who owned property. The fact that the president did not do these things and that he was opposed to their being done by the federal government did much to bring on military reconstruction in Louisiana and in other states of the South.[1]

This is not the place for a detailed history of events in Washington

---

1 *House Reports*, 39th Cong., 1st Sess., No. 30, *passim*; McKitrick, *Andrew Johnson and Reconstruction*, 153–54, 195–96, 212.

from the end of the war to the beginning of military reconstruction. But an understanding of developments in the nation's capital is essential to an understanding of events in Louisiana. Before the end of the war, Lincoln had established "governments" in Arkansas and Tennessee as well as in Louisiana. However, except for those elected from Louisiana in 1862, Congress had refused to seat representatives from these states. When Lincoln's assassination brought Johnson to the presidency, Congress was not in session. Johnson implemented his plan for Reconstruction under his executive powers and established governments in the other formerly Confederate states. The changes mentioned above that the president forced upon a reluctant South were not enough to satisfy the Radical Republicans led by Thaddeus Stevens in the House of Representatives and Charles Sumner in the Senate, but for the first months after the end of hostilities the president probably had the support of a majority in Congress. He certainly was not opposed by a majority.

However, the erosion of Johnson's position was almost constant. His being a southerner was a handicap, and his enemies had not forgotten how he had disgraced himself by his drunkenness on the day of his inauguration as vice-president. The 1865 elections in southern states which, as in Louisiana, restored former Confederates to power, weakened his position. When Congress met, it not only refused to seat representatives from the formerly rebellious states, it set up the famous Joint Committee on Reconstruction to investigate conditions in the South.

This was not an unbiased committee in the sense that it heard prosouthern and antisouthern witnesses in equal numbers and gave equal weight to "rebel" and "loyal" testimony. The Joint Committee on Reconstruction was an agency of the victorious North looking into conditions in the defeated South. In the spring of 1865, the South would have accepted this as one of the unpleasant consequences of unconditional surrender, but before the end of that year the South had allied itself with President Johnson against the Radicals. When the report of the joint committee was published in early 1866 Louisianians and other southerners could denounce it as biased because the point of view of the South and of the president was not confirmed by the committee's conclusions.

President Johnson's reputation has varied greatly through the years. During most of his term of office he was perhaps the most unpopular chief executive the nation has ever had. As is well known, he was impeached and escaped conviction by only one vote; there is no evidence that the public breathed a sigh of relief when he was so narrowly acquitted. When he left office, he had few friends outside the South. But after Radical Reconstruction failed, Johnson's reputation began to improve. The fall of Radical regimes in the South and the gradual disfranchisement and humiliation of Negroes by the southern and border states were accompanied by a rise in historians' estimates of Johnson's abilities and principles. By the 1930s, Johnson had become the voice of reason in an era of madness as well as the savior of presidential government. A reversal of this trend began in the mid-twentieth century, and Johnson, the president, has once more come under attack. It is no accident that the decline in his reputation coincided with the Civil Rights movement of the twentieth century.[2]

It is easy to say what Andrew Johnson did between his succession to the presidency and his return to Tennessee. It is not so easy to say why he did it. Although he had never been a Republican, before the war he had been the champion of freehold farmers against the planting aristocracy of the South and the political machines of the cities. The Radicals expected him to be more severe in his dealings with the defeated South than Lincoln would have been. Close scrutiny, however, reveals that the Radicals were unrealistic in their expectations.

---

2 Some of the earlier and favorable works dealing with Johnson are: George F. Milton, *The Age of Hate: Andrew Johnson and the Radicals* (New York, 1930); Lloyd P. Stryker, *Andrew Johnson: A Study in Courage* (New York, 1929); Robert W. Winston, *Andrew Johnson: Plebian and Patriot* (New York, 1928). Claude G. Bowers, *The Tragic Era: The Revolution After Lincoln* (Cambridge, Mass., 1929), was a very popular and extremely biased pro-Johnson and anti-Radical account of Reconstruction. J. G. Randall, *The Civil War and Reconstruction* (New York, 1937) gives probably the most balanced and scholarly pro-Johnson account of the years 1865–1867, but it should be noted that a revision of this work, J. G. Randall and David Donald, *The Civil War and Reconstruction* (2nd ed.; New York, 1967), has some significant changes in interpretation. More recent and critical works are Brock, *An American Crisis*; Cox and Cox, *Politics, Principle and Prejudice*; and McKitrick, *Andrew Johnson and Reconstruction*. Attention should also be given to Albert Castel, "Andrew Johnson: His Historiographical Rise and Fall," *Mid-America*, XLV (July, 1963), 175–84, and Willard Hays, "Andrew Johnson's Reputation," *East Tennessee Historical Society's Publications*, No. 31 (1959), 1–31; No. 32 (1960), 18–50.

In the first place, they were a minority in Congress. Secondly, Johnson was a southerner. He and the majority of his eastern Tennessee neighbors were Unionists, but their opposition to the planter leaders of the Confederacy was based as much upon Negrophobia as upon economic or class conflict. Johnson shared with practically all southerners, and with a vast majority of white Americans, an unquestioned belief in the innate inferiority of the Negro. Thus he could not advocate Negro suffrage with any enthusiasm. Also, Johnson apparently believed that eastern Tennessee was a microcosm of the South as a whole; that if the yeoman farmers of the South were given a chance they would unite in loyalty to the Union and take over control of their states from the old aristocracy. He also was a strict constructionist in his view of the United States Constitution. He wanted to restore a Union much like that which preceded the war, except that chattel slavery would no longer exist.[3]

Yet another development must be taken into account. Johnson's hatred of the planter class, if it did not disappear, was certainly diluted during 1865 and early 1866. His own proclamation made it necessary for higher Confederate officials and wealthier planters and merchants to procure pardons from him before their full civil rights were restored. As a result, the president was besieged by patrician southerners who desired pardons. One is almost forced to conclude that these gracious gentlemen and their ladies changed Johnson's mind as to the iniquities of the former slaveholders. Flattery from men who had despised him in 1860 had its effect, but more important than flattery, in all likelihood, was the fact that Johnson, who was not always a fool, came to see that he had more in common with the officially repentant slaveholders of the South than with the northern Radicals who already were making it clear that they planned to control the process of Reconstruction.[4]

3 The most important recent study of Johnson's attitudes is McKitrick, *Andrew Johnson and Reconstruction.* Also valuable is Brock, *An American Crisis;* see also New Orleans *Tribune,* November 13, 1866.

4 Jonathan Truman Dorris, *Pardon and Amnesty under Lincoln and Johnson: The Restoration of the Confederates to Their Rights and Privileges, 1861–1898* (Chapel Hill, N.C., 1953), 112, 146, 320–21; *Nation,* II (March 22, 1866), 353; Craven, *Reconstruction,* 110; John Hope Franklin, *From Slavery to Freedom: A History of Negro Americans* (3rd ed.; New York, 1969), 299–300; Stampp, *The Era of Reconstruction,* 54, 70–78; McKitrick, *Andrew Johnson and Reconstruction,* 142–89.

The Radicals failed to understand that Johnson sincerely believed that the Confederate states had never been out of the Union and that it was his duty to restore them to full participation in the Union as quickly as possible. Probably, if he had been willing to keep men of well-known Confederate sympathies out of office, and if he had required the conquered states to grant suffrage to a few Negroes, he would never have become engaged in a no-compromise struggle with Congress. Almost surely he could have kept enough congressional support to sustain his vetoes. But apparently Johnson had gone as far as he could go in his plan of Reconstruction. And he was one of those unfortunate men who looked upon those who disagreed with him as personal enemies. Thus he gradually forced moderate Republicans into alliance with Radicals.

Those people of Louisiana who had so meekly admitted defeat in April, 1865, were, by the end of that year, almost as defiant of the North—at least of the North represented by Radical Republicanism —as they had been in 1860 and 1861. The explanation is obvious. The South had found an ally in Andrew Johnson. By the late summer of 1865, conservative Louisianians had realized that President Johnson must be their defender against congressional Radicals. The *Picayune* proclaimed that "Radicals will make no headway threatening Andrew Johnson."[5] A few days later a Baton Rouge paper approved of Johnson's acceptance of former Confederate leaders as officeholders in the southern states: "Their past bravery and their frank submission to the government is the best guarantee of their future fidelity."[6] An assessment so erroneous as to be almost comical appeared in November, when an editorial writer in the *Picayune* said of Johnson's arguments: "There is a weight in [them] . . . that never fails to carry conviction with it, and there is an irresistible charm in his manner which often disarms enmity and converts opponents into supporters of his policy."[7] In reality, Andrew Johnson had a singular ability to convert supporters into opponents.

As Johnson's relations with Congress worsened, the confidence

5 New Orleans *Daily Picayune*, September 17, 1865.
6 Baton Rouge *Tri-Weekly Advocate*, September 29, 1865, quoted in McKitrick, *Andrew Johnson and Reconstruction*, 204.
7 New Orleans *Daily Picayune*, November 11, 1865.

Louisianians had in him increased. *De Bow's Review* printed what almost amounted to hymns of praise for the president. The people of Louisiana were also misled by the Washington correspondent of the *Picayune*, who in early 1866 repeatedly informed his readers that the Radicals could not possibly do the things they then proceeded to do. In 1866 the Louisiana legislature adopted one joint resolution condemning opponents of the president and another expressing enthusiastic support of his veto of the Freedmen's Bureau Bill.[8] Of this veto a Baton Rouge editor wrote: "The president has crushed the eggs of the serpents who were to be hatched and dashed upon the devoted South to disgorge their poison upon a helpless people. . . . [This is] the first gleam of light in the darkness of the long night of expectation."[9] In the same month, the historian Charles Gayarré wrote to a northern acquaintance: "President Johnson is doing more to consolidate the *New Empire* than three millions of bayonets."[10] When Johnson vetoed the Civil Rights Bill of 1866, an action often regarded as his most unwise one, the *Picayune* noted gleefully: "The President has taken his coat off. His veto of . . . [this bill] which was one of the most shameful a disordered or maddened brain ever conceived, is so unanswerable a document that even his bitterest foes are unable to bring a solid argument against it."[11] A hundred other examples could be given, but most ridiculous of all was the marketing, in New Orleans, of "Andy Johnson Whiskey." The seller was sure it would become a favorite of the president's supporters.[12]

Early in 1866, malaise began to pervade the North. The Confederate armies had surrendered, but where were the fruits of victory? Chattel slavery was ended, but daily accounts in the newspapers made it clear that the Negro could not enjoy his freedom in safety. The publication, in June, 1866, of the Report of the Joint Committee on

8 "President Johnson's Policy of Reconstruction," *De Bow's Review*, After the War Series, I (January, 1866), 16–25; New Orleans *Daily Picayune*, January–March, 1866; *Acts of Louisiana, 1866*, 84.

9 Baton Rouge *Weekly Advocate*, February 24, 1866.

10 Charles Gayarré to Evart Duyckinck, February 25, 1866, in "Some Letters of Charles Etienne Gayarré on Literature and Politics, 1854–1885," *Louisiana Historical Quarterly*, XXXIII (April, 1950), 231.

11 New Orleans *Daily Picayune*, April 7, 1866.

12 *Ibid.*, May 10, 1866.

Reconstruction went far to confirm, in the popular mind, the intransigence of the South.[13] So did the election to high office of military and civilian leaders of the Confederacy. So did the characteristic bombast of southern rhetoric. In October, 1865, the *Picayune* had suggested that the president might need military force to impose his will on Congress, "but if so, the bayonets will be there."[14] Less than a year later the *Weekly Advocate* at Baton Rouge proposed that the importation of Radical newspapers into the South be prevented, presumably as the importation of abolitionist papers had been halted before the war.[15] Later, during the impeachment trial, southerners offered military force to aid President Johnson. W. G. McDowell, of Greenville, Louisiana, said that he could raise two thousand "men who had never been whipped."[16]

Another fact which must not be forgotten is that the abolition of slavery had also abolished the Three-Fifths Compromise, which meant that the South would gain representation in the national House of Representatives and have a greater voice in the selection of the president. And if the governments established by President Johnson stood, the leadership of this politically stronger South would differ little from prewar southern leadership. Most northerners looked upon the Republican party as the party of the Union. The Democratic party outside the South stood on three legs: the midwestern Copperheads, who had sympathized with the Confederacy; Negrophobes from the border states; and corrupt big-city political machines. If a restored and unreformed South were added as a fourth leg, the Democrats, still looked upon as the party of disunion, might be invincible.[17]

Efforts have been made by some twentieth-century historians to fit the American of 1865–1867 into the Procrustean bed of conventional Leninism,[18] and much more impressive efforts have been made

13 *House Reports*, 39th Cong., 1st Sess., No. 30, *passim.*
14 New Orleans *Daily Picayune*, October 5, 1865,
15 Baton Rouge *Weekly Advocate*, September 29, 1866.
16 William A. Russ, Jr., "Was There Danger of a Second Civil War During Reconstruction?" *Mississippi Valley Historical Review*, XXV (June, 1938), 51; see also Beale, *The Critical Year*, 159.
17 Brock, *An American Crisis*, 65.
18 James S. Allen, *Reconstruction: The Battle for Democracy (1865–1876)* (New York, 1937), *passim*; DuBois, *Black Reconstruction, passim.*

to find an economic explanation for the events which took place.[19] But these efforts fail. If the treatment of the Negro in the South and the fear of restoration of Democratic dominance in the Union are removed, then it is seen that the Radicals had no program or ideology which would have united them against the president. Some wanted a strong Republican party in the South in order that the rights of the Negro might be protected. Others came to favor Negro suffrage so that there might be a strong Republican party in the South, strong enough to prevent a Democratic resurgence.

2

These Radicals were a minority in large part because Negro rights were not popular in the North. They were able to command a majority in Congress because the people of Louisiana and the other southern states unwittingly cooperated with them and because, in his own bullheaded way, Andrew Johnson was just as cooperative. As former rebels took control of the southern states and the Black Codes put the freedmen in a condition not far removed from slavery, it increasingly seemed that the fruits of victory, whatever they might be, were escaping. Southern leaders, allied with the president, were talking more like men who had won than men who had lost. Worst of all in northern eyes, the former rebels, the men responsible for the death of more than 300,000 Union men and the maiming of as many more, showed no sign whatsoever of penitence. The North was uncertain as to how to behave in victory. The South certainly did not know how to behave in defeat.[20]

The deterioration of the president's relations with Congress was rapid. During February, 1886, Congress passed a bill extending indefinitely the life of the Freedmen's Bureau, which had been established for one year in March, 1865. The president vetoed this bill, and

19 Beale, *The Critical Year*, *passim*; Howard K. Beale, "On Rewriting Reconstruction History," *American Historical Review*, VL (July, 1940), 807–27; Bernard Weisberger, "The Dark and Bloody Ground of Reconstruction Historiography," *Journal of Southern History*, XXV (November, 1959), 427–47; John Hope Franklin, "Whither Reconstruction Historiography?" *Journal of Negro Education*, XVII (Fall, 1948), 446–61.
20 *Nation*, II (May 1, 1866), 545; Beale, *The Critical Year*, 159; McKitrick, *Andrew Johnson and Reconstruction*, 21, 206; Schurz, *Reminiscenses*, 187, 199; Cox and Cox, *Politics, Principle and Prejudice*, 159–60.

his veto was upheld. People of the North remembered the Black Codes and the riots of 1865 and read newspapers which carried frequent accounts of the beating and murder of blacks by whites; to many, it seemed that the president, because of his insistence upon leaving domination of the freedmen to the "rebel"-controlled governments he had established, was practically a party to atrocities. Johnson did not help his cause when, sober, he delivered an impromptu and intemperate speech to a crowd which had gathered on Washington's Birthday, 1866. He said, in effect, that Radicals such as Stevens and Sumner were now the subversive element with which the nation must deal. Some northern Democrats agreed with Johnson's evaluation of the Radicals, but many more people of the North were dismayed that their chief executive should equate such loyal men as Stevens and Sumner with Confederate leaders as traitors to the United States. The most charitable interpretation of the president's remarks was that he was irritated by criticism of his recent actions and spoke in anger, without thought. Even this interpretation did not improve confidence in the chief executive.[21]

Atrocities, real and imagined; the Black Codes; the veto of the Freedmen's Bureau Bill; and the Washington's Birthday speech turned public opinion more and more against the president. Republican members of Congress who faced elections in 1866 were forced to disassociate themselves from the president's policies.[22] But—and this is important—in late 1865 and early 1866 most northerners did not see Negro suffrage as the answer to the problem of the South.[23]

The first solution devised by Congress was the civil rights bill of 1866. This bill was largely the work of Senator Lyman Trumbull, and it is significant that Trumbull was a former Democrat, one of the moderate Republicans, and, later on, one of those who voted to acquit Johnson in the president's impeachment trial. Whether or not the freedman needed protection, and he did, Republican voters had decided that he needed protection. Experienced politicians knew that some effort had to be made in this direction. James G. Blaine, a mod-

21 For a strongly pro-Johnson interpretation of the Washington's Birthday speech see Bowers, *The Tragic Era*, 103–106.
22 David Donald, *The Politics of Reconstruction, 1863–1867* (Baton Rouge, 1965), *passim.*
23 Cox and Cox, *Politics, Principle and Prejudice,* 159–60.

erate, later wrote that the Civil Rights Act of 1866 was drawn so as "to confer upon the manumitted Negro of the South the same civil rights enjoyed by the white man, *with the exception of the right of suffrage;* [italics mine] to give him perfect equality in all things before the law, and to nullify every law . . . that should be in conflict."[24]

President Johnson was certainly consistent. He promptly vetoed this act as an unwarranted intrusion by the federal government upon the powers of the states. By this veto he alienated the moderate Republicans who were seeking ground where they could stand between the president and their Radical peers. As practicing politicians, they had no choice but to vote to override the veto. Their success marked the first time in American history when a presidential veto had been overridden on a major political question. Johnson had earned the undying gratitude of southerners, and of a later generation of historians, but he was a leader who could no longer lead.[25] Georges Clemenceau wrote of the sequel:

> Mr. Johnson . . . shows a lack of wisdom in continually opposing the progressive decisions of Congress with his veto, but after all he is exercising a right which the Constitution confers upon him. Congress on the other side, being sure of a two-thirds majority, can pass its resolutions over the veto and make them laws. Thus the great American Revolution is being carried on without violence and accomplishing its results just the same. The only reason Mr. Johnson stands in its way is that he does not understand anything whatsoever about it.[26]

A new Freedmen's Bureau Bill was quickly brought forward, and this time it passed over the president's veto. Now the Radicals, with support from moderate Republicans, could legislate. President Johnson, of course, hoped for vindication at the polls in the congressional elections of November, 1866. The Republicans were not overly confident of the strength of their position. They especially doubted the constitutionality of the Civil Rights Act. Therefore they drew up a proposed Fourteenth Amendment to the Constitution embodying the basic provisions of the act.

The congressional elections of 1866 constituted one of the few

---

24 Blaine, *Twenty Years of Congress,* 173.
25 Brock, *An American Crisis,* 115; Cox and Cox, *Politics, Principle and Prejudice,* 231–32.
26 Clemenceau, *American Reconstruction,* 79.

times in American history when voters had a relatively clear-cut choice. They could choose between supporters of the Johnsonian concept of Reconstrution and supporters of the congressional concept. This simplification of the issue was aided by the Radical press, which played up every crime against Negroes reported from the South and made sure that northern readers remembered that southern leaders were secessionists and that many northern Democrats had opposed the war to preserve the Union and to end slavery. The Democratic press countered as best it could by playing upon the strong racial prejudice of the northern people. Southern Radicals, including Warmoth of Louisiana, went North to support their cause.

Last, but certainly not least, President Johnson undertook his famous "swing around the circle," attempting to bring his Tennessee stump-speaking technique to the support of Democratic candidates. It has been suggested that the technique was a mistake, but political speaking techniques were not so different in Indiana and Illinois from those in Tennessee. Johnson's first mistake was in breaking precedent: never before had a president campaigned openly in congressional elections. His second error was in losing his self-control when faced with hecklers, thus demeaning himself and his office. There were occasions when jeering crowds would not let him speak, a situation which would not recur for a century. Nonetheless the issues were made clear. As one student of the era says, "It is possible to maintain that the people were misinformed but not that they were uninformed."[27] In retrospect, it seems evident that the minds of the voters were already made up. If anything more had been needed to convince them that sterner measures were needed in the South, it was provided by the Memphis and New Orleans riots. When the election was over the Republican majority, already sufficient to override politically unwise vetoes, was sufficient to override almost any conceivable veto.

Louisianians were optimistic as the "swing around the circle" began, and they reported that Johnson was being received with enthusiasm. But uncomfortable reality soon imposed itself; by the end of September it had become apparent that the Republicans were

---

27 Brock, *An American Crisis*, 155–56; see also *ibid.*, 7, 62–63, 77, 157, 236, 244, 285–90; McKitrick, *Andrew Johnson and Reconstruction*, 47–48; Brodie, *Thaddeus Stevens*, 286–87; Bowers, *The Tragic Era*, 130–39.

winning and that Louisiana had put her faith in another lost cause. Now, it would seem, was the time to seek some sort of compromise. But Louisiana's white leaders were determined to resist, passively if not actively. A state senator spoke for many in 1867, even after the passage of the Military Reconstruction Acts, when he said that he was opposed "to meeting the North half way, which course of action had been our great misfortune since the termination of the war. The only true line of action was that of honor, dictated by our conscience."[28]

3

On June 13, 1866, the Fourteenth Amendment to the Constitution had been submitted to the states for ratification. It was basically a moderate Republican proposal. The first section reversed the Dred Scott decision by definitely declaring that Negroes were citizens of the United States and the state in which they lived. States were forbidden to interfere with their rights as citizens, but blacks were not given the right to vote. Another section attempted, however, to persuade the states to grant black suffrage by making it possible, but not mandatory, for Congress to reduce proportionately the representation in the national House of Representatives of those states which denied suffrage to adult male citizens. Federal or state officeholding was prohibited to any person who had ever taken an oath of loyalty to the United States and then participated in or aided the rebellion, which removed almost all prewar officeholders from eligibility. This disability could be removed only by a two-thirds vote of both houses of Congress. Other sections repudiated the Confederate debt, guaranteed the debt of the federal government, and gave power to Congress to enforce the amendment.

The true Radicals in Congress, among whom Thaddeus Stevens was the most outstanding figure, wanted far more for the Negro than the Fourteenth Amendment gave. They wanted, in the first place, Negro suffrage. Secondly, the most Radical and perhaps the most realistic of them desired the confiscation of plantations and the allotment of land to freedmen so that black political power would have some sort of foundation in economic power. Some few Radicals

28 New Orleans *Daily Picayune*, March 10, 1867.

dreamed, as did a few black men North and South, of true equality of the races in America immediately, but this was a dream of the impossible. Equality was rejected by the North as well as the South. Only the unintentional cooperation of President Johnson and southern whites made the adoption of the Fourteenth Amendment by Congress possible. The North in 1866 was not pro-Negro; it was antisouthern.[29]

It should have been clear to the leaders of the South that ratification of the Fourteenth Amendment was a prerequisite to the seating of United States senators and representatives from the South and the restoration of full statehood. It can be argued that ratification would not necessarily have assured readmission, but certainly there would be no readmission without ratification. President Johnson, however, made it plain to the legislatures of the southern states that he opposed the amendment. Only in Tennessee, where Johnson was better known and less popular than in other southern states, was ratification effected. This was accomplished on July 19, 1866. Four days later the president signed a congressional resolution fully restoring Tennessee to the Union.[30]

In Louisiana the legislature considered the Fourteenth Amendment when it convened in January, 1867. Governor Wells recommended ratification. He went further and suggested that the amendment alone was inadequate and that Louisiana should grant equal suffrage to all. Wells was, of course, speaking to a future audience; he was not enough of a political amateur to believe that ratification by the Louisiana legislature as then constituted was possible. When the final vote was taken, not a single vote was cast for ratification. Indeed, it was suggested that the governor should be impeached for recommending favorable consideration.[31]

It is difficult to explain irrational behavior in rational terms. Cer-

---

29 Woodward, "Seeds of Failure in Radical Race Policy," 1–9; C. Vann Woodward, "Equality, America's Deferred Commitment," *American Scholar*, XXVII (Autumn, 1958), 459–72; Stampp, *The Era of Reconstruction*, 122–23.

30 Stanley J. Folmsbee, Robert E. Corlew, and Enoch L. Mitchell, *Tennessee: A Short History* (Knoxville, 1969), 367; James W. Patton, "Tennessee's Attitude toward the Impeachment and Trial of Andrew Johnson," *East Tennessee Historical Society Publications*, No. 9 (1937), 65–76; Stampp, *The Era of Reconstruction*, 113–14; Blaine, *Twenty Years of Congress*, 247–49.

31 New Orleans *Daily Picayune*, February 7–9, 1867; Lowrey, "James Madison Wells," 1,085–86; Memelo, "The Development of State Laws Concerning the Negro in Louisiana," 35; Ficklen, *History of Reconstruction in Louisiana*, 184–85.

tainly the fact that President Johnson opposed ratification influenced the Louisiana legislature, but that body had not been influenced when the president had publicly expressed the belief that well-qualified Negroes should be given the right to vote. Some historians have concluded that the South's chief objection was to the exclusion of Confederate leaders from office. When the amendment was still before Congress, the *Picayune* had noted that it would give Louisiana increased representation in Congress if the state would grant suffrage to the blacks, but had concluded that black suffrage was too high a price to pay.[32]

The most obvious conclusion is that two years after losing the war, the white leaders of the South had concluded that they could win the peace. United by racial attitudes largely shared by people of the North, conditioned to a strict-construction interpretation of the Constitution, sure of executive support, they believed that they could successfully resist the Radical thrust toward political equality for the Negro. In the short run they were wrong; they brought on themselves the Military Reconstruction Acts and "Black Reconstruction." But although they may have been irrational in expecting triumph in the short run, in the long run they were right. By 1900 the political position of the Negro in Louisiana was not greatly different from what it had been in 1866. But, in the short run, the refusal of the southern states to ratify the Fourteenth Amendment led to stern measures; it was in anticipation of these that the New Orleans *Tribune* rejoiced at the failure of the former Confederate states to ratify.[33]

Certainly a majority of people in the North, and probably a majority of northern Republicans, hoped that the Fourteenth Amendment would be ratified and that the Reconstruction issue would thus be settled. Despite the Republican victory in the elections, the Sumner-

---

32 Stampp, *The Era of Reconstruction*, 113–14; Ficklen, *History of Reconstruction in Louisiana*, p. 176; Nash K. Burger and John K. Bettersworth, *South of Appomatox* (New York, 1959), 280–81; William L. Richter, "James Longstreet: From Rebel to Scalawag," *Louisiana History*, XI (Summer, 1970), 216–21; New Orleans *Daily Picayune*, February 2, October 2, 30, 1866; Dunning, *Reconstruction, Political and Economic*, 83–84; Beale, *The Critical Year*, 202–205; McKitrick, *Andrew Johnson and Reconstruction*, 358; Joseph B. James, "Southern Reaction to the Fourteenth Amendment," *Journal of Southern History*, XXII (November, 1956), 478.

33 New Orleans *Tribune*, October 23, 1866; Carl N. Degler, *Out of Our Past: The Forces That Shaped Modern America* (New York, 1959), 215.

Stevens type of Radicalism was apparently waning as 1866 drew near its end. Then it became evident that the southern states were not going to ratify the Fourteenth Amendment. At about the same time the Supreme Court ruled in *Ex Parte Milligan* that martial law could not be invoked where civil courts were open and functioning.[34] If the amendment was to be lost, and if the freedmen of the South were to be left to the protection of the state courts with no recourse to the military authorities, then President Johnson and the formerly Confederate southern leaders had won a complete victory. In fact, the president very quickly issued orders prohibiting the trial of civilians in military courts in the South.[35]

4

As a result, the Radicals succeeded in passing the Reconstruction Acts of 1867. These acts were not, as is sometimes assumed, the goals toward which the ultra-Radicals had striven. Apparently, however, almost all Republicans felt "that the States which had rushed into a rebellion so wicked, so causeless, and so destructive, should not be allowed to resume their places of authority in the Union except under such conditions as would guard against the outbreak of another insurrection."[36] These conditions did not exist. The treatment of Union troops in the South, where there was a real threat that civil action could be brought against officers in the state courts, had forced army commanders to the conclusion that stronger measures were needed. Insults and social ostracism directed at northerners in the South, military and civilian, still persisted. The fact of the matter was that, as northern Republicans saw it, the verdict of the Civil War was in danger of being set aside and the country might well return to something close to the antebellum status quo. If this was to be prevented, either there must be indefinite military occupation of the South or Negro suffrage must be imposed. The assumption was, of course, that with suffrage the freedmen would be able to defend themselves. Thus the Reconstruction Acts imposed black suffrage, but moderates lim-

34 D. Donald, *The Politics of Reconstruction,* 57; Charles Warren, *The Supreme Court in United States History* (Rev. ed.; New York, 1926), II, 442; *Harper's Weekly,* XI (January 19, 1867), 34.
35 Randall, *Civil War and Reconstruction,* 803n.
36 Blaine, *Twenty Years of Congress,* 303.

ited the acts to this and to the disfranchisement of former Confederate leaders. A program of confiscation and land reform favored by some Radical leaders was rejected. In the context of the situation which existed, the Reconstruction Acts were a compromise measure.[37]

The First Reconstruction Act was passed by the "lame duck" Thirty-ninth Congress; it became law on March 2, 1867, after the president's veto had been overridden. First it stated that no legal governments existed in those ten former Confederate states whose representatives had not been seated in Congress; nor was there adequate protection of life and property in those states. The ten states were divided into five military districts, Louisiana and Texas being the Fifth District. It was decreed that a general officer should be placed in command of each district and that military courts under their supervision should take precedence over state courts. The act also provided that each of the ten states could be fully restored to the Union when a constitution had been drawn up by a convention of delegates elected by all adult male citizens except those disfranchised for rebellion or other crimes. This constitution must provide for universal adult male suffrage and be approved by Congress when it had been ratified by a majority of the qualified electors. When state elections had been held, when the elected state legislatures should have ratified the Fourteenth Amendment, and when enough of all the states had ratified the Fourteenth Amendment for it to become part of the Constitution, the state concerned would be restored to full participation in the Union.[38] This law did not specify the procedure to be followed

---

37 Hyman, "Johnson, Stanton and Grant," 92; *Harper's Weekly*, XI (February 23, 1867), 14; Lawanda and John H. Cox, "Negro Suffrage and Republican Politics: The Problem of Motivation in Reconstruction Historiography," *Journal of Southern History*, XXXIII (August, 1967), 303–30; Hans Trefousse, "Ben Wade and the Negro," *Ohio Historical Quarterly*, LXVIII (April, 1959), 161–76; Stanley Coben, "Northeastern Business and Radical Reconstruction: A Reexamination," *Mississippi Valley Historical Review*, XLVI (June, 1959), 67–90; Peter Kolchin, "The Business Press and Reconstruction, 1865–1868," *Journal of Southern History*, XXXIII (May, 1967), 183–96; Glenn M. Linden, "Radicals and Economic Policies: The Senate, 1861–1873," *Journal of Southern History*, XXXII (May, 1966), 189–99; Craven, *Reconstruction*, 95–96; William Archibald Dunning, *Essays on the Civil War and Reconstruction and Related Topics* (New York, 1904), 251–53; D. Donald, *The Politics of Reconstruction*, 65–82; DuBois, *Black Reconstruction*, 198.

38 Robert W. Johannsen (comp.), *Reconstruction, 1865–1877* (New York, 1970), 90–92.

in organizing the new state governments, and some Radicals were concerned. However, Warmoth, for one, was assured that the Fortieth Congress would provide a procedure.[39]

The procedure was specified by the Second Reconstruction Act, which became law March 23, 1867. The new act required that a registration of qualified voters should be completed in the ten states concerned by September, 1867. Each registrant was required to take the following oath:

I, ——— ———, do solemnly swear (or affirm) in the presence of Almighty God, that I am a citizen of the State of ———; that I have resided in said State for ——— months next preceding this day, and now reside in the county of ———, or the parish of ———, in said State (as the case may be); that I am twenty-one years old; that I have not been disfranchised for participation in any rebellion or Civil War against the United States, or for felony committed against the laws of any state of the United States; that I have never been a member of any state legislature, nor held any executive or judicial office in any State, and afterwards engaged in insurrection or rebellion against the United States, or given aid and comfort to the enemies thereof; that I have never taken an oath as a member of Congress of the United States, or as any officer of the United States, or as a member of any State legislature, or as an executive or judicial officer of any State, to support the Constitution of the United States, and afterward engaged in insurrection or rebellion against the United States, or given aid and comfort to the enemies thereof; that I will faithfully support the Constitution and obey the laws of the United States, and will, to the best of my ability, encourage others to do so, so help me God.[40]

The commanding general of the district was then to call an election in which the voters should decide whether or not to hold a convention. A vote in favor of holding a convention was to be of no effect unless a majority of those registered voted in the election. In the same election, delegates to the convention were to be elected. In Louisiana the number of delegates was to be equal to the membership of the lower house of the legislature in 1860, but representation was to be apportioned according to voter registration in 1867.

The commanding general was empowered to appoint as many boards of registration as necessary, each to consist of three persons loyal to the United States. In Louisiana, it should be noted, there were

39 S. Shellebarger to Warmoth, March 2, 1867, in Warmoth Papers.
40 Johannsen (comp.), *Reconstruction*, 92–93.

many parishes where it was impossible to find three loyal men qualified to act as registrars. The registrars were to register voters, supervise the election, and report the returns to the commanding general.
It was the general's duty, if the vote favored a convention, to call the
convention into session within sixty days. The vote upon ratification
of the state constitution drawn up by the convention was to take
place at least thirty days after the convention had concluded its work.
For ratification, a majority of those voting was required, and a majority of those registered must vote. When ratification was completed
in the state, the commanding general was to forward the state constitution to the president of the United States, who would send it on
to Congress. If Congress found that the constitution met the conditions set forth in the First Reconstruction Act, then senators and representatives from the state would be admitted to Congress, providing,
of course, that the Fourteenth Amendment had been ratified.[41]

The Third Reconstruction Act, which became law July 19, 1867,
affirmed the almost absolute power of the military commanders in
their districts and made it clear that these commanders were under
the control of the General of the Army (Grant). It also gave registrars the power to refuse to register a person taking the oath if the
registrar believed that that person was not entitled to register. The
registrars were also given the power, two weeks before an election
under the acts, to review registration lists and to remove the names
of persons who should not have been registered and to add the names
of persons who should have been registered but were not. The act
also made it clear that the granting of a presidential pardon or amnesty did not qualify any person to vote.[42]

The Fourth Reconstruction Act was not passed until March 11,
1868, more than a year after the first act. It came about when the
conservative voters of Alabama refused to vote for or against ratification of the constitution drawn up by a Radical convention in that
state and thus brought about the constitution's defeat because the
total vote was not a majority of the voters registered. The new act of
Congress provided that the new constitutions should go into effect
if they were approved by a majority of those voting. A second part

41 *Ibid.*, 92–96.
42 *Ibid.*, 96–99.

stated that the election of state officials and United States representatives should take place at the same time as the vote upon the constitution.[43]

The Reconstruction Acts did not disqualify a white man in the South from voting unless he had previously held public office or a military commission under the United States and had then taken part in or given aid to the rebellion. The ordinary Confederate private soldier, and probably a majority of the commissioned officers of the Confederate army, did not come under these provisions. Probably, however, the discretion given to registrars resulted in the disqualification of some Democrats who were not disqualified under the letter of the law. In Louisiana, more than 48,000 votes were cast against ratification of the constitution of 1868, demonstrating clearly that large numbers of men opposed to Radical Reconstruction did register and vote.[44]

Louisianians objected to the Reconstruction Acts partly on constitutional grounds, partly because the natural leaders of the state were made ineligible for office, but primarily because of Negro suffrage. *De Bow's Review* first said that if the acts were put into effect the South would "be deserted and left to grow up as forests, as hunting grounds for savage tribes of Negroes."[45] When it was evident that the laws would be carried out, this publication claimed that the southern states would be governed by "an unprincipled, semi-barbarous and wholly ignorant but absolutely unmanageable majority" and that men would be put into power who were "as ignorant of the theory and practice of government as aurang-outangs [sic]."[46] There was some foolish talk of a new Civil War, but most Louisianians were more temperate in the expression of their views. One planter wrote to his brother: "I see by the papers that which we . . . expected has come to pass. We are now territories or military districts. Give much love to Auntie and family."[47] Charles Gayarré could only say, "I assure

---

43 *Ibid.*, 99–100.
44 Donald W. Davis, "Ratification of the Constitution of 1868—Record of Votes," *Louisiana History*, VI (Summer, 1965), 301–305.
45 *De Bow's Review*, After the War Series, III (April–May, 1867), 353.
46 *Ibid.*, After the War Series, IV (July–August, 1867), 153.
47 Dudley Avery to D. D. Avery, March 6, 1867, in Avery Family Papers, Southern

you we are in the saddest condition imaginable," but he was talking as much about the floods of 1867 as about political conditions.[48] The amazing thing about the Reconstruction Acts insofar as Louisiana is concerned is the absence of comment in the family letters of the period. Most private correspondents ignored the subject. One of the most bitter private comments came from a transplanted northerner, living in Baton Rouge, who wrote in June of 1867: "In respect to the politics of this state we are in the power of the radicals and there is a few low Whites who condescend to take the Negro by the arm to get his vote. We are entirely at the mercy of the Negroe as there is four Negroes to one white registered."[49]

The reaction of Louisiana newspapers to the passage of the Reconstruction Acts was mixed. The *Weekly Advocate* of Baton Rouge had highly praised the black population of that parish in October, 1866, but in March, 1867, the editor was less contented. He excoriated former governor and governor-to-be Joseph E. Brown of Georgia because "this extraordinary old fool . . . is out in a letter advising the acceptance of the situation, believing the Negro vote will be ultimately available and being a little lame (in character) he starts first in the race to infamy."[50] The *Picayune* was much more conciliatory in the beginning, even deploring the fact that Louisiana had not given suffrage to blacks before it was granted by the Congress. There was no halting of plans for the Louisiana State Fair scheduled for November, 1867, and *De Bow's Review,* which so deplored the rape of states' rights by the Reconstruction Acts, called on the federal government to restore Louisiana's broken levees.[51] Perhaps the best expression of white Louisiana's general reaction was a bulletin from

---

Historical Collection, University of North Carolina; see also Russ, "Was There Danger of a Second Civil War?" 10.

48 Gayarré to Duyckinck, March 29, 1867, in "Some Letters of Charles Etienne Gayarré," 239.

49 Payne to Mrs. Sterrett, June 16, 1867, in Barnhart (ed.), "Reconstruction on the Lower Mississippi," 393–94.

50 Baton Rouge *Weekly Advocate*, March 9, 1866.

51 New Orleans *Daily Picayune*, March 19, 22, 27, April 14, July 27, 1867; *De Bow's Review,* After the War Series, III (April–May, 1867), 469–72; Copeland, "The New Orleans Press and Reconstruction," 149–250; Ficklen, *History of Reconstruction in Louisiana*, 185–86.

Shreveport in March, reporting "rain, snow, sleet, frost, and gloom."[52] Perhaps it took an observer from abroad to comprehend what a great precedent was set by the granting of suffrage without color distinction.[53]

5

The New Orleans Riot, which brought about the death of several Radical leaders and showed how easily the use of force by whites could demoralize blacks conditioned by more than two centuries of bondage, was a low point in the Louisiana Unionist movement. But this apparent victory of the Conservatives was, as has been seen, really a defeat. It contributed to the victory of Congress over President Johnson, the defeat of the Democrats in the election of 1866, and, finally, to the passage of the Reconstruction Acts.[54]

As 1866 drew to a close, Louisiana Radicals became more and more hopeful that their cause might triumph in Washington. The *Tribune* was the voice of Republicanism in Louisiana at this time. In December it recommended editorially that a provisional government be established in Louisiana with ample powers for the governor. "It is useless to disguise the fact that a stronger resistance will be encountered today than would have been in 1865."[55] This paper supported Durant for the position of provisional governor. The *Tribune* also published accounts of every atrocity which came to its attention; no doubt some of these stories were based more on rumor than on fact, but the indisputable instances were enough to make it clear that in many parts of Louisiana blacks were, for all practical purposes, without legal protection.[56]

As the fortunes of Radicalism rose, adherence to the cause grew also. More and more whites became Republicans, although the number of native Louisianians was never large. Thomas J. Durant urged that converted rebels should be welcomed into the party. A branch of the Grand Army of the Republic was organized in Louisiana; since Warmoth was a leading spirit in the organization, it certainly had

---

52 New Orleans *Daily Picayune*, March 21, 1867.
53 Clemenceau, *American Reconstruction*, 65.
54 Uzee, "Republican Politics in Louisiana," 18–19; Warmoth Papers, 1866–67.
55 New Orleans *Tribune*, December 9, 1866.
56 *Ibid.*, November, 1866–March, 1867.

political implications. But it was obvious from the beginning that in Louisiana white Republicans would never be numerous enough to carry elections. Only with Negro suffrage could the party hope to be victorious. In mid-December, 1866, the Republican Central Committee of Louisiana, on the motion of Oscar J. Dunn, a Negro, decided to perfect its statewide organization. A state convention was called for July, 1867, with representation for Republican clubs in the country parishes based on the size of the clubs' membership. Also it was resolved that insofar as possible the delegates should be equally divided between whites and blacks.[57]

It is generally assumed that the Union League and the agents of the Freedmen's Bureau were the chief organizers of a statewide Republican party in Louisiana. Generals Philip Sheridan and Joseph A. Mower definitely encouraged Republican political activity on the part of bureau personnel. It is a fact that bureau officers were often named registrars in the country parishes because it was so difficult to find Unionists who were capable of performing this duty. Nonetheless, the two most recent studies of the bureau in Louisiana conclude that most agents were too busy to spend time on politics. Indeed, they generally found political activity by Negroes a nuisance because rallies, meetings, and elections all interfered with the work the agents were trying to get done. A few of them attempted to organize Democratic clubs in opposition to the Republicans, but the military administration in New Orleans put a quick stop to that.

The Union League might have been important in organizing the blacks politically in other southern states, but relatively few traces of this group can be found in Louisiana. Northern missionaries, religious and educational, contributed their bit toward political activation of the freedmen. The Grand Army of the Republic seems to have been especially influential, perhaps because many Union veterans were among the northerners who had settled in Louisiana after the war. At the top, Republican leadership was generally white, although Negroes such as Oscar J. Dunn and Dr. Joseph B. Roudanez were leaders from the beginning, and P. B. S. Pinchback was soon to join.

57 Durant to Warmoth, March 28, April 7, 1867, in Warmoth Papers, Warmoth Diary, February 27, 1867; New Orleans *Tribune*, December 4, 1866, in Martin Abbott (ed.), "Reconstruction in Louisiana: Three Letters," *Louisiana History*, I (Spring, 1960), 156.

In the plantation parishes, especially in southern Louisiana, a few blacks took a leading role in local organization.[58]

In the rural parishes, white recruits to Radicalism were hard to find. P. G. Deslondes, an educated black man who had been free before the Civil War, wrote to Warmoth from Bayou Goula, in Iberville Parish, that although the party was growing daily, there were only three white Republicans in the parish: "one a native of this parish— the other a native of South Carolina and the 3d from some Eastern State—therefore our task was a hard one."[59] But in the nonplantation parishes, recruiting seems to have been even more difficult. Another of Warmoth's correspondents wrote to him from Independence in what is now Tangipahoa Parish:

> You ask me to send you a list of the Radicals of my acquaintance in the country. . . . In reply I have to state that the subject of radicalism is not discussed in this section of the state. Mr. W. M. Wilder . . . [postmaster] at Amite comes the nearest to being a radical of anyone of my acquaintance, and he told me . . . that he was afraid to take sides with a Negro in any controversy with a White, that the Freedmen's Bureau was no advantage to the Negro, that the agent was drunk most of the time, and that his clerk in a drunken spree shot and killed a Negro without any provocation a few weeks since, for which he was bound over in the sum of 500 dollars, which it seems is the price of killing a Negro in this section of the state.[60]

Some Conservatives persisted in believing that they could control the Negro vote, and a few even joined the Republican party with this idea in mind. Duncan F. Kenner and General Beauregard, among others, urged Louisianians to accept the fact that blacks would vote and to work at influencing that vote.[61] General James Longstreet

58 J. Thomas May, "The Freedmen's Bureau at the Local Level: A Study of a Louisiana Agent," *Louisiana History*," IX (Winter, 1968), 5–19; John William De-Forest, *A Union Officer in the Reconstruction,* ed. James H. Croushore and David Morris Potter (New Haven, 1948), 100; Coulter, *The South During Reconstruction,* 127–28; Franklin, *From Slavery to Freedom,* 321; Shugg, *Origins of Class Struggle in Louisiana,* 220; Uzee, "Republican Politics in Louisiana," 19–20; J. D. Rich to Warmoth, April 12, 1867; William George to Warmoth, May 6, 1867, Richard Dickinson to W. R. Crane, May 11, 1867, all in Warmoth Papers; Grosz, "Pinchback," 531; New Orleans *Daily Picayune,* May 25, 1867; Morrow, "Northern Methodism in the South During Reconstruction," 197–218; Drake, "American Missionary Association and the Southern Negro," 220–21; Henry Lee Swint, *The Northern Teacher in the South, 1862–1870* (New York, 1967), 85–87.
59 P. G. Deslondes to Warmoth, May 7, 1867, in Warmoth Papers.
60 N. J. Hyler to Warmoth, March 27, 1867, in Warmoth Papers.
61 Ficklen, *History of Reconstruction in Louisiana,* 185.

went so far in urging obedience to the laws of the land that he suffered social and political ostracism and became a full-fledged Republican. The *Times* and the *Picayune,* among New Orleans papers, and many country papers, advised acceptance as gracefully as possible. In some parishes attempts were made to form biracial political organizations under the leadership of prominent white citizens, but these efforts were almost entirely in vain. In retrospect, it seems incredible that former masters should expect peacefully to lead their onetime slaves against the party which had freed them, but probably it was not harder to believe this than it had been a few years earlier to believe that the Negro was happier as a slave than he could be in any other condition. The blacks flocked to Republican meetings, however, and it was soon evident that the Radicals would control their vote.[62] George Washington Cable said that the black man could have found physical security beyond what could "be given him by Constitutional Amendments, Congress, [or] United States Marshals" by throwing "himself upon the old patriarchal tie with the former master." But even in slavery, said Cable, the black man had absorbed too much of the American belief in freedom to do this, and by his adherence to the Republicans "he . . . proved to us who once ruled over him that . . . he is worthy to be free."[63] The *Picayune* asserted: "The Negro has a very quick wit, and can soon discover who are and who are not his friends."[64] In any event, the Negro's wit told him that the Radicals were more nearly his friends than the men who had fought to keep him in bondage.

When registration was completed under the Military Reconstruction Acts, the vast majority of Louisiana Republicans were black. Nonetheless, there were thousands of white men who called themselves Republicans in 1867 and 1868. Exactly how many thousands we do not know. A study of the Scalawags, the native white Republicans in Louisiana, is badly needed. Undoubtedly, some native whites became Republicans from conviction. Some men who had been Whigs or Know-Nothings became Republicans because to them any-

62 *Ibid.,* 185–87; New Orleans *Daily Picayune,* March 27, April 11, 1867; Williams, "Analysis of Some Reconstruction Attitudes," 481.
63 George Washington Cable, *The Silent South: Together with the Freedmen's Case in Equity and the Convict Lease System* (New York, 1907), 15.
64 New Orleans *Daily Picayune,* March 27, 1867.

thing was preferable to being a Democrat. The idea expressed by William Z. Foster, that most of the Scalawags were upland farmers,[65] may fit Marxist dogma, but in Louisiana it simply was not true. The poorer hill parishes were the most determinedly Democratic in their politics. Very few of the yeoman-farmer class became Republicans. No figures are available, and apparently there is no way of arriving at a reasonably accurate estimate, but I have been convinced that the number of Scalawags among Louisiana Republicans was never large, that it was concentrated mainly in New Orleans, and that the number decreased rather rapidly with the passage of time.[66] Those who followed Warmoth into fusion with the Democrats in 1872 did not, as a rule, follow him back into the Republican fold afterward.

Thus the dominant element in the Louisiana Republican party was largely a group of so-called Carpetbaggers, men from the North who had settled in the South and who, for whatever reason, took advantage of the opportunities which the Reconstruction Acts and ten years of Radical domination of the national government afforded. Native white southerners and Negroes were to be found in positions of power in Louisiana throughout Radical Reconstruction, but the outstanding figures were men from outside the South, most of them Union army veterans who had known Louisiana during the war. Some were idealists, some were dutiful servants of the national Republican party, many were opportunists, and entirely too many were shamelessly corrupt.

General Philip Sheridan, one of Grant's favorite lieutenants, was put in charge of the Fifth Military District under the terms of the First Reconstruction Act. Military Reconstruction must not be looked upon as a military occupation in the usual sense. In Mississippi, for example, there were only 716 men and officers when Military Reconstruction began. In the Fifth District there were approximately 7,000 troops, but it must be remembered that Sheridan was responsible for the defense of the Mexican border and for protecting western Texas against the Indians. He had no excess of troops for overawing the people of Louisiana. Many of the men that he did have available for

---

65 William Z. Foster, *The Negro People in American History* (New York, 1957), *passim.*
66 See below, pp. 158–60.

duty were sent into areas with the largest Negro population, at least as much to protect whites against the freedmen as to protect the freedmen against the whites. But Sheridan was a Radical to the extent that he despised the men who had led the South into rebellion, and he had a great deal of sympathy for the Louisiana Negro.[67]

Sheridan pushed the registration of voters required by Congress. It was he who ordered registrars to refuse to register men whom they believed ineligible to take the required oath, and Congress, over the president's objections, upheld him in the Third Reconstruction Act. It was asserted that this led to the exclusion of half the whites legally entitled to register, but since the numbers of the two races were almost equal, and since a substantial number of whites certainly was ineligible, the final figure of 78,230 registered blacks and over 48,000 registered whites demonstrates that this assertion was incorrect. On the other hand, these figures certainly do show that the registrars were strict in their assessment of eligibility.[68]

General Sheridan had been horrified by the riot of July, 1866, and he was more ruthless than any of the other Reconstruction commanders in removing local officials from office. One of his first acts as district commander was to remove District Judge Edmund Abell, Louisiana Attorney General Andrew S. Herron, and New Orleans Mayor John T. Monroe. Abell, he said, had promised immunity to the rioters before the riot; Herron had prosecuted the victims rather than the perpetrators; and Monroe had used the city police to carry out the massacre. The general did not hesitate, either, to remove local officials for lack of cooperation. The *Tribune* wryly noted, however, that when Sheridan replaced the officials he ousted, color other than black seemed to be one of the qualifications.[69] This was exemplified in the reform of the New Orleans police force. Sheridan annulled a Louisiana

67 Special Order No. 48, Hq., District of Louisiana, April 14, 1867, quoted in New Orleans *Tribune*, April 17, 1867; New Orleans *Daily Picayune*, April 12, 1867; Patrick, *Reconstruction of the Nation*, 103; Franklin, "The Negro and Reconstruction," 70–71; Degler, *Out of Our Past*, 219; New Orleans *Tribune*, April 11, 1867.

68 Ficklen, *History of Reconstruction in Louisiana*, 187; Donald W. Davis "Ratification of the Constitution of 1868—Record of Votes," *Louisiana History*, VI (Summer, 1965), 301–305.

69 Philip Sheridan to U. S. Grant, April 19, 1867, in *Senate Executive Documents*, 40th Cong., 1st Sess., No. 14, p. 201; Sefton, *United States Army and Reconstruction*, 140; New Orleans *Daily Picayune*, March 27–31, 1867; New Orleans *Tribune*, June 18, 1867.

law which set five years' residence as a qualification for police officers because the act was obviously intended to reserve the force for Confederate veterans. He ordered Mayor Edward Heath, whom he had just appointed, to see to it that at least half the police were veterans of the Union army. Mayor Heath obeyed, but the *Tribune* complained that the order was carried out without the appointment of a single black man.[70]

Sheridan did give some satisfaction to Louisiana whites by removing Governor Wells from office. The legislature, in its 1867 session, had authorized a four-million-dollar bond issue for the restoration of the state's ravaged levees. The legislature named one set of commissioners to disburse this juicy plum, the governor named another. Sheridan disregarded both groups of appointees and named commissioners of his own. Wells's obduracy on this matter was the last straw as far as the commander was concerned. A special order declared the governor deposed. Sheridan first named Thomas J. Durant as a replacement; when Durant refused, Benjamin F. Flanders was appointed.[71]

No tears were shed. The New Orleans *Times* told its readers: "All's well that ends Wells."[72] Sheridan wrote the following to Secretary of War Edwin M. Stanton:

I say now . . . that Governor Wells is a political trickster and a dishonest man. I have seen him . . . when I first came to this command, turn out all the Union men who had supported the government and put in their stead rebel soldiers, some of whom had not yet doffed their gray uniform. I have seen him again during the July riot of 1866, skulk away . . . instead of coming out as a manly representative of the State and join those who were preserving the peace. I have watched him since, and his conduct has been as sinuous as the mark left in the dust by the movement of a snake.[73]

70 Special Order No. 33, Hq. 5th Military District, May 2, 1867, quoted in New Orleans *Tribune*, May 10, 1867; Lowrey, "James Madison Wells," 1,089; New Orleans *Daily Picayune*, July 29, 1867.
71 Special Order No. 34, Hq. 5th Military District, May 3, 1867, quoted in New Orleans *Tribune*, May 10, 1867; Highsmith, "Louisiana During Reconstruction," 143–44; Lowrey, "James Madison Wells," 1,090–91; Cox, *Three Decades of Federal Legislation*, 544–45; Sefton, *United States Army and Reconstruction*, 140–41.
72 Quoted in Ficklen, *History of Reconstruction in Louisiana*, 189.
73 P. Sheridan to Edwin M. Stanton, June 3, 1867, in *Senate Executive Documents*, 40th Cong., 1st Sess., No. 14, p. 213.

The removal of Wells was probably Sheridan's only action which pleased the Conservatives of Louisiana. He made numerous removals and appointments at lower levels of government, even filling vacancies on the town council of Grand Coteau. In New Orleans he removed the entire board of aldermen, twenty-two in number, and replaced them with men of his own choosing, some of whom were Negroes. The *Picayune* reported: "It is a mixed Board, in which there are whites . . . [others] genuinely black, and others . . . so largely tinged with white blood that among some of the zealots of African progress they might be pronounced inferior to their colleagues of pure blood."[74] White New Orleans was further outraged when the new board of aldermen named three Negroes as assistant recorders and two others as city physicians.[75]

In comparison with the 1950s in the South, the ease with which Sheridan handled the "star car" controversy in New Orleans is surprising. The horse-drawn cars on the street railways had been segregated since before the Civil War. Those cars "reserved" for blacks were marked with a star, and Negroes were expected to wait until a "star car" came along the tracks. In the spring of 1867 some blacks began forcing their way aboard the "white" cars. The presidents of the companies asked Sheridan to help them enforce segregation. He refused, perhaps because many of his troops were black. Without support from the military commander or from local government, the companies' practice of segregating cars had to be abandoned. Sheridan wired Grant on May 11 that all bitterness over his action had subsided, but he was over-optimistic. Two months later there were still complaints that nothing was being done to protect white passengers from the insolence of Negroes.[76]

Sheridan had never been a favorite of President Johnson, and the complaints of Louisiana Democrats were heard in the White House. Despite efforts by General Grant to prevent it, Johnson removed

74 New Orleans *Daily Picayune*, August 2, 1867.
75 Ficklen, *History of Reconstruction in Louisiana*, 190; Cox, *Three Decades of Federal Legislation*, 547; New Orleans *Tribune*, June 28, 1867.
76 New Orleans *Tribune*, May 1–10, 1867; P. Sheridan to Grant, May 11, 1867, in *Senate Executive Documents*, 40th Cong., 1st Sess., No. 14, p. 206; Ficklen, *History of Reconstruction in Louisiana*, 188; Highsmith, "Louisiana During Reconstruction," 155; Memelo, "The Development of State Laws Concerning the Negro in Louisiana," 40; New Orleans *Daily Picayune*, July 24, 1867.

Sheridan from command of the Fifth District. Sheridan gave up his command on September 5, 1867; General Winfield Scott Hancock was named his successor, but it was not until November 29 that Hancock was able to personally assume command. Temporary commander General Charles Griffen soon died and was replaced by General Joseph A. Mower. Mower was as unrelenting as Sheridan in his removals. The *Picayune* noted in one issue that Mower was "still mowing" and had removed Lieutenant Governor Albert Voorhies, Secretary of State H. H. Hardy, Treasurer Adam Giffin, Auditor Hypolite Peralta, Superintendent of Education Robert M. Lusher, and state Tax Collector Henry Bensel.[77]

Hancock was known to be a Democrat, and his appointment was welcomed by Louisianians. He completely won their hearts a week after his arrival by revoking an order of Sheridan's which required that Negroes be placed on the jury list for state courts. This was only a partial victory for lily-white justice, however, because federal District Judge E. H. Durrell the next day ordered that blacks should be used on federal juries in Louisiana.[78] Hancock's downfall resulted from his removal from office of New Orleans Recorder Arthur Gastinel. The Republican city council called an election to fill the vacancy, which was a violation of Sheridan's order that no election be held without the permission of the district commander. Hancock responded by removing from the council nine men, including seven Negroes, who had voted for holding the election. What was sauce for the Republican goose was not sauce for the Democratic gander in early 1868, and Grant ordered Hancock to restore the ousted officials. Hancock obeyed, but requested that he be removed from command. He departed on March 18, 1868, and after a few days interim, General R. C. Buchanan, also a Democrat, took command. By this time, however, the process of Reconstruction prescribed by Congress had almost been completed. The "reconstructed" state government went into office in late June.[79]

77 Hyman, "Johnson, Stanton and Grant," 98–99; William Best Hesseltine, *Ulysses S. Grant, Politician* (New York, 1935), 93; New Orleans *Daily Picayune*, November 22, 1867; Ficklen, *History of Reconstruction in Louisiana*, 191–92.
78 White, *Freedmen's Bureau in Louisiana*, 158; New Orleans *Daily Picayune*, December 7, 1867; New Orleans *Tribune*, December 8, 1867.
79 Cox, *Three Decades of Federal Legislation*, 549; Sefton, *United States Army and*

To carry out the terms of the Reconstruction Acts, Sheridan first had to register qualified voters, and this necessitated the appointment of three registrars for each parish. As noted earlier, it was difficult in many parishes to find loyal Unionist residents who were qualified to act as registrars. Few of those appointed were distinguished enough before or after 1867 to be identifiable, but many, probably most, were not residents of the parishes where they functioned. Probably the majority were Union soldiers who had settled in Louisiana at the end of the war. None of them was black.[80] From the Radical point of view, the selection of reliable men as registrars was essential, "for much will depend upon those officers, if it is left with the Parishes to make their own selections you may rely upon it, few if any radicals will be elected to the Convention, and the reconstruction policy of Congress will prove little better than that of the president."[81]

In April Sheridan informed Grant that in New Orleans registration was progressing well, "without trouble or ill feeling, colored and whites registering at the same offices."[82] It could hardly be said that there was no bad feeling in the parishes, but there also registration was satisfactory from the Radical point of view. A majority vote in favor of holding a convention and a majority of Radical delegates were certain.[83]

Probably, as noted earlier, the registrars discouraged native white registration. In 1860 there had been in Louisiana 94,711 white males age twenty-one or over. Making every allowance for war casualties, emigration, and disease, the number of whites registered was not more than one half of those qualified by age. It is not possible to estimate with any degree of accuracy how many of the white men of the state had held office of some kind or another before the war. The figure might possibly, assuming an almost Athenian degree of white

---

Reconstruction, 186–87; New Orleans *Daily Picayune,* December, 1867–June, 1868.

80 New Orleans *Daily Picayune,* April 21, 1867; Highsmith, "Social and Economic Conditions in Rapides Parish," 85–86; William R. Russ, Jr., "Registration and Disfranchisement Under Radical Reconstruction," *Mississippi Valley Historical Review,* XXI (September, 1934), 168–69; New Orleans *Tribune,* April 21, 1867.

81 Hyler to Warmoth, March 27, 1867, in Warmoth Papers.

82 P. Sheridan to Grant, April 16, 1867, in *Senate Eexcutive Documents,* 40th Cong., 1st Sess., No. 14, p. 198.

83 Dunning, *Essays on the Civil War and Reconstruction,* 188.

male democracy, have reached 10,000, including justices of the peace, police jurors, and municipal officers; but it certainly did not amount to 45,000, and approximately 45,000 white adult males did not register. This may be interpreted as evidence that the registrars rejected many qualified men, but in opposition to this interpretation stands the fact that only 2,169 persons were rejected by the registrars. It may be, of course, that so few applied because it was evident that they would be refused. It seems more likely, however, that apathy, preoccupation with making a living in a year disastrous for Louisiana agriculture, and racism which rejected the indignity of standing in line with Negroes were responsible.[84]

While whites were not registering, blacks were. Local leaders encouraged registration when local leaders were available, but in the main arousing the freedmen was the work of Radicals, black and white, who moved out from New Orleans. White northerners were more successful than southerners with the freedmen. It may be surmised that the rural blacks were able to sense the racial attitudes of southern Republicans; only a few of the well-educated and sophisticated men of color of New Orleans were beginning to realize that racism also existed among northern Radicals. Warmoth's expeditions into the country brought huge crowds, and a visit to New Orleans by Representative William (Pig Iron) Kelley of Pennsylvania aroused enthusiasm. The number of black registrants makes it clear that the Radicals were brilliantly successful. Efforts by Louisiana Conservatives to influence the Negro accomplished little or nothing.[85]

Even as registration was proceeding and preparations being made for the election of delegates, there was the beginning of a rift in Radical ranks. Men like Mayor Heath of New Orleans and the Roudanez brothers of the *Tribune* were demanding not only political equality

84 *Senate Executive Documents*, 40th Cong., 2nd Sess., No. 53, p. 11; New Orleans *Tribune*, July 23, 1867; New Orleans *Daily Picayune*, April 17, June 28, 1867; Cox, *Three Decades of Federal Legislation*, 546; Russ, "Registration and Disfranchisement," 176–77; Patrick, *Reconstruction of the Nation*, 104.
85 Deslondes to Warmoth, April 3, 1867, in Warmoth Papers; New Orleans *Tribune*, May 9, 10, 21, June 15, 1867; White, *Freedmen's Bureau in Louisiana*, 28–30; Cable, *The Negro Question*, 211–12; Blaine, *Twenty Years of Congress*, 304–305; Forrest G. Wood, "On Revising Reconstruction History: Negro Suffrage, White Disfranchisement, and Common Sense," *Journal of Negro History*, LI (April, 1966), 98–113.

for blacks but also integrated public schools and what would today be called "open accommodations," the right to patronize any public place, store, theater, saloon, or other establishment which was open to whites. Others—and Warmoth is the outstanding example—preferred to concentrate on politics and to leave other manifestations of equality to the future, preferably the distant future. For most blacks, only two years removed from slavery, the right to hold political meetings, to register, and to vote were excitement enough for the time being. So long as the Warmoth wing was in command of the party organization, it could depend upon the support of the vast majority of Louisiana freedmen. The "radical Radicals" protested against white domination of the Republican Central Committee and wondered publicly: "Have bad Republicans been put in because they are white, and good Republicans kept out because they are black?"[86] The factionalism manifested was to so divide and disrupt the Republican party in Louisiana as to be in large part responsible for its demise.[87]

There was no organized attempt at intimidation of Louisiana blacks in 1867. As is well known, the Ku Klux Klan was formed at Pulaski, Tennessee, in 1866, and was quickly converted from a social club into a terrorist group devoted to the thwarting of Radical Republicanism. The KKK may never have existed in Louisiana as an organized body during Reconstruction, but the shock of "Negro supremacy" and the threat to the "southern way of life" which impelled the Klan's activities in states to the north and east certainly did exist in Louisiana. Perhaps military government inhibited such terrorist activities in Louisiana in 1867, or perhaps it took time for Louisianians to believe the unbelievable.

There were other manifestations of white reaction. One form of this was avid reporting of instances of violence by Negroes against whites. The *Picayune*, taking items from country papers, was almost as fervid in reporting atrocities committed by blacks, or, in one case, by white Unionists, as the *Tribune* had been a year earlier in reporting violence by whites against blacks. The New Orleans *Times*, in-

86 New Orleans *Tribune*, June 30, 1867.
87 New Orleans *Tribune*, April–July, 1867; Kendall, *History of New Orleans*, I, 315–16; Cable, *The Negro Question*, 211; Highsmith, "Louisiana During Reconstruction," 145–46.

dulging in wishful demographic prophecy, said that in a few years the white vote would more than double that of the Negroes, "and the sins which the colored man now commits against equal rights and manhood suffrage will be remembered against him."[88] In May riots broke out in Galveston and Mobile, and when a fire alarm rang during a Republican meeting in Lafayette Square, it caused real fear of a repetition of the massacre of 1866. A man named Moore attempted to break up a Union meeting in Franklin Parish, but he was arrested by the military. At Baton Rouge a "Loyal League" meeting was dispersed when pistols were fired into the building where it was being held. During the election of delegates there was a riot in Jefferson City which resulted in one death and several injuries. But overall, by Louisiana standards, the campaign of 1867 preceding the election of delegates would have to be described as a peaceful one.[89]

General Sheridan set September 27 and 28, 1867, as the dates for voting on whether or not a constitutional convention was to be held and to elect delegates to the convention who would serve if the convention were called. It was apparent to Louisiana whites that they could not win this election. Newspapers which in the spring had urged whites to register grew silent as the election neared. In the meantime the Republicans held a party convention in New Orleans which adopted a platform advocating equality for all men, the opening of all public schools to all children, and an end to "class" discrimination. The platform declared the party's support of candidates who would divide the appointments within their power equally between white men and black, and it favored the same ratio in elective offices. On a more material level the platform demanded repeal of the federal tax on cotton, federal aid in repairing levees, payment of the national debt, and an eight-hour day for workers except those under special contract.[90]

The election was held as ordered. Apparently there were no sig-

88 New Orleans *Times*, September 1, 1867, quoted in Ficklen, *History of Reconstruction in Louisiana*, 192.

89 New Orleans *Daily Picayune*, April–December, 1867; see particularly the issues of April 4, 17, July 17, 27, September 11, 27, 29, 1867, January 9, 11, 1968; New Orleans *Tribune* May 19, July 25, 1867; Wharton, *The Negro in Mississippi*, 219; Craven, *Reconstruction*, 232.

90 New Orleans *Daily Picayune*, 21 April, May–August, 1867; New Orleans *Tribune*, July 7, 1867.

nificant disorders; if there were, contemporary newspapers and manuscripts ignored them. Organizers led, and sometimes marched, blacks to the polls. The few troops available could not guard all the polling places, but there seems to have been no need for them. The vote for the convention was 75,083, and only 4,006 voted against it. Ninety-eight delegates were elected, half of them black. All except two were Republicans. Obviously, most of the registered white voters did not go to the polls, but a majority of the voters registered did vote. Louisiana conservatives could not have elected a majority of the delegates, but they could have elected more than two. As Cable put it, the leading citizens were determined "to withhold the cooperation of society's best wealth, intelligence and power from all attempts to establish order and safety . . . and leave this colossal task to the freedmen, with no one to aid his clumsy hands save here and there a white man heroic enough or shameless enough to laugh at complete and ferocious ostracism."[91] In practice, the shameless rather than the heroic seem to have dominated among the few native white Republicans, to whom Negro suffrage and promises of equality were tactics to be used in gaining power, whereupon the black could be abandoned. What was true of the Scalawag seems to have been equally true of the Carpet-bagger. In Louisiana there were very few whites who were dedicated to Negro rights. Some, like General Longstreet, were certainly heroic, but Longstreet's loyalty was to the United States, not to the cause of racial equality.[92]

6

The constitutional convention of 1867–1868 met in Mechanics' Institute in New Orleans on November 23, 1867. As the delegates gathered, General John B. Hood wrote that the people of Louisiana were affected with a spirit of desperation; that their spirits, if any-

91 Cable, *The Negro Question*, 8.
92 New Orleans *Daily Picayune*, September 27, 1867; *Official Journal of the Proceedings of the Convention for Framing a Constitution for the State of Louisiana, 1867–1868* (New Orleans, 1868), 1–20; Highsmith, "Louisiana During Reconstruction," 147; Charles Vincent, "Negro Leadership in Programs in the Louisiana Constitutional Convention of 1868," *Louisiana History*, X (Fall, 1969), 341–42; Wood, "On Revising Reconstruction History," 109–10; Otto H. Olsen, "Reconsidering the Scalawags," *Civil War History*, XII (December, 1966), 317–18; Ficklen, *History of Reconstruction in Louisiana*, 190–93; Richter, "James Longstreet," *passim*.

thing, were degenerating rather than improving.[93] *De Bow's Review* raged that "This base conspiracy against human nature . . . will soon . . . leave no doubt. . . . The foolish and infuriate Negroes are already writing its history in secret leagues, riotous conventions, and cruel prescriptions. They will soon begin to write it in letters of blood, for they daily and openly threaten arson, rape, murder, rebellion, civil war, and extermination of the whites."[94] The New Orleans *Crescent* said that the only relief the South needed was from Radical administration which had brought into the cities mobs of blacks hostile to the common interest.[95] If whites exaggerated the possibilities of the convention for evil, the black-edited *Tribune* certainly overestimated its possibilities for good: "The time has come when any citizen should enjoy his full rights as well as every other citizen, without star schools, star juries, a star militia, and star witnesses before our courts of justice."[96] The *Republican* was vehement: "We would rather see another war, another revolution, had rather see every rebel from the Potomac to the Gulf proscribed, disenfranchised, their property confiscated, and every mother's son of them stripped naked and sent out into the world as they were born than the right of suffrage taken away from the loyal people of the South."[97]

The rhetoric on both sides was mostly bombast. Louisiana whites realized the futility of another riot like the one of 1866, and probably the farseeing ones hoped to see Louisiana fully restored to the Union in the expectation that they would soon take control of the state. The Radicals, on the other hand, white or black, had no "arson, rape, murder, rebellion" in mind. The changes they were planning were remarkably mild. A political revolution of sorts had already been accomplished by the Reconstruction Acts. The Radical leaders had no real intention of trying for further social or economic revolution.

The delegates who participated in the convention were equally divided between white and black.[98] James G. Taliaferro of Catahoula

93 John B. Hood to James Chesnut, November 22, 1867, in William-Chesnut-Manning Papers, Manuscript Department, University of South Carolina.
94 *De Bow's Review*, After the War Series, IV (December, 1867), 549.
95 New Orleans *Crescent*, January 3, 1868, cited in White, "Freedmen's Bureau in Louisiana," 84.
96 New Orleans *Tribune*, October 3, 1867.
97 Quoted in Ficklen, *History of Reconstruction in Louisiana*, 195–96.
98 Unless otherwise noted, information concerning the convention's deliberations is

Parish, who had been a strong opponent of secession, was elected president. He represented the best of the native white element at the convention. Some other whites, mainly newcomers, were sincere men who wished to make Louisiana over into a somewhat idealized version of the "progressive" states of the North. Others were political opportunists who saw the opportunities for power and plunder that the new dispensation might provide. The black delegates included educated men who had been free before the Civil War and who had long been struggling for Negro rights: others were former slaves. Some of the latter were surprisingly well-educated, considering the fact that it had been illegal to teach them to read or to write, but others were just what one would expect men only three years removed from slavery to be. A recent analysis of the records of the convention concludes that most Negro delegates were not pawns of white leaders; instead they participated actively in and contributed substantially to the work of the convention.[99]

No vote in the convention of 1868 strictly set off black against white. Enough blacks commonly voted with the whites to give the white leaders their way. On the other hand, there were a few whites so Radical that they frequently were to be found on the side of the Negroes when racial lines were drawn. One such was Dr. George M. Wickliffe, a dentist from East Feliciana Parish, who had edited an antiabolitionist newspaper before the war but who now had swung to the other side.[100]

On some issues most whites were to be found on one side, most blacks on the other. The *Tribune,* which advocated many policies more radical than the convention was willing to make into basic law, claimed in January, 1868, that the Republican leadership in Louisiana was made up of "white adventurers, who are striving to be elected to office by black votes. . . . Some of these intend, if elected, to give a share of office to colored men . . . but they will choose only docile

---

taken from the *Official Journal of the Proceedings of the Convention for Framing a Constitution for the State of Louisiana, 1867–1868* (New Orleans, 1868).

99 Vincent, "Negro Leadership in 1868," 339–51; see also Ficklen, *History of Reconstruction in Louisiana,* 193–94; Highsmith, "Louisiana During Reconstruction," 148; Frazier, *The Negro in the United States,* 137; Dunning, *Essays on the Civil War and Reconstruction,* 194–95.

100 Vincent, "Negro Leadership in 1868," 350–51; Ficklen, *History of Reconstruction in Louisiana,* 194.

tools, not citizens who have manhood."[101] In general the black delegates were more concerned with education, access to public accommodations, and state-supported public services than were the whites. In the field of education, and especially in public accommodations, where the proposed article for equal rights was introduced and pushed by the able P. B. S. Pinchback, the blacks were able to have their way. The *Picayune* noted with satisfaction that white Radicals seemed to be as opposed to these measures as any other white men.[102]

While winning these battles, the Radical blacks as represented by the *Tribune* were losing the war. This paper had favored Thomas J. Durant as governor on the Republican ticket even though he had refused the office when it was offered to him by General Sheridan. While the convention was in session, however, many blacks came to prefer Oscar J. Dunn, a Negro, as their candidate. But in the meantime Warmoth was clearly emerging as the leader of the white Radicals. Warmoth's victory was signalled when the convention changed the constitutional age of eligibility for the governorship from thirty-five to twenty-five years, and then simply to the same age (twenty-one) as for voting. Since Warmoth was only twenty-five, this was a fairly obvious move.[103]

One action of the convention of 1867–1868 was especially criticized, although it is difficult to see what else might have been done. The legislature elected in 1866 had adjourned in the spring of 1867 without making adequate provision for the finances of the state. This probably would have been impossible even if an attempt had been made. Louisiana was bankrupt as 1867 drew near its end, and there would be no new legislature to levy taxes and make appropriations until the convention had done its work and elections had been held. The delegates to the convention were not prosperous merchants and planters who could pay their own expenses. Therefore it became necessary to levy a one mill tax on assessed valuation of property with a penalty for failure to pay. Since the returns from this tax would not come in immediately, the convention decreed that its warrants

101 Quoted in Ficklen, *History of Reconstruction in Louisiana,* 196.
102 Vincent, "Negro Leadership in 1868," 339–51; New Orleans *Daily Picayune,* January 3, 1868.
103 New Orleans *Tribune,* December 10, 27, 1867; Stampp, *Era of Reconstruction,* 138–39.

should be issued to delegates for their per diem and allowances. To give these warrants value, they were made receivable as taxes. Thus the convention exercised a function properly belonging to the legislature.[104]

The constitution of Louisiana drawn up by the convention of 1867–1868 was probably the most radical of any of the constitutions which resulted from the Reconstruction Acts. It had provisions for universal desegregated education, a prohibition of racial discrimination in public places, and severe disfranchisement of "disloyal" voters. It should be noted here that in the convention the opposition to disfranchisement was made up largely of blacks led by Pinchback. Overall, nonetheless, one must term the convention moderate. A proposal that blacks be guaranteed a quota of state jobs was rejected on the grounds that appointments should be based on merit. Despite much talk in Congress and the *Tribune* of conficasting rebel estates and dividing the land among the blacks, these suggestions received no serious consideration at the convention. In fact, there seems to have been a general understanding among whites that the equal accommodations and integrated school clauses of the new constitution would not be enforced as, in fact, they were not for four years, and then not successfully. There is no evidence that ordinary social relationships between blacks and whites changed significantly during Reconstruction. The greatest change was universal adult male suffrage, and that came by decree from Congress long before the convention, which adjourned on March 9, 1868, had even begun its deliberations.[105]

The document drawn up was, by modern standards, an improvement over any basic law the state had ever had. If the amendments of 1870 be taken into consideration, and if honest administration be assumed, this constitution was probably superior to any of the five which have succeeded it. Certainly it was superior to the thousand-

104 Ficklen, *History of Reconstruction in Louisiana*, 196–97.
105 Vincent, "Negro Leadership in 1868," 339–51; Memelo, "The Development of State Laws Concerning the Negro in Louisiana," 48; Shugg, *Origins of Class Struggle in Louisiana*, 221–22; Grosz, "Pinchback," 535; New Orleans *Daily Picayune*, February 28, 1868; Russ, "The Negro and White Disfranchisement," 183; Ficklen, *History of Reconstruction in Louisiana*, 198; Stampp, *Era of Reconstruction*, 138–39, 170.

page monstrosity with which the state of Louisiana was burdened until 1974. Later constitutions were modeled largely on that of 1868, not including the accretions attached to the constitution of 1921.

A major concern of the delegates of 1867–1868 was the bill of rights. There had been no bills of rights as such in the constitutions of 1852 and 1864, but this was more than compensated for in 1868. Most of the bill of rights was what might be expected, outlawing slavery, guaranteeing peaceful assembly and petition, freedom of speech and press, freedom of religion, trial by jury, and the right to bail. There was also a guarantee of the right of private property. The Black Codes were specifically declared to be null and void.[106] After quoting the Declaration of Independence to the effect that all men were free and equal, the document introduced an unusual clause (and one highly offensive to Louisiana whites), which read as follows: "All persons shall enjoy equal rights and privileges upon any conveyance of a public character; and all places of business, or of public resort, or for which a license is required by either State, Parish, or Municipal authority, shall be deemed places of public character and shall be opened to the patronage of all persons, without distinction or discrimination on account of race or color."[107]

The constitution of 1868 borrowed wording from the Fourteenth Amendment and declared that all persons born or naturalized in the United States and residents of Louisiana were citizens of Louisiana. Suffrage was granted to all adult male citizens who had been residents of the state for one year and of the parish ten days except for those disfranchised by law. All voters were required to be registered. The disfranchising provisions were severe. Any person who had held office for a year or more under the Confederacy, persons who had registered as enemies of the United States, persons who had led guerrilla bands, persons who had written or published newspaper articles or preached sermons advocating and aiding rebellion, and all persons who had voted for or signed an ordinance of secession in Louisiana or elsewhere were excluded from voting. However, a man who was disfranchised under one or more of these provisions could

---

106 Material concerning the constitution of 1868 is derived from Thorpe, *The Federal and State Constitutions*, III, 1,449–71, unless otherwise noted.
107 *Ibid.*, 1,450.

nonetheless be registered as a voter if he had favored execution of the Reconstruction Acts before 1868 and had assisted in restoring Louisiana to the Union. Also, an otherwise disfranchised person would be registered if he signed an affidavit in which he admitted that the rebellion had been morally wrong and stated that he repented of any aid or comfort he had given to the Confederate cause. One historian referred to this clause as placing "a premium on perjury."[108] Many of the black delegates to the convention opposed this disfranchising clause. It did go into the constitution, however, and assured the election of a Republican state administration in 1868. In 1870 it was repealed by a constitutional amendment, so it was in effect for only two years.

The constitutions of 1852 and 1864 had specifically stated the principle of separation of powers. The 1868 constitution did not, and the powers of the governor were somewhat greater than they had been under previous constitutions. This was particularly true, taking subsequent legislation into account, of the power to fill newly created or vacant elective offices by appointment. It has been suggested that the great appointive powers of the governor were quietly sponsored by white delegates to the convention to prevent the election of too many Negroes to office in areas where blacks were in the majority.[109]

The qualifications for governor in four constitutions are revealing. The constitution of 1852 set a minimum age of twenty-eight and required four years residence. The White Unionist constitution of 1864 raised minimum age to thirty-five and time of residence to five years. The 1868 requirements, apparently drawn to Henry Clay Warmoth's specifications, required only that the governor be a qualified voter and a resident for two years. The constitution of 1879 demonstrated the reaction against Warmoth and Reconstruction, setting the minimum age at thirty and requiring no less than ten years residence.[110]

The constitution of 1868, like earlier ones, provided for a bicameral legislature. Members of the senate had to be residents in and qualified voters of the districts they represented, and, unlike the governor, they

108 Ficklen, *History of Reconstruction in Louisiana*, 200.
109 Patrick, *Reconstruction of the Nation*, 112–13.
110 Thorpe, *The Federal and State Constitutions*, III, 1,417, 1,436, 1,456, 1,481.

had to be at least twenty-five years old. They were elected to four-year staggered terms. The total number of senators was to be thirty-six, of whom nine could be from Orleans Parish, but two of the nine were shared, one with St. Bernard, the other with Plaquemines. It might be noted again that the prewar constitution of 1852 gave Orleans only five senators of a total of thirty-two. Members of the lower house of the legislature were required only to be qualified voters and residents of the districts they represented. Apportionment was according to total population, not according to registered voters as had been the case in 1864. Representatives were elected to two-year terms, which was probably an error in view of the fact that elections were almost always occasions for disorder. Members of both houses were to receive eight dollars per diem, the same as in 1864.[111]

Black delegates to the convention of 1868 were intensely interested in education. In this area the ideas of the more radical delegates seem to have prevailed. The constitution required that at least one free public school should be established in each parish, and that children from six to eighteen years of age should be eligible to attend regardless of race, color, or previous condition of servitude. The state superintendent of education was to be an elected official. Education was probably the most strongly opposed section of the new constitution. In practice, with rare exceptions, the desegregation provisions were to prove very difficult to put into effect.[112]

The constitution of 1868 provided for a supreme court whose members should be appointed by the governor to eight-year terms. Outside of New Orleans there were to be not less than twelve and not more than twenty district courts with both civil and criminal jurisdiction. The judges and clerks of these courts were to be elected to four-year terms. Seven district courts were set up in New Orleans, subject to change by the legislature. One was to hear criminal cases, one probate cases, one appeals from justice-of-the-peace courts, and the other four were to hear civil cases. The judges of these were to be elected to four-year terms. In each parish except Orleans there was to be a parish judge, elected for two years, with jurisdiction over cases in-

111 *Ibid.*, 1,430, 1,450.
112 Vincent, "Negro Leadership in 1868," 344–45; Memelo, "The Development of State Laws Concerning the Negro in Louisiana," 49.

volving more than a hundred but less than five hundred dollars. Finally, there were justices of the peace, elected to two-year terms, with jurisdiction over misdemeanors and civil cases involving less than a hundred dollars. The judicial system was to be completed by an elected state attorney general, a district attorney for each district court, and a sheriff and a coroner for each parish except Orleans, which was to have a civil sheriff and a criminal sheriff.

In evaluating the constitution of 1868, the first thing a Louisianian might note was that in readable print, including amendments, it was less than twenty-two pages in length. It was a more democratic constitution than any of its predecessors, and certainly more so than its two immediate successors. It provided the fundation upon which most features of the basic governmental machinery of Louisiana today have been erected. The public accommodations section and the public school section were a century ahead of their time, but both are in effect, though under federal law, at the time of this writing. It was a constitution under which the state could have lived in peace had good men held office and had Louisiana whites been willing to accept Negroes as free and politically equal citizens. But the office-holders were too often venal, and in their hearts Louisiana whites had made no real concessions. There is something pathetic in the expectation of the *Tribune* that the new constitution would cure the disorders of the state, and that "the sharks that preyed upon our state treasury will be kept aloof, and we may hope for a speedy restoration of our finances."[113]

113 New Orleans *Tribune*, December 1, 1867.

V *The Warmoth Ascendancy*

IN PREPARATION for the April election, the Republicans had held a nominating convention in January, 1868. On the first ballot Major Francis E. Dumas, a Negro, received forty-one votes and Henry Clay Warmoth received thirty-seven, with a lesser number going to George M. Wickliffe, W. J. Blackburn, and James G. Taliaferro. The nomination of P. B. S. Pinchback was proposed, but he refused on the ground that the candidacy of a black man would be ill-advised at the time. On the second ballot Warmoth won the nomination over Dumas by a vote of forty-five to forty-three. After Dumas had refused to run with Warmoth for lieutenant-governor, that honor went to Oscar J. Dunn, also a Negro. George E. Bovee for secretary of state, George Wickliffe for auditor, Simon Belden for attorney general, Antoine Dubuclet for treasurer, and Thomas M. Conway for superintendent of education completed the ticket. These nominations were not satisfactory to the ultra-Radicals whose views were expressed in the *Tribune*. Some of them bolted and nominated Taliaferro for governor and Dumas for lieutenant-governor.[1] The bolters received very little Republican support, and

---

1 Warmoth, *War, Politics and Reconstruction,* 54–56; Ficklen, *History of Reconstruction in Louisiana,* 201–202; F. B. Harris, "Henry Clay Warmoth," 548.

the *Tribune* was punished by loss of official printing, which now went to the New Orleans *Republican*—of which Warmoth was, or was soon to become, a major stockholder. The *Tribune* was forced to suspend publication in April, 1868.[2]

Louisiana Democrats and other anti-Radicals were still too crushed by the Reconstruction Acts and Military Reconstruction to field a ticket of their own, but they did seek to take advantage of the split in Republican ranks. Despite the fact that the Taliaferro splinter was considerably more "Radical" than the party led by Warmoth, Conservative leaders endorsed Taliaferro and worked for his election. Perhaps they preferred him because he was a native of Louisiana. As late as April 16, the first day of the election, the *Picayune* confidently predicted a Taliaferro victory.[3]

The campaigning of early 1868, it must be remembered, did not deal with the election of officials alone; the vote on ratification of the constitution was to be held at the same time. The effort to get out the Negro vote may not have been so intensive as it had been the previous September, but the Republicans still worked hard. The Grand Army of the Republic was now functioning well with Warmoth as Grand Commander. Presumably the Union League played a part, though this is not easy to prove. Some Freedmen's Bureau agents, encouraged by General Howard, worked at getting out the vote, and few Republican newspapers were established in the country parishes. Mass meetings were held, and the presence of some leading Radicals at these rallies almost guaranteed a good turnout. Last, but certainly not least, black ministers were enlisted wherever possible to direct their flocks to the polls with Republican tickets in their hands.[4]

In New Orleans the Democrats were rather halfhearted; frauds there, if any, were apparently the work of Radicals. In Calcasieu

2 Thomas W. Conway to Warmoth, March 15, 1868, in Warmoth Papers; New Orleans *Daily Picayune*, April 27, 1868; Uzee, "Republican Politics in Louisiana," 21.
3 New Orleans *Daily Picayune*, April 16, 1868; F. B. Harris, "Henry Clay Warmoth," 548.
4 Warmoth, *War, Politics and Reconstruction*, 51; Mortimer Smith to Warmoth, February 17, 1868, Charles Swenson to Warmoth, March 31, 1868, John Sims to Warmoth, February 13, 1868, all in Warmoth Papers; Henderson Hamilton Donald, *The Negro Freedman: Life Conditions of the American Negro in the Early Years after Emancipation* (New York, 1952), 201, 213; White, *Freedmen's Bureau in Louisiana*, 27–28.

Parish, according to one of Warmoth's correspondents, the sheriff, a disfranchised rebel, appointed a rebel deputy to oversee each polling place. According to the *Picayune*, disorder occurred in St. Bernard Parish a few days before the election when Negro Radicals attempted to break up a meeting of Negro Democrats. Another of Warmoth's correspondents reported that many blacks of Claiborne Parish were kept from the polls by threats that they would be driven from their homes; also, "many other bad and dirty act was done [*sic*]."[5] Only in East Baton Rouge, Caddo, Bossier, and DeSoto parishes was there evidence of systematic coercion and intimidation of the type that was to be so common in future elections. It should be noted that no troops were stationed at the polling places.[6]

The election for ratification of the constitution of 1868 and for electing state officials to serve under that constitution was held on April 16 and 17, 1868. The total vote in favor was 66,152 as compared to 48,739 against—a majority of 17,413 thus favoring the constitution. Of forty-eight parishes, twenty voted against ratification, but among the twenty were such small parishes as Catahoula with 529 votes against, Franklin with 413, Calcasieu with 363, and Sabine with 335. Orleans voted against ratification, but by only 452 votes out of 29,034. Only in East Baton Rouge, Caddo, and Jefferson parishes did as many as 500 Negroes vote against ratification, which probably indicates some intimidation on the part of white opponents. Even so, in Jefferson Parish a majority favored ratification. In plantation parishes with large black populations, the vote was overwhelmingly in favor, 1,384 to 363 in Carroll; 1,235 to 674 in Ouachita; 1,278 to 130 in St. Charles; 1,334 to 144 in Tensas; 1,948 to 828 in St. Mary; 1,215 to 386 in West Feliciana. The vote was not broken down by race in De Soto and Orleans parishes, but in the other forty-six, only 1,449 white votes were cast for ratification. In fact, only in Winn Parish were there more

---

5 William R. Meador to Warmoth, April 18, 1868, in Warmoth Papers.
6 W. G. Miefret to Warmoth, April 29, 1868, W. L. Lamb to Warmoth, April 30, 1868, W. C. Farquahar to Warmoth, April 26, 1868, T. H. Garret to Warmoth, May 28, 1868, all in Warmoth Papers; New Orleans *Daily Picayune*, April 14, 1868; Robert Joseph Aertker, "A Social History of Baton Rouge During the Civil War and Early Reconstruction" (M.A. thesis, Louisiana State University, 1947), 126; Kendall, *History of New Orleans*, I, 325; Sefton, *United States Army and Reconstruction*, 185.

than 100 favorable white votes—113 for compared with 393 opposed. Almost 6,000 of the voters who can be identified as black voted against ratification.

The south Louisiana sugar parishes, excepting East Baton Rouge, all had majorities favoring ratification, but here the relatively large number of small freeholders, particularly in Lafourche, Terrebonne, and St. Mary, gave a substantial minority of opposition votes. The majorities in the northeastern cotton parishes and in West Feliciana were overwhelming. The majority was not so great, however, in East Feliciana, which had a smaller number of plantations and more yeoman farmers. Of the parishes bordering on the Red River, Catahoula, Bienville, De Soto, and Caddo voted against ratification, but the vote was relatively close. Avoyelles ratified by a majority of only twenty-one votes and there was a substantial opposition minority in the parishes of Rapides and Bossier. Along the Red River only Natchitoches Parish was overwhelmingly in favor. Of the remaining parishes north of the Red River, Caldwell, Claiborne, Franklin, Jackson, Union, and Winn were all against, as were Sabine and Calcasieu to the west. Finally, in the nonplantation parishes east of the Mississippi, St. Tammany and St. Bernard voted for ratification by small margins. Livingston, St. Helena, and Washington voted against the document.[7]

A number of tentative conclusions may be drawn from this vote. In the first place, the term "black Republican" was not inaccurate. Overwhelmingly, the votes that ratified the constitution were black votes. Secondly, the hill, prairie, and pineflat parishes, most of which were overwhelmingly white in population, were opposed to the Radical Republicans from the beginning. They were to remain so throughout the Reconstruction period.[8] Also noteworthy is the very small number of whites in the country parishes who supported the constitution of 1868. If every white man outside of New Orleans who voted for ratification became an active and zealous member of the Republican party, there still would be only fifteen hundred white Republicans in the country parishes. We know that some of them were northern immigrants; it would be interesting to know how many. It cannot be

7 Davis, "Ratification of the Constitution of 1868," 301–305.
8 Howard, *Political Tendencies in Louisiana*, 71–81.

proved, but it can be assumed from the vote on ratification that at this time there were probably fewer than a thousand so-called Scalawags in Louisiana outside of New Orleans. It is doubtful that there were twenty-five hundred in the whole state. One final conclusion is that there was never any alliance between the Radicals and the poorer whites of the hill parishes. On the contrary, the people of such parishes were the most unbending in their opposition to Radicalism. In view of the truism that hatred of the Negro among southern whites is in inverse proportion to social and economic position, this is hardly surprising.

When the vote for state officials was counted, Warmoth had almost sixty-five thousand to slightly more than thirty-eight thousand for Taliaferro, and his entire ticket went into office with him. A substantial majority of Radical Republicans was elected to the legislature, although the Democrats made a good showing in the senate. Some Democratic legislators were successfully challenged, however; in the upper house M. L. Jewell was expelled and his seat awarded to his Republican opponent, Pinchback. The legislature elected J. S. Harris to the short term in the United States Senate and William Pitt Kellogg to the long term. Harris, a native of New York but a resident of Concordia Parish, seems to have been accepted by the press and the people with reasonably good grace. Kellogg, however, was a native of Illinois who had come to Louisiana as a federal officeholder.[9] He was not so well received. Two years after his election, the *Picayune* noted that "judge William Pitt Kellogg, Senator from this state, arrived in the city yesterday from his home in Illinois."[10]

The relatively acquiescent mood of the spring of 1868 was not to last long among Louisiana conservatives. The prevailing sentiment was expressed in the following editorial: "The black man has secured himself the right of suffrage and to hold office whenever he can get votes enough. We did our best to defeat this aspiration of his . . . but that contest is now over. . . . Yes it is certain that the constitution pre-

---

9 New Orleans *Daily Picayune*, May 5, July–August, October 6, 1868; Grosz, "Pinchback," 535–36; F. B. Harris, "Henry Clay Warmoth," 549; Ficklen, *History of Reconstruction in Louisiana*, 201–202; Dunning, *Reconstruction, Political and Economic*, 134–35; Blaine, *Twenty Years of Congress*, 447–48.
10 New Orleans *Daily Picayune*, October 5, 1871.

pared on Dryades Street has been adopted . . . and we must abide by it until we can throw it off and resume our original government, as it stood before the revolution."[11] White Louisianians truly felt that they were "ground to the dust by the iron heel of a . . . relentless oppression."[12] Therefore, they believed that revolutionary measures were justified in resistance to oppressors. But it was not Radical policy in economic and political fields which determined the southern attitude. Southerners might, as they later did, accommodate themselves to economic and political domination by the North. What they could not and would not accept was the idea of black men voting and holding office.[13]

2

The mood of white Louisiana became more belligerent when northern elections in early 1868 showed the Democratic party to be gaining ground. Perhaps a Democratic president could be elected, and if so, then a prompt end might be put to Radical Reconstruction. Professor William Best Hesseltine believed that had the Democrats concentrated their fire on either finance or Reconstruction, Grant could have been defeated. But Horatio Seymour, who headed the Democratic ticket, committed himself to nothing. The statements of his vice-presidential candidate, Frank Blair—that a newly elected Democratic president should declare the Reconstruction Acts null and void, order the army to disperse the Radical governments in the South, and allow the white people of the South to organize their own governments—lost badly needed votes in the North. Blair's words were music to white southern ears, however, and helped persuade southern leaders to make every possible effort to carry their states for Seymour.[14] In a fair election, the Democrats could not possibly carry Louisiana so long as the disfranchising provisions of the constitution

11 *Ibid.*, May 1, 1868.
12 W. T. Palfrey to J. G. Palfrey, September 20, 1868, in Frank Otto Gatell (ed.), "The Slaveholder and the Abolitionist: Binding Up a Family's Wounds," *Journal of Southern History*, XXVII (August, 1961), 390.
13 Copeland, "The New Orleans Press and Reconstruction," 190; Blaine, *Twenty Years of Congress*, 467–68; Patrick, *Reconstruction of the Nation*, 141.
14 Woodward, "Seeds of Failure in Radical Race Policy," 5; Hesseltine, *Ulysses S.*

of 1868 were in effect. It was only natural, therefore, that determined Democrats should turn to force and fraud to achieve their ends. For protection they formed secret or semisecret organizations.

The Ku Klux Klan already existed in Tennessee and the Carolinas; at the least it provided a model for Louisiana organizations. Although Walter Lynwood Fleming found evidence of the organization's existence in the Florida parishes, and Warmoth received a death threat purportedly from the Klan in April of 1868, the Klan probably did not exist as an organized entity. Rather, scattered groups of men, for political or other purposes, organized themselves into groups which they called the Klan. One such group which supposedly began as a patrol against hog thieves developed into a gang of horse thieves. Insofar as the national election of 1868 is concerned, the Klan had little or no impact in Louisiana.[15]

By far the most important secret anti-Republican organization in Louisiana was the Knights of the White Camellia. Obviously modeled after the Klan, this society was first established in St. Mary Parish in 1867. Its first leader was Judge Alcibiades DeBlanc. Whether DeBlanc continued to lead after the headquarters was reportedly transferred to New Orleans cannot be determined. According to Ficklen, who knew men who had belonged to the organization, new members, in addition to learning secret words, handshakes, and signals, swore a solemn oath to maintain white supremacy, to observe a marked difference between the races, and to do all in their power to prevent political power from falling into the hands of the inferior race. One member claimed that every man in St. Landry Parish belonged to the group except one, and that one was senile. Warmoth

---

Grant, Politician, 130–31; Clemenceau, *American Reconstruction,* 65; DuBois, *Black Reconstruction,* 474; Highsmith, "Louisiana During Reconstruction," 211–12.

15 [?] to Warmoth, April 27, 1868, in Warmoth Papers; Walter L. Fleming (ed.), "A Ku Klux Document," *Mississippi Valley Historical Review,* I (March, 1915), 575–78; Franklin *Planters' Banner,* quoted in New Orleans *Daily Picayune,* October 27, 1868; H. Oscar Lestage, "The White League in Louisiana and Its Participation in Reconstruction Riots," *Louisiana Historical Quarterly,* XVIII (July, 1935), 628–29; Dunning, *Reconstruction, Political and Economic,* 122–23; Susan Lawrence Davis, *Authentic History of the Ku Klux Klan, 1865–1877* (New York, 1924), 303; Coulter, *The South During Reconstruction,* 169; Ficklen, *History of Reconstruction in Louisiana,* 218, 222.

later maintained that he had paid informers in the ranks of the KWC, and the truth of this is borne out by a letter the governor received from one of these informants, accusing him of ingratitude.[16]

Scattered over Louisiana were a number of other organizations devoted to Democratic victory in November, 1868, by whatever means necessary. One club was known as the "298," and its members wore badges carrying that number. The significance of the numeral, if any, has been lost in time. All over the state Seymour Knights, usually mounted, and the Blair Guards, normally on foot, ostentatiously armed themselves and drilled. In New Orleans there was an organization of Sicilians known as the "Innocents," reportedly two thousand strong, much feared by the Negroes but also arousing trepidation in the breasts of old white residents. Also in New Orleans were the Crescent City Democratic Club, headed by Fred N. Ogden, and the Seymour Legion, each several hundred strong, which were paramilitary units.[17]

It should be clearly understood that, basically, all of these were terrorist organizations. A legend of long standing has it that the KKK and the KWC frightened blacks into staying away from the polls by playing upon their superstitions. No doubt this legend flourished because it fitted in so well with white southerners' smug belief in the superstitious ignorance of the black man. In reality, as events in Louisiana in 1868 demonstrated, the black man had something far more tangible than ghosts or spirits to fear. Masked men, riding through the countryside at night, brandishing weapons and often firing them, were enough to give second thoughts about the right to suffrage. So was the discovery of the lynched body of a neighbor hanging near a crossroads, or the disappearance forever of another neighbor who had dared assert his citizenship. It was fear which

16 Ficklen, *History of Reconstruction in Louisiana*, 215–18; Highsmith, *Louisiana During Reconstruction*," 248–49; Avary, *Dixie After the War*, 268; F. B. Harris, "Henry Clay Warmoth," 568; W. R. Evans to Warmoth, March 31, 1870, in Warmoth Papers; Allen W. Trelease, *White Terror: The Ku Klux Klan Conspiracy and Southern Reconstruction* (New York, 1971), 127–36.

17 Baton Rouge *Weekly Advocate*, August 1, 1868; Walter Prichard (ed.), "The Origin and Activities of the 'White League' in New Orleans (Reminiscences of a Participant in the Movement)," *Louisiana Historical Quarterly*, XXIII (April, 1940), 528–29; Highsmith, "Louisiana During Reconstruction," 302–303.

kept many blacks from the polls, but well-founded fear of the lash, the bullet, and the rope, not fear of spirits.[18]

The Republicans nominated General Ulysses S. Grant for president and Schuyler Colfax for vice-president. Warmoth's wartime experience with Grant had not been happy, and there was certainly some bad feeling between the two men. One of Warmoth's friends wrote: "[Grant's] military prestige rendered it, I suppose, a necessity to nominate him though . . . he seems one of the last men to be the leader of a great party at the head of a great nation."[19] The Republican platform statement on Negro suffrage was an excellent example of the "double standard" in racial morality: "The guarantee by Congress of equal suffrage to all loyal men at the South was demanded by every consideration of public safety, of gratitude and of justice, and must be maintained." In the loyal northern states, however, "the question of suffrage . . . properly belongs to the people of those states."[20] In July Senator Kellogg wrote: "Let it be understood that . . . [Louisiana] must be carried for Grant this fall and that those who expect official favors . . . must help to secure the success of the party."[21] Even so, Warmoth's correspondence leaves the impression that his enthusiasm for Grant was something less than overwhelming. On the other hand, he certainly did all that could reasonably be expected.[22]

If Louisiana was to go for Seymour, every possible Democratic vote had to be cast, and a large number of Negroes had to be persuaded or coerced to vote Democratic or stay at home on election day. Andrew Johnson made a contribution by issuing a full amnesty to all adherents of the Confederacy. Technically, this added no voters to the rolls, but it encouraged proscribed voters to register in defiance of state law in those parishes where registrars were willing. The old scriptural proslavery arguments were refurbished in an attempt to show that the cause of the South had been just, after all. Rumors of Negro insurrections abounded, creating more solidarity in the ranks

18 Grady H. McWhiney and Francis B. Simkins, "The Ghostly Legend of the Ku Klux Klan," *Negro History Bulletin*, XIV (February, 1951), 109–112.
19 "John" to Warmoth, May 25, 1868, in Warmoth Papers.
20 Quoted in Woodward, "Seeds of Failure in Radical Race Policy," 139–40.
21 William Pitt Kellogg to Warmoth, July 30, 1868, in Warmoth Papers.
22 Warmoth Papers, June–November, 1868; New Orleans *Daily Picayune*, September 22, 1868; Hesseltine, *Ulysses S. Grant, Politician*, 240.

of the white population. For the first time a serious Democratic effort was made to cultivate the vote of the German colony in New Orleans. The *Picayune* even revived the old arguments of 1864, saying that the constitutions of 1861, 1864, and 1868 were all illegal, and that Louisiana by right should still be governed under the constitution of 1852.[23]

The main effort at getting out the white Democratic vote was made in New Orleans for the simple reason that that was where the largest concentration of white voters was to be found. More than two months before the election a great parade was held in which more than fifteen thousand people were reported to have participated. No fewer than sixty-five pro-Seymour organizations took part in this parade, including the Blair Defenders of Carrollton, the Jackson Railroad Club, the Third Ward Democratic Club, the Seymour Southrons, the Second Ward Colored Club, the Minute Men of '68, the Algiers Club, and the Constitution Skimmer Club. The papers were full of announcements of meetings of Democratic organizations.[24] A country editor who visited the city during the summer, and who happened to be a leading member of the KWC, told his readers: "Every night something is done to strengthen the cause." He went on, "The true white people of New Orleans are strong and confident of . . . complete success, not only in November, but forever after."[25]

An effort was made to enlist as many Negroes as possible in the Democracy's ranks. The planter class had always felt that it should be able to control the vote of its former slaves, and now it set out to do so. One planter wrote in August:

Politics engages everybody's attention. We had three colored orators to address the sovereign freedmen and the "white trash" night before last. . . . The Democrats are effecting a foothold in the Radical camp. I shall start tomorrow on a collecting tour for funds to carry on the campaign. . . . I

23 Ficklen, *History of Reconstruction in Louisiana*, 213–14; Proclamation, July 4, 1868, in J. D. Richardson (ed.), *Messages and Papers of the Presidents*, VI, 656; Franklin *Planters' Banner*, quoted in New Orleans *Daily Picayune*, September 16, 1868; Marksville *Villager*, July 11, 1868, quoted in New Orleans *Daily Picayune*, July 19, 1868; New Orleans *Daily Picayune*, July 17, August 16, September 5, 19, 1868; Robert T. Clark, Jr., "Reconstruction and the New Orleans German Colony," *Louisiana Historical Quarterly*, XXIII (April, 1940), 504.
24 New Orleans *Daily Picayune*, August, 1868.
25 Franklin *Planters' Banner*, quoted in New Orleans *Daily Picayune*, August 1, 1868; see also Highsmith, "Louisiana During Reconstruction," 248–49.

have worked myself up to the height of political enthusiasm in this conflict. . . . I shall make speeches to the Negroes at the Barbecues—and hope they will be of service to the cause. I suppose you have received from home an account of the barbecue at Jenerette's [sic]—too much drunkenness marred the good effects it otherwise would have had.[26]

Negro votes were sought fairly whenever possible, even though the Opelousas *Courier* objected so strongly to Negro suffrage that it wanted no blacks at all to vote. Three leading white Democrats spoke to a rally for freedmen at Plaquemine in Iberville Parish. The Minden Democratic Colored Club proudly reported three hundred members. In Alexandria the Ice House Hotel made its ballroom available for a Democratic Negro ball. Use was made of Democratic black orators. W. H. Mills was active in Rapides Parish; another well-known black Democratic speaker was Willis Rollins, whose appearance almost brought on a riot in New Orleans. If blacks could not be persuaded, sometimes they could be bought. For the vast majority of Louisiana freedmen, however, a stronger measure—intimidation—was required to force them to vote Democratic or remain away from the polls.[27]

In many cases economic intimidation was enough. Whites still owned Louisiana, and the vast majority of freedmen were either paid laborers or sharecroppers on lands owned by whites. One newspaper suggested in the summer that Democratic landlords keep a record of how blacks had voted. At Clinton a meeting of planters agreed to employ no Negro who had voted the Radical ticket. When some employers attempted to discharge blacks for political activity in the summer of 1868, General Robert Buchanan called a halt, but the threat was still there for the following year. Doctors and lawyers

26 Donalson Caffery to Bethia Richardson, August 23, 1868, in Caffery Papers, Southern Historical Collection, University of North Carolina.
27 Ficklen, *History of Reconstruction in Louisiana,* 210–13; Williams, *Romance and Realism in Southern Politics,* 27; Lestage, "The White League," 626; Lonn, *Reconstruction in Louisiana,* 14–15; William Gillette, *The Right to Vote: Politics and the Passage of the Fifteenth Amendment* (Baltimore, 1965), 41; F. B. Harris, "Henry Clay Warmoth," 559–60; Coulter, *The South During Reconstruction,* 357–58; William E. Highsmith, "Some Aspects of Reconstruction in the Heart of Louisiana," *Journal of Southern History,* XIII (November, 1947), 483–84; Highsmith, "Social and Economic Conditions in Rapides Parish," 91–92; Charles L. Dufour, "The Age of Warmoth," *Louisiana History,* VI (Fall, 1965), 343; Baton Rouge *Weekly Advocate,* August 1, 1868; New Orleans *Daily Picayune,* July–September, 1868.

announced that they would not serve Radicals, millers that they would not grind their corn. New Orleans Democrats proposed a boycott of Radical barbers, draymen, and cabmen. Without doubt this economic coercion was effective in thousands of instances. On the other hand, Louisiana planters still needed more labor than was available, and many blacks realized that the demand for their labor would not end with the election. Thus fear greater than that inspired by economic threats was necessary to keep most black voters away from the polls.[28]

White Louisianians did not hesitate to resort to violence in the summer and fall of 1868. Andrew Johnson was still chief executive of the United States, so there was much less danger of federal interference than there would be later under Grant. Southerners hoped, of course, to keep Grant out of the White House. The violence of 1868 reached peaks in certain particular outbreaks, but it should be remembered that lesser incidents occurred daily; the pressure upon Negroes was constant. When Governor Warmoth spoke out against violence in August, he was castigated by the *Picayune*. Republicans were not murdered for political reasons, said the paper, but for personal reasons. That there was too much violence the *Picayune* was ready to admit, but "The cause of this is to be found in Radical teaching, Radical measures, and Radical threats against our population."[29]

There were a few instances when blacks apparently did instigate trouble. One affray broke out in New Orleans when someone, presumably a Radical black, fired a shot at a parade of the Italian-American Innocents. Some whites were killed by Negroes in St. Bernard Parish, and Governor Warmoth had to intercede to prevent the lynching of Democratic orator Willis Rollins by a Radical mob.[30] But Georges Clemenceau put his finger on a striking feature of the violence in Louisiana and elsewhere in the South in 1868: "In all events of the kind, the remarkable feature is that according to telegraphic

28 New Orleans *Daily Picayune*, September 15, October 20, 1868; Patrick, *Reconstruction of the Nation*, 158; Cox, *Three Decades of Federal Legislation*, 552–53; White, *Freedmen's Bureau in Louisiana*, 182; Williams, *Romance and Realism in Southern Politics*, 26–27; Highsmith, "Louisiana During Reconstruction," 247–48.
29 New Orleans *Daily Picayune*, August 8, 1868.
30 *Ibid.*, September 11, 1868; White, *Freedmen's Bureau in Louisiana*, 141; Ficklen, *History of Reconstruction in Louisiana*, 225–26.

reports, there is always a band of heavily armed negroes attacking a handfull [*sic*] of harmless whites. Then when it comes to counting the dead, a few negroes are always down, but of white men, not a trace."[31]

The summer and fall of 1868 saw numerous disturbances in Louisiana. In Bossier Parish there were two outbreaks, the first in September. According to white accounts, some two hundred blacks armed themselves for the purpose of seizing land belonging to whites. If any persons were killed, there is no record of it, but twenty-one blacks were found guilty, apparently of insurrection, by a jury which included eight blacks. Those convicted were sent to the penitentiary at Baton Rouge, but eventually all or most of them were pardoned by Warmoth. A bloodier battle broke out in Bossier several weeks later when several Negroes were shot to death by a white mob, supposedly from Arkansas. A group of Negroes arrested two white men accused of being members of the mob and, when it appeared that the captives might be rescued, killed them. Then more than a hundred armed white men assembled and began to shoot Negroes indiscriminately. The Democrats estimated that forty were killed; the Republicans said three times that many, with one hundred more wounded.[32]

In late September trouble broke out in St. Landry Parish when a group of Seymour Knights warned Radical blacks at Washington not to interfere with some of their peers who had joined the Democrats. At Opelousas the Republican *St. Landry Progress*, a bilingual paper, published a story critical of the Knights' action. The English-language editor was horsewhipped and driven from town; the French editor managed to get aboard a steamboat with a whole skin. Negroes, led by a former free man of color, attempted to come to the aid of the editors. In the resulting exchange of gunfire, three whites were wounded and four blacks killed. A dozen blacks were captured. The prisoners were taken out of jail and shot to death during the night, and the next day a general "Negro hunt" began all over the parish. The Democrats proudly admitted killing thirty freedmen; the Radi-

---

31 Clemenceau, *American Reconstruction*, 228–29.
32 Baton Rouge *Weekly Advocate*, September 19, 1868; New Orleans *Daily Picayune*, October 6, 17, 1868; Ficklen, *History of Reconstruction in Louisiana*, 226–27.

cals claimed that more than two hundred had been murdered.[33] The *Picayune's* account of the beginning of this tragedy is instructive:

NEGRO RISING IN ST. LANDRY
Program of Spoilation, Rapine, Conflagration, and Murder
The Radical Editor a Social Firebrand
Conciliatory Policy of the Whites
Opelousas Invested by the Negroes
They Are Driven Back and Disarmed[34]

Another outburst of violence, this time against white Republicans, took place at Franklin in St. Mary Parish. There a local Unionist named Chase, described by Warmoth as connected with some of the best families in the parish, had been elected parish judge under the constitution of 1868. At the same time H. H. Pope, a native of New York and a former colonel in the Union army, had been elected sheriff. On October 17, 1868, an editorial in Daniel Dennett's *Planters' Banner* described Pope as "the little rat" and predicted that because of bad health he would not live long. This was a startlingly accurate prediction. The night after this item appeared, a small group of disguised men shot and stabbed Sheriff Pope and Judge Chase to death on the gallery of the hotel where they lived; Mrs. Pope saw her husband murdered.[35] Dennett was active in the KWC.

In late October a riot broke out in St. Bernard Parish. Accounts of this affair are conflicting, but apparently an altercation began between an Italian storekeeper and some Negroes. One Negro was either killed or wounded, whereupon the store was besieged. The proprietor definitely was killed and also, according to an apparently reliable account, his son and his son's wife. The store was burned. This was reason enough for the Innocents to descend upon the parish and conduct a Negro hunt on the now familiar pattern. How many died is not known, but sixty blacks were jailed and held for sixty days with no charges made against them. The death toll was probably not high.

---

33 New Orleans *Daily Picayune*, October 6–10, 1868; White, *Freedmen's Bureau in Louisiana*, 182–83; Highsmith, "Louisiana During Reconstruction," 243–44; Ficklen, *History of Reconstruction in Louisiana*, 227–28; Lestage, "The White League," 626; Donald, *The Negro Freedman*, 195–96; Charles H. Coleman, *The Election of 1868: The Democratic Effort to Regain Control* (New York, 1933), 322–23.

34 New Orleans *Daily Picayune*, October 6, 1868.

35 Warmoth, *War, Politics and Reconstruction*, 68–69.

However, although the registration figures for St. Bernard Parish showed 700 Republicans and 325 Democrats, the Democrats carried the parish by an almost unanimous vote in November of 1868.[36]

New Orleans was far from immune to the violence of 1868. In addition to the Rollins incident, in late September several men were killed in a fight between Democrats and Radicals on Canal Street. Michael Hahn wrote that early in the campaign Republicans from the country parishes were seeking refuge in New Orleans, but that by autumn many were leaving the city in search of safety.[37] The worst disorder in the city since July 30, 1866, began on the evening of October 25, 1868. As usual, the accounts of the two sides are so much in conflict that the truth is hard to determine. However the trouble began, white anger was directed especially against Negro policemen, at least one of whom was killed. This may have been a premeditated action, because armed Democratic clubs immediately took over the task of patrolling the city. Now that black policemen had been driven from the streets, the Metropolitan Police Board proceeded to remove all of them from the police force. But this did not end the trouble, nor did a proclamation by Governor Warmoth, who counseled Republicans to stay off the streets. The Democrats accomplished their object. New Orleans had more than twenty thousand registered Republican voters, but the city cast only three hundred Republican votes in the election.[38]

The use of federal troops on a fairly extensive scale might have prevented the violence in the summer and fall of 1868. Warmoth and other southern Republicans had attempted to get the approval of Congress for the formation of a militia, but, according to Senator Kellogg, the northern Republicans "feared the effect of putting arms

36 New Orleans *Daily Picayune*, October 27–28, 1868; Ficklen, *History of Reconstruction in Louisiana*, 228–30.
37 New Orleans *Daily Picayune*, August 2–7, September 23, 1868; Warmoth, *War, Politics and Reconstruction*, 74–75; Ficklen, *History of Reconstruction in Louisiana*, 212; Kendall, *History of New Orleans*, I, 330; Richard N. Current, *Three Carpetbag Governors* (Baton Rouge, 1967), 47–48.
38 C. D. Lualke (?) to J. J. Williamson, October 27, 1868, in Warmoth Papers; New Orleans *Daily Picayune*, October 25–28, 1868; Warmoth, *War, Politics and Reconstruction*, 76; Prichard (ed.), "White League in New Orleans," 529; F. B. Harris, "Henry Clay Warmoth," 566–67; Clemenceau, *American Reconstruction*, 258–59; Highsmith, "Louisiana During Reconstruction," 245–46.

into the hands of the colored population."[39] Warmoth made a half-hearted effort to arm the police, even negotiating in the North for the purchase of arms, but he seems to have realized that this was a dangerous resort. As William A. Dunning was later to point out, "The appearance of a body of Negroes under arms, whether authorized by law or not, had for its almost certain result an affray, if not a pitched battle, with armed whites, in which the Negroes almost invariably got the worst of it."[40]

Warmoth turned instead to President Johnson. On August 1, 1868, a joint resolution of the legislature requested the president to "furnish civil authorities of this State such forces as shall be necessary to secure peace and good order in the State."[41] When John F. Deane, a personal emissary of Warmoth, appealed to Johnson, the president not only gave him no satisfaction but was sarcastic in his comments. A letter from the governor, detailing incidents which had occurred and predicting more violence to come unless prevented by the national government, had no effect. Johnson instructed the Louisiana troop commander, General Robert Buchanan, to preserve order if the need arose, but to clear any use of troops with Washington. This meant, of course, that acts of intimidation could be carried out before federal troops could possibly intervene. After the riot in St. Bernard Parish, Warmoth asked General L. H. Rousseau, in direct command at New Orleans, to request more troops. The War Department stated that reinforcements would have to come from Mississippi, which would bring them to New Orleans too late to preserve the peace. Rousseau refused to use Negro troops stationed on Ship Island because he believed them more likely to cause trouble than to prevent it. Indeed, the general had told Warmoth that he did not believe that any number of troops could protect Louisiana Republicans at the polls. Warmoth then urged Rousseau to take over Orleans, Jefferson, and St. Bernard parishes under martial law until after the election, but this request also was refused. Now, apparently, Warmoth realized that there was

39 Kellogg to Warmoth, July 30, 1868, in Warmoth Papers.
40 Dunning, *Essays on the Civil War and Reconstruction*, 356–57.
41 *Acts Passed by the General Assembly of the State of Louisiana at the First Session of the First Legislature, Begun and Held in the City of New Orleans, June 29, 1868* (New Orleans, 1868), 18–19.

no way to safely get Republican voters to the polls; he advised them to stay at home. [42]

The election was held on November 3, 1868. The *Picayune* reported: "The City Perfectly Quiet—The Negroes Abstain from Voting—Democrats Up and Doing." [43] In the country parishes the election was generally quiet, although in Bossier three Negro bodies were found floating in the Red River on the morning of election day. In Lafourche a cordon of white men surrounded each voting place. The supervisor of registration in St. Landry reported: "I am fully convinced that no man could have voted any other than the Democratic ticket and not been killed inside of twenty-four hours. [44] John L. Lewis wrote from Minden that the election there had been quiet, "owing I presume to the fact that no opposition was offered. The White Republicans as well as the freedmen were afraid to vote as they really desired—having had intimations before the election that they would suffer if they did not vote the Democratic ticket." [45] The results as counted showed 80,225 votes for Seymour and Blair, and 33,225 for Grant and Colfax. On November 7 the *Picayune* announced that Radical Republicanism had been killed in Louisiana and demanded that all Negro members of the legislature resign. [46]

Grant was elected without Louisiana's electoral vote, so the vote for Seymour was not seriously challenged. Congressional elections were the subject of contests, and Congress seated a number of Republicans on grounds of Democratic intimidation and fraud. One contest arose in the Second District where Congress declared Republican James Mann to have been the victor in the regular election. Mann died soon afterward, and a Negro, J. Willis Menard, was the Republican candidate in a special election. This election went before the national House of Representatives as a contest, and Menard, allowed to plead his own case, was the first black man to speak from

---

42 J. R. West to Warmoth, July 15, 1868, John Lynch to Warmoth, August 10, 1868, John F. Deane to Warmoth, August 5, 9, 1868, in Warmoth Papers; Cox, *Three Decades of Federal Legislation*, 433; Clemenceau, *American Reconstruction*, 227–28, 236; F. B. Harris, "Henry Clay Warmoth," 560–62.
43 New Orleans *Daily Picayune*, November 3, 1868.
44 Report of Board of Registration, January 10, 1869, in Appendix, *Legislative Documents, Louisiana, 1869* (New Orleans, 1869).
45 John L. Lewis to Warmoth, November 4, 1868, in Warmoth Papers.
46 New Orleans *Daily Picayune*, November 7, 1868.

the floor. The idea of a black man in Congress was still too radical for many Radicals, however, so neither Menard nor his Democratic opponent was seated.[47]

It might be interesting to speculate on how much bloodshed could have been avoided, how much the prosperity of Louisiana could have been improved, and how much antagonism between the races could have been reduced if white leaders had checked the Democratic excesses of 1868. But such speculation is profitless. White Louisianians of the nineteenth century were not willing to grant political equality to the Negro; they were not willing to accept it other than at the point of a bayonet. Whenever an opportunity arose, they would seek to do away with it. Eventually they would succeed.

3

Henry Clay Warmoth was twenty-six years old when he became governor of Louisiana on June 27, 1868. Congress had declared Louisiana restored to the Union two days earlier, and the state was at long last fully and without reservation back in the Union. The first act of the legislature when it met on June 29 was to approve the Fourteenth Amendment. John Hay wrote Warmoth from Vienna: "It is a most cheering indication for the South that the fresh young energy of the West is taking so large a share in the management of civil affairs."[48]

Many years later Warmoth wrote that he "found the state and city of New Orleans bankrupt. Interest on the state and city bonds had been in default for years; the assessed property . . . had fallen in value from $470,164,963.00 in 1860 to $250,063,359.63 in 1870; taxes for the years . . . [1861–1867] were in arrears. The city and state were flooded with state and city shinplasters which had been issued to meet current expenses."[49] In his inaugural address the young governor put chief emphasis on the restoration of order, urging the people

---

47 J. Willis Menard to Warmoth, November 19, 1868, J. Hale Sypher to Warmoth, December 5, 1868, in Warmoth Papers; *House Miscellaneous Documents*, 41st Cong., 2nd Sess., No. 152, pp. 703–18, No. 154, pp. 471–99, 530–40, 703–31, 754–59; Gillette, *The Right to Vote*, 40–41; Samuel Denny Smith, *The Negro in Congress, 1870–1901* (Chapel Hill, N.C., 1940), 131.

48 John Hay to Warmoth, July 12, 1868, in Warmoth Papers; see also Ficklen, *History of Reconstruction in Louisiana*, 202–204.

49 Warmoth, *War, Politics and Reconstruction*, 79.

to aid in this endeavor, but warning that he would provide strong
law enforcement from above if the people did not provide it from
below.[50]

The new government faced many obstacles. The vast majority of
the white people of Louisiana never accepted it as legitimate. In his
four years as governor Warmoth never used federal troops, although
he requested them during the presidential campaign of 1868, but the
background presence of federal military power was essential to the
survival of the Republican state administration. Warmoth's government contained no representatives of the dominant merchant-planter
class of Louisiana; a member of that class who joined Warmoth would
have forfeited his previous position in the eyes of his neighbors.[51] In
fact, few members of the new administration could even be described
as gentlemen. One Republican representing Louisiana in Congress
wrote to Warmoth about another:

Newsham is the same damn fool here that he was in La. . . . He gets
drunk, talks loud, lies like a Turk. I have spoken to him several times about
his conduct. . . . I can't keep him within the bounds of decency to say nothing about . . . propriety. . . . His general deportment is bad enough, but his
table manners are so damnable that I am ashamed to be seen . . . dining
where he is. . . . He talks loud enough, and in his boastful style, to be heard
over the entire hall, he eats sliced tomatoes and even meats with his
fingers, blows his *nose* on his napkin, and does other equally indecent and
outrageous things at the table.[52]

According to Warmoth's private notes, the Louisiana house of
representatives of 1868–1870 had sixty-five Republicans and thirty-
six Democrats. Thirty-five of the Republicans were black; none of
the Democrats were. The Senate had twenty-three Republicans, of
whom seven were black, and thirteen Democrats, all white. Obviously it would be incorrect to refer to this as "Negro rule." This legislature,
and others to follow during the eight years of Radical Reconstruction
in Louisiana, were vilified and ridiculed. If one's ideas of legislative
propriety are derived from an ordinary junior-high school civics text,

50 F. B. Harris, "Henry Clay Warmoth," 553; New Orleans *Daily Picayune*, July 14,
   1868; Burgess, *Reconstruction and the Constitution*, 198; Highsmith, "Louisiana
   During Reconstruction," 151; Ficklen *History of Reconstruction in Louisiana*,
   206; Current, *Three Carpetbag Governors*, 40–41.
51 Franklin *Planters' Banner*, quoted in New Orleans *Daily Picayune*, August 5, 1868.
52 Sypher to Warmoth, July 18, 1868, in Warmoth Papers.

he can conclude that the Louisiana legislatures from 1868 to 1877 ranked low indeed. But a researcher familiar with the procedure and protocol of modern state legislatures, and that of Louisiana in particular, will note that the legislators of 1868–1870 were a little uncertain as to parliamentary law, but that otherwise they suffer little in comparison with their modern counterparts. Allowance must be made for the bias of Democratic newspapers and the prejudices of observers, from North and South, to whom the presence of Negroes in the role of lawmakers seemed unnatural and monstrous. An interesting fact concerning this first Radical Republican legislature is that it proposed the repeal, by constitutional amendment, of disfranchisement of supporters of the Confederacy. It also appropriated five thousand dollars to aid in establishing a cemetery for the Confederate dead who fell at Fredericksburg, Chancellorsville, and the Wilderness.[53]

Like any politician in office, Warmoth sought to strengthen his position through his use of patronage. There was no lack of office seekers. As early as April of 1868 a minister wrote that he had given Warmoth "the weight of the *Church* for your election. God has been pleased to bless our efforts and you are governor of Louisiana. And now I ask for the *Church* two appointments." After naming the men and the offices desired, the writer added, "They are both members of my church . . . yet I am particularly anxious for our mutual friend, Captain Armstrong. He has the good sense to know he must pay something toward the late campaign if needed. . . . The Captain will hand you this note. . . . God bless you!"[54]

Letters concerned high offices and low. From Sugartown came a protest against the appointment as postmistress, which was not within Warmoth's province, of "a lady by the name of Hector . . . a most

53 Warmoth Papers, Item 00920; New Orleans *Daily Picayune*, June, 1868–June, 1870; Michael Hahn to Warmoth, May 9, 1868, in Warmoth Papers; Charles Nordhoff, *The Cotton States in the Spring and Summer of 1865* (New York, 1876), 48; H. H. Donald, *The Negro Freedman*, 219; F. B. Harris, "Henry Clay Warmoth," 551; Ficklen, *History of Reconstruction in Louisiana*, 203–204; Franklin, *Reconstruction After the Civil War*, 89–90; DuBois, *Black Reconstruction*, 471–72; Lonn, *Reconstruction in Louisiana*, 22–23, 25–27; *Acts Passed by the General Assembly of the State of Louisiana at the Third Session of the First Legislature, Begun and Held in the City of New Orleans, March 7, 1870* (New Orleans, 1870), 101–102.

54 J. P. Newman to Warmoth, April 26, 1868, in Warmoth Papers.

noted lady for her rebel sentiments."[55] A letter from John T. Ludeling informing the governor that he would accept a seat on the state supreme court brought results because Ludeling became chief justice. This appointment received less popular approval, however, than Warmoth's naming of his opponent in the gubernatorial election, James G. Taliaferro, to a seat on the supreme court, a position he had held under Wells. Warmoth aided his followers in obtaining federal office, as for example his recommendation that R. K. Howell be appointed to the federal circuit court. To increase the number of offices at his disposal, Warmoth secured passage of legislation giving him the power to fill all vacancies, local and otherwise, for which provision was not made in the state constitution, and providing for an inquiry into the eligibility of those already in office; the governor was to replace those found ineligible. Thus a number of good Republicans were accommodated and, probably, some Democrats converted to Republicanism.[56]

In September, 1868, Warmoth received the following charming letter from a friend in the Custom House:

Dear Henry,
The name of the bearer is J. F. Winston; he is part proprietor of a soda and cake stand in the rotunda of the Custom-House. He is however and moreover ambitious and patriotically desirous of serving the state—for a consideration—"his soul is above small beer:" the present and immediate object of his aspirations is a commissionership on the Metro-politan Police and he comes to me for a recommendation—I disclaim all powers to exercise authority . . . in any . . . field of your excellency's prerogatives.
I am free to say however and accordingly do say and say it boldly that this man sells me very decent sandwiches at a price which in this latitude is not unreasonable. . . . his cakes are also by no means bad and his coffee cannot in reason be called very bad.[57]

Warmoth realized that the white Republicans in Louisiana were a tiny minority of Louisiana white men. He also felt that Louisiana freedmen, so recently released from bondage, could not defend them-

55 H. Clay Farquahar to Warmoth, June 1, 1868, in Warmoth Papers.
56 John T. Ludeling to Warmoth, June 1, 1868, Warmoth to Ulysses S. Grant, April 5, 1869, James O. Fuqua to Warmoth, July 9, 1868, all in Warmoth Papers; New Orleans *Daily Picayune*, August 1, 1868; *Acts of Louisiana, 1868*, 27–28, 45–46; Lonn, *Reconstruction in Louisiana*, 45–46.
57 Deane to Warmoth, September 5, 1868, in Warmoth Papers.

selves against white aggression. The United States Army had been a most unreliable protector during the troubles preceding the election of 1868, and the governor had no reason to believe that President Grant, an old enemy, would go out of his way to keep his onetime subordinate in power in Louisiana. Therefore he promoted the passage of a militia bill and urged repeal of an act of Congress prohibiting the organization of militia in southern states. Congress was cooperative, and the Louisiana legislature authorized a militia of five thousand men, half white and half black. General Longstreet was made adjutant general, and a mission was sent North to buy arms. In the final analysis, however, Warmoth was most reluctant to equip, or even to organize, the militia. Louisiana troops half white and half black would almost surely be divided among themselves, and the white element would probably be unreliable for the defense of a Republican regime. Therefore the organization of the militia, though begun, was never wholly completed.[58]

While federal law still forbade a militia, Warmoth had arrived at another solution to the problem of providing a military force. After the St. Bernard Riot, the legislature made Orleans, Jefferson, and St. Bernard parishes into the Metropolitan Police District. Using the Republican members of the old city police as a nucleus, Warmoth enlarged the Metropolitan Police, provided it with arms, and made it into a military organization. A board of five commissioners appointed by the governor, three of them Negroes, supervised this force and was given the authority to levy taxes to pay its expenses. In reality it was a state militia under the governor's control. The city government of New Orleans had no power whatsoever over the Metropolitans, as they came to be called, and a statute was enacted specifically forbidding the mayor to exercise any police powers within the city. Thus Warmoth had a military force without relying upon a possibly disloyal statewide militia. Also, there was no burden on the state treasury because the taxpayers of the police district paid for the Metropolitans. The Metropolitan Police was to be the military arm of the Radical Republican regimes throughout Louisiana from 1869

58 *Acts of Louisiana, 1868,* 178; *Acts of Louisiana, Extra Session 1870,* 175–88; *Debates in the House of Representatives of the State of Louisiana, 1869* (New Orleans, 1869), 110; Lynch to Warmoth, May 3, 1870, James Longstreet to Warmoth, June 30, 1870, in Warmoth Papers.

through 1877, but they were never really effective after their defeat by the White League at Liberty Place in 1874.[59]

The Metropolitan Police Board was only one example of gubernatorial interference with the government of New Orleans. The Democrats had taken over control of the city government in 1868, but in 1869 the legislature enacted a new charter which enabled Warmoth to appoint new city officials to serve until the next election. Then in 1870 some of Jefferson Parish was joined to Orleans Parish and Jefferson City was consolidated with New Orleans. A group of leading citizens designated themselves as an "electoral jury" and nominated a number of men for each vacancy Warmoth had to fill. Of the seven officials Warmoth appointed, five were from the list proposed, and he named a member of the electoral jury as mayor. When this man declined, Benjamin F. Flanders was named to the post. Bernard Soulier, a Negro recommended by the citizens, was made director of the waterworks. The Radicals were firmly in control of New Orleans until the 1872 election.[60]

The city was in deep trouble financially before Radical Reconstruction began. In 1868 it owed some ten million dollars, about one-third of which was in the form of city notes which served as the chief circulating medium for ordinary transactions. In 1869 the legislature ordered the entire floating debt funded; this was to be accomplished by issuing five million dollars in twenty-five-year bonds bearing 7 percent interest, at least three million dollars of which must be sold for city notes. The remainder was to be used to meet judgments against the city, outstanding warrants, and other current obligations. An appropriation of twenty-nine thousand dollars a month used for redeeming bonds issued in 1852 was to be applied to the new bonds when the old had been paid off. Under these conditions, of course, the bonds sold at a considerable discount. The city had been ordered

---

59 *Acts of Louisiana, 1868,* 3, 16–17, 85–98; *Acts Passed by the General Assembly of the State of Louisiana at the Second Session of the First Legislature, Begun and Held at the City of New Orleans, January 4, 1869* (New Orleans, 1869), 60–61; *Acts of Louisiana, 1870,* 74–75, 102–103; Kendall, *History of New Orleans,* I, 330–31; F. B. Harris, "Henry Clay Warmoth," 566; Ficklen, *History of Reconstruction in Louisiana,* 208–209.

60 *Acts of Louisiana, 1870,* 2–4, 30–49; New Orleans *Daily Picayune,* November 30, December 19, 28, 1869, January 5, February 18, March–April, 1870; Kendall, *History of New Orleans,* I, 328–29; Lonn, *Reconstruction in Louisiana,* 46–47, 54.

to halt the issuance of city notes, but in practice this was not done until the state seized and destroyed the plates. Even then it turned out that the city had held a considerable amount in notes in reserve, so it was some time before they were entirely removed from circulation. The bonded indebtedness of New Orleans increased about two million dollars more when the waterworks was purchased by the city. Even as these transactions were being carried out, the gas company was threatening to cut off the gas if its bills were not paid. By 1870 the debt of the city had increased to about fifteen million dollars. Two-thirds of this amount antedated Warmoth's accession, and approximately one-third antedated the Civil War.[61]

Education was of prime interest to the Radical Republicans, especially the Negroes. As will be seen, significant progress had been made by the occupation authorities, the Freedmen's Bureau, and northern charitable organizations before the end of the war. However, the state government under the constitution of 1864 showed little interest in any schools, and none at all in the education of blacks. The constitution of 1868 provided for integrated schools, but Warmoth made no attempt to enforce this article. As he later explained, "The white people were opposed to mixed schools. The masses of the colored people loved their children and knew too well what would happen to them if any of them should attempt to force themselves into white schools."[62] Such efforts as were made at integration during the Warmoth regime were primarily political ploys rather than attempts at mixing the races. Educational legislation was enacted, but relatively little was accomplished.[63]

As time passed, Warmoth demonstrated that he was the ablest politician in Louisiana. Even so, he had a major problem to solve. How was the Republican majority to keep itself in power if the Democrats resorted again to the methods they had used in the presidential election of 1868? In December, 1869, he took a trip up the left bank

61 *Acts of Louisiana,* 1869, 45–47; *Acts of Louisiana, Extra Session, 1870,* 10–12; New Orleans *Daily Picayune,* January 28, 1870; Kendall, *History of New Orleans,* I, 316–17, 334.
62 Warmoth, *War, Politics and Reconstruction,* 92–93.
63 Report of the State Superintendent of Education, in *Legislative Documents, 1869; Acts of Louisiana,* 1869, 175–89; *Acts of Louisiana, Extra Session, 1870,* 12–31; Daspit, "Governors Messages," 42; Ficklen, *History of Reconstruction in Louisiana,* 207–208; Lonn, *Reconstruction in Louisiana,* 54–56, 80–82.

of the Mississippi to Baton Rouge and Bayou Sara. He was well-received, had a friendly conversation with former governor Wickliffe, was cheered by the cadets of the Louisiana Seminary when he spoke to them in Baton Rouge, and demonstrated his virility when horses ran away with his carriage on the way to Centenary College by somehow leaping from the carriage and halting the team.[64]

This tour seems to have acted as a tonic, preparing Warmoth to battle for registration and election laws which would prevent a repetition of the events of 1868 and which, incidentally, would greatly increase the power of the governor. The Registration and Election acts of 1870 represent the high point of Warmoth's political power. Although enacted separately, they may be considered together. They replaced an act of 1868 which had not been sufficient to control the situation of that year.[65] The Registration Act of 1870 created a state registrar, appointed by the governor, to serve for three thousand dollars a year under a ten-thousand-dollar bond. In each parish the governor was to appoint a supervisor who would be responsible for actual voter registration. In the older parishes the registration lists were merely to be brought up to date, but completely new registrations were to be made in newly created parishes. The parish supervisors could be removed by the governor at will. Each person who registered was to take the oath set forth in the constitution of 1868, and the decision of the supervisor as to eligibility was to be final, not subject to injunction or writ of mandamus. Registration was to be closed nine days before an election, and a list of qualified voters was to be posted in each polling place.[66]

The Election Act set forth the procedure to be followed in conducting elections. The supervisor of registration in each parish was empowered to designate polling places, and he was to name commissioners to oversee the voting at each poll. To preserve order, the commissioners had the power to imprison for the remainder of election day any person creating a disturbance. Liquor establishments within two miles of a polling place were to be closed on election day.

64 New Orleans *Daily Picayune*, December 16–17, 1869.
65 *Acts of Louisiana, 1868,* 65–70; Report of Board of Registration, January 10, 1869, in *Legislative Documents, 1869.*
66 *Acts of Louisiana, 1870,* 132–44.

All riots, tumults, violence, intimidation, bribery, or corrupt influences were to be reported to the supervisor, who would forward a copy to the governor. The Board of Metropolitan Police was given the duty of discovering and reporting to the supervisors of registration in Jefferson and Orleans parishes the names of all persons improperly registered in those parishes. The sheriffs of Orleans, Jefferson, and St. Bernard parishes were specifically forbidden to interfere with the conduct of any election.[67]

At the close of the voting, the commissioners were to count the votes and report them, along with any report of violence, intimidation, or fraud, to the supervisor, who would in turn report this information to the governor. Then, according to Section 54 of the act, "The Governor, the Lieutenant Governor, the Secretary of State, and John Lynch and T. C. Anderson, or a majority of them, shall be the returning officers for all elections in the State . . . and have the power to make returns of all elections."[68] Presumably Lynch and Anderson were named because they were considered reliable Republicans. A majority of this Returning Board could fill its own vacancies. This body was to compile the votes reported by the supervisors of registration, but it also had the authority, if it determined that fraud, violence, intimidation, or corrupt influence had materially interfered with the election at any polling place, to exclude the vote from such places from their returns.[69]

The Returning Board was, of course, the Republican answer to the Democratic intimidation which had been so disastrous for the Grant ticket in 1868. It was intended to prevent the stealing of elections by the Democrats, and as such it was well designed. As events were to prove, it could also be used to steal elections for the Republicans, and this was the main purpose it was to serve. The Louisiana Returning Board was to be a stench in the nostrils of the nation in 1872 and 1876. In all fairness, however, it must be said that even in those election years the Returning Board may have finally arrived at more accurate results than those reported from the polling places. These elections

67 *Ibid.*, 145–54.
68 *Ibid.*, 155.
69 *Ibid.*, 155–61.

were so corrupt on both sides that to this day it is impossible to come to any sure conclusion as to the results.

The legislature of 1868–1870 created a number of new parishes, Iberia, Grant, Tangipahoa, Richland, and Cameron. A new Atchalafaya Parish almost came into being, but this bill never achieved final passage.[70] In 1869 the legislature finally passed a vagrancy act, which was strengthened in 1870. It was not nearly so severe as the one enacted in 1865.[71] An 1870 law making certain actions illegal and punishable is important because it demonstrates what undesirable conduct was so prevalent as to demand special legislation. Specifically forbidden were theft of crops, stealing, killing, or misbranding cattle, giving short measures, conspiracy to commit rape, murder, robbery, and a number of other felonies. Also prohibited was forcing any person to leave any city, town, or parish by violence or threat of violence, shooting at any "school house, church house, out house, person, or persons," and it was forbidden to "take away, destroy, secrete, alter, falsify, mutilate, or deface any bill of indictment, bond," or other part or record of criminal proceedings.[72]

The legislature elected in 1868 also proposed four amendments to the state constitution. These were Warmoth proposals; some of them were opposed by the Republican Central Committee. One amendment made the governor eligible for a second term; another put a ceiling of twenty-five million dollars on the state debt; a third provided that no person who had had state funds in his possession could hold office or vote until he had turned the funds over to the proper office and received a receipt for them. The last, and most important, amendment did away with all constitutional restrictions on voting by former rebels. All of these amendments were to be voted on by the people in the election of 1870.[73]

70 *Acts of Louisiana, 1868*, 151–54; *Acts of Louisiana, 1869*, 79–81, 83–86; *Acts of Louisiana, 1870*, 168–69; New Orleans *Daily Picayune*, March 1, 1870; Maurine Bergerie, "Economic and Social History of Iberia Parish, 1868–1900" (M.A. thesis, Louisiana State University, 1956), 27.

71 *Acts of Louisiana, 1871*, 11–13 (actually enacted by the extra session of 1870, but promulgated too late to be bound with the acts of that year).

72 *Acts of Louisiana, Extra Session, 1870*, 49–51.

73 *Ibid.*, 53; Daspit, "Governors' Messages," 14, 35; New Orleans *Daily Picayune*, February 1, 18, 1870; Lonn, *Reconstruction in Louisiana*, 52, 57–58, 83–84.

4

There was no significant change in general white opinion in Louisiana between the election of 1868 and the beginning of 1870. Republicans received threatening letters, and a meeting of white veterans of the Union army at Lafayette Square protested "social equality." The Germans of New Orleans, who had been strongly Unionist and partly Radical began to drift into the Democratic party as Republicanism and the Negro became more and more inseparable. A Baton Rouge newspaper referred to President Grant as "one of those insignificant individuals whom God for some inscrutable purpose permits to occupy the White House, when better men are needed there."[74] The *Picayune* in March was bold enough to assert that the North had gone into the Civil War in defiance of "the plainest provisions of the Constitution protecting the seceding states in their sovereignty."[75] Municipal elections in Baton Rouge in April resulted in a Democratic victory. On the other hand, the strength of the Democrats in New Orleans was lessened when the Conservative city administration elected in 1868 proved to be shamelessly corrupt.[76]

Congress made it clear that it did not intend to permit in 1870 any repetition of the intimidation of 1868. The Enforcement Act provided fines and imprisonment for interfering with the civil or suffrage rights of citizens. Cases arising under this act would be tried in federal courts. This action by Congress encouraged the Republicans of Louisiana. Warmoth, in contrast to 1868, instructed parish sheriffs to take whatever steps might be necessary to preserve the peace. He also made it clear that he did not desire that any public meeting should be broken up on the pretense that its existence was a threat to the peace; thus he protected Republican rallies.[77]

74 Baton Rouge *Weekly Advocate*, February 26, 1870.
75 New Orleans *Daily Picayune*, March 6, 1870.
76 *Ibid.*, February 16, 19, March 6, April 20, May 24, 1870; Baton Rouge *Weekly Advocate*, April 9, 1870; R. T. Clark, Jr., "Reconstruction and the New Orleans German Colony," 1,011–12; Copeland, "The New Orleans Press and Reconstruction," 210.
77 Warmoth to [?], August 11, 1870, in Warmoth Papers; Baton Rouge *Weekly Advocate*, June 11, 1870; Everette Swinney, "Enforcing the Fifteenth Amendment, 1870–1877," *Journal of Southern History*, XXVIII (May, 1962), 202–203; Frank-

In 1870 an election was to be held to name all members of the Louisiana House of Representatives, half the members of the state senate, and, of course, representatives in the lower house of Congress.

The Republican convention of 1870 saw the beginning of a power struggle between Warmoth on the one hand and the so-called Custom House Ring on the other. Warmoth was defeated for the presidency of the convention, and the state executive committee of the party as appointed had a majority of anti-Warmoth members. As a result of this dissension there were opposing Republican tickets in several parishes. In general, however, most of the Republican candidates for the legislature were pro-Warmoth.[78]

All was not harmony in the ranks of the opposition. A "Conservative" convention was held at the St. Charles Theater in New Orleans on January 30, 1870, but a few days later a mass meeting in Lafayette Square demanded a Democratic convention. In March a meeting of editors of Conservative newspapers was held in New Orleans. There was much discussion at this gathering as to whether the opposition to the Radicals should unite around the Democratic standard or found a new party. Probably the advocates of a new party were old Whigs who could not stomach the idea of uniting with Democrats. However, although the term "Conservative" was frequently used, the Democratic party organization was the nucleus of opposition to Radicalism throughout Reconstruction in Louisiana. One concession was made. At the Democratic convention in September, 1870, a number of Negro delegates were present. When questioned about black participation in party affairs, the Democratic State Central Committee replied that "The interest of both black and white men are identical in this struggle. . . . The Democratic Party has always upheld and defended the Constitution . . . and will now, as ever in the past, protect and defend every citizen in the full and free exercise of all rights guaranteed by that instrument."[79] In effect, the Democratic hierarchy

lin, *Reconstruction After the Civil War*, 165; Dunning, *Reconstruction, Political and Economic*, 184–85.

78 New Orleans *Republican*, August 8–12, 1870; New Orleans *Daily Picayune*, January–March, September, October 15, 20, 1870; Baton Rouge *Weekly Advocate*, August 6, 1870; F. B. Harris, "Henry Clay Warmoth," 605.

79 Quoted in Lonn, *Reconstruction in Louisiana*, 69–70; see also New Orleans *Daily*

had accepted black suffrage so far as public statements were concerned.

Warmoth began planning early for the November, 1870, election. In March he saw to the creation of the Eighth District Court of Orleans Parish, which was given exclusive jurisdiction over all cases involving right to office. Obviously, with a loyal Republican on the bench of this court, the Radicals would have a distinct advantage. Likewise Warmoth made sure that registrars of voters were friendly to him. In sixteen instances he appointed Democrats, but in a number of parishes where he had neither Republican nor Democrat whom he could trust he named a friendly resident of New Orleans as registrar. In places like St. Landry Parish, where there was almost certain to be intimidation, the number of polling places was drastically reduced. A few registrars proved unreliable, some adhering to the Custom House Republicans, some to the Democrats. United States Marshal Stephen B. Packard later testified that in West Feliciana Parish Warmoth's registrar made a deal whereby Republican votes were counted for Democratic parish officials in return for enough Democratic votes to assure the election of a Republican state senator.[80]

The governor did much personal campaigning in 1870, perhaps because the Republican state committee, dominated by the Custom House, did very little. In general he was well received, although one paper advised the people of Baton Rouge to let him come and go "as one of those stinks which an ill wind sometimes brings from the filthy alleys of cities and sweeps through the streets to the momentary disgust and annoyance of its inhabitants."[81] The Democrats had no such central figure as Warmoth, and the local candidates who opposed Republicans were usually no match for the governor's oratory and wit. The usual mass meetings, torchlight parades, and rallies were

---

Picayune, January 30, February 8, March 3, September, 1870; Baton Rouge *Weekly Advocate*, March 12, 1870.

80 New Orleans *Daily Picayune*, March 22, 1870; Ludeling to Warmoth, October 24, 1870, W. R. McMillin to Warmoth, October 24, 1870, in Warmoth Papers; F. B. Harris, "Henry Clay Warmoth," 606–607; Lonn, *Reconstruction in Louisiana*, 70n.

81 Baton Rouge *Weekly Advocate*, October 22, 1870.

held, but Warmoth's control of the registrars, the availability of the Metropolitan Police to keep order, and the possibility of calling on the United States Army in an emergency probably had more influence on the outcome. Also, Pinchback campaigned energetically to get out the black vote. The Republicans won a sweeping victory. They won a working majority in the legislature; every Republican candidate for Congress was elected; Radical Benjamin F. Flanders was elected mayor of New Orleans; all four proposed constitutional amendments were adopted; and many Negroes were elected to local office.[82]

All in all, the election was a quiet, orderly, and reasonably honest one. There was a riot in Baton Rouge on election day, seemingly an attempt at intimidation. If so, it was unsuccessful, because Radical legislators and a Radical parish judge were elected. Two days after the election a bloody disturbance broke out at Donaldsonville. After whites fired shots at Negro militia, a large number of blacks from Ascension and St. James parishes marched on Donaldsonville with the avowed intention of burning the town. Two white Republicans, Judge W. C. Lawes and Max Schoumburg, who had recently been appointed mayor by Warmoth, went out to reason with the mob. They were shot to shreds by the blacks, but this was apparently enough violence. No attack on Donaldsonville was made. Some of the black leaders were arrested and imprisoned in New Orleans with the whites arrested at Baton Rouge. The Republican district attorney of Ascension Parish, according to the *Picayune,* announced after an investigation that a factional fight among Republicans was the basic cause of the disturbance. Several participants in the Donaldsonville killings were convicted, but they were later pardoned.[83] With the

---

82 O. H. Rice to Warmoth, October 26, 1870, Frank Morey to Warmoth, October 31, 1870, M. A. Southworth to J. H. Platt, Jr., November 3, 1870, in Warmoth Papers; New Orleans *Daily Picayune,* August–November, 1870; New Orleans *Republican,* November 8–12, 1870; Warmoth, *War, Politics and Reconstruction,* 96–97, 100–102; F. B. Harris, "Henry Clay Warmoth," 606; Kendall, *History of New Orleans,* I, 340; Dufour, "The Age of Warmoth," 350; Jean M. Eyraud and Donald J. Millet, *A History of St. John the Baptist Parish* (Marrero, La., 1939), 18; Lonn, *Reconstruction in Louisiana,* 71–72; Grosz, "Pinchback," 541; Cox, *Three Decades of Federal Legislation,* 554.

83 New Orleans *Daily Picayune,* November 7–27, 1870; New Orleans *Republican,* November 15–17, 1870; Sidney A. Marchand, *The Story of Ascension Parish* (Donaldsonville, La., 1931), 77.

election over, the state government could return to its preoccupation with internal improvements.

5

A fever for internal improvements had raged in Louisiana long before the Civil War. It persisted under the Johnson governments following the war. In general, it was believed that by internal improvements Louisiana could attain the economic strength that northern states had demonstrated in winning the war. Warmoth followed the course of action begun by his predecessors in promoting internal improvements. Party disagreement over specific measures existed, but there was no disagreement over the need for and the wisdom of internal improvements in general. Many of the projects undertaken involved corruption to a greater or lesser degree, and both parties were guilty. Probably, being in power, the Republicans profited as politicians more than the Democrats. On the other hand, the bankers, brokers, and entrepreneurs who gave the bribes and who profited at the expense of the taxpayers were more likely to be "Conservatives" than to be Radicals. Louisiana was not unique. The same sort of programs were being promoted, and the same sort of corruption practiced, in most, if not all, of the states of the Union at the time.[84]

One of the great commercial ambitions of New Orleans was for a ship channel to the Gulf of Mexico which would provide nearer access to salt water. This was an especially pressing problem before the construction of the Eads jetties because silting at the outlets sometimes kept deeper draft vessels waiting weeks, and even months, to enter the Mississippi River. The New Orleans and Ship Island Company was chartered in 1868 for the purpose of constructing a canal 150 feet wide and 12 feet deep from the Mississippi River to the Rigolets, with a shell road alongside. The next year the company was put in charge of drainage in Orleans and Jefferson parishes and was empowered to collect the taxes levied for drainage purposes. Money collected in excess of the costs of drainage was to be applied to the

---

84 Lonn, *Reconstruction in Louisiana*, 32, 36–37, 56–57; F. B. Harris, "Henry Clay Warmoth," 579–80; *Acts of Louisiana, 1871*, 39–42; Sam Mims, "Louisiana's Administration of Swamp Land Funds," *Louisiana Historical Quarterly*, XXVIII (January, 1945), 299; New Orleans *Daily Picayune*, March 10, 18, 1869.

canal. In 1870 the required width of the canal was reduced to a hundred feet, but the company was now required to erect a protection levee around Carrollton, Jefferson City, and New Orleans two feet above any known high water and to install pumps powerful enough to pump water out of the protected area to a depth at least ten feet below the average level of Lake Pontchartrain. This company accomplished nothing toward digging the canal, and its drainage work was unsatisfactory. How much was collected from the taxpayers of the drainage district is unknown, but one student suggests that it was not less than two million dollars. Much of this amount, of course, went to pay for such drainage as was accomplished, but much went into the pockets of the promoters.[85]

The Mississippi and Mexican Gulf Ship Canal Company had been chartered under the Democrats. In 1869 it was promised state aid for the construction of a canal from the head of English Turn on the Mississippi to Lake Borgne. The state was to grant $120,000 in bonds after the completion of the first mile, and a like amount for each of the next three miles, and a final $120,000 when the entire canal was completed. Since the canal was never dug, it was never necessary to issue any of these bonds. In 1871, because of the unsatisfactory performance of the Ship Island Company, the Mexican Gulf Company was given the responsibility for draining New Orleans. The company was to receive any drainage funds on hand and was to pay for its operations by a tax of two mills per front foot on lands drained. New Orleans was kept as dry as in previous years, which meant that much of the city was flooded after every heavy rain. The fact that Warmoth had owned $100,000 worth of stock in the Mexican Gulf Company since 1868 may have been influential in the replacement of the Ship Island Company. It must be emphasized, however, that both of these ventures had strong support from Democrats as well as Republicans.[86]

85 *Acts of Louisiana, 1868,* 185–98; *Acts of Louisiana, 1869,* 49; *Acts of Louisiana, 1870,* 134–35; *Acts of Louisiana, Extra Session, 1870,* 5–10; New Orleans *Daily Picayune,* December 12, 1868, January 5, September 12, 1869; F. B. Harris, "Henry Clay Warmoth," 576; Highsmith, "Louisiana During Reconstruction," 251–52.

86 *Acts of Louisiana, 1869,* 166–69; *Acts of Louisiana, 1871,* 75–79; Notice of Protest, October 3, 1871, in Warmoth Papers; Warmoth Notebook, March 24, 1874, in Warmoth Papers; New Orleans *Daily Picayune,* February 11, 1869; F. B. Harris, "Henry Clay Warmoth," 578; Lonn, *Reconstruction in Louisiana,* 32–34; Highsmith, "Louisiana During Reconstruction," 35–52; Joy Jackson, *New Orleans in*

These were not the only attempts to improve navigation. In 1868 up to $135,000 was voted to improve the navigation of the Red River. In 1869 the Mississippi and Atlantic Ship Canal Company was chartered to dig a canal from Fort St. Philip, below New Orleans, to Breton Island Sound. Also in 1869 the governor was authorized to issue $80,000 in bonds as a grant-in-aid to the Boeuf and Crocodile Navigation Company. Other acts could be cited, but these should suffice. Little or nothing was accomplished, and by 1871 the rage for navigation improvement was over. These enactments were not different in kind or overall purpose from many which had been approved before the Civil War. The chief difference was in the number, and in the amount of state aid given to, or proposed for, the companies chartered. Also, before the war, the state had done some such work itself. After the war private enterprise reigned supreme.[87]

Louisiana had nine railroads at the beginning of the Civil War, but only three of these—the New Orleans, Opelousas, and Great Western; the New Orleans, Jackson, and Great Northern; and the Vicksburg, Shreveport and Texas—were of any great significance. All had been subsidized by state bond issues before the Civil War, and both the state and the city of New Orleans owned substantial blocks of stock in the New Orleans, Jackson, and Great Northern.[88] All over the United States, as the war came to an end, railroads were looked on as the key to future prosperity. They were subsidized by federal, state, and local governments. Louisiana followed this trend during the Warmoth administration, and it was mainly in the subsidization of railroads that the much-deplored but little-understood contingency debt of the state was incurred. The contingency debt was a possible debt, contingent upon a subsidized corporation's meeting conditions, usually the completion of a certain amount of construction specified by the legislature.

Probably the most successful but also one of the more costly rail-

the *Gilded Age: Politics and Urban Progress, 1880–1896* (Baton Rouge, 1969), 147–52.

87 *Acts of Louisiana, 1868,* 72–76; *Acts of Louisiana, 1869,* 199–201; *Acts of Louisiana, 1870,* 21–23 (enacted in 1869, but bound with acts of 1870), 87, 116–17, 163–72; *Acts of Louisiana, 1871,* 125–27.

88 Merl E. Reed, *New Orleans and the Railroads* (Baton Rouge, 1966), *passim;* Lawrence E. Estaville, Jr., "Louisiana Railroads During the Civil War" (M.A. thesis, McNeese State University, 1970), *passim.*

roads subsidized was the New Orleans, Mobile and Chattanooga. Originally chartered in Alabama, this company set out first to connect Mobile with New Orleans. Its charter was recognized in Louisiana in 1868, and in 1869 the Louisiana legislature voted to grant $12,500 in bonds for each mile of track laid within the state. After the road reached New Orleans, the city gave it free use of certain streets to the riverfront. Warmoth, and probably a majority of Louisianians, had already decided that this road was their choice to connect New Orleans and Houston, a dream which had existed in Louisiana since the 1830s.

Therefore in 1870 the legislature authorized the issuance of up to $3,000,000 in second mortagage bonds to the New Orleans, Mobile and Chattanooga, of which $750,000 was contingent upon the track's being completed from Algiers to Donaldsonville, another $750,000 upon the road's reaching Lafayette, and equal amounts upon when the tracks reaching the Sabine River and Houston, respectively. The road was finished to Donaldsonville by June, 1871; after some delay caused by Charles Morgan, who now controlled the line to Morgan City, the Chattanooga Company received its $750,000 in bonds. But then an act of the legislature changed the method of subsidy. Now the state bought $2,500,000 in company stock and paid for it in bonds. Some roadbed was constructed, but the line did not really get beyond Donaldsonville before the Panic of 1873 struck. By the end of Reconstruction it had advanced only to Bayou Goula in Iberville Parish. In the end the stock was worthless, and Louisiana was obligated for the bonds issued.[89]

The chartering of railroads with subsidies to be provided upon completion of a given number of miles of construction was a frequent legislative exercise during the Warmoth administration. Among lines chartered were the Mandeville and Sulphur Springs; the North Louisiana and Texas (the former Vicksburg, Shreveport and Texas); the Louisiana Central; the New Orleans, Metairie and Lake; the Louisiana and Arkansas; and the New Orleans, Baton Rouge and

89 *Acts of Louisiana, 1868,* 28–38; *Acts of Louisiana, 1869,* 22–30; *Acts of Louisiana, 1870,* 55–63; L. A. Sheldon to Warmoth, March 5, 1871, in Warmoth Papers; New Orleans *Daily Picayune,* June 9, 1869, November 25, 1870, June 1, 1871, February 21, 1872; F. B. Harris, "Henry Clay Warmoth," 581–84; Nordhoff, *The Cotton States,* 58.

Vicksburg. In addition, stock purchases were authorized to aid in the repair and extension of the prewar Baton Rouge, Grosse Tete and Opelousas. The New Orleans, Baton Rouge and Vicksburg, often referred to as the "backbone line," attracted much attention, perhaps because its promoters included both leading Radicals and leading Democrats. Local governmental units were specifically authorized to buy the line's stock and bonds or to issue loans or warrants as grants-in-aid. The state itself never made any payments to this company because no track was ever laid.[90]

Another railroad matter with which Warmoth was closely connected was the sale of the 106,360 shares of stock in the New Orleans, Jackson and Great Northern owned by the state and by the city of New Orleans. This road, inoperable at the end of the war, was quickly repaired under the presidency of General P. G. T. Beauregard, and by 1870 was in full operation. In March of that year a bill was pushed through the legislature authorizing the sale of the state and city shares, and they were sold to Henry S. McComb of the Wilmington and Southern Railroad for four dollars a share. This was certainly a bargain price, but the stock was not worth the twenty-five dollars a share claimed by those who opposed the sale. The sale to McComb was followed by a rapid development of the road which pushed northward by construction and consolidation first to Humboldt, Tennessee, and then to a meeting with the Illinois Central at the Ohio River. It is doubtful that this could have been accomplished without the direction of some promoter-capitalist such as McComb. McComb failed financially in 1873, and eventually the New Orleans, Jackson and Great Northern became part of the Illinois Central system.

There can be no reasonable doubt that legislative votes were bought to secure passage of the bill authorizing the sale of the railroad to McComb. Evidence is rather conclusive that Pinchback got a thousand dollars for his vote, but that other legislators received only

90 New Orleans *Daily Picayune,* November 11, 1868, June 12, 1869; *Acts of Louisiana, 1868,* 125, 136–41, 179, 203–206; *Acts of Louisiana, 1869,* 205–207; *Acts of Louisiana, 1870,* 1–5, 7–21, 28, 192–94; Baton Rouge *Weekly Advocate,* March 19, 1870; Oakes Ames to Amos B. Merrill, November 11, 1871, in Warmoth Papers; *Acts of Louisiana, 1871,* 23–24, 66–72, 89–97; *Acts Passed by the General Assembly of the State of Louisiana at the Second Session of the Second Legislature, Begun and Held in New Orleans, January 1, 1872* (New Orleans, 1872), 7–21, 79–87, 139–40.

half as much. A real question is whether Warmoth's support for the sale was bought. Letters from McComb to the governor at this time are headed "My Dearly Beloved Friend." Thomas Conway, in a letter to Warmoth, quoted Richard Henry Dana as saying: "Warmoth got one hundred thousand dollars for his influence on the Jackson Railroad job."[91]

The practice of leasing the penitentiary to private companies had begun under Governor Wells, and the lease to Messrs. Huger and Jones was continued under Warmoth, although the governor let the bill become law without his signature. The state issued $500,000 in bonds to buy machinery for the penitentiary and was to receive half the profits in return. By 1871 no payment to the state had been made. The famous Slaughterhouse Bill passed the legislature in 1869, giving the Crescent City Live Stock Landing and Slaughterhouse Company a monopoly on the slaughter of animals for food in New Orleans. This was to be a matter of dispute for years, and the act did put scores of small butchers out of business. Before it is utterly condemned, however, it should be noted that many of these small-scale slaughtering enterprises were located upstream from the intakes for the city's water supply, and that they disposed of offal by throwing it into the river.[92]

The difference between urban life in the United States a century ago and urban life today was illustrated when the New Orleans Sanitary and Fertilizer Company was incorporated and given a monopoly of cleaning privies in the city. In 1870 the Mississippi River Packet Company was chartered. Pinchback and other leading black Radicals were among the promoters of this corporation, and one historian says that its purpose was to provide better traveling facilities on the Mississippi River for Negroes. In 1871 the act was amended to require the state to buy $250,000 worth of stock. Nothing was ac-

91 Conway to Warmoth, August 25, 1870, in Warmoth Papers; see also Henry L. McComb to Warmoth, April 8, May 13, June 22, 1870, in Warmoth Papers; *Acts of Louisiana, Extra Session, 1870,* 188–98; New Orleans *Daily Picayune,* March 3, 10, 15, 17, 22, April 5, 1870; F. B. Harris, "Henry Clay Warmoth," 578–81; Grosz, "Pinchback," 543; Kendall, *History of New Orleans,* I, 339–40; Lawrence E. Estaville, "A Strategic Railroad: The New Orleans, Jackson and Great Northern in the Civil War," *Louisiana History,* XIV (Spring, 1972), 135–36.

92 *Debates in the House of Representatives, 1869,* 144–46, 193–94; New Orleans *Daily Picayune,* June, 1869; *Acts of Louisiana, 1869,* 170–73; "Governor Warmoth's Message, January 4, 1869," in New Orleans *Daily Picayune,* January 4, 1869; Nordhoff, *The Cotton States,* 58; Lonn, *Reconstruction in Louisiana,* 42–44.

complished; the state received no return on its investment either in cash or in improved transportation facilities. An equally political measure was the chartering of the Louisiana Warehouse Company, which had such Radicals as L. A. Sheldon, J. R. West, and James F. Casey among its incorporators. This bill was vetoed by Warmoth but passed over his veto. On the positive side, the legislature in 1869 ordered a topographical and geographical survey of the state by professors of the Louisiana Seminary of Learning at Baton Rouge, and in 1870 the office of Registrar of State Lands was created.[93]

Neglect during and after the Civil War had left the levees which protected the alluvial lands along the rivers and bayous almost useless. The Democratic legislature had attempted to solve the problem and had authorized the sale of some four million dollars in levee bonds, but when the Radicals came to power almost nothing had been done. In 1868 a Board of Public Works appointed by the governor was established to oversee all public works, but primarily levees. In the same year the legislature ordered the sale of $1,586,000 in 1867 levee bonds which had not yet been sold, but half the proceeds were to go into the general fund rather than into the levee fund. In 1869 a joint committee reported that little or nothing had been accomplished toward repairing and improving the levees. In the same year $990,000 in state bonds was issued to cover $486,000 in debts owed by the pre-1868 Board of Levee Commissioners. Here, it should be noted, is an example of the way the state's debt grew so rapidly. Louisiana bonds, on the New York market, brought little more than half their face value. In 1870 the legislature authorized the sale of three million dollars in 8-percent bonds for levees and set a tax of two and a half mills to service these bonds. By early 1871 some repairs and improvements had been effected, but they were far from sufficient to afford protection from flooding.[94]

In 1871 a group of promoters and politicians organized the Louisiana Levee Company. This private corporation was to take over the function of levee building and upkeep, sell stock to the public, and be

93 *Acts of Louisiana, 1869*, 71–72; *Acts of Louisiana, 1870*, 128–30; *Acts of Louisiana, Extra Session, 1870*, 89–93, 216–18; *Acts of Louisiana, 1871*, 16–18, 72–75, 98–103; Grosz, "Pinchback," 540–41; Nordhoff, *The Cotton States*, 61.

94 *Acts of Louisiana, 1868*, 82–84, 177–78; *Acts of Louisiana, 1869*, 7–8, 190–91; *Acts of Louisiana, 1870*, 63–65, 83.

paid by the taxpayers. A commission was to estimate the total levee needs of the state at the rate of sixty cents per cubic yard of earth to be moved. Then a tax was to be levied on the assessed property of the state sufficient to bring in 10 percent of the estimate each year for twenty-one years. In addition a tax of two mills per year was to be levied on all property for twenty-one years to provide a levee repair fund. Finally, since no tax could be collected during 1871, the governor was to issue a million dollars in 8-percent bonds to the company so that work could begin immediately. A half-mill tax was to service these bonds.[95]

The Levee Company was intended primarily for the profit of its promoters, secondarily for the building and maintenance of levees. Apparently many legislators were bribed in order to assure their votes for the charter. Warmoth listed in his private papers eighty legislators who, he said, received a thousand dollars each for voting for the bill. The *Picayune* listed the names of eight Democrats whom it accused of accepting a thousand dollars apiece to support the bill. This was no doubt reprehensible, but it was not illegal. Louisiana had no statute against bribery.[96]

John Ray became president of the Levee Company, but Charles T. Howard and John A. Morris, leading spirits of the Louisiana Lottery, were reported to be the main promoters. Ray was richly rewarded, however, with a salary of ten thousand dollars a year. Warmoth stated his disapproval of the bill, but he did not veto it. He apparently hoped to get his friend McComb to take over the company. In a lawsuit instituted in March, 1872, by a stockholder of the company against the directors, the plaintiff stated that in the summer of 1871 the officers of the Levee Company "undertook a secret negotiation with Henry S. McComb of Wilmington, Delaware, and Thomas Scott of Philadelphia," McComb and Scott being represented by a man named Wilmon. The defendants, according to the complaint, "entered into a contract . . . by which the capital stock was to be raised from $3,000,000 to $10,000,000 . . . [the additional stock] to be delivered to Wilmon together with $370,000 in bonds of the company."

95 *Acts of Louisiana, 1871*, 29–38.
96 Warmoth Papers, February 24, 1871; New Orleans *Daily Picayune*, August 7, 1872; F. B. Harris, "Henry Clay Warmoth," 575–76; Mims, "Swamp Land Funds," 307–10.

After this contract was made, Scott and McComb failed to comply with its conditions. In the meantime, however, seventy-three thousand new shares of stock had been issued, of which Wilmon received thirteen thousand shares, the other sixty thousand being placed in the care of the governor.[97]

It is obvious from letters and telegrams sent to Warmoth by McComb and Senator J. R. West that McComb backed out of some sort of deal in regard to the Levee Company. Apparently his decision was made, or became known, in mid-October, 1872, because the stock of the company dropped from six to three dollars a share between October 18 and 26. West suggested to Warmoth that pressure be put on McComb through his railroad. On October 22, 1871, he sent a desperate telegram: "Can you make McComb protect my forty bonds [?]"[98] In a letter written the same day West denounced McComb and told Warmoth: "Whatever you do I trust will be for the best and if possible you should save your friends (Howard, Sherman and myself) who are in the company."[99] Warmoth was able to reach an accommodation with McComb, who in November agreed that the New Orleans, Jackson and Great Northern Railroad would take the Levee Company bonds owned by Warmoth and West if Warmoth would see to it that the Bonnet Carre Levee was fully repaired. This levee protected the railroad out of New Orleans, and during a flood the previous spring the tracks had been covered, making it necessary to transport passengers across Lake Pontchartrain by boat.[100]

The Levee Company proved much more efficient at collecting the taxes due to it than at building and repairing levees. Until 1874, in fact, it intercepted the taxes in the parishes, so that these funds did not even pass through the state treasurer's hands. Thus there is no certain record of how much revenue the company received during its first three years. It was estimated to be about $720,000 per year. The state certainly did not get value received for this money. On the

97 New Orleans *Daily Picayune*, February 24, 1871, March 31, 1872; McComb to Warmoth, October 9, 1871, in Warmoth Papers; F. B. Harris, "Henry Clay Warmoth," 574–76; Mims, "Swamp Land Funds," 307–10; Lonn, *Reconstruction in Louisiana*, 35.
98 West to Warmoth, October 22, 1871, in Warmoth Papers.
99 West to Warmoth, October 22, 1871, in Warmoth Papers.
100 McComb to Warmoth, June 29, October 30, November 6, 1871, West to Warmoth, October 15, 1871, in Warmoth Papers.

other hand, this was not adequate revenue for the work that needed doing, even if every cent had been applied to the levees. Between 1866 and the fall of 1876, approximately $10,500,000 was spent on Louisiana levees, and a total of 19,274,874 cubic yards of earth was moved. Much of this work was done by parish authorities, however, because before 1871 was over Warmoth found it necessary to ask police juries to do the best they could. Worst of all, no real protection from flooding was accomplished. A northerner who had purchased a sugar plantation wrote in 1874: "My loss in Louisiana by high water was very large, and I can but think unnecessary had the Levee Company done their duty; but how can you expect anything from a company organized for the sole purpose of stealing the people's money. It was the fruit of carpetbag rule."[101] The Levee Company Act was finally repealed in 1877, and the Board of State Engineers took over the levees. This board did little if any better at flood prevention, but it cost much less.[102]

6

There can be no question but that the Warmoth administration was corrupt. Much evidence to this effect has already been noted; much more is available than can be set forth here. However, attention needs to be given to corruption, because the Warmoth administration was not the first nor the last era of dishonesty in Louisiana history. The pattern has a modern design to it.

Probably the most notorious scandal of Louisiana Reconstruction and the years that followed was the Louisiana Lottery Company. The Democratic legislature of 1866 established a lottery to be owned and operated by the state. In 1868 the newly elected Radical legislature chartered a private corporation and gave it a monopoly on the sale of lottery tickets in Louisiana. The company was to have a capital stock of a million dollars but it could begin operations when one-tenth of the capital was paid in. In practice, the promoters borrowed

101 Thompson to Woodman, August 6, 1874; in Marquette (ed.), "Letters of a Yankee Sugar Planter," 527.
102 New Orleans *Daily Picayune*, March 26, May 21, September 29, 1871; Mims, "Swamp Land Funds," 323; F. B. Harris, "Henry Clay Warmoth," 574–76; Nordhoff, *The Cotton States*, 58–59; Hilda Mulvey McDaniel, "Francis Tillou Nicholls and the End of Reconstruction," *Louisiana Historical Quarterly*, XXXII (April, 1949), 357–513.

$100,000, deposited it in a New Jersey bank for one day, withdrew it and repaid the loan, and thus began operations with no capital paid in. The only investment was fifteen thousand dollars used to bribe legislators. Most did not demand cash and were satisfied with shares of stock in the company; they were wise because the lottery was highly profitable. Charles T. Howard, the first president, and John A. Morris, another promoter, rapidly became wealthy men. Not only was the company profitable; it also was powerful. In early 1877 Francis T. Nicholls' "government" was partially financed by the lottery. In 1879, when Nicholls proved able to resist lottery demands, the company was able to bring about the writing of a new constitution which cut short the redeemer governor's term. The Louisiana Lottery Company was powerful in politics for two decades, and its demise came from congressional action. The state, in return for the company's charter, received a fee of forty thousand dollars a year out of the millions in profits.[103]

The case of the Vicksburg, Shreveport and Texas Railroad (later renamed the North Louisiana and Texas) was unusual in that the fraud was eventually publicly proclaimed by the United States Supreme Court. This road, which had been profitable before the war, was almost destroyed during hostilities. Soon after the war was over the line was declared bankrupt and put up for sale at auction. John Ray, a native Radical, and John T. Ludeling, soon to be chief justice of the Louisiana Supreme Court, bought the railroad for $50,000 by means of legal skullduggery and, probably, bribing the agent of purchasers willing to pay a much higher price. Then Ray lobbied through the legislature a bond issue of $546,000 for repair of the road on which the company was to pay interest of $43,680 per year. Ludeling, by this time on the supreme court, declared the bond issue legal. The railroad never paid one cent of interest on the bonds. Eventually the United States Supreme Court declared the sale to Ludeling and

---

103 New Orleans *Daily Picayune*, August, 1868, November 25, 1869, August 11, 28, 1872; *House Miscellaneous Documents*, 42nd Cong., 2nd Sess., No. 211, p. 18; Berthold C. Alwes, "The History of the Louisiana State Lottery Company," *Louisiana Historical Quarterly*, XXVII (October 1944), 973–76, 981; Henry C. Dethloff, "The Alliance and the Lottery: Farmers Try for the Sweepstakes," *Louisiana History*, VI (Spring, 1965), 142–43; Richard H. Wiggins, "The Louisiana Press and the Lottery," *Louisiana Historical Quarterly*, XXI (July, 1948), 721, 725, 728, 754.

Ray null and void, but through five years of possession these two gentlemen harvested a comfortable profit.[104]

The case of George M. Wickliffe, a Louisiana resident who was elected auditor in 1868, received more attention than some more flagrant scandals. Wickliffe was apparently a forger who added to his income by forging state warrants and selling them on the market. However, when indicted by a grand jury and brought to trial, he was acquitted. After a comic-opera episode during which Warmoth barred him from his office in Mechanics' Institute, the house of representatives brought in articles of impeachment and, despite Wickliffe's resignation, he was convicted by the unanimous vote of the senate on March 3, 1870. In the meantime another grand jury indictment was returned and, after scattering more forged warrants abroad, Wickliffe fled the state and disappeared from history. His books were so carelessly kept that the amount of his embezzlements could not be determined; estimates range from $200,000 to $700,000. Of course state warrants were so heavily discounted that he realized no more than half the amount, whatever it was, in greenbacks.[105]

The cost of printing is one of the devils whipped most often in descriptions of Reconstruction corruption. Under a printing bill enacted in 1868, some $1,500,000 in state warrants were paid out for printing in three years. Allowing for the fact that state warrants were worth only about half their face value, this was nonetheless greatly in excess of the $60,000 a year or less expended on printing during the prewar years. Printing contracts were not outright theft, however, because they served two purposes. First, they were a form of patronage essential to the Republican party as it sought to establish itself. Second, the existing Louisiana papers were violently anti-Republican,

---

104 New Orleans *Daily Picayune*, August 25, 1872; F. B. Harris, "Henry Clay Warmoth," 589; Cox, *Three Decades of Federal Legislation*, 561; Nordhoff, *The Cotton States*, 47; A. M. Gibson, *A Political Crime: The History of the Great Fraud* (New York, 1885), 245–46.

105 *Acts of Louisiana, 1870*, 36, 79; New Orleans *Daily Picayune*, December 31, 1868, January 1, 6, 1869, February 2, March 4, 30, April 13, 15, 1870; George M. Wickliffe to Warmoth, August 5, 1868, Wickliffe to J. S. Harris, April 14, 1869; in Warmoth Papers; New Orleans *Republican*, March 5, April 12, 1870; Warmoth, *War, Politics and Reconstruction*, 85–86; Lonn, *Reconstruction in Louisiana*, 47–51; Cox, *Three Decades of Federal Legislation*, 559–60; Cortez A. M. Ewing, "Five Early Louisiana Impeachments," *Louisiana Historical Quarterly*, XXXI (July, 1948), 692–94, 698.

and a paper with a Republican editorial policy could not support itself with subscriptions and local advertising. Such newspapers had
to be nourished by official printing if the voice of the Republican
party was to be heard at all. On the discreditable side, there were
some papers which received printing fees from the state and which
never began publication. Also, after the quarrel between Warmoth
and the Custom House Republicans broke into the open, there were
sometimes rival Republican papers in sparsely settled rural parishes,
both of which might be getting some printing subsidies. Finally, Warmoth was a major stockholder in the New Orleans *Republican*, which
grew fat on state printing.[106]

One tragic result of the moral climate of the late 1860s and early
1870s was the outright theft of school funds. Usually this was done
at the local level as the treasurers of the parish school boards too often
yielded to temptation. The money provided for schools was little
enough when administered honestly; theft meant that there were no
schools in some parishes.

A more conventional type of dubious profit was made by United
States Senator West, Pinchback, and others when what is now Audu-
bon Park was created in New Orleans. After the legislature authorized
the purchase of land for a park and levied a tax to pay for it, Pinchback and West were among the park commissioners appointed. They
proceeded to buy up a tract of land for $600,000, paying $65,000
down, and then sold the land to the city for $800,000, receiving $65,000
in cash, $195,000 in bonds, and transferring their remaining indebted-
ness to the city. Another incident involved Secretary of State George
E. Bovee, who was accused of having promulgated laws which the
legislature had not enacted, selling books belonging to the state on his
own account, misappropriating state bonds, and offering bribes on
the floor of the senate. Warmoth suspended Bovee from office and
appointed Francis J. Herron as temporary secretary of state.[107]

106 Contract, May 6, 1871, Emerson Bentley to Warmoth, July 16, 1871, in Warmoth
      Papers; *Acts of Louisiana, 1870*, 85–86; Lonn, *Reconstruction in Louisiana*, 87;
      Lestage, "The White League," 633; F. B. Harris, "Henry Clay Warmoth," 555.
107 Thomas H. Harris, *The Story of Public Education in Louisiana* (New Orleans,
      1924), 39–40; DuBois, *Black Reconstruction*, 476–77; *Acts of Louisiana, Extra
      Session, 1870*, 196–200; New Orleans *Daily Picayune*, January 22, 1871; Nordhoff,
      The Cotton States, 62; Kendall, *History of New Orleans*, I, 341; Grosz, "Pinch-

Another means of profiting through political position was in the buying and selling of warrants. Throughout Reconstruction, and for years afterward, the income of the state of Louisiana was not equal to its expenditures. Many bonds were issued, but the state paid most ordinary expenses in warrants. Since currency was available to re-deem only a fraction of these obligations, they were heavily dis-counted. The only thing that gave them value was the fact that, with certain reservations, they were receivable for state taxes. This afforded many opportunities for sharp dealing. Tax collectors, for example, might collect taxes in currency, then buy warrants to turn over to the treasurer, reaping a profit of 50 percent in addition to the commission received for collecting the taxes. Even more reprehensible was the practice, when currency was available in the treasury, of letting in-siders cash warrants at face value, leaving those who had performed services for the state to bear the discount. Last, but not least, guber-natorial or legislative action could affect the value of warrants, and the temptation to buy them up and then take action to temporarily raise their value was not always resisted.[108]

Among other reported shenanigans of the Warmoth period were the insertion of a clause legalizing gambling houses in New Orleans into an act after the act had been passed, the sale of appointments to West Point by two Radical congressmen, the securing of appoint-ments as commissioners of the insane asylum at Jackson by bribery, and the extortion of three hundred dollars from the head of Charity Hospital before the money appropriated for that institution was made available. Scandal was not confined to Radical officeholders. When E. A. Burke ran against General Beauregard for administrator of im-provements in New Orleans in 1872, he was accused of seeking the office in order to cover up the frauds of the preceding three years. Whether or not this was true, and considering Burke's later career it does not seem improbable, it is definitely true that Burke's winning majority was announced before the votes had been counted.[109]

---

back," 543–44; F. B. Harris, "Henry Clay Warmoth," 589, 596–97; Daspit, "Governors' Messages," 44.

108 New Orleans *Daily Picayune*, June 1, August 20, 1872; F. B. Harris, "Henry Clay Warmoth," 591–92.

109 *Acts of Louisiana, 1869*, 5; New Orleans *Daily Picayune*, August 8, 1869, Febru-ary 10, 20, 1870, October 27, November 6, 1872; Stella O'Conner, "The Charity

The legislature elected in 1870 was undoubtedly corrupt. Not every man who served in this body was tainted, but almost certainly most of them were. But they were not criminals. They accepted bribes, but, as already noted, bribery was not forbidden by Louisiana law. They practiced pluralism, many holding positions in the Custom House, others being employed by companies which had an interest in legislation, some serving as tax collectors in their parishes, but none of these things was illegal. The expenses of the legislature were much higher than they needed to be because legislators padded their expense accounts and sat on interim committees which enabled them to draw a per diem between sessions. More clerks and pages than necessary were employed because this added to legislative patronage. But none of these things was contrary to law. Except that bribery was not so open, all these practices continued when Reconstruction was long past.

Not for an instant should it be assumed that wrongdoing was confined to Radical legislators. Negroes, with the exception of leaders such as Pinchback and C. C. Antoine, made less out of questionable practices than did whites because they were not so skilled at the game. And white Democrats were just as corrupt as white Republicans. This was admitted even by Democratic newspapers. In fact, Louisiana government has never been simon-pure, and the Reconstruction years were not much worse than those to follow. Warmoth was not far off the mark when he said: "These much abused members of the Louisiana legislature are at all events as good as the people they represent. Why, damn it, everybody is demoralized down here. Corruption is the fashion."[110]

When a public official is bribed, someone has done the bribing. The *Picayune* noted of two anti-Radical meetings held early in 1870 that Warmoth and the legislature were denounced, but that neither meet-

Hospital at New Orleans: An Administrative and Financial History, 1736–1941," *Louisiana Historical Quarterly*, XXXI (January, 1948), 64–65.

110 Cited in Shugg, *Origins of Class Struggle in Louisiana*, 227; see also New Orleans *Daily Picayune*, March 18, 1870, February 26, December 19, 1871, March 6, 1872; *House Miscellaneous Documents*, 42nd Cong., 2nd Sess., No. 211, p. 57, *passim*; Shreveport *Times*, December 31, 1871, January 31, 1872; Highsmith, "Louisiana During Reconstruction," 280–81; Lonn, *Reconstruction in Louisiana*, 19–20, 28–29, 86, 91–92; Current, *Three Carpetbag Governors*, 62; F. B. Harris, "Henry Clay Warmoth," 621.

ing gave "one word to the rings of lobbyists and brokers . . . in their infamous schemes of bribery and corruption."[111] In his 1871 message to the legislature, Warmoth warned against "schemes of plunder" designed to "fill the pockets of unprincipled speculators." He cautioned: "The persons who will probably importune you most pertinaciously for the most bare-faced of these speculations are well-dressed gentlemen, claiming to be representatives of the most respectable of our people. It is these pleasant gentlemen in broadcloth . . . and not the poor and needy applicants for some long-delayed but petty act of justice who have most depleted the public till in the past, and will endeavor to do so again."[112]

Earlier than this, when a committee of citizens had called on the governor to protest "obnoxious laws and financial schemes," Warmoth had pointed out that those who profited most from these measures were New Orleans' "very best people." Speaking of a bill to redeem Confederate bonds, which he had vetoed, Warmoth asked rhetorically. "By whom was it lobbied through? By your Carondelet Street brokers, who crowded the halls . . . suggesting bribes. . . . I walked into the Senate Chamber and saw nearly every prominent broker of the city lobbying that bill through." One of the delegates admitted that many Democrats were involved in corrupt schemes, but denied that they could be called "best people."[113]

7

Much has been written about the debts incurred by Louisiana during the Warmoth regime, not a little of it nonsense. The height of bad arithmetic was probably reached by John Burgess, who wrote that average expenditure under Warmoth was about $6,000,000 a year, and that the state debt rose from about $7,000,000 at the beginning of his administration to $50,000,000 when he went out of office. The best figures available show that Louisiana owned slightly over $10,000,000 in 1860. This increased during the war to $27,000,000, but much of this was classified as Confederate debt and therefore void, leaving a

111 New Orleans *Daily Picayune*, February 15, 1870.
112 Governor's Message, 1871, in New Orleans *Daily Picayune*, January 12, 1871.
113 New Orleans *Daily Picayune*, February 3, 1870.

legitimate debt of about $14,000,000, which was increased to about $17,500,000 before Radical Reconstruction began. In June, 1871, the bonded indebtedness had passed $22,000,000. By the end of 1872 the total of bonded indebtedness and unpaid bills was something over $25,000,000.[114]

Part of the misinformation in regard to the debt arises from the fact that the state had incurred approximately $12,000,000 in so-called "contingent debt." This was in the form of guarantees to railroads and canals to be paid in bonds when these companies had constructed a stipulated number of miles of road or canal. Until the construction was accomplished, no bonds were issued; therefore the state owed nothing. As it developed, very few such bonds were ever issued, and these mainly to the Chattanooga Railroad, and all before 1872, so none of the contingent debt of 1872 ever became actual debt. Therefore the figure of $42,000,000 total debt, often seen, is not at all accurate.

The actual debt was burden enough. In 1870 the state paid $963,000 in interest. It should be noted, however, that $215,000 of this was interest on the prewar debt, and $320,000 was interest on levee bonds authorized by the Democratic legislature which preceded the Warmoth regime. But the debt would have risen no matter who had governed Louisiana after the war. The great damage inflicted during hostilities had to be repaired, at the least. At the same time the value of taxable property was greatly decreased. Much of this decline resulted from the emancipation of slave property, but the value of the land itself was also significantly reduced. Yet at the same time internal improvements were promoted and new programs, such as the expansion of the public school system, were undertaken. The Chattanooga Railroad did connect Mobile and New Orleans and then move on upriver to Donaldsonville. The levees were not made proof against floods, but they were in far better condition in 1872 than in 1868. Much school money was embezzled, but a public school sys-

114 Burgess, *Reconstruction and the Constitution*, 263; Annual Message of His Excellency, H. C. Warmoth, Governor of Louisiana, January 1, 1872, in *Legislative Documents, Louisiana, 1872* (New Orleans, 1872); *Senate Reports*, 42nd Cong., 2nd Sess., No. 41, p. 189; Highsmith, "Louisiana During Reconstruction," 408–409; F. B. Harris, "Henry Clay Warmoth," 573.

tem for both races was established so firmly that the Bourbons were not able to destroy it even though they tried.[115]

Finally, it must be borne in mind that the face value of state obligations and the amount of purchasing power the state received had little relationship to one another. The interest on state bonds ranged from 6 to 8 percent, and the interest on good commercial loans ranged from 10 to 15 percent. The interest on well-secured mortgages was more than 10 percent. Louisiana bonds were secured by the credit of the state, and that credit was constantly growing worse as, year after year, the state government had to borrow to meet current obligations. In 1868 Louisiana had to pay $7,000 in interest to borrow $100,000 for ninety days to pay interest due on levee bonds and also had to give the lender an option to buy $100,000 worth of the bonds at sixty cents on the dollar. In 1869 Louisiana bonds sold in New York brought little more than fifty cents on the dollar. In 1870 8-percent bonds brought eighty-three cents, and 6-percent bonds brought sixty-five cents. Local government bonds usually fared even worse, as did state warrants. In 1872, bonds sold by Red River Parish to build a courthouse sold at half of face value. Charity Hospital was almost forced to close because it cost $85,000 a year to operate, and the $155,000 appropriation, paid over in state warrants, brought only about $40,000. Other examples could be given, but this should be enough to demonstrate that a large share of the state debt resulted from bad credit, not from fraud or extravagance. Furthermore, Louisiana's credit was no worse under Warmoth than it had been under the Democratic legislature which had preceded him.[116]

8

Taxation is another subject much discussed in connection with Reconstruction. The planters and merchants who ruled Louisiana be-

---

115 *Acts of Louisiana, Extra Session, 1870*, 77–85; *House Miscellaneous Documents*, 42nd Cong., 2nd Sess., No. 211, p. 521; New Orleans *Daily Picayune*, June 14, November 4, 1871; Carter, *The Angry Scar*, 183; Williams, *Romance and Realism in Southern Politics*, 26; Stampp, *The Era of Reconstruction*, 183.

116 New Orleans *Daily Picayune*, November 24, 1869, February 3, 1870, August 30, 1872; *Acts of Louisiana, Extra Session, 1870*, 52; *Acts of Louisiana, 1869*, 4, 44–45; Lonn, *Reconstruction in Louisiana*, 18–19; O'Conner, "Charity Hospital," 167; Lewinson, *Race, Class, and Party*, 49.

fore the Civil War were men of property who needed little that state government could give; therefore they kept taxes very low. In 1860, for example, property in Iberville Parish was valued at $14,000,000 and paid state taxes of only $44,000. St. James Parish paid $27,000 on an assessed valuation of $8,500,000. This was a rate of only three mills per hundred dollars valuation. Out of taxes collected at this rate all expenses of state government, including a small amount of state support of schools, were paid. Not only were the people of Louisiana accustomed to low taxes before the war; most of them, outside of New Orleans, paid no taxes whatsoever during the war. These back taxes were eventually demanded by the state, but they were payable in depreciated state warrants and, as late as 1871, no interest or penalty was assessed.[117]

After the war the tax rate grew steadily. The basic state tax was only 2.5 mills, but additional millage was levied to the amount necessary to pay interest and retirement of principal on bonded indebtedness. This was 3.75 mills in 1865, 5.25 mills in 1871, 21.5 mills in 1872. What this meant in terms of taxes levied can be seen from the following:

TABLE ONE

State Taxes Paid in Selected Parishes

Parish	1866	1870	1871	1872
Assumption	$20,201.24	$19,907.24	$38,536.65	$42,876.20
Caddo	$31,282.48	———	$68,044.35	$108,557.04
Concordia	$17,252.39	$27,208.11	$34,003.33	$42,937.92
Lafourche	$19,478.59	$31,475.71	$38,478.37	$43,605.55
St. Tammany	$5,620.09	$4,548.23	$6,899.20	$9,630.46
Tensas	$24,463.45	$24,963.45	$25,898.08	$38,303.23[118]

In addition to state taxes, citizens of Louisiana also had to pay

117 Shugg, *Origins of Class Struggle in Louisiana*, 130–51, 156; Walter Prichard (ed.), "A Tourist's Description of Louisiana in 1860," *Louisiana Historical Quarterly*, XXI (October, 1938), 1,110–75; Warmoth, *War, Politics and Reconstruction*, 84–85; *Acts of Louisiana, 1868*, 244; *Acts of Louisiana, 1871*, 19.

118 *Acts of Louisiana, 1868*, 149–50, 247–63; *Acts of Louisiana, 1869*, 66, 146–65; *Acts of Louisiana, 1870*, 63–65; *Acts of Louisiana, 1871*, 104–33; *New Orleans Daily Picayune*, November 12, 1868; Reports of Auditor of Public Accounts, 1866–72, in *Legislative Documents, Louisiana, 1867–1873*; DuBois, *Black Reconstruction*, 477.

parish taxes and, if they lived in a municipality, city taxes. Parish taxes varied, but at the height of Reconstruction ten to fifteen mills seems to have been a fair average. Parishes were forbidden to levy a poll tax. It is obvious that in most parishes the taxpayers were able to exert more influence toward keeping taxes down than they were able to exert in respect to state levies.[119]

In New Orleans, which was deeply in debt before Reconstruction began and which continued to live beyond its means under both Radical and Democratic administrations, city taxes were a considerable addition to state taxes. In 1867 the city tax was fifteen mills; in 1872 it was twenty-seven and a half mills. A New Orleans property owner paid almost fifty mills in state and local taxes, or almost five dollars on each hundred dollars of assessed valuation. Thus homeowners and businessmen of the city were taxed much more heavily than people of the countryside.[120]

Taxes were collected by collectors appointed by the governor. They were compensated by a commission on their collections. In most parishes this commission did not amount to a large sum, probably averaging about fifteen hundred dollars a year. The country collectors probably made more by exchanging what currency they collected for depreciated state warrants and then using the warrants at face value to settle their accounts. In New Orleans, however, the commissions could be most lucrative. General George A. Sheridan, friend of Warmoth and collector of the First District in the city, collected taxes on property assessed at over seventy million dollars, and his income was reported to be more than twenty thousand a year. In 1870 the office of assessor and collector was combined. This may have caused an increase in assessments so as to increase commissions, but in a number of country parishes the assessment went down rather than up. The costs of collection overall were high, amounting one year to almost 8 percent of the total collected. Also, so many collectors were delinquent in settling their accounts that, as noted earlier, a constitutional

119 New Orleans *Daily Picayune*, January 26, August 11, June 22, September 9, 1871; Baton Rouge *Weekly Advocate*, September 24, 1870; *Acts of Louisiana*, 1870, 47.
120 New Orleans *Daily Picayune*, September 15, 1871, September 3, 1872; Kendall, *History of New Orleans*, I, 335, 340–41; John Burnside Tax Receipts, 1869–72, in Gaudet Papers.

amendment of 1870 prohibited the holding of public office by any onetime tax collector whose accounts had not been settled.[121]

Throughout Warmoth's administration there were sporadic attempts at resisting the payment of taxes. In November, 1868, the *Picayune* heartily applauded the formation of a nonpartisan Taxpayers' Association "to resist the heavy taxation imposed on us by . . . bad legislation."[122] Similar groups were organized in several country parishes in 1868. In 1871 there was another effort, directed particularly against a new school tax. Tax resisting became fashionable again in the spring of 1872 but had little or no effect. The movement was to continue, however, and it would be significant under the Kellogg administration.[123] Under Warmoth perhaps the most extreme tax-resisting action was taken by Hephzibah Baptist Church, which excommunicated one James A. Merchant in 1869 for "dishonorable conduct in making a false assessment of the property in the Parish of East Feliciana."[124]

How high were taxes under Warmoth? The rates became high, it is true, but rates are meaningless unless the relation of the assessment to the true value of the property taxed is known. This has not been ascertained with any exactness for the Reconstruction years. However, an examination of the tax assessment rolls of a number of country parishes leaves a strong impression that assessed valuation of farm property was much less than the actual value. In New Orleans assessments were higher, but in 1872 the total assessed valuation of the city was, in round numbers, only $124,000,000. On a lot assessed at three thousand dollars, the taxes for 1871 were only sixty dollars.[125]

121 New Orleans *Daily Picayune*, October 16, 1869, May 18, September 3, 1872; *Acts of Louisiana, 1868*, 247–63; *Acts of Louisiana, 1869*, 15, 146–65; *Acts of Louisiana, 1871*, 104–33; F. B. Harris, "Henry Clay Warmoth," 572–73; Lonn, *Reconstruction in Louisiana*, 85–86.

122 New Orleans *Daily Picayune*, November 4, 1868.

123 New Orleans *Daily Picayune*, November 24, December 2, 1868, October 30, 1869, March 26, June 24, 1871, April–May, 1872; Shreveport *Times*, May 16, 1872.

124 Hephzibah Church Books, II, 1858–1898 (Merritt M. Shilg Memorial Collection, Department of Archives, Louisiana State University).

125 Ascension Parish Tax Assessment Rolls, 1870, 1880, Claiborne Parish Tax Assessment Rolls, 1871, 1876, East Feliciana Parish Tax Assessment Rolls, 1871, 1880, Rapides Parish Tax Assessment Rolls, 1871, 1880, St. Mary Parish Tax Assessment Rolls, 1877, Tensas Parish Tax Assessment Rolls, 1870, 1880, Winn Parish Tax Assessment Rolls, 1873, 1880, all on microfilm in Office of Comptroller, State of Louisiana; John Burnside Tax Receipt, 1872, in Gaudet Papers.

This was not a particularly high tax if the assessment was actual value or below. Another factor which must be considered is that most taxes, especially those paid by larger property owners, were paid with state warrants at face value when these warrants could be bought for much less than their face value. Likewise, taxes due to the city of New Orleans could be paid in several kinds of depreciated city paper. As for the state poll tax, it simply was not collected. Taxes during the late 1860s and early 1870s may have been a heavy burden to a people impoverished by war, but by any kind of absolute standard, they were not extraordinarily high. They did increase, but the idea of taxes being so high as to be confiscatory is simply another Reconstruction myth insofar as Louisiana is concerned.[126]

126 John Burnside Tax Receipts, 1870, 1872, in Gaudet Papers; *Acts of Louisiana, 1869*, 3; Robert Somers, *The Southern States Since the War, 1870–1871* (reprint; University, Ala., 1965), pp. 227–28; Tax Receipt, Plaquemines Parish, 1872 [for 1871 taxes], William P. Kellogg Papers; Department of Archives, Louisiana State University; New Orleans *Daily Picayune*, June 1, 1871, March 1, September 3, 7, 29, October 11, 1872; Lonn, *Reconstruction in Louisiana*, 84–85; L. Frank Paragoud to Warmoth, April 26, 1870, in Warmoth Papers.

VI   *The Fall of Warmoth*

BY MID-1870, Henry Clay Warmoth had more power than any of his predecessors as governor of Louisiana. Probably he was more powerful than any of his successors except Huey P. Long. But even as he achieved this pinnacle of power the process which was to bring about his political destruction had begun. The story of Warmoth's downfall is not an inspiring one, though it does have moments of high and low comedy, but it is a story which needs to be told.

In 1868 Warmoth had not received wholehearted support from black Republican leaders. After his election as governor he lost more black support by vetoing a civil rights bill passed by the legislature in 1868. This bill provided for enforcement of the equal-accommodations section of the state constitution and was opposed mightily by the conservative press: "This . . . social equality bill . . . is a sham and a snare. It is the convocation of a set of characterless adventurers from the North, who desire the extermination of the negro race . . . or mongrel mulattos, who have read the mischievous books of Fourier, Victor Hugo, and other ridiculous theorists of the French or German Red Republican and infidel schools; and of a small number of misguided black men, and very worthless and wicked white ones, the object of all being strife and subsequent bloodshed."[1]

Warmoth's public reason for vetoing the bill was that discrimination would gradually give way, and that such measures, by agitating the race question, delayed the disappearance of prejudice. In actuality, he seems to have realized that the bill could not be enforced if it passed; probably he did not desire its enforcement. By his veto he earned the praise of the conservative press at the cost of making enemies within his own party.[2]

Warmoth did other things which antagonized Republicans. He made no Radical friends when he appointed a number of Democrats to office, even though in many parts of the state qualified Republicans simply were not available. The submission and passage in 1870 of the constitutional amendment making him eligible for a second term as governor turned men with hopes of attaining that high office against him. Finally, according to Warmoth, many of his enemies within the Republican party had become foes after he had vetoed financial measures in which they had an interest.[3]

The United States Custom House became the center of Republican opposition to the governor. United States Marshal Stephen B. Packard was the leader of this faction, but in the early part of the Warmoth regime he remained in the background. The ostensible head of the Custom House Ring was James F. Casey, collector of customs and, more important, President Grant's wife's brother-in-law. Later William Pitt Kellogg was to become a leader of the Custom House faction, but until 1871 he and Warmoth apparently cooperated. Casey and Packard were in good position to strike at Warmoth's leadership from within the party, because they controlled extensive federal patronage. Casey cooperated with Warmoth on occasion, when necessary, but in the main they were bitter enemies. Warmoth said of

1 New Orleans *Daily Picayune*, September 22, 1868.
2 Veto Message, September 25, 1868, in *Legislative Documents, 1868*; New Orleans *Daily Picayune*, January 6, 1870; Baton Rouge *Weekly Advocate*, October 3, 1868; Althea D. Pitre, "The Collapse of the Warmoth Regime, 1870–72," *Louisiana History*, VI (Spring, 1965), 162–63; F. B. Harris, "Henry Clay Warmoth," 556–57; Ewing, "Early Louisiana Impeachments," 699.
3 John Scollard to T. W. Conway, June 6, 1871, C. Case to Warmoth, April 15, 1870, A. W. Smythe to Warmoth, April 19, 1870, in Warmoth Papers; F. B. Harris, "Heny Clay Warmoth," 604–605.

Casey in 1872: "My friend Jim Casey is a clever fellow. He hasn't sense enough to be a bad fellow. A man to be a bad fellow must have some character—he hasn't any."[4]

In 1869 the legislature once more voted to guarantee blacks equal accommodations in public places. Pinchback was the chief promoter of this bill. Warmoth could not politically afford a veto, so he let the measure become law without his signature. In 1871 the governor successfully vetoed another Pinchback bill, which made it a criminal offense for any person to discriminate unjustly on account of race. The futility of such a law at that time and place was demonstrated when McComb's Jackson Railroad refused to sell Pinchback a sleeping-car ticket, and all of Warmoth's efforts at intercession with McComb were useless. Public opinion had been aroused far more, however, in 1870 when a few black children entered the public schools. One result was that the schools were late in opening. Because he did not push integration of public accommodations and schools, Warmoth was losing support from the blacks of his own party, particularly Lieutenant-Governor Dunn and his followers. Warmoth apparently hoped that he would be accepted as governor by all the people of Louisiana, but in this he was disappointed. His enemies in the Custom House were quick to take advantage of his dilemma and ally themselves with Dunn.[5]

In early 1870 Warmoth went on the offensive and tried to secure the discharge of Collector Casey, apparently with the tacit consent of Packard and with the open cooperation of Kellogg. United States Representative J. Hale Sypher assured Warmoth that "We will make it so damned hot about the Customhouse, that Mr. C. will get out much quicker than he got in."[6] Senator J. S. Harris assured Warmoth that Casey was a Democrat at heart, and Senator Kellogg not only

4 *Senate Reports*, 42nd Cong., 2nd Sess., No. 41, p. 361; see also Sheldon to Warmoth, December 7, 1869, Kellogg to Warmoth, December 22, 1869, in Warmoth Papers; New Orleans *Daily Picayune*, April 8, 1869; Lonn, *Reconstruction in Louisiana*, 10.

5 *Acts of Louisiana, 1869*, 37; Henry L. McComb to E. L. Sewell, June 28, 1871, McComb to R. Pritchard, July 3, 1871, Warmoth to McComb, July 11, 1871, all in Warmoth Papers; New Orleans *Daily Picayune*, January 12, October 20, 1870; F. B. Harris, "Henry Clay Warmoth," 556–57; Lonn, *Reconstruction in Louisiana*, 40–41; Grosz, "Pinchback," 540.

6 Sypher to Warmoth, January 3, 1870, in Warmoth Papers.

believed that Casey would resign, but also that his resignation was necessary for the welfare of the Republican party in Louisiana.[7] Presumably someone suggested to Casey that he could mollify his opponents by making appointments acceptable to them, but he realized the real meaning of the attack upon him: "You can say to the President that it makes no difference who I appoint . . . I am the one they want removed."[8] By March Warmoth had learned that "Gen'l Grant is determined to stand by Casey to the bitter end."[9] How much of this determination resulted from family ties and how much from Grant's dislike of Warmoth dating back to the Vicksburg campaign, no one can say. The Custom House Ring, by 1870, had a rather significant advantage over the governor because he had, by that time, used up most of the state patronage at his disposal. Just as Warmoth, by statute, was seemingly almost dictator of Louisiana, he was beginning to lose control of his own party.

This loss of control was clearly demonstrated at the meeting of the state Republican convention in August, 1870. The black delegates were discontented because of Warmoth's lack of enthusiasm for civil rights, and Dunn, Packard, and Postmaster C. W. Lowell encouraged this attitude. Warmoth was elected temporary chairman of the convention, but when the vote was taken for permanent chairman the black delegates rejected Warmoth and gave the honor to Lieutenant-Governor Dunn.[10]

The legislature elected in 1870 met first on January 2, 1871. Dunn, as lieutenant-governor, presided over the senate, heading a group of Republican opponents of the governor. Before the session opened, Warmoth, to checkmate Dunn, had made a bargain with the Democrats in the senate to take the appointment of committees out of Dunn's hands. As payment, the Democrats received the chairmanship of several committees. In the house of representatives, Warmoth was able to secure the appointment of an ally, Mortimer Carr, as

7 Kellogg to Warmoth, July 23, 1868, January 17, 1869, March 6, 1870, J. S. Harris to Warmoth, January 6, 1870, in Warmoth Papers.
8 Casey to George A. Sheridan, March 15, 1870, in Warmoth Papers.
9 George A. Sheridan to Warmoth, March 21, 1870, in Warmoth Papers; see also F. B. Harris, "Henry Clay Warmoth," 608.
10 Pitre, "Collapse of the Warmoth Regime," 162–64; Harris, "Henry Clay Warmoth," 608; Lonn, *Reconstruction in Louisiana*, 73–74; New Orleans *Daily Picayune*, August 8–10, 1870; Rousseve, *The Negro in Louisiana*, 104–105.

speaker. The session seemed harmonious for a brief time after organization, but when the governor, who had called for the enactment of a statute against bribery, vetoed several acts in which legislators had financial interests, harmony disappeared. Colonel George W. Carter, representative from Cameron Parish, became the leader of the anti-Warmoth Republicans in the house.[11]

In March, 1870, Warmoth signed a bill creating Cameron Parish, mainly in order to get George W. Carter into the legislature. He appointed Carter parish judge and gave him blank commissions for other parish officials. This was sufficient leverage to assure Carter's election to the house of representatives from the new parish. Carter was a Virginian by birth, a former Methodist minister, former president of a school for girls, and former commander of a regiment of Confederate cavalry. In his busy career he had found time to read law and was a practicing attorney. Warmoth first looked on him as "one of the most gentle, simple, and attractive men that I have ever known."[12] As events proved, loyalty was not one of Carter's virtues. Discontented Republican representatives, with aid from the Democrats, forced Speaker Carr to resign and elected Carter to the office. The gentleman from Cameron promptly became the leader of the Custom House faction in the house of representatives. To assure himself an adequate livelihood, he accepted a sinecure as an employee of the Custom House. To assure a few luxuries, he refused to sign the bill obliging the state to buy stock in the Chattanooga Railroad until that company had retained him, at ten thousand dollars a year, as one of its attorneys.[13]

The legislature enacted no really important legislation during its 1871 session. Additional advantages were given to the Chattanooga Railroad and the North Louisiana and Texas. The purchase, with bonds, of stock in Pinchback's Mississippi River Packet Company added to the state's debt. Of more long-range importance was the creation of the State Board of Engineers which would function long

---

11 Pitre, "Collapse of the Warmoth Regime," 165–66; F. B. Harris, "Henry Clay Warmoth," 587; Lonn, *Reconstruction in Louisiana*, 75–76.
12 Warmoth, *War, Politics and Reconstruction*, 109.
13 *Ibid.*, 109–11; *House Reports*, 42nd Cong., 2nd Sess., No. 92, p. 27; New Orleans *Daily Picayune*, February 1, 1871; F. B. Harris, "Henry Clay Warmoth," 608–11; Lonn, *Reconstruction in Louisiana*, 76.

after Reconstruction was over. This legislature also created three new parishes, Red River, Vernon, and Webster. The legislators appropriated $500,000 for per diem, travel, and other expenses, in celebration of which Colonel Carter and the house apparently issued, at the end of the session, some warrants for monies which had not been appropriated.[14]

Perhaps the most significant action of the session of 1871 was the election of a United States senator to replace Harris, whose term expired March 4. There was no lack of candidates. Among the important ones were Casey, former governor Michael Hahn, J. R. West, Dunn, and Pinchback. A caucus of Negro Republicans chose Pinchback over Dunn as their candidate. Warmoth threw his support to West and with the aid of Democrats who preferred any white man to Pinchback he secured West's election. Packard, Casey, and Lowell fought Warmoth every step of the way, but to no avail. This election probably can be considered the point of no return in the progress of the quarrel between Warmoth and the Custom House.[15]

The legislature of 1871 was extravagant, contained leaders as well as rank-and-file members who were not above outright fraud, was rent by factionalism, and was lacking in decorum. It was certainly subject to influences such as the banquet for Democratic and Republican leaders given by Louisiana Lottery officials at the St. Charles Hotel. After numerous toasts, the guests enjoyed turtle soup, red snapper, fillet of flounder, two kinds of beef, salmon, chicken, rib of veal, Maryland terrapin, turkey, venison, crayfish, wild duck, beans, potatoes, asparagus, peas, tomatoes, and numerous desserts.[16] This was fine fare for lawmakers who, according to the *Picayune*, had filled minor positions with "renegades, escaped convicts, broken down gamblers, exhausted inebriates, panders of all sizes and colors . . . with some admixture of needy and seedy respectability, not imported."

14 *Acts of Louisiana, 1871*, 7–8, 29–42, 59–63, 66–70, 86–103, 134–36, 173–76, 211–16; New Orleans *Daily Picayune*, January–February, April 7, 1871; Lonn, *Reconstruction in Louisiana*, 78–79, 83.

15 New Orleans *Daily Picayune*, January 11, February 7, 1871; New Orleans *Republican*, January 12, 1871; Pitre, "Collapse of the Warmoth Regime," 165; F. B. Harris, "Henry Clay Warmoth," 610; Grosz, "Pinchback," 542; Lonn, *Reconstruction in Louisiana*, 76–77.

16 New Orleans *Daily Picayune*, February 8, 1871.

Even worse, "The corrupt influences have extended to classes once free from taint. Some of our most respected citizens are asking favors or taking privileges from them."[17]

As the session came to an end, Warmoth decided to make one more attempt to establish his primacy in the Republican party. He had attempted an alliance with Casey, but this had ended with the election of West to the senate. Since experience had proved that there was nothing to be gained by striking directly at the president's brother-in-law, Warmoth this time chose Postmaster Lowell as his target. General Longstreet was sent to ask his old friend in the White House to remove Lowell, and Senator West gave his support. Kellogg, on the other hand, seems to have decided that Warmoth's was the losing side. Of him West wrote: "It is really amusing to see Kellogg's ways that are dark and tricks that are vain. I breathe the very air of his Jesuitism."[18] Concerning Casey, who was in Washington supporting Lowell, West wrote: "I have seen Casey only once—alternately bespattered and bullied him—he is here just what he is in New Orleans, too weak to stand alone and don't know who to lean against."[19] West was not altogether correct; Casey knew very well how to lean on his wife's sister's husband.

For a time it seemed that Warmoth might succeed. Grant actually sent the nomination of a successor to Lowell to the Senate, but a visit by Lieutenant-Governor Dunn apparently changed his mind. He withdrew the nomination, but the Senate proceeded to reject it anyway. West's angry comment was: "The President shows no more stability than a pillar of jelly in an earthquake."[20] The end result was a definite victory for the Custom House. With almost every federal officeholder in Louisiana arrayed against him, the president hostile, and Dunn influencing the blacks, Warmoth could expect a difficult time remaining at the head of his party. To add to his difficulties, he suffered an injury to his foot while on a pleasure cruise; the wound became infected and he was incapacitated for much of the spring and early summer. For a time his life was in danger. When he went

17 *Ibid.*, March 1, 1871.
18 West to Warmoth, March 18, 1871, in Warmoth Papers.
19 *Ibid.*
20 West to Warmoth, March 24, 1871, in Warmoth Papers.

to the Mississippi Gulf Coast to recuperate, Dunn became acting governor and used such opportunities as he had to further the interests of the Custom House faction.[21]

2

It was necessary to hold a Republican party convention in 1871 to select a new state central committee. Packard dominated the existing committee, but he strongly suspected that Warmoth would control a majority of delegates to the convention. Disabled by his injury, Warmoth recommended that the convention not be held until November because during the summer many people were out of town and there was always danger of an epidemic. Packard called the convention for August 9; he did not name a place, however.

Throughout the state a contest for delegates began. Warmoth, who controlled the police in New Orleans and local officials in almost all Republican parishes, had advantages which he did not hesitate to use. Meetings of Custom House supporters were harassed and sometimes broken up. Packard counted on Dunn's influence with black voters, and he gained some additional support by increasing the Custom House payroll. Warmoth suggested that these employees were hired for "conventional" purposes. Packard's greatest strength, however, was outside Louisiana. He was confident now that he could depend upon Grant's support in a showdown with Warmoth.[22]

Warmoth wanted the convention to meet in the State House (Mechanics' Institute), and in order to ensure that it would not meet elsewhere he rented all the halls in New Orleans. Packard countered by naming the Circuit Court Room in the Custom House as the place of the meeting. To "prevent violence" he named forty or fifty deputy marshals, and as United States marshal he asked for federal troops to protect federal property. A company of troops with two Gatling guns was provided, from which the meeting at the Custom House

21 New Orleans *Daily Picayune*, March 14, 1871; West to Warmoth, March 14, 26, 1871, James Longstreet to Warmoth, January 19, 1871, in Warmoth Papers; Pitre, "Collapse of the Warmoth Regime," 165, 167; F. B. Harris, "Henry Clay Warmoth," 612–13.
22 Warmoth *et al.* to S. B. Packard, May 31, 1871, Jeff Thompson to Warmoth, July 13, 1871, J. W. Fairfax to Warmoth, July 14, 1871, all in Warmoth Papers; New Orleans *Daily Picayune*, July 25, 27, August 2–4, 1871; Pitre, "Collapse of the Warmoth Regime," 167–68; Lonn, *Reconstruction in Louisiana*, 96–99.

has been given the name Gatling Gun Convention. Packard ordered that no one was to be admitted except those certified by the existing central committee; Postmaster Lowell would issue the certificates. Since most delegations were contested, this rule almost assured a Custom House majority.

Warmoth, on crutches and running a temperature, led his followers to the Custom House and then, as instructed, went to Lowell for certificates. Only about half the Warmoth group received these "tickets." Even so, when they returned to the Custom House and went to the second floor, deputy marshals informed them that they could not enter the courtroom until noon. As they stood in the lobby, the door of the District Court Room, which connected with that of the Circuit Court, was opened long enough for Warmoth to see a caucus of his opponents in progress. He realized immediately that these adversaries would organize the convention and name a credentials committee which would exclude his delegates before they could get into the meeting room. Therefore he directed his followers, 118 strong, to follow him to Turner Hall, where they would hold their own convention. Warmoth's convention thus had the 118 delegates the rules called for; the Gatling Gun Convention had only 89. Obviously, many districts were represented in both conventions. Contemporary opinion in New Orleans was that a majority of the legally qualified delegates was made up of Warmoth supporters.[23]

Now began one of those comic-opera scenes which were more and more to be a feature of Louisiana Reconstruction. The Gatling Gun Convention and the Turner Hall Convention both claimed to represent the true Republican party, and both proceeded to name a new central committee. At the Custom House, Warmoth was read out of the party. Speaker Carter referred to him as "the greatest living practical liar." Warmoth accused Carter of "corruption, dishonesty, and licentiousness."[24] Indeed, Warmoth's final speech at Turner Hall was a delightful philippic in which he ridiculed all the major Custom

---

23 Warmoth, *War, Politics and Reconstruction*, 113–17; New Orleans *Daily Picayune*, August 9–11, November 22, 1871; New Orleans *Republican*, July 30–August 12, 1871; F. B. Harris, "Henry Clay Warmoth," 613, 615–19, 623; Lonn, *Reconstruction in Louisiana*, 100–104; Pitre, "Collapse of the Warmoth Regime," 167–68.
24 Quoted in Lonn, *Reconstruction in Louisiana*, 102–103.

House figures. Casey, he said, was led around by the nose by "that little native of Jerusalem, Felix Herwig. . . . Herwig sometimes says, 'upon my soul . . . I believe that there is a good deal said that is wrong against [Warmoth] . . . but, by G——d, he will not let Casey and me make any money!' "[25]

Packard and his friends were inevitably victorious in this contest, because they could be sure that their central committee would be recognized by the national party so long as Grant was president. The Turner Hall Convention sent a delegation of twenty to call upon Grant, but Packard had already persuaded the president that Warmoth must go if the Republicans in Louisiana were to keep the Negro vote. Presumably he did not tell him that Pinchback, almost if not entirely as influential with the black voters as Dunn, had remained loyal to Warmoth. Grant promised the Turner Hall delegation that he would investigate, but he did nothing. In November the Custom House faction established the *National Republican* as an anti-Warmoth newspaper. The Conservatives, as they observed the rupture in Republican ranks, began dreaming of voting the Radicals out of office in 1872.[26]

3

After the convention of 1871 was over, the Custom House Republicans began negotiating with the Democrats for the votes that they needed to impeach and convict Warmoth. There is a possibility that this move might have succeeded, although most Democrats would have had second thoughts about making Dunn governor with almost a year to serve. However this might have been, the issue never came to a test because on November 22, 1871, Dunn died, very suddenly, of "congestion of the brain." There were rumors that he was poisoned, but there seems to have been no real foundation for such a belief.[27]

25 New Orleans *Daily Picayune,* August 12, 1871; New Orleans *Republican,* August 10–18, 1871; full accounts of both conventions appear in the New Orleans *Daily Picayune,* August 10–14, 1871.
26 G. A. Sheridan to Warmoth, September 2, 1871, in Warmoth Papers; Warmoth, *War, Politics and Reconstruction,* 118; Pitre, "Collapse of the Warmoth Regime," 169; Copeland, "The New Orleans Press and Reconstruction," 212.
27 New Orleans *Republican,* November 23–24, 1871; New Orleans *Daily Picayune,* August 26, October 24, November 23, 1871, February 18, 1872; Warmoth, *War, Politics and Reconstruction,* 118–19; Grosz, "Pinchback," 546–47; DuBois, *Black*

Dunn was an anomaly among Reconstruction leaders in Louisiana in that he was never accused of dishonesty. Indeed, his incorruptibility made him, in the eyes of some Conservative leaders, far more dangerous than those white or black Radicals who could be bought. Dunn had been born into slavery, but he had bought his freedom after being allowed to hire out his own labor as a plasterer. He seems to have realized early that Warmoth was just as much a believer in white superiority, just as opposed to civil rights for blacks, as were the conservative whites who opposed him. His adherence to the Custom House which supported civil rights, or at least pretended to, was a means of opposing Warmoth's racism more effectively. He was a leader in obtaining anti-Warmoth delegates to the 1871 convention, asking "for your support and influence in behalf of the colored people. . . . An effort is being made to sell us to the Democrats by the Governor. . . . Now he seeks to force us to elect such delegates . . . as will . . . support him in this outrageous treatment of our race."[28]

Dunn's death brought a brief truce in political infighting. His funeral was reportedly one of the largest New Orleans had ever seen. Warmoth was among the pallbearers, but so were Lowell, Packard, Casey, and Kellogg. Even the conservative *Picayune* was able to speak well of the dead: "Not even the acerbity of political strife, nor the animosities so inseparable from politicians have ever changed the respectful and gentlemanly bearing which uniformly distinguished the deceased."[29]

Politically, Dunn's death was a blessing to Warmoth. If he could secure the election of some man who was not a part of the Custom House faction as lieutenant-governor, then the plans to impeach him would fall through because there would be nothing to be gained. On the other hand, he had to act quickly, because, with the office vacant, Carter, now the governor's archenemy, was next in line in the succession. But if the legislature was to be called into session to elect a suc-

---

Reconstruction, 479–80; Pitre, "Collapse of the Warmoth Regime," 169; Harris, "Henry Clay Warmoth," 624; Perkins, "Burch and Dunn in Louisiana," 327–29.

28 Oscar J. Dunn to John Sims, July 26, 1871, in New Orleans *Daily Picayune*, November 22, 1871; see also DuBois, *Black Reconstruction*, 469; Lonn, *Reconstruction in Louisiana*, 92–93.

29 New Orleans *Daily Picayune*, November 22, 1871; see also New Orleans *Republican*, November 23–24, 1871; F. B. Harris, "Henry Clay Warmoth," 624.

cessor to Dunn, then the house of representatives might bring in articles of impeachment before the senate could act to fill the vacancy left by Dunn. Under the constitution of 1868, when an official was impeached, he was suspended from office until after his trial. Thus, if the Democrats and the Custom House Republicans in the lower house cooperated, Warmoth might still find himself supplanted by an enemy.

His solution to this problem was simple but effective. On November 24, 1871, he issued a proclamation, calling the senate into session, but not the house of representatives. Thus no impeachment charges could be brought, and the senate could elect a successor to Dunn. Warmoth stated in his memoirs that he had consulted the chief justice of the Louisiana Supreme Court, the United States district attorney, Christian Roselius, and others, and that all these eminent jurists agreed that the senate alone could meet to fill the vacancy. Warmoth even considered appointing a lieutenant-governor, but apparently his legal advisers felt that this would be stretching the constitution too far. The senate therefore met in extra session, as one house, on December 6, 1871.[30]

There were protests when the senate met, but these were overruled. It was agreed that a president pro-tem must be elected first, then a lieutenant-governor. The Custom House candidate was T. V. Coupland, a white deputy collector of customs who had the support of seven Custom House Republicans, seven Democrats, and two Negroes. Warmoth had fourteen white senators on whom he could rely, leaving the balance of power in the hands of four remaining black senators. Thus, however he may have felt about it, Warmoth was almost forced to support Pinchback, Dunn's longtime rival as the leading Negro Republican in the state, as Dunn's replacement, so as to attract these black votes. Pinchback had usually supported Warmoth up to this time.

The election was extremely close. Whether an actual tie-vote was taken is uncertain, but in one way or another it became evident that a seventeen to seventeen tie was in prospect. Therefore Warmoth made a deal with an opposition senator who was a Custom House employee. This agreement, in writing, obligated the gentleman to vote as Warmoth directed in return for fifteen thousand dollars in currency and twenty thousand in state bonds. The money was to be placed in a metal box and left in charge of a bank president, Mr. Van Norden, for delivery after Pinchback had been elected and recognized by the regular session of the legislature. When this had come to pass, and the senator applied to Van Norden for his box, the banker refused to deliver it. The senator obtained possession only after going to court and only after Van Norden had several times been found guilty of contempt of court and equally as many times pardoned by Warmoth. The box, when delivered, contained no currency, no bonds, only the written agreement. Pinchback had been elected lieutenant-governor by a white vote bought but not paid for. The vote was eighteen to sixteen.[31]

Pinchback was one of ten children borne by Eliza Stewart, an emancipated slave, to her former owner, a white planter who lived first near Macon, Georgia, and then moved to Mississippi. The father sent his mulatto children north because he was afraid they might be enslaved by his heirs. Pinckney Benton Stewart Pinchback attended school in Cincinnati and then became a steward on a river steamer. In 1862 he quit this job at Yazoo City, Mississippi, and from there made his way to New Orleans. For the next five years he seems to have lived somewhat dangerously, serving for a time in the Union army and later being convicted of participation in a brawl. In 1869 he went into the factorage business with C. C. Antoine, who was to succeed him as lieutenant-governor, and the business was successful. By this time, too, he was in the state senate and making money where he could in the political arena. He founded a newspaper, the New Orleans *Louisianian*, which he sought to make into the voice of Louisiana blacks. Warmoth characterized Pinchback as "a restless, ambitious man . . . [who] had more than once arrayed himself against me.

31 New Orleans *Republican*, December 7, 1871; New Orleans *Daily Picayune*, December 7, 1871; Warmoth, *War, Politics and Reconstruction*, 119–20; F. B. Harris, "Henry Clay Warmoth," 626; Grosz, "Pinchback," 546–48, 550; Pitre, "Collapse of the Warmoth Regime," 170–71.

He was a free lance and dangerous and had to be reckoned with at all times."[32]

With Pinchback installed as lieutenant-governor, Warmoth canceled almost fifty printing contracts that Carter and Dunn had awarded. In his memoirs Warmoth refers to the money he saved the state, but it must be concluded that he cut off supporters of his opponents first, then served the state. During December, 1871, political action was fast and furious in preparation for the regular meeting of the legislature in January. The governor was threatened by an agreement between Custom House Republicans and the Democrats to sustain Speaker Carter, reject Pinchback, and carry on with their plan to impeach the chief executive. In return the Democrats were to get repeal of the Election Act and several other statutes they disliked plus a majority on seven senate committees. The dispute became more vitriolic when Warmoth let it be known that he would veto appropriations to pay certain warrants authorized by "statutes" Carter had included with acts of the previous legislature even though they had never been voted on. Warmoth had to tread warily, because he knew from his correspondents in Washington that Grant was sure to support Packard. Also, most of the Democratic papers in the state were supporting the Custom House plan; so eager were the Conservatives to defeat Warmoth that they failed to realize that his troubles came in large part from the fact that his racial attitudes were the same as those of most white Louisianians.[33]

The next regular session of the legislature was scheduled for January 1, 1872. Packard, assured of Democratic support, expected to carry articles of impeachment through the house and thus suspend Warmoth from office. He had no hope, however, of getting the two-thirds vote necessary for conviction in the senate. Therefore the strategy planned was to prevent a quorum in the senate while the governor was suspended. To make sure that a quorum would not be

32 Warmoth, *War, Politics and Reconstruction*, 120; see also New Orleans *Daily Picayune*, February 17, 1872; Grosz, "Pinchback," 527–42.

33 Warmoth, *War, Politics and Reconstruction*, 121–24; West to Warmoth, September 20, 1871, H. C. Dibble to Warmoth, September 22, 1871, in Warmoth Papers; Shreveport *Times*, December, 1871–January, 1872; New Orleans *Daily Picayune*, December 9, 23, 1871; Current, *Three Carpetbag Governors*, 50–51; F. B. Harris, "Henry Clay Warmoth," 625, 627, 635; Lonn, *Reconstruction in Louisiana*, 93, 106–107, 110–11; Grosz; "Pinchback," 548–49.

on hand, three Democratic and eleven anti-Warmoth Republican senators were embarked upon a federal revenue cutter, the *Wilderness*, and for a week disported themselves upon the Mississippi below New Orleans. Among the Republicans were two Negroes, with whom the Democrats ate and slept, cheek by jowl. After a week, the secretary of the treasury ordered the *Wilderness* to land, whereupon the senators aboard made their way to a hotel on the Mississippi Gulf Coast. During most of January, then, the battle between Warmoth and his enemies was confined to the house of representatives. The senate, without a quorum, could do nothing but adjourn from day to day.[34]

The house met first on January 1, but adjourned to the next day in tribute to Dunn. On January 2, by a vote of forty-nine to forty-five, a resolution of confidence in Speaker Carter passed. But Warmoth then busied himself, and the next day, when the minutes of January 2 were offered for approval, approval was postponed by a vote of forty-nine to forty-six. Carter then took the floor to defend himself against the charge of issuing warrants without authorization during the confused closing hours of the 1871 session. At the close of his speech, amidst great tumult and confusion, a motion was made to declare the speaker's chair vacant. Carter refused to put the motion, whereupon a number of Warmoth Republicans, led by former Speaker Mortimer Carr, moved toward the chair. Carter was prepared for this move, and a dozen or so armed men came out from behind the dais to defend the speaker. The house then adjourned, having received, according to Warmoth, assurances that Carter would step down at the next day's session. Whether or not this last assertion was correct, Carter most definitely had lost control of the house.[35]

Carter's loss of control was obvious to Packard and Casey, and probably to Carter himself. Packard asked General W. H. Emory to bring troops into the city from Jackson Barracks to preserve order. Then Warmoth, Pinchback, four state senators, and eighteen pro-Warmoth house members were put under arrest on charges of violat-

---

34 New Orleans *Daily Picayune*, January, 1872; New Orleans *Republican*, January, 1872; Warmoth, *War, Politics and Reconstruction*, 125–26; Lonn, *Reconstruction in Louisiana*, 112–13.

35 Warmoth, *War, Politics and Reconstruction*, 127–29; New Orleans *Republican*, January 4–5, New Orleans *Daily Picayune*, January 4–5, 1872; Pitre, "Collapse of the Warmoth Regime," 172; F. B. Harris, "Henry Clay Warmoth," 627–28; Lonn, *Reconstruction in Louisiana*, 113–19.

ing the laws of Louisiana and the United States. The object of this ploy was to leave the house with an anti-Warmoth majority. But the plan did not work; when Warmoth and his fellow prisoners left the State House, his supporters who were not under arrest also departed, leaving the Custom House–Democratic coalition without a quorum.

Bail for those under arrest was delayed as long as possible, but Carter had only fifty-one members, less than a quorum, when he called the house into session. To remedy this, seven Warmoth men, all of whom had served unchallenged through the 1871 session, were expelled on the grounds that they had not met the sixty-day residence requirement in the parishes from which elected. This was a weak case, because Carter himself had spent far less than sixty days in Cameron Parish. The vote on expulsion was forty-two to eight, which was a quorum if the legislature had only ninety-nine members.

This maneuver was not nearly enough to stop Warmoth. As soon as bail had been arranged for those arrested, he called a special session of the legislature for that afternoon, January 4, 1872, at 4:30 P.M. All pro-Warmoth representatives were informed of this special session. Custom House partisans were welcome to attend if they accidentally happened to learn that the session was being held. When the legislature met according to call there was still no quorum in the senate, but a bare quorum was present in the house. This was all that was necessary. The action of the morning session was reversed, and the seven pro-Warmoth representatives were reseated. Then the speaker's chair was declared vacant, and O. H. Brewster, a native of Illinois, former Union soldier, former teacher in a Freedmen's Bureau school, and representative from Madison Parish, was named speaker.[36]

Warmoth now had control of the house of representatives and occupied the State House. To make certain that he continued to hold the State House he called out both the militia and the Metropolitan Police. Carter had been defeated, but he was not ready to give up. He and the Custom House rump of the house of representatives met in a hall over the Gem Saloon on Royal Street. General Emory's

---

36 New Orleans *Daily Picayune*, January 5, March 27, 1872; New Orleans *Republican*, January 4–10, 1872; Warmoth, *War, Politics and Reconstruction*, 130–32; F. B. Harris, "Henry Clay Warmoth," 628–30; Grosz, "Pinchback," 549–50; Dufour, "The Age of Warmoth," 354; Pitre, "Collapse of the Warmoth Regime," 173.

United States troops remained on hand, but the general was careful to confine their efforts to preserving order, not favoring either faction in the dispute. As a result, there was little violence. A mob of Warmoth opponents broke into the United States Arsenal on the night of January 7 and seized a number of weapons, but these arms were never used. The Democratic Executive Committee of Orleans Parish called a meeting in Lafayette Square for the night of January 8, and many violent words were spoken. None of these was translated into action. Most of the effort expended was by the sergeants-at-arms of the two legislatures, each of whom sought to arrest members of the opposing body and force their attendance where they did not want to go. One tragedy occurred when Walter R. Wheyland of Sabine Parish, a Warmoth supporter, was shot to death while resisting arrest by Carterite officials. Overall, from January 5 through January 10, the Warmoth legislature was slowly but surely gaining ascendancy.[37] The murder of Wheyland gave Warmoth a reason for breaking up the meetings over the Gem Saloon. Carter and three of his followers were accused of murder and a force of three hundred Metropolitan Police went to the Gem to make the arrests. They did not find Carter, who was cleared of all charges when he appeared in court on January 12, but the Gem was no longer used as a meeting place. Carter and about twenty others met elsewhere, including the Custom House, for ten or twelve more days.[38]

Carter now was at wit's end. Three times he organized forces with which to take over the State House by force. Three times General Emory, whose performance during this trying period was superb, made it clear that he could permit no violence by either side. The Conservative newspapers, although they dutifully denounced Warmoth, nonetheless give the impression that people in general were disgusted with Carter. Also, businessmen were surely growing weary

37 W. H. Emory to E. D. Townsend, January 8, 10, 1872, in *House Executive Documents*, 42nd Cong., 2nd Sess., No. 209, pp. 6–7; Francis J. Herron to Warmoth, February 10, 1872, in Warmoth Papers; New Orleans *Daily Picayune*, January 6–10, 1872; Lonn, *Reconstruction in Louisiana*, 121–28; Warmoth, *War, Politics and Reconstruction*, 131–35; F. B. Harris, "Henry Clay Warmoth," 630–31; Kendall, *History of New Orleans*, I, 343; Grosz, "Pinchback," 549–50.

38 New Orleans *Daily Picayune*, January 9–12, 1872; New Orleans *Republican*, January 8–12, 1872; Lonn, *Reconstruction in Louisiana*, 125–26.

of the continuing tumult. One planter wrote home from the city as early as January 11 that "The political excitement is giving way slowly to the pressure brought against it by the moneyed men of the city."[39] As the days passed it became clear that Warmoth had solid support from the Republican leaders in the country parishes. Carter finally overplayed his hand when he distributed leaflets calling on the blacks of New Orleans to arm themselves and rid the state of Warmoth.

Members of the Carter house had already begun to slip over to the Mechanics' Institute to join Warmoth, and on January 24 the remainder went over and demanded their seats. They were gravely informed that they were excluded from the floor because only members were allowed there. Each one's case was discussed separately as they waited in the lobby, but eventually all were seated except two white men and one Negro. The Negro was J. Henri Burch, who could be classified as a Carpetbagger. After the war he moved from his home in New England to Louisiana and became a leader among the blacks of East Baton Rouge Parish. He was later to marry Dunn's widow. His expulsion in 1872 did not put an end to his political career in Louisiana.[40]

In the meantime, Warmoth had achieved a quorum in the senate. Senator T. C. Anderson had appeared on January 8, giving the governor's senate exactly half the elected membership. Warmoth then learned that the Democratic senator from Bossier Parish, one Thomas, was en route from his home to join the other exiles at Bay St. Louis, Mississippi. Promising immunity from arrest, Warmoth arranged a conference in which he relied on two Conservatives, Dr. Newton Mercer and former Confederate General Richard Taylor, to persuade Senator Thomas that it was his duty to take his seat in the Warmoth senate. Also, Warmoth apparently promised to see to the repeal of the Election Act which the Democrats found so distasteful. Senator Thomas made a quorum, so now both houses of the legislature could proceed to business. On January 20, the holdouts from Bay St. Louis arrived and took their seats. They tried to oust Pinchback as lieuten-

---

39 L. A. Bringier to Stella Bringier, January 11, 1872, in Bringier Family Papers.
40 *House Reports*, 42nd Cong., 2nd Sess., No. 92, p. 7; New Orleans *Daily Picayune*, January 12–14, February 17–18, 1872.

ant-governor, but the vote was a tie and Pinchback's casting vote defeated the motion.[41]

Before the Mississippi exiles returned, bills repealing the Election Law, the Registration Law, and the Constabulary Law were rushed through both houses. Despite his apparent promises to the Democrats, Warmoth did not sign them. He said that he had concluded that the senate at the time of their passage did not have a legal quorum after all. Eventually new registration laws and election laws were enacted, but they were not what the Democrats wanted. The new election statute, which Warmoth did not immediately sign, provided that the Returning Board should be named by the senate. This was to be of great importance following the election of 1872.[42] One interesting postlude to these events was that Carter and General A. S. Badger of the Metropolitan Police went across the border into Mississippi to fight a duel, with rifles, at sixty paces. Both emerged unscathed. The *Picayune*, perhaps disappointed, suggested that neither "of them could hit a barn unless they were to go inside and shut the door."[43]

4

Before the end of 1871, the people of Louisiana had begun to discuss the election of 1872. One reason was the real need for reform; notorious scandals existed both in Louisiana and in the nation. Another factor was the schism in the Republican party, locally and nationally. With the Republicans divided, the possibility of a Democratic victory in 1872 seemed very real. At first it was assumed that Warmoth would be the Radical candidate for governor; he was denounced from all sides as various groups sought to unite the opposition to his government.

The Reform party was the first to make a formal appearance upon the scene. It had its beginning, seemingly, in the New Orleans German colony in November, 1871. On December 1, 1871, a committee of fifty-one people met to consider the condition of the city. Christian Roselius was one of the speakers, and I. N. Marks was the leading

---

41 New Orleans *Daily Picayune*, January 8–20, 1872; Warmoth, *War, Politics and Reconstruction*, 140–41; Lonn, *Reconstruction in Louisiana*, 132–33.
42 New Orleans *Daily Picayune*, February, 1872; F. B. Harris, "Henry Clay Warmoth," 633; Lonn, *Reconstruction in Louisiana*, 132–33.
43 New Orleans *Daily Picayune*, February 20, 1872.

spirit of the meeting. In the main, the Reform party members seem to have been men of substance, many, if not most, being former Whigs who did not want to have to choose between Carpetbag Republicans on the one hand and John Slidell Democrats on the other. After the legislative session of 1872 had demonstrated its incapacity, the Committee of Fifty-one called a mass meeting which in turn called for a convention of the people of the whole state to meet in New Orleans for the purpose of adopting a platform and nominating candidates. The Reformers were careful to do nothing which might antagonize black voters, and their speakers made it clear that the party recognized fully the rights of blacks under the Reconstruction amendments and the Louisiana Constitution of 1868. It is difficult to determine how much support the Reform party had outside of New Orleans. The *Picayune* thought it rather extensive, but the Shreveport *Times* said that the *Picayune* lied. In northern Louisiana there certainly was much opposition to the Reform party's racial policy.[44]

On the national scene early in 1872 those Republicans repelled by the corruption of the Grant administration and by Grant's imperialistic foreign policy formed the Liberal Republican party and called for a nominating convention to meet at Cincinnati in May. This gave Warmoth somewhere to go, because he was *persona non grata* with the Grant wing of the Republican party in Louisiana at the same time that the conservative press was attacking him more severely than ever before. The German faction of the Reform party quickly went over to the Liberal Republicans, but it was careful to keep itself separate from Warmoth. The young governor went north to look over the situation, then returned to Louisiana to urge the establishment of a Liberal Republican movement there.[45]

In May Warmoth led a delegation of one hundred people, about

---

44 *Ibid.*, December 2, 17, 1871, February 18, March 12, 18, April 7, 1872; Shreveport *Times*, March 27, 31, April 6, 14, 1872; John Edmond Gonzales, "William Pitt Kellogg: Reconstruction Governor of Louisiana, 1873–1877," *Louisiana Historical Quarterly*, XXIX (April, 1946), 398; F. B. Harris, "Henry Clay Warmoth," 638; Kendall, *History of New Orleans*, I, 344–50; Clark, "Reconstruction and the New Orleans German Colony," 516.

45 Warmoth, *War, Politics and Reconstruction*, 161; Lonn, *Reconstruction in Louisiana*, 142–43; Nau, *The German People of New Orleans*, 43–47; R. T. Clark, Jr., "Reconstruction and the New Orleans German Colony," 508, 517–18; F. B. Harris, "Henry Clay Warmoth," 635.

twenty of them black, to the Liberal Republican convention. Eight were German delegates who did not consider themselves part of the Warmoth group. Warmoth supported Lyman Trumbull for the nomination, but he seems to have had no difficulty in accepting Horace Greeley. This was not true of other conservative residents of Louisiana, many of whom recalled Greeley's abolitionist background. The *Picayune* did remember in Greeley's favor that he had advocated the release of Jefferson Davis from prison.

The Liberal Republican movement gave the voters of Louisiana another choice besides the corruption of the old Slidell machine on the one hand and the equally corrupt Casey-Packard-Kellogg ring on the other. Warmoth's presence in the Liberal Republican ranks prevented a clear-cut choice between darkness and light, however. Among prominent Louisianians who came out in favor of Greeley were the former Confederate general D. B. Penn, Major E. A. Burke of New Orleans, later to be the prince of Bourbon thieves, Major Andrew Hero of New Orleans, T. C. Manning of Rapides, W. W. Pugh of Assumption, Warmoth's friend Effingham Lawrence of Plaquemines, Thomas J. Foster of St. Mary, George A. Sheridan, Chief Justice Ludeling, John Lynch, Francis J. Herron, and General Longstreet. The last four had been strong Radicals. It presumably was obvious to Warmoth and these other leaders that the Liberal Republican party could not carry the state alone. However, with Warmoth in control of the electoral machinery, if it could join forces with the Campbell-Pinchback wing of the Republican party on the one hand, or with the Democrats on the other, the prospects of victory were bright.[46]

As implied, those Republicans who did not follow Warmoth were far from united. The Custom House group was strongly pro-Grant and, probably more important, had the support of the national administration. The other faction, as indicated, was led by Pinchback and General Hugh J. Campbell. Pinchback had told Warmoth that

46 New Orleans *Daily Picayune*, May 1, 1872; Warmoth, *War, Politics and Reconstruction*, 164–65, 186, 200; Lowrey, "James Madison Wells," 1,092; F. B. Harris, "Henry Clay Warmoth," 635; Clark, "Reconstruction and the New Orleans German Colony," 518; Matthew T. Downey, "Horace Greeley and the Politicians: The Liberal Republican Convention in 1872," *Journal of Southern History*, XXXIII (March, 1967), 731–32.

he would support the Liberal Republicans only if Charles Sumner were that party's nominee. Greeley's nomination left Pinchback in the unenviable position of supporting Grant but opposing the Grant organization in Louisiana. Even so, Pinchback could not be ignored. He was the nearest thing to a recognized leader of Louisiana Negroes. It was a convention of Custom House Republicans, however, which selected Louisiana's delegates to the Philadelphia convention that was to nominate Grant for a second term.[47]

The Louisiana Democratic party was in a quandary in the spring of 1872. Most of its oral and written ammunition had been fired at Warmoth; then, suddenly, with the break between Grant and the Liberal Republicans and Warmoth's seizure of control of the Liberal Republican movement in Louisiana, the young ogre at the governor's desk had become a possible ally against the Grant ticket. In early 1872 this was too much to swallow, but when the national Democratic convention endorsed Greeley, the pressure for accommodation increased. It was the old Slidell Democrats of New Orleans who were most opposed to any compromise. A Democratic convention met in April and adopted a resolution condemning Warmoth, then it adjourned without making nominations because of the probability of an alliance with him. A fusion of the Democratic and Liberal Republican tickets was really essential; if both parties participated in the election separately, a Grant–Custom House victory in Louisiana would be assured. But already the Democrats, or many of them, were earning the name Bourbon, because they had learned nothing and forgotten nothing. Although always hopeful, they could expect very few black votes. Their national leaders were so bitterly anti-Negro that there was not a single black delegate or spectator at the national Democratic convention.[48]

In early 1872 the Shreveport *Times* commented, "It is repugnant to the fitness of things that such a reptile as Warmoth should longer . . . curse the people of Louisiana. It is arraigning the wisdom of God . . .

---

47 New Orleans *Daily Picayune*, May 1–2, 23, 1872; New Orleans *Republican*, May 1, 1872; Warmoth, *War, Politics and Reconstruction*, 178–79; Lonn, *Reconstruction in Louisiana*, 144–49; Harris, "Henry Clay Warmoth," 637; Grosz, "Pinchback," 551–52.

48 New Orleans *Daily Picayune*, April, July 4, 10, 1872; Warmoth, *War, Politics and Reconstruction*, 166–74; Stampp, *The Era of Reconstruction*, 194–95; Lonn, *Reconstruction in Louisiana*, 141–42, 159–60; Harris, "Henry Clay Warmoth," 635.

to believe that he will permit it."[49] By midsummer of that same year Warmoth was earning praise, however reluctant, from Democrats all over the state for his efforts to defeat the regular Republican nominees. But this was characteristic of the 1872 political campaign in Louisiana which in complexity of shifting alliances might be compared to the Italian peninsula during the Renaissance or China during the 1920s and 1930s. Postelection events were not greatly different.

The so-called Pinchback Republicans met in convention in New Orleans in late May of 1872. Led by Pinchback and Campbell, this group may have represented a majority of Louisiana Republicans. Basically it was loyal to Grant but opposed to the Custom House. Pinchback expressed some sympathy for the Liberal Republicans, but he recognized the delicate situation of Louisiana blacks: "As a race [we] are between the hawk of Republican demagogism and the buzzards of Democratic prejudices. The aspirants for position in our party threaten us with excommunication if we do not follow every jack o'lantern who raised his feeble light, and the Democrats invite us to annihilation if we turn away from those Republican jack o'lanterns."[50] The convention declared itself in favor of reconciling the discordant elements of the party, something Pinchback had been trying to do for months. When the time came for nominations, the delegates chose Warmoth for governor and Pinchback for lieutenant-governor. However, and significantly, the convention adjourned only until June 19, when it was to reconvene at Baton Rouge at the same time the Custom House convention was meeting there. This made it fairly obvious that Pinchback and Campbell hoped to effect some sort of compromise with the Custom House; as a result Warmoth rejected the nomination. The governor may have been influenced by the fact that, in May, nearly all the state's newspapers were supporting Greeley. Warmoth certainly wished to do nothing which might contribute to Grant's success.[51]

What to do about Warmoth was the chief problem facing the

49 Shreveport *Times*, January 12, 1872.
50 Quoted in Elsie M. Lewis, "The Political Mind of the Negro, 1865–1900," *Journal of Southern History*, XXI (May, 1955), 197.
51 P. B. S. Pinchback to J. R. West, March 20, 1872, in Warmoth Papers; New Orleans *Republican*, May 24, 1872; New Orleans *Daily Picayune*, May 15, 29–31, 1872; Grosz, "Pinchback," 552–54; Pitre, "Collapse of the Warmoth Regime," 174–75.

Democrats of Louisiana as they met in convention at New Orleans on June 3, 1872.[52] The convention, it developed, was dominated by the New Orleans delegates, so much so that some of the country representatives went home in disgust. Galleries packed with partisans of the Orleans Parish "Last Ditch" Democrats made it difficult for the opposition even to be heard. After six days and nights of wrangling, John McEnery of Ouachita Parish was nominated for governor, Daniel Dennett of St. Mary Parish for auditor, with all others on the ticket being from Orleans Parish. McEnery, especially, seems to have been forced upon the delegates. Many country papers were definitely unhappy, maintaining that the Bourbons had attempted to make all anti-Radicals into the tail of the Orleans kite.[53]

The Reform party convention met in New Orleans on June 5. The intention of the party's leaders, obviously, was to effect some sort of compromise alliance with the Democrats. The Democrats, however, were not particularly interested, apparently believing that the Reformers would vote the Democratic ticket because they had no other choice. Some earlier Reform meetings, in fact, had been broken up by Democratic hoodlums. Even so, a committee of eleven men from each convention was appointed to reach agreement on a joint ticket, and this committee suggested George Williamson as the gubernatorial candidate. The Democrats rejected the committee's recommendation and insisted on McEnery for governor. They did consent to sacrifice Dennett, but otherwise the Reformers got nothing. The Reform convention then proceeded to nominate Williamson for governor but to name Democratic candidates for lesser offices. Finally the Democratic leaders dropped their candidates for two lesser offices and accepted Reform nominees, both of whom happened to be Democrats. By July 18, the Democratic and Reform parties had been united at the state level.[54]

52 Warmoth Papers, April–May, 1872; Clinton *Patriot*, May 10, 1872, quoted in New Orleans *Daily Picayune*, May 17, 1872; New Orleans *Daily Picayune*, May, 1872.
53 Shreveport *Times*, June 13, 1872; J. E. Scott to Warmoth, June 15, 1872, in Warmoth Papers; New Orleans *Daily Picayune*, May 3, June 4–8, 16, 25, 1872; Lonn, *Reconstruction in Louisiana*, 143–44.
54 New Orleans *Daily Picayune*, March 26, June 5, 9, 18, 1872; Shreveport *Times*, August 8, 1872; Lonn, *Reconstruction in Louisiana*, 152–54; F. B. Harris, "Henry Clay Warmoth," 634.

The two factions of the Republican party met at Baton Rouge on June 19. A few days earlier, Warmoth had announced that he would not accept the Republican nomination for governor and that he no longer considered himself a member of that party. This was apparently sincere, because messages from the convention practically guaranteed him the nomination if he would come to Baton Rouge. Hugh J. Campbell telegraphed him on the second day: "The convention will nominate you and Pinchback if you will accept [and] ignore national questions."[55] This was the first of numerous messages to the same effect. Packard's inability to keep order among the delegates seems to have added to Warmoth's strength. The governor made no favorable response to any of these overtures. Probably he believed that the Custom House faction would put up candidates in any case, which would make a Democratic victory certain. Warmoth was well informed, because he was receiving copies of some of the correspondence between Packard and Kellogg. Packard had his way. Kellogg was nominated for governor, and C. C. Antoine, a Negro from Caddo Parish, for lieutenant-governor. The Pinchback convention rejected this ticket and adjourned once more, this time until August.[56]

The Liberal Republican state convention met on August 5. Warmoth was the unquestioned leader of this party, because of his control of the electoral machinery if for no other reason. He was still extremely unpopular, however; to many white Louisianians he represented the essence of Carpetbag government at its worst. In June, in fact, the insurance on his house in New Orleans had been canceled because it was subject to "extraordinary hazards." Under the constitutional amendment of 1870 he was eligible to succeed himself as governor, and he had some personal support. One backer wrote him: "I know there has been and is [sic] bad men in office. I am somewhat acquainted with the morals of this state, and I know you would have to go beyond the limits of this state to find enough honest men for

55 Campbell to Warmoth, June 20, 1872, in Warmoth Papers.
56 Kellogg to Packard, December 7, 1871, P. B. Darrell to L. E. Bentley, April 28, 1872, J. W. Fairfax to Warmoth, June 20, 21, 1872, Harris to Warmoth, June 20, 1872, all in Warmoth Papers; New Orleans *Daily Picayune*, May 25, June 15, 1872; Baton Rouge *Weekly Advocate*, June 15, 1872; Shreveport *Times*, June 23, 30, 1872; New Orleans *Times*, June 20, 1872, quoted in Gonzales, "William Pitt Kellogg," 401; Lonn, *Reconstruction in Louisiana*, 150, 154–56.

your appointees."[57] A letter from the hamlet of Greensburg presented the dilemma, probably unconsciously. "All the white Republicans here are with you. And all the Blacks are against you except a few that have got good sense which I have under my controll. I controll them [because] I tell them that Pinchback is with you and that he is the smartest Black man in the state."[58]

The crucial point, of course, was that Pinchback was not with Warmoth. Also, Warmoth was realist enough to know that Louisiana freedmen would almost certainly vote the regular Republican ticket no matter what he might do. Therefore, if the Liberal Republicans were going to win, they had to have white support, and this meant coming to terms with the Democrats. And if Warmoth were on the ticket, no accommodation with the Democrats would be possible. Senator West, who believed in June that Greeley would defeat Grant, advised the governor to put together as strong a Liberal Republican ticket as possible, but not to be a candidate himself. Warmoth took this advice; he wrote to his personal friend, Effingham Lawrence, that he would not accept any nomination. He said the same thing before the convention in a speech which was enthusiastically received, promising also to do everything within his power to bring success to the new party. Already the Liberals were conferring with the Democrats, and in the letter to Lawrence, Warmoth said: "If you can induce the . . . Conference Committee to accept Colonel D. B. Penn as the fusion candidate for Governor and can put . . . Pinchback on the ticket as our candidate for Congressman-at-large, we will carry the state by a 30,000 majority. Governor Pinchback tells me he will accept this nomination."[59]

At the moment neither the Pinchback Republicans nor the Democrats were prepared to make significant concessions, so the Liberal convention proceeded to nominate Penn for governor; John S. Young of Claiborne Parish for lieutenant-governor; Francis E. Dumas of Orleans, the Negro who had been Warmoth's rival for the Republican

57 A. Coates to Warmoth, July 14, 1872, in Warmoth Papers.
58 W. D. Floyd to Warmoth, June 11, 1872, in Warmoth Papers; see also Sam P. B. Blyden to E. E. Morgan, June 24, 1872, in Warmoth Papers; New Orleans *Republican*, August 6–11, 1872.
59 Warmoth to Effingham Lawrence, August 6, 1872, in Warmoth, *War, Politics and Reconstruction*, 186–87.

nomination in 1868, for secretary of state; James Graham of Orleans Parish as auditor; W. F. Kernan of East Feliciana for attorney general; J. W. McDonald of Webster for superintendent of education; and George A. Sheridan for congressman-at-large. It is significant that Pinchback was not nominated.[60]

Among those already committed to McEnery, there was much resentment of the Liberal ticket. A Warmoth-favoring tax assessor, Henry Heideshain, was stabbed as the culmination of a political argument with a Democratic attorney in a saloon on Bienville Street.[61] After Penn's nomination, the *Picayune* said he was "the alter ego, the catspaw and tool of Governor Warmoth. If he does not know it now, he will soon."[62] But support for Penn began to manifest itself all over the state. One doubtless overenthusiastic supporter assured Warmoth that the Democrats did not have a single partisan in Natchitoches Parish. Another wrote, "Your wise choice is to go for Horace Greeley . . . and let the Grant officeholders go to hell."[63] Penn's support outside New Orleans was obviously greater than the Democrats had expected. The Baton Rouge *Weekly Advocate*, the Opelousas *Journal*, and the Shreveport *Times*, among other country papers, preferred Penn to McEnery. Then, on August 9, the Pinchback Republicans met for the third time. Negotiations effected a union with the Custom House faction with Kellogg and Antoine remaining at the head of the ticket. Pinchback was nominated for congressman-at-large, and two of his followers, P. G. Deslondes and William G. Brown, both black, were nominated for secretary of state and superintendent of education, respectively.[64]

Thus by mid-August the five parties of the spring had been reduced to three. With the Pinchback and Custom House Republicans now united, and because the Liberal Republican movement was unexpectedly strong, the Democrats became more amenable to compromise. On either August 27 or 28, a joint Democratic–Reform–Liberal

60 *Ibid.*, 180–96; West to Warmoth, June 16, July 3, 1872, in Warmoth Papers; New Orleans *Republican*, August 6–11, 1872.
61 New Orleans *Daily Picayune*, August 7, 1872.
62 *Ibid.*, August 11, 1872.
63 L. M. Grears to Warmoth, August 13, 1872, in Warmoth Papers.
64 Baton Rouge *Weekly Advocate*, August 17, 24, 1872; Shreveport *Times*, August 15, 1872; Lonn, *Reconstruction in Louisiana*, 142–43, 156–58, 162–64.

Republican slate was agreed upon. McEnery remained the gubernatorial candidate, but Penn went on the ticket for lieutenant-governor, Graham for auditor, and Sheridan for congressman-at-large. A Negro, Samuel Armistead of Caddo Parish, was named candidate for secretary of state. The only three original Democratic nominees who remained in contention were McEnery, H. N. Ogden for attorney general, and R. M. Lusher for superintendent of education.[65]

Warmoth showed good political judgment in urging that Penn rather than McEnery head the joint ticket. Anti-Custom House or anti-Grant Republicans found it almost impossible to support a last-ditch Bourbon Democrat, especially McEnery. Such men as Longstreet, Wells, Chief Justice Ludeling, and John Lynch, all of whom had been Liberals, went over to Kellogg.[66] The New Orleans *Republican*, which owed Warmoth money, nonetheless announced that it could not support McEnery: "We regard the McEnery ticket as representing the negro-hating, schoolhouse burning, fire-eating Bourbonists. . . . Good these last ditchers cannot learn, and bad they will not forget."[67]

Naturally Warmoth was assailed by the Custom House Republicans, but old friends also expressed their disappointment. One wrote: "I can scarcely believe that *you* would consent to an arrangement which does not preclude . . . a renewed Bourbon domination and secure the objects for which we were striving."[68] Pinchback, writing from Boston where he was campaigning for Grant, said:

Political preferment can only be obtained in Louisiana by the votes of the colored people therefore you should act as not to forfeit their confidence and support. You may entertain the idea that the white people of Louisiana are willing to accord you perfect political equality, but take my word for it, just as soon as your power is gone they will have nothing to do with you politically or otherwise. All you have politically you owe to the Republican

65 New Orleans *Daily Picayune*, August 28–30, 1872; Warmoth, *War, Politics and Reconstruction*, 197–99.
66 Dudley Avery to D. D. Avery, July 22, 1872, Minnie Avery to Mrs. D. D. Avery, August 16, 1872, Dudley Avery to D. D. Avery, September 13, 1872, all in Avery Family Papers; Warmoth, *War, Politics and Reconstruction*, 199–200; Lowrey, "James Madison Wells," 1,092; Baton Rouge *Weekly Advocate*, August 24, 1872.
67 New Orleans *Republican*, July 26, 1872.
68 Durant DaPonte to Warmoth, September 6, 1872, in Warmoth Papers.

party and especially the colored people of Louisiana and I hope and trust that a sense of the obligation will prevent you from putting their enemies in power merely to get your revenge upon Packard, Casey, Kellogg, and company.[69]

Warmoth had, of course, made his decision to use the power of his office to support the Fusion ticket, and these powers were formidable. In the event, they probably secured for McEnery a majority of the votes cast, but McEnery was never to be governor of Louisiana. As for Warmoth's motives, revenge against Grant and the Custom House was certainly a factor. However, if his memoirs, written in his old age, are to be believed, he was also fearful of the "Africanization" of Louisiana.

The Fusionists could not use in 1872 the tactics which the Democrats had used so successfully in 1868. Since then the Fifteenth Amendment to the Constitution had made the Enforcement Acts of 1870 and 1871 possible. These empowered the president to use the armed forces to enforce the Fifteenth Amendment and to suspend habeas corpus if necessary. Furthermore, all cases concerning suffrage under the Fifteenth Amendment were to be tried in federal courts. In a few years it would be demonstrated that these acts could not accomplish the ends for which they had been enacted, but this was not so apparent in 1872. Thus it was necessary to devise more subtle forms of fraud and intimidation than had been used four years earlier.[70]

The campaign, for Louisiana, was relatively moderate. Kellogg denounced the Fusion ticket as an attempt to restore the Slidell Bourbons to power. The *Picayune* accused Kellogg of stealing enough money to make himself rich since coming to Louisiana. The country papers carried some threats against Negroes who might vote Republican, but there was little of the armed intimidation of early years. In New Orleans the union between Democrats and Reformers proved weak. The hardest-fought battle in the city election was between

69 Pinchback to Warmoth, September 11, 1872, in Warmoth Papers.
70 Swinney, "Enforcing the Fifteenth Amendment," 202–18; Woodward, "Seeds of Failure in Radical Race Policy," 1–9; Ficklen, *History of Reconstruction in Louisiana,* 221; Dunning, *Reconstruction, Political and Economic,* 186–87, 203–204.

E. A. Burke and General Beauregard for head of the Department of Public Works.[71]

One amusing event of the campaign took place in September. The legislature of 1872, it will be remembered, had passed a new election law, but had then adjourned within five days; under the constitution of 1868 the governor had until the next meeting of the legislature, January 1, 1873, to sign or veto. The act was regarded as giving the governor less power over the state electoral machinery. Pinchback had been campaigning for Grant in the North, and he and Warmoth met on the street when Warmoth went to New York on business. Pinchback accepted an invitation to visit the governor at his hotel that evening. When this engagement was not kept, Warmoth realized that the lieutenant-governor was probably on his way to Louisiana to sign the election bill as acting governor, which he could do with Warmoth out of the state. Major Burke was at that time a railroad official. Warmoth sent a telegram to Burke, who then arranged to have Pinchback called off his train for a "message" at Canton, Mississippi. He was left standing on the platform. After spending the night at the station, he caught the next southbound train at 10:00 the next morning and was welcomed aboard by Warmoth. They rode together to New Orleans.[72]

No political campaign in nineteenth-century Louisiana could be completely without violence. Indeed, few issues of New Orleans newspapers between elections failed to carry accounts of one or more homicides in or out of the city. This was an era when many men preferred to settle their own difficulties with knife, pistol, or shotgun rather than depend upon the law. Law enforcement left much to be desired; white killers of white men were seldom convicted, white killers of Negroes almost never. The legislature in 1870 felt it necessary to authorize the governor to issue warrants for the arrest of persons accused of crimes punishable by death or imprisonment if the appropriate parish officials had failed, or had been unable, to make the arrest. With

---

71 New Orleans *Daily Picayune*, September–November 2, 1872; Baton Rouge *Weekly Advocate*, June 8, 1872; Lonn, *Reconstruction in Louisiana*, 166–67; T. K. Fauntleroy to Warmoth, September 27, 1872, in Warmoth Papers; Gonzales, "William Pitt Kellogg," 408.

72 Warmoth, *War, Politics ad Reconstruction*, 201–202; DaPonte to Warmoth, September 27, 1872, in Warmoth Papers; F. B. Harris, "Henry Clay Warmoth," 640.

violence a commonplace between elections, it certainly could not be completely avoided during a campaign.[73]

One incident was an all-Republican shooting and stabbing brawl at a Grant-Wilson rally in New Orleans in August. According to the *Picayune*, it was caused by Negro dislike of Carpetbaggers. In Grant Parish about three hundred Negroes were forced to vote the Fusion ticket, almost at gun point. In Jackson Parish, after the vote for federal offices had been counted, the United States supervisors who were on hand under the provisions of the Enforcement Acts were compelled to flee the polls by shots accurate enough to wound two of them. On the other side, the registrar of Terrebonne Parish, a Warmoth man, claimed to have been terrorized by a mob of drunken Negroes urged on by Republican officeholders. But compared to 1868, or 1878, the election of 1872 was not violent.[74]

If violence played a small part, fraud and trickery played a large one. The registrars in the parishes were Warmoth appointees. Some of them went over to the regular Republicans, but most of them remained loyal to the governor. The anti-Kellogg people realized early that only by taking advantage of Warmoth's control of the election machinery could the Republicans be defeated, and full advantage was taken.[75]

One tactic of the Fusionists was to reduce the number of polling places in strongly Republican parishes and to locate those remaining in places as inconvenient as possible for black voters. For example, in Natchitoches Parish there were normally twelve polling places, but in 1872 there were only four. One of the four was on an island and could be reached only by boat. In the town of Natchitoches, where the voters were mainly white, the polling place was easily available. Even before the election, Warmoth's registrars had registered as many Fusionists as possible and as few Negroes as possible. This was accom-

73 Reports of Coroners' Inquests, in *Legislative Documents, Louisiana, 1870*; *Acts of Louisiana Extra Session 1870*, 94–96; Baton Rouge *Weekly Advocate*, September 10, 1870; Franklin, *Reconstruction After the Civil War*, 161–63; *House Executive Documents*, 41st Cong., 2nd Sess., No. 142, p. 14.

74 *Senate Reports*, 42nd Cong., 3rd Sess., No. 457, pp. 1,044–45; New Orleans *Daily Picayune*, August 2, 1872; Lonn, *Reconstruction in Louisiana*, 171; Allie Bayne Windham, "Methods and Mechanisms Used to Restore White Supremacy in Louisiana, 1872–1876" (M.A. thesis, Louisiana State University, 1948), 21, 38–39.

75 New Orleans *Daily Picayune*, July 20, 1872; Warmoth Papers, October, 1872.

plished by opening the books at odd hours, then closing them as soon as the blacks became aware that they were open. Another tactic was to register whites rapidly but to require time-consuming oaths from blacks. In mainly black Rapides Parish the registrar insisted on alternating whites and blacks, then closed his books when no more whites sought to register.

On election day some commissioners prevented Negro voting by sending would-be black voters to another poll or by rejecting them because they appeared to be under age. United States supervisors were expected to prevent such tactics, but normally they were not familiar with the local area, and the commissioners were. In heavily Republican districts such as Bossier Parish, the vote was delayed as much as possible; only 415 votes were cast in twelve hours, and polls closed with 300 Republicans still in line. In West Baton Rouge Parish, T. T. Allain, the Negro United States supervisor, cooperated with the Fusionist commissioners and gave illiterate freedmen Democratic rather than Republican ballots. In some other parishes Democratic ballots were deliberately printed so as to resemble Republican ballots, with the same result.

Nor were the Fusionists above simple stuffing of ballot boxes. In East Baton Rouge Parish one box containing the votes cast was discarded, and an already-prepared box, filled with Democratic ballots, was substituted. In many other instances the commissioners, after the ballots for federal office were counted, excluded the United States commissioners and reported whatever state vote they chose. In New Orleans, which had had scores of years of practice in electoral trickery, minors voted without registration papers, and repeating was common. One man was caught after voting seventeen times. Finally, according to Republican charges which apparently were well founded, the Fusionists engaged in deliberate and unconcealed fraud in a number of sure Republican parishes, especially Iberville, Iberia, St. James, St. Martin, and Terrebonne, with the intention of getting the entire vote thrown out. This election was as notable an example of fraudulent election practices on a statewide basis as is likely to be found before the introduction of the Australian ballot.[76]

76 *Senate Reports*, 42nd Cong., 3rd Sess., No. 457, contains hundreds of pages of testimony concerning this election. Windham, "White Supremacy in Louisiana,"

5

The election of 1872 was so shot through with fraud that no one ever had any idea who had actually won. There is no question that the vote, as reported, elected the Fusionist ticket, but it is impossible to determine how closely the vote reported corresponded with the vote cast. Certainly fewer Fusionist votes were cast than were reported. On the other hand, since some white Republicans had followed Warmoth into the Fusionist party, since the disfranchising provisions of the constitution of 1868 had been repealed, and since at least a few blacks voted the Fusion ticket, the actual vote may well have favored McEnery. But it is equally possible that a majority of the votes were for Kellogg. The election was dishonest, the count was dishonest, and there was no honest way in which the result could be decided. A committee of the national House of Representatives, in ruling on the contest between Pinchback and Sheridan for representative-at-large for Louisiana, concluded that neither contestant could establish a valid claim.[77]

If the campaign and election of 1872 in Louisiana smelled of fraud, the events from election day, November 4, to the end of the year reeked of it.[78] Under the election law of 1870, the governor; the lieutenant-governor; the secretary of state, John Lynch; and T. C. Anderson made up the Returning Board. Under the same law, however, Pinchback and Anderson were ineligible to serve because they had been candidates for office in the election. Earlier Warmoth had removed Secretary of State Bovee from office and replaced him with

---

1–46, is an excellent description based largely on the above. See also Lonn, *Reconstruction in Louisiana,* 167–79; New Orleans *Daily Picayune,* November 13, 1872; New Orleans *Republican,* November 8–17, 1872.

77 *House Miscellaneous Documents,* 45th Cong., 2nd Sess., No. 52, pp. 196–233; Warmoth Papers, November, 1872; Windham, "White Supremacy in Louisiana," 2–3; Kendall, *History of New Orleans,* I, 346–48; *Senate Reports,* 42nd Cong., 3rd Sess., No. 457, *passim;* Dunning, *Reconstruction, Political and Economic,* 200; Lonn, *Reconstruction in Louisiana,* 180; Burgess, *Reconstruction and the Constitution,* 269–72.

78 The account of the Returning Board battle which follows is derived primarily from the following sources: New Orleans *Daily Picayune,* November–December, 1872; New Orleans *Republican,* November 21–December 30, 1872; *House Executive Documents,* 42nd Cong., 3rd Sess., No. 457, *passim;* Warmoth, *War, Politics and Reconstruction,* 203–20; Pitre, "Collapse of the Warmoth Regime," 178–87; Lonn, *Reconstruction in Louisiana,* 181–205.

Francis J. Herron. Thus Warmoth, Lynch, and Herron presumably made up a majority of the board, could fill the two vacancies, and could canvass the returns.

Nationally, Grant had been overwhelmingly reelected. If the Louisiana Republicans could somehow manipulate the returns, they could anticipate support from Washington. Warmoth was approached by his old comrades; according to his memoirs he was offered the United States senatorship being vacated by Kellogg if he would cooperate.[79] As might be expected, since the Republicans had returned to power nationally, many men who had supported Greeley and McEnery now went over to the Kellogg camp. Herron, as Warmoth discovered, was now a Kellogg man.

In the meantime, from many parts of the state, United States Marshal Packard and other Kellogg supporters were gathering affidavits from black, and some white, Republicans stating that they had been prevented from voting by intimidation, fraud, or force. Thousands of these affidavits had been prepared at least fifteen days before the election and were ready for signatures. Obviously, there were many voters who could legitimately make such statements, but there probably was not enough time to get enough legitimate affidavits to overturn McEnery's election, so forgery was used to increase the number. One of the men who admitted to this before a United States Senate investigating committee testified that signing another man's name for money was considered criminal in Louisiana, but that doing so for political purposes was an accepted practice.[80] By legitimate and illegitimate means, enough affidavits were secured to make a case.

After a preliminary meeting on November 13, the Returning Board met formally on November 14. Warmoth was prepared. He had secured from the state auditor a statement that Herron, who had formerly served as tax collector for a New Orleans district, had not settled his accounts. Therefore the governor wrote an order for Herron's removal and appointed Jack Wharton as secretary of state and hence a member of the Returning Board. Herron was not informed of his removal when Wharton was sworn into office on the morning of the fourteenth.

79 Warmoth, *War, Politics and Reconstruction*, 205.
80 *Senate Reports*, 42nd Cong., 3rd Sess., No. 457, pp. 541–42.

Benjamin F. Butler

Nathaniel P. Banks

Michael Hahn

James Madison Wells

Henry Clay Warmoth

Oscar J. Dunn

P. B. S. Pinchback

William Pitt Kellogg

Francis T. Nicholls

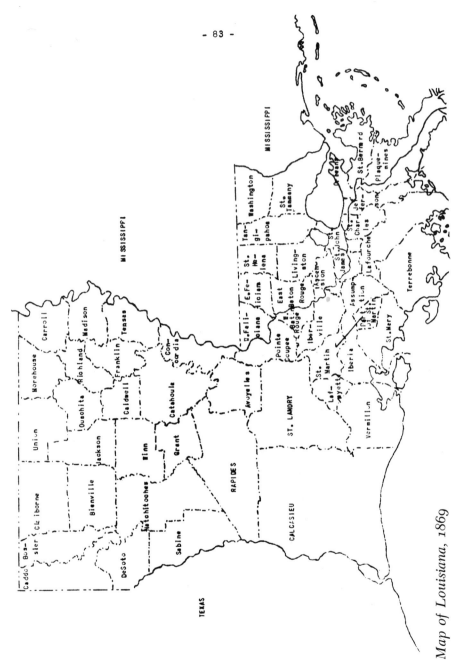

Map of Louisiana, 1869

There are two versions of what happened in Warmoth's office when the board met officially at noon on the fourteenth. Lynch stated that Herron made a motion to name General Longstreet and Jacob Hawkins to fill the vacancies on the board, that he and Herron voted for the motion, and that Warmoth voted against it. According to Warmoth's account, which seems more plausible, though it must be remembered that Warmoth was always plausible, Wharton handed Herron a copy of his (Wharton's) commission as secretary of state before any motions were made. Warmoth then moved to elect Frank H. Hatch and Durant DaPonte to fill the vacancies. He and Wharton voted for the motion, Herron voted against it, and Lynch remained silent. Then Herron moved to elect Longstreet and Hawkins, but Warmoth pointed out that Herron was no longer a member of the board and therefore could not make a motion. At this point Lynch and Herron, declaring the meeting irregular, left the executive office. Thus there were two sets of men claiming to be the legal Returning Board. Warmoth and Lynch were on both boards, but the Lynch Board had Herron, Longstreet, and Hawkins as additional members; the Warmoth Board had Wharton, DaPonte, and Hatch.

Herron now went before Judge H. C. Dibble of the Eighth District Court of Orleans Parish, which had jurisdiction over all election contests. Dibble ruled on November 19 that Warmoth had no power to remove Herron from office, which is interesting inasmuch as Warmoth's removal of Bovee had brought Herron into office. The judge then declared the Lynch body to be the legal Returning Board.[81] Warmoth made some sort of proposition to Dibble, to which the judge replied on November 20: "I cannot do what you ask. . . . I am convinced that it would be treason for me to act as you suggested. I hold a trust which was given me by a party . . . [which] I must not surrender except to those who gave it to me or the one entitled by law to succeed me."[82]

Warmoth was not yet at the end of his resources. Now he took from his safe the Election Bill of 1872, which he had prevented Pinchback's signing by the September railroad race to New Orleans, and signed it

---

81 New Orleans *Daily Picayune*, November 20, 1872; F. B. Harris, "Henry Clay Warmoth," 641–42.
82 Dibble to Warmoth, November 20, 1872, in Warmoth Papers.

into law. Under the terms of this bill the existing Returning Board was abolished and replaced by a board elected by the state senate.[83] Lest Dibble, who had been defeated in the election, interfere again, Warmoth declared his opponent, W. A. Elmore, elected, and installed Elmore on the Eighth District Court bench by force. Elmore immediately ruled that both the Warmoth Board and the Lynch Board were abolished.[84] On the same day, Warmoth called a meeting of the newly elected legislature for December 9, 1872.

Under the constitution of 1868, the governor had the power to fill all vacancies which occurred while the legislature was not in session. Therefore, on December 3, 1872, Warmoth appointed a new Returning Board, the third to make its appearance, with Gabriel DeFeriet as chairman of a sure Fusionist majority. On December 4 the new board certified that Greeley and the McEnery ticket had carried Louisiana, and Warmoth so proclaimed. It probably should be noted that when the state senate met, it elected a fourth Returning Board, called the Forman Board, but it was to report the same returns as the DeFeriet Board.

In the meantime the Lynch Board had canvassed no returns because it had no returns to canvass. But with the passage of time some action became imperative because the state's electoral vote had to be cast in December. In the meantime, Herron had been ousted from the Lynch Board in favor of Bovee. Also in the meantime, Collector Casey had gone to Washington where he apparently received assurance of support if some means could be found to declare Kellogg elected. On December 4, without any returns in its possession, the Lynch Board declared the Grant electors elected.

Next Packard and Kellogg turned to the only power which could sustain them, the United States courts. Federal Circuit Judge Edward H. Durell was old, infirm, and probably alcoholic. He was, according to Warmoth, much under the influence of E. C. Billings, an attorney who had been a rival of Kellogg's for the Republican guber-

---

83 *Acts Passed by the General Assembly of the State of Louisiana at the First Session of the Third Legislature, Begun and Held in New Orleans, January 6, 1873* (New Orleans, 1873), 15–29.

84 New Orleans *Daily Picayune*, November 22, 1872; F. B. Harris, "Henry Clay Warmoth," 642.

natorial nomination and who had not supported Kellogg in the election. But Kellogg, or his emissaries, pointed out to Billings and other friends of Durell that an opportunity existed to become favorites of the Grant administration. It was also called "to Billings' attention that . . . Judge Durell was old and feeble" and that by cooperating with Kellogg and Packard, Billings could become his successor.[85] This was no idle promise; it was later made good.

On the evening of December 5, 1872, from his residence, Judge Durell issued an order to Marshal Packard instructing him to take possession of the State House and to prevent illegal assemblies there, meaning, of course, that in Durell's view the legislature reported as elected by the DeFeriet Board was an illegal assembly. Packard was, however, to allow people who were entitled to enter and leave the building to do so.[86] There can be little doubt that this coup was planned in advance, with the knowledge of the national administration, because on December 3 Attorney General George H. Williams had told Packard by telegraph that he was "to enforce the decrees and mandates of the United States courts, no matter by whom resisted, and General Emory will furnish you with all necessary troops for that purpose."[87] Packard did not wait. Using two companies of federal troops, he took possession of Mechanics' Institute at 2:00 A.M. on December 6. In court that same morning Durell declared the DeFeriet Board illegal and ordered the returns from the election turned over to the Lynch Board. Warmoth did not comply with this order, so the Lynch Board still had no returns to canvass.

The lack of returns proved no serious handicap to the Lynch Board. The affidavits gathered after the election were available, and they were enough. Lynch later stated to a congressional committee: "We had not the technical evidence before us. We were what I considered in the midst of a revolution, and in order to get at the results of the election as near as we could, as an officer acting, I availed myself of every kind of information within my reach, not only the affidavits, but my former knowledge of the political divisions of the inhabitants of

85 Warmoth, *War, Politics and Reconstruction*, 209.
86 *Senate Reports*, 42nd Cong., 3rd Sess., No. 457, xvii.
87 George H. Williams to Packard, December 3, 1872, quoted in Warmoth, *War, Politics and Reconstruction*, 210.

the State as corroborative of the evidence placed before us."[88] Lynch lost no time in making the board's reports. By December 9 Kellogg and his ticket had been declared elected as had state senators and representatives. Results in all contests in the state were promulgated before the end of December.

The house of representatives, as counted in by the Lynch Board, contained 77 Republicans and 32 Fusionists; the senate had 28 Republicans and eight Fusionists. Of the 145 legislators, 68 were black. The legislature reported by the Forman Board, which replaced the DeFeriet group, had a house of representatives made up of 75 Fusionists and 35 Republicans, with seven seats undecided. There were 15 senators held over, and the Forman Board reported that 15 Fusionists and 4 Republicans had been elected. This would have given a Fusionist majority in the senate, but not nearly so great as in the house. The Forman Board returned 56 Negroes. A total of 66 men was declared elected by both boards, 58 in the house, 8 in the senate.[89]

The Lynch Board legislature met according to Warmoth's call on December 9. The senate had 29 members present of 36, but some of those on hand had refused to take the oath, so the actual number participating is difficult to determine. The house met with 69 present out of 110, 14 of whom were listed as Democrats. Both houses organized, but they were unable to find the governor to notify him of their organization. Some of the Fusionists claiming legislative seats met at Lyceum Hall on December 9 and were joined by seceders from Mechanics' Institute. On the evening of December 12 they had a quorum, according to the Fusionist version of the returns, and organized. This was when the Forman Board was created. Then this McEnery legislature adjourned until the first Monday in January.[90]

6

Warmoth, whose term would expire in mid-January, 1873, had learned from an informant in Washington that the Grant administration was "firmly determined to sustain decisions of the United States

88 *Senate Reports*, 42nd Cong., 3rd Sess., No. 457, p. 155, quoted in Lonn, *Reconstruction in Louisiana*, 202.
89 Lonn, *Reconstruction in Louisiana*, 204–205.
90 *Ibid.*, 211–13.

Court at all hazards. Republican congressional opinion strongly ap-
proves this course while the opposition is apathetic."[91] He was a re-
sourceful man, however, and the Kellogg legislature was unable to
feel secure so long as he was governor. On December 9, when the
Kellogg legislature met, Pinchback announced that Warmoth had
offered him fifty thousand dollars to organize the legislature as the
governor should direct. Warmoth had made some sort of proposal,
because Pinchback wrote to him on that same day: "I have slept on
the proposition you made to me last night and have resolutely de-
terminded [*sic*] to do my duty to my state, party, and race by declining respectfully to do the same. I am truly sorry for you, but I cannot
help you."[92]

Kellogg and Packard were now in a position to accomplish the impeachment of Warmoth which they had sought so long. The Kellogg
house of representatives elected the governor's old adversary, Postmaster Lowell, as speaker. On the day the legislature met, December
9, the house impeached Warmoth of high crimes and misdemeanors
and notified the senate of that fact. Under the constitution, the impeachment suspended Warmoth from office until after trial before
the senate. Therefore Pinchback assumed the office of governor. Not
until later did the house draw up specific articles of impeachment,
which charged the governor with (1) having illegally removed Bovee
from office in 1871; (2) having illegally appointed a tax collector in
Tangipahoa Parish in 1870; (3) commissioning officers when no
official returns had been made by the Returning Board; (4) attempting to bribe the supervisor of elections of St. Charles Parish; (5) attempting to bribe Pinchback; and (6) attempting to exercise the
powers of governor after being impeached. Warmoth, on the thirteenth, wrote a letter of resignation to the chairman of a joint meeting
of senators and representatives of the McEnery legislature, but his
resignation was refused.[93]

91 Morey to Warmoth, December 7, 1872, in Warmoth Papers.
92 Pinchback to Warmoth, December 9, 1872, in Warmoth Papers.
93 New Orleans *Daily Picayune*, December 9–14, 1872; New Orleans *Republican*,
December 10, 1872; Warmoth to J. W. Moncure, December 13, 1872, in Warmoth Papers; Ewing, "Early Louisiana Impeachments," 702–703; Grosz, "Pinchback," 560–61; Lonn, *Reconstruction in Louisiana*, 206–13; F. B. Harris, "Henry
Clay Warmoth," 646–47; Pitre, "Collapse of the Warmoth Regime," 182–83,
186–87.

The Democrats of New Orleans, having participated in stealing an election, now were outraged that it was being stolen back. Charles Gayarré wrote: "We are completely under the rule of ignorant and filthy negroes scarcely superior to the orang outang. The Republic of Greece had their solons, we have Sambo."[94] Warmoth made one last attempt at judicial action. He went before the Eighth District Court and asked for an order restraining Pinchback from acting as governor on the grounds that he could not have been lieutenant-governor because his term as state senator had not expired. This was a weak case, because Warmoth himself had secured Pinchback's election as lieutenant-governor and had recognized him as such. Judge Elmore issued the injunction requested, but Pinchback ignored it. The judge then fined Pinchback fifty dollars and sentenced him to ten days in jail for contempt of court. This decree was also ignored. When the question finally came before the Louisiana Supreme Court, in March, 1873, that solidly Republican bench ruled that Pinchback had indeed been lieutenant-governor and that he had become governor when Warmoth was suspended. Thus was dashed the last hope of Warmoth and the Fusionists for legal action to block Kellogg's accession to the governorship.[95]

In the meantime the telegraph wires between New Orleans and Washington were kept busy. On December 9 Packard sent four telegrams to his superior, Attorney General Williams, reporting Radical progress. On December 10 a mass meeting of Fusionists was held in front of City Hall, and a committee of one hundred leading citizens was selected to present a petition to General Grant. On December 11 Warmoth declared the Pinchback-Kellogg legislature illegal. On the same day Pinchback asked Washington that he be authorized to call on federal troops to preserve order if such action became necessary. Also on that day Casey and Kellogg appealed to Grant for recognition by him of Pinchback and the legislature sitting at Mechanics' Institute.[96] On December 12, Attorney General Williams sent Pinchback

94 Gayarré to Duyckinck, December 18, 1872, in "Some Letters of Charles Etienne Gayarré," 247–48.
95 Lonn, *Reconstruction in Louisiana*, 213–14; Pitre, "Collapse of the Warmoth Regime," 183–85; Grosz, "Pinchback," 561–64.
96 Warmoth, *War, Politics and Reconstruction*, 213–17; Pitre, "Collapse of the Warmoth Regime," 184–85; Grosz, "Pinchback," 564–65.

the letter he had been waiting for: "Let it be understood that you are recognized by the President as the lawful executive of Louisiana, and that the body assembled at Mechanics' Institute is the lawful legislature of the State . . . and also that all necessary assistance will be given to you and the legislature herein recognized to protect the State from disorder and violence."[97]

Grant's recognition of Pinchback settled the matter. The Committee of One Hundred, despite notification that the president's mind was made up and would not be changed, made a fruitless trip to Washington. Pinchback removed General Hugh Campbell as commander of the militia and named Longstreet to the post, but the militia officer in command of the state armory, where a number of white militiamen had gathered, refused to surrender the armory to representatives of Pinchback's administration. When faced with a demand from federal officers, however, the militiamen marched out of the armory. Pinchback was governor of Louisiana until the expiration of Warmoth's term on January 13, 1873. He required Fusionists who had been elected to office to come to him for their commissions, thus recognizing his authority. The legislature passed a number of bills which he signed and which were thereafter part of the law of Louisiana. One of these abolished Judge Elmore's Eighth District Court and created a new Superior District Court in its place. Jacob Hawkins, member of the Lynch Returning Board, was named to preside over this court. Warmoth's day in Louisiana politics was over.[98]

7

On May 9, 1864, Warmoth wrote in his diary: "I am twenty-two years of age today. I have determined to persist in my course and not drink liquor of any kind nor smoke cigars or use tobacco in any way."[99] Before he was thirty-one he had served a full term, less thirty-five days, as governor of Louisiana and had become nationally known as a corruptionist. He also took a drink and smoked cigars. By the middle

97 Williams to Pinchback, December 12, 1872, quoted in Warmoth, *War, Politics and Reconstruction*, 217.
98 New Orleans *Daily Picayune*, December 11, 1872–January 13, 1873; Grosz, "Pinchback," 567–89; Lonn, *Reconstruction in Louisiana*, 212–13, 216–17.
99 Warmoth Diary, May 9, 1864, in Warmoth Papers.

of his four-year term he had made himself into the most powerful governor Louisiana was to have until the advent of Huey P. Long, whom Warmoth lived to see in office. Yet Warmoth was suspended from office and powerless when his term came to an end.

There is no doubt that as governor Warmoth made money by means which a moralist would have to define as corrupt. On the other hand, it is not true that he went into office penniless. Two years before he became governor he was able to lend $6,000 on good security.[100] Whether or not he took bribes can be debated. Historian Ella Lonn was unable to discover any firm evidence that he did so, and she would have been convinced by relatively little evidence. We do know that he was offered a $50,000 bribe by one John A. Walsh, which he refused; Walsh, however, said that Warmoth would not take the $50,000 because he wanted $75,000. Warmoth never admitted having offered Pinchback a bribe.[101]

No necessity exists for establishing bribery as a source of income for Warmoth. He vetoed a great many bills whose promoters would have been happy to pay substantially for his approval. It must be noted, however, that he was accused of vetoing bills and then encouraging the legislature to override his veto. But there were many ways for his fortune to increase without his having to accept bribes. He speculated in state and city bonds and in 1874 listed $361,000 worth, face value, in his portfolio. Also, while he was governor, the New Orleans *Republican* did state printing, and Warmoth was the largest stockholder. He could buy state warrants on the open market at discounts up to 50 percent, and he was in a position to redeem them at face value when the state treasury accumulated currency. Probably, also, he got what would today be called kickbacks from men he appointed to office. He himself is reported to have said, not long after becoming governor: "I don't pretend to be honest . . . I only pretend to be as honest as anybody in politics, and more so than those fellows who are opposing me now."[102] One historian concludes, with some reason, "In short, if Warmoth was corrupt, it would be nearer the truth to say that Louisiana corrupted him than to say that he cor-

100 Warmoth Diary, June 11, 1866, in Warmoth Papers.
101 Lonn, *Reconstruction in Louisiana*, 90–91; Current, *Three Carpetbag Governors,* 61–62.
102 New Orleans *Daily Picayune*, November 27, 1868.

rupted Louisiana."[103] This may be going too far. Probably a more accurate assessment would be that the man and the state were made for one another. Louisiana state government was corrupt before Warmoth's administration and was corrupt afterward. It was corrupt when Republicans were in power and was corrupt when Democrats held the reins. "When in Rome" may not be an excuse in the eyes of the recording angel, but it must certainly be taken into account by the historian.

Obviously Warmoth had a remarkable degree of personal charm. This was one of his greatest assets. Even Grant, who referred to him as "the shrewdest, boldest, ablest and most conscienceless young man he ever knew,"[104] seems to have felt his charm. Certainly the ladies of General Banks's coterie were aware of it. One suspects that other ladies of New Orleans were aware of it, too, because Warmoth did not marry until he was thirty-five. His bride was a beautiful, accomplished young lady, nineteen years old, from New Jersey. "She also had a very wealthy father."[105] They lived together fifty-three years, had three children and at least one grandchild. At eighty-seven Warmoth was alert enough to write his memoirs which, although they always show him in a favorable light, are full of valuable information and are interesting reading. He was aware enough of his place in history to preserve his personal and political records, though one suspects that a few items showing him in a bad light may have been removed.

It says something about him that in 1874, when he was forced to kill a man in self-defense on the streets of New Orleans and was jailed for several days until a coroner's jury freed him, he received dozens of letters of sympathy, one from his old adversary of the Returning Board quarrel, Francis J. Herron. A stream of visitors came to visit him in prison, including such partisan Demo Louis Wiltz of New Orleans and old enemies like visitor was Bishop Joseph Wilmer of the Episcopal

103 Current, *Three Carpetbag Governors*, 63; see also H
    ments, 42nd Cong., 2nd Sess., No. 211, pp. 283–422
    24, 1874, in Warmoth Papers; New Orleans *Daily F*
    7, June 6, 1872.
104 Morey to Warmoth, December 4, 1872, in Warmoth
105 Current, *Three Carpetbag Governors*, 44.

visit resulted in Warmoth's becoming a communicant in that faith. Other Carpetbaggers fled North when their power ended. Warmoth spent the rest of his life as a resident of Louisiana.[106]

One question remains. Gifted with youth, charm, and ability, unhampered by too many scruples, why did Warmoth fail—and in the final analysis he did fail—as governor of Louisiana? One answer, of course, is that in the long run the failure of Radical Reconstruction as a whole was inevitable, but Warmoth might still have had a successful four years and been elected to a second term. Another reason for failure was the personal enmity of General Grant, leading to the long contest with the Custom House Ring. But internal feuds broke out among the Radicals in other states where Grant was not personally involved. Warmoth checkmated the Custom House faction again and again before 1872. It was only after he had allied himself with the Democrats—and that is what Fusion amounted to—that he was brought down. One is almost forced to the conclusion that Warmoth's failure to sympathize with or even to understand the aspirations of the black people of Louisiana caused his downfall. His actions and memoirs indicate that he largely shared the attitude of the Democrats in regard to the Negro. This was, of course, true of many of his Custom House rivals, but he had already demonstrated his racist attitudes, and they, in order to combat him, had to conceal theirs. Thus they made concessions to blacks which Warmoth had not made and McEnery certainly would not have made. It is perhaps understandable why Warmoth remained in Louisiana when other Carpetbaggers left. He felt at home in Louisiana because he shared so many attitudes, including racial ones, with the white people of the state.

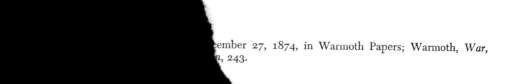

cember 27, 1874, in Warmoth Papers; Warmoth, *War,* n, 243.

VII *The Kellogg Era*

T HE "EXTRA SESSION" of the Pinchback legislature adjourned on January 6, 1873, but the new
legislature certified by the Lynch Returning Board, largely the same
men, convened immediately. Kellogg was inaugurated as governor
at Mechanics' Institute on January 13. McEnery was being inaugurated at Lafayette Square at the same time, and a McEnery legislature held its sessions in Odd Fellows' Hall. For almost two months
the rival legislatures went through the motions of legislating. The
vast majority of Louisiana whites considered the Kellogg government
illegitimate, but it was the legislation enacted by the Kellogg legislature which went into the statute books.[1]

Kellogg was far more hated than Warmoth had ever been. The
Democratic newspapers of the state vilified him constantly. One
reputable work uses him as an example of the worst sort of Carpetbagger.[2] It is true, of course, that Kellogg played the dirty game of
nineteenth-century politics, and Louisiana politics at that, without

---

1 New Orleans *Daily Picayune*, January 14, 1873; Shreveport *Times*, September 23,
1873; Grosz, "Pinchback," 575–76; Lonn, *Reconstruction in Louisiana*, 222–23.
2 Garner (ed.), *Studies in Southern History and Politics*, 164; Joe Gray Taylor,
"New Orleans and Reconstruction," *Louisiana History*, IX (Summer, 1968),
198–200.

scruple, but there is no evidence that he was personally dishonest. Furthermore, he effected reforms, especially in finance, which improved Louisiana government. The manner of his election accounts partly for how much he was hated; but more important, he either lacked Warmoth's contempt for the Negro, or he managed to conceal it better. Blacks were not dominant in his administration, but they had a much larger role in Louisiana government than they had under Warmoth. Thus race was the major factor in white Louisiana's opinion of Kellogg.

The Kellogg administration, assured of support from Washington, could afford to wait, which was exactly what McEnery could not do. Hindsight makes it obvious that McEnery had no chance to succeed so long as Grant was president, but this was not so evident in 1873 as it is today. The voice of the people that McEnery heard came from nearby. Louisianians emphasized theories and ignored the realities of power. The *Picayune,* for example, pontificated, "It is not in the nature of things that an attempted outrage so flagrant, as subverting a popular election through the usurped power, exercised by a United States . . . judge, can secure more than temporary success."[3] The Shreveport *Times* raged that "The sovereignty of Louisiana had been outraged; her government overthrown by the fiat of a federal judge and a negro gambler."[4]

Influenced by such incitement and support at the state level, McEnery decided to resort to force. On February 27, 1873, he appointed Fred N. Ogden brigadier general of the First Division of Louisiana militia. With this militia, acting in an "unofficial" capacity, the Fusionists, who can by now be called Conservatives or even Democrats, sought to seize control of the major police stations of New Orleans. This resulted in the "Battle of the Cabildo" on March 5, 1873. The Metropolitan Police under General Longstreet kept command of the situation and arrested sixty-five of the attackers. Those arrested were quickly set free, but now Kellogg had justification for taking action against the Fusion legislature. On March 6, the Metropolitans took possession of Odd Fellows' Hall. The federal com-

---

3 New Orleans *Daily Picayune,* January 1, 1873; see also New Orleans *Daily Picayune,* February, 1873.
4 Shreveport *Times,* January 1, 1873.

mander in New Orleans viewed this as a valid assertion of authority by Kellogg and refused to interfere. The McEnery legislature continued a shadowy existence, but the failure of the coup of March 5 and the dispersal on March 6 cost it sympathy in the rest of the country and prestige in Louisiana.[5]

From 1873 through 1875, Louisiana Democrats writhed in impotent rage because Kellogg remained in power. Refusal to pay taxes, attempted compromise, even armed revolt, failed to shake the hated Radical regime. Over much of the state there was no government, and a partial state of guerrilla warfare prevailed. Congressional investigations aroused hope but did not oust Kellogg. So much turmoil existed that in March, 1873, a man wrote that he had come to Louisiana with "a view to settling. I am going away on Saturday with a view of keeping out of such a mudhole."[6] Three days later, however, Warmoth had opened negotiations with Kellogg, because it was evident that Kellogg could not be ousted so long as Grant was president. By late 1873, New Orleans newspapers were admitting that Kellogg could not be ousted and urging Democratic legislators who had refused to attend the Radical legislature to take their seats. By January of 1874 some Democrats had gone over to the Radical legislature; others were said to be going home.[7]

The tumult regarding the rightful government of Louisiana was not confined to the state most concerned. By 1873 Grant's popularity in the North had decreased as the scandals of his administration came to light, but he was still president of the United States, and as president he had awesome powers. He was influenced in regard to Louisiana by his wife's brother-in-law, Casey, who wired him soon after the election that the Democrats "are making desperate efforts to array the people against us. . . . our members are poor and the opposition is rich. . . . The real underlying sentiment is with us if it can be en-

5 New Orleans *Republican*, March 5–6, 1873; New Orleans *Daily Picayune*, February 22, 28, March 6–7, 13, 1873; Sefton, *United States Army and Reconstruction*, 238–39; Highsmith, "Louisiana During Reconstruction," 283; Kendall, *History of New Orleans*, I, 356–58; Lonn, *Reconstruction in Louisiana*, 228–29.
6 Archibald Goodson to Warmoth, March 8, 1873, in Warmoth Papers.
7 Warmoth to L. Texada, March 11, 1873, John Cockreny to Warmoth, May 25, 1873, in Warmoth Papers; Shreveport *Times*, July 9, 1875; New Orleans *Daily Picayune*, December 24, 1873, January 11, 1874; Hesseltine, *Ulysses S. Grant, Politician*, 346.

couraged."[8] Grant had already recognized Pinchback as the rightful governor and so, in effect, had recognized Kellogg's government when it assumed office. However, in his fourth annual message to Congress, the president stated plainly that the Louisiana election had been so fraudulent that it was not possible to tell who had been elected. He urged Congress to take action, but he also made it clear that if Congress made no decision, he would continue to recognize Kellogg as the rightful governor.[9]

Congress took note of the president's message, but it took no action except to investigate Louisiana once again. The investigation committee, controlled by Republicans, found that it could not, on the evidence, conclude that either McEnery or Kellogg had been elected. The majority then concluded that no state government existed in Louisiana and went on to recommend that a new election be held. This, of course, brought up a real constitutional question. Did the federal government have the power to discard a state election and order another, presumably to be held under federal supervision? In the end, those doubtful of such federal power and Radicals satisfied to leave Kellogg in office prevented any action. Northern Democrats probably were not too dissatisfied; Kellogg was a club with which they could strike the administration at will.[10] But white Louisianians were not satisfied. The Shreveport *Times* concluded: "We are justified by recent events in the opinion that there are not a half-dozen members of either the Senate or House, or in the cabinet, or on the Supreme Bench, all combined, who could not be readily bought . . . at a moderate price."[11] Kellogg was secure for the time being. In June he requested and received from the federal government two howitzers, two Napoleon guns, two Gatling guns, plus rifles, muskets, and cavalry equipment. Soon he would need these arms.[12]

As a result of the rival legislative sessions of 1873, Pinchback was the subject of a controversy which was to last for three years. As noted

---

8 James F. Casey to Grant, December 11, 1872, in *House Executive Documents*, 42nd Cong., 3rd Sess., No. 91, p. 19.

9 Ulysses S. Grant, Fourth Annual Message, February 25, 1873, in Richardson (ed.), *Messages and Papers of the Presidents*, VII, 212–13.

10 *Senate Reports*, 42nd Cong., 3rd Sess., No. 457, pp. xiv, l–li; Lonn, *Reconstruction in Louisiana*, 235–39.

11 Shreveport *Times*, March 2, 1873.

12 *Nation*, XVI (June 5, 1873), 379.

earlier, he had been a candidate for United States representative-at-large in the election of 1872; he claimed to have won that election, but he was not allowed to take the seat. In the meantime, however, J. R. West's term as United States senator had expired, and the Kellogg legislature elected Pinchback to replace West. This seems to have been a demonstration of independence on the part of Negro members of the legislature, because the prospect of Pinchback's election caused six members of the Kellogg senate to go over to McEnery. This gave the McEnery legislature a quorum in both houses, and it proceeded to elect William T. McMillan to replace West.[13]

McMillan was never considered by the United States Senate, but Pinchback was never seated. The contest over the seat dragged on from session to session with final rejection coming in 1876. The reason for rejection is not fully clear. Warmoth took credit for it, having informed some Radical senators of unsavory facts concerning Pinchback. Ella Lonn and Agnes Grosz have concluded that Pinchback was rejected because of his race, more particularly because the wives of senators did not wish to associate with Mrs. Pinchback. This may well have been true of the Senate, but Negro representatives and their wives danced at Grant's inaugural ball in 1873; in addition, a black man, Hiram R. Revels of Mississippi, had already sat in the Senate. Pinchback was no doubt comforted when Congress awarded him $16,096.90 for his expenses. His followers were aroused over the long delay and final rejection. It may be that this contributed significantly to black defections to the Democrats in 1876.[14]

2

The legislature which went into office with Kellogg was not one of outstanding ability, but it did not deserve the abuse heaped on it by

13 *House Reports*, 43rd Cong., 1st Sess., No. 597, *passim*; New Orleans *Daily Picayune*, January 26, March 25, 1873; Grosz, "Pinchback," 575, 589–603; Smith, *The Negro in Congress*, 131–32.

14 Warmoth, *War, Politics and Reconstruction*, 233–36; W. T. McMillan to Warmoth, March 4, 1873, in Warmoth Papers; Grosz, "Pinchback," 589–603; New Orleans *Daily Picayune*, November 23, 1875, January 13, February 1, March 9, 1876; *Nation*, XVI (March 13, 1873), 173, XVIII (February 5, 1874), 84; *Acts Passed by the General Assembly of the State of Louisiana at the Second Session of the Third Legislature, Begun and Held in New Orleans, January 5, 1874* (New Orleans, 1874), 37; Lonn, *Reconstruction in Louisiana*, 308–38; Smith, *The Negro in Congress*, 27, 131–32.

the Conservative press. The real, though not often stated, objection to this legislature was the large proportion of black members. The hostile *Picayune* believed that Speaker Lowell and former Governor Hahn were the ablest members of the house of representatives. However, John Gair, a mulatto, was the best orator. Other able black members were G. W. Murrell of Lafourche Parish, an elderly minister; David Young of Concordia; George Devizen of New Orleans; and T. T. Allain of Iberville. There was corruption in the Kellogg legislatures, but in ability and integrity his legislators seem to have been no worse than those who went before or those who came after.[15]

The Kellogg administration attempted reforms, but many of the attempts were failures. Among the administration's accomplishments was the enactment in 1874 of a new registration and election law intended to prevent the abuses of the campaign of 1872. This act retained the Returning Board, however, and was unacceptable to Louisiana Conservatives. In 1876, when the lower house of the legislature had a Democratic majority, there was a strong effort to pass yet another election law. The senate, however, insisted on retaining the Returning Board, the house refused to have it, a conference committee could not agree, so no new law was enacted. This same legislature of 1876 adopted a new apportionment act. The senate remained unchanged, but the 119 house members were so distributed that the number of Republican districts was increased. The Democratic majority in the house consented to this bill, perhaps because the Bourbon Democrats were farsighted enough to realize that many sure Republican districts under Reconstruction could be made into sure Bourbon districts in the years to come.[16]

Kellogg was responsible for a number of lesser, but long-needed, reform measures. More money was provided for the insane asylum at Jackson and for Charity Hospital in New Orleans, and a new Charity

---

15 New Orleans *Daily Picayune*, January 11, 1874, January–February, 1875.

16 *Acts Passed by the General Assembly of the State of Louisiana at the First Session of the Fourth Legislature, Begun and Held in the City of New Orleans January 4, 1875, and at the Extra Session, Convened April 14, 1875* [New Orleans, 1875 (actually passed by the 1874 session, but bound with 1875 statutes)], 5–15; *Acts Passed by the General Assembly of the State of Louisiana at the Second Session of the Fourth Legislature, Begun and Held in the City of New Orleans, January 3, 1876* (New Orleans, 1876), 12–15; New Orleans *Daily Picayune*, July 30, 1874, February 2, 4, 11, 12, 1876; Lonn, *Reconstruction in Louisiana*, 227–28, 250, 388–92.

Hospital was established at Shreveport. The Bureau of Immigration was given the power to exclude unfit immigrants. Bribery at last became a crime, as did the usurping of public office. Some of the five million acres of state lands were disposed of, though at a price of only twelve and a half cents per acre. The lessee of the state penitentiary was forbidden to employ convicts outside the walls of the prison; this act would have prevented a tragic chapter in Louisiana history had it remained in effect. An ingenious, though futile, measure of 1874 provided that the expense of calling out militia or police to quell a riot should be borne by the parish where the disturbance took place. Kellogg asked for, but did not get, an item veto, which could have saved many dollars. He was not able, however, to comply with a request from Shreveport that called attention to the excess of adultery and the excessive number of illegitimate children and demanded that fathers of these unfortunates be identified and required to support them.[17]

A stronger civil rights act than the one previously enacted over Warmoth's objections passed the legislature and was approved by the governor in 1873. Basically, this was a public accommodations act, making it illegal to discriminate on grounds of race or color in public places or on public conveyances. Penalties were provided for interstate common carriers which did not comply. This act, like the previous one, was ignored outside of New Orleans, and little attention was paid to it in the metropolis. It had been so disregarded by 1877 that the post-Reconstruction legislatures did not bother to repeal it until 1902. The Kellogg legislature was much aware of the civil rights issue, however, and a joint resolution in 1875 tendered thanks to the United States House of Representatives in general and Benjamin F. Butler in particular for the House's passage of the national bill. This resolution also urged passage by the United States Senate.[18]

17 *Acts of Louisiana, 1873*, 42–46, 80–81; *Acts of Louisiana, 1874*, 163–68, 271–76; *Acts of Louisiana, 1875*, 16–17 (enacted in 1874), 54; *Acts of Louisiana, 1876*, 16, 77–79; O'Conner, "Charity Hospital," 68; Daspit, "Governors' Messages," 67; W. C. Adams, W. M. G. Calvin, D. Morgan to Kellogg, January 9, 1875, in William P. Kellogg Papers, Department of Archives, Louisiana State University; Lonn, *Reconstruction in Louisiana*, 253.
18 *Acts of Louisiana, 1873*, 156–57; *Acts of Louisiana, 1876*, 8 (enacted in 1875); Memelo, "The Development of State Laws Concerning the Negro in Louisiana," 84–86, 144.

Kellogg's greatest accomplishment was funding the state debt. This was the beginning of the retreat from early Radical extravagance, a retreat which was completed by the Bourbons. It is significant that in Louisiana and at least two other former Confederate states, this movement toward fiscal responsibility began under Republicans. The confusion attending Kellogg's accession, and the refusal of many to pay their taxes, made it impossible to pay the interest on the bonded indebtedness due January 1, 1873. During the year interest payments were brought up to date, except for some bonds of doubtful legality, but it was obvious that the state could not continue to operate on the existing financial basis. A committee of nine businessmen appointed by the governor reported to him that the total indebtedness, including $30,500,000 of contingent debt, was, in round numbers, $53,000,000. This left slightly more than $23,000,000 in interest-bearing debt, obviously more than the state could manage, especially after its income was reduced by the depression which began in 1873. In addition, day-to-day expenses were being paid in warrants, not all of which could be redeemed. As of July 2, 1873, the auditor reported over $1,750,000 in outstanding warrants. The auditor's policy was to pay warrants for a given year with taxes collected in that year; therefore more than $850,000 in warrants issued before 1872 were, for all practical purposes, not redeemable.[19]

The result was the Funding Act of 1874. Under the terms of this act all grants-in-aid which had lapsed or otherwise been forfeited were annulled; thus in one stroke the contingent debt was abolished. This act also provided that outstanding obligations of the state should be funded at the rate of 60 percent of face value and replaced by new forty-year bonds, soon known as consols, bearing 7 percent interest. The act also established a Board of Liquidation, made up of the governor, the lieutenant-governor, the auditor, the treasurer, the secretary of state, and the speaker of the house, which had the power, subject to review by the courts, to decide which obligations were valid for refunding and which were not. A tax of five and a half mills on assessed value of property was levied to pay the interest on these

19 New Orleans *Daily Picayune*, July 2, 1873, January 6, 1874; Woodward, *Origins of the New South*, 86–87; Gonzales, "William Pitt Kellogg," 464–65; Lonn, *Reconstruction in Louisiana*, 247–51.

consolidated bonds. The maximum total of the state debt was fixed at $15,000,000. In 1875 the legislature listed eighteen bond issues, more than $14,000,000 in face value, which were not to be refunded until their validity had been established by the courts. As of April, 1876, the courts had rejected almost $4,000,000 in bonds as invalid, and another $1,500,000 remained in litigation. Among the issues held invalid was $2,500,000 granted to the Mobile and Chattanooga Railroad. On the other hand, the state supreme court, presided over by a major figure in the North Louisiana and Texas Railroad (formerly the Vicksburg and Shreveport), decided that the Board of Liquidation must fund the bonds issued to that line. By the close of Kellogg's term, funding and invalidation had reduced the bonded indebtedness of Louisiana to approximately $12,000,000. Many issues remained in litigation after the Radicals went out of office. The interest rate on the new consolidated bonds was considered usurious by many Louisianians, but it should be pointed out that in 1874 farm mortgages were almost impossible to obtain and that commercial paper on the New Orleans market was discounted at more than 12 percent. Despite the interest rate on the market, the bonds were bringing only sixty-six cents on the dollar in the spring of 1876.[20]

Kellogg managed also to bring about a reduction in the rate of taxation. He found that property in Orleans Parish was assessed much nearer its real value than property in the country parishes and advocated equalization. To what extent this was attained it is difficult to say. He did, however, secure a reduction in the levee tax from four mills to three and, in all, brought state taxes down from 21½ to 14½ mills. So much were taxes reduced, in fact, that in 1876 the *Picayune* commented that taxes were "burdensome not so much on account of . . . amount as for the misapplication of revenue."[21] Indirectly, this provided relief from parish (not municipal) taxes, because it was illegal for parish taxes to exceed those levied by the state. In New

20 *Acts of Louisiana, 1874,* 39–42; *Acts of Louisiana, 1875,* 55–56; *Acts of Louisiana, Extra Session, 1875,* 110–12; *Acts of Louisiana, 1876,* 130–31; New Orleans *Daily Picayune,* August 22, December 2, 11, 1875, February 22, April 11, 18, 1876; A. Dubuclet to Kellogg, December 16, 1875, quoted in New Orleans *Daily Picayune,* December 23, 1875; *Nation,* XVIII (February 5, 1874), 84; Gonzales, "William Pitt Kellogg," 466–67, 469–70; Highsmith, "Louisiana During Reconstruction," 409–10; Caldwell, *Banking History of Louisiana,* 103.
21 New Orleans *Daily Picayune,* February 11, 1876.

Orleans the tax for the support of the Metropolitan Police was low-ered. Special tax concessions were made to planters whose property had been flooded. Stern measures were taken against defaulting tax collectors so that all taxes paid to state officials could be used by the state. State warrants were specifically made receivable for taxes. This enabled citizens to pay their taxes at lower actual cost and at the same time built up the value of state warrants. In early autumn of 1874, Kellogg claimed to have retired more than $900,000 of the "floating" debt (mainly warrants) of Louisiana. During the depression which began in 1873 it was difficult for most people in Louisiana to pay any taxes, but certainly the burden was not nearly so great under Kellogg as it had been under Warmoth.[22]

While refunding the state debt and reducing taxes, Kellogg also managed to reduce expenditures. For this he himself must receive the chief credit, because he had little cooperation from his legislatures. The legislature of 1873 investigated expenditures, but took no action to reduce them. Total general appropriations of the legislature in 1874 were slightly larger than those of 1873. Kellogg used his executive powers, however, to revoke printing contracts, saving some $100,000. By 1876 the general appropriations bill, which had amounted to more than $2,000,000 in 1873, was reduced to $1,353,265. These figures do not give a complete picture, because the bill of 1873 included interest on bonds; that of 1876 did not. Even so, there was a significant reduc-tion, primarily in printing and in salaries. In 1876, $500,000 went for public education; $20,000 for the insane asylum; $88,400 for charity hospitals; and lesser amounts for the school for the blind, the deaf-and-dumb asylum, and nine orphanages. The conservative *Picayune* often felt compelled to support the governor's policies, though it sel-dom found any good in Kellogg himself.[23] In October, 1874, when

---

22 *Acts of Louisiana, 1874,* 41, 82, 95–96, 154–55; *Acts of Louisiana, 1875,* 35–39; *Acts of Louisiana, 1876* (enacted during the extra session of 1875), 10; Shreveport *Times,* November 22, 1877; New Orleans *Daily Picayune,* March 14, 1873, April 14, 27, 1875, June 6, 1877; Gonzales, "William Pitt Kellogg," 468–69; Lonn, *Reconstruction in Louisiana,* 388.

23 *Acts of Louisiana, 1873,* 108–15; *Acts of Louisiana, 1874,* 40–48; *Acts of Louisiana, Extra Session, 1874,* 102; *Acts of Louisiana, 1876,* 40–43, 61–66, 128–29; Report of the Auditor of Public Accounts, 1877, in *Legislative Documents, Louisiana, 1877;* New Orleans *Daily Picayune,* March 19, 1874, April–May, June 19, 1875; Lonn, *Reconstruction in Louisiana,* 225–26; Gonzales, "William Pitt Kellogg," 468–69.

Kellogg responded to a charge that he had not reduced public expenditures by proving that he had, the *Picayune* sputtered: "It is an illustration of the craft and ingenuity with which the Radical system of spoilation had been arranged that such replies as the above can be made to charges of extravagance and oppression."[24]

The city of New Orleans, with a debt of $23,000,000, was in worse condition than the state, and this condition had further deteriorated after Democratic administrations took control of city hall. Partly this was because the city had no control of its police or schools, yet supported them financially; partly it was because property was assessed more nearly at its actual value in the city than in the country. Mainly, however, mismanagement, extravagance, corruption, and the depression of 1873 were responsible. It probably should be noted that the tax resistance movement, which will be discussed presently, gave New Orleans taxpayers an excellent opportunity to be proudly delinquent in payment of their city taxes. By 1875 delinquent taxpayers, for one reason or another, owed the city $4,000,000, and the municipality's debt increased $1,500,000 that year.[25]

Kellogg tried to help New Orleans. He sought to make Orleans Parish tax assessors salaried officials so that they would not benefit from high assessments. He succeeded in giving the city control of its own drainage, and limits were placed on the amount of money to be expended on the state-controlled Metropolitan Police. New Orleans sought its own financial salvation, however, by means of the remarkable "premium bond" scheme. Under this plan the bonded indebtedness of the city was to be replaced by one million bonds of twenty dollars face value, bearing interest at 5 percent. These bonds were to be divided into ten thousand series of one hundred bonds each. Each quarter the numbers of the series to be redeemed were drawn from a lottery wheel. Normally this would be fifty series, or $100,000 worth of bonds, to be redeemed at face value. As an extra attraction, prizes up to $5,000 could be won at these drawings. Eventually bondholders traded in over $13,000,000 worth of the old bonds for premium bonds, reducing the annual interest owed by some $300,000, which helped.

24 New Orleans *Daily Picayune*, October 4, 1874.
25 *Ibid.*, April 15, June 23, July 20, 1875, February 8, 1876; Nordhoff, *The Cotton States*, 63; Gonzales, "William Pitt Kellogg," 474–75; Kendall, *History of New Orleans*, I, 351–52, 381–82.

On the other hand, the credit of the city was not significantly improved. From the time they were issued through 1878, premium bonds were normally worth from thirty to thirty-five cents on the dollar on the bond market.[26]

The taxpayers of the city were unable to obtain any direct relief from city taxes during the Kellogg administration. Democratic city officials were as determined as the Radicals had been to satisfy bondholders. The large amount of city scrip and other outstanding obligations in circulation helped taxpayers, however. First they were made receivable for part of the taxes owed the city, then by 1876 for all. Thus the property owner was really able to achieve a sizable discount, sometimes as much as 50 percent, when he paid his taxes.[27]

Kellogg was a Radical governor in a state which contained few Republicans who were qualified for public office. He appointed Radicals when he could, sometimes unqualified ones and too often men who proved to be dishonest when the temptation was strong enough. Nonetheless, he named a great many Democrats to office, especially in northern Louisiana. The number of blacks he selected was far too great from the point of view of white Louisianians, but they were few in proportion to the importance of the black vote to his party. Even so, he appointed many more blacks than Warmoth. Apparently Kellogg sought to name the best men available, but in the final analysis he yielded to the pressure of legislators from the parish involved, especially if those legislators were Republican.[28]

During Kellogg's governorship the chartering of hoped-for railroads continued, but no subsidies were paid. Likewise a telegraph company, the New Orleans and Rio de Janeiro Steamship Company, a slack-water navigation company to operate in Avoyelles Parish, a

26 *Acts of Louisiana, 1874*, 35–36; *Acts of Louisiana, 1875*, 32–34; *Acts of Louisiana, 1876*, 35–36, 54–58; New Orleans *Daily Picayune*, January 30, 1874, February 2, October 7–8, 26, November 3, 1875, March 8, April 9, 1876, December, 1878; Kendall, *History of New Orleans*, I, 383–84.

27 New Orleans *Daily Picayune*, June 19–20, October 26, 1875, March 18, 1876; Gonzales, "William Pitt Kellogg," 473–74.

28 E. Weber to Kellogg, April 10, 1876; in Kellogg Papers; New Orleans *Daily Picayune*, 1874–1876; Shreveport *Times*, March–June, 1875; Sidney A. Marchand, *The Flight of a Century (1800–1900) in Ascension Parish, Louisiana* (Donaldsonville, La., 1936), 177.

new Sanitary Excavating Company to clean New Orleans privies, and scores of "benevolent" societies received state charters. The Levee Company's charter was amended in the public interest, but the efficiency of the corporation was not increased. Lincoln Parish was created in 1873, Carrollton was annexed to New Orleans in 1874, and Brashear City was renamed Morgan City in 1876.[29]

3

Corruption existed during Kellogg's administration, but the flamboyant thievery of the Warmoth days was past. The most celebrated scandal involved auditor Charles Clinton, but it is difficult to this day to decide whether or not Clinton was actually guilty of wrongdoing. Early in Kellogg's term a power struggle broke out between Clinton and treasurer Antoine Dubuclet, a black whose honesty was never questioned. Clinton apparently was auditing accounts of tax collectors, then sending them on to the treasurer with their collections accompanied by favored warrant holders. These warrant holders were thus able to cash their warrants at once for face value. Also, Clinton was accused of embezzling some twenty thousand dollars. He was impeached by the house of representatives in April, 1875, but was never brought to trial before the senate. He was indicted by a grand jury, however, but at his trial the jury was unable to agree, reportedly being divided eleven to one for conviction. In the meantime a committee appointed by the governor investigated the auditor's office and reported some apparent instances of fraud, but none involving culpability on the part of Clinton. Nonetheless on July 23, a few days after his trial, Clinton resigned effective December 15. In accepting the resignation, Kellogg expressed his confidence in Clinton's integrity. All was not right in the auditor's office; when the Nicholls administration took over in 1877, some important records were missing.[30]

The Kellogg legislatures were ridiculed in the press and in books written by visitors almost as much as the South Carolina assemblies of

29 *Acts of Louisiana, 1873–1876.*
30 New Orleans *Daily Picayune,* July 10–12, 1873, August 12, 1874, April 22, June, December 15, 1875, January 21, February 16, 18, 1876, May 31, 1877; Gonzales, "William Pitt Kellogg," 448–49, 470–71; Ewing, "Early Louisiana Impeachments," 703–705.

the same time. An objective observer must conclude that they were not as bad as they were painted. This is not to say that the legislatures were completely honest. A number of members, Democratic and Republican, were known to be in the service of the Louisiana Lottery. The purchase of the St. Louis Hotel as a state house, passed over the governor's veto, was probably accomplished by not altogether honorable means. The most barefaced fraud, or attempt at fraud, was the alteration of the general appropriations act of 1875 after it had passed the legislature. The fraudulent bill was promulgated by the secretary of state before Speaker Michael Hahn and Lieutenant-Governor C. C. Antoine discovered the alterations. The appropriation bill actually adopted was included in the printed statutes of 1875.[31]

Most Louisiana stealing from 1873 through 1876 was petty peculation. Various kinds of fraud were practiced in the parishes. In Carroll the tax collector collected the tax in currency then settled with the police jury by presenting near-worthless parish scrip. In Plaquemines some fraudulent bonds were issued. The threat to raise tax assessments was used for blackmail, and in other instances assessments were arbitrarily raised, whereupon for a consideration "fixers" could get them reduced again. Pluralism and absenteeism were common. "The officials of this state nearly all fill one or two [other] offices. Members of the legislature are rewarded . . . by appointment to tax-collectorships. . . . If the Governor cannot take care of them, the Custom House is open."[32] One extreme case was the East Baton Rouge sheriff who appointed a deputy to look after the jail. The deputy then hired a substitute for part of his salary. The substitute then put the custody of the jail into the hands of a prisoner who, as compensation, was allowed to come and go as he pleased. The most tragic corruption during the Kellogg regime was the embezzlement of parish school funds. The embezzlers were in many instances black men. This perhaps made the offense worse because outside of New Orleans the public schools were almost entirely schools for black children. The money was hon-

---

31 Wiggins, "The Louisiana Press and the Lottery," *Louisiana Historical Quarterly,* XXXI (July, 1948), 742–53; Alwes, "Louisiana State Lottery," 991–1,047; *Acts of Louisiana, 1875,* 27–28, 39–40; New Orleans *Daily Picayune,* March 31, April 6, 1875.
32 New Orleans *Daily Picayune,* April 16, 1874.

estly apportioned and distributed by the state superintendent; it was in the parishes that it was stolen. Most of the sums involved were under $5,000, but Senator Dave Young of Concordia Parish was indicted for making away with $31,000 of school money.[33]

Kellogg was so generous in granting pardons that Democratic newspapers accused him of abusing the pardoning power. No doubt many pardons were granted for political reasons, but there is no evidence that pardons were sold. Most of the prisoners pardoned were blacks, which probably accounted for some indignation in the press. But the punishment of black offenders did not cease; lynchings were common and gruesome public hangings were reported in the papers. In August, 1874, five men, one white, were legally hanged on one day in the little village of Napoleonville. In practice it was not the Negro offender who escaped punishment; those who went unpunished were "respectable" white Conservatives who turned to violence to achieve political ends.[34]

4

Grant Parish had been created from territory formerly in Winn and Rapides parishes while Warmoth was governor. The parish seat, located on the farm of a good Republican, was named Colfax in honor of Ulysses S. Grant's first-term vice-president. This little village was to be the scene in 1873 of one of the bloodiest events in Louisiana history, the famous, or infamous, Colfax Riot. To what extent this event developed spontaneously from local causes and to what extent it was planned is difficult to say. Certainly the ingredients for racial conflict were present. Grant Parish was made up of two distinct areas, the narrow alluvial plain of the Red River, occupied by cotton plantations and with a largely black population, and the adjacent hill country, inhabited largely by Negro-hating white yeoman farmers. But it should also be noted that in the neighboring state of Mississippi it had

33 *Ibid.*, February 28, March 6, April 12, August 21, October 6, 1874, February 5, July 28, August 18, October 23, 1875, February 2, 1876; Lestage, "The White League," 649–52; Nordhoff, *The Cotton States*, 47, 51; DuBois, *Black Reconstruction*, 476–77.
34 New Orleans *Daily Picayune*, August 22, 1874, May 16, 1877; Gonzales, "William Pitt Kellogg," 482–83; Copeland, "The New Orleans Press and Reconstruction," 228.

been discovered as early as 1871 that the freedmen, "economically dependent, and timid and unresourceful after generations of servitude, would offer no effective resistance" to violence.[35] Furthermore, unless the blacks were propped up by outside help, resistance to white domination in an area collapsed after "riots" had killed some freedmen and frightened many more.[36] This was known in Louisiana.

After the election of 1872, the Warmoth Returning Board had commissioned Alphonse Cazabat as parish judge and Christopher Columbus Nash as sheriff, and these men had taken office. Early in March, 1873, however, Kellogg named R. C. Register as judge and Daniel Shaw as sheriff. On March 23, 1873, Kellogg's people, including William Ward, a black state representative and former officer in the Grant Parish militia unit, took possession of the courthouse at Colfax. According to the *Picayune*, when arms had been sent to the Grant Parish militia, Ward, over General Longstreet's protest, had issued the weapons to individual freedmen who took them home. Anticipating the use of force by whites of the parish, blacks armed with Enfield rifles and other miscellaneous firearms came out to guard the Kellogg officials at the courthouse. Trenches were dug, and some "artillery," which probably would have been most dangerous to fire, was made from old steam pipes. The assembled blacks were drilled daily by Ward, by a northern-born Negro named Flowers, and by Levi Allen, a black Union veteran. All three of these men had served in the Union army during the Civil War. It is impossible to determine how many blacks were in Colfax guarding the courthouse. Contemporary estimates range from less than two hundred to more than four hundred.[37]

Early in April pickets were placed at all approaches to Colfax, and whites were not allowed to enter the town without reasons satisfactory to the pickets. On April 1, a Judge Rutland of Colfax was ordered to leave town, which he proceeded to do, followed within a few hours by his wife and children. He left within his house a casket containing the remains of one of his children who had died in Calcasieu Parish

---

35 Wharton, *The Negro in Mississippi,* 189.
36 *Ibid.,* 188–89; Manie White Johnson, "The Colfax Riot of April, 1873," *Louisiana Historical Quarterly,* XIII (July, 1930), 398.
37 Johnson, "The Colfax Riot," 399–401; New Orleans *Daily Picayune,* March 8, April 5, 10, 1873; Gonzales, "William Pitt Kellogg," 419–20.

six years earlier; the body had been exhumed and brought to Colfax for reburial. That night Judge Rutland's house was ransacked and the casket thrown into the road. Other white men were forced to depart, as was a freedman named Butler, who had become a merchant in Colfax. Officers and passengers of steamboats coming into New Orleans reported that Colfax and the riverbank for several miles above and below the town were occupied by armed Negroes. Judge Register, Flowers, and Ward soon left Grant Parish for New Orleans, leaving Allen in command.[38]

Some ten miles north of Colfax lay the white village of Montgomery. Concerned about the state of affairs in Colfax, a group of Montgomery citizens, unarmed, went into town for a conference on April 1, but soon left in fear of their lives. Another parley was arranged a day or two later, but this broke up when it was learned that a black farmer near Colfax had been shot to death by a group of white men as he worked on a fence. The stage was thus set for tragedy in Grant Parish, and the tragedy came on Easter Sunday, April 13. The thirst for blood was not confined to white Conservatives, however; the New Orleans *Republican* stated on April 12: "The local majority of Grant Parish is prepared to clean out the minority . . . in twenty-four hours or less. . . . The time is past, if ever it existed, when a handful of whites could frighten a regiment of colored men."[39]

The *Picayune*, in an editorial published after the massacre but set in type before the news reached New Orleans, said: "We have been waiting to hear that the white men of Grant and the adjoining parishes had taken care of the lawlessness in their neighborhood."[40] Judge Rutland appealed to Kellogg for help, but got no response. The governor at this time was under attack by black members of his party, and there is evidence that the armed blacks at Colfax were almost as hostile to white Republicans as to white Democrats. An appeal to federal authorities also was rejected. In the meantime "Sheriff" Nash had summoned a posse. Hundreds of men reported to him, coming from all the neighboring parishes, including, according to the memory

38 *House Reports*, 43rd Cong., 2nd Sess., No. 261, p. 15, cited in Johnson, "The Colfax Riot," 400; New Orleans *Daily Picayune*, April 5–12, 1873.
39 New Orleans *Republican*, April 12, 1873.
40 New Orleans *Daily Picayune*, April 15, 1873.

of an aged participant, the "Old Time Ku Klux Klan" from Sicily Island, which rushed to the support of white supremacy "when that Tytantic [*sic*] Black hand was sweeping over the Red River Valley in 1873."[41] Nash secured warrants for the arrest of a number of Negroes, presumably from the Conservative parish judge who had, like himself, been ousted from office.[42]

On Easter morning Nash led his posse, deployed in line of battle, into Colfax. Under a flag of truce he conferred with Allen, who apparently was a man of great courage, and demanded the surrender of the men for whom he had warrants. According to one chronicler, when Allen refused this demand, Nash warned that "we are going to get 'em." Allen laconically replied, "I'll see you when you get 'em."[43] Nash gave Allen half an hour to get women, children, and men who did not want to fight out of town.[44]

The accounts of the fighting at Colfax are conflicting, but apparently an exchange of fire went on for several hours. Black casualties during this phase are not known, but one of the white attackers was killed and eight or nine were wounded. Of the wounded men, a Mr. Hadnot who was a member of the McEnery legislature, died. Eventually the black defenders abandoned their fortifications and took refuge in the courthouse. From there some of them continued to return fire; others tried to hide under the building. Nash's posse then set the courthouse on fire. Some Negroes were killed as they fled from the building, some burned to death inside, a few escaped, and thirty-seven were taken prisoner. That night the prisoners were taken out and shot in cold blood; a few of them, left for dead, managed to make their escape and were able to testify in court against members of the posse. One white man, Kellogg's Sheriff Shaw, was reported killed fighting against Nash's posse. The total number of blacks killed is unknown. Some bodies were taken away by relatives. A deputy United States marshal who reached Colfax on April 14 or 15 found sixty-nine Negro bodies and buried them in a common grave. Among the dead was

---

41 Quoted in Johnson, "The Colfax Riot," 409.
42 New Orleans *Daily Picayune*, March 6, 1874; Gonzales, "William Pitt Kellogg," 425; Johnson, "The Colfax Riot," 402–403, 407.
43 Johnson, "The Colfax Riot," 410.
44 *Ibid.*

Alexander Fellman, who had been a delegate to the constitutional convention of 1868. The available reports do not make clear whether Levi Allen was killed or escaped. It seems probable that he perished.[45] Metropolitan Police arrived a day or two after the riot, and within a week they were reinforced by United States troops. Kellogg officials were restored, but they seem to have made little or no effort to exert the powers of their offices. To the extent that it was not under military rule, Grant Parish was in a state of anarchy, but within a year this was to be true of much of the state. The Metropolitans set about arresting as many of the participants in the riot as they could identify and find, a total of nine. Nash escaped by swimming his horse across Red River under fire and supposedly took refuge in Sabine Parish. During the ensuing year, he appeared fairly often on the middle reaches of Red River.[46]

The effect of the Colfax Riot upon northern public opinion was certainly adverse to the cause of Louisiana Conservatism. The Republicans had a new issue, though it was not well-timed for electioneering. The northern reaction was not nearly so strong, however, as it had been after the New Orleans Riot of 1866. An anti-Grant publication regarded the "horrible massacre" as "a not unnatural consequence of the position in which Congress left the dispute . . . over the government of the state."[47] Among Louisiana whites the most common reaction was to deplore the necessity for the killing but not to question that necessity. Undoubtedly the violence at Colfax encouraged more violence. In August Kellogg's appointee as mayor of Shreveport, Joseph Taylor, was forced to resign when "he found affairs getting complicated."[48] In September District Attorney Arthur H. Harris, a Democrat, and District Judge T. S. Crawford, a Republican, were murdered from ambush in Franklin Parish; in No-

---

45 *Ibid.*, 410–18; New Orleans *Daily Picayune*, April 26, 1873; Shreveport *Times*, April 26, 1873; New Orleans *Republican*, April–May, 1873; Gonzales, "William Pitt Kellogg," 419; Highsmith, "Louisiana During Reconstruction," 309–10; Highsmith, "Some Aspects of Reconstruction in Louisiana," 485.

46 New Orleans *Daily Picayune*, April–May, August 2, December 5, 21, 1873, January 18, 1874; Johnson, "The Colfax Riot," 424; Carter, *The Angry Scar*, 208; Garner (ed.), *Studies in Southern History and Politics*, 197–98.

47 *Nation*, XVI (April 24, 1873), 277.

48 New Orleans *Daily Picayune*, August 9, 1873.

vember four blacks accused of rape there were lynched. In many parts of the state persons whom Kellogg selected for office feared to accept the appointments.[49]

The most important effect of the Colfax Riot upon Reconstruction as a whole was in the realm of court decisions. In 1871 a federal circuit court had ruled that despite the Fourteenth and Fifteenth amendments to the United States Constitution, the right to vote was derived from the states, not from the federal government.[50] The trial of the white men arrested for participation at Colfax dealt another blow to the power of the United States government to enforce the Fifteenth Amendment.

The nine men accused of taking part in the Colfax Riot went on trial in federal court in New Orleans on February 23, 1874, charged with violating the "Ku Klux" Act, which provided that the punishment for crimes committed to prevent the exercise of rights and privileges by citizens of the United States should be the same as the punishment provided for the same crime by the state in which the crime was committed. Since the Grant Parish prisoners were charged with murder, they were not admitted to bail. The prosecution proved that the killings had taken place and produced numerous Negro witnesses who specifically identified the accused as having been participants. The defense, on the other hand, produced witnesses who swore to an alibi for every one of the accused. The alibies still suggest perjury after almost a century—well-meant, but perjury nonetheless. The jury acquitted one of the accused, but brought in a mistrial for the other eight. The eight were denied bail, despite a plea by prominent citizens, but the presiding judge promised an early trial. This second trial began in May, 1874, with a jury of three blacks and nine whites. This time four of the accused were acquitted, but the remainder, including William B. Cruikshank, were found guilty of conspiracy against

49 *Ibid.*, September 10, October–November, 1873, June 12, 1874; Shreveport *Times*, April 26, May 14, 1873; Lonn, *Reconstruction in Louisiana*, 243–45; Robert Barnwell Rhett to William Porcher Miles, August 27, 1873, in William Porcher Miles Papers, Southern Historical Collection, University of North Carolina; Gonzales, "William Pitt Kellogg," 427; S. H. Cardill to Kellogg, October 20, 1873, in Kellogg Papers; Kellogg Papers, 1873–1874, *passim*.

50 Richard Claude, "Constitutional Voting Rights and Early U. S. Supreme Court Decisions," *Journal of Negro History*, LI (April, 1966), 116.

a peaceful assemblage, not of murder. Also, the jury recommended mercy. Those convicted appealed to the United States Circuit Court, which heard the case shortly afterward.

The Federal Circuit Court of Appeals was made up of the original trial judge and Associate Justice Bradley of the United States Supreme Court. Bradley's opinion was that the power of Congress to enforce the Fifteenth Amendment did not include the power to provide punishment for crimes punishable under the laws of the state where they were committed. Judge Woods, the trial judge, disagreed, so the case was certified to the United States Supreme Court. In the meantime the prisoners were admitted to bail, and white Louisianians realized that they no longer needed to worry about the Enforcement Acts. In 1876, the Supreme Court agreed with Justice Bradley. Already, in the famous Slaughterhouse Cases of 1873, the Supreme Court had held that the privileges and immunities clause of the Fourteenth Amendment did not protect those rights derived from the states under the concept of dual citizenship. Then, in 1875, in *United States* v. *Reese*, the court had declared certain parts of the Enforcement Acts unconstitutional. The decision in the Cruikshank case left the federal government almost powerless to protect the freedmen except by the use of troops, and these ordinarily had to be requested by the legislature or the governor of the state concerned. The Supreme Court was probably responding to northern public opinion as well as to an extremely strict interpretation of the Constitution. Most of the money spent to enforce the Enforcement Acts had been spent in the North, leading one historian to wonder "how much Radical Reconstruction was really concerned with the South and how much with the party needs of Republicans in the North."[51] An avowed Radical such as Ben Wade of Ohio could say in a private letter in 1873 that he was "sick of niggers."[52]

---

51 Woodward, "Seeds of Failure in Radical Race Policy," 9.
52 Patrick W. Riddlebarger, "The Radicals' Abandonment of the Negro During Reconstruction," *Journal of Negro History*, XLV (April, 1960), 91; see also Claude, "Constitutional Voting Rights," 119–20; New Orleans *Republican*, May 19–June 11, 1874; New Orleans *Daily Picayune*, February 28–March, May–June, 1874, March 29, 1876; Dunning, *Essays on the Civil War and Reconstruction*, 366–67; Dunning, *Reconstruction, Political and Economic*, 260–65; Franklin, *Reconstruction After the Civil War*, 206–209; Garner (ed.), *Studies in Southern History and Politics*, 199, 207, 225–27; Swinney, "Enforcing the Fifteenth Amendment," 208.

5

After their first attempt forcibly to take over the state government had failed and their legislature had been dismembered, the McEnery forces turned to "Tax Resistance" as a means of opposing Kellogg. The plan, obviously, was to bring down the Kellogg government by denying it revenues. McEnery issued a proclamation warning the people of Louisiana against paying their taxes to persons pretending to be tax collectors under Kellogg, and he wrote a letter to each parish, recommending a mass meeting of citizens "with a view to resistance of collection of taxes by the Kellogg Government." The people were assured that "It is impossible that the Kellogg usurpation can survive beyond the meeting of Congress in December next."[53]

The response to this suggestion was widespread. After all, it appealed to the dislike of property owners for Radicalism and gave them an excuse for holding on to money which otherwise would have gone for taxes. There were few, if any, instances of taxes being tendered to McEnery officials, but mass meetings were held, fierce speeches were made, and solemn resolves to pay no taxes to the usurping regime were adopted. In many parishes attorneys offered free representation to tax resisters.[54]

Kellogg was characterized by some as a weak man, but there was nothing weak about his response to this Tax Resistance movement. In St. Martin Parish the ubiquitous Colonel Alcibiades DeBlanc led the resisters. Kellogg ordered a detachment of the Metropolitan Police under General A. S. Badger to proceed to St. Martinville, install the officials named by the Returning Board, and preserve order. Badger landed 125 men at New Iberia on May 3 and marched on St. Martinville two days later. DeBlanc was reported to head 600 men, but, if so, he kept them under good control. There was much shooting, but casualties were light; only two Metropolitans were killed and only a

---

53 New Orleans *Daily Picayune*, March 22, 1873; see also New Orleans *Daily Picayune*, March 15, 1873; Highsmith, "Louisiana During Reconstruction," 274–85; Gonzales, "William Pitt Kellogg," 423; Roger W. Shugg, "Survival of the Plantation System in Louisiana," *Journal of Southern History*, III (May, 1937), 311–12.

54 New Orleans *Republican*, May 6–14, 1873; New Orleans *Daily Picayune*, March–April, 1873; Shreveport *Times*, April–May, 1873; Opelousas *Courier*, March 22, 1873, cited in Windham, "White Supremacy in Louisiana," 42.

few men wounded on each side. Reinforcements went to Badger from New Orleans, but they were delayed for a time at Morgan City when no steamer would transport them to the Teche. They arrived, about 75 strong, on May 8. On May 9, according to Badger's report, De-Blanc's men had dispersed into small groups and were heading home.

DeBlanc himself was arrested, along with a few of his followers. He was brought to New Orleans on May 16 and received a hero's welcome from a crowd at the waterfront. He and his fellows were charged with violation of the Enforcement Act of 1871 by intimidating Negroes. This charge was hardly applicable; DeBlanc was trying to intimidate the Kellogg government. Before a United States commissioner for a preliminary hearing, all the witnesses, including nine Negroes, testified that DeBlanc's forces had resisted the Metropolitan Police to the point of killing two of them, but they were unanimous in denying that any Negroes had been intimidated. The commissioner ruled that since only Louisiana law had been violated, the federal courts had no jurisdiction. Kellogg was probably satisfied. The insurrection in the Attakapas country had been put down, and taxes were being collected there. Two hundred federal troops landed soon after the "battle," so there was no danger of further resistance in that area.[55]

Kellogg used force in other areas. On their way back from New Iberia, the Metropolitan Police stopped over in Terrebonne Parish long enough to install Kellogg officials there and, according to one account, to get drunk. The same procedure was applied to Tangipahoa Parish, and when citizens of Catahoula Parish refused to pay licenses, they were brought to New Orleans in custody. Seldom if ever were such offenders brought to trial, and apparently none was ever convicted. But the inconvenience of being arrested and brought to New Orleans and the expense involved in obtaining bail and legal assistance were significant deterrents.[56]

The most effective way of dealing with tax resisters, however, was simply to seize their property and sell it for taxes. The large number

55 New Orleans *Daily Picayune,* May, 1873; Opelousas *Courier,* May 10, 1873, quoted in Windham, "White Supremacy in Louisiana," 42.

56 New Orleans *Daily Picayune,* April 29, May 14–15, 1873; Gonzales, "William Pitt Kellogg," 423.

of tax sales reported by observers and later chroniclers was a result, first, of tax resistance, and second, of the depression of 1873, rather than of high taxes and corruption. In 1873, at least, much of the property advertised for sale was redeemed before the sale took place. Even the *Picayune*, scheduled to go under the sheriff's hammer in early May, 1873, decided to pay up before being sold out.[57]

President Grant added to Kellogg's power to combat tax resistance by a proclamation of May 22, 1873, in which he explicitly recognized Kellogg and his legislature as the rightful government of Louisiana. Kellogg had already had support from Washington, but this proclamation made it clear that he could continue to have it. At the next session of the Louisiana legislature a law was enacted which gave a person whose property was sold for taxes only six months to redeem it, and for redemption he had to pay the full price the purchaser had paid plus taxes, penalties, and costs, plus 50 percent of such taxes, penalties, and costs. In one instance, a tax of $58, due in 1873 and delinquent for one year, became $116.03. By June of 1873, however, the backbone of the tax resistance movement had been broken. By October, Kellogg had proved more successful than any governor since the war in collecting taxes due to the state.[58] It is quite possible that if it had not been for the depression, Kellogg might have achieved balanced budgets for the years 1874 through 1876.

6

When it became evident that Kellogg's government had the full support of Grant's administration, the more sophisticated businesmen of New Orleans, with some support from surrounding parishes in south Louisiana, launched what came to be known as the Unification Movement. Before 1873, as has been noted, there had been efforts to enlist Negroes in political activity opposed to the Radicals, but the Conservatives had sought to deal from Mount Olympus, and the blacks were offered little more than the privilege of cooperating with their

---

57 A. S. Herron to Warmoth, April 26, 1873, in Warmoth Papers; Nordhoff, *The Cotton States*, 59–60; New Orleans *Daily Picayune*, April 20, 25, 29, 1873.

58 New Orleans *Daily Picayune*, June, October 23, 1873, July 7, 21–22, 1875; Shreveport *Times*, November 27, 1873, March 26, 1875; *Acts of Louisiana, 1874*, 154–55; Lonn, *Reconstruction in Louisiana*, 244–45; Gonzales, "William Pitt Kellogg," 461.

white superiors. Not surprisingly, the blacks had chosen to cast their lot with the Radicals, who offered them something, if only a few scraps.

Probably the chief motive of the Unification Movement of 1873 was economic. The disorders and uncertainty which had followed the election of 1872 had hurt New Orleans business, and it was mainly businessmen who led and promoted unification. Most of the city's newspapers gave support, and a committee of one hundred black and white leaders was formed to draw up specific proposals. The real white leader was Isaac N. Marks, a prominent businessman, but General P. G. T. Beauregard became the spokesman of the movement, no doubt because he was a local hero. Marks, Beauregard, and the other white Unificationists were willing—and in the Louisiana of their day this was quite a concession—to recognize the validity of the Fourteenth and Fifteenth amendments to the United States Constitution. The resolutions advocated, among other things, the recognition of every civil and political right guaranteed by the Constitution, that public places be open to all regardless of race and color, integration of the public schools, and equal employment opportunities for both races. Rural blacks were to be encouraged to become landowners, violence was condemned, and public offices would be divided equally between the two races. The black members of the committee agreed that as soon as discrimination in public accommodations was ended and a feasible plan for dividing political offices adopted, they would give their support to plans to reduce taxation, to "correct" the public debt, and to secure the establishment of an "honest, economic and patriotic government."[59] The black signers of this statement were mainly from the old property-holding class of New Orleans free Negroes. They included Aristide Mary, P. Bonsegneur, Dr. Roudanez, and William Randolph. Also a signatory, however, was Lieutenant-Governor C. C. Antoine, who had been a slave before the Civil War.[60]

The conservative newspapers of New Orleans supported the Unification Movement. The Donaldsonville *Chief* and the Opelousas *Courier* expressed some sympathy with Unification, but such sym-

59 Unification Movement Papers, 1873, in Department of Archives, Louisiana State University.
60 *Ibid.*; New Orleans *Republican*, July, 1873.

pathy was rare in the country. How the people of the city felt is more difficult to determine, but it is doubtful that they were as willing as businessmen to make concessions to the blacks. Whatever the popular feeling inside New Orleans, where one later writer referred to Unification as a "Quixotic scheme,"[61] public sentiment in the country parishes, especially those north of Baton Rouge, was definitely hostile. The Shreveport *Times* was strongly opposed: "Let our people realize that the salvation of Louisiana does not depend on the negro, but on railroads and white immigration."[62] Later this paper spoke more strongly: "The hope of Louisiana is in the white race; in its increase and in its dominion within her borders, and we hold as folly all political movements that have not that object in view."[63] Parish officials of Catahoula insisted that all other questions must be subordinated to racial separation: "If the political death of the state must be the consequence, let us accept it."[64]

While the Democrats of northern Louisiana were damning Unification from one side, the Radical Republicans were belaboring it on the other. Former senator West and Governor Kellogg both dismissed the movement as a plot against the Republican party. Unification was almost certainly doomed by disapproval from the northern, Protestant parishes of the state, but it was the Radicals who dealt the death blow. A great mass meeting was held in New Orleans on July 15, 1873. Marks presided and spoke; three of the other four speakers were black men. T. T. Allain's address was conciliatory, but J. Henri Burch, who had married Oscar Dunn's widow, took a very different line. Burch, a black Carpetbagger, noted that southern whites had refused to recognize the right of Negroes to freedom and citizenship.

> Year after year we have waited and hoped for the consummation of the last closing act of our great life's drama, the full and unconditional recognition of our civil rights.
> Year after year you who have kept us from the full enjoyment of them have been swimming in the charmed circle of policy and temporary expedients. . . .

61 Prichard (ed.), "White League in New Orleans," 531.
62 Shreveport *Times*, July 2, 1873.
63 *Ibid.*, July 15, 1873.
64 Quoted in Williams, *Romance and Realism in Southern Politics*, 39.

You, gentlemen of Louisiana, cannot stand still and indulge in constitutional hair-splitting as to the legality of laws enacted for the protection of the blacks, nor the right of our national Congress to enact such laws.[65]

At this July 15 meeting, Negro leaders pledged themselves to join with the whites to secure better government only when "the existing opposition against the enjoyment of our rights to be admitted on an equal footing with other citizens in places of public amusement and public resort, to receive equal accommodations in public conveyances, steamboats, and in public hotels, admission in public schols and other public institutions of learning shall have ceased, and so soon as our fellow citizens will be disposed to divide the Governmental powers equally between the two races."[66]

Burch and other black leaders, if their words be accepted at face value, were only demanding what the Unificationists had already proposed to give. But there was a vast difference between the granting of rights by patriarchial whites and the demanding of those same rights by black politicians. Unification was already sick unto death for lack of statewide white support. The refusal of Negro leaders to subscribe wholeheartedly was enough to cut off the last breath. In the climate of the time, Unification probably had no chance of success, but it does seem tragic that neither white nor black was willing to try it. One thing was made clear. The problem of race overrode all other Louisiana problems, political or economic. This would be evident in the next stage of Louisiana Reconstruction, the formation of the famous—or infamous—White League.[67]

7

There was a change in temper among white Louisianians in 1873 and 1874. Colfax was the first of a series of violent episodes of greater

65 New Orleans *Daily Picayune*, July 16, 1873.
66 *Ibid.*
67 Williams, *Romance and Realism in Southern Politics*, 21–43, provides the best account of the Unification Movement. See also Unification Movement Papers, 1873; New Orleans *Daily Picayune*, June–July, 1873, October 8, 1874; New Orleans *Republican*, July, 1873; *Nation*, XVI (June 26, 1873), 426; Shreveport *Times*, June 26, July 2, 1873; Vincent J. C. Marsala, "The Louisiana Unification Movement of 1873" (M.A. thesis, Louisiana State University, 1962), 51, 54, 60–64, 70; Gonzales, "William Pitt Kellogg," 426–27.

magnitude than had occurred since the New Orleans Riot of 1866. Many factors contributed to this change in temper. Resentment of the Kellogg "usurpation" played a major role. The success of violence against blacks in other states, particularly Mississippi, contributed to similar actions in Louisiana. The depression which began in 1873 probably accentuated the reckless abandon with which acts of violence were committed, but the mood which brought violence, as at Colfax, was present before the depression began. The fact that so few of the participants in the Colfax Riot were arrested, and that these were eventually freed, encouraged others to go and do likewise.

What happened was that the race hatred which had long existed among most white Louisianians, but which had to some extent been held in check by fear of federal authority and by some leading Conservative politicians who clung to the hope of using the Negro vote, broke out into the open. General approval of Colfax had been expressed immediately after the event, and almost a year later the Shreveport *Times* returned to the subject: "We shall not pretend to conceal our *gratification at the summary and hopeful lesson* the Negroes have been taught in Grant Parish. . . . The wonder is not that there was one Colfax, *but that there is not one in every parish.*"[68] A transplanted northerner who had been a Radical in 1866 wrote from St. Mary Parish in March, 1873: "You can hardly form an idea of the condition we are now in down here and altho I am a law and order man I think it is about time to resort to extreme measures."[69] A businessman wrote north from Baton Rouge: "Our Government is a Negroe one we are entirely under the command of the Negroe. . . .the prosecuting attorney the sheriff the Clerk assessor and Collector Marshal of the town and all the Constables Treasurer [are Negroes] and the Balance are Carpet Baggers."[70]

In June of 1874, even a Catholic church publication could state "That . . . the colored people are and have been carrying on a relent-

68 Shreveport *Times*, July 10, 1874; see also Williams, "Analysis of Some Reconstruction Attitudes," 484.

69 Thompson to Woodman, March 2, 1873, in Marquette (ed.), "Letters of a Yankee Sugar Planter," 526.

70 Payne to Mrs. Sterrett, September 10, 1873, in Barnhart (ed.), "Reconstruction on the Lower Mississippi," 395.

less war on the whites. . . . There is but one way now to manage the Negro. He is, as a class, amenable to neither reason nor gratitude. He must be starved into the common perceptions of decency."[71] And George Washington Cable, who was to be driven from the South because he championed the rights of black men after the end of Reconstruction, and who was not a hater of blacks, wrote in later years: "In the practical daily experiences of life I saw the Freedman in all his offensiveness, multitudinous, unclean, stupid, ugly, ignorant, and insolent. Maybe it was not as bad as it looked to me. I am telling how it looked. If the much feared war of races should come . . . I was going to be in the ranks of the white race fighting for the subjugation of the blacks."[72]

The formation of the White League in Louisiana can probably be said to have begun with the publication of a newspaper, the *Caucasian*, at Alexandria on March 28, 1874. The publishers were three former Confederate officers, and they argued from the beginning that the Radicals had already made politics in Louisiana a matter of race. They demanded that all previous party labels be forgotten, and that the issue be the simple one of white man against black man. DuBois suggests that a meeting was held in New Orleans in May, 1874, of representatives from all the states still under Radical control to arrange for a final drive against Radical regimes in the South, and that this meeting led to the White League of Louisiana and similar organizations in other states. This seems doubtful. Rather, the alignment of white against black seems to have been an idea whose time had come.[73]

The *Caucasian* set no limits to the tenor of its attempts to arouse white against black: "There will be no security, no peace, and no prosperity for Louisiana until the government of the state is restored to the hands of the honest, intelligent, and tax-paying masses; until the superiority of the Caucasian over the African in all affairs pertain-

71 New Orleans *Catholic Messenger*, June 14, 1874, quoted in Stuart Omer Landry, *The Battle of Liberty Place: The Overthrow of Carpetbag Rule in New Orleans—September 14, 1874* (New Orleans, 1955), 47–48.
72 Cable, *The Negro Question*, 7.
73 Lestage, "The White League," 637; Coulter, *The South During Reconstruction*, 684–85; Highsmith, "Louisiana During Reconstruction," 300–301; DuBois, *Black Reconstruction*, 684–85.

ing to government, is acknowledged and established."[74] This and like appeals led to the organization at Opelousas on April 27, 1874, of what can be considered the first White League. The resolutions adopted at this meeting were to serve more or less as a model for dozens of others adopted elsewhere before the end of the year.

WHEREAS, the colored people of . . . Louisiana . . . have had undivided control of the legislation of the state since 1868 . . . although abundant opportunity has been given them to demonstrate their capacity as lawmakers it can no longer be questioned that the capacity . . . has not been used for the good of the country, but . . . for its degradation—morally, socially and politically, and

WHEREAS, the Republican party being composed almost entirely of Negroes . . . the black people are responsible for the abuse of office and corrupt legislation. . . .

Therefore

Be it resolved, 1st, That we hold the colored people responsible for most of the evils arising from fraudulent and corrupt legislation. . . .

Resolved, 2nd, that our experience with the colored people demonstrates their utter incapacity for good government. . . .

Resolved, 4th, That the issue in the next campaign is not between Republicans and Democrats or Liberals, but between the whites and blacks, and that the issue is: Shall the white people of Louisiana govern Louisiana? . . .

Resolved, 5th, That the conduct of the black man, as a politician, alone has forced upon the white man the necessity of making the issue in self defense, and . . . we can and will unite as a race to protect ourselves against . . . the other race. . . .

Resolved, 7th, That we recognize the necessity of union among ourselves . . . and that we earnestly invite all white men, without regard to former party affiliations, to unite with us under the banner of the White League; which alone can rescue us from dessention [*sic*] and defeat.[75]

The next organization apparently was effected at Mansfield, but the League rapidly swept over the state. An organizational meeting was held in Breaux Bridge on June 14, and another at Franklin before the end of that month. When the new League was challenged by the Republican *Attakapas Register*, that paper's press was destroyed.

74 Alexandria *Caucasian*, April 4, 1874, quoted in Windham, "White Supremacy in Louisiana," 48.
75 Resolutions Adopted at Organization of White League at Opelousas, April 27, 1874, quoted in Lestage, "The White League," 641–42.

By July many, if not most, of the parishes had White Leagues. A leader at Vermilionville was the familiar Alcibiades DeBlanc. Riots at Vicksburg, Mississippi, in August, 1874, in which the Mississippi White Line was clearly victorious, promoted the success of the White League in Louisiana. There never was, so far as can be determined, any overall state organization. Parish and local leagues, although they were much alike, were not uniform. The statements of purpose drawn up were meant to deal with the local as well as the statewide situation.[76] On the other hand, none of the White League resolutions disagreed with the following editorial in the Shreveport *Comet* in October, 1874:

> While we are willing and always have been to give the Negro everything he needs and should have . . . *we are not and never will be in favor of his ruling the state of Louisiana any longer and we swear by the Eternal Spirit that rules the universe we will battle against it to the day of our death* . . . Let each man make it his special duty to watch the pothouse scalawagers, as they have spotted skins and black hearts. . . . *Somebody ought to make these black-hearted villains angels at once*, for . . . the quicker such monumental liars take . . . wings and fly away, the better.[77]

The White League swept into New Orleans in June of 1874. There was some reluctance among the city's Conservatives, but the city as a whole followed the lead of Opelousas. Action in New Orleans was hastened by reports, seemingly without foundation, that Black Leagues were being formed to enforce civil rights. The *Picayune*, a few days after announcing the existence of Black Leagues, blandly noted that "if there never was such a plot, our article will only have

76 New Orleans *Republican*, June 12, August 29, 1874; Lestage, "The White League," 638–39, 643, 653, 657; Breaux Bridge *Attakapas Sentinel*, June 4, 11, 1874; White League Documents, in Paul Deballion Papers, Department of Archives, University of Southwestern Louisiana; New Orleans *Daily Picayune*, June 27, July 7, August 5, 8, 1874; White League Resolutions, Winn Parish, July, 1874, quoted in Carter, *The Angry Scar*, 224–25; New Iberia *Sugar Bowl*, July 19, 1874, quoted in Landry, *Battle of Liberty Place*, 54; New Orleans *Times*, August 4, 1874, quoted in Windham, "White Supremacy in Louisiana," 50; Highsmith, 'Some Aspects of Reconstruction in Louisiana," 489; Sidney James Romero, "The Political Career of Murphy James Foster, Governor of Louisiana, 1892–1900," *Louisiana Historical Quarterly*, XXVIII (October, 1945), 1,139; Kathryn Reinhart Schuler, "Women in Public Affairs in Louisiana During Reconstruction," *Louisiana Historical Quarterly*, XIX (July, 1936), 745.
77 Quoted in Landry, *Battle of Liberty Place*, 47.

the effect of promoting on the part of the whites an organization which all must admit to be immediately necessary."[78]

No mass organizational meetings such as were common in the country parishes took place in New Orleans. On the contrary, the Crescent City Democratic Club, a paramilitary organization which had been formed to influence the election of 1868, was simply converted into the New Orleans White League. Other Democratic clubs in the city followed suit. The leading figures in the New Orleans movement were Fred N. Ogden and F. R. Southmayd; the constitution adopted was consistent with those adopted in other parishes. The *Picayune* rejoiced: "It is plain to our mind . . . that the white man's party as now developed is the party we have been seeking, lo! these many years."[79] The New Orleans White League had a military cast from the beginning. A participant wrote that "shortly after its birth . . . the organization became a military body to defend our people from the depredations of the Republicans."[80]

The only incidents of large-scale organized violence by the White League during 1874 were the Coushatta Massacre in Red River Parish and the Battle of Liberty Place in New Orleans. This was not because the League eschewed violence; on the contrary its members, or a part of them, acted as vigilance committees. Economic pressure was used, and used successfully, but so was intimidation. The social ostracism of white Republicans was sterner than ever, but the final resort of the League—encouraged by Judge Bradley's opinion in the Cruikshank case and by President Grant's refusal to use United States troops during the riot at Vicksburg—was violence. In July, 1874, four men were "advised" to leave Iberia Parish and wisely took the advice. "Even if there should have been mistakes made . . . we hope the lesson will have its effect on others."[81] Five Negroes were reported lynched near Lafayette in late July, and a "notoriously bad Negro" was "tried"

78 New Orleans *Daily Picayune*, July 1, 1874; see also New Orleans *Daily Picayune*, June 17, 25, 30, July 17, 1874; Windham, "White Supremacy in Louisiana," 51.
79 New Orleans *Daily Picayune*, July 18, 1874.
80 Prichard (ed.), "White League in New Orleans," 534; see also 529, 532–33; Kendall, *History of New Orleans*, I, 359–60; New Orleans *Daily Picayune*, July, 1874; W. O. Hart, "The New Orleans *Times* and the New Orleans *Democrat*," *Louisiana Historical Quarterly*, VIII (October, 1925), 583.
81 New Iberia *Sugar Bowl*, July 20, 1874, quoted in New Orleans *Daily Picayune*, August 13, 1874.

before a jury of some two hundred citizens near Ile Piquant in August: "The jury decided that the best way to get rid of the villain . . . was to hang him."[82] There were many other reports of "executions" and admitted lynchings of blacks from all over Louisiana during July and August of 1874, yet a leading newspaper asserted seriously on September 1 that "nothing could be more utterly false than to say that any animosity or aggression has been shown the negroes as a race."[83] The Shreveport *Times* promised: "If a single hostile gun is fired between the whites and blacks, every carpetbagger and scalawag that can be caught will in twelve hours be hanging from a limb."[84] Things went so far that a few frightened groups of Negroes announced their adherence to the White League.[85]

The most effective work of White League organizations was in forcing Radical parish officeholders to resign. Here violence was usually not necessary. This tactic seems to have originated at Natchitoches, where on June 27 a mass meeting drew up a petition asking Kellogg to remove four Radical police jury members. July 6 was set as the date for the last meeting of the existing police jury. Then, on July 4, the whites broke up a meeting of black Republicans at Natchitoches. Perhaps significantly, Captain T. W. Abney of Red River Parish was a participant in these activities. The offending police-jury members resigned, so emboldening the White League that it demanded the resignation of the parish judge and the parish tax collector. These two gentlemen did not resign, but they left Natchitoches Parish in haste.[86]

Other parishes followed the example of Natchitoches. Colonel Alcibiades DeBlanc led several hundred White Leaguers in forcing the retirement of Radicals in St. Martin Parish, and he seems to have participated with some seven hundred others in the same activity in Iberia Parish. Forced to leave Iberia were "Judge Kreider and son," who were charged with drilling Negroes. The *Sugar Bowl* com-

82 New Iberia *Sugar Bowl*, August, 1874, quoted in Landry, *Battle of Liberty Place*, 48.
83 New Orleans *Daily Picayune*, September 1, 1874.
84 Shreveport *Times*, quoted in Lonn, *Reconstruction in Louisiana*, 258; see also New Orleans *Daily Picayune*, July–August, 1874; Windham, "White Supremacy in Louisiana," 67–68, 72–73.
85 Lestage, "The White League," 644.
86 *Ibid.*, 653–66.

mented: "We have known the Messrs. Krieder for years, and can scarcely believe that they could be guilty . . . yet we believe more justice has been done in Attakapas by these . . . [White Leagues] than by all the courts in Louisiana."[87]

Radical officials resigned under pressure in Lincoln and Avoyelles parishes. The *Picayune* reported Radical resignations in Claiborne Parish, also, but scalawag Republican W. Jasper Blackburne informed the paper that this was not probable, since there were no Radical officials in Claiborne. Perhaps, he suggested, it was Democratic officials who had stepped down, inasmuch as they had doubled taxes since coming into office. Forced resignations were few during the last few months of 1874, but in late 1875 and early 1876 there were many more such incidents. An unusual note was struck by the parish judge of St. Mary, whose resignation was requested by six leading members of the parish bar. He replied that since none of the petitioners had voted for him, he felt free to retain his office.[88]

The resignation of local officials weakened the Kellogg government. Many officials resigned before the White League could threaten them. Many appointees refused to accept positions. A perusal of Kellogg's correspondence shows, however, that the thirst for office was not altogether quenched by danger. There were applicants for most vacancies as soon as they developed. But the local officials who remained in office, as well as new appointees, functioned with the knowledge that they could be ousted at almost any time. Thus they did as little as possible. As a result, Kellogg ceased to govern most areas of Louisiana, except where his writ was enforced by federal troops or, to a lesser extent, by the Metropolitan Police.[89]

---

87 New Iberia *Sugar Bowl*, August, 1874, quoted in Landry, *Battle of Liberty Place*, 48; see also New Orleans *Daily Picayune*, August 18, 1874; Lestage, "The White League," 656.

88 New Orleans *Daily Picayune*, August 12–13, 21, 1874, August 13, November 9, 30, 1875, January 21–22, 29, 1876; Joseph W. Armstead to C. C. Antoine, May 1, 1876, in Kellogg Papers; Shreveport *Times*, December 23, 1875; E. M. Violette, "Donelson Caffery—a Louisiana Democrat Out of Line," *Louisiana Historical Quarterly*, XIV (October, 1931), 522; Fanny Z. Lovell Bone, "Louisiana in the Disputed Election of 1876," *Louisiana Historical Quarterly*, XIV (October, 1931), 552–53; Thomas R. Landry, "The Political Career of Robert Charles Wickliffe, Governor of Louisiana, 1856–1860," *Louisiana Historical Quarterly*, XXV (July 1942), 709–10.

89 Kellogg Papers, 1874–75.

8

One of the most senseless outbreaks of violence in Louisiana history took place near the little village of Coushatta in August, 1874. Marshall F. Twitchell, a native of Vermont who became a Union army captain, was stationed in Bienville Parish in 1867 as provost marshal. He married a young lady of the parish and, when discharged, settled just across the Red River from Coushatta. In 1870 he was elected to the state senate. Complying with the wishes of the white people of the district, he succeeded in getting the legislature to create Red River Parish out of portions of De Soto, Caddo, Bossier, and Bienville parishes. Once the new parish was formed, members of Twitchell's family began to arrive.[90]

His brother Homer arrived in 1871, and his brothers-in-law George A. King, Clarke Holland, and M. C. Willis followed soon after. In addition, a number of friends of the family came to Coushatta. These immigrants completely dominated the parish government. Marshall Twitchell, in addition to being senator, was president of the police jury and the parish school board. Homer Twitchell became recorder, treasurer of the school board, and tax collector. King was a member of the police jury, constable, and mayor of Coushatta. Clarke Holland was supervisor of registration, and M. C. Willis was justice of the peace. Marshall Twitchell made a formidable enemy, however, of an old resident, Captain T. W. Abney, when the courthouse of the new parish was located to Twitchell's advantage and Abney's disadvantage. Testimony before congressional committees accused Twitchell, his relatives, and his friends of numerous corrupt contracts, including $40,000 in warrants for the construction of the courthouse, which cost only $15,000. This might not have been as profitable as it may seem at first glance: the warrants were heavily discounted, and it is quite possible that no more than $15,000 was realized from their sale. Yet Marshall Twitchell was worth very little in 1869 and was well-to-do in a few years. His relatives also prospered.

90 This account of the Coushatta Massacre is based mainly upon Ida Waller Pope, "The Coushatta Massacre" (M.A. thesis, McNeese State College, 1968), *passim;* see also New Orleans *Republican,* August 30–September 5, 1874; Jimmie G. Shoalmire, "Carpetbagger Extraordinary: Marshall Harvey Twitchell, 1840–1905" (Ph.D. dissertation, Mississippi State University, 1969), *passim.*

Naturally the old inhabitants of Red River Parish resented the political control that these Carpetbaggers had established. Their discontent grew much greater when, for 1873, the cultivated lands of the parish were assessed at forty dollars an acre and uncultivated lands at five dollars per acre. Thus, though Red River Parish had a low tax rate, landowners actually paid greater taxes than in neighboring Caddo, where cultivated lands were assessed at fifteen dollars or Natchitoches, where the tax rate was much higher, but the assessment only five dollars per acre. This significant increase in taxes came in the same year that the panic of 1873 began to spread destitution over the land.

Thus the white Democrats of Red River Parish were more than ready for the organization of the White League in their area. As noted, leaders from the parish, including Abney, were in the crowd which forced Radical officials in Natchitoches Parish to resign. Soon afterward a White League was organized in Red River Parish. The Republican sheriff wrote to Senator Twitchell, who was in New Orleans. "I am certain we are on the verge of a Civil War. A drunken or crazy man is liable to start it at any moment."[91]

Next the deputy postmaster at Coushatta was killed, and the postmaster, a Negro, was driven away. This gave members of the White League an opportunity to read Twitchell's letters to his followers in Coushatta. One letter told Sheriff F. S. Edgerton: "As soon as some overt act has been committed, a United States Marshall can be sent up there and will doubtless take . . . troops with him. . . . In case a demand is made for your resignation . . . be certain first that violence is to be used in case you do not, and to save your life resign."[92] In the meantime Kellogg was asking that federal troops be sent to Coushatta, but without success.

At Brownsville, eight miles south of Coushatta, a quarrel took place between two white men and several Negroes on the night of August 25, 1874. One of the white men decided to take his family away, and that evening the blacks with whom he had quarreled were reported to have entered his house, armed. The next night an im-

91 F. S. Edgerton to M. H. Twitchell, undated, quoted in Pope, "The Coushatta Massacre," 60.
92 Twitchell to Edgerton, August 4, 1874, quoted in Pope, "The Coushatta Massacre," 60.

promptu white "posse" arrested Dan Winn, one of the Negroes, and went to the house of one Tom Jones to arrest him. Jones resisted and killed one of the whites before he was shot dead. Then Winn was shot down. These events aroused the blacks, and on the night of August 27, while a dance was going on in a new brick store in Coushatta, word spread that a crowd of armed Negroes was gathering at Brownsville.

Probably this was a false rumor, but a number of armed blacks did come to Coushatta, probably called by Homer Twitchell to resist an anticipated attempt by the White League to force the resignation of Radical officeholders. They concealed themselves under Twitchell's house. When it seemed that there would be no trouble, Twitchell told his black supporters to go home. Just as they were leaving, two young white men, patrolling against possible danger from Brownsville, rode by. They were fired upon by two of the blacks, and one of the horsemen was seriously wounded. The Coushatta White League leaders thought that this was the beginning of a general attack and sent out a call for help to neighboring parishes.

The next day almost a thousand White League members gathered at Coushatta. Some were said to have come from as far away as Texas, but most were from neighboring parishes. Toward the end of the day there was drinking; the mob grew more and more unruly and began to threaten Republican officeholders. The white citizens of Coushatta then "took into custody" Homer Twitchell; Sheriff Edgerton; Bob Dewees, the tax collector of De Soto Parish; W. R. Howell, a Republican attorney of Coushatta; registrar Clarke Holland; United States marshal Henry A. Scott; deputy sheriff Gilbert Cone; and six Negroes. The citizens' announced purpose was to protect these men from the mob.

All day Saturday, August 29, was spent in investigating the prisoners' part in the assumed Negro insurrection. Captain Abney, who had just returned from Shreveport, headed this inquiry. Marshal Scott and Deputy Cone were released. The remaining whites, realizing that their lives were in danger, agreed to resign their offices and leave the state if their safety was guaranteed. M. C. Willis decided to accompany those who were leaving.

They departed on Sunday morning, August 30, with an escort of about twenty men. That afternoon they were intercepted by a mob, and the five prisoners and Willis were shot to death in cold blood. Whether all the "citizens" of Coushatta had been party to the plot is uncertain, but some of them certainly were. The interception was carefully planned and timed so that the prisoners had no possible chance to escape. The murderers may have been from Texas, or Shreveport, but most of them were probably White League members from De Soto Parish. The leader apparently was Dick Coleman, known at the time only as "Captain Jack."

An end to the summary executions at Coushatta was not yet in sight. A thorough investigation into the wounding of the white picket on the night of August 27 continued. The investigators released all the blacks arrested except two, one of whom had reportedly confessed and implicated the other. The two Negroes were being returned to jail after questioning, late on September 2, when they were seized by a mob of seventy-five or a hundred men—again led by Captain Jack—taken into the nearby woods, and hanged.

Even this was not the end of the story. Almost two years later Senator Twitchell dared return to his plantation opposite Coushatta. On the morning of May 6, 1876, he and his brother-in-law, George A. King, started across the Red River in a skiff rowed by a black man, to attend a police-jury meeting in Coushatta. (By this time United States troops had restored tenuous Kellogg control of the parish.) On the Coushatta side of the river stood a man in a long raincoat, his hat pulled down over his eyes, wearing goggles and a false beard. As the boat neared shore, the man pulled a repeating rifle from under his raincoat and shot Twitchell in the leg. Twitchell jumped or fell into the water but held on to the side of the skiff. King drew a revolver, whereupon the diguised attacker shot him through the body and the head, killing him instantly. The rifleman then calmly shot Twitchell first through one arm, then the other. Believing his work accomplished and ignoring the Negro, he rode away. Somehow the wounded senator managed to remain afloat until the black rower, who must have been a man of great courage, pulled him from the water. Both Twitchell's arms had to be amputated, but he survived the assault and lived for thirty more years. He was later appointed consul at Kingston, Canada, by President Hayes. Testifying before congressional investigators, leading men of Red River Parish professed to have no idea of the assassin's identity. In reality, most of them seem to have known that he was Dick Coleman, alias Captain Jack. Many years later when the Coushatta Massacre was an heroic episode in Louisianians' memory of Reconstruction, Coleman, then living in Arkansas, returned to Coushatta an honored guest.

The Coushatta Massacre received wide attention in the North and destroyed any impression that the White Leagues were peaceful organizations. Undoubtedly it damaged the Conservative cause in Congress and in the nation; it did not even free Red River Parish from Republican officeholders.[93] The impact of Coushatta was short-lived, however; two weeks later came the Battle of Liberty Place in New Orleans.

9

As previously noted, the White League was born in New Orleans in June, 1874, and it was a military organization from the beginning. In effect it became a regiment, organized into battalions and companies, under the overall command of Colonel Fred N. Ogden. During the same summer the "First Louisiana Regiment," four companies under Colonel John B. Angell, was formed. This regiment was not part of the White League but was, rather, supposed to be a part of the McEnery government's militia. The objectives of the two forces were the same, however: to rid Louisiana of the Kellogg administration. Volunteers flocked to these units, including Confederate veterans with experience on the battlefield. They drilled at night, in warehouses and other secret places and, as the results would indicate, achieved satisfactory military proficiency. At the time no federal troops, except a skeleton housekeeping unit, were in Louisiana.[94]

Although Ogden and Angell had no problem obtaining men, getting suitable weapons was more difficult; the Metropolitan Police were well aware that trouble was brewing, and they looked out for

93 *Nation*, XIX (September 3, 1874), 145.
94 Special Message, U. S. Grant to the Senate of the United States, January 13, 1875, in Richardson (ed.), *Messages and Papers of the Presidents*, VII, 309; Frank L. Richardson, "My Recollections of the Battle of the Fourteenth of September, 1874, in New Orleans, La.," *Louisiana Historical Quarterly*, III (October, 1920), 498–501; Kendall, *History of New Orleans*, I, 360–61; Landry, *Battle of Liberty Place*, 63; Lonn, *Reconstruction in Louisiana*, 259–268.

arms shipments. About September 1, a carload of weapons came into New Orleans, labeled as machinery. The arms were taken inside a foundry; Ogden's and Angell's men came there at night, drew arms, and took them home. Some rifles and Navy revolvers were purchased from the Great Western Gun Works at Pittsburgh, which had bought up large quantities of surplus arms at the close of the Civil War. Other small shipments came up or down the Mississippi.

The Metropolitans seized cases containing seventy-two rifles on September 8; others were seized on September 9 and 10. Some weapons were confiscated from citizens who were carrying them on the streets. On September 12 it became known that the steamboat *Mississippi* had arrived carrying a large consignment of arms. The determination of the Metropolitan Police to prevent the landing of these weapons, and the determination of Angell and Ogden to have them, set the stage for the Battle of September 14.[95] Fighting would probably have broken out sooner or later, however, even if the *Mississippi* had never arrived. Lieutenant-Governor Penn of the McEnery government, Angell, and Ogden had made plans to secretly infiltrate men into the State House, take it over, seize Kellogg and other Radical officials, rush them aboard a ship, and transport them to some foreign port. They hoped in this way to install McEnery firmly in the governor's chair before there could be any reaction from Washington.[96] One almost regrets that this mad scheme was not attempted. It could not have succeeded permanently, and the lives lost on September 14 might have been saved.

When news spread that the Metropolitans planned to prevent the landing of arms from the *Mississippi*, a call went out for a mass meeting at the Henry Clay statue at Canal and St. Charles streets on Monday morning, September 14. A crowd of some five thousand men gathered, heard fiery oratory, and adopted resolutions which affirmed the political rights of Negroes, denounced Kellogg as a usurper, and demanded his abdication. This meeting was not attended by Angell's and Ogden's regiments; these two leaders had already made their

95 New Orleans *Daily Picayune*, September 1–3, 1874; Prichard (ed.), "White League in New Orleans," 534; Landry, *Battle of Liberty Place*, 65, 77, 80, 82.
96 Kendall, *History of New Orleans*, I, 361–62.

plans, and their men were assembling at appointed positions. The meeting served two purposes. First it aroused an already excited public opinion. Second, there was probably a faint hope that Kellogg might resign, as country parish Radicals had done when faced with the threat of force. During the meeting, Penn, Ogden, and Angell made their final decision to go ahead with the planned attack, and Ogden was made commander-in-chief. President Grant was informed of the situation early on the morning of the fourteenth and ordered that troops stationed at Brookhaven, Mississippi, be rushed to New Orleans. Probably the troops could not have arrived on time under any conditions, but the story was told, and believed, that Major E. A. Burke arranged with the engineer to delay the train.[97]

When it became evident to General Longstreet that the attempt would be made to unload the *Mississippi* by force, he sought to prevent it. He had about 500 Metropolitan Police, 100 more armed police, and about 3,000 Negro militia. In addition, he had two Gatling guns and a battery of artillery. He faced about 8,400 men, including Ogden's White League, Angell's regiment, and volunteers. Longstreet established a line with his back to the river, extending from Jackson Square to Canal Street; the Custom House, in which most state officials took refuge, formed the left anchor of his line.

Ogden, accompanied by Angell and Penn, made his headquarters at 58 Camp Street, just below Poydras. McEnery had gone to Baton Rouge several days earlier, then on to Vicksburg, Mississippi. There can be but little doubt that his absence was deliberate. Probably it was feared that the civilian leaders of the uprising would be arrested, and therefore it was better to have the claimant to the governor's office safe from arrest.

It was late in the afternoon before Ogden's forces advanced, and the fighting did not last long. The Gatling guns and artillery were not well served; apparently the artillery was not used at all. The Metropolitans, who bore the brunt of the attack, fell back, and this demor-

97 New Orleans *Daily Picayune*, September 13, 15, 1874; Robert Cinnamunde Tucker, "The Life and Public Service of E. John Ellis," *Louisiana Historical Quarterly*, XXIX (July, 1946), 721; Hart, "The *Times* and the *Democrat*," 580; Lonn, *Reconstruction in Louisiana*, 169–71; Landry, *Battle of Liberty Place*, 86–91; Kendall, *History of New Orleans*, I, 359, 362–67, 372–73.

alized the militia. As thousands of spectators watched from windows, rooftops, and boats on the Mississippi, Ogden's men drove to the river. General A. S. Badger, commander of the Metropolitan Police, had been critically wounded. Kellogg troops still held the Custom House and Jackson Square, but Penn rejected the idea of an attack, believing, correctly, that the militia at Jackson Square would disperse during the night. There was no thought of attacking the Custom House, which was federal property. Casualties were not heavy considering the number of men engaged. Of the Metropolitans, who did almost all the fighting on the Kellogg side, eleven were killed and sixty wounded. Six of the Metropolitan dead were white. One of these was John Kennedy, a veteran of the Mexican war, a Confederate officer, and a leader in the Masonic order and the Episcopalian church. Two of the others had been officers in the Union army. The McEnery forces suffered more men killed—twenty-one—but only nineteen wounded.[98]

The *Picayune* somewhat prematurely announced on September 16: "So ends the Kellogg regime. Big, inflated, insolent and overbearing, it collapsed at one touch of honest indignation and gallant onslaught. Its boasted armament dissolved before the furious rush of our citizens, its sneering, thieving, unscrupulous chieftains hid like moles, and its mercenaries fled like stampeded cattle."[99]

On September 15, Kellogg wired Grant a request for federal aid to suppress domestic violence beyond the control of state authorities. On the same day the New Orleans *Bulletin* referred to Grant as "The thing who disgraces the office formerly held by Washington, Jefferson, and Madison"[100] which would seem to have been poor judgment under the circumstances. A church paper went even further, stating that one of Grant's messages went "far to confirm the unpleasant rumor that the intemperate habits of the president have begun to impair his mind."[101] Grant issued a proclamation ordering turbulent

98 New Orleans *Daily Picayune*, September 15–16, October 2, 1874; New Orleans *Republican*, September 15–19, 1874; Prichard (ed.), "White League in New Orleans," 536–37; F. L. Richardson, "Recollections," 126; Lonn, *Reconstruction in Louisiana*, 271–73; Kennedy, *History of New Orleans*, I, 365–72.
99 New Orleans *Daily Picayune*, September 16, 1874.
100 New Orleans *Bulletin*, September 15, 1874, quoted in Lonn, *Reconstruction in Louisiana*, 273.
101 *Southwestern Presbyterian*, December 10, 1874.

persons in Louisiana to disperse and to submit to the constituted authorities of the state. In addition to the troops on the way from Brookhaven, General Emory and three naval vessels were ordered to New Orleans.[102]

Penn announced the deposition of the Kellogg government late on September 14, and soon afterward the troops from Brookhaven arrived. It might be noted that Penn recognized Republican treasurer Dubuclet as holding office legally; the *Picayune* referred to the treasurer as "a highly respected colored man who is the legal treasurer of the State, and his orders will be promptly executed."[103] Colonel Brooke, who was in command of the first federal troops to arrive, met with Ogden, and the two of them agreed that nothing more should be done on either side until orders arrived from Washington. Ogden's men, it should be noted, had taken possession of the arms aboard the *Mississippi.*

On September 16 the victorious Louisiana forces under Ogden's command held a victory parade. They reportedly were cheered by federal troops who watched them march past. That evening McEnery and General Emory arrived in New Orleans at approximately the same time. The next morning Emory demanded that McEnery surrender all state property captured by the insurgents, and McEnery complied. Emory did not restore Kellogg at once. For one day Colonel Brooke was military governor of New Orleans. On September 18 the reins of authority were restored to Kellogg, and the insurrection was seemingly at an end.[104]

When news of the events of September 14 reached the country parishes, many of those which had not already driven their Radical officials out proceeded to do so. The Shreveport *Times* said on September 22 that although Kellogg had been reinstated in New Or-

---

102 Proclamation of the President of the United States, September 15, 1874, in J. D. Richardson (ed.), *Messages and Papers of the Presidents*, VII, 276–77; New Orleans *Daily Picayune*, September 16, 1874; S. B. Packard to [George S.] Williams, September 14, 1874, in *Senate Executive Documents*, 43rd Cong., 2nd Sess., No. 13, p. 14; Lonn, *Reconstruction in Louisiana*, 274–75; Kellogg to Grant, September 15, 1874, in Kellogg Papers.
103 New Orleans *Daily Picayune*, September 17, 1874.
104 Kendall, *History of New Orleans*, I, 373–75; Landry, *Battle of Liberty Place*, 149, 166; Cox, *Three Decades of Federal Legislation*, 568; New Orleans *Daily Picayune*, September 18, 1874.

leans, "he has not an official in authority in North Louisiana, nor will he have until Federal troops are present to compel compliance in the country as in the city."[105] The *Times* did not have long to wait. Before the end of September, federal troops, including the famous Seventh Cavalry, were moving into north Louisiana. They gave special attention to Grant and Red River parishes, but Shreveport was not neglected. The *Picayune* pointed out that persons arrested by the troops were innocent under Judge Bradley's ruling in the Cruikshank case, which proved to be true. Nonetheless, Kellogg officials were restored to power wherever the standards of United States Army units flew. Before January 1, the work of the White League in forcing resignations was largely undone.[106]

It would not be correct, however, to say that the events of September 14 had no lasting result. President Grant was embarrassed by having to use federal troops once more. It is quite possible, although not at all certain, that events in Louisiana helped the Democratic party win a victory in the congressional elections of November, 1874, which gave it a majority in the House of Representatives. Furthermore, the White League had demonstrated beyond contradiction that the Kellogg administration could not govern Louisiana without the support of federal bayonets. Kellogg officials were restored in most of the parishes where they had been ousted, but they were very careful in asserting their authority. And the Conservatives were well aware that once more, if necessary, they could oust Radicals in parish and state if they were not protected by United States troops. Last, but not least, Ogden's and Angell's troops continued as organized entities; they were armed and they drilled frequently. They were to be available to support Francis T. Nicholls in the winter and spring of 1877.[107]

---

105 Shreveport *Times*, September 22, 1874.
106 *Senate Executive Documents*, 43rd Cong., 2nd Sess., No. 13, 1–8; Attakapas *Sugar Bowl* [New Iberia?], quoted in Lonn, *Reconstruction in Louisiana*, 276n; New Orleans *Daily Picayune*, September 17–18, 20, 22, 27, October 9, 21, 25, 31, December 4, 1874; Lestage, "The White League," 686–88; Landry, *Battle of Liberty Place*, 177–78.
107 Kendall, *History of New Orleans*, I, 375–77; Hesseltine, *Ulysses S. Grant, Politician*, 347–48.

10

In preparation for the election of 1874, the White League proved to be in control of white sentiment in Louisiana. The Democratic party in New Orleans sought to hold leadership of the Conservative forces, and it called for a convention of white people at Alexandria on September 1. The New Orleans Democrats saw that the time had come to compromise, especially when the "Committee of Seventy" of New Orleans brought pressure. What amounted, in effect, to a White League convention was called to meet at Baton Rouge on August 24, 1874. The purpose of this convention was to unite all anti-Republican forces, Democrats, old Whigs, Liberal Republicans, and Independents against Kellogg's Radicals in the upcoming legislative and congressional elections.[108]

The White League convention met in Baton Rouge as scheduled. It made nominations for the national House of Representatives, but its primary effort was a set of resolutions. These resolutions declared the Kellogg administration to be fraudulent, claimed that the Radicals, by "inflaming" the blacks, had forced the whites to unite, stated that the rights of both races must be preserved, but insisted that the Civil Rights Acts passed by Congress were unconstitutional. These resolutions once more declared Kellogg a usurper, and announced that the election laws were intended to perpetuate fraud, but insisted that there was no intent to carry the forthcoming election by violence. The convention declared that the white people of the state would not recognize fraudulent state obligations, but would punctually pay legitimate debts. The resolutions invited all whites to join them, and in effect rejected Negro support by stating that needed reforms could be achieved only by the election of white men to office. These resolutions reflected the sentiment of most white Louisianians accurately, and they won approval all over the state, including the endorsement of a mass meeting of ten thousand men in New Orleans. The professional politicians, however, realized that the clause excluding black

108 New Orleans *Daily Picayune*, July 19, 31, August 5, 11, 22, 1874; Thompson to Woodman, April 15, 1873, in Marquette (ed.), "Letters of a Yankee Sugar Planter," 526–27; Lonn, *Reconstruction in Louisiana*, 253–54, 262–63; Lestage, "The White League," 645–66.

candidates was a sure road to defeat. In the campaign which followed, the Conservatives nominated black candidates when they could get them. Few were elected, but the Conservatives had prevented complete alienation of the black vote. This was to be important two years later.[109]

The Republican party in Louisiana did not approach the 1874 elections as a united body. Black Republicans were becoming more and more dissatisfied with their white leaders. This was noticeable during the legislative session of 1874. In July the state Republican convention, well managed by Packard, chose him over Pinchback as chairman. The *Picayune* looked on this as a defeat for the "more corrupt and dangerous element of the Radical party."[110] Blacks were not content to accept defeat, however. At a meeting in New Orleans on October 9, it was pointed out that the North had no "great love for the Negro. . . . It was only a matter of dollars and cents, a question of office and party." The murder of Negroes brought no federal troops, "but as soon as five white officials were killed at Coushatta, and the white Republicans frightened at New Orleans, the whole Navy and Army were ready for Louisiana." Unfortunately, Louisiana blacks had no place to turn: "We deeply regret, in the progress which the nation has made . . . raising us from servitude to citizenship, that we are so little indebted to the white people of Louisiana. . . . our association and connection with them have been painful and bitter."[111] This hostility between black and white Republicans was manifest in the country parishes, particularly St. James and the Felicianas, as well as in New Orleans. By mid-October it was obvious that Kellogg represented only a small coterie of officeholders.[112]

In 1874 the Louisiana Conservatives used every tactic they had used in elections since that of 1868. Despite the Baton Rouge plat-

---

109 New Orleans *Daily Picayune*, August 26, September 2, 1874; New Orleans *Republican*, August 25–30, 1874; Nordhoff, *The Cotton States*, 67; Tucker, "E. John Ellis," 717–18; Lestage, "The White League," 647–48.
110 New Orleans *Daily Picayune*, August 4, 1874.
111 *Ibid.*, October 9, 1874.
112 *Ibid.*, October, 1874; Highsmith, "Social and Economic Conditions in Rapides Parish," 104; *Nation*, XIX (October 29, 1874), 275; Nordhoff, *The Cotton States*, 41, 50, 66; Lonn, *Reconstruction in Louisiana*, 255–56; Lewis, "Political Mind of the Negro," 197–98; Gonzales, "William Pitt Kellogg," 428; William B. Hesseltine, "Economic Factors inn the Abandonment of Reconstruction," *Mississippi Valley Historical Review*, XXII (September, 1935), 208–209.

form, they sought to appeal to black voters and to the German and Irish minorities as well.[113] Basically, however, intimidation, economic and physical, was the main weapon of the Conservatives. Economic coercion seems to have been particularly intense along the Red River. In Shreveport, United States troops were ordered to arrest ninety merchants who had threatened to discharge any of their employees who voted Republican. Many blacks decided that discretion was the better part of valor. They did not vote Conservative; rather they remained in the fields and did not vote at all. It seems probable that the depression which began in 1873 made economic coercion all the more effective in 1874.[114]

Physical intimidation, however, seems to have been more suited to the preferences of white Louisianians. The Colfax and Coushatta massacres fall into this category in an extreme sense, and the latter certainly had some effect on the election. The Red River area was once more the most active center of political violence. More than two hundred Republicans in Caddo Parish asked Kellogg for protection, claiming that within three weeks sixteen Radicals in that parish had been shot, hanged, or burned to death by the whites. Freedmen, they said, were afraid even to gather for church services. Violence was common enough all over the state that potential black voters got the message.[115]

Though United States troops were in Louisiana during the election of 1874, they really could do very little to protect black voters from violence and intimidation. They could make arrests, but the persons arrested were invariably set free. The Enforcement Acts could not be enforced. Also, a great many of the officials whose duty it was to enforce the acts were southerners who, although they were Republicans for various reasons, did not feel called upon to protect Negroes

113 Thompson to Woodman, September 14, 1874, in Marquette (ed.), "Letters of a Yankee Sugar Planter," 528; New Orleans *Daily Picayune*, August 7, 22, 1874; Hahn to Kellogg, September 5, 1874, in Kellogg Papers; Tobias Gibson to Mrs. S. G. Humphrey, October 28, 1874, in Gibson-Humphrey Papers.

114 New Orleans *Daily Picayune*, July 14, October 23, 25, 1874; Windham, "White Supremacy in Louisiana," 60–79; Highsmith, "Louisiana During Reconstruction," 306–307; Highsmith, "Some Aspects of Reconstruction in Louisiana," 286–88; Lonn, *Reconstruction in Louisiana*, 280–81.

115 New Orleans *Daily Picayune*, July 18, August 21, 1874, January, 1875; Windham, "White Supremacy in Louisiana," 88–92; Dunning, *Reconstruction, Political and Economic*, 267–69; Lonn, *Reconstruction in Louisiana*, 280.

against their white neighbors. Furthermore, the federal court system was not adequate to handle the vast number of cases which would have gone on the docket if full enforcement had been intended. Not enough money was made available for prosecutions under the acts. Public opinion had no effect, because people in the North who had been interested in the Negro were rapidly losing that interest. By autumn of 1874, moreover, it had become fairly obvious that the Supreme Court looked on some of the Radical interpretations of the Reconstruction amendments with a jaundiced eye. The General Amnesty Act of 1872, which restored the right to hold office to almost all previously excluded former Confederates, damaged the credibility of the Enforcement Acts. In fact, there is some doubt that the prime purpose of these acts was to protect the black voters of the South; more money was allocated to cases arising in Democratic strongholds in the North. Certainly the Louisiana freedmen in Caddo or De Soto Parish, or along the Teche, could expect little protection from the federal authorities in November, 1874. A subsequent congressional investigation might expose the crimes committed, but it would do nothing to aid the victims of those crimes.[116]

The Radical campaign in Louisiana in 1874 depended more on tactics than on convictions. Bad feeling between Pinchback supporters and regular Republicans made for a divided party. Nonetheless, registration was carried out so as to register as many Republicans and as few Conservatives as possible. Supervisors of registration were instructed plainly to "keep your office open at the Court House for as short a period as necessary and then remove to the localities most thickly populated by the colored voters."[117] In Winn and De Soto parishes, no new voters at all were registered. The state attorney general, A. P. Field, ruled that the Louisiana courts had no authority to naturalize aliens, which disqualified about six thousand potential

116 Swinney, "Enforcing the Fifteenth Amendment," 202–18; Drake, "American Missionary Association and the Southern Negro," 175; Woodward, "Seeds of Failure in Radical Race Policy," 1–9; James A. Rawley, "The General Amnesty Act of 1872: A Note," *Mississippi Valley Historical Review*, XLVII (December, 1960), 480–84; Lewis, "Political Mind of the Negro," 195; DuBois, *Black Reconstruction*, 683–84; Dunning, *Reconstruction, Political and Economic*, 270–72.
117 Thomas Lynne to Supervisors of Registration, August 31, 1874, quoted in Lestage, "The White League," 632.

Conservative votes in New Orleans. Observers reported that a greater number of blacks than whites, in proportion to population, were registered.[118]

The Republican convention met in New Orleans on August 4, 1874. Since there was no gubernatorial contest, the task of this gathering was to nominate candidates for state treasurer and for the national House of Representatives. A test of strength between the black followers of Pinchback and Packard's delegates came on the evening of August 6. When the Pinchback faction lost, a fistfight broke out on the floor of the convention, much to the delight of the Conservatives. Packard was named permanent chairman on August 7, and thereafter the old Custom House Ring was firmly in control of the convention. Antoine Dubuclet, "a man of property, of education, and in all his associations a fit companion for the best class of our citizens,"[119] was renominated for state treasurer. The nominees for Congress were all Carpetbaggers except for C. E. Nash, a former slave destined to be Louisiana's only black representative in Washington during Reconstruction.[120]

In a number of south Louisiana parishes, despite the militant pronouncements of the Baton Rouge convention, the Conservatives sought a compromise. This led to the "Terrebonne Plan," named for the first parish in which it was attempted. This was a local adaptation of the Unification Movement and proposed to divide offices between Democrats and Republicans, whites and blacks. Such moderate black leaders as T. T. Allain preached the virtues of compromise, but Pinchback was opposed. The idea nonetheless spread into Jefferson and St. Mary parishes; in the latter the White League was the chief promoter of compromise. In each case, however, there were Conservative tickets on the one hand, Radical on the other, opposing the compromise candidates. In Tangipahoa Parish the white Radicals nominated an all-white ticket, disregarding the fact that "without the

118 New Orleans *Daily Picayune*, August 26, October 11, 21–23, 1874; James D. Houston to Warmoth, October 12, 1874, in Warmoth Papers; W. R. Murphy to William Wright, September 29, 1874, in Kellogg Papers; New Orleans *Republican*, June 25, 1874; Nordhoff, *The Cotton States*, 66; Kendall, *History of New Orleans*, I, 379.
119 New Orleans *Daily Picayune*, August 8, 1874.
120 *Ibid.*, August 5–9, 1874; Lonn, *Reconstruction in Louisiana*, 261–62.

colored vote there are not 100 Radicals out of the 1500 voters in the Parish."[121]

It is difficult to assess the effect of the presence of federal troops upon the election of 1874. If the situation in Louisiana was comparable to that in Mississippi, many of the army officers, although they dutifully carried out orders, were nonetheless sympathetic with the Conservatives and let their sentiments be known. Probably, however, the sight of blue uniforms gave some blacks the courage to go to the polls on election day—courage they might not have had otherwise.[122]

Both parties seem to have desired a peaceful election in 1874. In September an agreement was reached between the executive committees of the two parties that an advisory committee on registration should be established, to consist of two Democrats, two Radicals, and a nonpartisan umpire. Kellogg agreed to be bound by the recommendations of this committee, and the Conservatives promised to give up intimidation. Former lieutenant-governor Albert Voorhies and future embezzler E. A. Burke were the Democratic members. Packard and Representative B. F. Joubert represented the Radicals, and Dr. M. F. Bonzano, a conservative Republican, was the "umpire." This committee lasted only three weeks before Bonzano's resignation broke it up. Kellogg up to this time had accepted a number of recommendations from the committee, and it is stated by at least one historian that hasty action by the Democratic members was responsible for its demise.[123]

There is no way short of black magic to determine who won the election of 1874 in Louisiana. As the votes were counted and reported from the parishes, the Conservatives claimed to have won a majority in the state house of representatives. This probably was a reasonably

121 New Orleans *Daily Picayune*, October 29, 1874; see also New Orleans *Daily Picayune*, September 24–29, October 18, 20, 1874; Kendall, *History of New Orleans*, I, 378–79.
122 New Orleans *Daily Picayune*, October 27, 29, November 10, 1874; Blaine, *Twenty Years of Congress*, 643; Sefton, *United States Army and Reconstruction*, 240; Lonn, *Reconstruction in Louisiana*, 281–82, 286–87; Wharton, *The Negro in Mississippi*, 139.
123 Kendall, *History of New Orleans*, I, 376; see also Kellogg to E. A. Burke, October 28, 1874, in Kellogg Papers; New Orleans *Daily Picayune*, September 30, October 1–21, 1874; Gonzales, "William Pitt Kellogg," 437–38; Lonn, *Reconstruction in Louisiana*, 284–86.

correct report of the votes cast: there is evidence that some blacks voted the Conservative ticket and that many others did not vote at all. But no one can say how many of those who did not vote were intimidated. Yet it was the task of the Louisiana Returning Board to determine how many were kept from the polls by intimidation. The Conservatives could take comfort from the fact that the Democrats had won control of the national House of Representatives. The whites of Louisiana were particularly gratified because Benjamin F. Butler was defeated for reelection in Massachusetts.[124]

On November 12, 1874, the *Nation* reported: "In Louisiana the process is going on which we took the liberty of predicting. . . . Kellogg and his friends are considering the amount of fraud they can safely commit to give the state to the Republicans."[125] The Returning Board consisted of James Madison Wells, Gadane Cassanave, Louis M. Kenner, John Lynch, and General Longstreet. Longstreet was replaced by one Arroyo, a Democrat, but Arroyo soon resigned in disgust. When the Conservatives demanded representation, Wells announced that he was a Conservative. There can be no doubt that the board manipulated the returns so as to insure a Republican majority in the lower house of the state legislature. Even returns certified by Wells's son were rejected. The compromise candidates, white and black, elected under the Terrebonne Plan were rejected in favor of Radicals. Returns from no less than nine north Louisiana parishes were rejected in whole or in part on the ground that black voters there had been intimidated by the Colfax Riot, the Coushatta Massacre, or lesser incidents. When the returns were finally promulgated on Christmas Eve, Dubuclet had been reelected treasurer in the only statewide vote. Democrats won once more in New Orleans, and Democrats were certified as having been elected to Congress from the First and Second districts. In the state senate, where staggered terms decreed a carry-over, there was a safe Republican majority. In

124 New Orleans *Daily Picayune*, November, 1874; *Nation*, XIX (November 12, 1874), 293, XX (February 25, 1875), 123; Albert L. Grace, *The Heart of the Sugar Bowl: The Story of Iberville* (Plaquemine, La., 1946), 140; D. W. Harris and B. M. Hulse, *The History of Claiborne Parish, Louisiana* (New Orleans, 1886), 247–49; Uzee, "Republican Politics in Louisiana," 140; Smith, *The Negro in Congress*, 88; Tucker, "E. John Ellis," 724; Alrutheus A. Taylor, "Negro Congressmen a Generation After," *Journal of Negro History*, VII (April, 1922), 131, 139.
125 *Nation*, XIX (November 12, 1874), 310.

the house of representatives, however, despite all its manipulations, the board could certify only fifty-three Republicans to face fifty-three Conservatives. Five seats were left to be decided by the house itself. A great many Radicals were certified as having been elected to local offices in north Louisiana, but many of them did not dare assume the offices. Those elected to the legislature from north Louisiana, according to an army officer stationed at Shreveport, could never return home. He added, "The leading Radicals have left. The usual worrying and harassing of Negroes goes on with little intermission."[126] The threats made before the election were being carried out.[127]

11

As 1874 came to an end, it was apparent that Radicalism was weakening in the nation as a whole. The Democratic victory in the congressional elections was one indicator. President Grant's annual message in December showed "perceptible indications of wavering and uncertainty in his southern policy."[128] National scandals and scandals in the South tended to discredit Radicalism. In Louisiana the Metropolitan Police, after September 14, were no real threat to Conservative ambitions. Thus Conservative politicians were emboldened to attempt another coup, this one parliamentary rather than military.[129] They laid careful plans for taking control of the house of representatives. Three Republican members temporarily "disappeared." At least one of them, A. J. Cousin from St. Tammany Parish, was "arrested" by White League members on a charge of embezzlement, only to be released when the conflict in the legislature was over.[130]

Police were stationed about the State House when the legislature

126 Major Lewis Merrill to Adjutant General, Department of the Gulf, December 30, 1874, in *Senate Executive Documents*, 43rd Cong., 2nd Sess., No. 13, pp. 23–24.
127 New Orleans *Republican*, November 3–December 22, 1874; New Orleans *Daily Picayune*, September 30, November 15, 24, December 24, 1874, January 1, 5, 1875; Shreveport *Times*, January 7, 1875; Lowrey, "James Madison Wells," 1,093–96; Lonn, *Reconstruction in Louisiana*, 263–64, 287–98; Lestage, "The White League," 689.
128 Dunning, *Reconstruction, Political and Economic*, 269.
129 *Ibid.*, 213–14, 269–70; New Orleans *Daily Picayune*, November–December, 1874; William Hepworth Dixon, *White Conquest* (London, 1876), II, 101–106.
130 New Orleans *Republican*, January 8, 1875; New Orleans *Daily Picayune*, January 3, 1875; *Senate Executive Documents*, 43rd Cong., 2nd Sess., No. 13, pp. 26–27.

met on January 4, 1875, but the Conservatives managed to infiltrate a large number of supporters into the building. Fifty-two Republicans and fifty Democrats answered the roll. Thereupon a Democrat nominated Louis Wiltz as temporary speaker. The clerk declared this nomination out of order, but Wiltz rushed to the stand, pushed the clerk aside, was sworn in by a conveniently available Democratic justice of the peace, and began accepting the nominations of Democrats for legislative offices. In the confusion he declared them elected. Then Wiltz named assistant sergeants at arms, and these materialized with labels on their coats. The Republicans now tried to withdraw so as to prevent a quorum, but enough were forcibly detained to keep the house in session. The Democratic majority then present proceeded to name Democrats to all the seats left undecided by the Returning Board. There was a tremendous hubbub outside the meeting room, and Wiltz called upon Colonel P. Regis de Trobriand, who commanded a detachment of federal troops at the State House, to clear the corridors. The officer persuaded the crowd to disperse, and then he left the building. For the moment, the Conservative coup was successful—but only for the moment.[131]

Colonel de Trobriand returned about an hour later. Governor Kellogg had formally requested him to eject those persons in the legislature who had been illegally seated. Followed by a file of soldiers with fixed bayonets, the colonel ejected the five newly seated Democrats. Republicans were named to replace them. The Democrats now sought to set up a separate house, but they could not achieve a quorum. Once more a Conservative coup had been frustrated by federal arms. The *Picayune* fulminated: "For the first time in the history of the United States, armed soldiers have invaded a legislative hall, and bayonets have been used to expel the representatives of the people from their seats."[132]

In late 1874, President Grant sent a man in whom he had full confidence, General Philip Sheridan, to inspect conditions in the South.

131 New Orleans *Daily Picayune*, January 5, 1875; Dixon, *White Conquest*, II, 54–64; Lonn, *Reconstruction in Louisiana*, 293–96; Sefton, *United States Army and Reconstruction*, 241.
132 New Orleans *Daily Picayune*, January 5, 1875; see also New Orleans *Republican*, January 5–7, 1875; Lonn, *Reconstruction in Louisiana*, 297–98; Sefton, *United States Army and Reconstruction*, 241.

Sheridan had arrived at the St. Charles Hotel on January 1, 1875, and was in New Orleans during the coup and countercoup of January 4. He had been empowered by Grant to take over command where it was necessary, and in New Orleans he found it necessary. As a result he assumed command of the Department of the Gulf. He wrote Secretary of War W. W. Belknap that "The lives of citizens have become so jeopardized that unless something is done to give protection . . . all security usually afforded by law will be overridden."[133] The next day he wrote his famous "banditti" letter, suggesting that the president or Congress declare terrorists in Louisiana, Arkansas, and Mississippi to be "banditti" subject to arrest, trial, and punishment by military courts.[134]

Colonel de Trobriand's action and Sheridan's proposal were violently denounced. South and north Louisianians, male and female, deploring the "Stuart Tyranny" of de Trobriand, took pride in terming themselves "banditti." In New Orleans Protestant ministers, the Catholic archbishop, and the Jewish rabbi protested with equal vehemence. The Louisiana Grange appealed to all members of that order everywhere for help in ending Louisiana's suffering.[135] One Louisiana newspaper said: "President Grant seems to have thrown off even the flimsy pretense of being the chief Civil Magistrate of the people, and grasping the sword essays to play the role of Caesar. If the people of the United States, and if the army and navy are prepared to support him in his treasonable designs, then is the doom of the Republic sealed and liberty is dead."[136]

The North's reaction to Grant and Sheridan was almost as hostile as the South's. Democratic newspapers published condemnatory editorials; Republican papers, in the main, were discreetly silent.

---

133 Sheridan to Belknap, January 4, 1875, in New Orleans *Daily Picayune*, January 5, 1875.
134 Sheridan to Belknap, January 5, 1875, in *Senate Executive Documents*, 43rd Cong., 2nd Sess., No. 13, p. 23; New Orleans *Daily Picayune*, January 1, 6, 1875; Dixon, *White Conquest*, II, 65; Lonn, *Reconstruction in Louisiana*, 292, 298–99; Sefton, *United States Army and Reconstruction*, 244.
135 New Orleans *Daily Picayune*, January 6, 19, 1875; Dixon, *White Conquest*, II, 75; Lonn, *Reconstruction in Louisiana*, 302.
136 New Orleans *Bulletin*, January 7, 1875, quoted in Lonn, *Reconstruction in Louisiana*, 301.

Democratic members of the Congress demanded investigation and impeachment. The *Nation* said of Grant: "The very obstinacy of temper which made him so formidable in the field now . . . combined with . . . his reelection and the flattery of his adherents not only makes him impervious to public opinion, but makes all criticism of him seem an act of insolent hostility."[137] In reality, Grant was not impervious to public opinion. On January 13 he sent a special message on Louisiana to the Senate in which he pointed out that de Trobriand had acted without his knowledge. He declared his support of Sheridan, but weakly, and he did not issue or suggest any sort of "banditti" proclamation. In the Republican Senate, at least, he found support in a resolution approving his actions in protecting the "lawful" government of Louisiana.[138]

In retrospect, de Trobriand's actions would seem to have been justified by the fact that the legislators whom he expelled had been seated by violence. Kellogg's government was recognized by the president of the United States, and Kellogg requested the army to act. The colonel's actions probably were not strictly legal, but Wiltz had not become speaker legally. As for the "banditti" message for which Sheridan was so roundly condemned, he was absolutely correct if the political rights of black men were to be preserved in Louisiana. In the face of the force used against the blacks by the White League, only the countervailing force of federal troops could protect them. Further, since state courts would not take action against murder, assault, fraud, and intimidation committed by whites against Radicals, black and white, and since the federal courts had been declared powerless, only military courts could have brought offenders to account. Louisiana was in a state of guerrilla insurrection against federal and state authority, and this insurrection could not be quelled by due process. Since Sheridan's proposal was not adopted, and in the face of nationwide opposition it could not be adopted, the life expectancy of Radical government in Louisiana was short.

137 *Nation*, XX (January 14, 1875), 17.
138 *Ibid.* (March 25, 1875), 197–98; Presidential Message to the Senate of the United States, January 13, 1875, in J. D. Richardson (ed.), *Messages and Papers of the Presidents*, VII, 310–12; Dunning, *Reconstruction, Political and Economic*, 272–74; Hesseltine, *Ulysses S. Grant, Politician*, 351.

12

While these events took place, steps toward a compromise were taken. Kellogg had sought recognition of his government by the Conservatives since 1873, and McEnery reportedly had proposed arbitration of the disputed election of 1872. No agreement had been reached, but on December 30, 1874, Kellogg proposed a solution to the dispute over the election of 1874. He put this in a published letter on January 2, 1875. Four days later McEnery and Penn proposed that the congressional investigating committee decide the election of 1872. In the end, the subcommittee dealing with Louisiana did make a proposal. The four members of the subcommittee were William A. Wheeler, William P. Frye, George F. Hoar, and Samuel S. Marshall, but Wheeler was the main agent in effecting the compromise, and it has taken his name.[139]

The agreement took the form, almost, of a treaty between nations. Recognizing that doubts existed as to the result of the election of 1872 and 1874, the resolution drawn up by Wheeler to be passed by both houses of the Louisiana legislature had two basic parts. First, the legislature, while not approving the Kellogg government, would not disturb it, would not impeach Kellogg for any past acts, and would give the governor all necessary support in maintaining law and order. Secondly, the committee would review the election returns of 1874, and the house of representatives as determined by the committee would remain unchanged until the next general election. Obviously, it was understood by all that the Democrats would be awarded a majority of the members of the house of representatives.[140]

Proposal of the Wheeler Compromise and the accepting of it were two entirely different things. Opposition was strong in both Radical and Conservative camps. On February 24, 1875, a caucus of Democratic legislators approved the compromise by a majority of only one vote. In the final analysis, Wheeler brought enough pressure on re-

---

139 New Orleans *Daily Picayune*, January 1–7, February 7, 12, 1875; Lonn, *Reconstruction in Louisiana*, 358–64; Dunning, *Reconstruction, Political and Economic*, 276–77.

140 *Acts of Louisiana, Extra Session, 1875*, 99; *Nation*, XX (February 11, 1875), 17–18; New Orleans *Daily Picayune*, February 7, 1875; Ewing, "Early Louisiana Impeachments," 706–707.

calcitrant Radicals to force them to accept the compromise. A substantial minority, it not a majority, of Democrats was opposed, but New Orleans businessmen weighted the scales in favor of acceptance. On April 14 the Republican Central Committee announced its agreement. The same day the last Conservative holdouts took their seats in the Kellogg legislature. The legislature met in extra session for the purpose of confirming the compromise, which was consummated by a joint resolution that passed the senate on April 12 and the house on April 14.[141]

In the meantime the congressional committee was reviewing the returns from the election of 1874. It concluded that the Returning Board had erred in seating eleven Republican representatives from Assumption, Bienville, De Soto, Jackson, Rapides, Terrebonne, and Winn parishes. This gave the house sixty-three Conservative versus forty-seven Radical members. In the senate the Republicans retained a majority of twenty-seven to nine. The house, it should be noted, proceeded to expel four Republicans who had not been designated by the Returning Board but who had been sworn in to take seats that Democrats refused to occupy. Kellogg's position may have been strengthened a bit when the lame duck House of Representatives of the Forty-third Congress passed a resolution recognizing him as governor. He probably got more satisfaction, however, from preventing Wiltz from obtaining the Louisiana speakership, which went to E. C. Estilette, "a man of little personal presence and slightly deaf."[142] The extra session of the legislature was then adjourned, and Louisiana had a few months of comparative political peace. Enough hope was abroad that state bonds went up in price, though they were still worth less than sixty cents on the dollar.[143]

As noted, those Democrats opposed to the Wheeler Compromise may have been a majority of the Conservatives in the spring of 1875.

141 New Orleans *Republican,* January 8, April 11, 15, 1875; New Orleans *Daily Picayune,* January 8, 10–14, 27, February 1–2, 7, 12, 25–27, March 16, April 13–17, 1875; Shreveport *Times,* March 7, 12, 1875; Tucker, "E. John Ellis," 726; Lonn, *Reconstruction in Louisiana,* 364–68, 372–75; *Acts of Louisiana, 1875,* 99.
142 Lonn, *Reconstruction in Louisiana,* 375.
143 New Orleans *Daily Picayune,* April 15–16, 1875; *Nation,* XX (April 22, 1875), 268, (April 29, 1875), 285, (May 13, 1875), 321; Uzee, "Republican Politics in Louisiana," 24; Lonn, *Reconstruction in Louisiana,* 370, 375–77; Gonzales, "William Pitt Kellogg," 446.

Certainly they gained strength during the year that followed. Despite the opposition of the businessmen of New Orleans, they were in control of the Conservative majority in the house soon after the legislature reconvened in January of 1876. In February, 1876, a special committee of the house recommended the impeachment of Kellogg and of state treasurer Dubuclet for misuse of public funds during 1874, when funds designated for interest payments had been used to pay the police. No question of personal dishonesty was involved, because the money had been restored from police taxes soon afterward. Since the act had taken place in 1874, impeachment would be a clear violation of the compromise. Nonetheless, on February 28, 1876, as the session was drawing to a close, the house by a strictly partisan vote of sixty-one to forty-five voted to impeach Kellogg. It was thought that the senate would adjourn before hearing charges, and thus Kellogg could be suspended as Warmoth had been suspended. The senate however, when informed of the impeachment, organized itself into a court, and gave the house until 7:00 P.M. of that day to present specific articles of impeachment. Within less than five hours of the impeachment Kellogg was acquitted by a vote of twenty-five to nine, securing him his office, for what it was worth, to the end of his term.[144]

13

In summary, it can be said of Kellogg's administration that it was remarkably free of corruption at the statewide level when compared with Warmoth's four years. There was petty stealing at the local level, but in state offices there were no scandals to compare with the previous administration. One commentator has said that the fault of the Radical governments in the South was that they were not Radical enough.[145] A contemporary observer, on the other hand, said that Kellogg appeared to be "a stirring and fanatical person, strongly wedded to his opinions and ready to spend and be spent in what he deems the

---

144 Shreveport *Times*, February 16, 29, March 3, 26, 1876; New Orleans *Daily Picayune*, October 22, February, March 3, 1876; Harry Swords to Warmoth, April 22, 1875, in Warmoth Papers; Ewing, "Early Louisiana Impeachments," 707–10; Lonn, *Reconstruction in Louisiana*, 380–85, 393–98; Highsmith, "Louisiana During Reconstruction," 322–23.

145 Olsen, "Reconsidering the Scalawags," 317.

good cause."[146] The most severe indictment of Kellogg, outside the local partisan press, is to be found in Charles Nordhoff, *The Cotton States in the Spring and Summer of 1875,* but a student familiar with Louisiana finds Nordhoff wrong on so many counts—for example, the safety of Union men and Negroes in Louisiana—that it is difficult to accept his conclusions on any aspect of Louisiana Reconstruction.[147]

The primary criticism to be made of the Kellogg regime is that it was unable to govern the state. There were many reasons why this was true. First, by the time Kellogg became governor, northern support for Radical regimes in the South had greatly declined. Only when the national administration would benefit could Kellogg expect support from the North. Northern Democrats gave full support to resistance throughout his term, especially so after the national victory of the Democrats in 1874.[148]

Second, Kellogg took office with the Republican party in Louisiana disunited. This meant that he had to depend almost entirely on the Negro vote, which made it necessary to give more offices to black Republicans. But the more black officeholders there were, the stronger the objections of white Louisianians, and many northerners, to the regime. A third fact was the national depression which began in 1873 and persisted throughout the remaining Reconstruction years. It was all too easy for white Louisianians to blame a state government which they already despised for their economic plight. In fact, the idea of impersonal or far-removed economic forces seems hardly to have existed in Reconstruction Louisiana. In retrospect, it is amazing that Kellogg was able to finish out his term; only the stubborn determination of General Grant made it possible.[149]

146 Dixon, *White Conquest,* II, 108.
147 Nordhoff, *The Cotton States, passim.*
148 *Nation,* XVI (May 15, 1873), 325; Brock, *An American Crisis,* 286–87; James M. McPherson, "Abolitionists, Woman Suffrage, and the Negro, 1865–1869," *Mid-America,* XLVII (January, 1965), 40–47; Patrick, *Reconstruction of the Nation,* 290, 295; DuBois, *Black Reconstruction,* 684; Stampp, *The Era of Reconstruction,* 194–95; Swinney, "Enforcing the Fifteenth Amendment," 205–206; Blaine, *Twenty Years of Congress,* 470.
149 New Orleans *Daily Picayune,* April 8, 1873, January 13, 1876; *Nation,* XIX (October 15, 1874), 241; C. M. Selph to Warmoth, April 26, 1875, Jack Wharton to Warmoth, May 8, 1875, in Warmoth Papers; G. W. Cochran to Kellogg, January 30, 1876, in Kellogg Papers; Shreveport *Times,* November 2, 1875; Edward S. Godfrey to Assistant Adjutant General, Department of the Gulf, November 16,

Fourth, the years when Kellogg attempted to govern Louisiana were a time of almost unbridled violence. To some extent this was endemic. The *Nation* noted of southern riots in 1875: "Such incidents have been common at the South ever since the settlement of the country. What people used to say about them was that they were a product of a low state of civilization, to be cured by time, religion, and education."[150] Thus the situation at Shreveport described by Major Lewis Merrill in autumn, 1874, was not so much out of the ordinary then as it might seem today:

It is to be borne in mind that this whole community is practically an armed mob . . . and that for months no . . . authority save individual will has been recognized. There has been no attempt . . . to enforce any law . . . local, state, or national, and the whole community seems to have become impressed with the notion that it is in practically a state of war, in which all law is to be ignored, and is fast drifting into a state of anarchy in which any crazy fool could precipitate a condition of things which it is fearful to contemplate.[151]

Louisiana was a violent place before and during the Civil War, and it was to be a violent place after Reconstruction was over. Hundreds, and probably thousands, of incidents of violence unconnected with politics could be cited for the Kellogg years. Nonetheless, during these years there was a large measure of deliberate terrorism, terrorism different from that of rebellious Irishmen or Communist guerrillas in southeast Asia mainly in its efficiency and in the immunity of the terrorists from any retaliation. Bloody affrays at Colfax, Coushatta, and Liberty Place have been described. These have frequently been noted by historians because of their magnitude and because of the national publicity they received. But all over the state lesser in-

---

1874, Henry A. Morrow to Assistant Adjutant General, Department of the Gulf, December 24, 1874, in *Senate Executive Documents*, 43rd Cong., 2nd Sess., No. 17, pp. 22, 72; Jack B. Scroggs, "Southern Reconstruction: A Radical View," *Journal of Southern History*, XXIV (November, 1958), 407–29; Robert Dabney Calhoun, "A History of Concordia Parish, Louisiana," *Louisiana Historical Quarterly*, XVI (April, 1933), 322; Cable, *The Silent South*, 12–13, 50–52; Clay, "Economic Survival of the Plantation," 94–95; Stampp, *The Era of Reconstruction*, 195–96; Nordhoff, *The Cotton States*, 59; Robert Somers, *The Southern States Since the War* (Rev. ed.; University, Ala., 1965), 227.
150 *Nation*, XXI (September 23, 1875), 193.
151 Merrill to Assistant Adjutant General, Department of the Gulf, October 25, 1874, in *Senate Executive Documents*, 43rd Cong., 2nd Sess., No. 17, pp. 4–5.

cidents took place almost daily. A sharecropper who had served as foreman of a grand jury which dared to investigate political murders was run out of town. Whites organized themselves into groups of "regulators" to prevent and punish, even by death, thefts by Negroes, and an amazing number of the thieves were Radicals. Negro churches were burned. A Radical editor and legislator was shot dead. The white Republican tax collector of Grant Parish, who had the courage and lack of judgment to stay on, was gunned down in the streets. A Radical Negro legislator, arrested on an obviously trumped-up charge of having conspired with his sister-in-law to poison a white family, was seized from officers taking him to trial and lynched; the sister-in-law suffered the same fate. Hundreds of other incidents could be noted.[152]

The Shreveport *Times* was more bloodthirsty and intemperate than most Louisiana newspapers, but its columns are nonetheless instructive. On Christmas Eve, 1875, it noted that "White men may have burned and killed in Louisiana, but the responsibility belongs to the Radical government of the State." Earlier this paper had asserted that there could be no peace or safety until "the liberty of speech and action" had been so limited that "unscrupulous scoundrels" could not incite "the worst classes of our society." The editor could not understand why the people of the North would not comprehend that what was happening in the South was "the natural and irresistible organization of . . . conservatism and intelligence . . . against Communism in its worst and most dangerous phase."[153] Against such a sanctimonious reign of terror, the Radical regime in Louisiana could sustain itself only so long as it could count on armed support from Washington.

---

152 New Orleans *Daily Picayune*, June 22, October 15, November 24, 1875, January 19, 1876, 1873–1876, *passim*; Shreveport *Times*, December 28, 1875; Register to Kellogg, July 20, 1875, in Kellogg Papers; Gonzales, "William Pitt Kellogg," 450.
153 Shreveport *Times*, December 24, August 2, June 19, 1875.

VIII *The General Economy of Louisiana, 1865–1877*

T HE PEOPLE now residing in the late rebellious states are generally impoverished," wrote a northerner soon after the close of the Civil War. "They have little money, and . . . their stock and valuables of all kinds have been swept away. Their farms are without fences, and their farming tools worn out, disabled, or destroyed. Their system of labor is broken up . . . and the transition from bondage to freedom will affect for a time, the producing interests."[1] This description certainly applied to Louisiana. Although the oft-made comparison between per capita wealth before and after the war is invalid—since Negroes were counted as property before the war and as people after it[2]—the most fertile regions of Louisiana had been devastated or so disorganized by the movement of armies that the production of staple crops was either halted or greatly reduced.

One obvious result was a drop in land values. One reason for this was the deflation which struck the South when surrender made Confederate currency utterly worthless. Equally important, however, were such factors as the deterioration of the levees during the war,

---

1 Thomas W. Knox, "Beckoning Fields of Cotton," in William B. Hesseltine (ed.), *The Tragic Conflict* (New York, 1962), 452.
2 Franklin, "Whither Reconstruction Historiography?" 452.

uncertainty as to what could be accomplished with free labor, and loss of tools and work animals. Many fields, neglected for several years during the conflict, had, in Louisiana's semitropical climate, so grown up in weeds and scrub that they had almost returned to wilderness. Much land was to remain abandoned for years after the war, and some would never be restored to cultivation.[3]

The drop in land values has been somewhat exaggerated by the comparison of assessed valuation of land and slaves before the war with the assessed value of land alone after 1865. Nonetheless there was a decided decline in value. Some less desirable sugar lands sold for as little as five dollars an acre during Reconstruction, but others, with fields in good shape, well-drained, and with a sugar house in good working order, brought from thirty-five to as much as seventy-five dollars per acre.[4] Cotton lands had not been so valuable as sugar lands before the war, but they did not lose as much of their value. The price of cotton was high when peace came, and not nearly so much capital was needed to put in a cotton crop as was needed for sugar planting. Cotton was planted on rich land and on poor land, so lands were available to a purchaser at any price he could pay. Some of the poorer tracts were not worth working at any price. On the other hand, a Madison Parish plantation which had sold for sixty dollars an acre in gold before the war was offered for thirty dollars an acre in greenbacks in 1866. As the price of cotton went down, the price of cotton lands declined, but not in proportion.[5] Lower prices did not bring about any significant increase in sales. Indeed, voluntary sales seem to have been rare. The planter was loath to part with acres

3 George L. Anderson, "The South and the Problems of Post–Civil War Finance," *Journal of Southern History*, IX (May, 1943), 184; Engelsmen, "Freedmen's Bureau in Louisiana," 208; Henry Skipworth, *East Feliciana, Louisiana, Past and Present* (New Orleans, 1892), 15; New Orleans *Daily Picayune*, June 3, 1866, February 10, 1873.

4 Report of the Auditor, *Legislative Documents, Louisiana, 1864–65*; Coulter, *The South During Reconstruction*, 220; New Orleans *Daily Picayune*, December 16, 1866, April 24, 1867; Knox, "Beckoning Fields of Cotton," 445; J. Carlyle Sitterson, *Sugar Country: The Cane Sugar Industry in the South, 1753–1950* (Lexington, Ky., 1953), 295.

5 Baton Rouge *Weekly Advocate*, March 16, 1866, quoted in New Orleans *Daily Picayune*, March 19, 1866; *De Bow's Review*, After the War Series, II (December, 1866), 667; Agreement between Samuel Davis of Natchez and John S. Harris of Milwaukee, January 18, 1864, in Joseph Vidal Papers, Department of Archives, Louisiana State University.

which had yielded him luxury before the war. He believed that his land would soon be worth more. "It was the only capital by which he could hope to regain his former wealth; and to own a plantation still carried a social prestige."[6]

Sugar production as the war ended was only a fraction of what it had been. The crop of 1861, the largest on record, had been 459,000 hogsheads, that of 1860 almost 229,000 hogsheads. The crop of 1864 was only 7,000 hogsheads, that of 1865 only 15,000. More than the standing crop of cane would have been needed to provide seed for acreage comparable to prewar years. Northern travelers noted "the dilapidated buildings and the general air of neglect"[7] on sugar plantations. A man familiar with East Baton Rouge, Ascension, and Iberville parishes observed in 1865 that the existing sugar crops looked good, but that "thousands of acres are idle where ten are cultivated."[8]

Because cotton prices were high as the war ended, this staple was planted on lands that normally would have been devoted to sugar. In Baton Rouge vacant lots, orchards, and even the racetrack were planted in cotton. The plantations above Red River on the west side of the Mississippi, many leased by northerners and a few by freedmen, were once more beginning to plant on a fairly large scale. Along Red River, where Banks's armies had marched, little cotton was planted; the crop of 1865 was reported to be less than four hundred bales in Natchitoches Parish, less than three hundred in Rapides. Only in the Shreveport area was production close to normal, and there many growers did not benefit because United States Treasury agents, honest and otherwise, seized many bales as they came on the market. The Treasury agents, who were a hazard to farmers and

6 Shugg, *Origins of Class Struggle in Louisiana*, 261; see also Clay, "Economic Survival of the Plantation," 153; Theodore Saloutos, "Southern Agriculture and the Problems of Readustment, 1865–1877," *Agricultural History*, XXX (April, 1956), 61.

7 Reid, *After the War*, 269.

8 New Orleans *Daily Picayune*, August 18, 1865; see also New Orleans *Daily Picayune*, September 6, 1865; *De Bow's Review*, After the War Series, I (February, 1866), 201; W. G. Eliot to John Sherman, February 25, 1867, in James G. Randall, "John Sherman and Reconstruction," *Mississippi Valley Historical Review*, XIX (December, 1932), 386; Highsmith, "Louisiana During Reconstruction," 199–204; Sitterson, *Sugar Country*, 231–32; Frank Otto Gatell (ed.), "The Slaveholder and the Abolitionist: Binding Up a Family's Wounds," *Journal of Southern History*, XXVII (August, 1961), 368–91.

planters all over the state in 1865, not only impoverished producers; their activities also prevented the arrival of more cotton on the market.[9]

Food was more important than staples. No exact figures are available for Louisiana, but the South as a whole had lost twenty-nine horses out of a hundred, thirty-two cows out of a hundred, and thirty-five swine of every hundred according to the census of 1870. The deficit was undoubtedly greater in 1865. The deterioration on agricultural tools was even more drastic. Without "horses, mules, agricultural implements, and negroes,"[10] farmers and planters were more concerned with corn, sweet potatoes, and vegetable gardens than with cotton gins or sugar houses.[11]

Today it is difficult to imagine how bad Louisiana roads were in 1860, but even so, before the war, some effort was made to keep the roads passable. From 1861 to 1865, very few roads had any maintenance at all. Bridges were carried away by floods or rotted until they fell into the creek or bayou. When a mudhole became impassable, traffic moved to one side or the other until a morass wide enough and long enough to halt all passage by wheeled vehicles had been created. In the hill parishes, freshets cut great trenches across roadways on hillsides, and the same road might offer quicksand in the next valley. Only on the prairies, where the flat terrain made it possible to go almost anywhere, was travel relatively easy, and there was little traffic on the thinly populated prairies. Farther north, in the Caddo-Bossier area, farmers bringing goods to market had to contend not only with mud and the scarcity of draft animals; there a convoy system was necessary to deal with bandits.[12]

9   New Orleans *Daily Picayune*, August 25, 28, 1864, July 1, 8, August 9, 18, September 9, 12, December 13, 1865; Reid, *After the War*, 579; Engelsmen, "Freedmen's Bureau in Louisiana," 208–209; Statement of T. J. Mackay, U.S. Provost Marshal in Louisiana, in Fleming (ed.), *Documentary History of Reconstruction*, I, 30–31; Elaine Holmes Brister, "A History of Pineville, Louisiana" (M.A. thesis, Louisiana State University, 1948), 33; Sefton, *United States Army and Reconstruction*, 38.

10 New Orleans *Daily Picayune*, August 6, 1865.

11 *Ibid.*, September 6, October 2, 1865, May 20, 1866; Baton Rouge *Weekly Advocate*, March 24, 1866; Bayside Plantation Records, II, February–March, 1864; Stock Inventory, Pittsfield Plantation, January 19, 1864, in Vidal Papers; Eugene M. Lerner, "Southern Output and Agricultural Income," *Agricultural History*, XXXIII (July, 1959), 117.

12 Warmoth, *War, Politics and Reconstruction*, 79–80; Baton Rouge *Weekly Advocate*, March 24, 1866; New Orleans *Daily Picayune*, August 10, November 7, 1865.

Louisiana had about 386 miles of railroad when the Civil War began. The most important line was the New Orleans, Jackson, and Great Northern, which extended north from New Orleans to Canton, Mississippi. Subject to destruction by both sides during the conflict, it was for all practical purposes without track, rolling stock, or bridges as hostilities ended. The ambitiously named Vicksburg, Shreveport and Texas extended from opposite Vicksburg to Monroe before the war, about seventy-five miles; it too was in useless condition when the war ended. The Baton Rouge, Grosse Tete, and Opelousas ran twenty-eight miles from Baton Rouge westward toward the Atchafalaya River. During the war high water floated the crossties and rails off the roadbed, and emancipation cost the company $115,000 which it had invested in slaves. The Mexican Gulf Railroad from New Orleans to Lake Borgne was not damaged so much by war as by neglect. A legislator complained in 1864: "It is and has been for the last fifteen years . . . a public nuisance. . . . The cars run off the track, and have now been stuck in the ditch for the past five days."[13] The Southern Pacific, running westward into Texas from near Shreveport, was in fair condition at war's end, but it contributed little to the economy of Louisiana. The West Feliciana Railroad and the Clinton and Port Hudson were useless in the spring of 1865. The New Orleans, Opelousas, and Great Western, which ran from Algiers to Brashear City, was in relatively good condition because it had been maintained by the Union army, but it remained under military control during 1864.[14] Louisiana's waterways had not been destroyed by war, but the number of steamboats available for moving goods over the waterways had been drastically reduced. Water transportation could be restored more rapidly than the railroads, but it definitely was insufficient in the summer and fall of 1865 to meet the commercial needs of the state. Common articles of merchandise were often not avail-

---

13 *Debates in the House of Representatives, 1864–65*, 189.
14 Estaville, "Louisiana Railroads During the Civil War," *passim*; Walter Prichard (ed.), "A Forgotten Engineer: G. W. R. Bayley and His 'History of the Railroads of Louisiana,'" *Louisiana Historical Quarterly*, XXX (October, 1947), 1,179–83, 1,209–13; Report of the Baton Rouge, Grosse Tete, and Opelousas Railroad Company, in *Legislative Documents, 1865–66*; Daniel Dennett, *Louisiana As It Is: Its Topography and Material Resources* . . . (New Orleans, 1876), 221; Highsmith, "Louisiana During Reconstruction," 403–404; Coulter, *The South During Reconstruction*," 189.

able, but spasmodic mail delivery caused the most vocal discontent.[15]

Deranged communications added greatly to the costs of getting goods to market. Quotations for cotton prices in New Orleans may have been high, but the farmer upriver on the Mississippi paid dearly for moving his crop to New Orleans. Farmers on the Red River or those who had no access to river transportation were at a much greater disadvantage. Here the scarcity of horses, mules, and oxen aggravated the problem. Comparative prices are deceptive, because the gold value of greenbacks varied, but quotations for middling cotton at Shreveport in late 1865 and early 1866 were, on the average, about twenty-five cents per pound below New Orleans prices of the same date. Presumably the cost of transportation accounted for most of the difference.[16]

Probably the longest-lasting physical damage suffered by Louisiana was the deterioration of the levees along the rivers and bayous near which farms and plantations were located. Before the war, landowners had been responsible for keeping up the levee fronting their own property. Crevasses, breaks in the levee, had come rather frequently, but usually they were closed before major damage was done. During the war the contending armies seldom actually cut levees, but breaks went unrepaired; as flood waters poured through these crevasses, the shoulders were pushed ever farther apart until miles of levee disappeared. For all practical purposes, Louisiana had no levee system when the war ended. Under the new labor system, the state proved incapable of repairing old damage as fast as new damage occurred. Louisiana spent more than twenty-three million dollars on levee work between 1865 and 1903, but it was not until the federal government took over flood control that the levee system once more became effective—and there were costly floods in the twentieth century. Flood waters were a threat, and often more than a threat, to Louisiana agriculture throughout the Reconstruction years.[17]

The Houma *Civic Guard* of November 18, 1865, noted that Colonel

---

15 New Orleans *Daily Picayune,* August–December, 1865.
16 Natchitoches *Times,* August 12, 1865, quoted in New Orleans *Daily Picayune,* August 19, 1865; Shreveport *Southwestern,* December 27, 1865, quoted in New Orleans *Daily Picayune,* January 1, 1866; New Orleans *Daily Picayune,* November, 1865–January, 1866.
17 Mims, "Swamp Land Funds," 323; New Orleans *Daily Picayune,* February 10, November 7, 1866; Highsmith, "Louisiana During Reconstruction," 399–400.

J. R. Bisland, Captain W. A. Bisland, Colonel D. S. Cage, Dr. Boykin, Major J. C. Potts, and other members of prominent planting families had returned from the wars.[18] These men and others like them were "laboring under the severest embarassments, partly reduced to absolute poverty. . . . the nervous anxiety which such a state of things produces extends to those classes of society which . . . were always in close business connexion with the planting interest."[19] Not only were such men in financial straits; those who had held political office or high military rank, or who owned property worth more than twenty thousand dollars, were disfranchised in every sense of the word until pardoned by the president. This could be a most severe handicap where court action was required to recover property, foreclose a mortgage, or for one of many possible reasons. Under these conditions some gave up and sold their holdings for whatever they could get; others sought to lease lands to northerners with money. Others grimly went to work, using those of their former slaves who had remained on the plantation and often toiling with their own hands.[20]

The planter's condition in 1865 was bad in contrast to his affluence in 1861, but in absolute terms the ordinary man in Louisiana was in far worse condition than the planter. First, it should be remembered that many husbands, sons, and brothers did not return from the war. Louisiana had contributed her share of the Confederate dead. Many of the ordinary soldiers who did come home found "their homesteads destroyed, their farms devastated, their families in distress . . . at all events, [they found] an impoverished and exhausted community which had but little to offer them. . . . They must do something, honest or dishonest, and must do it soon to make a living."[21] A resident of Baton Rouge noted in September, 1865: "I find the country is going to be very poor Negroes will not work and White people think they can't and I fear very much the Whole will starve . . . want is staring

---

18 Cited in New Orleans *Daily Picayune*, November 23, 1865.
19 *Senate Executive Documents*, 39th Cong., 1st Sess., No. 2, pp. 38–39.
20 A. C. Myers to Andrew Johnson, March 13, 1866, in Williams-Chesnut-Manning Papers; Aertker, "A Social History of Baton Rouge," 108; Engelsmen, "Freedmen's Bureau in Louisiana," 207; J. Carlyle Sitterson, "The McCollams: A Planter Family of the Old and New South," *Journal of Southern History*, VI (August, 1940), 347–67; Gatell (ed.), "The Slaveholder and the Abolitionist," 368–91.
21 *Senate Executive Documents*, 39th Cong., 1st Sess., No. 2, p. 39.

so many . . . in the face."[22] In New Orleans more than fourteen thousand poor people, many of them white, were being supported by the federal government, and in Orleans Parish more than six thousand taxpayers were listed as delinquent. The people of Alexandria and Pineville welcomed Union occupation because the troops had greenbacks to spend. In the final analysis, however, few starved, most worked, and with help from neighbors, the Freedmen's Bureau, and the presence of fish and game, the poorer farmers and workers of Louisiana managed to survive the hard closing months of 1865.[23]

However desperate the condition of whites, it was far better than that of Louisiana freedmen. Tens of thousands of Louisiana slaves had run away when the federal armies came near, and others left home when they realized that they had a right to do so. The actual reduction in the number of blacks on the land between 1860 and 1865 cannot be determined, but there was a definite decline. Southerners probably tended to exaggerate the decrease. One writer estimated in 1869 that the decline in the sugar parishes was from one fourth to one third. "To what extent they have migrated it is impossible to ascertain. Some have come . . . others have gone, nobody knows where."[24]

Planters and military authorities made an effort to keep freedmen at work. In June of 1865 the Union commander at Natchitoches informed "All freedmen . . . that they will not be allowed to straggle from the premises to which they belong without written permission from their former owners."[25] A planter wrote from the Teche that his former slaves had suffered many deaths, but that the survivors had "remained together and behaved remarkably well. . . . They are working along under my direction managing to raise enough to eat."[26]

22 Payne to Mrs. Sterrett, September 3, 1865, in Barnhart (ed.), "Reconstruction on the Lower Mississippi," 391.
23 New Orleans *Daily Picayune*, April 25, 1865; *Nation*, II (June 4, 1866), 705; Constantin, "Louisiana Black Code," 6; Brister, "History of Pineville," 31; Ficklen, *History of Reconstruction in Louisiana*, 102–103.
24 *De Bow's Review*, After the War Series, VII (January, 1869), 92.
25 General Order No. 3, Hq. U. S. Military Forces, Natchitoches, Louisiana, June 6, 1865, in *St. Martin Democrat* (St. Martinville, La.), June 17, 1865.
26 W. T. Palfrey to J. G. Palfrey, June 29, 1865, in Gatell (ed.), "The Slaveholder and the Abolitionist," 373.

Probably on the larger, more prosperous, and more patriarchal plantations freedmen were more inclined to be "loyal," less likely to seek for greener pastures.[27]

Certainly many freedmen enjoyed a period of loafing after their liberation. On the other hand, the impression that the vast majority of them were idle is false. Probably the reduction in numbers and the labor shortage thus brought about convinced many who were in need of labor that most freedmen were not working. Nor did a crowd of idle Negroes in a town such as Baton Rouge or Shreveport, where no such sight had been seen on weekdays in slavery times, have to be very large to convince a man in need of labor that tens and even scores of thousands of blacks were living a life of ease in towns. In fact, Butler and Banks had done what they could to restore black labor to the fields. As the war ended, economic necessity drove back most of those who would have liked to be idle; a black man hoping for forty acres and a mule at Christmas still had to eat during the months that remained before Christmas. However, many of those who worked chose not to work too hard, nor did they hesitate to take a day or two off if they felt so inclined. To former masters accustomed to the forced labor of slavery this was a maddening experience, but it was one they had to accept if they were to get any work done at all.[28]

Among those who worked, some became independent. Most of these were tradesmen in New Orleans or smaller communities, but there were those who established themselves independently on the land. Before the war, of course, free men of color had owned land, some being planters by any system of classification. The number of black landowners obviously did not increase significantly in 1865, but blacks did lease land. The *Tribune* reported in November that there were fifty-eight "plantations" in Louisiana leased by freedmen. Fourteen of these were subsidized to some extent by the New Orleans Freedmen's Aid Association, but others, singly or communally,

27 *Senate Executive Documents*, 39th Cong., 1st Sess., No. 2, p. 15; Houma *Civic Guard*, November 18, 1865, quoted in New Orleans *Daily Picayune*, November 23, 1865; Ficklen, *History of Reconstruction in Louisiana*, 126–27; Ellis, "The Transition from Slave Labor to Free Labor," 24; White, *Freedmen's Bureau in Louisiana*, 113n.

28 Harrington, *Fighting Politician*, 104–105; Highsmith, "Some Aspects of Reconstruction in Louisiana," 490; McRae, *The Americans at Home*, 313; New Orleans *Tribune*, August 23, 1865.

were on their own. The independence of freedmen must not be over-emphasized, however. The vast majority became agricultural labor-ers, as did their children and their children's children.[29]

Even if every man in Louisiana had been able and willing to work, there would have been much hardship and hunger in 1865. One result was an epidemic of theft. Some of this was organized; the jayhawkers of central and northern Louisiana continued to raid, burn, and kill for some time after the surrender of the Confederacy. Most theft, however, was of foodstuffs. Some of this was a carry-over from the pilfering which had gone on under slavery, but most seems to have been prompted by sheer hunger. One planter noted in October, 1865: "Some unknown person dug potatoes and cut cane today between breakfast and 2 o'clock." The same man wrote in December: "Rode over neighborhood in search of missing cattle but found none[.] 8 or 10 missing in last three months."[30] William Taylor Palfrey wrote to his brother: "The country is overrun with a vile, suddenly eman-cipated set of worthless Negro slaves, who will sooner steal than work."[31] In East Baton Rouge Parish, according to one resident, thieves made it impossible to grow fruit or vegetables or to keep any sort of animals. "They are now tearing up valuable bridges . . . for fuel."[32] Significantly, there was another outbreak of thievery after the depression beginning in 1873 had brought renewed destitution.

The Freedmen's Bureau did much to reduce the pangs of hunger and thus to prevent more theft. The bureau was not a cornucopia from which all who desired could draw largesse. The Louisiana bu-reau had no appropriation; it derived its income from seized rebel property and from a tax of three dollars per laborer, two dollars from the planter, and a dollar from the freedman. The bureau issued rations on the basis of one bushel of corn and eight pounds of pork per month for adults, half as much for children, plus occasional issues of vinegar, sugar, vegetables, and coffee. No able-bodied adult could draw ra-

29 New Orleans *Daily Picayune,* August 23, 1865; New Orleans *Tribune,* November 14, 1865; Eaton, *Grant, Lincoln and the Freedmen,* 163–64.
30 Bayside Plantation Papers, II, October 13, December 2, 1865.
31 W. T. Palfrey to J. G. Palfrey, October 4, 1865, in Gatell (ed.), "The Slave-holder and the Abolitionist," 377.
32 Baton Rouge *Weekly Advocate,* January 13, 1866; see also Sitterson, *Sugar Country,* 235–36; Clay, "Economic Survival of the Plantation," 54; Patrick, *Reconstruction of the Nation,* 36–37.

tions for more than one week. Indeed, the policy was to issue rations only to children and sick or disabled adults, but this could not be followed consistently in the dark days of 1865 and 1866. At one time two thirds of the freedmen and many whites in Avoyelles Parish were receiving rations, and a substantial proportion of those issued in the state went to hungry white people. The total number of adult rations issued between June 1, 1865, and June 1, 1866, was slightly less than 378,000; this was enough food to have fed 378,000 adults for one month, or 12,500 adults for one year. There were 195,000 black old people and children in Louisiana. The complaints of planters that freedmen were being spoiled were certainly not justified.[33]

2

Labor was the great problem of Louisiana planters throughout the Reconstruction years. Southerners had defended slavery so long that they simply did not believe that Negroes would work without compulsion. There was no particular bitterness in this attitude; the southerner took its correctness for granted. One young man, writing from Louisiana to his sweetheart in the Southeast, expressed the prevailing idea. The freedman, he said, "is a docile, indolent, sluggish, unambitious, sensual, brutish being with no wish above eating corn bread, keeping a poor dog, and sleeping with his face in the broiling mid-day sun."[34]

Once Louisiana state government was functioning on a statewide basis, demand for legislative action to force blacks into the fields increased. This was the primary purpose of the so-called Black Codes. In the event, the codes had no effect because of hostile northern reaction, but even if they had functioned, they could have accomplished little because there were not that many idle Negroes to be coerced. However, the cause of compulsory labor was not entirely lost. The

33 New Orleans *Tribune*, September 16, 1865; Engelsmen, "Freedmen's Bureau in Louisiana," 73–75, 84–86; DeForest, *A Union Officer in the Reconstruction*, 88; John Cox and Lawanda Cox, "General O. O. Howard and the Misrepresented Bureau," *Journal of Southern History*, XIX (November, 1953), 76–77; Highsmith, "Louisiana During Reconstruction," 115.

34 J. F. King to Lin Caperton, January 31, 1867, in Thomas Butler King Papers, Southern Historical Collection, University of North Carolina; see also Payne to Mrs. Sterrett, April 3, 1866, in Barnhart (ed.), "Reconstruction on the Lower Mississippi," 391; Avery Family Papers, 1865–1866; Baton Rouge *Weekly Advocate*, October 6, 1866; Schurz, *Reminiscences*, III, 199–200.

Freedmen's Bureau had as one of its functions keeping blacks on plantations and requiring them to fulfill agreements made with planters.[35]

Comparison of population figures for 1860 and 1870 gives some insight into the extent of the labor shortage in Louisiana. The total population of the state had increased from less than 650,000 in 1860 to slightly more than 725,000 in 1870. However, in 1860 there were 160,468 males between the ages of fifteen and forty, as compared to only 136,753 males between eighteen and forty-five in 1870. In the parishes outside of Orleans there were 118,735 males between fifteen and forty in 1860, but only 99,936 males age eighteen to forty-five in 1870. The number of men in the most productive age group had definitely declined. Part of this resulted from Confederate casualties, but part resulted from the deaths of young blacks in the Union army and in contraband camps. The shortage of productive men was surely considerably greater in 1865 than in 1870, because from 1865 to 1870 there was a substantial migration of freedmen into Louisiana.[36]

The census of 1870 cannot tell the whole story for 1865–1866. A high official of the Freedmen's Bureau stated in early 1866 that nine-tenths of the former slaves in Louisiana were employed, but that many of them refused to work on plantations. It was so difficult to get agricultural labor that many once-thriving acres remained abandoned. The reasons for this labor shortage, in addition to a decline in the number of men of working age, were multiple, as will be seen, but the fact that there was a shortage indicates that agriculture was being revived. In fact, it seems evident that one reason for the shortage was that free labor was not as efficient as slave labor had been. In part this was a result of the absence of the close controls and the threat of the lash which had existed under slavery. Also to be considered, however, is the fact that planters and farmers, unaccustomed to dealing with free labor, were far less efficient as managers than they had once

---

35 New Orleans *Daily Picayune*, July 8, November 26, 1865; White, *Freedmen's Bureau in Louisiana*, 51; Constantin, "Louisiana Black Code," 40–42; May, "The Freedmen's Bureau at the Local Level," 11; Sitterson, *Sugar Country*, 233–34; Franklin, *Reconstruction After the Civil War*, 48–49.

36 *Population of the United States in 1860: Compiled from the Original Returns of the Eight Census . . .* (Washington, D.C. 1864), 188–93; *The Statistics of the Population of the United States . . . Ninth Census* (Washington, D.C. 1872), I, 629.

been. It is probable, also, that the high price of cotton in the months just after the close of hostilities encouraged planters to persist in inefficient methods.[37]

A new feature of the New Orleans scene was the number of Negroes working or loafing about the levee. The same phenomenon was to be observed at Baton Rouge, Shreveport, and other towns. This is not surprising. Free Negroes had congregated in towns, North and South, before the Civil War. Most of the migrating freedmen were not idle. Before the war was over, the *Tribune* noted: "The freedman knows that he can make from $1 to $2 a day in New Orleans, enjoy there his freedom and circulate at liberty—without a pass. . . . To retain the laborers on the plantations, it will be necessary to offer them better inducements."[38]

Not all the freedmen who moved from the plantation went to town. Many tested their freedom by moving to another plantation. Some blacks desired to work for their former owners; others were determined not to do so. And whether it was economically wise or not, it was proof of freedom to choose a new employer each year, or even to break a contract in the middle of the harvest season. Most blacks obviously were self-supporting in one way or another. As free men they felt no obligation to stay where a former master, or any other white man, wanted them to stay. The fact that their labor was in such demand made it ever easier for them to move.[39]

A major factor in the labor shortage was the fact that some Negro women chose not to work in the fields. The black woman and her husband had noted that upper-class white women did not cut cane

---

37 Bayside Plantation Papers, II, January 28, February 20, 1866; King to Caperton, February 13, 1866, in King Papers; Thomas P. Street to A. Batchelor, January 11, 1867, in Albert A. Batchelor Papers, Department of Archives, Louisiana State University; Payne to Mrs. Sterrett, April 3, 1866, in Barnhart (ed.), "Reconstruction on the Lower Mississippi," 391; Saloutos, "Southern Agriculture, 1865–1877," 69; Henry Latham, *Black and White: A Journal of a Three Months Tour in the United States* (London, 1867), 153; White, *Freedmen's Bureau in Louisiana,* 114–15; Coulter, *The South During Reconstruction,* 92–93; Wilson, *Black Codes,* 81–83.

38 New Orleans *Tribune,* November 30, 1864; see also Wesley, *Negro Labor in the United States,* 194–95.

39 New Orleans *Daily Picayune,* December 1, 1865; *Senate Executive Documents,* 39th Cong., 1st Sess., No. 2, p. 30; White, *Freedmen's Bureau in Louisiana,* 109–10; Engelsmen, "Freedmen's Bureau in Louisiana," 178–79, 185.

or pick cotton. With the coming of freedom, women whose husbands' earnings were enough to support the entire family chose to be house-keepers. A few refused even to accept employment as house servants. Those women remaining on the plantations would soon return to the fields, but in town many became independent, being heads of families in their own right.[40]

The idea that Negroes refused to work at harvest time in 1865 because they expected to be given "forty acres and a mule" at Christmas was once generally accepted, but examination of contemporary sources casts doubt upon this idea, at least as far as Louisiana is concerned. There is no evidence that a great deal of cotton was left in the fields in 1865; one suspects that, at the high prices which prevailed, the relatively few acres to be harvested were gleaned most carefully. Nor was there enough sugar standing for any great difficulty to be encountered in cutting, grinding, or planting. A small fraction of the labor available could have dealt with the crop. Certainly the rumor of a division of land did circulate to some extent, but its effect was not upon the work to be done in 1865, but rather upon the willingness of the freedmen to sign contracts for 1866. It was natural for the freedman to wait until after the first of the year to commit himself even if there had been no rumor of free land. He had more time to bargain and to compare possible employers and their offers.[41]

Competition for labor was keen. Labor agents, whose main business was bringing in workers from other states, were not all above persuading workers under contract to seek better terms elsewhere. In early 1866 planters around Thibodaux were accused of offering freedmen a dollar a day or fifteen dollars a month with housing, clothing, and food provided. Cotton planters around St. Martinville were re-

---

40 Lee to Laney [last names unknown], April 4, 1865, in Gibson-Humphrey Papers; [?] to "Cousin Hal," February 7, 1867, in Slack Family Papers, Southern Historical Collection, University of North Carolina; Sitterson, *Sugar Country*, 235; Wilson, *Black Codes*, 51–54; *De Bow's Review*, After the War Series, I (May, 1866), 556; George Campbell, *White and Black: The Outcome of a Visit to the United States* (London, 1879), 144–45; Ellis, "The Transition from Slave Labor to Free Labor," 30; Highsmith, "Louisiana During Reconstruction," 361.

41 Oscar Zeichner, "The Transition from Slave to Free Agricultural Labor in the Southern States," *Agricultural History*, XIII (January, 1939), 22–23; Lowrey, "James Madison Wells," 1,065; Caskey, *Secession and Restoration*, 196.

ported to be offering half the crop, an obvious early stage of share-cropping, or to be offering each half-dozen workers all they produced above twenty bales. This competition for workers was responsible for the provision in the Black Code which forbade the employment of a freedman without the consent of his former employer, but the competition continued. In 1867 one planter was going to the unheard of length of providing mosquito netting for the hands in his employ. Wage competition was never brought completely under control during the Reconstruction years.[42]

The labor shortage persisted in Louisiana despite the arrival of black workers from other states. A large number of freedmen moved east from Texas to Louisiana, claiming that in Texas their diet had too much beef and not enough pork. Many of them had been taken to Texas during the war by refugee masters. At the end of 1865 the blacks coming into Louisiana from Texas, meeting a larger number of whites moving to Texas, was estimated at three hundred per day. Planters sought to recruit out-of-state workers themselves, or by employing agents to act for them. General St. John R. Liddell sent an agent into Mississippi; others sent them as far as the East Coast. At Brokenburn plantation Kate Stone's brother employed discharged Negro soldiers who proved to be rather intractable plantation workers. The main recruiters of new labor, however, were men who undertook this task for a profit, replacing the slave trader of the prewar years.[43]

When eastern lands were producing one bale of cotton to four acres of land and field hands were paid seven dollars per month, the better Louisiana acres were producing three quarters of a bale to the acre, and first-class field hands were worth fifteen dollars per month. Thus the westward migration of blacks was natural. Field hands could earn more in Louisiana during Reconstruction for the same reason that slaves were worth more in Louisiana before the Civil War. There would have been voluntary migration without the labor agents, but

42 New Orleans *Daily Picayune*, January 7, 10, 26, 1866; Constantin, "Louisiana Black Code," 74; Mrs. D. D. Avery to her husband, April 12, 1867, in Avery Family Papers; Plaquemine *Iberville South*, February 3, 1866, quoted in New Orleans *Daily Picayune*, February 13, 1866.
43 New Orleans *Daily Picayune*, November 28, 1865, February 3, 1866, December 26, 1869, February 1, 1870; Stone, *Brokenburn*, 368; White, *Freedmen's Bureau in Louisiana*, 115–16; Clay, "Economic Survival of the Plantation," 60–61.

the agents certainly added to the number of those who were willing to go.[44]

The labor agent might have an order from a planter for a given number of hands, or he might himself contract with workers to go west, depending on planters to pay high enough fees to make his venture profitable. The fee varied; frequently as low as ten dollars per laborer, it was sometimes as high as forty dollars. The profits in this business were greatest in 1866, and some agents were guilty of sharp practices. Sometimes Negroes were kidnapped and taken so far from home that they had to work to earn enough money to return. Agents might contract with freedmen to work in one area, say in the neighborhood of Memphis, then deliver them to the Teche. One conservative estimate is that fifteen thousand adult Negroes came into Louisiana from elsewhere between 1865 and 1871. Eastern planters, while they proclaimed to the world how worthless black labor had become, complained bitterly that these same workers were being lured away.[45]

General Butler began forcing Louisiana freedmen to work for wages, and General Banks followed with a "work or fight" policy for able-bodied black men. Banks's labor edict of February, 1864, set forth a scale of wages and prescribed working conditions and was a definite forerunner of Freedmen's Bureau regulations.[46] In the alluvial parishes along the Mississippi north of Red River, more generous regulations allowed first-class hands twenty-five dollars per month, but they had to provide their own clothing and rations. This regulation was quickly violated in practice, and wages were reduced to ten dollars per month plus rations. One advantage on the northern Louisiana plantation was a requirement that the Negro family be given a plot of ground for growing vegetables. Neither planters nor freedmen were satisfied with these military regulations, whether in north Louisiana or in the Department of the Gulf. The *Picayune*

---

44 *Nation*, II (April 2, 1866), 516; New Orleans *Daily Picayune*, April 6, 1866; Coulter, *The South During Reconstruction*, 99–100.

45 King to Caperton, May 17, 1866, in King Papers; DeForest, *A Union Officer in the Reconstruction*, 102, 130; New Orleans *Daily Picayune*, February 2, 1867; Wharton, *The Negro in Mississippi*, 108; Bentley, *The Freedmen's Bureau*, 124; Saloutos, "Southern Agriculture, 1865–1877," 66; Robert H. Woody, "The Labor and Emigration Problem of South Carolina, During Reconstruction," *Mississippi Valley Historical Review*, XVIII (September, 1931), 196–97.

46 See below, pp. 332–33.

maintained that it was impossible for the planters to pay the prescribed wages. The *Tribune,* which sought to be the voice of the freedmen, demanded that some system be devised to break up the old gang-labor system of slavery days, and it urged that a part of the laborer's pay should be a share of what he had produced.[47]

On March 3, 1865, little more than a month before Lee's surrender, Congress created the Freedmen's Bureau to protect the interests of freedmen in the South. The coming of the bureau brought no radical change. It was a branch of the War Department, and it took over from the military authorities in the occupied areas. It was fairly common for the provost marshal who had been in charge of Negro labor in an area to become the local representative of the new agency. The bureau has been condemned by many historians, primarily for interfering with the natural development of "normal" relationships between planters and freedmen. Before it had run its course, it was roundly condemned by southern whites, but it should be pointed out that in mid-1865 it was welcomed by many.

The role of the bureau has been overemphasized. The total number of employees was never more than nine hundred, certainly not enough to earn all the criticism heaped upon the agency. In Louisiana the employees probably did not exceed one hundred, and not all of these dealt with planter-freedman relations. One recent study concludes that even the most friendly students of the bureau emphasized its weaknesses and underestimated its accomplishments. Another concludes that the great failure of the bureau was not in overprotecting the freedmen, but rather in issuing regulations which, to some extent, were a continuation of the Black Codes. The bureau prevented reenslavement and attempted to protect freedmen from violence, but it also sought to keep them on the plantations and to force them to work.[48]

47 Capers, *Occupied City,* 224–25; Ficklen, *History of Reconstruction in Louisiana,* 131–32; General Order No. 23, Hq. Department of the Gulf, March 11, 1865; New Orleans *Tribune,* March 15, 1865; Tobias Gibson to B. F. Flanders, December 1, 1864, in *Senate Executive Documents,* 39th Cong., 1st Sess., No. 2, pp. 85–86; Eaton, *Grant, Lincoln and the Freedmen,* 159; *House Reports,* 39th Cong., 1st Sess., No. 30, p. 159; *House Reports,* 39th Cong., 1st Sess., No. 30, p. 143; New Orleans *Daily Picayune,* June 25, 1865; New Orleans *Tribune,* January 28–29, March 18, 1866.
48 Caskey, *Secession and Restoration,* 142–43; White, *Freedmen's Bureau in Louisi-*

In Louisiana the bureau was never particularly popular with either planters or spokesmen for the freedmen. In Opelousas the return of the bureau agent was welcomed in December, 1865, "as before his return we were without any authority whatever that could regulate labor,"[49] but this was not the usual reaction. As early as November, 1865, a resolution of the Louisiana house of representatives asked that the bureau be withdrawn from the state. Points of opposition were numerous, including objection to the allowing of plots for gardens, to the amount of rations specified, to permitting blacks to move about freely when they were not at work, and to certain bureau officials. Thomas M. Conway, state head of the bureau, was particularly disliked, and the planters, through Governor Wells, secured his removal in autumn, 1865. Many planters who would admit that free labor was productive were nonetheless opposed to the bureau. Probably the fact that it was opposed by President Johnson influenced many Louisianians.[50]

White opposition to the bureau also resulted from the previously noted belief that blacks would not work without compulsion. Obviously there were many blacks, as there were many whites, who found work distasteful and who avoided it as much as possible. But, as one writer put it, "Lazy shiftless white men were judged as individuals, but lazy, shiftless Negroes were judged as types and representatives of the group."[51] Closely related to the conviction that the black would not work without compulsion was a deep and perhaps unconscious refusal on the part of the white southerner to accept the fact that the Negro was really free. Carl Schurz noted that "Although it is admitted that . . . [the Negro] has ceased to be the property of a master, it is not admitted that he has the right to become his own master."[52] The

ana, passim; Shreveport *Southwestern,* June 28, 1865, quoted in New Orleans *Daily Picayune,* July 9, 1865; Bentley, *The Freedmen's Bureau,* 71, 136; Cox and Cox, "Howard and the Bureau," 428; Wilson, *Black Codes,* 57–59.

49 Opelousas *Sentinel,* December 16, 1865, quoted in New Orleans *Daily Picayune,* December 24, 1865.

50 New Orleans *Daily Picayune,* December 1, 21, 1865; Engelsmen, "Freedmen's Bureau in Louisiana," 182–83; *Nation,* I (November 30, 1865), 676; Franklin, *Reconstruction After the Civil War,* 39; Cox and Cox, "Howard and the Bureau," 435–36.

51 Wesley, *Negro Labor in the United States,* 135; see also New Orleans *Daily Picayune,* August 25, 1865; Saloutos, "Southern Agriculture, 1865–1877," 67.

52 *Senate Executive Documents,* 39th Cong., 1st Sess., No. 2, p. 21.

Louisiana white was just as unable in 1865 as in 1861 to conceive of the Negro as a truly free man.

The freedmen left few records of their reaction to the Freedmen's Bureau. Some of them did realize that the bureau was a means of compelling them to work. There was grumbling among them that when disputes arose the white officials of the bureau tended to take the side of the white planter. The recorded complaints about trifling work, sabotage, and contract-breaking on the part of the freedmen blame such behavior on ignorance and natural black laziness. Almost surely, many such incidents were protests against a system which forced the black into a position which resembled too much the status he had had before emancipation.[53]

Contracts enforced by the Freedmen's Bureau varied greatly, but when General Absalom Baird became assistant commissioner in charge of Louisiana in November, 1866, he set forth twenty rules which were to apply to agreements between freedmen and their employers. The employer was to take whole families, and the wage scale should take the aged and infirm into consideration. The working day was to be ten hours in winter, nine in summer, and there were to be twenty-six working days a month. Freedmen were to be paid extra for overtime. On Sundays only absolutely necessary work was to be done. Workers who received rations as part of their pay were to get five pounds of pork and a peck of corn per week, and each family was to have half an acre for a garden plot. If freedmen received a share of the crop rather than money wages, one twentieth was to be used for schools for their children. If wages were in money, one half was to be paid at the end of each month, the remainder at the end of the year, except that 5 percent was to go for schools. A laborer who broke his contract should lose all wages due to him, and if he wasted time he could, with the consent of the bureau agent, be fined double his wages for that time or forced to leave the plantation. Fines were to go to other workers or into the bureau school fund. The employer was

---

53 Andrew McCollam Papers, VII, March 23, 1863, in Southern Historical Collection, University of North Carolina; *Senate Executive Documents*, 39th Cong., 2nd Sess., No. 6, p. 70; *Nation*, II (March 22, 1866), 369; New Orleans *Tribune*, April 17, October 31, 1867; *Senate Executive Documents*, 39th Cong., 1st Sess., No. 2, p. 91; McRae, *The Americans at Home*, 324; White, *Freedmen's Bureau in Louisiana*, 120–21; Bentley, *The Freedmen's Bureau*, 81–82, 84–86.

to pay one dollar a month per employee for the support of the bureau. Last, but not least, the wages due to the freedmen were to constitute a first mortgage on the employer's property, including the crop.[54]

In general, money wages prevailed in 1865 and 1866, but as early as January, 1865, some freedmen made agreements for maintenance and a share of the crop they produced. Wages varied. On the McCollam sugar plantation in Terrebonne Parish a man and his wife were hired for $20.00 and $14.00 per month, respectively, in 1865. On the Shaffer plantation in the same parish top men drew $19.50 per month with rations, $26.00 a month without. During grinding, women feeding the presses made $12.60 a month with rations, $15.60 without. In general, wages were higher in the sugar parishes than in north Louisiana. In Assumption Parish one planter paid prime men only $13.00 and rations, women $8.00, but each family was given about three acres of land for its own use and was encouraged to keep hogs and chickens. To the north the practice of sharing the crop was beginning, but no standard system was accepted and there were many variations. In 1866, between January 1 and October 1, 2,262 contracts were recorded by the Freedmen's Bureau, and there were others with which the bureau had nothing to do.[55]

The shortage of workers remained so acute that although planters were denouncing the bureau as an unwarranted interference between employer and employee, they nonetheless called upon it to provide laborers from elsewhere when the local supply was exhausted. In 1868 the bureau did act as a labor agent by bringing workers to Louisiana from areas where they were not in such demand. Transportation costs were to be deducted from the workers' pay and paid to the

54 Engelsmen, "Freedmen's Bureau in Louisiana," 176–77, 181–82; White, *Freedmen's Bureau in Louisiana*, 24–25, 112.
55 Batchelor Papers, January 15, 1865; McCollam Papers, VII, February, 1865; Bayside Plantation Papers, II, September 16, 1865, February 1, 1867; John Avery to D. D. Avery, January 17, 1866, Dudley Avery to D. D. Avery, July 2, 1866, in Avery Family Papers; Freedmen's Contract, June 4, 1867, in Slack Family Papers; Shaffer Papers, VII, 1866; *Senate Executive Documents*, 39th Cong., 2nd Sess., No. 6, p. 71; Agreement with Freedmen on Monot Plantation, March 10, 1866, in C. Bordes and Company Papers, Department of Archives, Louisiana State University; Plaquemine *Iberville South*, January 27, 1866, quoted in New Orleans *Daily Picayune*, February 2, 1866; Bentley, *The Freedmen's Bureau*, 81, 148; White, *Freedmen's Bureau in Louisiana*, 116, 187; Highsmith, "Some Aspects of Reconstruction in Louisiana," 469–70; Martin Abbott, "Free Land, Free Labor, and the Freedmen's Bureau," *Agricultural History*, XXX (October, 1956), 155.

bureau by the new employer. This was the last year that the bureau had a part in labor contracting; in 1869 the freedmen dealt with planters as best they could. The transition was not hard, because from 1866 on most laborers had done their own negotiating. By and large the laborers seem to have been satisfied where floods or insects did not destroy the crops. Examination of one rather complete set of plantation books for 1865 indicates that prime workers there cleared about ten dollars per month. Most of the disputes settled by bureau officers were between freedmen, not between employers and freedmen.[56]

Aside from the routine denunciations required by the exigencies of national and sectional politics, the Louisiana reaction to the Freedmen's Bureau seems to have been determined mainly by the characteristics of the local agent with whom whites dealt. Some of these local officials were convinced that southerners sought to reenslave the Negro and therefore would not deal fairly with him. Such men naturally were unpopular and could write truthfully that "The life of a northern man who is true to his country and the spirit and genius of its institutions, and frankly enunciates his principles, is not secure where there is not a military force to protect him."[57] Other bureau agents leaned so toward the planter that, in effect, they were his agents in obtaining employees and forcing them to work. Most agents were somewhere between these two extremes. Contrary to the long-prevailing impression, relatively few of them were corrupt. They were young men, nearly all former officers in the Union army, attempting to deal with an unprecedented situation. Some of them were Democrats, and almost all thought it their primary duty to keep the freedmen at work. Insofar as possible they discouraged political gatherings which interrupted work. They protected the freedmen against unfair dealings by the planter, but they also tried to see to it that he earned his pay. Some of them were remarkably popular with the planters in their bailiwick. In fact, one suspects that most of them,

---

56 White, *Freedmen's Bureau in Louisiana,* 117, 130–31; Vermilionville *Advertiser,* January 29, 1866, quoted in New Orleans *Daily Picayune,* February 2, 1866; Sitterson, *Sugar Country,* 236; Bayside Plantation Papers, II, 1865; Ellis, "The Transition from Slave Labor to Free Labor," 23; Engelsmen, "Freedmen's Bureau in Louisiana," 170–71.

57 Stickney to Conway, August 26, 1865, in *Senate Executive Documents,* 39th Cong., 1st Sess., No. 2, p. 91.

unaccustomed to dealing with the freedman, were disappointed to discover that the Negro was not a northern farm hand with a black skin; as a result they tended to be partial to the planter to the extent that they were partial at all.[58]

One little-publicized effort of the Freedmen's Bureau in Louisiana was to settle blacks on abandoned plantations. The seizure of such lands was authorized by an act of Congress during the war, and the Freedmen's Bureau Act gave the head of the agency authority to assign confiscated land to freedmen. Heads of families could get forty acres at a rent not greater than 6 percent of the assessed value of such lands. The freedmen could purchase whatever title the United States could convey by paying the assessed valuation. The catch phrase, of course, was whatever title the United States could convey. The owners of such land were presumably traitors, and their property could be confiscated. The United States Constitution provided, though, that an attainder of treason affected only the traitor, not his heirs. Thus John Slidell, if unpardoned, could not regain possession of his property, but when he died the claim of his heirs was valid. Most Confederates who had abandoned their property were pardoned by President Johnson, and this presidential pardon enabled them to personally reclaim their land.

In 1865 freedmen cultivated 62,528 acres of land in Louisiana on their own; almost as much more was available to them but not cultivated. A number of large places, the McHatton estate near Baton Rouge, the Rost estate in St. Charles Parish, the Sparks estate in Jefferson Parish, and General Bragg's plantation near Thibodaux became "home colonies" for freedmen. Reports on these ventures varied with the bias of the reporter, but since they served as much as a refuge for the old, the orphaned, and the maimed as attempts at viable economic operations, the prospects for success were not good. Combined, the colonies had 9,650 acres of land, and in 1865 they produced for sale $175,000 worth of goods. Of the 1,902 Negroes on

58 May, "The Freedmen's Bureau at the Local Level," 8–19; Franklin *Planters' Banner*, quoted in New Orleans *Daily Picayune*, January 23, 1865; DeForest, *A Union Officer in the Reconstruction*, 74, 100; Reid, *After the War*, 577; White, *Freedmen's Bureau in Louisiana*, 33–34, 38; Cox and Cox, "Howard and the Bureau," 431–32; Dunning, *Reconstruction, Political and Economic*, 33–34; Franklin, *Reconstruction After the Civil War*, 37–38; Bentley, *The Freedmen's Bureau*, 73.

the land, 609 were sick or disabled. It is doubtful that they could ever have succeeded, but the question can never be finally answered because in 1866 all the colonies except Bragg's plantation were returned to their former owners, and Bragg's place was sold into other hands.[59]

The Federal Homestead Act of 1866 was another attempt to aid freedmen. Under this act, any man over twenty-one years of age, white or black, who had not supported the Confederacy could obtain eighty acres of land by paying a five-dollar filing fee and by living on the land for five years and making improvements. Very few black men ever took advantage of this act. One obvious reason was that much of the nationally owned land in Louisiana was worthless. Secondly, homesteading in Louisiana, as on the Great Plains, required more capital than most freedmen possessed. Last, but not least, there was strong white opposition to Negro homesteading. In 1866 General Baird warned freedmen that those who took up land should act in groups of families strong enough to protect themselves. Among the few settlements made by freedmen was Hilaryville, southwest of Gonzales, established by a group of black Virginians who had come together to the Burnside Plantation. This settlement lasted for more than a generation, but by the early 1930s the inhabitants had moved to New Orleans.[60]

An impartial evaluation of the role of the Freedmen's Bureau in Louisiana makes it clear that this much maligned agency was essen-

59 New Orleans *Tribune,* February 11, 1865; *Nation,* II (April 19, 1866), 484; White, *Freedmen's Bureau in Louisiana,* 47, 107–109; Bentley, *The Freedmen's Bureau,* 89–90; Engelsmen, "Freedmen's Bureau in Louisiana," 205–206, 211–12; Clay, "Economic Survival of the Plantation," 22; Edgar L. Erickson (ed.), "Hunting for Cotton in Dixie: From the Civil War Diary of Captain Charles E. Wilcox," *Journal of Southern History,* IV (November, 1938), 494; Lawanda Cox, "The Promise of Land for the Freedmen," *Mississippi Valley Historical Review,* XLV (December, 1958), 418.

60 Hyler to Warmoth, March 27, 1867, in Warmoth Papers; *Senate Executive Documents,* 39th Cong., 2nd Sess., No. 6, p. 72; Baton Rouge *Weekly Advocate,* July 28, 1866; New Orleans *Tribune,* October 20, 1866, White, *Freedmen's Bureau in Louisiana,* 58–62; Bentley, *The Freedmen's Bureau,* 145; Marchand, *The Story of Ascension Parish,* 117, 163–64, 189; Engelsmen, "Freedmen's Bureau in Louisiana," 210–11; Paul W. Gates, "Federal Land Policy in the South, 1866–1888," *Journal of Southern History,* VI (August, 1940), 307; Rachael Edna Norgress, "The History of the Cypress Lumber Industry in Louisiana," *Louisiana Historical Quarterly,* XXX (July, 1947), 979–1,059; Frederick B. Goddard, *Where to Emigrate and Why: Homes and Fortunes in the Boundless West and the Sunny South* . . . (Philadelphia, 1869), 575–76.

tial. It succored hungry whites as well as hungry blacks, and the bureau agents were just as concerned as the planters to get freedmen to work in the fields. To some extent the bureau agent did protect the freedmen from unscrupulous planters, but it also protected planters from unreliable black workers. The labor shortage in Louisiana was not ended by these officials because there were not enough hands available to do all the work that needed to be done, but the exertions of the bureau and the economic needs of the freedmen had put the vast majority of able-bodied blacks back into the fields by 1866. In a sense the Freedmen's Bureau did replace the Black Codes as a means of coercing the labor force into working. It succeeded so well that it had presided over the creation of a workable, though far from perfect, labor system by 1869, and to that extent had worked itself out of a job. Unwillingness of the available labor force to work was never really a handicap to Louisiana's Reconstruction agriculture after 1865, certainly not after 1866.

3

Postwar restoration of communications was rapid. Water transportation was quickly revived. New Orleans had been open to traffic from the sea from the beginning of Union occupation, and travel by the Gulf and the Atlantic to the Northeast was reasonably regular and convenient thereafter. The fall of Vicksburg and Port Hudson in 1863 opened New Orleans to traffic down the Ohio and the Mississippi. The Red River and the Arkansas, however, remained largely under Confederate control. Within Louisiana regular steamer service to the Lafourche plantations was available in 1864, and there was shipping, though apparently irregular, to the Teche.

In 1866 there was a strong revival of New Orleans' upriver trade, especially with St. Louis. New low-pressure engines were so successful that at least six lines were operating up and down the Mississippi by 1868. Despite railroad competition, the number of landings at New Orleans continued to increase until a peak was reached in 1880. Seaborne traffic was handicapped by the difficulty of crossing the bars at the mouths of the Mississippi, so the increase in sea traffic was not very great. Transportation on the tributaries of the Mississippi was very expensive when it was first revived after the war. As noted, in late 1865 and early 1866 cotton in Shreveport was worth about one third less than in New Orleans, mainly because of high freight rates.[61]

Roads were seldom good anywhere in the nineteenth century, and those of Louisiana were as bad as, and in alluvial sections probably worse than, in the rest of the United States. At the end of the war there had been little or no maintenance for four years. Four years later there had been little improvement; most bridges had not yet been replaced. In 1873 a carriage could not go from Shreveport to Minden, a distance of thirty-three miles; only a wagon drawn by six strong horses or mules could make it through the Red River mud. In what is now Evangeline Parish there were reportedly no publicly maintained roads whatsoever before 1872. Land travel was so difficult that as late as 1874 persons going from Shreveport to Monroe preferred, even though there was a stage line, to go down the Red River and the Mississippi to New Orleans, then up the Jackson Railroad to Jackson and west to Vicksburg and Monroe, or, alternatively, by rail to Galveston, then by steamer to Morgan City, by rail to New Orleans, and then northward on the Jackson Railroad.[62]

Where railroads did not run, and where water traffic was impossible, a network of stagecoach lines, running on infrequent and usually unreliable schedules, spread thinly over Louisiana. In the Florida parishes one line ran from Baton Rouge to Clinton as early as October, 1865. The next year another was in operation from Clinton to Tangipahoa, on the Jackson Railroad, making the round trip three times a week. Before the end of 1866 a number of stage lines converged at Alexandria, which had become a mail distribution center. In 1870 a stage ran from Winnsboro to Delhi, where it made connections with the Vicksburg railroad. The line from Shreveport to Monroe has already been mentioned, and another ran from Shreveport to Natchi-

---

61 New Orleans *Daily Picayune*, February 3, 1864, December 7, 25, 1865, January 19, April 10, 1866; *Acts of Louisiana, 1867*, 315–19, 323–25; Highsmith, "Louisiana During Reconstruction," 401–402; Oscar Osburn Winther, *The Transportation Frontier: Trans-Mississippi West, 1865–1890* (New York, 1964), 75, 84–85, 90; J. E. Hilary Skinner, *After the Storm: Or Jonathan and His Neighbors in 1865–6* (London, 1866), 51–52.

62 New Orleans *Daily Picayune*, July 3, 1869, July 21, 1874; Shreveport *Times*, April 11, August 31, 1873; *Acts of Louisiana, 1867*, 243–45; Bergerie, "Economic and Social History of Iberia Parish," 104–105.

toches by way of Mansfield. There were, in addition, other shorter and shorter-lived lines.[63]

A necessary task at the end of the war was to restore postal service. One difficulty was in obtaining postmasters who could take the necessary loyalty oath. By the end of 1865 mail from Shreveport was being delivered to Monroe, and routes existed from Minden to Homer, Louisiana, and El Dorado, Arkansas. Letters from Shreveport were delivered to Washington three times a week, and scheduled delivery existed from Shreveport and from Natchitoches to various towns in Texas. Interestingly enough, it was not until March, 1866, that a weekly delivery of mail to Plaquemines Parish, just below New Orleans, was established. By the end of that year, however, mail delivery had become approximately as efficient as before the war, but this was not particularly efficient. Complaints of the slowness and unreliability of the mails were frequent; on the other hand, a letter from New Orleans to New York in 1876 arrived in sixty-one hours, which was at least as fast as surface mail traveled between the same points ninety-six years later.[64]

Telegraphic communication between New Orleans and cities in the Northeast had existed before the war and was restored soon after it was over. During hostilities, Confederate authorities had built a line from Shreveport to Houston. After the war this line was extended southward to Galveston and northeastward until messages could go from Galveston to the national capital by way of Shreveport. By the late 1870s such communities as Opelousas, Natchitoches, and Thibodaux, to name a few, were connected to the rest of the United States by telegraph. On March 29, 1877, there was an omen of the future in the exhibition of Alexander Graham Bell's telephone at Grunewald Hall in New Orleans.[65]

As noted earlier, the repair of existing railroads and the construction of new ones was looked upon from the end of the Civil War to the beginning of the Panic of 1873 as the means by which the pros-

63 New Orleans *Daily Picayune*, October 15, 1865, April 19, 1866, July 29, 1870, June 25, 1877; Baton Rouge *Weekly Advocate*, December 15, 1866.

64 New Orleans *Daily Picayune*, September, 1865–December, 1866, November 24, 1869, September 7, 1871, August 16, 1876, April 17, 1877.

65 *Ibid.*, August 8, 1865, May 29, 1876, March 22, April 1, May 8, 1877.

perity of the South was to be restored. But no matter how many bonds were issued, the capital to accomplish this work did not exist in the South. Therefore most Louisiana rialroads rapidly came under the control of northern capitalists. The Southern Pacific connected Shreveport and Marshall, Texas, soon after the war, and in a relatively short time Shreveport had connections with Dallas, Houston, and Galveston. Another short line, the Clinton and Port Hudson, ran its first passenger train on February 8, 1867, but did not open its track all the way to Port Hudson until after midsummer of that year.[66]

In 1865 two Louisiana Scalawags, John T. Ludeling and John Ray, by means of blatant skulduggery, had obtained control of the Vicksburg, Shreveport and Texas Railroad for $50,000. With it they received 300,000 acres of a prewar land grant, a generous state subsidy, and some $57,000 from Vicksburg. In 1879, when the original stockholders finally got their railroad back, the name had been changed to the North Louisiana and Texas Railroad Company and the prewar tracks from Delta to Monroe had been restored. Floods cut the line occasionally, but from 1870 on it was normally open. It was not until after Reconstruction was over, however, that progress was made westward from Monroe, and it was not until 1884 that the tracks reached Shreveport. Only then was Vicksburg truly connected with Texas by rail.[67]

The floods of 1866 and 1867 hampered rebuilding of the Baton Rouge, Grosse Tete, and Opelousas Railroad, and it was not until October, 1868, that a determined effort to put the road back into commission began. In December of that year handcars were carrying passengers and light freight over the line. In 1869 the line had two locomotives and a number of cars in operation, and in August of that year a locomotive went all the way to Rosedale on Bayou Grosse

66 *Ibid.*, January 11, February 15, July 10, 1867; Stampp, *The Era of Reconstruction*, 181–82; John F. Stover, "Northern Financial Interests in Southern Railroads, 1865–1900," *Georgia Historical Quarterly*, XXXIX (September, 1955), 205–20; Fred A. Shannon, *The Farmer's Last Frontier: Agriculture, 1860–1897* (New York, 1945), 106–107.

67 Prichard (ed.), "A Forgotten Engineer," 1,183–207; New Orleans *Daily Picayune*, July 8, 1870, May 17, June 12, 1877; E. Dale Odom, "The Vicksburg, Shreveport and Texas: The Fortunes of a Scalawag Railroad," *Southwestern Social Science Quarterly*, XLIV (December, 1963), 277–85; Highsmith, "Louisiana During Reconstruction," 402–403.

Tete. In December the track was operational to Livonia, thirty-two miles from Baton Rouge, which was as far as it would go during Reconstruction.[68]

The New Orleans, Opelousas, and Great Western Railroad fell into the hands of Charles Morgan, and Morgan's main activity was operating steamships on the Gulf. He nonetheless greatly improved the railroad, changing to standard gauge, raising the roadbed so as to make it safe from overflow, establishing a freight yard on the New Orleans side of the Mississippi, and introducing a steam ferry which transported as many as ten loaded cars at a time back and forth across the river. On the other hand, he was not particularly interested in pushing the railroad on westward. The road fed freight and passengers to his steamships, which made regular runs from Berwick Bay to Indianola and Galveston, Texas. Morgan built some roadbed west of the Atchafalaya, but he laid no track on it. It was not until after he was dead and Reconstruction was over that tracks were laid from Morgan City along the Teche and across the prairies to meet tracks running out from Houston to the Sabine.[69]

Rebuilding of the New Orleans, Jackson, and Great Northern, usually referred to simply as the Jackson Railroad, was rapid. As early as June, 1865, regular service was available from New Orleans to Ponchatoula, and farther north the one locomotive to survive the war on this line was pulling damaged cars from Brookhaven to Jackson and back. By October the entire line was open to Canton, its prewar northern terminus, with daily trains each way. This established connections with Grand Junction, Tennessee, making it possible to travel from New Orleans to New York by rail. In 1866 passengers had to change cars only twice on this journey. Much of the credit for this rapid recovery must go to General P. G. T. Beauregard. As noted earlier, the Jackson Railroad fell into the hands of Henry S. McComb, who began the process of consolidation which resulted, eventually,

68 Prichard (ed.), "A Forgotten Engineer," 1,214–15; Baton Rouge *Weekly Advocate*, November 10, 1866, September 5, October 10, December 5, 1868, June 26, August 21, 1869; New Orleans *Daily Picayune*, December 17, 1869.
69 Prichard (ed.), "A Forgotten Engineer," 1,078, 1,164–65, 1,177; New Orleans *Daily Picayune*, September 6, 1865, July 3, 1867, April 6, 1869, December 23, 1871; Kendall, *History of New Orleans*, I, 299; James P. Baughman, *Charles Morgan and the Development of Southern Transportation* (Nashville, 1968), 127–28, 130, 147–49, 155–56, 159–62.

in the unbroken tracks of the Illinois Central from Chicago to New Orleans.[70]

The one new line to appear in Louisiana soon after the war was the New Orleans, Mobile and Chattanooga.[71] The tracks from Mobile to New Orleans made relatively little economic contribution because they ran through rather barren country from one port to another. This corporation was favored by Radical political powers in Louisiana, however, and was heavily subsidized to build westward to Texas. It reached Donaldsonville before being halted by mismanagement and the Panic of 1873. One lasting memento of its existence and ambitions is its starting point on the west side of the Mississippi. It was named *West We Go* and remains Westwego to this day. It was to be many years before this line—finally combined with the Baton Rouge, Grosse Tete, and Opelousas and extended westward as the Kansas-Pacific— was significantly to benefit the economy of Louisiana.[72]

4

The Civil War had a devastating effect upon the economy of New Orleans, but probably the damage would have been much greater had it not been for the Union occupation beginning in 1862. Even so, the total value of exports, $155,863,000 in 1860–1861 had declined to $29,766,000 in 1862–1863. The cotton trade, amounting to $92,000,-000 in 1860–1861, was down to $46,000,000 in 1863–1864, when cotton was bringing much higher prices. The sugar trade suffered worst of all, declining from 459,110 hogsheads worth $25,000,000 in 1861, an extraordinarily large crop, to 9,800 hogsheads worth $2,000,000 in 1864. Some planters within Confederate lines were able to continue to deal with their New Orleans factors, but it is obvious that the occupation forces were the city's chief source of revenue from 1862 until the end of the war.[73]

As the war ended old inhabitants returned, new men with new

70 New Orleans *Daily Picayune*, June–November, 1865, July 26, 1868; Highsmith, "Louisiana During Reconstruction," 404–405; T. Harry Williams, *P. G. T. Beauregard: Napoleon in Gray* (Baton Rouge, 1955), 273–78.

71 See above, pp. 189–90.

72 Warmoth, *War, Politics and Reconstruction*, 81–83; Beale, *The Critical Year*, 339; Baughman, *Charles Morgan*, 159–60, 165.

73 Capers, *Occupied City*, 147–48; Woodman, *King Cotton and His Retainers*, 211–12; New Orleans *Daily Picayune*, January 17, 1864.

capital arrived, and a degree of prosperity was restored. Immigration was encouraged by the fact that occupation had left New Orleans a cleaner and more healthful city. This prosperity was artificial, based in roughly equal parts on hope and the high, but declining, price of cotton. Rents doubled in 1865, partly because there had been no construction during the war. Real estate worth $50,000 before the war was reported to bring $75,000 in early 1866. Of $875,000 in state taxes collected from October 1, 1864 to January 1, 1866, New Orleans paid $666,000. James D. B. De Bow wrote in early 1866:

> *In New Orleans again!* It is nearly four years since our departure was hurried by . . . Farragut's fleet. . . . The old residents have returned. The young men of the army who have survived are here, and all at work with vigor and energy. There are, too, hundreds and thousands of strange faces. The levee is crowded with steamers and ships and merchandise and busy men, and the shops are filled with goods. Chartres Street and Canal Street make a marvelous display of beautiful women. The newspapers publish triple and quadruple sheets of advertising. . . . Still, it does not equal the New Orleans of former times.[74]

Visitors from North and South noted that the people of New Orleans were better dressed than elsewhere in the South. Some sort of culmination was reached with the Second Grand State Fair which opened on January 7, 1868. A brave show was made, but the newspaper accounts seem a little dispirited, perhaps because the truth had struck home that the railroads of the Northwest were diverting eastward traffic that would otherwise have come to the Crescent City. Gradually the realization grew, though never admitted, that New Orleans would never again "equal the New Orleans of former times."[75]

5

The years 1866 and 1867 were disastrous for Louisianians. Sugar planters usually had not the capital or the seed cane to plant any

---

74 *De Bow's Review*, After the War Series, I (February, 1866), 219.
75 *Ibid.*; New Orleans *Daily Picayune*, May–December, 1865, January 10, 28, February 4, March 1, April 25, 1866, January 8–10, 1868, June 4, 1869; J. H. L. Hull to Martha Holland, November 4, 1866, in Martha Holland Papers, Southern Historical Collection, University of North Carolina; Henry Deedes, *Sketches of the South and West or Ten Months Residence in the United States* (Edinburgh, 1869), 136; Caldwell, *Banking History of Louisiana*, 96–97; Shugg, *Origins of Class Struggle in Louisiana*, 281–82, 287–88, 298–99; Franklin, *Reconstruction After the Civil War*, 10; Somers, *The Southern States Since the War*, 29.

significant amount of sugar. Those who could, leased their plantations; others found a partner to provide capital. Most planted what sugar they could, mainly for seed in many instances, then attempted to grow cotton. Those unfamiliar with this crop sought guidance as to varieties and methods of cultivating. A Mr. Stafford from Grand Chenier in what is now Cameron Parish instructed the Averys of Avery Island in cotton farming. Experienced cotton planters found it easy to obtain financing in 1866. Kate Stone noted: "Mama had little trouble getting advances in New Orleans to plant. Cotton is so high that merchants are anxious to advance [money] to put in a crop."[76] Many men who had never worked before now developed calloused hands from axes, plow handles, and hoes.[77]

More than a million acres were planted in cotton in Louisiana in 1866, but only some 131,000 bales were harvested. As early as April the waters of the Mississippi were beginning to flow through the myriad breaks in the levee, and by May 23 at least eight parishes along the great river were inundated. But this was only the beginning. Fed by heavy rains and checked by the swollen Mississippi, the Red River at the end of May flooded its narrow valley from Indian Territory down to its mouth. Alexandria was reported to be under three to six feet of water. Monroe on the Ouachita was not flooded, but a newspaper noted that although the fields looked green, the color came from grass and weeds, not from cotton and corn.[78]

By June 9 the waters were receding rapidly; those whose lands had been flooded hastened to replant their cotton, hoping to make at least a partial crop in the short season remaining. These hopes were largely doomed. Before the end of July cotton worms were reported from almost every section of the state; the voracious caterpillars proceeded to destroy most of the cotton which had survived the flood or which had been planted afterward. Thousands of people, black and white, were left destitute; hundreds of thousands of rations issued by the

76 Stone, *Brokenburn*, 368.
77 R. E. Butler to Margaret Butler, September 17, 1866, January 25, 1867, in Butler Papers; J. W. Avery to D. D. Avery, January 21, March 1, 1866, in Avery Family Papers; Bayside Plantation Papers, II, January 19, 1866; Coulter, *The South During Reconstruction*, 201.
78 New Orleans *Daily Picayune*, April 6, May 23, 29–30, June 5, 1866; Highsmith, "Social and Economic Conditions in Rapides Parish," 31–32.

Freedmen's Bureau preserved many of both races from actual starvation. The legislature, which had suspended taxes due for the years from 1860 through 1864 until 1868, acted in early 1867 to extend the suspension to 1870.[79]

Cotton prices remained high in the spring of 1867, but many marginal planters and farmers had been wiped out by the disaster of 1866. Also, costs of operation went up. Good mules, essential to both sugar and cotton planting, were worth up to $250. As a result, fewer acres were planted than in the previous year. This was just as well, because in March the Mississippi River began pouring through crevasses from one end of Louisiana to another; Bayou Lafourche swept over the sugar fields from Thibodaux southward. All of Pointe Coupee Parish was flooded, and as late as May it was possible to go by boat directly from Franklin to Plaquemine, in Iberville Parish, passing over flooded cane fields part of the way.

As in 1866, an infestation of army worms followed the flood, destroying most of the cotton which had escaped flooding. To make things worse, the price of cotton dropped sharply as the small surviving crop came to market. Then in September an epidemic of yellow fever struck the state. Tens of thousands of people were utterly destitute. In Assumption Parish alone the Freedmen's Bureau asked for rations for fifteen hundred white people and six hundred Negroes. The agent in Pointe Coupee needed four thousand rations. Deaths by starvation were recorded, and an army medical officer reported that many of the deaths reported were caused in part by malnutrition. To the everlasting credit of Louisiana planters, they cared for more than thirty-six thousand destitute freedmen, mainly old people and children, in this crisis. This was a far larger number than was fed by the Freedmen's Bureau.

The disasters of 1866–1867 in Louisiana were more harmful than they might otherwise have been because a business recession affected the entire nation. The price of lands went down still more, and often it was difficult to find buyers at any price. Undoubtedly many planters

79 Shreveport *News*, June 9, 1866, quoted in New Orleans *Daily Picayune*, June 12, 1866; New Orleans *Daily Picayune*, July 24, 28, 1866, January 11, 1867; *Acts of Louisiana*, 1866, 44–46; *Acts of Louisiana*, 1867, 79–81; C. L. Price to D. D. Avery, September 3, 1866, in Avery Family Papers; White, *Freedmen's Bureau in Louisiana*, 67–68; Shannon, *The Farmer's Last Frontier*, 79–80.

who had worked hard to restore their fortunes were broken in spirit by these successive catastrophes. The freedmen, many of whom received no wages or income at all, were demoralized as well as impoverished. Caterpillars did not attack corn, and fairly good crops were made, but much of it was stolen by hungry freedmen. As might have been expected, cattle and hogs disappeared with alarming frequency.[80]

There were some bright spots in the gloom. Because there had been little building during the war, the owners of rental housing prospered. In Shreveport lack of space was said to be the chief obstacle to more business, and a building boom led to the establishment of several brick kilns and sawmills. A Monroe newspaper commented on the large amount of machinery being brought into north Louisiana, particularly sawmills and gristmills. Lumber was assuming increased importance. A reporter traveling from New Orleans to Grand Isle by way of Harvey's Canal and Bayou Barataria noted three large steam sawmills in operation, one of which had a railroad running into the swamp to bring out the logs. Finally, an omen of Louisiana's future appeared with the discovery of petroleum in Calcasieu Parish.[81]

6

The Civil War years were inflationary in Louisiana. The story of the depreciation of Confederate currency is well known, but there was also inflation in those parts of the state occupied by Union troops. The occupation brought in greenbacks, but it did not significantly increase the supply of goods available. Thus New Orleans prices, which had been high before the war began, rose to such a height that the ordinary necessities of life were beyond the means of working-class citizens. This condition was only partially corrected when the fall of Vicksburg opened the Mississippi to goods from the Northwest.

80 New Orleans *Daily Picayune*, March, 1866–December, 1867; Engelsmen, "Freedmen's Bureau in Louisiana," 167–69; Bentley, *The Freedmen's Bureau*, 14; White, *Freedmen's Bureau in Louisiana*, 66–73; Vidal Papers, 1867; Batchelor Papers, 1866–67; Anderson, "The South and Post–Civil War Finance," 188; Clay, "Economic Survival of the Plantation," 157; Highsmith, "Some Aspects of Reconstruction in Louisiana," 467.

81 Shreveport *News*, June 24, 1865, quoted in New Orleans *Daily Picayune*, July 7, 1865; Shreveport *Gazette*, quoted in New Orleans *Daily Picayune*, February 3, 1866; Monroe *Intelligencer*, quoted in New Orleans *Daily Picayune*, April 5, 1866; New Orleans *Daily Picayune*, March 18, June 3, September 19, 1866; William G. Peterkin to D. D. Avery, May 5, 1866, in Avery Family Papers.

For several reasons the end of the war did not bring immediate deflation. Some federal troops remained in Louisiana, adding to the money in circulation. Of much greater significance was the flow of northern capital southward. Some, as noted earlier, was for investment in land. Probably more important to Louisiana's economy, however, were the advances made by northern banks and businesses to New Orleans merchants and factors. Northern businessmen were eager to restore the cotton trade with the South and appreciated the need of capital to bring about this restoration.

Louisiana had had a strong prewar banking system, partly because the state had issued bonds to provide capital for the banks. Thirteen were in business at the beginning of the Civil War, but the loss of four million dollars in specie to the Confederate government, General Butler's requirement that deposits made in Confederate money be paid off in more acceptable currency, and his assessments upon the banks had weakened the system. By the end of February, 1863, when the first National Bank Act was enacted, only six New Orleans banks remained.

The First National Bank of New Orleans opened its doors in 1864, and by the end of the war ten banks were operating in the city. They were not in healthy condition, however; the value of their stock, all of which was a hundred dollars per share par value, ranged from eight to seventy-six dollars except for the First National, which sold for ninety-nine dollars. Another national bank, James Robb's Louisiana National, was chartered in late 1865. The banking situation gradually improved until by 1870 the eleven banks then in business in New Orleans had capital of almost seven-and-a-half million dollars, still far less than before the war, and deposits of fifteen million dollars. Probably more money was available for lending in Louisiana than in any other southern state. Even so, the resources available were only a fraction of the capital needed. Interest rates, naturally, were high.[82]

82 Capers, *Occupied City*, 151–52, 168, 171–77; Anderson, "The South and Post–Civil War Finance," 189–90; Woodman, *King Cotton and His Retainers*, 243, 246–47, 252, 319–20, 348; Franklin, *Reconstruction After the Civil War*, 10–11; Caldwell, *Banking History of Louisiana*, 96–98, 102; New Orleans *Daily Picayune*, June 18, December 29, 1865; Reid, *After the War*, 230–31; Somers, *The Cotton States Since the War*, 210; George Ruble Woolfolk, *The Cotton Regency: The Northern Merchants and Reconstruction, 1865–1880* (New York, 1958), 108–

The National Bank Act was a wartime measure intended to sell United States bonds as much as to set up a new banking system. A companion act taxed state bank notes out of existence. The amount of currency national banks could issue was strictly limited by their capital invested in United States Bonds, providing an inadequate and almost completely inflexible money supply. This was true over the whole nation, but the South had been out of the Union when the act was passed and for sixteen months thereafter. When the war ended there was little southern capital for investment in national banks. The sectional malapportionment was striking. By 1872 an additional five national banks had been established in New Orleans. This was an improvement, but inadequate banking facilities handicapped Louisiana throughout Reconstruction. As late as 1880 the South had one bank for every 22,603 people as compared to one for every 3,699 in New England, one for every 6,906 in the Middle West, and one for every 5,452 in the Far West. It may be added that national banks were forbidden to lend money with real estate as security. By the end of Reconstruction most articulate Louisianians realized that the national banking system was a disadvantage to Louisiana, but protests were of no avail.[83]

Two other kinds of national money were nominally in circulation, gold and greenbacks. Events abroad during the late 1860s and early 1870s resulted in a flight of gold to Europe, making it so scarce that speculators paid as much as $1.67 in greenbacks for one dollar in gold. Obviously this was a perfect environment for the working of Gresham's law, and gold did not circulate. This left greenbacks— United States Treasury notes backed only by the federal government's improved but still questioned credit. It was national financial dogma, accepted even by those who were injured by it, that "hard" money was somehow good, and fiat money, such as greenbacks, somehow

---

109; Report of the Board of Currency to the General Assembly of the State of Louisiana, January, 1866, in *Legislative Documents, 1865–1866.*

83 New Orleans *Daily Picayune*, March 2, 15, 1870, April 9, 1873; Shreveport *Times*, August 7, 1878; Saloutos, "Southern Agriculture, 1865–1877," 64–66; Caldwell, *Banking History of Louisiana*, 100–101; Anderson, "The South and Post–Civil War Finance," 194; Robert P. Sharkey, *Money, Class and Party: An Economic History of Civil War and Reconstruction* (Baltimore, 1959), 235–38; Walter T. K. Nugent, *The Money Question During Reconstruction* (New York, 1967), 32–33.

bad. Therefore, at the end of the war, President Johnson's secretary of the treasury, Hugh McCulloch, began to reduce the amount of greenbacks in circulation. This brought drastic deflation which was particularly disastrous to the capital-starved South. From 1868 to 1873, the money supply in the South improved, but it was at no time adequate, and then the Panic of 1873 began another period of deflation. Had financial policy and the trend of the national economy been designed to do as much harm as possible to Louisiana and the South, they would not have been greatly different.[84]

If Gresham's law kept greenbacks in circulation nationally, in Louisiana it tended to keep them out of circulation, because there they were the soundest currency available. As a result, other types of paper circulated. Baton Rouge issued city bonds of one-dollar denomination. Several of the state banks continued to issue notes during the last months of 1865 and early 1866. They were negotiable despite the federal tax, although not at face value. The notes of these banks were never worth more than eighty cents on the greenback dollar, and they soon disappeared.

Treasury notes issued by the city were the main circulating medium in New Orleans. They also passed in the country, but there state treasury notes seem to have been more common. In 1865 the city treasury notes were discounted less than 1 percent in relation to greenbacks, but by the end of 1866 the discount rate was beginning to rise. State treasury notes were discounted much more heavily, from 3 percent to more than 10 percent at various times in 1865 and 1866, although retail merchants usually accepted them at face value. Both state and city notes had value because they were receivable as tax payments, but the value of neither was improved by the fact that the city would not accept state notes, nor the state city notes.

In 1867 there was a substantial increase in the volume of notes, and by August the discount on New Orleans paper had risen to as much

84 New Orleans *Daily Picayune*, March 15, 1870; Sharkey, *Money, Class and Party*, 67, 82–86; Irwin Unger, *The Greenback Era: A Social and Political History of American Finance, 1865–1879* (Princeton, 1964), 35–37, 42, 61, 142, 264–65; Nugent, *The Money Question During Reconstruction*, 29–30; Herbert S. Schell, "Hugh McCulloch and the Treasury Department, 1865–1869," *Mississippi Valley Historical Review*, XVII (December, 1930), 403–21; *Nation*, II (March 29, 1866), 399.

as 5 percent. In that month General Sheridan ordered a reduction in circulation, but it would seem that new notes were printed as fast as the old ones were burned. By November notes of five-dollar or larger denominations were discounted 10 percent, but so great was the demand for small bills for everyday business that notes of one-, two-, and three-dollar denominations were discounted little at the banks and not at all by retailers. For a time five-dollar bills were made more valuable by being issued with the treasurer's signature across them and then being cut diagonally in half.

State notes were depreciating at the same time. By December, 1867, small city notes were discounted 3 percent, large city notes 17 percent, and state treasury notes 35 percent. The downward path continued gradually until February of 1868, at which time General Hancock ordered that all taxes be paid in greenbacks. By mid-March city notes were worth only seventy cents on the dollar, state notes as little as fifty cents. Gradually greenbacks began to circulate, but never in adequate quantity. State and city warrants served to some extent as a circulating medium throughout Reconstruction, but not in retail trade.[85]

Obviously, the South had many problems other than deflation during the Reconstruction years, but the scarcity of currency, which was far more pronounced than in other parts of the nation, certainly made conditions worse. No sooner had some relief developed in the early 1870s than the depression of 1873 made the situation worse than ever. Louisiana, because of the existence of New Orleans, was probably better off than other southern states, but Louisiana was impoverished. The great need was credit, and this could not be made available except upon exorbitant terms.[86]

7

From late 1868 through most of 1873, Louisiana had four years which, compared with those immediately before or those which came af-

---

85 New Orleans *Daily Picayune*, 1864–1869; Baton Rouge *Weekly Advocate*, June 30, 1866; Aertker, "A Social History of Baton Rouge," 107–108; Saloutos, "Southern Agriculture, 1865–1877," 63; Kendall, *History of New Orleans*, I, 316–17.
86 Nugent, *The Money Question During Reconstruction*, 31–32, 93–94, 100–101; Unger, *The Greenback Era*, 125; Shannon, *The Farmer's Last Frontier*, 78–79; William E. Lair and James E. Rinehart, "Post–Civil War South and the Great Depression: A Suggested Parallel," *Mid-America*, XLVI (July, 1966), 206–207.

ter, must be described as prosperous. Middling cotton, which had dropped as low as fifteen cents a pound in New Orleans in late 1867, climbed to more than thirty cents by late May of 1868; thereafter there was a decline, but middling quotations did not fall below twenty-four cents for the remainder of the year. The cotton crop planted was less in acreage than in either of the two preceding years, but production was much higher, and value higher still. The sugar crop was more than twice that of any one of the previous four years, and corn, the staff of life for people and animals, prospered. A few cheerful agricultural voices were heard for the first time since 1865. Some planters in St. Mary Parish who had been eager to sell their land for almost any price in late 1867 and early 1868 now demanded more than most potential buyers would pay. Even rice production improved; in 1869, well before the beginning of the rice industry in southwestern Louisiana, Louisiana produced more than South Carolina and Georgia combined. In late 1870 the price of cotton was low, but production of more than 600,000 bales and a high yield per acre more than compensated. Prices were better in 1871 and for most of 1872, but before the end of the latter year they had begun the long decline which would continue with hardly a break for the remaining years of Reconstruction. Overall, nonetheless, the years from 1868 through 1872 were the best Louisiana farmers were to know for a generation.[87]

During this period of relative prosperity, communications and transportation facilities continued to improve. As noted earlier, the New Orleans, Mobile and Chattanooga Railroad came from Mobile to New Orleans then up the west side of the Mississippi to Donaldsonville. Much work was done, using convicts leased from the state penitentiary, to push this line across the Atchafalaya swamp, but the Panic

---

87 New Orleans *Daily Picayune*, 1868–1872, August 31, 1873; *De Bow's Review*, After the War Series, VIII (September, 1870), 790; Thomas Butler to Margaret Butler, March 26, 1868, in Butler Papers; F. D. Richardson to F. L. Richardson, January 30, 1869, in Caffery Papers; White, *Freedmen's Bureau in Louisiana*, 76, 130; Sitterson, *Sugar Country*, 244–45; Rendigs Fels, "American Business Cycles, 1865–1879," *American Economic Review*, XLI (June, 1951), 330–31; Clay, "Economic Survival of the Plantation," 128–29; Engelsmen, "Freedmen's Bureau in Louisiana," 191; Lerner, "Southern Output and Agricultural Income," 125; Richard W. Griffin, "Problems of Southern Cotton Planters After the Civil War," *Georgia Historical Quarterly*, XXXIX (June, 1955), 111.

of 1873 halted this effort. In the northwestern part of Louisiana, direct rail connections were established between Shreveport and Galveston by way of Marshall, Texas. Meanwhile, McComb extended the New Orleans, Jackson, and Great Northern to Humboldt, Tennessee, by purchase of an existing line. Late in 1872 an agreement was reached by which the Jackson road moved on toward a connection with the Illinois Central at the Ohio River. Finally a branch line was built from Terrebonne Station (Schriever) to Houma by the New Orleans, Opelousas, and Great Western. Planters along this branch subscribed from three to four thousand dollars each, according to one report, but the rails saved each of them from a thousand to fifteen hundred a year in transportation costs.[88]

Agricultural prosperity brought prosperity to the steamship lines which still transported most goods to New Orleans. Shreveport may serve as an example. During the year ending September 1, 1871, some 104,776 bales of cotton came into that city, and 91,821 came in during the next twelve months. In the latter year 5,500 came to Shreveport by steamer, 37,356 by rail, and the remainder, about 49,000, by wagon. Until rail connections with Galveston were complete, all of this cotton went downstream to New Orleans. In the year ending September 1, 1872, five thousand bales passed Shreveport without stopping. Keen competition usually kept freight rates down. The steamer *John T. Moore* carried 2,200 bales of cotton to New Orleans in December, 1871, at a rate of $1.50 per bale. In the autumn of 1872 the steamboat operators attempted to raise rates by collusion, but the competition was too intense for any such agreement to be fully successful. On one day in 1873 there were sixteen steamers docked at Shreveport.[89]

Two natural calamities hampered communications during these years of prosperity. High water caused a great number of crevasses in 1871. The damage to crops was not nearly so great as in 1867, but New Orleans itself was partially flooded, one half of the city being reported under water in mid-June. A break in the levee at Bonnet

---

88 R. E. Butler to Margaret Butler, November 13, 1871, in Butler Papers; New Orleans *Daily Picayune*, January 11, 1869, August 30, 31, October 27, 1872, February 5, 19, June 29, August 1, 1873.

89 Shreveport *Times*, December, 1871–1873; C. A. Ives, *As I Remember* (Baton Rouge, 1964), 19–20.

Carre washed away the tracks of the Jackson railroad. This crevasse, eventually more than a third of a mile wide, cut off through-rail-traffic north for three months. Passengers and freight were transported across Lake Pontchartrain by steamer. The next year an epizootic killed or temporarily disabled horses over much of Louisiana and New Orleans' other trading regions. In December all streetcars in the city were halted, and throughout the affected region special arrangements had to be made for the transportation of cotton. The arrival of the crops at market was probably delayed significantly.[90]

New Orleans rapidly regained her position as the leading port for American exports. Between the year beginning September 1, 1865, and the year ending August 31, 1874, exports never fell below $60,000,000; the lowest year was after the 1867 crop failure. In 1870–1871 and 1872–1873 exports exceeded $100,000,000. Cotton made up most of the exports but tobacco and grain from upriver contributed also to the upsurge in commerce. The city's trade was unbalanced, however. Imports never amounted to as much as $20,000,000 during these years.

New Orleans' great advantage, of course, was its location near the mouth of the Mississippi. One great disadvantage was the fact that the mouths of the Mississippi were frequently obstructed, sometimes for more than a month at a time, by silt deposits, known as mud bars, which made the channels too shallow for most oceangoing vessels. The Eads jetties were to solve this problem near the end of the Reconstruction era. More difficult to correct was the high cost of shipping in and out of New Orleans. Labor costs, wharfage fees, taxes for those who owned property, and other costs were so high that steamers based at St. Louis could take cotton from Red River ports and send it from St. Louis to New York by rail about as cheaply as the cotton could be transported to New Orleans and on to New York entirely by water. The costs of doing business in New Orleans were so great that Charles Morgan eventually transferred the headquarters of his Opelousas railroad and Louisiana-to-Texas steamship lines to Morgan City, taking more than seven hundred jobs with him. Of Louisiana railroads only the Jackson line transported significant amounts of goods, mainly cotton, to New Orleans. This counted, however; in

90 New Orleans *Daily Picayune*, May–July, 1871, November–December, 1872.

1871–1872, 28,500 bales were shipped from Memphis to New Orleans by rail, and 12,000 bales which would otherwise have gone to Memphis came directly to New Orleans. One informed observer maintained, however, that the main effect of the railroads was not to increase the amount of cotton coming to New Orleans but rather to speed its arrival. Cotton which once would have arrived in May now was unloaded in December and January. Despite drawbacks such as floods, epidemics, epizootics, mud bars, protective tariffs, and bad municipal government, New Orleans commerce prospered from 1868 through nearly the end of 1873. [91]

New Orleans' banks were adequate to finance the commercial activities of the city. New ones were set up, and in 1872, after a runner was robbed of sixty thousand dollars, a clearinghouse was established. The banks, under the inflexible National Bank system, lacked the capital needed to finance the agriculture which was the primary basis for the city's commerce. Each November the supply of currency became stringent. As the crops moved to market, the producers had to be paid. The planters, moreover, had to have large amounts of currency because they had to pay off their hands at the end of the year. Interest rates would have been high in any case, but this annual shortage of currency probably kept interest higher than it would otherwise have been. The banks prospered, however, as did almost all of about two dozen insurance companies which operated, without regulation of any sort, out of New Orleans. From 1868 to 1873 an investment in the stock of banks or insurance companies in New Orleans was usually a good investment. Finance was still centered in the city, however; there were no banks in Louisiana outside of New Orleans during Reconstruction.[92]

These years of relative prosperity brought a definite increase in the value of real estate. "Mechanics and laboring men are all busy . . . and the demand constantly increasing," stated the Thibodaux *Sentinel* in

91 *Ibid.*, 1868–1873; Edward King, *The Great South: A Record of Journeys in Louisiana, Texas, the Indian Territory, Missouri, Arkansas, Mississippi, Alabama, Georgia, Florida, South Carolina, North Carolina, Kentucky, Tennessee, Virginia, West Virginia, and Maryland* (Hartford, Conn., 1875), 54; Somers, *The Southern States Since the War*, 191, 197, 199–201; Highsmith, "Louisiana During Reconstruction," 347–48; Baughman, *Charles Morgan*, 129, 175–76.

92 Highsmith, "Louisiana During Reconstruction," 211–12; Caldwell, *Banking History of Louisiana*, 100–101.

June, 1870. "Not a room in town but what is occupied, and houses are sought after daily."[93] The same sort of news came from most towns. In 1870 rents in New Orleans were so high that many small dwellings were built in the suburbs. Two years later an observer was annoyed that so much building was going on despite heavy taxation. A Shreveport editor was amazed at the number of dwellings being erected in that city in 1872, and that same year it was reported that twenty new buildings had gone up at Marksville in the preceding two years. From Monroe it was reported that property bought for $20,000 in 1866 had just sold for $54,000. What was true in town was true in the country. Tensas Parish plantations far enough back from the river to be subject to overflow were nonetheless bringing up to $25.00 an acre. Around Shreveport river lands were worth $18.50, and even in less fertile De Soto Parish some lands sold for $15.00 an acre. This was a notable advance over 1866 and, especially, 1867.[94]

Other than agriculture, lumber was the most important industry in Louisiana during Reconstruction. In 1870 there were fewer sawmills in the pine forests of the Florida parishes than had been there in 1860, but elsewhere in the state cypress logging had become important. The Atchafalaya swamps were a major source of cypress logs; it was estimated in 1869 that twenty thousand such logs had been rafted out of the area between Maringouin and the Atchafalaya River between 1867 and 1869. Among the leading lumbermen was John N. Pharr, who went into the business at Opelousas in 1868, then built a sawmill at Pattersonville, on the Teche, in 1874. Francis Bennet Williams began lumbering in 1870. He became a partner of Pharr and was soon one of the wealthiest men in the state. On the Mississippi River, Plaquemine, in Iberville Parish, which had water access to the Atchafalaya swamps, became an important sawmill center. It is difficult today to comprehend how many cypress trees were cut. One raft arrived at New Orleans made up of 350 logs, none less than fifty feet in length, amounting to more than a million feet. Lake Charles, on the Calcasieu River, was shipping large amounts of lumber to Galveston

93 Quoted in Baton Rouge *Weekly Advocate*, July 3, 1870.
94 Shreveport *Times*, May 30, 1872; New Orleans *Daily Picayune*, July 15, December 22, 1869, October 28, 1870, February 1, April 14, May 18, 1871, May 22, June 16, 1872.

by 1871, but its great days as a yellow-pine center were to begin later in the 1870s.[95]

There was some mineral activity in Louisiana from 1868 through 1873. The salt deposits on Avery Island had been worked during the Civil War, and afterwards efforts were made to begin commercial production. This was not accomplished until 1878. In Shreveport a well that was being dug for water struck natural gas in 1870. The gas was used for lighting for a time, but nothing more was done about it. The most intensive effort in mineral exploitation was in Calcasieu Parish. Men digging for oil in 1870 discovered sulphur deposits some four hundred feet below the surface. After some legal maneuvering, a company was established to exploit this resource, and in 1872 a well eighteen inches in diameter was begun, and a five-hundred-horse-power steam engine was installed. Whether the sulphur mines ever got into commercial operation before 1874 is questionable. At any rate, the depression which followed the Panic of 1873 ended the project until after Reconstruction.[96]

There were no large-scale industries in Louisiana during Reconstruction, but there was an abundance of entrepreneurs who sought to satisfy demands for raw materials and manufactured goods. A factory at Independence produced thirty railroad cars for the Jackson railroad in 1866. In Baton Rouge in 1869 the Steam Plow and Wagon Factory sought to hire a dozen blacksmiths and as many wheelwrights, and there was a foundry and a brick kiln at the penitentiary. Ice was always in demand, and by 1872 one of the three ice companies in New Orleans was making its own ice rather than importing it from Philadelphia. New Iberia boasted a foundry, until it was destroyed by fire in 1871, and Donaldsonville's Scard and Creissen manufactured "first

95 New Orleans *Daily Picayune,* July 3, 1869, June 18, October 20, 1871, February 5, 1873; Baton Rouge *Weekly Advocate,* June 19, 1869; Shreveport *Times,* May 18, 1872; Nollie W. Hickman, "The Yellow Pine Industries of St. Tammany, Tangipahoa, and Washington Parishes, 1840–1915," *Louisiana Studies,* V (Summer, 1966), 75–88; Norgress, "The History of the Cypress Lumber Industry in Louisiana," 1,009–10; Donald J. Millet, "The Lumber Industry of 'Imperial' Calcasieu, 1865–1900," *Louisiana History,* VII (Winter, 1966), 51–60.

96 Avery Family Papers, 1868–1873; New Orleans *Daily Picayune,* February 16, 26, March 15, 1870, July 11, August 30, 1872; *Acts of Louisiana, Extra Session, 1865,* 22; Gerald Forbes, "A History of Caddo Oil and Gas Field," *Louisiana Historical Quarterly,* XXIX (January, 1946), 59; Coulter, *The South During Reconstruction,* 273–74.

class" wagons, buggies, and carts. Cotton gins and sugar refineries were, of course, common, and New Orleans boasted five rice mills. Cotton presses were found at Shreveport and New Orleans. The former in 1872 had an icehouse, a factory making cotton gins, another making carriages, three machine shops and foundries, a steam laundry, a cottonseed-oil mill, a soap factory, three breweries, and three brick kilns. New Orleans, though primarily a commercial city, obviously had hundreds of similar establishments. Nearby residents of the Crescent City probably did not appreciate the construction near the slaughterhouse of a plant manufacturing fertilizer from the blood and offal formerly thrown into the Mississippi. At a more primitive level, a Jewish entrepreneur set up a factory for baling moss at Brashear City, and a Mr. Guidry of Raceland employed fifty people to hunt the marshes between bayous Lafourche and Terrebonne, making a daily shipment of waterfowl to New Orleans by way of the New Orleans, Opelousas, and Great Western Railroad. His was only one of many commercial hunting enterprises.[97]

Despite political turmoil, the people of Louisiana were hopeful from 1868 through most of 1873. "Public gambling is increasing rapidly throughout the length and breadth of our fair city," said the *Picayune* in 1869. "The rattle of the ivory checks of faro banks can be heard, with the click of the roulette ball . . . while the voice of the keno dealer, as he sings out numbers with his nasal twang is unceasing at night below Canal Street."[98] In the spring of 1871 the people of Shreveport gave a thousand dollars for French relief after the Franco-Prussian War. That fall I. N. Marks was chairman of a New Orleans committee to raise money to help victims of the great Chicago fire. Good whiskey was available at $2.50 a gallon. In the fall of 1871 the state fair in New Orleans was a gala occasion. Compared to the dark days of 1865–1867, times were indeed good.[99] Louisianians hoped that

97 New Orleans *Daily Picayune*, December 15, 1866, May 19, 1867, July 25, October 18, 28, 1871, May 2, October 2, 1872, February 1, 1873, March 18, August 8, 1874; Baton Rouge *Weekly Advocate*, July 24, 1869, February 26, April 23, 1870; Shreveport *Times*, April 25, September 3, 1872; Bergerie, "Economic and Social History of Iberia Parish," 56.
98 New Orleans *Daily Picayune*, February 12, 1869.
99 Clinton and Port Hudson Railroad Company Account Book, 1867–1870, Department of Archives, Louisiana State University; New Orleans *Daily Picayune*, March 29, October 11, November 18–23, 1871.

their economy would continue to improve. In this hope they were to be sadly disappointed.

8

The depression which began in 1873 was almost as long in duration as the Great Depression of 1929; it lasted until 1879, and agriculture really did not recover until after 1900. Since Louisiana was an agricultural state whose metropolis depended largely upon agriculture for a livelihood, it was very severely affected. The economic hardships which have been so often ascribed to the corruption, extravagance, and high taxes of Reconstruction governments were in large part a result of the depression. This made good propaganda against the Kellogg regime in Louisiana, but redemption brought no end to economic hardships.

New Orleans financial interests were uneasy as the spring of 1873 began. During 1872 the best commercial paper had brought 8 to 10 percent interest, and the best mortgages 9 to 10 percent. Farm mortgages ordinarily were not good mortgages, and when they were available at all, the interest rates were higher. There was no appreciable change in rates in early 1873, but the *Picayune* felt it necessary to assure uneasy readers that "the merchants and bankers of New Orleans . . . are in a thoroughly healthy condition. . . . There is no ground whatever for apprehension, here or abroad."[100] Nonetheless, the failure of the Crescent City Bank did cause uneasiness, and a few days later the same paper admitted that the money supply was "perhaps not as plentiful as the season of the year would justify."[101]

In April McComb's Jackson Railroad issued a statement showing net earnings of $850,000. Close examination revealed, however, that interest on almost $3,000,000 of debt and other costs were not included. Actually the road had lost money. By May currency was becoming increasingly scarce, and late in the month news arrived of panic on the bourse in Vienna. In August workmen were reported to be complaining of want of employment in New Orleans. In early September lenders were more and more reluctant to lend money. Thus

100 New Orleans *Daily Picayune*, March 21, 1873; see also Fels, "American Business Cycles," 348–49; Walter T. K. Nugent, *Money and American Society, 1865–1880* (New York, 1968), 59–59.
101 New Orleans *Daily Picayune*, March 26, 1873.

a depression psychology was developing in New Orleans well ahead of the panic.

On September 14 Louisianians learned of the failure of Kenyon, Cox, & Co. in New York, but it was the failure of Jay Cooke, four days later, which began the panic. On September 20 and 21, most of the front page of the *Picayune* dealt with New York business failures. On September 23, however, this paper announced that the panic was over, and two days later it stated that since "there is no reason to believe that the disturbance will extend beyond a day or two, the loss to New Orleans cannot be very great."[102] The very next day, New Orleans banks suspended currency payments, and on October 10 the *Picayune* admitted that business was unsatisfactory. Banks continued to renew notes which came due, but made no new loans. Planters were urged to hurry their cotton to market so that New Orleans merchants could pay debts they owed in the North. The existence of hardship could not be denied, but the *Picayune* believed that "bad government is the sole cause of the universal wretchedness of the people of Louisiana."[103]

Economic activity gradually slowed from September of 1873 through 1874. High interest rates helped slow the pace of business. Two days before Jay Cooke's failure, mortgages could not be placed at all, the best commercial paper was at 12 percent, and much good paper was discounted 24 percent. It was practically impossible to make any new loans at all for the remainder of the month. By early October the stringency had eased enough that the best commercial paper could be discounted, but at an annual rate of 30 percent! By the middle of the month this had risen to 36 percent. Thereafter there was a gradual decline in discount rates until, in December, some gilt-edged paper could be placed at 18 percent. By March, 1874, the damage done, good commercial paper was discounted at 9 to 15 percent, and mortgages, when obtainable at all, were 10 to 12 percent.[104]

No statistics are available on the number or proportion of unemployed workers in New Orleans or in Louisiana. In Iberville Parish

---

102 *Ibid.*, September 25, 1873; see also New Orleans *Daily Picayune*, March–September, 1873; Dunning, *Reconstruction, Political and Economic*, 235–37; Fels, "American Business Cycles," 336.
103 New Orleans *Daily Picayune*, October 29, 1873.
104 *Ibid.*, September, 1873–March, 1874.

some black workers literally starved. Crop prices did not drop sharply, but they began a slow decline which was to continue steadily for the remainder of the nineteenth century. No new capital came in; in fact, many of the economic Carpetbaggers left the South with what they could preserve of their investments. The state could not afford to repair breaks in the levees, and New Orleans saved an estimated hundred thousand dollars a year by turning off the gas lights when the moon was bright.[105] Perhaps the seriousness of the depression is best illustrated by the wave of suicides which took place in New Orleans from March through September of 1875. Someone killed himself almost every day, and in September the *Picayune* printed an editorial lamenting this "mania for self-destruction."[106] In the city property worth fifty thousand dollars a few years earlier could be bought for ten thousand, and one fourth of the taxes due in January, 1875, could not be collected. Ships came to New Orleans and could find no cargo. Construction came to a halt. Those freedmen who had best followed the teachings of their Yankee liberators, worked hard, and saved their money, suffered along with the rest. When the Freedmen's Savings Bank, which had branches at New Orleans and Shreveport, failed in 1874, some $300,000 in savings belonging to Louisiana blacks vanished into thin air. The end of Republican rule in 1877 brought no relief. A sugar planter who visited New Orleans after losing $8,000 on his crop in 1877 wrote that every face he saw indicated hard times. To add to the distress, in 1874 and 1876 floods as bad as that of 1867 played havoc with crops, persons, and property all along the Mississippi and its southern tributaries.[107]

Louisiana agriculture did not suffer as much immediate damage as New Orleans. Sugar planters, in fact, benefited when the tariff, which had dropped from three to two cents in 1869, was raised a half cent

---

105 *Ibid.*, March 26, July 19, September 23, November 27, 1874, January 19, April 1, 1875; Unger, *The Greenback Era,* 228; Woodward, *Origins of the New South,* 29–30.

106 New Orleans *Daily Picayune,* September 24, 1875.

107 King, *The Great South,* 33; *Legislative Documents, 1874*; Shaffer Papers, VIII, December 19, 27, 1877; New Orleans *Daily Picayune,* September 1, 1874–May, 1876; Shreveport *Times,* February 27, 1876; Woolfolk, *The Cotton Regency,* 112; Engelsmen, "Freedmen's Bureau in Louisiana," 218; Fleming, *The Freedmen's Savings Bank,* 38, 51, 74–75, 98; Richard J. Amundson, "Oakley Plantation: A Post–Civil War Venture in Louisiana," *Louisiana History,* IX (Winter, 1968), 37.

in 1873. Cotton prices went down so gradually that 1874 was only a little worse than 1873, 1877 only a little worse than 1876; but 1877 was much worse than 1873. The most immediate effect left by farmers was that interest rates were exorbitant in 1874 and that credit was hard to get under any circumstances in 1875. Land prices dipped once more. By the late 1870s white farmers were complaining bitterly at processing and transportation costs, and there were occasional outbreaks of violence directed against merchants. Black agriculturists stole vegetables, poultry, swine, and cattle to satisfy very real hunger, and they resorted more and more to the mobility which emancipation had given them to look for better times. Agriculture had entered that long period of depression and discouragement which was to last the remainder of the century. In 1876 Daniel Dennett published a book intended to encourage immigration into Louisiana. Read carefully, however, this book describes a poverty-stricken state inhabited by discouraged people.[108]

Probably no city in the nation fared worse than New Orleans. One historian concluded that five thousand familes were threatened with starvation there in 1874 and 1875 as a result of unemployment. In 1875 the city's administrator of improvements reported that he had received more than three thousand applications for jobs from men of all classes. So much property was seized for unpaid taxes that in 1874 more than six hundred tenants were paying their rent to the sheriff. In the face of this situation, the *Picayune*'s only recommendation to the unemployed was: "Work! Earn an honest day's living, and remember that working does not necessarily mean over-seeing, and that farming is not planting."[109] This must have given great comfort to the workman, unable to find a job, who saw his children go hungry.

At one time during the 1873–1874 harvest, merchants in the Crescent City held 300,000 bales of cotton worth perhaps $25,000,000 but they were unable to borrow money on it. Currency payments by the

108 New Orleans *Daily Picayune*, June 25, 1874, June 17, September 1, 1875, May 23, August 24, 1876, March 27, April 5, 18, May 6, 1877; Shreveport *Times*, April 4, 1876; Nordhoff, *The Cotton States*, 70; Dennett, *Louisiana As It Is, passim*; Sitterson, *Sugar Country*, 305; Clay, "Economic Survival of the Plantation," 131–32, 136–40, 161; Griffin, "Problems of Southern Cotton Planters," 112.
109 New Orleans *Daily Picayune*, April 17, 1876; see also New Orleans *Daily Picayune*, March 10, 31, 1874, April 29, May 3, 1875; Shugg, *Origins of Class Struggle in Louisiana*, 296–97; Lonn, *Reconstruction in Louisiana*, 339–40.

banks remained suspended for months. Goods coming to New Orleans from upriver dropped $30,000,000 in value between 1873 and
1874, and still lower the next year. Exports to foreign ports amounted
to over $104,000,000 in 1872–1873; $93,000,000 in 1873–1874; and only
$71,350,000 in 1874–1875. During the same years imports from abroad
dropped from almost $20,000,000 to $14,350,000 and $12,350,000.
Obviously, the merchants and bankers of New Orleans could do very
little to help farmers, black or white, as their own economy went from
bad to worse.[110]

As bad as economic conditions were in the middle and late 1870s
in Louisiana, there were some signs of hope. The lumber industry
grew by leaps and bounds after the repeal, in 1876, of the Homestead
Act of 1866 and the passage of the Timber Act of 1876 opened huge
new areas of cypress and yellow pine for exploitation. Shreveport
joined Plaquemine and the towns along the Teche as a cypress milling
center, using logs floated down the Red River. More important was
the rapid exploitation of yellow-pine lands. One member of Congress
bought more than a hundred thousand acres of Louisiana timber. The
greatest devastation of yellow-pine forests was to take place in southwestern Louisiana, where the Calcasieu and Sabine rivers offered easy
access to the Gulf of Mexico and the markets of the world. One result
of this, somewhat comical in retrospect but no doubt deadly serious
to those involved, was the "Log War" in Calcasieu Parish in 1877 and
1878. Enterprising men could acquire small tracts in the middle of
the forest, quickly cut the timber from their own land, then continue
cutting from adjacent lands owned by the federal government. Naturally the central government sought to halt this practice, and in May,
1877, "war" was reported between federal marshals and Calcasieu
lumbermen. The marshals found that they had met their match and
called for a posse to aid them. This conflict continued until March,
1878, at which time a boom was stretched across the Calcasieu River
to prevent any more logs' being floated downstream. Early that spring
a settlement was reached, and the mills began running again. It should
be noted that the Louisiana lumber industry was still in its infancy
as Reconstruction ended. Production in 1880 amounted to less than

110 New Orleans *Daily Picayune,* September 1, 1874, September 1, 1875.

two million dollars. By 1900 it exceeded seventeen million dollars.[111]

During the same years work very important to the future of the port of New Orleans was being carried on. As oceangoing ships grew larger and of increased draft, constant dredging proved inadequate to keep a channel to New Orleans open through the mud bars at the mouths of the Mississippi. At one time in March of 1874 forty-seven ships, some seeking to go upstream to New Orleans, others seeking to reach the Gulf, were held up at the bar. In that same year Captain James B. Eads was commissioned to carry out his proposal to deepen the channel by means of jetties which would narrow the stream of flowing water, thus increasing its velocity and scouring a deeper channel through the bars. By 1875 it was obvious that the jetties Eads was constructing at South Pass were accomplishing their object. Each week the channel was a little deeper, twenty-two feet in late 1877, and thirty feet when the work was completed in 1879. As might be expected in Louisiana, some pilots insisted on running ships aground at Southwest Pass in 1877 despite a good channel through and past the jetties at South Pass.[112]

111 *Ibid.*, July 4, 1876, May 17, 22, 27, July 24, October 23, 1877, March 8, 20, 1878; Shreveport Times, July 4, 1876; Norgress, "The History of the Cypress Lumber Industry in Louisiana," 996; Woodward, *Origins of the New South*, 116–18; Millet, "The Lumber Industry of 'Imperial' Calcasieu," *passim.*
112 New Orleans *Daily Picayune*, March 31, 1874, September 1, 1875, 1876–1877; Shannon, *The Farmer's Last Frontier*, 104; Caldwell, *Banking History of Louisiana*, 99; Walter M. Lowrey, "The Engineers and the Mississippi," *Louisiana History*, V (Summer, 1964), 233–55.

IX   *Labor, the General Merchant, and the Crop Lien*

SUGAR PLANTING was a semiindustrial operation. The capital investment required was much more than was needed for planting cotton. The fields had to be carefully ditched and drained, an item of considerable expense. The work force for a sugar plantation had to have a larger proportion of young and vigorous men, men who could demand and get higher wages than the blacks in the cotton fields. Another major factor in cane production was seed; between one fourth and one third of a year's crop had to be saved as seed for the next year.

More than this, a sugar plantation required far more equipment than a cotton plantation. A sugarhouse, where the juice was pressed from the cane, boiled down, then crystallized into brown sugar, was far more expensive than a cotton gin. In addition, wood had to be gathered to provide fuel for the sugarhouse. Also necessary were many carts to haul wood in the summer and cane to the sugarhouse during the harvest. Oxen, horses, and mules had to draw these carts and the plows used in cultivation. Because the soil in the sugar-producing regions was normally heavier than elsewhere, bigger and stronger work animals were needed. Finally, sugar was a crop which involved great risks. It was not so subject to insect damage as was cotton, but it was just as susceptible to flood. But the greatest danger came as harvest time approached. The longer the crop stood in the fields, the more sugar it would produce. But the longer the planter waited before cutting it, the more danger there was of a hard freeze which might ruin the crop completely.

After the Civil War it was exceedingly difficult to make money planting sugar. John Burnside remained the largest sugar planter, in terms of acres, for a decade after Appomattox. In 1869, which was a relatively good year for sugar, three of Burnside's seven plantations showed profits totaling $30,732.80, but the other four lost $161,964.89, for a net loss of $131,232.09. Two northerners who bought Oakley Plantation in Iberville Parish found that expenses exceeded income by about $12,000 per year. In January, 1873, it was estimated that a third of the sugar plantations in the state were no longer planting cane. The 4,291 sugarhouses in Louisiana in 1861 had been reduced to 817 by 1869. It is obvious that sugar planting was unprofitable during Reconstruction, but one of the leading students of the sugar industry concluded that the inability of the planters to manage their enterprises efficiently was the single most important reason for failure.[1]

So difficult was it to resume sugar planting, and so unprofitable were operations which were undertaken, that many planters and, especially, smaller farmers in the sugar region turned to cotton or rice. South central Louisiana was not well adapted to cotton culture, especially in the years before insecticides, but cotton prices were high, and not nearly so much capital was required to put in a cotton crop. Plaquemines Parish had produced rice in some quantity before and during the Civil War, but afterward the cultivation of this grain was taken up temporarily in other parishes, especially Lafourche. Rice culture had not yet reached the prairies west of present-day Lafayette —that would come about after Reconstruction was over.[2]

Some people, including newspaper editors, hoped that the end of

1 John Burnside's Income Report, 1869, in Gaudet Papers; Amundson, "Oakley Plantation," 38; New Orleans *Daily Tribune*, September 24, 1864; Somers, *The Southern States Since the War*, 198–99; New Orleans *Daily Picayune*, February 1, 1866, May 6, 1870, January 3, 1873; White, *Freedmen's Bureau in Louisiana*, 113; Ulrich B. Phillips, "Plantations with Slave Labor and Free," *Agricultural History*, XII (January, 1938), 92; Highsmith, "Louisiana During Reconstruction," 397; Sitterson, *Sugar Country*, 251, 259, 304–306, 313–14.
2 Bergerie, "Economic and Social History of Iberia Parish," 30–33; New Orleans *Daily Picayune*, November 28, 1872; *Nation*, II (June 4, 1866), 706.

slavery would break up sugar plantations into smaller productive units worked by white men. A few sincere Radicals wanted them broken up into freeholds for former slaves. These hopes were not realized. Some of the already-present small farms in the sugar region began planting cane, but the plantations were not divided. The false impression given by the census of 1870, which listed sharecropper plots as separate farms, is now well known to historians. What really happened, as Roger Shugg has shown, was that the number of plantations in Louisiana increased almost 300 percent between 1860 and 1890. In the same years, although the number of landholdings increased 89 percent, the number of small farms decreased by 14 percent. A reporter traveling from Thibodaux to New Orleans in 1869 noted that "The desire to hold on to large bodies of land is so great that the owners will never consent to part with any portion until under the sheriff's hammer."[3] Legislation which required foreclosed plantations to be broken up into smaller farms when sold had no lasting effect.

The fact that sugar plantations were not subdivided did not mean that they remained in the same hands as before the war. The pervading scarcity of capital forced more and more planters into voluntary or involuntary sales. Northerners began acquiring sugar plantations at war's end. They were joined by banks, corporations, country merchants, and enterprising individuals. John N. Pharr, a steamboat operator in 1875, owned eight sugar plantations by 1903. Leon Godchaux, who had come to Louisiana as a peddler in the 1830s, purchased his first plantation in 1862 and by 1896 owned more than thirty thousand acres. One student estimated that one half of all the sugar plantations in the state had changed hands by 1869. This is probably a conservative estimate, because a check of planters who owned fifty or more slaves in 1860 against tax assessment rolls after the war shows that of thirty such planters in Ascension Parish in 1860, only thirteen still owned large tracts of land in 1871. Of ninety who had owned fifty or more slaves in St. Mary Parish in 1860, only twenty-five still held

3 Baton Rouge *Weekly Advocate*, June 12, 1869; see also New Orleans *Daily Picayune*, May 6, December 30, 1870, October 11, 1875, March 27, 1877; Shugg, "Survival of the Plantation System," 313–15; Highsmith, "Louisiana During Reconstruction," 396–97; Bergerie, "Economic and Social History of Iberia Parish," 38; Sitterson, *Sugar Country*, 240.

on in 1877. Thus the process of eliminating the prewar sugar-planting families was continuing throughout Reconstruction.[4]

One partial solution to the problem of lack of capital was some form of sharecropping, so that the worker would be obliged to wait for the harvest for part of his reward for a year's labor. On one place, blacks were cutting wood on shares in 1863, and that year on another sugar plantation the planter agreed to give his workers one twentieth of the crop—presumably in addition to food, clothing, and shelter. Some form of division of the crop became more common in 1864. In the sugar region the trend toward sharecropping was so pronounced by the end of 1865 that the Freedmen's Bureau encouraged this type of contract. After the sugar crop failed in 1866, the bureau advocated a return to monthly wages, but many of the freedmen preferred to stay with sharecropping.[5]

The early enthusiasm for sharecropping on the sugar plantations did not endure. The industrial nature of sugar production made centralized direction more essential than was the case on cotton lands. Reliable and thrifty croppers could benefit both themselves and the landowner, but most were just as careless with ditching, fences, stock, and tools as were wage workers, and they could not be supervised as closely. Another important obstacle to sharecropping in the cane fields was the difficulty of accurately separating the sugar made from one tenant's cane from that made from another's. Some sharecropping continued, especially when white tenants could be had, but by 1870 most plantations were firmly fixed on a system of contract labor for wages. The employees lived in what had been the slave quarter, and gang labor was the rule. Adventurous planters might experiment with

4 New Orleans *Daily Picayune,* May 6, 1870; Shugg, "Survival of the Plantation System," 319–20; Sitterson, *Sugar Country,* 312; Highsmith, "Louisiana During Reconstruction," 396–98; Joseph Karl Menn, *The Large Slaveholders of Louisiana, 1860* (New Orleans, 1964), 122–24, 327–36, 380–89; Ascension Parish Tax Assessment Rolls, 1870, Rapides Parish Tax Assessment Rolls, 1877, all on microfilm in Office of Comptroller, State of Louisiana.

5 Bayside Plantation Papers, II, November 17, 1863; McCollam Papers, VII, March, 1863; *Nation,* I (August 31, 1865), 259; Baton Rouge *Gazette and Comet,* November 30, 1865, cited in Constantin, "Louisiana Black Code," 44–45; Saloutos, "Southern Agriculture, 1865–1877," *passim*; Bentley, *The Freedmen's Bureau,* 85; May, "The Freedmen's Bureau at the Local Level," 13; White, *Freedmen's Bureau in Louisiana,* 121; Bergerie, "Economic and Social History of Iberia Parish," 36–37; Caskey, *Secession and Restoration,* 142–43.

various sharecropping arrangements, especially in Terrebonne Parish, but this type of tenure was not to become the rule in the sugar fields as it did in the cotton regions.[6]

If the vast majority of blacks in the sugar regions was fated to be contract laborers, they were also fated to be relatively well paid because scarcity of labor assured good wages. As the acreage under cultivation increased, additional imported laborers, estimated at about twenty thousand in five years, were absorbed, but pay did not go down. The Panic of 1873 did force wages down somewhat, but less than might have been expected. Planters held meetings at various times to seek agreement on wage ceilings; such agreements did not last. Some planters in dire need of labor would always offer more than the ceiling in order to save their crops.

It was reported in 1866 that freedmen in the sugar fields were receiving ten to twelve dollars per month on the average, some as much as eighteen dollars, plus shelter, food, fuel, medical care, and clothing. Those who provided their own clothing and food received twenty-five dollars. Wages seem to have reached their height in 1869. The average field hand in St. John the Baptist Parish earned ten to twelve dollars a month, food, clothing, shelter, and a plot of land on which to grow corn, vegetables, swine, and poultry of his own. In St. Mary Parish the same year the going wage for field hands was reported to be twenty dollars a month plus cabin, rations, and fuel. In 1870 a number of whites labored in the cane fields of West Baton Rouge Parish, and on the Teche, during grinding, white cotton-farmers were said to have left their own crops in the fields in order to earn two or three dollars a day making sugar. Even after the panic occurred, wages of twenty-five dollars a month plus cabin and rations were not unheard of. Also, workers usually received a garden plot and time to work it. The most thorough student of sugar culture concludes that the freedman, working for wages, was as productive as the slave had been.[7]

6 New Orleans *Daily Picayune,* September 4, 1868, January 27, July 23, 1869, January 21, December 11, 1870, April 12, 1871, September 11, 1872, October 26, 1873, March 22, April 14, 1874, July 12, 1876, March 28, 1878; Nordhoff, *The Cotton States,* 71; Sitterson, *Sugar Country,* 233–34, 239–41; Sitterson, "The McCollams," 361–62; Bergerie, "Economic and Social History of Iberia Parish," 37–38; Highsmith, "Louisiana During Reconstruction," 438.
7 Sitterson, *Sugar Country,* 237, 242–43; Shaffer Papers, VII, 1876; Bayside Planta-

In general the black laborers of the sugar region seem to have lived better lives in a material sense than sharecroppers on cotton plantations. Ordinarily, their wages were given in addition to housing and rations, and sometimes in addition to clothing. Thus they were not forced into debt as, too often, the freedmen on cotton plantations were. Probably they did not like living in the old slave quarter or having their rations passed out to them in the same fashion as under slavery, but the rations were at least as adequate as in the cotton fields, and the housing on sugar plantations was usually better. Furthermore, there was a plantation commissary, or a merchant nearby, where whiskey and modest luxuries could be bought at outrageous prices; there the worker could go into debt and, sometimes, be cheated. In general, life for the sugar plantation workman was better than life had been under slavery. He had access to a church, and his children usually had access to a school. He could, with thrift and foresight, save money. Many did not go to church; most did not send their children to school; and few saved money; but the opportunities existed. Complaints that planters and merchants cheated their workmen were heard; no doubt some of these complaints were valid, but most of them were not.[8]

Probably the most important development in sugar during the Reconstruction period was the beginning of the separation of sugar cultivation and harvesting from the refining process. Before the Civil War a few planters may have processed the cane of neighbors who cultivated so few acres that they could not afford to build sugarhouses, but in general each production unit had its own refinery. This was inefficient, because as the machinery for refining was improved, one refinery would handle the cane from a number of plantations. In

---

tion Papers, II, May 6, 1875; Nordhoff, *The Cotton States*, 70; *Nation*, II (March 8, 1866), 305, (March 15, 1866), 334; Phillips, "Plantations with Slave Labor and Free," 92; Francis William Loring and C. F. Atkinson, *Cotton Culture and the South Considered with Reference to Immigration* (Boston, 1869), 5–6; New Orleans *Daily Picayune*, February 26, September 4, 1868, January 14, March 31, July 23, November 19, 1869, December 10, 1870, January 3, July 29, 1873, December 28, 1874; Shugg, *Origins of Class Struggle in Louisiana*, 250–51; Sitterson, "The Transition from Slave to Free Economy," 221.

8 Shaffer Papers, VII, 1876; *Nation*, II (March 22, 1866), 365–66; New Orleans *Daily Picayune*, January, 1875; Loring and Atkinson, *Cotton Culture and the South*, 26; Sitterson, *Sugar Country*, 323.

1868, D. C. Avery agreed with one John Hayes to grind Hayes's cane "or as much as he can," for which Avery was to receive half the sugar produced, Hayes to get one barrel of molasses for each hogshead of sugar. Each man was to supply his own hogsheads and molasses barrels.[9] The immigration of small-scale white farmers to the sugar region gave impetus to the consolidation movement because the immigrants were forced, if they grew sugar, to depend upon some planter's sugarhouse for grinding. John Dymond of Plaquemines Parish began buying cane by the ton in 1871, and he was so successful that he sent boats up and down the river in 1872 to buy cane for his mill. The consolidation of sugar refining had only begun when Reconstruction ended, but it most definitely had begun.[10]

TABLE TWO

Sugar Production During Civil War and Reconstruction[11]

Year	Hogsheads	Price	Value
1860	228,753	$ 63.25	$14,468,647
1861	459,610	84.62	25,097,271
1862	87,231	83.84	7,749,602
1863	76,801	179.70	13,801,139
1864	10,387	208.50	1,994,300
1865	18,079	157.50	2,847,442
1866	39,000	137.50	5,360,500
1867	37,647	154.00	5,797,638
1868	84,256	137.80	11,610,476
1869	87,090	140.00	12,442,251
1870	144,881	102.26	14,260,326
1871	128,461	97.16	12,487,020
1872	108,529	91.68	10,027,717
1873	89,496	86.50	8,122,575
1874	116,867	95.82	11,269,767
1875	114,146	95.90	11,265,000
1876	169,331	83.00	11,578,000
1877	194,964	95.50	15,646,000
1878	149,469	72.00	9,007,000

9 Contract, December 19, 1868, in Avery Family Papers.

10 New Orleans *Daily Picayune*, August 31, 1872, April 15, 1876; King, *The Great South*, 80; Highsmith, "Louisiana During Reconstruction," 204; Sitterson, *Sugar Country*, 251, 257–59.

11 New Orleans *Daily Picayune*, September 1, 1874–September 1, 1878. The *Picayune* published a commercial summary each September 1 during Reconstruction.

As may be seen from Table Two, the Civil War brought a drastic decline in sugar production. In only two years of Louisiana's antebellum history did production come within 100,000 hogsheads of the 1861 crop, and only the crop of 1858 came close to its value. The average crop of the 1850s was about 250,000 hogsheads, and the average price about sixty dollars. Production during Reconstruction never reached the average of the 1850s, but the total value of the crop of 1870 was greater than the total value of the very poor crops of 1850, 1851, and 1856. Furthermore, as the table shows, production was generally improving during Reconstruction. Although it was not until 1893 that the crop equaled that of 1861, from 1881 on the crop exceeded the average for the 1850s except in very bad years.[12]

Improved technology contributed to the gradual increase in sugar production. Louisiana sugar planters were aware of the potentialities of labor-saving machinery, but the machines which would help them overcome the postwar labor shortage did not have a great effect until after Reconstruction was over. The steam plow, which made use of two movable steam engines to draw a plow back and forth across a field, was the great hope of the immediate postwar years, and at least three were put into operation on Louisiana plantations. The most famous example was on Magnolia Plantation in Plaquemines Parish, partly owned by Henry Clay Warmoth. In the long run the steam plow was not successful. The initial cost was large, firm beds had to be established on which the two heavy engines could move the length of the field they were plowing, and shutdowns for repairs were frequent and expensive.[13]

Other failures were the use of the diffusion process for separating the sugar-bearing juices from the cane by dissolving them in water, and the use of coal as fuel for sugar mills. The real advances came in relatively simple horse-drawn tools such as cultivators and stubble

---

12 New Orleans *Daily Picayune*, May 1, 1870, September 1, 1874, September 1, 1878; Highsmith, "Louisiana During Reconstruction," 203–204, 397–98; Somers, *The Southern States Since the War*, 230–31.

13 New Orleans *Daily Picayune*, February 16, 1864, May 6, October 9, 16, 1870, January 14, 1872; Sitterson, *Sugar Country*, 274–75; King, *The Great South*, 81; Horace Greeley, *Mr. Greeley's Letters from Texas and the Lower Mississippi: To Which Are Added His Address to the Farmers of Texas and His Speech on His Return to New York, June 19, 1871* (New York, 1871), letter of May 17, 1871 (pages not numbered).

diggers; such implements designed especially for use in cane cultivation were on the market by 1875. They were to have their greatest effect after Reconstruction, but the beginning of mechanizing what was to become one of the most highly mechanized crops in the nation was made before 1877.[14]

2

If wage labor was to prevail in the sugar industry, sharecropping was to triumph decisively in the cotton fields. Cotton lands were prepared for planting as early in the spring as rainfall and temperature permitted, and the seed was planted when the danger of cold weather was past. As cotton plants grew, they required much cultivation with plow and hoe, but ordinarily by July the crop could be "laid by." Then there was relatively little work to be done until late August or early September, when it was time to pick, that is to harvest the white cotton from the newly opened bolls. After being picked, the cotton was "ginned" to separate seed from lint, and then the lint was pressed into five-hundred-pound bales. After the harvest was complete, six weeks to two months might elapse before there was more work in the fields. This very routine of cotton cultivation, involving two fairly long periods when little besides "make work" tasks could be assigned to laborers, militated against the wage system. This was not, however, the only reason the wage system did not prosper.

Except in a few sanctuaries such as Bossier and Caddo parishes, the effect of contending armies on cotton plantations and their labor supply had been at least as harmful as in the sugar regions. But cotton continued to be king, the major source of income for Louisiana and all the South. High prices resulting from the scarcity during the war years gave hope that the old monarch would restore prosperity, but this was a short-lived hope. High prices did not last long, and the cotton grower was just as dependent as the cultivator of sugar upon northern capital with which to produce his crop. Thus King Cotton was a figurehead, masking the real rule of northern financial interests. But the scarcity of capital was not all. Labor was as scarce in the cot-

---

14 New Orleans *Daily Picayune*, December 26, 1869, September 1, 1874, September 1, 1875; Sitterson, *Sugar Country*, 257, 275–76, 279–80.

ton fields of Concordia Parish as it was along the Teche, and cotton-planters also had to learn from experience how to manage free labor. The costs of getting cotton to market were high, amounting to from 4 to 10 percent of the value of the crop. Just after the war the cotton planter feared, with considerable justification, that his crop might be seized by a Treasury agent as the property of the Confederate government. Even if not seized, it was subject to a punitive federal tax of three cents a pound. In general cotton planters and farmers were far from content with their lot. The Grange was popular in Louisiana in the 1870s, but the race question prevented its becoming effective politically. Such movements as the Knights of the White Camellia and the White League can be understood partly as expressions of the cotton farmer's discontent with his economic lot.[15]

The wage system was also tried in cotton cultivation. A few cotton planters, apparently very few, were able to raise enough capital to pay monthly wages. Even in these cases, however, the normal practice seems to have been to pay the workers only half the month's wages at the end of the month, and if the plantation had a store, purchases during the month were deducted from this half. The remainder of wages due, if any, was paid at the end of the year. Thus the workers were constrained to remain on the place and not go elsewhere when harvest time might have driven wages upward. Some planters worked as much of their land as they could with the laborers they could afford to hire; the remainder they left idle rather than subdivide it even into sharecropper plots. But most planters did not have the money to hire laborers; to survive economically they had to work their fields. At the same time, as most contemporary accounts agree, most freedmen preferred sharecropping to wages. Some planters sought to compromise by working their most fertile lands with wage labor and letting

15 New Orleans *Daily Picayune*, December 5, 1872, July 13, 1873, January 8, 1874; Tax Notices, January, 1867, in Vidal Papers; Somers, *The Southern States Since the War*, 206; Dennett, *Louisiana As It Is*, 50; Garner (ed.), *Studies in Southern History and Politics*, 294–95; Clay, "Economic Survival of the Plantation," 89; Woodman, *King Cotton and His Retainers*, 359; Highsmith, "Louisiana During Reconstruction," 206–10; Coulter, *The South During Reconstruction*, 217–18; Shannon, *The Farmer's Last Frontier*, 80; Saloutos, "Southern Agriculture, 1865–1877," 71; Theodore Saloutos, "The Grange in the South, 1870–1877," *Journal of Southern History*, XIX (November, 1953), 473–87.

out poorer tracts to sharecroppers. But in the long run sharecropping was to prove the rule, wages the exception, on cotton farms and plantations.[16]

If the planter was constrained to sharecropping by scarcity of labor, scarcity of capital, and the rhythm of cotton culture, he quick-ly discovered that the system had some advantages. He could no longer rely upon the lash, and a share in the crop was a form of in-centive. Furthermore, cotton farming was always a gamble, and in the alluvial regions after the war, protected hardly at all from over-flow, the risks were greatly increased. From the planter's point of view sharecropping had the virtue of forcing the freedmen to share the risk.[17]

Sharecropping was being practiced across from Vicksburg to some extent in 1863, and in the Felicianas and East Baton Rouge and Con-cordia parishes in 1865. Some, perhaps all, of this early sharing was between the landowner on the one hand and the whole body of freed-men working the place on the other. Various forms of sharing were attempted in 1866, a year in which the crop was largely a failure. It has been asked whether sharecropping was voluntarily accepted by the freedmen or whether it was a device of the planters to exploit black labor.[18] Obviously the planters desired to exploit the workers to the extent that they hoped to profit from their labor, but it is equally obvious, insofar as Louisiana is concerned, that the black worker welcomed the new arrangement. He favored it more strongly after the crop failures of 1866 and 1867 than before. This may have been because he knew that the planter probably could not pay wages, but there is no evidence that Louisiana blacks were coerced or intimidated into sharecropping to any greater extent than were planters. The

16 New Orleans *Daily Picayune,* January 11, 1867, February 10, 20, June 5, 1869; Knox, "Beckoning Fields of Cotton," 550; *Senate Executive Documents,* 39th Cong., 1st Sess., No. 2, pp. 28–29; Nordhoff, *The Cotton States,* 73; Woodman, *King Cotton and His Retainers,* 308–309; Clay, "Economic Survival of the Planta-tion," 97, 99; Bentley, *The Freedmen's Bureau,* 150; Shannon, *The Farmer's Last Frontier,* 87; Zeichner, "The Transition from Slave to Free Agricultural Labor," 29–30.

17 Phillips, "Plantations with Slave Labor and Free," 90; Ellis, "The Transition from Slave Labor to Free," 30; Zeichner, "The Transition from Slave to Free Agricultural Labor," 31; Lerner, "Southern Output and Agricultural Income," 121.

18 August Meier, "Comment on John Hope Franklin's Paper," in Harold M. Hyman (ed.), *New Frontiers of the American Reconstruction* (Urbana, Ill., 1966), 80–81.

Freedmen's Bureau offered no opposition. Many planters, in fact, deplored the system even as they practiced it. There was much experiment and variation in sharecropping practices before a more or less common system came into use, but under the conditions that existed, some sort of sharecropping was inevitable. Vernon Wharton has suggested that whenever "a large class of landless laborers, a shortage of money or ready credit, and general dependency upon a cash crop which requires a long growing season" exist together, sharecropping "seems to develop naturally."[19]

In December, 1869, the *Picayune* could report that all farm hands in Richland Parish were working on shares, and that some had "got rich and quit," leaving cotton in the fields.[20] Middling cotton brought about thirty cents a pound much of the time in New Orleans during 1869, making it a prosperous year. The basic plan of sharecropping had now become fixed. The planter provided a cabin, as much land as the sharecropper and his family could work, teams, tools, seed, and supervision of varying degrees of intensity. The sharecropper provided the labor of himself and his family and assumed the responsibility for feeding and clothing himself and his family. Obviously the cropper had to have credit to obtain this food and clothing. This was provided by the planter or by a nearby merchant, but the credit system will be discussed later.[21] Any extra expenses, such as fertilizer, or the cost of extra hands for hoeing or picking the crop, normally were divided equally between landlord and sharecropper.

When the crop was harvested, the proceeds were divided equally. There are some accounts of sharecroppers on very fertile land who received only a third or a fourth of the crop, but these reports are questionable. It seems probable that in such cases the landlord was providing rations for the tenant's family as part of the sharecrop agreement. In other instances, observers possibly confused share rent,

19 Wharton, *The Negro in Mississippi*, 68–69; see also *Nation*, II (March 22, 1865), 368; *House Reports*, 39th Cong., 1st Sess., No. 30, Part IV, p. 141; New Orleans *Daily Picayune*, May 25, June 12, October 19, 1867; Baton Rouge *Weekly Advocate*, February 24, 1866; Skinner, *After the Storm*, 51–52; DeForest, *A Union Officer in the Reconstruction*, 97; Clay, "Economic Survival of the Plantation," 46, 68–69, 75, 97–98; Engelsmen, "Freedmen's Bureau in Louisiana," 210; Degler, *Out of Our Past*, 198; Highsmith, "Louisiana During Reconstruction," 112.
20 New Orleans *Daily Picayune*, December 5, 1869.
21 See below, pp. 400–406.

described below, with sharecropping. Certainly in all but a fraction of agreements, the division was on a half-and-half basis. From his half the freedman had to pay at high prices increased by high interest for the food and clothing consumed by his family during the year. The planter had to repay the money he had borrowed to finance the crop. Both landlord and sharecropper might end the year in debt, and neither was likely to become rich. It should be emphasized that not all sharecroppers were black. As early as 1866 there were some white sharecroppers in the Red River Valley, and eventually, though not during Reconstruction, white croppers would outnumber black ones in the South as a whole.[22]

Some cotton lands in Louisiana were rented for cash, or for a promissory note, but these cash renters then normally became, in effect, landlords who let out the land to sharecroppers. The more prosperous landless farmers, white and black, usually made a share-rent agreement. This was a definite step above sharecropping, because the tenant provided his own work stock, animal feed, fertilizer, and tools as well as the labor of himself and his family. He probably bought on credit at the same general store or plantation commissary as the sharecropper, at the same high prices and high interest, but he had much greater control over what he planted and how he worked his crop. The agreement between landlord and tenant might be anything they could agree upon, but the general practice was for the share renter to pay in rent one fourth of the cotton and one third of the corn he produced. This system was used both for parts of plantations and for entire small farms. Evidence in newspapers and travel accounts, such as it is, indicates that from 1869 to 1872 a fairly large number of sharecroppers were managing in one way or another to become share renters. The depression which began in 1873 reversed this trend; sharecroppers who had advanced to share-renter status dropped back to become sharecroppers, and some white renters who had

22 Loring and Atkinson, *Cotton Culture and the South*, 25–26; *De Bow's Review*, After the War Series, VI (February, 1869), 269–70; New Orleans *Daily Picayune*, August 2, 7, 1868; *Nation*, II (March 1, 1866), 269–70; Natchitoches *Times*, January 16, 1869, quoted in New Orleans *Daily Picayune*, January 23, 1869; Campbell, *White and Black*, 149; Saloutos, "Southern Agriculture, 1865–1877," 67, 70–72; Patrick, *Reconstruction of the Nation*, 233; Shannon, *The Farmer's Last Frontier*, 88–89; Wharton, *The Negro in Mississippi*, 69–70.

never before been sharecroppers descended to that economic level.[23]

Roger Shugg has shown that the myth that cotton plantations were broken up into small farms after the Civil War resulted from a misinterpretation of the inaccurate census of 1870. Shugg's findings have been reinforced by Floyd M. Clay, who clearly demonstrates the survival and in many cases the growth of plantations in the Felicianas. The superior economic resources, superior managerial skills, and perhaps the loyalty of some freedmen who had been their slaves before emancipation all gave an advantage to prewar planters. The fact that plantations had cotton gins and small farmers did not, gave the planters another advantage. Some "public" gins, owned by general merchants, were coming into operation during Reconstruction, but they did not advance the small farmer's ability to compete.

The tax assessment rolls, as demonstrated by Shugg, show that landholding was becoming more and more concentrated. Also, the prewar owners of cotton plantations were able to maintain possession to a greater degree than sugar plantation owners. In East Feliciana Parish, where fifty families owned fifty or more slaves in 1860, the same families owned thirty-seven large tracts of land in 1871, and seventeen plantations remained in the same name in 1880. Claiborne Parish, not a fertile area, had eight families with more than fifty slaves in 1860, but only one of these families, unless marriage had changed a female heir's name, still held on in 1876. In fertile Tensas Parish, 118 families owned fifty or more slaves in 1860, and sixty of these still held their lands in 1870. Overall, the actual percentage of plantations retained by prewar families is probably higher than the above would indicate, because there is no way of determining from tax assessment rolls whether a new name is that of a son-in-law or grandson of the 1860 owner.[24]

---

23 New Orleans *Daily Picayune*, April 14, 18, 1871, January 19, 1872; Loring and Atkinson, *Cotton Culture and the South*, 26; Clay, "Economic Survival of the Plantation," 76, 102–103.

24 Pointe Coupee *Pelican*, quoted in New Orleans *Daily Picayune*, September 4, 1878; Claiborne Parish Tax Assessment Rolls, 1871, 1876, East Feliciana Parish Tax Assessment Rolls, 1871–1880, Tensas Parish Tax Assessment Rolls, 1871, 1880, all on microfilm in Office of Comptroller, State of Louisiana; Shugg, "Survival of the Plantation System," 311–25; Clay, "Economic Survival of the Plantation," 106–107, 111–12, 129–30, 167–68; Menn, *Large Slaveholders of Louisiana*, 194–95, 218–23, 399–412; Griffin, "Problems of Southern Cotton Planters," 112.

TABLE THREE

Cotton Production in Louisiana, 1866–1880[25]

Year	Acres Planted	Bales	Pounds per Acre
1866	1,020,000	131,000	57
1867	844,000	167,000	88
1868	652,000	248,000	169
1869	767,000	351,000	183
1870	932,000	567,000	269
1871	868,000	337,000	172
1872	980,000	503,000	228
1873	1,039,000	454,000	194
1874	975,000	536,000	242
1875	1,000,000	689,000	306
1876	899,000	564,000	276
1877	991,000	586,000	266
1878	961,000	462,000	215
1879	865,000	509,000	267
1880	920,000	274,000	187

As is evident from Table Three, the number of acres of cotton under cultivation followed no definite trend, but if an average is struck for three five-year periods, something more emerges. Despite the fact that more than a million acres were planted in cotton in 1866, the

TABLE FOUR

Cotton Production in Louisiana by Five-Year Periods, 1866–1880[26]

Years	Average Acres in Cultivation	Average Number of Bales Produced	Average Yield per Acre
1866–70	843,000	291,600	153.2
1871–75	972,000	503,800	226.4
1876–80	927,000	499,000	242.5

average of 1866–1870 is 129,000 acres less than the average for 1871–1875, and 84,000 less than the average for 1876–1880. The production figures for 1866–1870 are much lower than for the next two five-year periods, but it must be remembered that floods and cotton worms made disasters of the crops of 1866 and 1867. If production per acre was an indication of efficiency, then the trend was toward greater

25 "Statistics on Cotton and Related Data," *Statistical Bulletin* 99 (Washington, D.C., 1951), 51, 53, 55.
26 *Ibid.*

efficiency, because the average number of pounds per acre was increasing. However, it is doubtful that this measure of efficiency is particularly accurate. After the Civil War, as before, labor was expensive and land was cheap. Thus the desire of the planter was to obtain the greatest yield possible per laborer, and this could best be done by extensive rather than intensive farming. When this is borne in mind, it casts considerable doubt upon the many learned statements regarding the inefficiency of free labor. Furthermore, this may explain why sugar, which had been cultivated intensively before the war, was so much slower than cotton in recovering from the dislocation of the conflict.

In 1875, the alluvial lands north of the mouth of the Red River, 16 percent of the state's areas, produced 43.5 percent of the entire cotton crop. Alluvial lands south of that point had 12 percent of the total. Finally, the narrow alluvial valley of the Red River itself produced almost 8 percent of the crop. Thus the alluvial lands contributed over 63 percent of the total production. They averaged over 350 pounds to the acre. The loess soils of East Baton Rouge Parish and the Felicianas produced 5.6 percent of the state's cotton on less than 3 percent of the state's area. The oak uplands of northwestern Louisiana produced about 21 percent of the state's total. The prairies and pine lands contributed the small remainder. Production per acre was highest in the alluvial parishes along the Mississippi north of Red River. East Carroll averaged 425 pounds, Concordia 395 pounds. The average in the Felicianas, where the lands had been long under cultivation, was only slightly more than two hundred pounds to the acre. The oak uplands averaged almost exactly two hundred pounds, the Attakapas region less than two hundred pounds.[27]

The chart showing acres planted in cotton, yield in bales, and price per pound permits few significant conclusions. There was no real correlation, after 1865, between the price of cotton and the acreage planted. Indeed, there was little the farmers could do to adjust planting to the price they would receive, because when the spring crop was planted they could not know what the price would be in the fall. There

27 E. W. Hilgard, "Report on the Cotton Production of the State of Louisiana, with a General Discussion of the General Agricultural Features of the State," *U.S. Census, 1880, Report on Cotton Production* (Washington, D.C., 1883), 111–39.

is, after 1870, some rough correlation between decline in prices and decline in total production, but the number of acres planted did not decline, so the reduction in production was not intentional. Obviously, farmers, planters, and sharecroppers, as the price of cotton went down, attempted to cover their fixed costs by planting as many acres as they could, leading to lower production per acre. It also is evident that there was no significant decline in the efficiency of Louisiana labor or, if there was a decline, it cannot be proven, because the prewar practice of extensive cultivation persisted. The low production of 1866 and 1867, often used to demonstrate the inefficiency of free labor, was caused by floods and army worms.[28]

3

Most white people in Louisiana outside of New Orleans were neither planters nor sharecroppers, but rather yeoman farmers working their own land. In south Louisiana they might be Acadians or other gallicized peoples. In north Louisiana, southwestern Louisiana, or the Florida parishes they were more likely to be of "Anglo-Saxon" heritage. Some of them had owned a slave or a few slaves. After the Civil War a few of them had one or two sharecropper families who worked lands they themselves could not work, but most of them worked their own acres. Surprisingly little is known about these people as individuals because they did not keep diaries, preserve the few letters they received, or attract the attention of travelers. Not all of them lived on the pine flats, in the hills, or on the prairies. Their small holdings were interspersed among the plantations both in the sugar parishes and farther north, but the planters' economic advantages, which had been slowly eliminating them from the better lands before the Civil War, continued after the war. In the oak hill regions of north Louisiana, however, their numbers increased during Reconstruction as a result of migration from worn-out lands of the southeastern states.

This was the class which had suffered most during the Civil War. The replacement of lost, worn-out, or destroyed tools and livestock

28 "Statistics on Cotton and Related Data," 51, 53, 55; Rosser H. Taylor, "Fertilizers and Farming in the Southeast, 1840–1950," *North Carolina Historical Review*, XXX (July, 1953), 305–28; Loring and Atkinson, *Cotton Culture and the South*, 50–55; Clay, "Economic Survival of the Plantation," 1, 130–31; Shreveport *Times*, May 30, 1872.

CHART 1
Cotton Prices, Acreage, and Bales Produced, 1866–1877

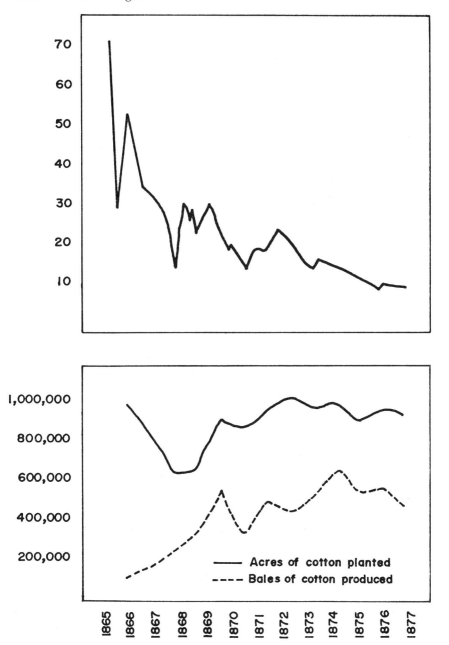

was more difficult for them than for the planters. They had never been subsistence farmers in the pure sense of the word. Before 1860 they had depended on cotton, sugar, rice, or in a few instances, tobacco, citrus fruit, or cattle as a source of ready money. Apparently this dependence was intensified after the war. To obtain the goods necessary to sustain life, they were as dependent upon the merchant as was the lowliest sharecropper. To guarantee the credit they received, they were forced to put more and more of their acres into a money crop, usually cotton, and into corn to feed their families and their animals.

Frederick Law Olmstead's prewar description of these people shows them to have been poor by national standards. After the war they were poorer than ever. The little recovery they experienced in the late 1860s and early 1870s was reversed by the Panic of 1873. Turning in blind anger to the White League, they provided the enlisted ranks for the war of intimidation waged against the Negro in the middle 1870s. Contrary to their economic interests, they allied themselves with the Bourbon Democrats, though it must be admitted that the Republicans probably would have done no more for them. There was a fairly strong Granger movement in the middle 1870s, going so far as to establish cooperative stores here and there, but the Grange was already declining in the North, and it was never a threat to the Louisiana planter-merchant oligarchy. Louisiana's yeoman farmers were destined to remain poor throughout the nineteenth and early twentieth centuries—so long as they remained yeoman farmers.[29]

Few Negroes succeeded in becoming landowners. As noted earlier they were seldom able to take advantage of the Homestead Act. In Concordia Parish one former slave was said to have bought three hundred acres from his onetime master and to have paid for it with

29 T. H. Harris, *The Memoirs of T. H. Harris, State Superintendent of Public Education in Louisiana, 1908–1940* (Baton Rouge, 1963), 1–19; Woodman, *King Cotton and His Retainers*, 317, 334–35; Nordhoff, *The Cotton States*, 73; Shreveport *Times*, July 7, 9, October 12, 1875; New Orleans *Daily Picayune*, December 12, 1866, February 15, 1868, July 4, 1869, May 6, June 20, 1875, May 30, 1877; *Acts of Louisiana*, 1874, 102–103; Shannon, *The Farmer's Last Frontier*, 82–83; Woolfolk, *The Cotton Regency*, 95–100; Coulter, *The South During Reconstruction*, 231; Shugg, *Origins of Class Struggle in Louisiana*, 266–73, 305–306; Samuel H. Lockett, *Louisiana As It Is: A Geographical and Topographical Description of the State*, ed. Lauren C. Post (Baton Rouge, 1970), *passim*.

one crop, but there were only two other freedmen in the parish who owned land. Poor as white farmers might be, they were more accustomed than blacks to independent farm operation, and generally they had better access to the capital needed even for small-scale cotton or subsistence production. Along the bayous in the south and in the hills to the north, the small farmers were almost entirely white. The black man who achieved independence, and few did outside of New Orleans, did so as an artisan or laborer in town.[30]

The black artisan in Louisiana has received little attention. Sterling D. Spero and Abram L. Harris estimate that in 1865 there were a hundred thousand black mechanics in the South as compared to twenty thousand white. One suspects that this was a conservative estimate insofar as blacks were concerned. Charles Wesley lists thirty occupations at which New Orleans blacks worked after the Civil War, but he sets the total number of such workers at 1,792. This is almost certainly too low for the decade following the Civil War. His count of 335 carpenters, 156 cigar-makers, 213 masons, and 82 tailors seems reasonable enough, but there were obviously more than seven stevedores. Such skilled men as draymen, barbers, and waiters, many of whom were black, are not listed. In the smaller towns there were almost always a Negro blacksmith, a carpenter or two, and men in other trades. However, the white resentment of black artisans which had existed before the Civil War continued afterward, and white opposition was so effective that from the end of the Civil War to the midtwentieth century the proportion of blacks engaged in skilled trades in Louisiana declined. Probably there was an absolute decline. There was also, however, a trend toward small business, black-operated and catering to the black community. These were not numerous enough during Reconstruction to be important, but they were to grow in number.[31]

30 *House Executive Documents*, 41st Cong., 2nd Sess., No. 142, *passim; House Miscellaneous Documents*, 44th Cong., 2nd Sess., No. 34, pp. 215–16; Coulter, *The South During Reconstruction*, 108; Ellis, "The Transition from Slave Labor to Free Labor," 62; Highsmith, "Louisiana During Reconstruction," 40–41; Frazier, *The Negro in the United States*, 596–97.

31 Sterling D. Spero and Abram L. Harris, *The Black Worker: The Negro and the Labor Movement* (Port Washington, N.Y., 1966), 16–17, 31–32; Wesley, *Negro Labor in the United States*, 596; Meier, "Comment on John Hope Franklin's Paper," 81; Baton Rouge *Weekly Advocate*, October 6, 20, 1866; Nordhoff, *The Cotton*

4

Class consciousness definitely existed among white and black workers in Louisiana during Reconstruction. As noted earlier, the constitutional convention of 1864 was dominated by the laboring class of New Orleans whites. Wages of skilled labor in New Orleans, $2.00 per day before the war, rose to $3.25 during the war. Some unions already existed, and others were formed, but the federal authorities refused to permit strikes. In 1864 the legislature set daily wages for cartmen, mechanics, and foremen at $3.50 and wages for common laborers at $2.00. It must be emphasized, however, that this was action by and for white workers. These workers and their representatives were strongly opposed to black competition which they believed, correctly, could be used to force wages down.[32]

Thus Negro competition aligned the white workers of New Orleans with the Conservatives who flocked into the state legislature in 1865. From that time until the end of Reconstruction, the white working class of New Orleans was as reliable a group of Democratic voters as was to be found in the state. They continued their organizations and in a few instances engaged in strikes. The coopers, at least, organized their black competitors into a separate local union. But racism was stronger than whatever common economic interests existed between black and white workers. Indeed, except in a Marxist sense, black and white workers had few common interests. Not only did Negro artisans compete with whites; the hundreds of thousands of blacks on the plantations were potential competitors. White workers were well aware that blacks from the plantations could move to town, work for lower wages than whites received, and yet be better off than they were on the plantations.[33]

The blacks themselves, rural or urban, were not completely passive. As noted, wages were good during the early years of Reconstruc-

States, 72; Brister, "History of Pineville," 56–57; C. W. Tebeau, "Some Aspects of Planter-Freedman Relations, 1865–1880," *Journal of Negro History*, XXI (April, 1936), 130–50.

32 *Acts of Louisiana, 1864*, 6; *Debates of the Senate of Louisiana, 1864*, 94; Shugg, *Origins of Class Struggle in Louisiana*, 300–305; Capers, *Occupied City*, 152–53; Spero and Harris, *The Black Worker*, 15.

33 New Orleans *Daily Picayune*, March 26, 1874; Shugg, *Origins of Class Struggle in Louisiana*, 302–303; Spero and Harris, *The Black Worker*, 32.

tion. As more lands were brought into production, more and more hands were needed. After the bad years of 1866 and 1867, the wages paid to field hands were high until 1874. Annual wage contracts were rare in the cotton parishes, but extra workers were frequently needed for cotton picking, and these laborers received what the traffic would bear. Pickers were paid by the pound, and the better pickers in Caddo and Bossier parishes were reported in 1869 to be earning four dollars a day. Probably the average adult picker was making two dollars a day at the same time, and this was the amount sugar planters were paying extra hands for grinding from 1869 through 1873. Wages fell some in 1874, but by 1877 they were as high as before.

Although most laborers worked in the cane or cotton fields, there were other opportunities for employment, such as levee and railroad construction. These opportunities continued despite the use of convict laborers. Some black workers had learned the uses of mobility. In spite of the constant importation of workers into Louisiana the demand for labor was never satisfied. Within the state workers migrated to areas where wages were highest or, if sharecroppers, to more fertile lands. Thus there was a rush from De Soto to Red River Parish in 1871, and throughout the 1870s there was a steady migration of blacks away from the impoverished Felicianas to the better lands west of the Mississippi. Some white commentators ridiculed the wagons loaded with pitifully sparse household belongings which crowded the roads in early January, but they were evidence that the freedmen were trying to improve their economic status. Probably most of them failed, but they made the effort.[34]

In January, 1874, planters in many of the sugar parishes held meetings and agreed among themselves to reduce wages. Generally they agreed to pay fifteen dollars a month, but in Terrebonne Parish the figure was set at thirteen dollars. This led to labor discontent everywhere, but the strongest reaction, naturally, came from Terrebonne. On January 14, 1874, the *Picayune* carried a headline of which yellow journalists twenty years later might have been proud:

---

34 John F. Pollock to Thomas O. Moore, August 14, 1869, quoted in Highsmith, "Social and Economic Conditions in Rapides Parish," 41; Wesley, *Negro Labor in the United States*, 132; Abbott, "Free Land, Free Labor, and the Freedmen's Bureau," 156; Loring and Atkinson, *Cotton Culture and the South*, 23; Baughman, *Charles Morgan*, 178–79.

WAR IN TERREBONNE
The Negroes Murdering, Outraging, and Burning
Gov. Kellogg and the Militia to the Rescue[35]

In fact a group of freedmen had decided to resist the reduction in wages and had formed an organization intended to halt work on sugar plantations in the parish. Most of them probably would have been happy to have obtained a restoration of wages, but the leaders demanded that each be allowed to rent a separate plot of ground and that the planter supervise the growing, grinding, and sale of their sugar crop. They were asking, in effect, for what cotton sharecroppers already had.

They got nothing. Radical Republicans were as horrified as Bourbon Democrats by a restive labor force. A posse of whites and blacks, led by the black sheriff of the parish, halted the strikers when they sought to persuade workers to leave the fields of the Henry W. Minor plantation near Houma. When state troops arrived Minor charged twelve of the labor leaders with violating his civil rights. Those charged were arrested and taken to New Orleans where, apparently, they were released soon afterward. It should be noted that the agreements on wage ceilings among planters did not last out the year. The demand for labor was too great.[36]

New Orleans workers, black and white, were more activist than rural laborers. Car drivers struck twice, coopers at least once, and cigar-makers once during the Reconstruction years. There were numerous strikes when wage reductions followed the Panic of 1873, and the discontent resulting from the depression was still manifest as Reconstruction ended. New Orleans labor seems to have been particularly outraged in 1877 when the city council decided to contract out city work rather than hiring directly, as had been the previous practice.

The most militant of all New Orleans workers were the black longshoremen. The loading and unloading of ships had been "white" work before the Civil War, but blacks took it over during the occupation. When white workers returned to the docks in 1865, they joined with

35 New Orleans *Daily Picayune*, January 14, 1874.
36 *Ibid.*, January 14–21, 1874; Shugg, *Origins of Class Struggle in Louisiana*, 252–53; Sitterson, *Sugar Country*, 247–48.

the blacks in a strike for higher wages, but the effort was a failure. From this time on, there was little cooperation between whites and blacks on the docks, but black militance worked to the benefit of whites since black wages constituted a floor.

No significant labor trouble occurred on the docks in 1866, but short-lived disturbances broke out in May, 1867, with dissidents claiming that leaders showed favoritism in choosing workers out of the lineup. Longshoremen shared the general prosperity from 1868 to 1873, but there was a short strike in October, 1872, and another in May, 1873, when a group of armed Negroes refused to permit unloading at Algiers by workers who had agreed to accept less than the prevailing wage. When the panic struck in the autumn, white workers sought to persuade General Badger of the Metropolitan Police to arrest as vagrants "low, ignorant negroes, who slept under tarpaulins and in barrel houses, and who . . . could afford to work at lower than regular rates."[37]

On September 14, 1873, black longshoremen met at Melpomene and White streets and adopted resolutions declaring that they were inadequately paid and demanding higher wages. They went out on strike on October 13, and they enjoyed some early successes. On October 25, however, General Badger announced that his Metropolitan Police would protect all who wished to work at the wages offered by employers. The Metropolitans were used, many blacks were arrested, and the strike was broken. Nonetheless, as late as October 29 the strikers could temporarily halt all work on the levee. Another walkout was reported on November 23.

The first full year of depression, 1874, saw much labor activity on the levee. Two black longshoremen were arrested in March for leading a group which sought to halt the unloading of a ship. That year the workers were successful in obtaining passage of a legislative act which forbade the employment of sailors in loading and unloading their ships. This act was described as a "monstrous absurdity," but the longshoremen enforced it and held their wages at three to four dollars per day. The same Radical legislature incorporated the Longshoremen's Protective Benevolent Association. In May, however, the state supreme court declared the law forbidding sailors to load and unload

37 Shugg, *Origins of Class Struggle in Louisiana*, 302.

ships unconstitutional. The winning attorney in pleading the case was John A. Campbell, former associate justice of the United States Supreme Court, who had resigned when the South seceded.

The black longshoremen did not give up. In June, 1874, they attacked nonunion black workers in a coal yard in Algiers and were driven off by the Metropolitan Police after a number of them had been wounded. In July a meeting advocated the establishment of a central employment agency to serve all the unemployed. In September a "mob" of workers temporarily halted the loading of a steamer, and another "riot" was reported from the levee in late January of 1875. On April 17 workers struck for $2.50 a day, but soon went back to work for the prevailing $2.00. In 1876 and 1877 the black longshoremen were once more struggling for higher wages. Labor militancy, white and black, continued in the Crescent City; it eventually culminated in a general strike of workers of both races in 1892.[38]

5

Negrophobia and the labor shortage led to much talk and some real effort to attract immigrants other than blacks to Louisiana during the Reconstruction years. In response to urging by Governor Wells and newspapers, the legislature in 1866 established a Bureau of Immigration and enacted a statute for the protection of immigrants. Carl Schurz recommended the continuation of northern military occupation on the ground that the preservation of order would encourage immigration from the North and abroad, but the *Nation* had some doubt whether the Yankee race could settle in warm climates and retain its greatness![39]

Entrepreneurs were importing white immigrants into Louisiana before the end of 1865. Most of them were newly arrived from abroad, and Germans outnumbered other Europeans. European peasants had

---

38 New Orleans *Daily Picayune*, July 15, December 28, 1865 (numerous other incidents are reported in 1873–1877); Shugg, *Origins of Class Struggle in Louisiana*, 301–304; *Acts of Louisiana*, 1874, 123–24, 131–32; Woodward, *Origins of the New South*, 231–32.

39 Communication from His Excellency, J. Madison Wells, Governor of Louisiana, in Relation to Immigration, in *Legislative Documents, 1865–66; De Bow's Review*, After the War Series, I (January, 1866), 10–13, 58–59; *Acts of Louisiana, 1866*, 198–202, 242–52; *Senate Executive Documents*, 39th Cong., 1st Sess., No. 2, pp. 40–41; Woolfolk, *The Cotton Regency*, 95; *Nation*, I (August 3, 1865), 136.

not been slaves in their homeland, however, and they refused to be treated as slaves in Louisiana. Also, they had an eye for economic opportunity, and many of them broke labor contracts before they left New Orleans or soon after arriving on plantations. On the other hand, German colonies in St. Landry and Acadia parishes, where the immigrants worked their own land, were successful, so much so that descendants of the original settlers live on the same lands today. The total number of Germans who moved to rural Louisiana during Reconstruction was probably less than a thousand, and some of these may have already been residents of New Orleans. None of them remained plantation workers long; quickly they made their way to New Orleans or the Middle West.[40]

From time to time other European immigrants arrived. Twenty-four Danes and Norwegians were reported at work in West Feliciana Parish in 1869, and a group of Swedes came in 1870. Some or all of these Swedes went to work on Oakley Plantation where they did well for a time but then became discontented. All of them departed except one who was too drunk to walk. Some Irishmen worked on the railroads and on the levees, but there is no record of them as field workers. In 1870 a St. Landry Parish planter contracted with a wealthy Canadian landlord for a hundred French-Canadian families. References are found to Portuguese workers, and in May of 1878 fifty Polish families, 277 persons, arrived on the Teche for work in the sugar fields at ten dollars a month for men, less for women and boys. Just as Reconstruction was coming to an end, planters turned to southern Italy as a source for labor. More Italians came to the sugar country than Europeans of any other nationality, but pride and industriousness prevented their staying long as plantation workers. Also, if the experience on Oakley was typical, they were prone to violence and were dangerous when crossed.

Despite editorials, immigration conventions, the State Bureau of Immigration, and numerous local immigration organizations, Louisiana attracted few European immigrants and the plantations kept

---

40 King to Caperton, January 1, 9, 13, 1866, March 4, 1867, in King Papers; New Orleans *Daily Picayune*, January 7, 1866, February 5, April 2, 1871; Baton Rouge *Weekly Advocate*, March 13, 1867; Sitterson, "The Transition from Slave to Free Economy," 223; Clark, "Reconstruction and the New Orleans German Colony," 513–14; Highsmith, "Louisiana During Reconstruction," 340–41.

almost none. Daniel Dennett could write that white labor was increasing and Negro labor decreasing every year in Louisiana, but saying so did not make it true. European immigrants did not come to America to be poverty-stricken and underemployed agricultural laborers; they were that in their homelands. They came to improve their economic lot, and the opportunities for the common man were far greater in the North and West than in the South.[41]

Throughout Reconstruction there was a trickle of immigration into Louisiana from the North and West and from other southern states. This movement usually was one family at a time and therefore did not attract attention from newspapers. It is known, as noted earlier, that many veterans of the Union army elected to stay in Louisiana when the war ended. Some of these, like the Twitchells in Red River Parish, were later joined by friends and relatives. A church paper in 1869 welcomed "immigration of intelligent and protestant families from Northern states"[42] to the Teche country; that same year four hundred white workers from the West arrived on the Teche to help with the sugar harvest. In 1871, twenty-five families from Kentucky arrived in St. Landry Parish on a steamboat they had chartered for the voyage. It was suggested after the Chicago fire that displaced laborers in that unfortunate city would be welcome in Louisiana, but none took advantage of the opportunity. Early in 1872 a number of white families from Alabama, bringing Negroes with them, settled in Richland Parish, and a group of farmers from Ohio established a "colony" near Mansfield in 1873. The Grange was active in promoting native white immigration to Louisiana and apparently enjoyed some success. Probably migration from the North would have been greater had it not been that Republicans were despised and ostracized in much of Louisiana, and if Louisiana had not had such a well-deserved reputation for lawlessness.[43]

41 New Orleans *Daily Picayune*, March 4, 1867, November 25, 1869, February 16, June 9, 1870, December 21, 1873, July 16, 1876, December 26, 1877, May 15, 1878; Baton Rouge *Weekly Advocate*, February 4, 1871; Amundson, "Oakley Plantation," 27–32; Dennett, *Louisiana As It Is*, 161; Sitterson, *Sugar Country*, 238–39, 315; Coulter, *The South During Reconstruction*, 104; Shugg, *Origins of Class Struggle in Louisiana*, 258–59.
42 *Southwestern Presbyterian*, April 22, 1869.
43 Goddard, *Where to Emigrate and Why*, 335–36; New Orleans *Daily Picayune*, October 26, November 6, 1869, January 11, October 14, 1871, January 10, July 2,

Much attention was given to the possibility of using Chinese coolies in the fields; the pros and cons were debated from 1866 on. Proponents held that Chinese were hard working, docile, and accustomed to a low standard of living. Opposition was based first on racism. A writer from Plaquemines Parish said in 1866 that a state "with a black population of over three hundred thousand groveling in ignorance and darkness" would be indulging in the height of folly to bring in "another race of human beings more ignorant and degraded than we already possess in our midst."[44] Yet the shortage of labor and dissatisfaction with free black workers did encourage a number of Louisianians to experiment with Chinese laborers. Coolies were working on a plantation near Natchitoches in 1867, and a Dr. Kittridge in Assumption Parish was faced with about fifty Chinese employees who refused to work in September of the same year. Delegates from Louisiana attended a Chinese Labor Convention at Memphis in July, 1869, and returned enthused at the prospect of cheap Oriental labor. In 1870 Chinese on a sugar plantation received fourteen dollars a month, in gold, and daily rations of two pounds of meat, two pounds of rice, and an ounce of tea. For Chinese this was sumptuous fare, but these Cantonese workers were not so docile as had been expected; they insisted on the observance of the letter of their contracts. It is impossible to say how many Chinese came to Louisiana, but assuming that most arrivals were publicized, the total was probably under fifteen hundred from 1865 to 1877. Most planters seemed not to like the coolie, of whom one wrote: "He can't plow, he can't run a cultivator, he can't steer a mule, but otherwise his performances are admirable."[45] By 1890 only 372 Chinese were left in Louisiana.[46]

Thus the immigration movement was an abject failure. Louisiana was not to get Europeans, northerners, or Orientals who would com-

---

1872, August 2, 1873, March 16, September 30, 1874, May 5, 1875; Woolfolk, *The Cotton Regency*, 104.

44 New Orleans *Daily Picayune*, November 13, 1866.

45 Quoted in Sitterson, *Sugar Country*, 250.

46 New Orleans *Daily Picayune*, 1866–67; Baton Rouge *Weekly Advocate*, June 5, 1869, October 29, 1870, May 13, 1871; *Southwestern Presbyterian*, July 14, August 5, 1869, January 20, 1870, July 1, 1875; Sitterson, *Sugar Country*, 236–38; Rowland T. Berthoff, "Southern Attitudes toward Immigration, 1865–1914," *Journal of Southern History*, XVII (August, 1951), 329; Loring and Atkinson, *Cotton Culture and the South*, 93; Coulter, *The South During Reconstruction*, 105.

bine the industry of the midwestern family farmer and the docility of the freedman. Louisiana plantation agriculture would depend almost entirely upon the Negro, and on a growing number of white sharecroppers who worked on the same terms and at the same pace as the Negro until the twentieth century brought mechanization. And even as the fourth quarter of the twentieth century draws near, practically every sugar or cotton plantation has its corps of black workers.

6

Before the Civil War planters had carried on their business through commission merchants or factors. The factor bought for the planter the items the planter chose to buy during the year; for this service he received a commission, normally 2½ percent, and, of course, he charged interest on the funds advanced. At the end of the crop year the crop, sugar or cotton, was shipped to New Orleans. There the factor sold for the best price he could obtain, and once more he received a commission for his services. From the proceeds of the crop he collected the advances made to the planter and the interest thereon. What was left, if any, was the planter's money profit for the year. Usually this money was left with the factor, and the planter drew on it as necessary. More often than not, however, the planter had bought so much during the year that he was in debt to the factor even though his farming operations might show a profit.

The Civil War did great damage to New Orleans factors. Most of their customers remained within Confederate lines, so accounts went unsettled. The high price of cotton at the end of the war did bring a revival of some of the old firms and the establishment of many new ones. They served a most necessary function in the first years of peace, providing credit to get Louisiana agriculture started once more. The capital advanced was northern or English, but the agents were usually southerners with some experience in factoring. The almost complete failure of the crops of 1866 and 1867, however, meant that the factors received little or no return on their investments for the first two years of postwar operation; they were almost forced to advance more credit, if they could, in order to have a chance to retrieve the funds already advanced. This was more than the weaker firms could endure, so they failed. Those who survived found themselves in a different business world from that of antebellum times. The telegraph and the cable had made world prices known at any point the wires touched. Decisions which once could be made at leisure now had to be made hurriedly. The advent of exchanges with future markets added to the tension under which the factor must work.

More harm was done the factor, however, by the rise of the general store and the cotton buyer in the interior. If a planter operated his own commissary, he could buy directly from a wholesale merchant, often one in the North. If he did not, he could get terms from a local merchant which were as good as those available from a factor in New Orleans. The telegraph made it possible for a keen businessman in a small town to buy and sell cotton just as effectively as the New Orleans factor. Thus the business of the cotton factor was reduced each year; many of them went into the country to compete with local cotton buyers, but when they did this they were competing with the commission-merchant side of their own operations. Factorage continued to be the rule for sugar planting, but by the end of Reconstruction the cotton factor had gone out of business or had developed into a cotton buyer who dealt primarily with major purchasers on the cotton exchange.[47]

There had been country stores in Louisiana before the Civil War, but generally they did not flourish. With rare exceptions, their patronage was limited to yeoman farmers of the immediate neighborhood. The planter dealt directly with New Orleans, and only a few crumbs from his table went to the local storekeeper. On the other hand, the local storekeeper did extend credit, often for six months or more, and the debts farmers owed him were secured by a lien on the debtor's crop. No doubt many of the general merchants of the postwar years had received their training in business before the war.[48]

---

47 Woodman, *King Cotton and His Retainers,* 254–55, 259–60, 263–65, 267, 269–74, 278–80, 282–84, 287, 330–31, 357–58; New Orleans *Daily Picayune,* December 8, 1868, October 24, 1872; Capers, *Occupied City,* 149–50; Shugg, *Origins of Class Struggle in Louisiana,* 391–93; Sitterson, *Sugar Country,* 293; Shannon, *The Farmer's Last Frontier,* 89–90.
48 Raleigh A. Suarez, "Bargains, Bills, and Bankruptcies: Business Activity in Rural

When slavery was a thing of the past, the planter could not deal with his work force as he had before the war. Even if he worked contract labor and provided the necessities of life, his workers had some cash to spend. If he engaged in sharecropping with his tenants, the croppers had to buy food, clothing, and any luxuries they wanted and could afford from somewhere on credit. It was to the planter's advantage to open a store, or commissary as it was usually called, on his own plantation. By so doing he added to whatever profit he might make from farming the profits, often greater, of his mercantile business. Charles Nordhoff found plantation stores widespread in Louisiana in 1875. In 1866 the legislature had authorized planters and farmers to operate stores for their employees without buying a retail merchant's license, but this act was repealed in 1868. However, the planter with a large work force on his own plantation who could also get the trade of his neighbors, usually yeoman farmers and small planters and their tenants, could well afford the cost of a license. His chief difficulty was in obtaining trustworthy employees to keep the store, supervise his sharecroppers, operate the cotton gin, and deal with suppliers.[49] It was far more than one man could do.

Some planters did not have the inclination to open stores, and others did not have the credit. As a result the country storekeeper—who, if he was successful, came to be classified as a general merchant —took over the business of furnishing supplies for sharecroppers, renters, yeoman farmers, and even planters. These were men who in one way or another had access to credit, usually northern credit. Many of them were Jews, others Yankees, but many were southern-born, the Snopeses of William Faulkner's novels. A northern-born man who had moved to Baton Rouge before the war realized early that land per se would not be a profitable investment after peace came. He was shrewd enough to lend Confederate money with land as security, however, and in the spring of 1866 he was vigorously pressing his claims. At the same time he had agreed to furnish twenty farmers or planters

Antebellum Louisiana," *Louisiana History*, VII (Summer, 1966), 189–99; *De Bow's Review*, After the War Series, VII (February, 1869), 24; Clay, "Economic Survival of the Plantation," 72–73.

49 *Acts of Louisiana, 1866*, 119; *Acts of Louisiana, 1868*, 119; Nordhoff, *The Cotton States*, 38; Woodman, *King Cotton and His Retainers*, 309, 330–31.

with supplies. He noted that he now charged 12 percent interest. Whether or not this man had a store is uncertain, but he had by 1866 gone into the "furnishing" business as it was to be practiced in the South for almost a century.[50]

It is often difficult to make a distinction between the planter and the merchant. If the landowning planter opened a store and became a merchant, the successful merchant soon became a landowner. However, whether the landowner became a merchant or the merchant became a landowner, the prewar planter had disappeared. One planter wrote in 1869: "The Negroes, since they have become producers on their own account . . . consume on a much larger scale than formerly, which makes the business of supplying them as lucrative, if not more so, than planting or renting."[51] The new landowner derived his income from his store, his gin, the profits he made from buying and selling cotton, and only indirectly from his land. The land was no longer an estate; it was simply another investment. The planter of sugar or cotton had become a businessman.[52]

A very significant change in the cotton business during the Reconstruction period was the development of cotton buying in the interior, away from New Orleans. The decline of the factor has already been noted. One of the ironies of southern history is that the country merchant often began as a buyer for the factor and bought his initial stock of goods on the factor's credit. At first this did send more cotton through the factor's hands, but soon the merchant began to bypass the factor and to sell directly to those who had been the factor's customers. A Springfield, Massachusetts, newspaper noted that the country merchants bought cotton "and shipping it to New Orleans insist upon the most rapid and economical realization of the proceeds . . . in

50 Payne to Mrs. Sterrett, February 18, 1865, June 10, 25, 1866, in Barnhardt (ed.), "Reconstruction on the Lower Mississippi," *passim*; Woolfolk, *The Cotton Regency,* 182; Woodman, *King Cotton and His Retainers,* 304–305, 314, 358; Coulter, *The South During Reconstruction,* 202–203; Griffin, "Problems of Southern Cotton Planters," 110.
51 Quoted in Loring and Atkinson, *Cotton Culture and the South,* 75.
52 Woodman, *King Cotton and His Retainers,* 282, 313, 329–31; King, *The Great South,* 53; Shannon, *The Farmer's Last Frontier,* 89–90; Highsmith, "Louisiana During Reconstruction," 394; New Orleans *Daily Picayune,* August 28, 1877; Coulter, *The South During Reconstruction,* 202.

every possible way they make themselves disagreeable. . . . They live to make money, not to spend it."[53]

From 1868 on, the number of local buyers increased rapidly. Apparently at least one cotton buyer could be found in every country town, and some new towns developed around the store, gin, and office where a local merchant carried on his business. In the South as a whole the construction of new railroads increased the number of merchants and buyers, but there was little of this in Louisiana where the only new line paralleled the Mississippi and ran through cane fields. On the other hand, older railroads did perform this function. The Jackson Railroad certainly encouraged cotton buyers in Mississippi; the Vicksburg and Texas encouraged buyers in Monroe and along the tracks to the Mississippi; and the Southern Pacific helped Shreveport buyers tap the cotton fields of eastern Texas.[54]

The buyer had to take into consideration the costs of selling the cotton he had bought. Transportation was one major cost, insurance another. Students of the subject agree that transportation costs were higher after the Civil War than before. In 1865 all costs, including transportation, were enormous. In June, 1865, cotton worth thirty-six cents in New Orleans was bringing only fourteen cents in Shreveport. One suspects that the Shreveport price was in gold, and the New Orleans price in greenbacks, but that would account for only a few cents difference. This difference in price between the interior and New Orleans declined steadily until in 1869 it amounted to only three or four cents at most.

The cotton planter whose fields were not on the banks of a major stream or near a railroad had a serious problem getting his crop off the plantation and to a shipping point over Louisiana's atrocious roads. A traveler in the back country near Trenton wrote in February 1873, that not more than half the crop of the area had been moved to the wharves over roads which were "so superlatively bad that the traveler sometimes stops to see how many of the next wagon train will miss turning over in passing a given point."[55] This same observer

53 Springfield (Mass.) *Republican,* quoted in New Orleans *Daily Picayune,* April 25, 1871; see also Woodman, *King Cotton and His Retainers,* 305–307.
54 New Orleans *Daily Picayune,* November 14, 1867, February 12, 1871; Woodman, *King Cotton and His Retainers,* 272, 300–301.
55 New Orleans *Daily Picayune,* February 10, 1873.

estimated that it cost farmers in this area three cents a pound to get their cotton to the dock, plus another three cents to get the goods they had ordered from New Orleans or elsewhere back to their homes. This, if true, was a transportation cost of six dollars per ton mile. Historian Fred A. Shannon estimated the cost of road transportation in 1873 at twenty cents per ton mile. Such figures are irreconcilable, so much so that the historian cannot honestly compromise by saying that the truth must lie somewhere in between. One is forced to conclude that for Louisiana, between the fall and the summer, Shannon's figure was far too low. The average cost of road transportation may not have been as high as six dollars a ton mile, but it should be expressed in dollars, not in cents.[56]

The cost of shipping freight by water declined as the Reconstruction years passed. There were complaints as early as 1869 that freight costs between Baton Rouge and New Orleans were frequently higher than those between Baton Rouge and St. Louis, Louisville, or even Pittsburgh. In August of 1870 transportation and insurance costs made cotton that was worth seventeen cents in New Orleans worth only fourteen cents in the Felicianas. Undoubtedly the cost would have been greater from the Black River region. There, a traveler wrote, "The steamboat drawing eight or ten inches gets anchored in the mud; the bayous are so narrow that the bushes on the banks look like cotton patches from the quantity scratched out of the bales." Furthermore, he said, "the streams are so crooked that . . . it would break a fish's back to travel up one of them."[57] Along the broad Mississippi the freight charges were lower. A merchant paid only $12 freight and $11.68 insurance on five bales worth $531 shipped from Madison Parish in 1870, and only $18.75 for freight, $12.59 in insurance on fifteen bales shipped in 1879. The decline in prices had been such that the net return from fifteen bales was only a hundred dollars more than the net return from five bales nine years earlier.[58]

56 *Ibid.*, June 30, 1865, August 24, 1869, February 10, 1873; Saloutos, "Southern Agriculture, 1865–1877," 73; Woodman, *King Cotton and His Retainers*, 271; Shannon, *The Farmer's Last Frontier*, 103.
57 New Orleans *Daily Picayune*, February 10, 1873.
58 Baton Rouge *Weekly Advocate*, March 13, 1869; New Orleans *Daily Picayune*, August 7, 1870; Statements, February 5, 1870, February 5, 1879, in W. E. Rapp Papers (MS in private possession).

On the Red River freight was higher than on the Mississippi, averaging perhaps $3.00 a bale from Shreveport and $1.25 a bale from Alexandria. There was a tendency for river freight to go up when railroads were flooded out and an even more pronounced tendency for the railroads to raise their rates when the rivers were too low for navigation. The big Mississippi steamers could offer much cheaper rates. It cost only a dollar a bale to ship cotton from Memphis to New Orleans, but then the Memphis shippers had an option of shipping to New York by rail. Insurance costs depended, of course, on the value of the cotton. Money spent on insurance was certainly not wasted. Steamboats hit snags and sank; boilers exploded, and in 1876 the *Katie*, carrying three thousand bales of cotton, was swept through a crevasse at Bonnet Carre.[59]

"There is no convincing evidence . . . that railways have ever carried freight at lower costs to shippers or to society than . . . waterways. . . . It was far more important that the railroad brought transportation to areas that without it could have had scarcely any commercial existence at all."[60] This was certainly true of Louisiana, where the main economic service of the railroads was to tap areas which otherwise would have had great difficulty in getting goods to market. They did make it possible for the new merchants–ginners–cotton buyers to do business and prosper in such areas. The railroads obviously charged what the traffic would bear. It has been suggested that national anti-railroad sentiment of the 1870s did not exist in the Gulf South, but in Louisiana such sentiment did exist, even while the state was subsidizing hoped-for new railroads. The merchants of Amite complained of the "onerous" rates charged by the Jackson Railroad in 1869, and Southern Pacific freight charges were condemned at Shreveport in 1872. In 1873 there were bitter complaints that the railroads discriminated against Shreveport, the freight on a bale of cotton from Dallas to Shreveport being $4.00 for 186 miles, compared with $4.50 for 300 miles from Dallas to Galveston, $3.50 for 250 miles from Sherman to Galveston, or $3.00 for 622 miles from Denison to St. Louis. Three years later, after a reduction in rates, it cost $2.75 to ship a bale of

59 Shreveport *Times*, 1873–76; New Orleans *Daily Picayune*, 1870–77.
60 Leland L. Jenks, "Railroads as an Economic Force in American Development," *Journal of Economic History*, IV (May, 1944), 12–13.

cotton 200 miles from Jackson, Mississippi, to New Orleans, $2.00 to ship a bale from nearby Hammond, Louisiana, to New Orleans. An extreme example of railroad gouging took place in the fall of 1877 when the Ouachita River fell so low that steamers could not reach Monroe. Before this, freight per bale of cotton from Monroe to New Orleans had been $1.25, but the railroad quickly went up to $3.00 until a rise in the water made river traffic practicable again.[61]

The new cotton buyers also had to be concerned with the processing costs on cotton. After freight and insurance were paid, port charges, drayage, classing fees, storage fees, and weighing fees had to be met when the cotton reached New Orleans or other domestic destinations. If the cotton was to be shipped abroad, the bales had to be compressed, that is pressed more tightly so that they would occupy less space. It was estimated that every bale of cotton which came to New Orleans left seven dollars in the city. This was probably not true after the Panic of 1783, but there were frequent complaints that the various charges were so much higher than at other ports that they put the city at a competitive disadvantage.[62]

Cotton buying in the interior was such a commercial success that the activities of the merchants-ginners-buyers became the nucleus of a very noticeable growth in southern towns. This was not in any way an industrial revolution. These new towns, or old towns grown larger, existed to serve the farmers and sharecroppers within trading distance. The merchants furnished necessities, ginned cotton, and bought and sold cotton. A drugstore provided medicines and soda water, and a physician provided such medical service as he and the times were able to provide. Usually there was a school which operated four to eight months of the year. Saloons provided euphoria on Saturday night, and church provided a place for repentance on Sunday morning. Most of these towns remained small and would gradually fade away in the twentieth century. Others, like Alexandria, Shreveport, and Baton Rouge grew into lesser cities. As early as 1869 a Baton Rouge newspaper urged farmers to sell their cotton in that city: "No middle men, no brokers, weighers, bulls or bears . . . .When it is

61 New Orleans *Daily Picayune*, August 21, 1869, July 2, 1870, October, 1877; Shreveport *Times*, February 4, December 11, 1872.
62 New Orleans *Daily Picayune*, 1871–72.

weighed there is no dustage, wetage, rotage, or any other 'edge' to cut down the weight."[63] As a matter of fact the country merchant who in buying cotton usually simply credited the seller's account, could afford to pay paper prices as good as, and sometimes better than, those quoted in the major markets. The season of 1874 was a depressed one, but Shreveport nonetheless received 25,695 bales by rail, 8,868 by water, and 47,715 by wagon. Almost 28,000 bales were shipped out by rail, some to Galveston, some to St. Louis; of the 54,000 bales shipped by river, most were directed to New Orleans, but over 7,000 bales were consigned to northwestern ports, and 3,000 were consigned to Liverpool.[64]

As the merchant grew in economic importance, he also grew in political importance, but his newfound prominence made him a natural target for criticism when hard times struck. As prices went ever lower, farmers and planters forgot that the local merchant provided them with a return on their crops much earlier than would have been the case had they had to consign it to New Orleans. They forgot, or chose not to remember, that he provided them with the only credit available. However, except for a few isolated cases of violence, the merchants were not harmed. The fact that they controlled the only available source of credit made them invulnerable. They were harmed more, probably, by the new futures market in cotton which had come into being. This provided a means whereby the man who bought or sold cotton could hedge and avoid risk, but the temptation to speculate, to sell cotton one did not own, or to buy cotton for which one could not pay, was often irresistible; yielding to the temptation often led to ruin.[65]

7

As has been said more than once in these pages, credit was the basic problem of Louisiana at the close of the Civil War. The capital of the state had been so depleted that the money to finance the resumption of cotton and sugar production had to come almost entirely from the

---

63 Baton Rouge *Weekly Advocate*, July 24, 1869.
64 Woodman, *King Cotton and His Retainers*, 276, 326, 333; Shreveport *Times*, July 3, 1875.
65 New Orleans *Daily Picayune*, 1877; Woodward, *Origins of the New South*, 185–86; Woodman, *King Cotton and His Retainers*, 290–91, 332–33, 335–36.

North and abroad. This money did not come in the form of a federal grant or foreign aid; it came through the channels of commerce, and lenders demanded security. Land had so decreased in value that it was inadequate security. One man wrote in 1873: "A good deal of property has . . . [fallen] into my hands and the Taxes almost make property of No value but the heavy Interest I get Counterballances and Keeps the amount about square."[66] If land would not serve as security, the lender must look to the crop. The factors of prewar Louisiana had had what amounted to a lien upon the crop of the planters with whom they dealt, but this had been between factor and planter. The postwar lien affected every level of rural society, and it was reinforced by statutes as binding as legislatures could make them. The system was well established in 1867, when a landlady cautioned all persons against "advancing money or supplies to the freedmen working on the plantation known as 'The Oaks' as I hold liens on all products raised by these persons."[67]

The rather large amount of northern and foreign capital invested in Louisiana agriculture soon after the war mostly was wasted on the abortive crops of 1866 and 1867. This credit had not come cheaply, but with its exhaustion, additional charges to cover the great risk of lending on the security of an unharvested crop, sometimes even an unplanted crop, was as great or greater than true interest. The larger planters were usually able to obtain from New Orleans funds needed to operate their plantations and "furnish" their tenants. Very little of what they borrowed came as cash money. They received seed, fertilizer, farm tools, work stock, pork, and a few other food items for sale in their commissary. If the planter's credit was exceptionally good he might deal directly with a bank, but ordinarily he dealt with a factor or wholesale merchant on the same basis as his

66 Payne to Sterrett, September 10, 1873, in Barnhart (ed.), "Reconstruction on the Lower Mississippi," 394.
67 Quoted in Schuler, "Women in Public Affairs in Louisiana During Reconstruction," 695; see also *Acts of Louisiana, 1867*, 351–53; *Acts of Louisiana, 1874*, 114–15; New Orleans *Daily Picayune*, February 12, March 23, September 20, 1867; Saloutos, "Southern Agriculture, 1865–1877," 72; Jacqueline P. Bull, "The General Merchant in the Economic History of the New South," *Journal of Southern History*, XVIII (February, 1952), 37–38; Woodman, *King Cotton and His Retainers*, 296–97, 345–47, 351; Engelsmen, "Freedmen's Bureau in Louisiana," 190–91; Woodward, *Origins of the New South*, 183; Bentley, *The Freedmen's Bureau*, 143; White, *Freedmen's Bureau in Louisiana*, 121.

tenants dealt with him. He paid very high interest rates because the only security he could offer was his unharvested crop. The capital required for producing an acre of cotton in the 1870s was about forty dollars. If the acre produced three hundred pounds of lint cotton at twenty cents a pound, the planter could pay 25 percent interest and still profit. However, when cotton dropped to fifteen cents per pound and below, no profit could be made on it. Profits, if any, must come from charging tenants higher interest on their debts than the planter paid on his.[68]

The opportunity to partially recoup by charging tenants and share-croppers high rates did not exist for the lesser planter or the yeoman farmer. These men had no credit in New Orleans, and to secure supplies they had no choice but to resort to the large planter or to the general merchant who often were indistinguishable from one another. If they had sharecroppers, their sharecroppers were furnished by the general merchant who thus made the profit to be made from them. The yeoman farmer was no better off than the sharecropper; he might be said to be worse off, because he had a farm to lose. In north Louisiana many a yeoman farmer, through bad luck, lack of industry, sickness, extravagance, or some other misfortune, lost his small tract of land and became a sharecropper. Naturally the small planter and the yeoman farmer resented the general merchant; this resentment was reflected to some extent in the Grange, and after Reconstruction it was to be expressed more explicitly in the Farmer's Alliance. Sometimes smothered anger gave way to violence, perhaps with a touch of anti-Semitism. In 1871 a Jewish merchant was murdered at Tigerville, in Terrebonne Parish. Later a mob of small farmers burned stores at Delhi belonging to men named Hirach, Blum, Weil, and Risenfield.[69]

Almost the entire superstructure of the crop lien system was erected upon the back of the sharecropper, black or white. The planter, large

68 Monroe *Ouachita Telegraph,* quoted in New Orleans *Daily Picayune,* September 27, 1871; Sitterson, *Sugar Country,* 291–93; Highsmith, "Louisiana During Reconstruction," 405, 439; Clay, "Economic Survival of the Plantation," 65; Woodman, *King Cotton and His Retainers,* 322; Coulter, *The South During Reconstruction,* 194–95.

69 Shugg, *Origins of Class Struggle in Louisiana,* 241; Degler, *Out of Our Past,* 198–99; New Orleans *Daily Picayune,* October 28, 1871; Woodward, *Origins of the New South,* 188.

or small, might go broke, but if so it was because the sharecroppers on his place did not produce enough in market value to meet his obligations. But at least the planter had some knowledge of the risk he faced; his managerial skill, if it existed, could be used to advantage; and he might make a profit on his dealings with his sharecroppers. The cropper, on the other hand, was at the absolute bottom of the heap. Except perhaps by stealing, he could profit from no other person in the crop lien chain of command. He had only his knowledge of farming and the strength of himself and his family to offer. He was not a tenant in the true sense, because he worked under supervision. This supervision might be strict or it might be lax; generally the stricter the supervision the greater was the production.

Obviously the Louisiana sharecropper had no capital. He hoped to begin the year with an adequate supply of rough clothes which he had bought from his earnings on the previous year's crop. For food he depended upon the landlord's commissary or upon a general merchant designated by the landlord. When the crop was harvested, half went to the landlord for rent. Theoretically, the other half belonged to the sharecropper, but most of it actually belonged to whomever had furnished him with food and his other purchases during the year. It was not at all unusual for him to end the year in debt, and when this happened he was as much bound to the land, at least until the debt was paid, as any medieval serf. Frequently he went into debt because in addition to such necessities as meat, meal, and molasses he had bought such luxuries as tobacco, candy for his children, canned goods, and even an occasional bottle of whiskey, but who can blame him? Emancipation had not brought real freedom; it had put him on an economic treadmill; he and his descendants worked hard to stay in the same place for three generations.[70]

The high interest rates under the crop lien system were a source of wry humor among the lien's victims. General merchants, for example were said to "charge from 25 per cent to grand larceny."[71] A supposed epitaph read:

70 Shreveport *Times*, December 3, 1874; Batchelor Papers, December 25, 1866; Wharton, *The Negro in Mississippi*, 71; Sitterson, *Sugar Country*, 244; Wesley, *Negro Labor in the United States*, 209.
71 Quoted in Bull, "The General Merchant," 47.

> Here lies thirty-six per cent,
> The more he got the more he lent;
> The more he got, the more he craved—
> Good God! Can such a soul be saved![72]

Interest rates paid by planters and merchants varied, but after 1867 they were never below 10 percent even for those with the best credit, and 25 percent was not unknown. The interest charged at the commissary or general store was almost astronomical. Exact rates are almost impossible to calculate, because interest per se was seldom figured by the merchant. Instead the merchant charged for goods a "credit price" which was far above the normal retail price. In fact, merchants often quoted no cash price because all their sales were on credit. One study of the entire South showed that the credit price for eleven staples was 55 percent higher than the prevailing cash price. Fatback, the cheapest salt pork, was seldom if ever more than ten cents a pound in retail groceries. Sharecroppers, small farmers, and planters often paid as much as twenty-five cents a pound. No firm average figure of the cost of credit to sharecroppers can be fixed, but estimates range from as low as 30 percent to as high as 110 percent. Examples of rates this low and this high probably can be found, but charges in the neighborhood of 40 to 50 percent seem to have been the norm in Louisiana.[73]

The crop lien has now been damned for three generations. Because the farmer had to grow enough cotton to cover his obligations, the lien has been blamed for the South's concentration on cotton and for blocking diversification on the one hand and improved agricultural methods on the other. In 1870 in north Louisiana the proportion of arable land planted to cotton did run from 30 percent in Winn Parish to 90 percent in Concordia. Probably the planter did require that his sharecroppers plant as much cotton as they could work, because his economic survival depended upon his cash crop. However, a serious student of the general merchant has not found a single lien which specifies the planting of any certain amount or proportion of cotton.

---

72 Quoted in Coulter, *The South During Reconstruction*, 194.
73 Shreveport *Times*, January 22, 1877; Monroe *Ouachita Telegraph*, quoted in New Orleans *Daily Picayune*, September 27, 1871; Somers, *The Southern States Since the War*, 198; Woodman, *King Cotton and His Retainers*, 302–303, 347–48; Bull, "The General Merchant," 49–50; Woodward, *Origins of the New South*, 180–81.

The farmer planted as much cotton as he could because he needed it to cover his fixed costs. He continued to do so until the federal government paid him to plant less and to practice improved agriculture. The crop lien continued to be standard even after the New Deal of the 1930s had effected its changes in southern agriculture, and it persists to some extent to the date of this writing.

It is not accurate to say that the crop lien forced sharecropping on Louisiana and the South or that it required its continuation. Sharecropping, as noted already, developed as a system under which the labor of the penniless freedman and the land and managerial skill of the penniless landowner could be combined most efficiently in the cotton fields. But wage labor prevailed in the sugar parishes, and the crop lien flourished there also. Much has been said about how the merchant-planter cheated the farmers and sharecroppers who dealt with him, but research into the existing books of general merchants does not bear out this accusation. The charges were inordinately high, or the interest high, or both, but the buyer knew, or could have known, what the cost was going to be when he bought the goods.

The misfortune of Louisiana planters, farmers, and sharecroppers in Reconstruction and after was not the existence of the crop lien. Rather their misfortune was to live in an underdeveloped agricultural economy which, because of its poverty and peculiar labor system, had never developed adequate credit facilities, and which had been further impoverished by war. Since land was not a satisfactory security for loans, only the crop was left as security. But a loan on a newly planted crop, with harvest six to eight months away, subject to destruction by flood, prolonged rains, drought, labor trouble, hail, insects, or a combination of any or all of these, was a risky loan indeed. The burgeoning American industrial revolution offered many opportunities for profitable investment at much less risk. A capitalist who could earn a safe 10 to 12 percent on commercial paper or good real-estate mortgages had to charge the planter-merchant much more to insure against the great risk he took. The planter-merchant then had to add enough to cover his own risks, which were also great. The cost of crop lien credit as practiced during and after the Reconstruction can be called exorbitant, but no other credit was available. Probably the costs of the crop lien did keep Louisiana agriculture poor, but without the lien there would have been no Louisiana agriculture beyond the eking out of a bare subsistence, probably with hand tools.[74]

The political developments of Reconstruction in Louisiana were short-lived. After 1877 in practice, and after 1898 in law, the same classes that had controlled antebellum Louisiana were once more in control. Politically, the power of the Negro vanished as quickly as it had risen, and it had never risen very high. But the economic results of Reconstruction were to show much more endurance. Sharecropping, the planter-merchant, and the crop lien were to be the basis of agriculture in the state until the New Deal, World War II, and mechization at last brought changes. Even with those changes, and despite oil wells and northern-owned industries, Louisiana remained one of the poorest states in the Union.

74 New Orleans *Daily Picayune*, January 22, 25, 1871, September 24, 1873; Woodman, *King Cotton and His Retainers*, 298–99, 334–45; Garner (ed.), *Studies in Southern History and Politics*, 296; Shannon, *The Farmer's Last Frontier*, 92–94, 99–100; Woodward, *Origins of the New South*, 181–85; Shugg, *Origins of Class Struggle in Louisiana*, 241–42; Highsmith, "Louisiana During Reconstruction," 394–95; Saloutos, "Southern Agriculture, 1865–1877," 72–73; Bull "The General Merchant," 39–42; Clay, "Economic Survival of the Plantation," 79–80, 153–54, 164, 166.

X   *Social and Cultural Developments*
               During Reconstruction

WHEN THE Civil War was over, the people of Louisiana held to every belief, every prejudice, every habit of prewar days that the exigencies of defeat and Reconstruction would permit. In 1876 the anniversary of the Battle of Shiloh was a day of memorial for Confederate dead; a few days later, on the anniversary of Lincoln's death, an editorial described the late president as uncultured, coarse, selfish, an infidel, and a sensualist. This editorial was particularly critical of northern churches which looked on the stage as an abomination and yet believed that Lincoln went straight to Heaven from a theater box.[1] A perceptive visitor from abroad noted: "The South in almost everything is conservative. The battles that are over . . . in the North have scarcely begun in the South. . . . the old creeds . . . bind her churches. . . . The same conservatism is visible in social relations. Servants are under control, children [likewise], and woman stands just where she used to."[2]

Social life seems to have remained very much as it had been before the war. During Reconstruction northern officers normally were not accepted socially, and northerners who moved permanently to Loui-

1 New Orleans *Daily Picayune*, April 6, 14, 1876.
2 McRae, *The Americans at Home*, 272–73.

siana had to accept southern social, religious, and political standards if they were to be received. But Louisianians did not sulk in their tents. Peace brought an active social whirl to Baton Rouge, and in 1868 New Orleans social life was described as most active. Visitors gaped at elegantly dressed ladies who promenaded on Canal Street on Saturday. On the sugar plantations social life was much the same from 1865 to 1900 as it had been in the 1850s.[3] Those with social position could still be gay. A young woman visiting in New Orleans wrote to her sister in the country seeking to borrow an evening wrap: "I need one for we are out constantly. Every night we have been out or had company until two or three o'clock. Balls, parties, and dinners until Leita and I are almost tired of it. We have, of course, lost our hearts a half a dozen times—but as yet with no one in particular. All are handsome, intelligent, and fascinating."[4]

If there was a significant change in eating habits, it was toward greater emphasis upon the prewar staples, pork and cornbread. This was the diet of Negroes and poorer whites, supplemented to a greater or lesser degree by vegetables, fish, and game. Many went hungry in 1865 and 1866, and again in 1874, but in general the quantity of food was adequate. The Latins of south Louisiana, of course, had their own diet, with less emphasis on pork and corn meal, more on beans, rice, and sea foods. In New Orleans the good restaurants continued to offer fine fare. A guest at a good hotel noted that dinner consisted of ten courses, that the diner had a choice of fifty-four items, and that if he had the capacity he could eat a portion of each item.[5] A North Carolinian wrote the following to a friend who had just returned from a trip to the Crescent City:

3 Aertker, "A Social History of Baton Rouge," 45–48; Capers, *Occupied City*, 201–202; John M. Avery to D. D. Avery, January 23, 1868, in Avery Family Papers; New Orleans *Daily Picayune*, October 31, 1869; Sitterson, "The McCollams," 365.
4 [?] to [?] (names of sender and addresses unknown; presumably members of the Gibson family), January 22, 1871, in Gibson-Humphrey Papers.
5 Mother Hyacinth to her family, June 25, 1865, October 20, 1871, September 29, 1876, in Sister Dorothea Olga McCants (ed. and trans.), *They Came to Louisiana: Letters of a Catholic Mission, 1854–1882* (Baton Rouge, 1970), 174–75, 218, 237; McRae, *The Americans at Home*, 391; Coulter, *The South During Reconstruction*, 313; H. H. Donald, *The Negro Freedman*, 47; Clay, "Economic Survival of the Plantation," 32–33; Joe Gray Taylor, "The Food of the New South (1875–1940)," *Georgia Review*, XX (Spring, 1966), 9–28.

I felicitate you on your pleasant trip to New Orleans. . . . But I was surprised to hear of such abounding good cheer. I had figured to myself N. O. as a perfect pandemonium, at least to good old Confederates—and that one of their torments would be to see all the good things you speak of in the clutches of the carpetbagger—while they would have to content themselves with the smell of the cooking and the aroma of the wines. I am glad to know there is one place at least where a Confederate gentleman can live as he desires to do. As to your eulogy on bacon and cornbread . . . all I have to say is I am glad you like it.[6]

Historians have been guilty, by indirection, of creating a false impression of the South during Reconstruction. Recounting the frenetic political activity and describing economic developments, they create the impression that the struggle between the forces of darkness and the forces of light was the chief preoccupation of almost everyone in the South from 1865 through 1877. This was not the case. The outstanding impression gained from scores of collections of family papers, particularly letters and diaries, is that little attention was paid to political development by those whose papers have been preserved. People were mainly concerned with family affairs, making a living, and their relations with their neighbors. In other words, life went on very much as usual. The destruction of war had had far more effect on everyday life than did the politics of Reconstruction.

There were, of course, some changes. Those who had died in the war were gone forever, and women had to do some things they might not have done in 1860. One reporter noted how much more often one saw a lady driving her own buggy or carriage. As always, fashions in dress changed. The hoop skirt prevailed just after the war, but it was shortened enough that a titillating glimpse of a lady's feet might be had now and again. In the late 1860s the "Grecian bend" became high fashion, featuring a corset laced so tightly that the body was thrown forward and the head back, so as to retain balance on high-heeled shoes. Men were practically required to grow mustaches, and fashion dictated tight-fitting trousers with a long-tailed coat and broad-brimmed hat. Obviously, only the reasonably prosperous could keep up with such fashions. The working-class white of the cities and the

6 William Gordon to W. Porcher Miles, June 21, 1873, in William Porcher Miles Papers.

yeoman farmer wore wool trousers with a cotton shirt and wool over-coat in winter, heavy cotton work clothing in summer. Most Negroes, unless they had hand-me-downs, wore the same type of garments as poorer whites, only of lower quality.[7]

New Orleans continued to be the metropolis of Louisiana and of parts of other states, hated and loved for its gaiety, sinfulness, and opportunities for unusual adventure. Angry editorials complained of the reckless driving of drays, wagons, and heavy cotton floats through the city. Visitors wished to see the St. Charles and St. Louis hotels, Carondelet Street, the Mechanics' Institute if the legislature was in session, the Vieux Carre with its famous restaurants and other attractions, and Canal Street during the evening promenade. The French Opera House and the St. Charles Theater were always attractions; also attractive was the more popular entertainment to be found at the Academy of Music, the National Theater, and the Olympic Varieties.

The fact that the city was a filthy pesthole apparently made no difference. Few streets were paved, and the sewers were the ditches beside the streets. Until the slaughterhouse monopoly came into being, refuse from the shambles was thrown into the river just above the main water intake. Butler's cleaning of New Orleans was to be the last until the turn of the century, and yellow fever and cholera were only two of the diseases which threatened residents and visitors alike.

The government of the city was corrupt no matter which party was in control. The police were as busy blackmailing their own victims as they were pursuing other criminals. Gambling houses, bars, and bawdy houses catering to every taste were to be found in abundance; they were patronized by both residents and tourists. All of these attractions made the city a Mecca for those who could afford it. It was the goal of thousands, black and white, who flocked in from the country seeking to improve their lot. Probably nothing in history was more futile than the Sunday-closing law—affecting saloons, theaters, and gambling houses—enacted by the legislature in 1874. Court action was not needed; the attorney general gave it as his opinion that it had not been legally enacted, and that was that.[8]

7 Beale, "On Rewriting Reconstruction History," 814; New Orleans *Daily Picayune*, July 13, 1871; Coulter, *The South During Reconstruction*, 310–11.

8 New Orleans *Daily Picayune*, January 7, 1865, May 19, June 1, 1866, March 31, 1867, July 28, 1873, March 27, April 1, 1874; New Orleans *Tribune*, May 28, 1867;

Insofar as entertainment was concerned, spectator sports still took a back seat compared with those in which people participated directly. Outdoor sports such as hunting, fishing, and swimming attracted most males. Women did not hunt, seldom fished, and—in the Victorian climate of nineteenth-century Louisiana—certainly did not swim in mixed company. Swimming, in fact, seems to have been a prerogative of boys, white and black, who swam unencumbered by garments when weather and opportunity permitted.[9]

Fishing was posible within a reasonable distance of most Louisianians. In the northern part of the state bass (alway called trout), crappie, bream, and catfish were sought after. To the south these were still fished for, but in brackish or salt water spotted weakfish (speckled trout), channel bass (redfish), drum, croaker, and crabs were also found. A fishing excursion was a gala affair which, if luck was good, ended in a fish fry enjoyed by all. It should be remembered that in the 1870s a fishing trip five miles from home was a more difficult and time-consuming outing than an excursion of fifty to seventy-five miles in the twentieth century.

Hunting was probably not as popular as fishing, but nonetheless the amount of game killed was almost unbelieveble. Today it is difficult to imagine the abundance of waterfowl in the midnineteenth century. Added to myriads of duck and geese were veritable clouds of wild pigeons, soon to become extinct as a result of unrestricted hunting. Also hunted were quail, snipe, woodcock, dove, wild turkey, grosbec (a water bird much esteemed as table fare), and robins. The latter, shot or caught in traps, were reported to be delicious eating.

As for animals, squirrel and rabbit were hunted as they had been throughout American history. Deer, common in most parts of the state, were the favorite big game. The wildness of Reconstruction Louisiana is evident in the killing of predators. A cougar weighing 180 pounds was reported killed in Livingston Parish in 1867 after being tracked down by a one-legged Confederate veteran. A still

Warmoth, *War, Politics and Reconstruction,* 80–81; McRae, *The Americans at Home,* 535; Somers, *The Southern States Since the War,* 192–93; Coulter, *The South During Reconstruction,* 304; Highsmith, "Louisiana During Reconstruction," 351–52; Schuler, "Women in Public Affairs During Reconstruction," 688.

9 New Orleans *Daily Picayune,* July 16, 1871.

larger "panther" was slain in St. Tammany Parish only seven miles from Covington in 1878. Nine wolves were reported killed near Jackson in 1869, and in 1877 wolves were wreaking havoc among swine in Richland Parish. In that same year a 350-pound black bear was killed in Gentilly Woods in Orleans Parish. Perhaps most noteworthy was a "tiger" (jaguar?) killed by a party of deer hunters in St. Landry Parish in 1872. Louisiana was still not far removed from the frontier.[10]

Another form of recreation, especially for residents of New Orleans, was the railway or steamboat excursion. This might be only to Lake Pontchartrain, six miles away. Those who could afford it drove by way of Shell Road, past the racetrack, but the great majority rode the Pontchartrain Railroad. On one June Sunday in 1866 this line carried over six thousand passengers; rates were not unreasonable, because total receipts were only a little over fourteen hundred dollars. A more elaborate excursion might be north to Brookhaven, Mississippi, or west to Morgan City. After construction of the Mobile and Chattanooga Railroad, one could ride upriver to Donaldsonville on the west bank or east to the Mississippi Gulf Coast. The utmost in excursions was still a steamboat ride up or down the river, and the *Natchez* seems to have been the most celebrated boat, fast, elaborately decorated, and serving excellent meals. The Mississippi Gulf Coast and Grand Isle had become favorite resorts where the affluent went to spend a week or two.[11]

Gambling was a favorite pastime, if it may be called that, in all of south Louisiana, and it certainly was not unknown in other parts of the state. The celebrated Louisiana lottery was the most notorious gambling scheme, and its operations extended far beyond Louisiana. This was a private business, operating as a monopoly under state law. It advertised in the newspapers, and one advertisement suggested that one could cure the blues by purchasing a lottery ticket. It continued to operate into the 1890s. The owners grew wealthy, but it should be

10 Baton Rouge *Weekly Advocate*, May–June, 1869; Shreveport *Times*, 1871–1876; New Orleans *Daily Picayune*, November 13, 1867, July 13, 1869, March 29, 1871, January 19, May 2, 1872, January 30, November 18, 1877 March 9, 1878; Highsmith, "Louisiana During Reconstruction," 338–39.

11 Somers, *The Southern States Since the War*, 193–216; New Orleans *Daily Picayune*, June 26, 1866, December 24, 1869, March 1, 1870, August 2, 1872; Shreveport *Times*, May 17, 1876; Coulter, *The South During Reconstruction*, 300–306.

noted that among them was the Howard family which donated Metairie Cemetery, where the racetrack was located before 1872, the old Howard Memorial Library, and the Confederate Memorial Building to the use of the people of New Orleans and Louisiana.

Almost any imaginable form of gambling was to be found in New Orleans. The competition between houses led to the employment of men to go out into the streets and "rope in" customers. In fact, the competition became so keen that the larger houses went before the legislature and secured the passage of a bill outlawing gambling. Thereafter they had to pay police bribes somewhat heavier than the taxes they had previously paid, but the police earned their money by shutting down the small-time operators and thus increasing the profits of the protected establishments.[12]

Gambling and drinking frequently went together, often to the distress of the "sucker" in the gambling den, but Louisianians drank on almost any occasion for almost any reason. On a cold day they drank to keep warm; on a hot day they downed iced drinks to keep cool. Apparently most of the ice manufactured in or imported into Louisiana was used for cooling alcoholic drinks. In August, 1865, one popular saloon was using more than a hundred dollars worth of ice a day: "Our people . . . must have their drams. . . . They would rather let their meat and fish spoil than miss their cooling (!) drink."[13] Drinking establishments ran the gamut from ornate saloons to "Radical social equality whiskey shops," which "generally propose to poison the bodies of . . . 'sovereign electors' of African descent, at the rate of five cents a drink."[14] A Colfax paper noted in 1878: "Marksville has four drinking saloons and one church. In another year Colfax will catch up. We have three . . . saloons now and as soon as another is able to exist we'll have the church."[15] Unrestrained drinking by freedmen was a problem after the restrictions of slavery were removed, but the freedmen were only following the example their former masters had set. Daniel Dennett was exaggerating when he

12 Alwes, "Louisiana State Lottery," 970–1,061; New Orleans *Daily Picayune*, May 25, 1870, September 10, 1872, 1865–78, *passim*; Highsmith, "Louisiana During Reconstruction," 354–55.
13 New Orleans *Daily Picayune*, August 16, 1865.
14 *Ibid.*, September 10, 1872.
15 Colfax *Chronicle*, quoted in New Orleans *Daily Picayune*, April 13, 1878.

said that the value of alcoholic drinks consumed in Louisiana was equal to the value of the sugar and cotton produced, but consumption was heavy.[16] On the other hand, David McRae stated that he had visited the "lowest" parts of New Orleans, "but never saw such sickening and hideous exhibitions of drunkenness as are to be seen every Saturday night in almost any Scotch or English city."[17]

Temperance organizations sought to combat the evils of drink during Reconstruction as they had before the war. In 1870 delegates met at Homer and effected a statewide organization. This movement was most active, as might be expected, in the northern, Protestant parts of the state, but temperance activity was publicized in New Orleans in 1871 and continued for a number of years. A Catholic Total Abstinence Society was established in 1871, and it was said to be making great strides in Terrebonne Parish in 1875. The consumption of alcohol, however, does not seem to have been greatly affected by either Protestant or Catholic temperance efforts.[18]

Dancing was frowned upon by some Protestant churches, but most Louisianians of the Reconstruction years loved to dance. Mardi Gras was an occasion for masquerade balls, of course, but balls, masked or otherwise, were a frequent occurrence during the rest of the year, and in other towns as well as in New Orleans. No doubt such entertainments were still held in private homes, but not so frequently as in the more prosperous days before secession. Blacks also danced, although there certainly were no "integrated" social functions. On the other hand, the Shreveport *Times* did recommend a black dancing teacher named Peter Bonner. The New Orleans Presbytery worried lest young people were taking "reprisal upon the sorrows of the past" and fleeing "from the gloom of the present by plunging recklessly into every form of earthly pleasure."[19] So far as one can tell from newspapers and pri-

16 New Orleans *Daily Picayune*, March 4, 1864, December 18, 1867, December 16, 1869, October 6, 1872; Baton Rouge *Weekly Advocate*, February 20, 1869; Shreveport *Times*, April 27, 1872; Coulter, *The South During Reconstruction*, 336.

17 McRae, *The Americans at Home*, 535.

18 New Orleans *Daily Picayune*, November 4, 1870, April–May, 1871, July 23, 1872, April 1, 1874, January 10, 1875.

19 St. Amant, *Presbyterian Church in Louisiana*, 120; see also Baton Rouge *Weekly Advocate*, January 13, 1866; Shreveport *Times*, May 1, 1872, January 26, February 4, 1876; New Orleans *Daily Picayune*, March 23, 1867; Highsmith, "Louisiana During Reconstruction," 336–37.

vate letters, there was a definite decline in social functions for a year or two after the beginning of the Panic of 1873.

Organized sports provided entertainment for participants and spectators. By 1869 baseball had become popular with white and black. New Orleans had the Southerns, who defeated the Robert E. Lees for the city championship by a score of twenty-five to nine and then went on the road, playing as far away as Brooklyn. Baton Rouge's leading team, naturally, was called the Red Sticks; the two favorite teams at Shreveport in 1876 were the Quicksteps and the Country Boys. The continuing popularity of baseball gave the lie to the writer in Shreveport who asserted in 1872 that "no longer will thousands of people of all classes, ages, sizes, and sexes stand for hours under a burning sun to watch eighteen men who could not be persuaded to undergo the most ordinary manual labor, undergo the greatest physical exertion."[20]

The tournament was a holdover from the South's prewar love affair with Sir Walter Scott. No clash of arms took place, but the "knights would ride at full gallop while trying to thrust their long lances through a small ring which was suspended by a string. . . . The knight who collected the largest number of rings was the winner and had the privilege of naming the queen of honor for the ball which invariably followed."[21] These affairs were widespread. One at Opelousas pitted bachelors against married men. Tournaments with black knights were a Fourth of July feature in Rapides Parish. In 1876 one of the contenders dubbed himself the "Knight of the Fifteenth Amendment"; another was the "Enchanted Knight of the Packard Guards."[22]

Boxing was beginning to attract attention, primarily in New Orleans. In 1872 a bout between Jim Mace and Joe Coburn, staged just across the Mississippi line, attracted a large number of Louisianians. The fight lasted three hours and thirty-eight minutes and was declared a draw. Another "fight" was between a coon and a dog, usually with the coon fastened to a log in the water. One such at Shreveport in 1872 had an admission price of fifty cents, half price for children and ministers. At another extreme was the New Orleans Cricket Club

20 Shreveport *Times*, April 11, 1872; see also Baton Rouge *Weekly Advocate*, July 17, 1869; New Orleans *Daily Picayune* 1869–78; Shreveport *Times*, July–August, 1876; Coulter, *The South During Reconstruction*, 302.

21 Highsmith, "Louisiana During Reconstruction," 338.

22 *Ibid.*, 160; New Orleans *Daily Picayune*, May 26, 1868, March 17, 1870.

which existed for a time in 1873. Croquet was popular in the spring but did not flourish under the hot summer sun. For fun, there were student high jinks: the faculty at Centenary, for example, was concerned with prankish young men who were shaving horses' tails.[23]

Another sport which aroused keen interest was racing. Horse racing news occupied an important place in New Orleans papers during the season, but lesser towns also had racetracks. The Caddo Race Course at Shreveport was operating on a fairly regular basis by the mid-1870s. At Baton Rouge there seems to have been no set schedule, but races did take place from time to time. The height of racing, of course, was a contest between two steamboats—the greatest excitement of all was the famous race between the *Natchez* and the *Robert E. Lee* in July of 1870. The course was from New Orleans to St. Louis, and the *Robert E. Lee* won with a time of three days, eighteen hours, and fourteen minutes.[24]

Circuses and other exhibitions relieved the tedium of life. The George W. DeHaven Circus played Baton Rouge in autumn, 1865. The same town had Mike Lepman's Circus and Trained Animals in December, 1866; admission was one dollar for adults, white or black, fifty cents for children under ten. Howe's Great London Circus was in Shreveport in late 1875, and early the next year General Tom Thumb made his appearance there. In 1866 in New Orleans Messrs. Hay and Adams offered "excursions" up to a thousand feet in a captive balloon. "Fairs" were occasions for entertainment as well as education. Then, as now, there were stock shows, but there was more emphasis on such varied items as new farm implements, churns, lacework, sugar boiling equipment, and ornamental chocolate. State fairs seemingly were held only at Baton Rouge or New Orleans, but lesser towns had lesser fairs. For example, an agricultural fair was held at Homer in December, 1874, at which the master of the Louisiana Grange was the main speaker.[25]

23 New Orleans *Daily Picayune*, March 20, 1869, December 1, 1871, March 25, April 6, 1873; Shreveport *Times*, April 16, 1872; Highsmith, "Louisiana During Reconstruction," 337; Faculty Minutes, Centenary College of Louisiana, 1840–90.
24 New Orleans *Daily Picayune*, July 1–6, 1870, 1865–78; Shreveport *Times*, 1875–76; Baton Rouge *Tri-Weekly Advocate*, January 11, 1867; Coulter, *The South During Reconstruction*, 302–303.
25 Baton Rouge *Weekly Advocate*, December 29, 1866; Shreveport *Times*, December 4, 1874, November 21, 1875, February 8, 1876; New Orleans *Daily Picayune*,

Opera and the theater had been popular in New Orleans long before the Civil War, and their popularity continued during the occupation and Reconstruction years. It is doubtful that an opera was performed in Louisiana outside of the Crescent City, but traveling theatrical groups had made circuits of the larger country towns before the war, and they gradually resumed their travels. The Cripps family was one such group, offering Shakespeare as well as other drama. More popular performances, such as those offered by the Gaîté Comique Troupe from New Orleans drew larger crowds. A performance could be too "popular." In April, 1872, a troupe danced the cancan in Brewers' Hall at Shreveport, an exhibition, according to the local newspaper, "which no lady could attend and where a gentleman should be ashamed to be seen."[26] Amateur dramatic companies were often formed—Opelousas had two in 1872—but they tended to be short-lived.[27]

Louisianians were always ready to celebrate. Christmas was a joyous time, but in the country the end of slavery may have reduced the holiday flavor of the season. Plantation hands still were released from work for a week at Christmas, or when the grinding ended on sugar plantations, but the paternalistic prewar celebration apparently had come to an end. Independence Day, which had been a holiday for all before the war, became a freedman's holiday during Reconstruction. Whites might not work on the Fourth of July, but it was blacks who held parades, picnics, and dances. The greatest holiday of all in New Orleans and the small towns of Catholic Louisiana was Mardi Gras. This festive season was somewhat muted in 1863, but thereafter, if newspaper accounts are to be trusted, it aroused all the enthusiasm of prewar years. Only in 1875, when the depression and the political situation combined to dampen spirits, was Mardi Gras largely ignored, and the celebration was renewed in succeeding years.[28]

Some Louisianians read. Most confined their reading to newspapers

---

March 16, 1866; Highsmith, "Louisiana During Reconstruction," 333; Coulter, *The South During Reconstruction*, 296–97.

26 Shreveport *Times*, April 11, 1872.

27 *Ibid.*, 1871–76; New Orleans *Daily Picayune*, 1863–1878; Baton Rouge *Weekly Advocate*, 1866–67; Highsmith, "Social and Economic Conditions in Rapides Parish," 148–49; John S. Kendall, *The Golden Age of the New Orleans Theater* (Baton Rouge, 1952), 486–572.

28 New Orleans *Daily Picayune*, 1863–1878; Biddle, *A Soldier's Wife*, 56–57; Shreveport *Times*, July 6, 1875; Coulter, *The South During Reconstruction*, 299.

or the Bible, but the educated read both for information and for entertainment. A town as small as Houma had a circulating library, and so, probably, did a number of others. In Carroll Parish a group of black people formed a literary society. Some Louisianians were writing. The *Crescent Monthly*, published in New Orleans by William Evelyn, lasted only two years despite the high quality of its content. Perhaps one reason for its demise was that its reviews described mediocre and worse southern literature as mediocre and worse. Charles Gayarré, now an old man, was still working on his histories; William Preston Johnston was writing the biography of his father, Albert Sidney Johnston; and George Washington Cable was producing his "Drop Shot" column for the *Picayune*. Louisiana was not New England, but neither was it a complete literary desert.[29]

In Louisiana both whites and blacks joined fraternal organizations. An 1864 issue of the *Picayune* carried three and a half columns listing Masonic lodges in the state and the districts to which they were assigned. Black Masonic lodges also were active; several of them cooperated in holding a picnic at Pass Christian, Mississippi, in 1875. Blacks had other secret organizations and "benevolent societies." In these groups, as in his church, the black man had a freedom of expression which he did not enjoy elsewhere. The Louisiana Grange, despite its efforts to improve the lot of the farmer, probably should be considered more a social organization than a politico-economic pressure group. It was fairly active in Louisiana from 1870 through 1876.[30]

2

This narrative has already recounted much violence, but no account of life in Reconstruction Louisiana would be complete without further attention to this feature of the times. Not all violence was politically motivated. The formal duel was on its way out, but "affairs of honor" took place from time to time. Two Sicilian immigrants killed

29 New Orleans *Daily Picayune*, January 13, 1872, October 25, 1877; Bergerie, "Economic and Social History of Iberia Parish," 82–83; Calhoun, "Concordia Parish," 97; Highsmith, "Louisiana During Reconstruction," 341–44.
30 New Orleans *Daily Picayune*, 1864–78; Shreveport *Times*, March 22, 1872, July 12, 1873, June 30, 1875, March 8, 1876; Breaux Bridge *Attakapas Sentinel*, June 11, 1874; *Acts of Louisiana, 1874, passim*; Frazier, *The Negro in the United States*, 371–75; E. Franklin Frazier, *Black Bourgeoisie* (Glencoe, Ill., 1957), 90; Saloutos, "The Grange in the South," 473–87.

one another in a formal duel at Algiers in 1864; an encounter with swords resulted in serious injury to one of the duelists in 1870; a formal exchange with shotguns, each loaded with a single ball, was fatal to a man just across the Mississippi line near Bay St. Louis in 1874; and a formal duel, results unknown, was fought at Jeanerette in 1877. Some "honor" was still attached to dueling. One paper insulted white Republicans by saying that they fought duels with blank charges and then went off to drink together.[31]

In the main, however, the shoot-out had replaced the duel. One man told David McRae in 1868: "I am as good a Christian, sir, at times, as any man in God's creation; but, sir, I am also a gentleman. And if any man insults me, I will call that man out, and if he refuses to come out, I will shoot him on sight, sir."[32] Usually no call preceded the shooting on sight. The *Picayune* noted in 1871 that "There is no town west of the Allegheney Mountains, or south of the James River which is without its notorious scoundrel whose hands are steeped in slaughter, yet who stalks free and unharmed through the village streets with a gang of admirers hanging around him."[33]

This was a society in which the carrying of arms was not only acceptable but also expected. In 1866 there were complaints in Baton Rouge because boys, white and black, were shooting pistols in the street, endangering the lives of all within range. One British traveler noted that to put one's hand behind one's back was the same as striking the first blow, and had resulted in the death of many an unarmed man. Homicides among "gentlemen" in New Orleans were almost weekly at times, but one suspects that the per capita rate was lower there than in the more sparsely settled country parishes. The most celebrated murders were the killing of General St. John R. Liddell by a Colonel Jones and his two sons and the subsequent killing of Jones and one of his sons and the almost miraculous escape of the other, but these were among hundreds of incidents involving men of family and standing which had no apparent connection with politics. In general, society approved of this method of defending one's honor. A St. Landry Parish newspaper stated in rather poor syntax that "the

31 New Orleans *Daily Picayune*, November 8, 1864, March 15, 1870, April 5, 1874, May 7, 1877; Shreveport *Times*, March 28, 1872.
32 McRae, *The Americans at Home*, 274.
33 New Orleans *Daily Picayune*, August 27, 1871.

idea of one man putting another one under a peace bond is the most cowardly act a man can do."[34] Looking back on this welter of blood, it is encouraging to read of Drozin Miguez and Theogene Viator of New Iberia, who fired twenty-two shots at one another, then clubbed away with empty weapons, yet did no serious damage.[35]

Foreign visitors to Louisiana were struck by the prevalence of lynch law, especially when the accused persons were black. It must not be thought, however, that only blacks were victims of illegal summary justice. In 1871 a white man accused of murder was hanged by a mob in Bossier Parish. In 1873 a dozen rustlers were reported to have been lynched in Vermilion Parish, and the next year two white men accused of robbing and murdering two German traders were summarily hanged at Delhi. A supposed horse thief was seized in De Soto Parish in 1875 and carried across the Texas line to be killed. In 1876 a man named Moore, accused of murder after a shoot-out in Shreveport, was riddled with shots by masked men as he lay in a hospital bed. In Monroe in 1877 unknown persons broke into the jail and with a sledgehammer beat out the brains of a man accused of incest. None of these instances, as far as can be determined, had any political significance whatsoever.

Negroes, of course, were lynched for political reasons, as has been amply demonstrated. However, the most apolitical black might face a mob for killing a white man, no matter what the justification, and for a black to be accused of the rape of a white woman meant almost certain death. Few, if any, instances of torture are recounted in Reconstruction newspapers; that was to come after the political threat to white supremacy had been removed, but lynch justice for blacks was already an established custom. For that matter, the difference between a lynching and a formal execution were not that great. Public hangings were a regular feature of justice, for black and white, and they were attended by large crowds. Some of these hangings, techni-

---

34 Washington (La.) *Enterprise,* quoted in New Orleans *Daily Picayune,* November 5, 1877.
35 Baton Rouge *Weekly Advocate,* February 24, 1866; Latham, *Black and White,* 161; R. E. Butler to Margaret Butler, November 13, 1871, in Butler Papers; S. M. Thomas to Warmoth, September, 1872; in Warmoth Papers; Dixon, *White Conquest,* II, 99; New Orleans *Daily Picayune,* January–February, 1866, April 5, May 26, 1871, March 5, 1876, 1864–1878, *passim;* Woodward, *Origins of the New South,* 158–59.

cally bungled, were so grisly that their horror is still apparent in newspaper stories a century old.[36]

From the end of the Civil War until well into the twentieth century there was, for all practical purposes, an open season on adult black males in Louisiana. The end of slavery took away from the Negro the protection that his pecuniary value had given him as a slave. Planters could give some protection to the workers on their plantations, but they did not have the backing of the community which they had had before emancipation. No jury would convict a white man of murdering a black man, and when this did happen, once, the convicted murderers simply stood up and walked out of the courtroom; no attempt was made to stop them. Under the circumstances, although the killing of black men by white men was all too frequent, it is remarkable that there was not more. Undoubtedly there were a few bloodthirsty psychopaths who sought opportunities to shed black men's blood, but most white men avoided violence entirely, and most of those who did kill Negroes had provocation according to the mores of the time.

The student of Reconstruction must remember also that most violence inflicted upon black people in Louisiana, and elsewhere for that matter, was inflicted by black people. In this area of behavior the freedman had been an apt pupil of his former master. Conservative newspapers emphasized intraracial violence in times of interracial political stress, but incidents were so abundant that they often received little notice. No statistical comparison is possible, but this student is convinced that for every black man killed by a white man, for political or other reasons, two were killed by other black men. The ratio would probably be greater in instances of violence where injury, rather than death, was the result. Obviously this conclusion does not excuse white violence, but neither must it be overlooked.[37]

Theft and robbery were common crimes as the war ended. A resident of Baton Rouge noted that at night he walked down the middle

---

36 Campbell, *White and Black*, 171; New Orleans *Daily Picayune*, June 20, 1871, September 14, 1873, July 21, 1874, May 12, 1876, December 9, 1877, 1865–77; *passim*; Shreveport *Times*, July 9, 1875, 1871–76, *passim*; Coulter, *The South During Reconstruction*, 300–301.

37 New Orleans *Daily Picayune*, 1864–78, *passim*; Shreveport *Times*, 1871–76, *passim*; Baton Rouge *Weekly Advocate*, 1866–77, *passim*; *Senate Executive Documents*, 39th Cong., 1st Sess., No. 2, p. 20; Nordhoff, *The Cotton States*, 49; May, "The Freedmen's Bureau at the Local Level," 14.

of the street with his knife in his hand. The frequency of armed robbery and burglary decreased, if one may judge by the newspapers,
during the prosperous years from 1868 through 1872. The panic
brought on an increase, however, accompanied by a vigilante movement which was almost, if not quite, as dangerous as the criminals
it sought to combat. In 1876 residents of Shreveport were advised to
keep their doors locked and a loaded shotgun at hand if they expected
to preserve their property from bad Negroes and worse white men. In
Terrebonne Parish a planter, after his storeroom was robbed repeatedly, set a gun trap and shot the thief in the leg.[38]

Most crime was simple theft. All accounts agree that many, if not
most, freedmen had no compunctions about stealing food, clothing,
or other everyday items on the plantation or in the homes of those who
employed them. This was partly a holdover from slavery days, when
masters had not been overly concerned if their slaves appropriated
food, and partly a result of the very real hunger which existed among
freedmen from 1865 through 1867, and in 1874 and 1875. Planters
were concerned with pilfering by freedmen after the war was over,
and the habit of stealing, brought on by hunger, could continue when
the hunger had been assuaged. Poultry, swine, and cattle were fair
game, and from 1865 through 1867 it was almost impossible to rear
such animals in much of the state. Plantation storehouses had to be
stoutly constructed, and locks had to be strong. Especially exasperating was the stealing of cotton. In various cotton areas, but especially
in the Felicianas, small merchants became, in effect, "fences" for
stolen cotton and thus provided the thieves with a cash market. Perhaps some retribution for slavery was involved in this stealing, but
it was certainly a handicap to farmers, and it tended to confirm in
many minds the already present opinions as to the moral inferiority
of the Negro.

The farmer or planter who decided to inflict summary justice on a
thief had to be careful. The offended black seldom resorted to violence
against a white man, but he could and did exact revenge for injury,

38 Payne to Mrs. Sterrett, February 18, 1865, Barnhart (ed.), "Reconstruction on
the Lower Mississippi," 390; Baton Rouge *Weekly Advocate*, 1866–77, *passim*;
New Orleans *Daily Picayune*, 1865–78, *passim*; Shreveport *Times*, 1871–76, *passim*; Lafayette *Advertiser*, August 5, 1876, quoted in New Orleans *Daily Picayune*,
August 10, 1876; Shaffer Papers, VIII, October 10–11, 1877.

real or fancied, by burning storehouses, cotton gins, barns, and other buildings. Arson was a serious crime, but arsonists were not often caught. Often the setting of a fire was a last gesture of defiance before a laborer or sharecropper departed for places unknown. Later, when white sharecroppers became more numerous, barn burning became a weapon they would use.[39]

The Louisiana State Penitentiary at Baton Rouge had had relatively few inmates before the Civil War, and relatively few of those confined had been blacks. Deeds by slaves which might have led to imprisonment were more often than not punished on the plantation where the offense took place, so that the master would not be deprived of the labor of his slave. In 1856, for example, only 94 blacks were in the penitentiary, and only three of these for any form of theft. After the war the Negro prison population increased rapidly, to 170 out of a total of 228 in 1866, about as large a proportion of 449 in 1874, and of 625 in 1877.[40] Even so, a double standard of justice prevailed. A black man was punished more severely for a crime against a white man than for the same crime against a black, and a white man received a lesser punishment for a crime against a black than if another white man had been the victim.

3

The greatest social changes during Reconstruction came in the lives of black people. The first thing that freedom meant to most blacks was freedom of movement. As noted, blacks tended to follow the northern armies while the war continued; when the war was over one of the tasks of the Freedmen's Bureau was to attempt to reunite families— often without success. The contrabands who flocked to the army camps suffered greatly, but very few were willing to return to slavery,

---

39 New Orleans *Daily Picayune*, 1865–77, *passim*; Baton Rouge *Weekly Advocate*, 1866–67, *passim*; Shreveport *Times*, 1871–76, *passim*; Reid, *After the War*, 273–74; Mother Hyacinth to her family, April 13, 1872, in McCants (ed. and trans.), *They Came to Louisiana*, 220; H. H. Donald, *The Negro Freedman*, 180–83; Coulter, *The South During Reconstruction*, 51–52.

40 J. G. Taylor, *Negro Slavery in Louisiana*, 209–10; Reports of the Board of Control of the Louisiana State Penitentiary, in *Legislative Documents, 1867, 1874, 1877*; Mark T. Carleton, "The Politics of the Convict Lease System in Louisiana, 1868–1901," *Louisiana History*, VIII (Winter, 1967), 5–10; Woodward, *Origins of the New South*, 212.

even though they might have lived more comfortably in the quarter. Freedmen continued to move about when peace came. In general they moved from country to town, from poor hill land to rich alluvial land, and from the older states of the Southeast to the newer states of the Southwest.

Some blacks did choose to remain on the plantations where they had been slaves, and those who had been taken to Texas to prevent their falling into the hands of the Union army were apparently happy to return to their homes in Louisiana. On cotton plantations, where sharecropping was the rule, the black moved from the old slave quarter to a cabin on the acres he worked. On sugar plantations, where the gang labor system was almost always followed, the central Negro quarter continued to exist.[41]

As thousands of blacks came to Louisiana from states to the east and upriver, almost three thousand black families were migrating from Louisiana to Texas. Within the state there was much movement from plantation to plantation. In part this resulted from a black determination not to be bound to one place. In part it was a movement from poorer to richer soil, as was the case between the Felicianas and Pointe Coupee in 1875. In January of each year wagons passed to and fro, loaded with the belongings of laborers and sharecroppers going from one plantation to another. Some improved their status; some were worse off because of the move; most found little change.[42]

In 1865 a man who had journeyed from New Orleans northward into Mississippi wrote: "I met droves of Negroes making their way to the city. Eastern Louisiana and the adjoining counties of Mississippi are depopulated of their laboring population."[43] New Orleans, which

41 Eaton, *Grant, Lincoln and the Freedmen*, 207–208; New Orleans *Tribune*, November 16, 1864; Woodward, *Origins of the New South*, 207; John T. Trowbridge, *A Picture of the Desolated States and the Work of Restoration, 1865–1868* (Hartford, Conn., 1868), 320; Francis B. Simkins, "New Viewpoints of Southern Reconstruction," *Journal of Southern History*, V (February, 1939), 52–53; E. Franklin Frazier, *The Negro Family in the United States* (Chicago, 1939), 164–65.

42 Wadley Diary, November 4, 1865; Pointe Coupee *Echo*, January 21, 1871, quoted in New Orleans *Daily Picayune*, January 29, 1871; Pointe Coupee *Republican*, December 25, 1875, quoted in New Orleans *Daily Picayune*, December 29, 1875; W. T. Palfrey to J. G. Palfrey, June 29, 1865, in Gatell (ed.), "The Slaveholder and the Abolitionist," 373; Campbell, *White and Black*, 151; Homer L. Kerr, "Migration into Texas, 1860–1880," *Southwestern Historical Quarterly*, LXX (October, 1966), 189–90; Coulter, *The South During Reconstruction*, 50–51.

43 New Orleans *Daily Picayune*, June 14, 1865.

had a sizable prewar black community, was probably better able to cope with this migration than were smaller towns. In Shreveport it was reported that many freedmen died during the winter of 1865–1866 for lack of food and shelter. The Negro population of Baton Rouge increased from 1,735 in 1860 to 3,356 in 1870. Developments in Louisiana were in accord with a sectional trend; in fourteen southern cities the black population increased 90.7 percent between 1860 and 1870 as compared to an increase of only 16.7 percent in the white population. Obviously, this created problems. Blacks in the towns had greater opportunities than the countryside afforded them, but they came more and more into conflict with the white laboring class and, with the passage of years, were excluded more and more from skilled occupations. On the other hand, they were unwittingly preparing the way for the great migration of the twentieth century which would make the urban ghetto the normal habitat of the black man in the United States.[44]

The former free men of color of New Orleans, many of whom were prosperous and well educated, constituted with a few mulatto freedmen something of an aristocracy of Louisiana blacks at the end of the Civil War. They were usually Catholic in religion, and they accepted the Christian institutions of marriage and the family; their standards of behavior were generally those of middle-class, white, south Louisiana Catholics. They were far from typical of the freedmen in general. George Washington Cable was forced to leave the South because of his pro-Negro views, but he wrote that "the vast majority of colored people in the United States are neither refined in mind nor very decent in person."[45]

Family life among Louisiana slaves had been far from the ideal of American Christians. Legal marriage had been impossible. A few

---

44 *Senate Executive Documents,* 39th Cong., 1st Sess., No. 2, p. 16; Payne to Mrs. Sterrett, September 3, 1865, in Barnhart (ed.), "Reconstruction on the Lower Mississippi," 391; Aertker, "A Social History of Baton Rouge," 66; White, *Freedmen's Bureau in Louisiana,* 115; Coulter, *The South During Reconstruction,* 261–62; Roussève, *The Negro in Louisiana,* 135–38; Frazier, *The Negro in the United States,* 190.

45 Cable, *The Negro Question,* 139; see also Skinner, *After the Storm,* II, 74; Mother Hyacinth to her family, January 27, 1871, in McCants (ed. and trans.), *They Came to Louisiana,* 213–14; Frazier, *The Negro in the United States,* 274–75; Coulter, *The South During Reconstruction,* 54.

planters encouraged religious marriages, but most slave pairings were highly informal and as impermanent as they were informal. Furthermore, the parents were not primarily responsible for the care of their children; this responsibility belonged to the owner-master. Customs built up over generations of slavery could not be ended overnight. Disregard of the marriage tie was encouraged by the fact that tens of thousands of couples were separted by the migration of black people during and after the war.

Probably nothing was more shocking to the missionaries, teachers, and Freedmen's Bureau agents who worked with the freedmen than the casual nature of sex relations. The solution seemed to be simple; require those who wished to live together to contract legal marriages. The Freedmen's Bureau sent out such an order, and in Louisiana General Baird issued a proclamation requiring either a civil or religious wedding with a license. This, and the preachings of northern missionaries, brought a flurry of formal marriages, but this was a short-lived phenomenon. Most black men found formal marriage entirely too confining. They preferred a system similar to that under slavery, except that men and women lived together of their own will, not by the consent of a white man. The arrangement might last a lifetime or it might not last a year; a man and woman were husband and wife only so long as they chose to live together. Once the cohabitation came to an end, each party was free to seek a new partner. Thus formal marriage was limited, largely, to the black middle class; most blacks had a common-law marriage or practiced serial polygamy.[46]

Negro men, by virtue of their physical strength and because a family relationship similar to that of whites was thought desirable, often actively asserted their power as head of the family during the early years of peace. Many insisted on the right to beat their wives. As a result, some marriages became patriarchial unions, and the family which resulted a patriarchial family. This was not the usual development, however. Men found the responsibility more than they could

46 Baton Rouge *Weekly Advocate*, April 14, 1866; Campbell, *White and Black*, 133–34; W. E. Burghardt DuBois, *The Negro Church* (Atlanta, 1903), 5; Engelsmen, "Freedmen's Bureau in Louisiana," 217–18; Frazier, *The Negro Family in the United States*, 97; Wharton, *The Negro in Mississippi*, 43–44; White, *Freedmen's Bureau in Louisiana*, 153–54; H. H. Donald, *The Negro Freedman*, 56–64; Frazier, *The Negro in the United States*, 627–28.

or would bear. Thus women, who had had far more responsibility
than men for child care under slavery, came more and more often to
head a matriarchal unit.

Because she might have had several husbands, and children by each
of them, the woman was the unifying element in the family. Also,
probably as a result of slavery, no stigma was attached to the bearing
of illegitimate children. Thus a young woman might have a family
dependent upon her before she had ever had a husband. Not to be
discounted was the influence of the "grandmother," whose age and
experience made her the head, almost, of a clan. She was the reposi-
tory of wisdom for a simple people. She was, as often as not, a midwife
of greater or lesser ability. She took the responsibility of seeing to it
that orphaned children were placed in homes, often in her own cabin
if she was not too old. In Louisiana the Freedmen's Bureau discovered
that it did not have to care for many orphans; the freedmen took care
of their own.[47]

4

Readers of the last half of the twentieth century may have difficulty
in comprehending how primitive the practice of medicine and surgery
was a century ago. Half the physicians practicing in some parishes
had no sort of medical degree, and many of those who boasted degrees had obtained them from highly questionable sources. If all factors were taken into consideration, the person who became ill may
have been better off without a physician than with one. He almost
certainly was better off at home than in a hospital. Many practitioners
still believed in bleeding as a treatment for fever. Almost all looked
on a massive dose of calomel as the beginning of any course of treatment. It was not until 1865 that the clinical thermometer, invented
during the Renaissance, was introduced to medical practice in Louisiana, and its use was not widespread until the century was nearly over.

In Europe Koch and Pasteur had demonstrated the existence of
bacteria, and in 1878 Pasteur proved conclusively that some diseases
were spread by bacteria. Even so, many Louisiana physicians of the

---

47 Frazier, *The Negro Family in the United States*, 95, 106, 125–26, 147–48, 153–54,
163, 165–66; Frazier, *The Negro in the United States*, 313–14; H. H. Donald,
The Negro Freedman, 64–66; White, *Freedmen's Bureau in Louisiana*, 81.

1880s continued to believe in the spontaneous generation of germs, and they refused to believe that tuberculosis could be transmitted from one person to another. Puerperal (childbed) fever was widespread in hospitals, its cause unknown and no cure available. Surgery was so often followed by fatal infection that the knife truly was a last resort. A few converts to Lister's belief in antiseptic treatment of the operating theater practiced in the 1870s with considerable success, but their teachings were ignored or forgotten in the 1880s. Anesthesia was in limited use, but it was probably more practical for tooth extraction than for surgery.

Charity Hospital in New Orleans was the largest hospital in Louisiana in the 1870s. During Reconstruction another Charity Hospital was established at Shreveport, and yet another was authorized for Baton Rouge. The last seems never to have gone into operation. Also in New Orleans was the United States Marine Hospital and, in sequence, Anfoux's Hospital and the Luzenburg Hospital, both for smallpox cases, supported by public funds. Private hospitals, all small, included Hotel Dieu, Stone's Infirmary, the Orleans Infirmary, and the Circus Street Hospital. There was a "madhouse" in New Orleans, and the state hospital for the insane at Jackson was as horrible a bedlam as can be imagined.[48]

During Reconstruction the health of the people of Louisiana was adversely affected, to say the least, by an almost complete disregard of sanitation. This was most apparent in a crowded, swampy city like New Orleans, but the concept of sanitation really did not exist anywhere in the state. Small towns probably could not become as filthy as New Orleans, but the people of smaller communities achieved conditions as unsanitary as was possible for them. Many farmers lived in filth comparable to that of the towns. In fact, after steps were taken to clean up New Orleans and larger country towns, about the turn of the century, small towns and some farms continued to be Asiatic in their disregard of sanitation well into the twentieth century. The

48 John Duffy (ed.), *The Rudolph Matas History of Medicine in Louisiana* (Baton Rouge, 1962), II, 327, 335, 338, 341–55, 360–67, 497–524; Shreveport *Times*, March 25, 1875, February 2, 1876; *Acts of Louisiana, 1874*, 248–49, 268–70; O'Conner, "Charity Hospital," 65–68; New Orleans *Daily Picayune*, December 16, 1869; Gonzales, "William Pitt Kellogg," 480–81.

freedmen, obviously, had less comprehension of the need for sanitation than better-educated whites.

Examples come primarily from New Orleans, because that city was visited by so many travelers who wrote books, and because newspapers there were aware of conditions. The city gradually returned to its former state after General Butler's cleansing. In 1867 the legislature forbade the disposal of offal or "feculant matter" from privies in the river above the city's water intake. Baton Rouge in 1866 required the emptying of privies to be performed after eleven o'clock at night, and property owners were required to keep open the gutters adjoining their property. Open gutters, of course, were the means of disposing of sewage. In 1870 a newspaper reporter in New Orleans noted a vegetable peddler freshening heads of lettuce by washing them in water from the gutter. Guano was unloaded from ships near the thickly settled portions of the city. In 1871 it was noted that the streets of the city in late summer were "very offensive to the eyes and exceedingly offensive to the nostrils and lungs."[49] Later, in 1876, it was noted that "Summer has come suddenly upon us. . . . All over the city, even in Camp and Canal streets the gutters are reeking with accumulated mud and stagnant water upon which a green scum floats offensive to the sense of smell as well as the sight."[50] Most residents of the city seemed not to care. In 1876 a dead dog lay on Chippewa Street between St. Mary and Felicity for days.[51]

Under the slavery regime it was in the interest of the master to keep his slaves alive and well, so most bondsmen received medical care as good as was available. The disorganization brought on by the war led to a decline in the quality of medical care on the plantations. More noticeable, however, was the death rate among blacks who left the plantations and gathered at army camps and in the towns. These unfortunates sickened and died by the thousands. Many southerners, in fact, became convinced that blacks were doomed to extinction in

---

49 New Orleans *Daily Picayune*, September 16, 1871.
50 *Ibid.*, June 1, 1876.
51 *Ibid.*, August 11, 1865, November 4, 1870, March 8, 1871, August 10, 1876; *Acts of Louisiana, 1867,* 207–209; Leland A. Langridge, Jr., "Asiatic Cholera in Louisiana, 1832–1873" (M.A. thesis, Louisiana State University, 1955), 93–94, 107–108; Woodward, *Origins of the New South,* 480–81.

the United States. It was not until the publication of the census of 1870 that it became evident that the black birth rate was far exceeding the death rate.

The Freedmen's Bureau did what it could to care for the health of black people in Louisiana; in fact, the Union army had begun such efforts in New Orleans well before the end of the war. The "Contraband Hospital," actually the old Marine Hospital, had nearly three thousand black patients in 1863 and 1864. Nonetheless, the first Freedmen's Bureau tabulation put the death rate among blacks in Louisiana at 167 per 1,000 per year. The bureau claimed to have brought this number down to 140.2 by 1866. It would be a mistake to overestimate the effectiveness of the bureau's medical service. It employed only seven physicians in the whole state, and the salary paid them, $97.50 per month, is probably indicative of their abilities. Freedmen's Bureau medical services came to an end in 1869. Thereafter the medical service received by freedmen in the country depended upon their landlords or the conscience and ability of the available physicians. Care certainly was not good, but it probably was no worse than that received by whites in similar economic circumstances. The death rate of blacks was much higher than that of whites, and the disparity, though lessening, was to continue for more than a century, but in the nineteenth century this high death rate was caused as much by poverty and ignorance as by discrimination.[52]

Louisiana was notorious for her epidemics, but other diseases took far more lives than smallpox, cholera, and yellow fever. In the first place, the infant death rate was horrifying. Few statistics are available, but evidence indicates that between 25 and 50 percent of all babies born died in infancy. Fevers, dysentery, diphtheria, whooping cough, and measles were just a few of the afflictions which carried off babies and small children.

Among older children and adults, dengue fever was not uncommon,

52 New Orleans *Daily Picayune*, August 20, 1865, March 31, 1866; Baton Rouge *Weekly Advocate*, March 31, 1866; H. H. Donald, *The Negro Freedman*, 154–55, 160; Clay, "Economic Survival of the Plantation," 33; DuBois, *Black Reconstruction*, 226; White, *Freedmen's Bureau in Louisiana*, 86–100; Engelsmen, "Freedmen's Bureau in Louisiana," 171–74; Frazier, *The Negro in the United States*, 568–69.

but it was seldom fatal. Malaria was omnipresent; it was so taken for granted that people in most parts of the state expected a bout of chills and fever between spring and winter as a normal feature of existence. Fortunately, it was known that quinine was a specific cure, or at least a suppressant, of malaria. Unfortunately, many victims of the disease preferred to let it run its course, so deaths were not uncommon. Blacks were not so susceptible to malaria as whites, but they certainly were not immune. Typhoid fever was just beginning to attack Louisiana on a large scale as the Civil War ended. In Europe it had been scientifically established that this disease was spread by means of human excrement, but this fact was denied by many New Orleans physicians, and most rural physicians had never heard of the experiments involved.

Respiratory diseases were probably more dangerous to blacks than to whites; influenza, pneumonia, and tuberculosis were common to both races. Pneumonia, before the day of antibiotics, was fatal as often as not, especially if treatment included the usual hot plasters, strong laxatives, and other weakening remedies. At least, however, the pneumonia patient reached a "crisis," at which time he died or began a recovery which, barring a relapse, would eventually be complete. There was no recovery from tuberculosis; the common name, consumption, described the progress of the disease. It was the chief killer of blacks. Heart disease, stroke, and cancer had their victims of course, but they were not such frequent causes of death as later because potential victims so often died of something else first.[53]

The best history of medicine in Louisiana asserts that smallpox probably killed more people than yellow fever in the state from 1865 to 1900. This disease was always present, but it was especially virulent in 1866, 1870, and 1877. Generally freedmen were more seriously affected than whites, but the epidemic of 1866 seems to have been equally deadly to victims of both races. In 1870 the disease was at its worst in Orleans and Jefferson parishes, but it was bad enough statewide that a bill was introduced into the legislature which would have

53 Duffy (ed.), *History of Medicine in Louisiana*, II, 342, 445–50; New Orleans *Daily Picayune*, September 28, 1873, February 6, 1877; H. H. Donald, *The Negro Freedman*, 161; Coulter, *The South During Reconstruction*, 262–63.

had the state buy vaccine, distribute it to physicians, and pay the physicians fifty cents for each vaccination. This bill never became law, and the disease continued to kill and disfigure throughout the Reconstruction years and afterward. The means of preventing smallpox was known, and it had been known for many years, but even some reputable physicians denied that cowpox vaccine was effective.[54]

The *Nation* noted in November, 1866, that cholera had "at last reached our shores."[55] This publication was far behind the event, because Asiatic cholera had been raging in Louisiana for months. A few cases appeared among freedmen in July, and during the first week of August, 29 deaths were reported in New Orleans; before the end of the month 569 people were dead of cholera in the Crescent City. From New Orleans the dread symptoms spread out over the city's trade routes, striking in Concordia Parish and the valley of the Red River. Baton Rouge was spared in August, but in September the pestilence appeared; at its height it killed 20 people between sunset and sunrise on September tenth and eleventh. Thereafter there was a decline. Over the whole state there were 456 deaths in September, 166 in October, 47 in November, and only 26 in December. The epidemic had not quite run its course, however. It attracted little attention until the yellow fever epidemic of 1867 was over, but in November, 1867, cholera killed 234 people in New Orleans, and in December 210 more. Thereafter the state had six years of respite.

On February 8, 1873, a German sailor on the levee at New Orleans, working at unloading a ship, collapsed at 2:00 P.M. He died at 9:00 A.M. the next morning. Two more people died of cholera before February was over, 16 more in March, 90 in April, and 125 in May. Before the end of 1873, 259 victims were counted in New Orleans. In April the disease was prevalent upriver in St. James and Ascension parishes. On a plantation in St. James, thirty-five white laborers contracted the pestilence, and every one of them perished. A number of black families, father, mother, and children, were completely wiped out. West of New Orleans, Thibodaux and Raceland suffered greatly, and to the

54 Duffy (ed.), *History of Medicine in Louisiana*, II, 437; Baton Rouge *Weekly Advocate*, February 24, 1866; New Orleans *Daily Picayune*, July 23–24, 1866, January 11, March 22, May 31, 1870, February 16, 1871, February 17, March 27, 1877.
55 *Nation*, I (November 9, 1866), 577.

north about sixty people died in Monroe. This was, however, the last major cholera epidemic to strike Louisiana.[56]

Yellow fever, which had stayed away from New Orleans during the war, returned in 1867. As compared to 1873 in Shreveport or 1878 in New Orleans, the epidemic of 1867 was mild, but it was terrible enough. During August there were seventy-two deaths in New Iberia, and seventy-five other cases were under treatment. New Orleans newspapers always pretended that yellow fever did not exist until it had reached epidemic proportions, so its beginnings there in 1867 cannot be traced exactly. By early September, however, deaths in the city were running from forty to sixty per day. The *Picayune* tried to offer a word of comfort on September 14, pointing out that of thirty-nine yellow fever victims buried the previous day, only seven were Louisiana born, and only five were born elsewhere in the United States. This did not alter the fact that burials were so numerous and so hurried that an odor of human decay pervaded the neighborhood of New Orleans cemeteries. Yellow fever would make its presence known again in 1870 and 1871, but the next serious epidemic was in 1873.

The yellow fever onslaught of late summer and autumn, 1873, killed 226 people in New Orleans, but the upper Red River valley in general and Shreveport in particular suffered the worst ravages. The disease appeared in Shreveport in early September, causing an exodus from the growing little city. Eventually almost half of the residents moved out. Of the 4,500 or so who remained, 3,000 contracted yellow fever, and 759 died. Deaths ran from 10 to 30 per day, and business reached such a standstill that the beginnings of the Panic of 1873 got no notice in the local newspaper. Towns such as Mansfield, Washington, Port Barre, and Ville Platte suffered greatly. Five Catholic priests died as they sought to comfort others, and the nuns of the Convent of St. Vincent were sorely afflicted. It should be noted, however, that only one person out of four who contracted yellow fever died. The scarcity of physicians meant that most victims received no treatment. If they remained in bed and were given all the liquids they wanted, the

---

56 New Orleans *Daily Picayune*, July–December, 1866, 1867, March–July, 1873; Baton Rouge *Weekly Advocate*, August 25, September 15, 1866; Langridge, "Asiatic Cholera in Louisiana," 96–113, 118–23; Duffy (ed.), *History of Medicine in Louisiana*, II, 443–44.

chance of survival was much greater than if a medical practitioner gave the medicines most commonly used.

In 1878, as Reconstruction ended, yellow fever returned for the most disastrous epidemic in the last half of the nineteenth century. This pestilence was not, of course, confined to Louisiana; it almost depopulated Memphis, far up the Mississippi. Shreveport enforced a strict quarantine with shotguns and avoided this attack. The proportion of deaths to cases of yellow fever was low in most instances. Baton Rouge reported 2,435 cases, but only 193 deaths, and Donaldsonville had only 83 deaths out of 484 cases. In Thibodaux only 65 died out of 750 who sickened, but Morgan City lost 109 out of 586. New Orleans suffered terribly. The city became so disorganized that accurate statistics were hardly attempted, but estimates are that the city had 27,000 cases and that more than 4,000 died. This, fortunately, was to be the last major epidemic before the cause of yellow fever was discovered and effective preventive measures taken.[57]

5

The years of Reconstruction saw a radical change in that blacks ceased to be slaves and began to participate in politics, but there was no radical change in day-to-day relations between the races. Physical segregation, begun under slavery, continued and perhaps grew stronger. Those regulations of freedmen adopted in 1865 by such towns as Opelousas, Franklin, and Monroe were intended to prevent the inconvenience of contact with blacks as much as to regulate their conduct. By and large, such attitudes were shared by the white Union soldiers who were stationed in the South during Reconstruction and by northerners at home. The American Colonization Society continued to operate for a time, and, as is well known, President Lincoln long hoped that some colonization scheme could solve the American race prob-

57 New Orleans *Daily Picayune*, July–October, 1867, September–October, 1873, August–October, 1878; Duffy (ed.), *History of Medicine in Louisiana*, II, 424–30; Shreveport *Times*, September–October, 1873, July–October, 1878; Mother Hyacinth to the Daughters of the Cross at Lanbezzelec, September 19, 1873, to her brother Joseph, November 15, 1873, to her family, December 2, 1873, February 11, 1874, November 6, 1878, all in McCants (ed. and trans.), *They Came to Louisiana, passim.*

lem. He went so far as to sponsor one attempt at colonization in the Caribbean.[58]

In Louisiana there had never been any thought of permitting blacks to patronize restaurants, bars, theaters, hotels, and other public accommodations on an equal basis with whites. They did belong to the same churches, but well before the Civil War they had been relegated to some separate sitting area except in Catholic sanctuaries. Such segregation was not required by law, but it was enforced by custom and public opinion just as effectively as by law. New Orleans blacks, as noted earlier, were restricted to certain streetcars, identified by a star, and this practice was continued under the military occupation until General Sheridan ended it. In general blacks were segregated on other public carriers. A British traveler, going from Morgan City to New Orleans by rail, noted that "By law the Negro is the white man's equal, by railway company he is charged the white man's fare. Is he allowed to exercise the simplest of his rights—to travel in which car he pleases? Never."[59] In 1871 not even Lieutenant-Governor Pinchback could buy a ticket for a sleeping car on the Jackson Railroad, but in the coaches on this line blacks and whites evidently did sit in the same cars. Likewise, on steamboats, whites and blacks mingled physically, though not socially, on the decks, but any sharing of cabins was in the nature of master or mistress and servant.[60]

Evidence indicates that just as physical segregation of the two races had been increasing during the last quarter-century of slavery, it con-

58 New Orleans *Tribune,* July 30, August 17, 1865; New Orleans *Daily Picayune,* September 11, 1866; Memelo, "The Development of State Laws Concerning the Negro in Louisiana," 176; Millard Whitfield Warren, Jr., "A Study of Racial Views, Attitudes and Relations in Louisiana, 1877–1902" (M.A. thesis, Louisiana State University, 1965), 104–105; Willis Dolmond Boyd, "Negro Colonization in the Reconstruction Era, 1865–1870," *Georgia Historical Quarterly,* XL (December 1956), 360–82.
59 Dixon, *White Conquest,* II, 354.
60 Adamoli, "Letter from America," 276; New Orleans *Tribune,* January 13, August 20, November 24, 1865, May 22, 1867; McComb to Sewell, June 28, 1871, McComb to R. Pritchard, July 3, 1871, Warmoth to McComb, July 11, 1871, all in Warmoth Papers; New Orleans *Daily Picayune,* February 28, 1865, July 24, 1867; Sheridan to Grant, May 11, 1867, in *Senate Executive Documents,* 40th Cong., 1st Sess., No. 14, p. 206; Cable, *The Silent South,* 65; Reed, "Race Legislation in Louisiana," 387–88; Henry C. Dethloff and Robert R. Jones, "Race Relations in Louisiana, 1877–1898," *Louisiana History,* IX (Fall, 1968), 312–14.

tinued to increase during Reconstruction. In the towns, ghettos already were developing, although the lines were not so tightly drawn as they were to become. Any commingling of races on any sort of basis of equality was regarded as an enormity. Civil rights laws, enforced halfheartedly or not at all, made no changes in this pattern.[61]

The constitutional convention of 1864 made no provisions for increasing the civil rights of blacks, and the Black Codes enacted under that constitution made it clear that their status was considered to be far below that of white people. The Constitution of 1868 contained a strong civil rights article, but it was not until 1873, after Warmoth was out of office, that a strong statute to enforce these rights could be enacted. An earlier act of 1869 had been declared invalid insofar as it applied to interstate commerce, and state officials had made no effort to enforce it. Outside of New Orleans, there was little if any attempt on the part of blacks to exercise these rights, and in the Crescent City officials and the proprietors of places of business were usually able to ignore them. One tactic was to serve a Negro if he entered a saloon or restaurant, but to refuse to serve the white man who accompanied him.

The national Civil Rights Act of 1875 made little difference. It had been greatly weakened before passage, and it had been enacted by a lame-duck congress. Two blacks who demanded service at a Canal Street saloon were ejected by the customers. A black senator and a black tax collector did attend the St. Charles Theater without interference in September of 1875, but they were effectively isolated, and no additional instances were reported. Peter G. Deslondes, another Negro official, sued the proprietor of a saloon on Lake Ponchartrain for refusing to serve soda water to Deslondes and his wife, but no result of this suit was reported in the newspapers. Negroes had won, for a time, the right to vote and to serve on juries, but that was as far as their progress toward equality extended outside the schools.[62]

61 Shreveport *Times*, March 8, 1876; Philip A. Bruce, *The Plantation Negro as a Freeman: Observations on His Character, Condition and Prospects in Virginia* (New York, 1889), 44–60; Cable, *The Silent South*, 65; Wharton, *The Negro in Mississippi*, 129–30.
62 New Orleans *Tribune*, August 27, 1864, May 16, 1867; Reid, *After the War*, 421–22; New Orleans *Daily Picayune*, May 16, 1867, February 3, 1870, January 6, 1873, May, 1874, March–September, 1875; Copeland, "The New Orleans Press and Reconstruction," 168; *De Bow's Review*, After the War Series, IV (November,

Mixing of the blood of the two races continued during Reconstruction. This is an area in which no statistics are available, so no conclusive proof of any assertion regarding black-white sexual relations can be offered. This writer has formed a distinct opinion that the amount of miscegenation declined with the end of slavery. Certainly it is plausible to conclude that black women were in a better position to reject the advances of white men after 1865 than they had been in 1860. Probably, also, white men had fewer opportunities to make demands of black women. This is not to say that sexual contacts between the races came to an end, but the end of slavery almost certainly reduced these contacts.

Certainly miscegenation was frowned upon by society, and in 1864 it was regarded as a crime in Recorder's Court in New Orleans. In the first legislature under the constitution of 1864, a bill to permit white-black marriages was defeated by the decisive vote of fifty-seven to five, and in 1866 a bill to permit a white father to leave his property to his illegitimate black children failed to pass. In 1870 the legal ban against interracial marriages was removed, but a few such marriages, common-law or otherwise, had existed before this date. The Tensas *Gazette* reported in 1868 that one of the newly elected white Radical officials of that parish had "proved his faith by his works by marrying a colored lady."[63] A number of other marriages between white men and black women were reported. In 1867 two young white women from near Baton Rouge, eighteen and nineteen years of age, eloped with two Negro men. They were arrested in New Orleans, where it was established that intimacy had existed for two years and that one of the girls had borne a mulatto child. The women were fined ten dollars each and returned to their parents. In 1874 a marriage between a white woman and a black man was reported from the Attakapas region, but no details were given. Obviously, formal marriages between blacks and whites were few.[64]

1867), 382; Shreveport *Times*, March 18, 1873, January 4, 1876; James M. McPherson, "Abolitionists and the Civil Rights Act of 1875," *Journal of American History*, LII (December, 1965), 493–510; White, *Freedmen's Bureau in Louisiana*, 182; Reed, "Race Legislation in Louisiana," 381–82; Highsmith, "Louisiana During Reconstruction," 149; Memelo, "The Development of State Laws Concerning the Negro in Louisiana," 155–56.

63 Quoted in New Orleans *Daily Picayune*, May 21, 1868.

64 *Debates in the House of Representatives, 1864–65*, 139; New Orleans *Tribune*,

The end of slavery brought no noticeable change in the southern white's belief in white superiority and black inferiority. Emancipation was grudgingly accepted as permanent, and political equality was endured until it could be overthrown, but the Louisiana white was unwilling to make any concession toward social equality. In 1876 an editorial stated: "We forget nothing. We apologize for nothing. We simply take things as we find them and make the best of them."[65] Nor was the attitude of the Carpetbagger or Scalawag significantly different. As previously noted, Warmoth shared Louisiana social attitudes fully, and he was not greatly different from other Radicals in that respect. Even the much hated Radical superintendent of education, "Parson" Conway, believed that the destiny of American Negroes was to return to Africa and Christianize that dark continent.

Poorer whites in general and north Louisianians in particular seem to have been more outspoken in their Negrophobia than whites south of Red River, but this was only a matter of degree. The northern part of the state had been more recently settled, and there had not been time for the development of the more patriarchal attitude which existed among long-established planter families. The planter, it must be understood, was just as much a believer in white supremacy as the hill farmer. He simply did not feel the same compulsion to vocally or violently assert his supremacy.[66]

In 1866 a resident of Baton Rouge wrote: "Mrs. Nelson . . . and Mrs. Knox have Great trouble with their servants. They want to treat

May 23, 1865, November 3, 1867; New Orleans *Daily Picayune*, May 3, 1864, February 3, 1866, March 12, 20, 1867, June 18, 1868, August 15, 1874; Baton Rouge *Weekly Advocate*, October 2, 1871; Shreveport *Times*, August 28, 1875; *Southwestern Presbyterian*, September 9, 1875; *De Bow's Review*, After the War Series, IV (October, 1867), 294; Reed, "Race Legislation in Louisiana," 389; Dethloff and Jones, "Race Relations in Louisiana," 314–15.

65 New Orleans *Daily Picayune*, May 12, 1876; see also New Orleans *Daily Picayune*, November 8, 1870, June 16, 1872; Cable, *The Negro Question*, 7; May, "The Freedmen's Bureau at the Local Level," 13; Stampp, *The Era of Reconstruction*, 196; Lewinson, *Race, Class, and Party*, 27.

66 *House Miscellaneous Documents*, 42nd Cong., 2nd Sess., No. 211, p. 459; New Orleans *Tribune*, December 5, 1867; New Orleans *Daily Picayune*, September 1, 1873, January 28, 1875; Shreveport *Times*, June 8, 1875, January 6, July 28, 1876; Simkins, "New Viewpoints of Southern Reconstruction," 56; Capell Diary, December, 1866, in Capell Papers.

the Negro as of old and they won't put up with it."[67] More commonly, however, the freedman did put up with it. Undoubtedly the free Negro aristocracy of Louisiana had strong reservations concerning white supremacy, and undoubtedly, also, there were former slaves scattered throughout the state who were conscious of their worth as men and women. Nonetheless, one is forced to the conclusion that the great majority of Louisiana freedmen had been conditioned to accept the white man's evaluation of them. In fact, most of the freedmen were educationally, economically, and politically inferior. After up to six generations of slavery, they could hardly have been otherwise.

As a result the etiquette of race relations, which expressed a caste of race which transcended slavery, was little changed by emancipation. In general, "the Southern people of both races lived as quietly and as normally . . . as in any undisturbed period before or after. . . . No attempt was made to destroy white superiority. . . . The political aggressiveness of the Negroes . . . did not extend to other phases of social relations. . . . Negro officeholders . . . were known to observe carefully the etiquette of the Southern caste system."[68] This etiquette, of course, involved subordination of the black, but it had the advantage, at least in many instances, of preserving peace. Also, it often preserved genuine friendship and concern between individuals of the two races. As a result, "The social activities of both races remained relatively wholesome and happy; there was little of the misery, hatred, and repression often sweepingly ascribed to . . . [Reconstruction] by writers."[69]

---

67 Payne to Mrs. Sterrett, June 10, 1866, in Barnhart (ed.), "Reconstruction on the Lower Mississippi," 393.
68 Simkins, "New Viewpoints of Southern Reconstruction," 52.
69 *Ibid.*, 53–54; see also New Orleans *Tribune*, December 23, 1865, May 25, 1867; Baton Rouge *Weekly Advocate*, October 20, 1866; New Orleans *Daily Picayune*, January 1, 1866; Faculty Minutes, Centenary College, May 17, 1876; Minutes of the Louisiana [Methodist] Conference, January 11, 1865 (printed minutes and typescripts of minutes bound into one volume), Centenary College Library; *Southwestern Presbyterian*, October 28, 1869; *Senate Executive Documents*, 39th Cong., 1st Sess., No. 2, pp. 30–31; Woodward, *Origins of the New South*, 209; Franklin, *Reconstruction After the Civil War*, 91; Spero and Harris, *The Black Worker*, 14; New Orleans *Times*, January 3, 1867, quoted in Copeland, "The New Orleans Press and Reconstruction," 157; Reid, *After the War*, 10; Highsmith, "Louisiana During Reconstruction," 156.

6

Louisiana was far from being completely evangelized by Christian sects before the Civil War. The Catholic church was the longest-established in the state; descendants of early French and Spanish settlers; the Acadians; the Irish who had come to New Orleans during the 1840s; and many of the Germans who had arrived during the same decade—all were Catholic. Generally Catholics were found in south Louisiana; the area north of Red River was Protestant country. In addition to the white members of the Roman community, some 160,000 blacks, freedmen, and slaves, had at least been baptized as Catholics, although the majority of slaves had received only such religious instruction as the master and his family would or could give. Not enough priests were stationed in Louisiana to supply the needs of white communicants; neglect of the blacks was almost inevitable. On the other hand, the Catholic church did not formally segregate black worshippers before, during, or immediately after the Civil War. The Catholic clergy, profiting from centuries of experience, avoided conflict with the occupation authorities during the war, and yet managed to hold the loyalty of their largely rebel parishioners.[70]

The two largest Protestant denominations in Louisiana were the Methodists and the Baptists. The first Baptist church in Louisiana had been established by a free black evangelist, and the church attracted large numbers of Negro worshippers. Most of these were members of the same churches to which their masters belonged, but where slaves had a choice, they seem to have preferred the more emotional services of the Baptists or Methodists even though their masters might prefer another faith. Probably it should be noted here that most white Louisiana Christians also preferred the more emotional, and more lively, Baptist and Methodist congregations. Baptist churches emerged from the Civil War impoverished and somewhat reduced in membership, but poverty was nothing new to them, and they were quick to recoup the decline in membership.[71]

70 John T. Gillard, *The Catholic Church and the American Negro* (Baltimore, 1929), 37–38, 42; Roussève, *The Negro in Louisiana,* 108–109; Highsmith, "Louisiana During Reconstruction," 175–76; Capers, *Occupied City,* 184–85.

71 Hephzibah Church Books, II, 1858–98; Highsmith, "Social and Economic Conditions in Rapides Parish," 167; Highsmith, "Louisiana During Reconstruction,"

The Methodist churches in the South underwent the usual trials which resulted from a lost war, and they had an additional cause of complaint in the fact that many of their buildings were quite literally occupied by northern Methodists. Methodists had separated over the slavery question in the 1840s, but when New Orleans was captured, northern Methodist ministers acted on the assumption that military occupation brought southern churches back under control of the northern Methodist hierarchy. A Baton Rouge resident wrote that the Methodist sanctuary there had been wholly taken over by Negroes. "None of the good citizens ever think of going into it and lots of School Marms here go side by side with the Negroes."[72] In August of 1865 the bishops of the southern Methodist church issued a pastoral address deploring the intrusion of northerners into places of worship, and added: "While some talk of reunion of the two churches, we forewarn you of a systematic attempt . . . to disturb and if possible disintegrate and then absorb our membership individually."[73] The Louisiana Methodists did eventually regain control of their property, and few southern white Methodists ever became communicants of the northern church.

The Presbyterian and Episcopalian churches also suffered from federal occupation to some extent. Neither of these denominations had had a large membership before secession, and a great number of their communicants had been slaves. The occupiers took over Grace Episcopal Church in New Orleans almost completely; a Union chaplain served as rector, and the vestry was made up mainly of northerners. The leading Presbyterian minister in Louisiana, Benjamin F. Palmer, had been more responsible than any other man for the state's secession; his church could hardly expect preferential treatment. The Presbyterian Synod of Mississippi, which included Louisiana under its jurisdiction, asserted in 1862 from behind Confederate lines that in occupied Louisiana there was "spiritual desolation. The churches are closed, the ministers are generally fugitives, and the people of God

---

173–74; Aertker, "A Social History of Baton Rouge," 70; C. Penrose St. Amant, *A Short History of Louisiana Baptists* (Nashville, 1948), 38.

72 Payne to Mrs. Sterrett, February 18, 1865, in Barnhart (ed.), "Reconstruction on the Lower Mississippi," 390.

73 New Orleans *Daily Picayune*, August 30, 1865; see also Coulter, *The South During Reconstruction*, 333–34; Sweet, "Methodist Influence in Southern Politics," 546–47.

are left as sheep without a shepherd."[74] The Episcopalians and Presbyterians recovered their property soon after the close of hostilities, but they had lost most of their black membership, and poverty and the scarcity of clergymen hampered their efforts.[75]

Thus, though the northern Methodist church and the northern Presbyterian church came to be established in Louisiana at war's end, they were not hospitably received. The southern Presbyterians had not separated themselves from the Old School Presbyterians of the North until after the Confederacy had been established, but when the war ended, they were determined to maintain their separateness. In 1865 the general assembly warned pastors and laymen against "all members or other agents [of the northern church] who may come upon us to sow the seeds of disunion and strife."[76] The northern Methodists claimed to have at least one hundred missionaries in each southern state, but in Louisiana they made few white converts. Rejected by whites, they turned to the blacks. Their Negro membership in the South grew from 18,000 in 1864 to 88,000 in 1871. Growth in white membership came almost entirely from the border states and the Appalachian region. Congregationalism was another northern import. Before 1861 there were only two Congregational churches in all the South, but by 1879 there were twenty-seven. Fourteen of these were in or around New Orleans, and their membership was almost entirely black.[77]

74 *Minutes of the Synod of Mississippi from 1861 to 1867* (Jackson, Miss., 1880), p. 25 (microfilm in possession of Austin Presbyterian Theological Seminary, Austin, Tex.).

75 *Ibid.*, 59; Minutes, New Orleans Presbytery, October 12, 1865 (microfilm in possession of Austin Presbyterian Theological Seminary, Austin, Texas); Minutes, Red River Presbytery, September 22, 1866 (microfilm in possession of Austin Presbyterian Theological Seminary, Austin, Texas); Pastoral Letter of the [Southern] General Assembly of 1865 (microfilm in possession of Austin Presbyterian Theological Seminary, Austin, Texas); Carter and Carter, *So Great a Good*, 140, 148, 153–54; St. Amant, *Presbyterian Church in Louisiana*, 117–18; Sweet, "Methodist Church Influence in Southern Politics," 550; Ernest Trice Thompson, *Presbyterian Missions in the Southern United States* (Richmond, Va., 1934), 188; Andrew E. Murray, *Presbyterians and the Negro—a History* (Philadelphia, 1966), 148–49; White, "Freedmen's Bureau in Louisiana," 56–57.

76 *Distinctive Principles of the Presbyterian Church in the United States*, 61.

77 Sweet, "Methodist Church Influence in Southern Politics," 548; J. C. Hartzell, "Methodism and the Negro in the United States," *Journal of Negro History*, VIII (July, 1923), 313; Morrow, "Northern Methodism in the South During Reconstruction," 203–205; Drake, "American Missionary Association and the Southern Negro," 14, 123–24, 130.

Christianity was not the only religion among southern Negroes. One group had a premature belief that God was dead, but it probably did not extend into Louisiana. Voodoo was widely practiced in the state, however. In New Orleans Dr. Jean, a black immigrant from the West Indies, grew wealthy through an extensive practice among whites and blacks. Marie Laveau and Melvina Latour presided over voodoo rites in the years following the war and had great influence over the black population and some whites. Voodoo was not confined to the Crescent City. Rural Hephzibah Baptist Church refused to grant a letter of dismissal to a black member who had moved to Bossier Parish because he had been "a conguerer [*sic*] and an adulterer."[78] In 1874 there was much publicity about a voodoo ceremony scheduled to take place on the shores of Lake Pontchartrain. Crowds gathered, but the whole affair was a hoax, perhaps inspired by the saloon proprietors who did a land-office business.[79]

Insofar as religion was concerned, the most notable event of Reconstruction was the separation of blacks from the white churches. As noted, nearly all blacks who attended church as slaves attended the church to which their masters belonged. In these churches they were inferiors, under white supervision and, except in Catholic churches, almost always physically segregated either in a balcony or in some corner of the church set aside for them. When the church was Catholic, Episcopalian, or Presbyterian, all but a few of the blacks found the service unsatisfying. Even in Methodist and Baptist churches dominated by whites there frequently was not enough fervor to satisfy the suppressed black man's need for emotional arousal through words and the rhythm of music. When the chance came for them to gather together and form churches of their own, they leaped at the opportunity. It has been suggested with considerable truth that only in their own churches did the former slaves find true freedom.[80]

---

78 Hephzibah Church Books, II, July 22, 1871.
79 Swint, *Northern Teacher in the South,* 75; Highsmith, "Louisiana During Reconstruction," 171–73; New Orleans *Daily Picayune,* June 26, 1874; Blake Touchstone, "Voodoo in New Orleans," *Louisiana History,* XIII (Fall, 1972), 371–86.
80 *De Bow's Review,* After the War Series, III (February, 1867), 182; Carter G. Woodson, *The History of the Negro Church* (Washington, 1921), 167; Frazier, *The Negro in the United States,* 338–39; DuBois, *The Negro Church,* 33; Robert Moats Miller, "Southern White Protestantism and the Negro, 1865–1965," in Wynes (ed.), *The Negro in the South Since 1865,* 236–37; Gillard, *The Catholic*

Long before the Civil War two independent Negro Methodist churches, the African Methodist Episcopal Church and the African Methodist Episcopal Church Zion, had been organized by free Negroes in the North, and an African Methodist Episcopal congregation had existed in New Orleans before secession. Both denominations grew rapidly in the South after Lee's surrender, attracting more freedmen than either the northern or southern white-dominated Methodist churches. As early as February, 1865, there were at least five African Methodist Episcopal churches in New Orleans; a conference was established in March of that year, and there were more than 10,000 communicants in Louisiana by 1871. The northern Methodist church discovered that blacks objected to integrating its black and white members. A number of black congregations of this sect were served for a time by white pastors, however. The southern Methodist church had boasted of 207,000 Negro communicants in 1860, but when the general conference of this denomination met in 1866 it was discovered that only some 78,000 black members remained. To avoid additional losses, separate congregations, districts, and annual conferences were established for freedmen. In 1870 the black members made it clear that they preferred complete separation, whereupon the Colored Methodist Episcopal church was organized and two Negro bishops were consecrated. Thus the Methodists attained practically complete separation of black and white.[81]

Most freedmen in Louisiana preferred to be Baptists. As the Methodists were hesitating over what recognition should be extended to the freedmen and whether they should be set apart as a separate body,

---

Church and the American Negro, 259–61; J. G. Taylor, *Negro Slavery in Louisiana*, 133–52; Thompson, *Presbyterian Missions*, 190; Roussève, *The Negro in Louisiana*, 109.

81 Hartzell, "Methodism and the Negro," 307, 311, 313; Harry V. Richardson, *Dark Glory: A Picture of the Church among Negroes in the Rural South* (New York, 1947), 13; Morrow, "Northern Methodism in the South During Reconstruction," 208–209; New Orleans *Tribune*, February 2, May 13, 1865; W. E. Burghardt DuBois, "Reconstruction and Its Benefits," *American Historical Review*, XV (July, 1910), 781–82; Highsmith, "Louisiana During Reconstruction," 176–77; Sweet, "Methodist Church Influence in Southern Politics," 550–51; Woodson, *The Negro Church*, 168–71, 173; Eugene Portlette Southall, "The Attitude of the Methodist Episcopal Church, South, toward the Negro from 1844–1870," *Journal of Negro History*, XVI (October, 1931), 359–70; Franklin, *From Slavery to Freedom*, 305; DuBois, *The Negro Church*, 47.

the Negro Baptists were using the new freedom which made possible the enjoyment of greater democracy in the church. "Every man was to be equal to every other man and no power without had authority to interfere."[82] In Louisiana most white Baptist churches made some attempt to hold their Negro members, but under Baptist policy the freedmen could not be held against their will. A Free Mission Baptist Church, and probably others, functioned in New Orleans as early as May, 1865. The black members of Boggy Bayou Baptist Church in Caddo Parish separated themselves from the whites as early as June, 1865. This process went on, seemingly, in every Baptist church with black members; by 1871 there were three Negro Baptist Associations in the state. Louisiana's black Baptists had been represented at the African Missionary Baptist Convention in Richmond in 1868, and a state convention met in New Orleans in 1873. These black Baptists had some help from the North, mainly from northern Baptists, until after Reconstruction, but they were mainly self-supporting. It must be emphasized that the membership in the black Baptist churches was not confined to those who had been communicants of a Baptist church before the war. On the contrary, Baptist congregations included many former Catholics, Methodists, Presbyterians, and persons who had belonged to no church at all.[83]

The Episcopalian church in Louisiana had relatively few black members, and the leaders of the denomination seemingly realized the futility of attempting to hold those they had. In 1875, Episcopalian Bishop Joseph Pere Bell Wilmer said that he wanted Negroes to become "intelligent Christians—prepared to Christianize Africa after being defeated in their frantic efforts to Africanize Louisiana."[84] The southern Presbyterians made a more determined effort to retain the black members of their Louisiana churches, but to little avail.

82 Woodson, *The Negro Church*, 174–75.
83 Minute Book, Boggy Bayou Baptist Church (Caddo Parish), September, 1860, to February, 1885, June, 1865, in University of Texas Archives, provided by the late Tom Henderson Wells, Northwestern State University, Natchitoches, La.; Walter H. Brooks, "The Evolution of the Negro Baptist Church," *Journal of Negro History*, VII (January, 1922), 19–20; M. W. Warren, "A Study of Racial Attitudes in Louisiana," 109–10; New Orleans *Tribune*, May 7, 1865; Highsmith, "Social and Economic Conditions in Rapides Parish," 169; Highsmith, "Louisiana During Reconstruction," 177–79; Gillard, *The Catholic Church and the American Negro*, 35; Thompson, *Presbyterian Missions*, 191–92.
84 M. W. Warren, Jr., "A Study of Racial Attitudes in Louisiana," 105–106.

Throughout most of Reconstruction the Good Hope Church in De Soto Parish remained integrated, but in 1877, upon petition from the black majority of the membership, Good Hope became all black and a new church, Kingston, was established for the white members. Good Hope continued to get financial support from the general assembly of the southern Presbyterian church. In Shreveport black and white Presbyterians used the same building, but they did not worship together. Apparently, also, a Negro Presbyterian congregation existed in New Orleans, but it was not a member of the New Orleans Presbytery until the war had ended. Some white Presbyterian ministers continued to preach to blacks, but the Louisiana Presbytery noted as early as 1868 that "generally the African race . . . prefer preachers of their own color, and do not discriminate in regard to their qualifications in a manner common to other communities of man."[85]

The prewar Louisiana religious denominations did not prosper during Reconstruction. The Louisiana Presbytery expressed the general mood in 1868: "Every picture has its dark and bright colors, and in . . . the state of religion the dark colors seem to preponderate. Desolated fields, impoverished people and wasted fortunes meet you on the threshold—while the deep shaded background presents a scene of dead and dying churches."[86]

The Catholic church attempted to ignore Reconstruction. An attempt by the Freedmen's Bureau to have seating in the church at Opelousas put on a nonsegregated basis failed; high bids for pews by black men were ignored, and the pews were sold to whites at low prices. In 1873 a pastoral letter of the bishops of the Province of New Orleans was primarily concerned with preventing Protestant-Catholic marriages, preventing Catholics' joining the Masonic order, and urging Catholics to send their children to parochial schools. The hierarchy

---

85 Minutes, Louisiana Presbytery, VIII, March 21, 1868, Presbyterian Historical Foundation, Montreat, North Carolina (microfilm in possession of Austin Presbyterian Theological Seminary, Austin, Tex.); see also New Orleans *Daily Picayune*, January 5, 1866; Minutes, Red River Presbytery, April 28, October 19–21, 1877; B. Charles Bell, *Presbyterianism in North Louisiana to 1929* (N.p., 1930), 16–32; Thompson, *Presbyterian Missions*, 189–90, 192–95, 199–200; Bruce, *The Plantation Negro as a Freeman*, 106–107; Coulter, *The South During Reconstruction*, 338–39.

86 Minutes, Louisiana Presbytery, September 26, 1868.

was strongly opposed to public schools, and to this extent was openly opposed to Reconstruction policies.[87]

Even so, the Catholic church was growing. New churches were built at Ponchatoula, Shreveport, Loreauville, Jeanerette, and Mansura, as well as at other places during Reconstruction. Catholics were a minority, however, and the church to some extent was on the defensive. New Orleans, where the Protestant Sunday was largely ignored, continued to be thought of as the American Sodom. Protestants were, of course, delighted when a Catholic priest in Baton Rouge forsook celibacy in 1876 and married a churchwarden's daughter in an Episcopalian ceremony. It must be emphasized, however, that the Roman church continued to be the spiritual home of almost all Louisianians of Latin descent, all Irish, and many Germans. Its failure to take a stand on Reconstruction probably served it better than the Protestant denominations were served by their outright partisanship.[88]

As noted previously, northern churches which sent missionaries to the South after the war had little success with southern whites. The northern Methodist church in 1871 had 88,000 black members and 47,000 white in all the South. In Louisiana the membership of the conference which was organized in 1869 was nearly all black. This was hardly surprising when church papers as late as 1873 urged freedmen to support the Republican party. The Congregationalists had twelve churches with 995 members in 1871, but these largely died on the vine when northern financial support dried up as a result of the Panic of 1873. The northern Presbyterian church established a few congregations, including for a time two German Presbyterian churches in New Orleans, but its success was modest and, in Louisiana, short-lived.[89]

87 New Orleans *Tribune,* April 23, 1867; New Orleans *Daily Picayune,* February 24, 1873; Gillard, *The Catholic Church and the American Negro,* 145.
88 New Orleans *Daily Picayune,* October 16, 1872, May 13, 1876; Gaillardit, *L'Aristocratie en Amerique,* 153; Mother Hyacinth to her family, February 11, 1874, October 5, 1875, to her brother Joseph, February 16, 1868, in McCants (ed. and trans.), *They Came to Louisiana, passim; Southwestern Presbyterian,* November 18, 1869; Bergerie, "Economic and Social History of Iberia Parish," 86.
89 *Southwestern Presbyterian,* March 30, August 31, 1871, July 11, 1872; Sweet, "Methodist Church Influence on Southern Politics," 548; Morrow, "Northern Methodism in the South During Reconstruction," 214; Richard B. Drake, "Freed-

A false impression may be given by talk of separate denominations in rural Louisiana. In New Orleans, and to a lesser degree in Baton Rouge and Shreveport, separate denominations were served by separate sanctuaries. In the country the same building often served two or more sects, and the Sunday schools were union efforts more often than not. Doctrine usually was not compromised, but in sparsely settled areas believers seem to have felt that any Protestant service was better than no service at all. In fact, the differences in social attitudes among the various Protestant groups were minute, and although persons might make nice theological distinctions, the ordinary member was seldom concerned with doctrine beyond being for or against infant baptism and total immersion. On the other hand, each denomination built its own separate place of worship as soon as it could afford to do so.[90]

In Louisiana the southern Methodist church lost not only black members but also suffered a slight decline in white communicants during the Reconstruction years. The Baptists seem to have had more success than the Methodists, perhaps because they had more recourse to "protracted meetings" for evangelistic purposes. There was some embarrassment in 1870 when a leading preacher deserted his wife and children and fled from the state with a young widow, but this had no real effect on the growth of the church. By 1876 there were in Louisiana eighteen white Baptist associations, consisting of 289 churches with over 13,000 members served by 142 ministers. Even so, white Baptists were less than half as numerous as black Baptists. Obviously, many of the Baptist congregations were small and poor. Hephzibah Baptist Church raised only $234.75 for the support of its pastor in relatively prosperous 1871.[91]

men's Aid Societies and Sectional Compromise," *Journal of Southern History*, XXXIX (May, 1963), 182; Minutes, New Orleans Presbytery, April 9, 1868.

90 *Southwestern Presbyterian*, March 30, 1871; New Orleans *Daily Picayune*, May 15, 1877; Minutes, Red River Presbytery, October 27–29, 1870, March 30–31, April 1, 1871; Carter and Carter, *So Great a Good*, 155; Brister, "History of Pineville," 42.

91 Minutes of the New Orleans District Conference, Methodist Episcopal Church, 1869–1880, in Centenary College Library; Manuscript Minutes of the Louisiana Conference of the Methodist Episcopal Church, South, 1875–1879, in Centenary College Library; New Orleans *Daily Picayune*, November 16, 1871, January 9, 1873, March 3, May 10, June 26, 1877; Robert Henry Harper, *Louisiana Methodism* (Washington, D.C., 1949), 93–94; New Orleans *Tribune*, February 22–23,

The Presbyterian church in Louisiana dissolved its connection with the General Assembly of the Confederate States after the war ended, but it rejected all efforts of the northern Presbyterians to effect reunion. In 1877 Louisiana Presbytery (one of three in the state) urged that "fraternal relations" be deferred until the northern Presbyterians "see their way clear to comply with the terms stated by our church."[92] Obviously, the southern Presbyterians had not surrendered at Appomattox. On the other hand, ministers from the northern church were welcomed at meetings of the New Orleans Presbytery, and they were welcomed into the Louisiana organization when they had suitable letters of dismissal from northern presbyteries.

The Presbyterians suffered from a great scarcity of pastors. In 1870, Louisiana Presbytery, which extended from Baton Rouge westward to the Texas line, but did not include Bayou Lafourche, the Teche, or the Red River Valley, did not have a single minister west of the Mississippi. As late as 1880 the churches of the presbytery had a combined membership of only 991, and the average annual contribution was only $8.52. Even so, the number of Presbyterian churches was increasing. At Centerville in 1871 there was a congregation of twenty-five with no building. The church at Thibodaux had seven families. In 1878 New Orleans Presbytery, which included the city and nearly all the sugar-growing region, had over 2,000 members in the city, 361 in the country. This small number was a significant increase in country membership, and it is not without significance that expansion was along the railroads running north and west from the city. Perhaps the Presbyterians were not properly grateful to the railroads, because in addition to gambling, intemperance, and attendance at theatrical performances, they condemned Sunday rail excursions.[93]

1865; Shreveport *Times*, July 12, 1876; Hephzibah Church Books, II, August 21, 1869, February 10, 1872, May 1, 1873.

92 Minutes, Louisiana Presbytery, VIII, April 21, 1877.

93 Minutes, New Orleans Presbytery, April 12, 1862, March 9, 1864, April 10, 1868, October 13, 1869; Minutes, Louisiana Presbytery, October 15, 1866, October 1, 1870, April 17, 1875, April 21, 1877; Minutes, Red River Presbytery, April 22–24, 1880; *Reverend Dr. Bullock's Address to His Congregation at the Franklin Street Presbyterian Church, Baltimore, Giving His Reasons for Dissolving His Connection with the Old School General Assembly of the Presbyterian Church, June 12, 1866* (Baltimore, 1866), 51 (microfilm provided by Austin Presbyterian Theological Seminary, Austin, Tex.); Baton Rouge *Weekly Advocate*, February 19, 1870; Shreveport *Times*, January 14, 1871; *Southwestern Presbyterian*, April 29,

The Episcopal church followed about the same course as the Presbyterian. As the Reverend Benjamin Palmer was the Louisiana voice of Presbyterianism, Joseph Wilmer, a Virginian who became Bishop of Louisiana in 1866, was the leading spirit of Episcopalianism. Despite the ravages of war, his diocese had thirty-two clergymen by 1873. New parishes, Lake Providence, St. Joseph, Washington, and Laurel Hill among others, came into being, and outmoded parishes, such as Point Celeste and Arcola, were abolished. The total number of communicants was decreasing, however, from over four thousand in 1873 to slightly over three thousand in 1878. Like the Presbyterians, Episcopalians were concentrated in New Orleans. One out of every seven in the state belonged to the Crescent City's Christ Church.[94]

Though white churches did not thrive during Reconstruction, the picture was not altogether dark. The cornerstone of a synagogue was laid at Shreveport in 1869, and by 1871 the building was in regular use. In the latter year a Jewish society was formed at Natchitoches for the purpose of erecting a house of worship at that place. When the congregation of the Episcopal church at Thibodaux was unable to meet mortgage payments in 1876, people of all faiths gave money to prevent foreclosure. Perhaps the strongest evidence of the basic strength of religion came from Baton Rouge. A resident wrote in May of 1867 that the city "can't support a preacher there is no Presbyterian or Episcopalian and the Methodist is the only one here and he is about to starve out and I think will have to leave."[95] Yet, ten years later, the same town was said to be "overflowing with the theology" as Methodists, Episcopalians, Baptists, and Presbyterians competed with Catholics and one another.[96]

During Reconstruction years white churches made some efforts at evangelization of Negroes. The effort of the Catholic church, as it saw

1869, January 4, 1872, June 1, 1875, April 20, 1876; New Orleans *Daily Picayune,* June 28, 1874, December 7, 1877; St. Amant, *Presbyterian Church in Louisiana,* 120–21, 123, 126–29.

94 New Orleans *Daily Picayune,* April 18, 1874, November 6, 1877; Shreveport *Times,* February 12, 1876; Carter and Carter, *So Great a Good,* 148, 161, 168, 176.

95 Payne to Mrs. Sterrett, May 20, 1867, in Barnhart (ed.), "Reconstruction on the Lower Mississippi," 393.

96 New Orleans *Daily Picayune,* January 28, 1877; see also New Orleans *Daily Picayune,* August 5, 1869, April 13, 1871; Shreveport *Times,* December 17, 1871, February 12, 1876.

its black communicants disperse into Protestant congregations, was rather intensive. Almost a hundred Redemptionist priests landed in New Orleans for missionary work among the blacks of the South. Not all of them remained in Louisiana, but most did. A few parish priests attempted to convert blacks, and at least one incurred a reprimand from his bishop by urging blacks to demand civil and political rights. Most Catholics, however, lay and clerical, shared common southern attitudes toward the black man, and a Protestant newspaper was not being completely unfair when it asserted that the Roman church discovered that Negroes had souls at the same time it discovered that they had votes. To the credit of the Catholic church, however, is the fact that it made no effort to segregate black parishioners during Reconstruction. That was to come much later. Yet the Catholic missionary effort had small success. The emotional appeal of all-black Baptist and Methodist congregations was too strong.[97]

The Presbyterians and Episcopalians enjoyed no more success than the Catholics. As previously noted, the Presbyterians until 1869 attempted to hold blacks in white churches and thus under white supervision. By the time this policy was abandoned, nearly all black communicants had gone elsewhere. Resolutions declaring the necessity for missionary work among the freedmen were passed from time to time; ministers preached to black audiences occasionally; and here and there Sunday schools were conducted for black children. In Red River Presbytery there were two black candidates for the ministry; one of them died; the other apparently was never recognized as a full member of the presbytery. He served on no committees. A school for training Negro Presbyterian ministers was established at Tuscaloosa, Alabama, in 1876, and it received moral support, though very little money, from Louisiana Presbyterians. The Episcopalians established a mission church for blacks, with an ordained black deacon in charge, in New Orleans, but it had only thirty-one communicants. The most meaningful evidence of the attitude of these two churches toward the Negro is silence. Meeting after meeting of governing bodies con-

97 Shreveport *Times,* May 29, 1872; *Southwestern Presbyterian,* January 17, 1878; New Orleans *Daily Picayune,* March 31, May 22, 1872; Gillard, *The Catholic Church and the American Negro,* 34, 36–37, 85, 259–62; Highsmith, "Louisiana During Reconstruction," 174–75; Dethloff and Jones, "Race Relations in Louisiana," 315.

vened, conducted their business, then adjourned with no mention, or only perfunctory mention, of the freedmen.[98]

As noted, the Louisiana blacks who remained members of the southern Methodist church were permitted to form a separate conference. For a time some white supervision was exercised, and ministers were ordained by the white conference. Nonetheless, the minutes of the Louisiana Conference of the Methodist Episcopal Church, South, for the Reconstruction years show the same indifference to the spiritual welfare of the black that is revealed by the minutes of the presbyteries. Once the Negroes were in separate churches, the arrangement proved to be so convenient to the whites that they made no effort to change it. It must be noted, however, that some blacks continued to attend white churches until well into the twentieth century.[99]

The jealous autonomy of Baptist congregations made complete separation of white and black Baptist churches an easy, almost an inevitable, development. In 1872 the Southern Baptist Sunday School Board stopped counting Negro congregations in its reports of membership. By 1880 Negro Baptist churches in the South were no longer looked upon as belonging to the Southern Baptist Convention. There is no evidence that blacks resented this. Probably they preferred to go their own way. A few continued to adhere to white congregations. Hephzibah Church in East Feliciana Parish baptized a number of Negro women in the early 1870s, and in 1873 it excluded a black man for communing with Methodists. By 1880, however, there seem to have been no more blacks in this congregation.[100]

The black churches formed during Reconstruction, mainly Baptist

---

98 Minutes, New Orleans Presbytery, 1854–78; Minutes, Louisiana Presbytery, 1866–82; Minutes, Red River Presbytery, 1863–81; *Minutes of the Synod of Mississippi*, 1861–80 (published annually in the city of meeting); *Southwestern Presbyterian*, October 19, 1876; Carter and Carter, *So Great a Good*, 169; Bell, *Presbyterianism in North Louisiana*, 32; Thompson, *Presbyterian Missions*, 196–97; Murray, *Presbyterians and the Negro*, 145–46, 194.

99 Recommendations for Ordination, Louisiana Conference, Methodist Episcopal Church, 1868, in Centenary College Library; Minutes of Louisiana [Methodist] Conference, 1865–68, in Centenary College Library; New Orleans *Tribune*, December 28, 1865.

100 Brooks, "The Evolution of the Negro Baptist Church," 17; Kenneth K. Bailey, "Southern White Protestantism at the Turn of the Century," *American Historical Review*, LXVIII (April, 1963), 620; Alfred B. Sears, "Slavery and Retribution," *Southwestern Social Science Quarterly*, XLI (June, 1960), 10; Woodson, *The Negro Church*, 94–95, 175–76; Hephzibah Church Books, II, 1858–98.

and Methodist, became the central institution in social as well as spiritual life for black people. The church, at least as much as the plantation, became the center of social life. In Louisiana, as in most of the South, Negro communities as often as not took their name from the name of their local church. Dinners on the grounds, Sunday-school picnics, and other church-sponsored activities provided perhaps the most wholesome recreation available to the freedmen.

The black congregation was emotional in its approach to religion. An English traveler noted: "They are inclined to take Christianity in a more literal sense than their more civilized fellow Christians, who have managed to explain most of it away to their own satisfaction."[101] There was excitement in their churches. The minister considered it his duty to reach his hearers emotionally, and if he was successful, they groaned, shouted, jumped, and even danced. In short, they acted as whites had acted the length of the frontier during the Great Awakening, Presbyterians included, and as whites of the lowest social and economic level in the rural South, and in many urban areas also, behaved through the third quarter of the twentieth century.[102]

The Negro church finished the Christian evangelism which had begun during slavery times. Not every black became a good churchman, but to a far greater degree than before the Civil War the teachings of Christianity were brought to blacks on the plantation and in the town. The evangelists may have been ignorant and untutored men, but they were in earnest. Their emotional appeals were hard to resist, especially when these appeals were reinforced by social pressure from friends and family. The mushrooming growth of black churches in the last third of the nineteenth century is evidence enough of their successful missionary endeavor.

The black church was probably the most effective measure of social control over the blacks. One student concludes that the Puritanism of the black Protestant denominations took all the joy out of Negro life. A noted southern historian, on the other hand, chides the black churches because "religion had no relation to morality," and goes on

101 Campbell, *White and Black*, 129.
102 *De Bow's Review*, After the War Series, II (July, 1866), 94–95; Shreveport *Times*, June 22, 1878; Frazier, *Black Bourgeoisie*, 117; McRae, *The Americans at Home*, 357–58; Nordhoff, *The Cotton States*, 73; Highsmith, "Social and Economic Conditions in Rapides Parish," 174–75.

to point out that some blacks who attended church stole watermelons and drank whiskey.[103] No doubt this was true; it was also true that whites who attended church fornicated and embezzled. The church existed for sinners, not for perfect human beings, and it was in restraining the tendency toward evil and in strengthening the tendency toward good that the black church, like the white, served a useful social purpose.[104]

Religion was the one field in which the former slave achieved complete emancipation. No white man could oversee his religious life. The people of the church ran their own affairs. Whites may have laughed at some grotesque features of Negro worship, but they may have been secretly envious of the fervor of exhortation and response and the beauty of congregational singing. Foreign visitors and northerners otherwise hostile to Reconstruction recognized the unique nature of the black man's religious experience and its value in training black people to manage their own affairs.

Under the circumstances, it was only natural that the leadership of the Negro community should arise in the churches. The ministers were the leaders in black society, but they did not impose their leadership; on the contrary they were more often than not chosen by the congregation. As one observer noted, the ministers "are rather preachers because they are leaders than leaders because they are preachers."[105] These preachers often were political as well as religious leaders, and for this they were criticized. It is, however, difficult to see how, if they had the welfare of their people at heart, they could do other than to urge them to support the Radicals.[106] For that matter, it is doubtful if any ten black ministers were as important to the cause of Radicalism in Louisiana as Presbyterian Benjamin F. Palmer and Episcopalian Bishop Joseph Wilmer were to the cause of conservatism.

103 Coulter, *The South During Reconstruction*, 337–38.
104 Woodson, *The Negro Church*, 197, 256; Frazier, *The Negro in the United States*, 347–48; Highsmith, "Louisiana During Reconstruction," 171; H. H. Donald, *The Negro Freedman*, 112, 115; Murray, *Presbyterians and the Negro*, 139.
105 Campbell, *White and Black*, 139.
106 *Ibid.*, 129, 132–33; Nordhoff, *The Cotton States*, 73; Thompson, *Presbyterian Missions*, 194; Trustees of Mt. Zion M. C. Church to Kellogg, March 31, 1875, in Kellogg Papers; H. H. Donald, *The Negro Freedman*, 129; Ruby F. Johnston, *The Development of Negro Religion* (New York, 1954), 38–39; Frazier, *The Negro in the United States*, 542–43; Murray, *Presbyterians and the Negro*, 137–38; Highsmith, "Louisiana During Reconstruction," 168–69.

7

Louisiana had established a system of public schools on paper during
the antebellum years, but outside of New Orleans these schools were
few, far-between, and short-lived. In New Orleans, where municipal
rather than state control was exercised, the public schools were much
more successful than in the country. In 1862, when the Union occupation began, the Crescent City had eight high schools, one for boys
and one for girls in each of the municipal districts, and thirty-nine
grammar schools. The school year was almost nine months, and 16,862
pupils were enrolled. Imitating the Boston system, Butler consolidated the schools under one superintendent and appointed boards
of visitors made up of ardent Unionists. Teachers who were overly
disloyal to the Union were discharged and replaced by more loyal
men and women. It should be emphasized, however, that Butler
basically dealt with the system as it was. He apparently made no effort
to establish a school for blacks, and he certainly admitted no blacks
to the city school system.[107]

Education for freedmen received attention when Banks replaced
Butler. Would-be teachers for blacks were arriving from the North,
both in New Orleans and in the occupied areas along the Mississippi
in north Louisiana. In October, 1863, several schools were already in
existence in the Vicksburg area, and by the end of the month at least
seven were in operation in Louisiana. After thus testing the water,
Banks plunged in by issuing a general order in March, 1864, which
established a board of education for the Department of the Gulf with
the purpose of providing basic education for freedmen. A tax on both
real and personal property financed these schools. The board reported
ninety-five schools in operation in December, 1864, with 162 teachers
and almost 10,000 pupils. During this early period, blacks displayed a
pathetic belief in the power of education. Grandfathers and grand-
mothers, fathers and mothers, joined the children in school, some

107 Raleigh A. Suarez, "Chronicle of a Failure: Public Education in Antebellum Louisi-
ana," *Louisiana History,* XII (Spring, 1971), 109–22; Leon Odom Beasley, "A
History of Education in Louisiana During the Reconstruction Period, 1862–1877"
(Ph.D. dissertation, Louisiana State University, 1957), 49–50, 56; White, *Freed-
men's Bureau in Louisiana,* 166–69; Capers, *Occupied City,* 186–87; Doyle,
"Nurseries of Treason," 161–79; Caskey, *Secession and Restoration,* 51–52; Thomas
H. Harris, *The Story of Public Education in Louisiana,* 23–24.

simply hoping to learn to read the Bible, others with more secular ambitions.[108]

In July, 1865, when the Freedmen's Bureau took control of schools for freedmen in Louisiana, there were 126 schools, 230 teachers, and some 19,000 pupils. Most of these were in or near New Orleans, but some black children were in classes in Baton Rouge. A number of northerners visited the New Orleans schools at the end of the war, and their reports were generally favorable. Whitelaw Reid, perhaps the most acute of these observers, noted that the quality of the school varied directly with the quality of the teacher. The teachers were mostly white, and mostly southern, but there were some blacks, and a few from the North. The apparent success of the schools in New Orleans was not matched in the country parishes. In the country, freedmen's schools were opposed by Catholics who objected to public education in general, by some Negro preachers, and by a large number of whites who did not believe in education of any kind for blacks. Some planters who favored black education in principle were alienated by the tax they had to pay. Teachers of freedmen had an especially hard time. At best they could expect social ostracism. At worst they might encounter violence. One planter who had two women teachers from the North quartered in his house by military order was reported to have sent his family away, "and then turned his home into a sort of bawdy-house that presented scenes which these ladies could not witness and to which they were invited to participate. Thus compelling the ladies to move [sic]."[109] It should be noted that while schools for blacks were flourishing, schools for whites were having the opposite experience. By 1864 attendance at the New Orleans public schools had decreased to about 12,500 students.[110]

The provision of education for black children in the South is often

108 J. L. M. Curry, *Education of the Negroes Since 1860* (Baltimore, 1894), 9–10; Eaton, *Grant, Lincoln and the Freedmen*, 194–95; Murray, *Presbyterians and the Negro*, 23, 26; H. H. Donald, *The Negro Freedman*, 98; DuBois, *Black Reconstruction*, 158; Doyle, "Nurseries of Treason," 175–76; Engelsmen, "Freedmen's Bureau in Louisiana," 192; Banks, *Emancipated Labor*, 10–11.

109 New Orleans *Tribune*, September 13, 1864.

110 *Ibid.*, December 2, 1864; White, *Freedmen's Bureau in Louisiana*, 169–71; Reid, *After the War*, 246–55; Betty Porter, "The History of Negro Education in Louisiana," *Louisiana Historical Quarterly*, XXV (July, 1942), 739–42; Caskey, *Secession and Restoration*, 144; Engelsmen, "Freedmen's Bureau in Louisiana," 193; Beasley, "Education in Louisiana During Reconstruction," 59.

considered one of the Freedmen's Bureau's greatest accomplishments. Unfortunately, however, congressional appropriations for the bureau were never enough to pay for the educational program. In Louisiana some income was derived from property seized from Confederates, but President Johnson's pardons quickly dried up this source of funds. The tax which the military had levied on property for educational purposes brought in perhaps $40,000 in 1865, but property owners complained so bitterly of this tax that General Fullerton cancelled it in November, 1865. Since the cost of freedmen's schools was almost twenty thousand dollars a month, it was necessary to close the schools as of January 31, 1866. This brought an outcry from those who favored black education. General Baird attempted to restore the tax, but his action was vetoed by President Johnson upon request of the Louisiana legislature. Raffles, contributions, entertainments, and like activities, primarily by the free Negro class of New Orleans, raised some money, but not nearly enough. There was considerable doubt that the black schools would be able to open in the fall of 1866.[111]

Forbidden to tax, General Baird resorted to a tuition system. In the towns, black parents paid $1.00 per month tuition per child for primary education, $1.50 per month for higher grades. In the country a 5 percent payroll charge was collected, first on all Negroes, then only on those with children in school. Blacks objected to this levy, and it brought in too little money for the work to be done. A significant decline in black enrollment followed. The Freedmen's Bureau was relieved of a significant part of its burden in autumn, 1867, when the New Orleans School Board took over the Freedmen's Bureau schools in the city and administered them as part of the public school system.[112]

Probably the most important factor in keeping the bureau schools in operation, even before 1866, was the help given by the various freedmen's aid societies sponsored by northern churches. These so-

111 New Orleans *Tribune*, November 3, 1865; Franklin *Planters' Banner*, September 3, 1865, quoted in New Orleans *Daily Picayune*, September 29, 1865; *Nation*, II (March 8, 1866), 305; Skinner, *After the Storm*, II, 79; Franklin, *Reconstruction After the Civil War*, 38; Engelsmen, "Freedmen's Bureau in Louisiana," 194–96, 200; Curry, *Education of Negroes Since 1860*, 13; Bentley, *The Freedmen's Bureau*, 171–72; *Senate Executive Documents*, 39th Cong., 2nd Sess., No. 6, p. 74; Porter, "Negro Education in Louisiana," 743–45.
112 White, *Freedmen's Bureau in Louisiana*, 176.

cieties, especially the American Missionary Association of the Congregational Church, the Methodist Freedmen's Aid Society, the northern Presbyterian church, and the Free Mission Baptist Church, provided some financial help. Their main contribution, however, was in providing teachers. Many of these teachers were from the North, but a surprising number were southern "schoolmarms." Usually the bureau provided a building and the charitable associations provided a teacher, but the federal agency and the societies worked so closely together that it is often impossible to distinguish the effort of one from that of the other. No separate figures are available for Louisiana, but between 1868 and 1870 in the whole South the bureau spent $3,521,934 for Negro education, the aid societies spent $1,572,287, and the freedmen themselves provided $78,700. In Louisiana the system was fairly successful. In October, 1867, the bureau reported 246 Louisiana schools with 8,435 students under its supervision. In 1870, just before the Radical state government took over most education, the bureau reported 404 day and night schools with 467 teachers and over 17,000 pupils. In addition there were 136 Sunday schools with 266 teachers and 7,088 pupils.[113]

Between 1864 and 1870 the Union army and then the Freedmen's Bureau and northern aid societies sought to make up for two centuries of deliberate neglect in the education of southern blacks. Because this effort did not succeed in bringing former slaves up to the educational level of their former masters, it is sometimes spoken of as a failure. It is a fact, of course, that their schools reached only a fraction of black youth; that many teachers were incompetent and that others were more interested in teaching "loyalty" than in imparting the three R's; that many blacks became disillusioned when a

113 W. A. Durant to "Cousin Hal," December 19, 1867, in Slack Family Papers; Woodson, *The Negro Church*, 188–89; Morrow, "Northern Methodism in the South During Reconstruction," 206; Engelsmen, "Freedmen's Bureau in Louisiana," 195, 202–203; Beasley, "Education in Louisiana During Reconstruction," 104; *House Executive Documents*, 41st Cong., 2nd Sess., VI, No. 142, p. 24; Murray, *Presbyterians and the Negro*, 132–33, 164, 170; Swint, *Northern Teacher in the South*, 94–101, 131–32, 141; Porter, "Negro Education in Louisiana," 745–46; Bentley, *The Freedmen's Bureau*, 64, 87, 172–74; H. H. Donald, *The Negro Freedman*, 97; Thomas H. Harris, *The Story of Public Education in Louisiana*, 40; Drake, "Freedmen's Aid Societies and Sectional Compromise," 176–77; Drake, "American Missionary Association and the Southern Negro," 156.

smattering of learning did not lead from the cotton patch or the cane field to a better life; that Congress was stingy almost beyond belief in providing funds for the education effort. It is a fact that seventy-five southern Negroes in every hundred were still illiterate in 1880, but it is also a fact that this was a *23 percent increase* in literacy since 1865. Obviously much had been accomplished in the rudiments of education. It was even more important, however, that the idea of black education had become so widely accepted that it could not be destroyed.[114]

The constitution of 1864 provided for the education of children at public expense, but the makers of the constitution thought only of white children when they included this provision. It would be three years before the city of New Orleans took over responsibility for black schools in the city, and almost four years before the state government accepted responsibility for black education. Indeed, the dominant whites of Louisiana had strong reservations concerning public education in general. The idea of compulsory education was indignantly rejected, and state appropriations for public education amounted to only $250,000 in 1866, only $257,000 in 1867. In his 1865 message to the legislature, Governor Wells advocated the abolition of public education outside New Orleans. Wells would later change his tune, but only after he had turned to the Radical point of view.[115]

In 1864 there were nine thousand children in the New Orleans public schools, a considerable increase over the previous year. By February, 1865, the total enrollment was over ten thousand, of whom 338 were in secondary schools. In August of 1865 a city school board of twenty-four members was established, and $250,000 was appropri-

114 *Senate Executive Documents*, 39th Cong., 2nd Sess., No. 6, pp. 75–76; White, *Freedmen's Bureau in Louisiana*, 195–96, 199–200; Porter, "Negro Education in Louisiana," 739; May, "The Freedmen's Bureau at the Local Level," 12; Engelsmen, "Freedmen's Bureau in Louisiana," 203; Highsmith, "Louisiana During Reconstruction," 184–85; Carter, *The Angry Scar*, 188–89.
115 Memelo, "The Development of State Laws Concerning the Negro in Louisiana," 178–79; Highsmith, "Louisiana During Reconstruction," 103; Harris, *The Story of Public Education in Louisiana*, 24–25; New Orleans *Tribune*, November 30, 1865; New Orleans *Daily Picayune*, January 26, 1866; *Debates in the House of Representatives, 1864–1865*, 190–94, 358–59; *Acts of Louisiana, 1866*, 224; *Acts of Louisiana, 1867*, 223–35; Beasley, "Education in Louisiana During Reconstruction," 87.

ated for schools. These schools did not reach nearly all white children. It was estimated in June, 1866, that two thousand white boys and girls of school age were attending no school at all. Negro children were in Freedmen's Bureau schools, or one of the very few private schools for blacks, if they were in any.

If the attitude of white Louisianians toward public education for whites was ambivalent, the attitude toward Negro education was decidedly hostile. Carl Schurz concluded, after hearing men acknowledge the need for Negro education but strongly oppose any tax support for it, that opposition to the education of blacks was as strong as it had been under slavery. Probably this was not altogether true. After 1865 there were a few whites willing to see freedmen in school, but there were practically none willing to pay for it. Acts of the legislature pertaining to public schools specified that these schools were for white children only. The state superintendent of education elected in 1865, Robert M. Lusher, made no attempt to conceal his opposition to education for Negro children.[116]

As noted, the New Orleans Board of Education decided that it should provide, or at least administer, schools for black children in the fall of 1867. This was after passage of the Military Reconstruction Acts, and the probable motivation of the board was to prevent the establishment of racially mixed schools. Two schools, one for boys and one for girls, were opened in October, and in November the Freedmen's Bureau schools were taken over by the city. There were an estimated ten thousand black children of school age in New Orleans, but provision was made for no more than five thousand of them. The board of education justified this by pointing out that none of the existing schools for blacks was crowded and by suggesting that the novelty of education had worn off insofar as the Negro population was concerned. Whether or not this was true, there were only about two thousand black pupils in New Orleans schools in December, 1867.[117]

116 *Senate Executive Documents,* 39th Cong., 1st Sess., No. 2, p. 25; *Acts of Louisiana, 1867,* 61, 203; *Debates of the Senate of Louisiana, 1864,* 193; White, *Freedmen's Bureau in Louisiana,* 185–86; Beasley, "Education in Louisiana During Reconstruction," 91–92; Memelo, "The Development of State Laws Concerning the Negro in Louisiana," 10.

117 New Orleans *Daily Picayune,* November 9, 1864, February 15, 1865, June 5,

In the rural parishes it could almost be said that there were no public schools during the period of presidential Reconstruction. In 1865, in all the country parishes, there were about five thousand white children attending school, but almost none of these schools was tax-supported. A Freedmen's Bureau official declared in 1868 that outside of New Orleans educational opportunities for black children were better than for poor white children. A Houma newspaper declared in 1866 that "not a single white child in . . . [Terrebonne] Parish . . . has learned to read and write . . . at the public schools."[118] Superintendent Lusher said that the situation in the country was almost hopeless insofar as education was concerned, but he opposed any tax on planters to improve it. Obviously, outside of New Orleans, public education lacked influential support.[119]

The advent of Radical government in Louisiana brought increased support for the idea of public education for all, though it would be difficult to prove that there was a great increase in accomplishment. The constitution adopted in 1868 required at least one public school in each parish, and ruled further that these schools were to be open to children of both races. The first legislature under the new constitution set up an administrative system, probably on some northern model, much better suited to a thickly settled area than to the thinly populated rural parishes of Louisiana. Each police jury ward was to be a separate school district. The parishes were authorized to levy a school tax to be distributed to the wards in addition to the fund provided from state taxes. The administration provided was topheavy for the limited facilities to be administered; it was simplified somewhat in 1874, but it continued to be unrealistic. In practice the state superintendent of education, subject to the political power of the governor, gave the public schools such little direction as they received. Local

---

1866, August 13, September 6, 17, 1867; New Orleans *Tribune*, July 24, 1867; Kendall, *History of New Orleans*, I, 298, 320; Porter, "Negro Education in Louisiana," 751; Beasley, "Education in Louisiana During Reconstruction," 108–109; White, *Freedmen's Bureau in Louisiana*, 180–81.

118 Houma *Civic Guard*, quoted in New Orleans *Daily Picayune*, September 12, 1866.

119 Baton Rouge *Weekly Advocate*, May 26, December 8, 1866; Report of the Superintendent of Education, in *Legislative Documents, 1865*; Daspit, "Governors' Messages," 41; Aertker, "A Social History of Baton Rouge," 78–79; Thomas H. Harris, *The Story of Public Education in Louisiana*, 29; White, *Freedmen's Bureau in Louisiana*, 183–84; Brister, "History of Pineville," 37–38.

police juries and school boards demonstrated little interest in the schools beyond their use for patronage.[120]

A few Radical leaders, white and black, sought to make school attendance compulsory. Thomas Conway, the first Radical superintendent, recommended compulsory attendance for children between the ages of eight and fourteen in 1868, but to no avail. J. Henri Burch proposed such a measure in 1876. Opposition seems to have been caused by fear of high costs on the one hand and fear of the compulsory mixing of the races on the other. When the idea was advanced in 1868, the *Picayune* tearfully protested "Tearing the infant from its mother's arms to educate it . . . no matter what the mother's anguish, or her desire to keep her little girl as solace for the last months of a life which may be slowly fading."[121]

The state levied a two mill school tax which produced less than $500,000 a year. New Orleans paid more than 70 percent of this tax, and got back little more than 30 percent. The state funds were distributed on the basis of educable children. In 1870, out of a total of $315,778 distributed, St. Landry Parish received $16,592 and Terrebonne $13,086. At the other end of the scale, Winn Parish received only $2,279, and St. Charles was granted only $2,101. The face value of the distribution increased in subsequent years, but inasmuch as state paper depreciated so rapidly, it is doubtful that the amount distributed increased in terms of United States currency. In theory, the monies disbursed by the state were to be supplemented by local tax revenues, but in practice the police jury usually did not levy a tax; if it did, the tax collector did not collect it. In 1874 Governor Kellogg stated that at least $1,500,000 was needed to operate the school system, that not more than half this amount was available, and that much of the money allocated to the parishes had been wasted. Radical school superintendent W. G. Brown thought that more than $1,500,000 was needed. After the panic which began in 1873 made itself felt, there were no state funds from January to September, 1874,

---

120 *Acts of Louisiana, 1868–1869*, 175–89; *Acts of Louisiana, 1874*, 215–16; Thomas H. Harris, *The Story of Education in Louisiana*, 32–35, 47–48; Porter, "Negro Education in Louisiana," 229.
121 New Orleans *Daily Picayune*, August 23, 1868; see also New Orleans *Daily Picayune*, February 7, 1874, February 10, 1876; Porter, "Negro Education in Louisiana," 754; Copeland, "The New Orleans Press and Reconstruction," 229.

and most schools remained closed. In a few isolated instances parents, white or black, raised enough money to keep a community school in operation until state funds became available.[122]

As could be predicted, teachers suffered second only to children from inadequate financing. In 1866 a large amount owed them for the previous year was yet unpaid in March. In 1869 teachers in New Orleans were four months behind in pay even though they were paid in depreciated city notes. Newspapers reported the teachers unpaid again in 1871, and in 1874, when most country schools were closed, New Orleans teachers kept the city schools open by dropping five months behind in their pay. Since the salaries ranged from less than fifty dollars to considerably under a hundred dollars per month, and since the payment was in depreciated state or city paper which had to be discounted substantially before it could be spent, a rule that women and blacks should receive the same pay as white men guaranteed only equal poverty.[123]

Obviously, lack of funds was not the only problem of the public schools during the years of Radical control. The greatest handicap was the constitutional and legislative requirement that the schools be open to children of both races. In many rural parishes this law was ignored, but where offices were held by Radicals determined to enforce the law, white parents simply would not send their children to school. White parents objected to black teachers as much as they objected to black children. In a few parishes black and white parents reached an accommodation, usually on the basis of one school, or one room, for whites, another for blacks, and when this was done the schools were more successful in reaching children who needed schooling.[124]

122 New Orleans *Daily Picayune*, December 21, 1870, August 25, 1871, August 30, 1872, March 21, 1874; Gonzales, "William Pitt Kellogg," 481; Thomas H. Harris, *The Story of Public Education in Louisiana*, 35–36, 44–45, 51, 60; Beasley, "Education in Louisiana During Reconstruction," 205–206; Bergerie, "Economic and Social History of Iberia Parish," 75–76.

123 *Senate Reports*, 44th Cong., 2nd Sess., No. 501, II, p. 1,477; Baton Rouge *Weekly Advocate*, March 31, 1866; New Orleans *Daily Picayune*, April 10, 1870, December 12, 1871; Schuler, "Women in Public Affairs During Reconstruction," 706–707.

124 B. Sears to Robert C. Winthrop, January 8, 1874, in J. L. M. Curry, *A Brief Sketch of George Peabody and a History of the Peabody Education Fund through Thirty Years* (Cambridge, Mass., 1898), 65; James A. Gla to William G. Brown, July 7,

Louisiana whites objected to public schools on grounds other than racial mixing. Many white taxpayers resented having to pay taxes used for Negro education. Others, with some reason, objected that the schools as operated were a part of the Radical political organization. The textbooks used were published in the North and often presented a point of view objectionable to southerners. When a state official attempted to organize a school at St. Martinville, the mayor informed him that the people of that village did not obey any law enacted by the Radical legislature. Last, but certainly not least, the Catholic clergy were opposed to all public education. A few Louisiana whites told questioners that they accepted the principle of public education for all so long as the schools were segregated, but probably many of them were telling northerners what they thought the yankees wanted to hear.[125]

Another handicap faced by the schools was the low quality of many teachers and administrators. Warmoth damned "young men . . . ignorant of the rudiments of English or other education, [who] foisted themselves upon the school boards."[126] Normal schools and special teacher institutes sought to remedy this condition, and they no doubt succeeded in part. Black teachers, in general, were less prepared than whites for their task.[127]

Not all Louisiana parents were interested in sending their children to school. Poverty was one reason—poor farmers, black and white, needed whatever labor their children could perform during most of the growing and harvest seasons. The state sought to help by pro-

1876, in Kellogg Papers; New Orleans *Daily Picayune*, January 31, February 4, December 27, 1871; Brister, "History of Pineville," 38; Highsmith, "Social and Economic Conditions in Rapides Parish," 122; Aertker, "A Social History of Baton Rouge," 79–80; James William Mobley, "The Academy Movement in Louisiana," *Louisiana Historical Quarterly*, XXX (July, 1947), 838–39; Schuler, "Women in Public Affairs During Reconstruction," 710; Edwin Lewis Stephens, "Education in Louisiana in the Closing Decades of the Nineteenth Century," *Louisiana Historical Quarterly*, XVI (January, 1933), 46–47.

125 New Orleans *Daily Picayune*, October 17, 1871; Nordhoff, *The Cotton States*, 50; Avary, *Dixie After the War*, 305; Highsmith, "Louisiana During Reconstruction," 370–72; 374–75; Porter, "Negro Education in Louisiana," 761, 766–77.

126 Daspit, "Governors' Messages," 41–42.

127 Porter, "Negro Education in Louisiana," 756–59; Lonn, *Reconstruction in Louisiana*, 356–57; Highsmith, "Louisiana During Reconstruction," 375–78.

viding some free textbooks, but this made little difference. Teachers noted that illiterate parents thought that their children had learned enough when they acquired the bare rudiments of reading and writing. In St. Landry Parish, for example, there were several public schools attended by white children only, but nonetheless, according to Robert M. Lusher, in 1875 there were hundreds of white children who were completely illiterate and who were attending no school whatsoever.[128]

Last, but certainly not least, the fact that the schools were pawns in politics damaged their effectiveness as well as preventing their acceptance. Calcasieu Parish, according to one chronicler, had 2,536 children of school age in 1869 but had no public school at all. This was remedied the next year, however. In Natchitoches Parish a black Republican state senator, reportedly illiterate himself, dominated the school board and had himself appointed as a teacher. Then he did nothing to earn the salary he collected. About one hundred teachers in New Orleans lost their jobs in 1875, but their refusal to accept black students might well be interpreted as insubordination. It is significant, however, that black as well as white parents were reported as complaining of political debasement of the schools.[129]

Without question there was much stealing of school funds in Louisiana during Radical Reconstruction. Thomas Conway himself agreed to restore some two thousand dollars which could not be accounted for after his term as state superintendent had ended. By 1873, according to Superintendent Brown, school funds had been misappropriated in St. Tammany, Tangipahoa, Plaquemines, Caddo, and St. James parishes. One parish treasurer took the school funds to New Orleans and invested them in merchandise; teachers had to do without their pay until the merchandise had been sold. School directors at Morgan City informed Brown that the local treasurer "has left for

128 New Orleans *Daily Picayune*, August 31, 1875; Marchand, *The Flight of a Century*, 170–85; Annual Report of the Superintendent of Education for the Year 1871, in *Legislative Documents, Louisiana, 1872* (New Orleans, 1872); Porter, "Negro Education in Louisiana," 766.
129 Nordhoff, *The Cotton States*, 72–73; New Orleans *Daily Picayune*, February 10, 1871, September 12, 1875, April 19, 1876; Lestage, "The White League," 651; Theodore John Ratliffe, "The Life and Service to Public Education of John McNeese" (M.A. thesis, Louisiana State University, 1933), 4.

parts unknown," leaving the school-fund books out of balance by some $622.95.[130] G. W. Foster, tax collector for Jefferson and Orleans parishes, made away with several thousand dollars in school money, leaving his books in such disarray that no one was ever able to tell exactly how much was missing. The greatest publicity was given to the supposed embezzlement of $31,000 in school funds by Dave Young, Negro state senator from Concordia Parish. Another black school board member and state legislator, accused of soliciting contributions from teachers whose appointments he had obtained, pleaded before a congressional investigating committee that he was insane. Perhaps the champion of all school fund embezzlers, however, was white state senator T. C. Anderson of St. Landry Parish, who was accused of making away with $85,000. Certainly the stealing of school money by Radical politicians greatly reduced the effectiveness of Radical efforts to provide free public education for all the children of the state.[131]

Too much attention given to opposition and to corruption in the school system can result in neglect of real educational accomplishments. Before 1870, schools outside of New Orleans were few indeed. It was in that year that the first public school was opened in Donaldsonville. Fourteen months later Ascension Parish had twelve tax-supported schools with seventeen teachers and from fifty to seventy-five pupils per school. In 1872 about eleven hundred pupils were attending public schools in Lafourche Parish; a year earlier newly created Iberia Parish boasted eleven public schools. According to one account, there were only one hundred public schools in the state in 1868, eleven times that many in 1872. In 1874 there were an estimated 280,387 educable children in the state, of whom 74,309 were enrolled in public schools. Total public school revenues were $789,069, or about $11.00 per child enrolled. Obviously, at this per capita expenditure, the school terms were short, but when attendance at private schools is taken into consideration, it is clear that more than half of the children in Louisiana were exposed to some degree of education. Furthermore, in spite of complaints that the law in effect prevented

130 Porter, "Negro Education in Louisiana," 758.
131 New Orleans *Daily Picayune*, February 5, 1875, February 8, 1876, April 13, 1877; Shreveport *Times*, July 20, 1877; Porter, "Negro Education in Louisiana," 757–58; Lonn, *Reconstruction in Louisiana*, 356; White, "Freedmen's Bureau in Louisiana," 33–34.

white children's attending school, there were always more white than black children in the public schools during Radical Reconstruction. The Radical school system was not a good one by modern standards, but it was better than the "Redeemers" would provide for many years after Reconstruction ended.

In a state where, in 1874, three fourths of all voters were illiterate, every bit of effort expended on education was certainly worth its cost. It is significant that the Bourbons, who probably would have been happy to end all public education, and who certainly would have liked to halt Negro education, did not dare to do so. Too firm a foundation had been established during the Radical years.[132]

An account which dealt only with public schools would give a false impression of education in Louisiana. The large Catholic minority had always preferred parochial schools. The fact that New Orleans was a prosperous urban center and that planters and merchants could afford to send their children to private schools had created a tradition which emphasized parochial and private education. During the war, nonpublic schools suffered, but it is estimated that there were 140 such schools in New Orleans in 1864, enrolling almost 5,000 pupils. Before the end of Reconstruction there were 222 private schools in the city, boasting 666 teachers and 19,401 pupils. No firm figures are available for nonpublic schools in the country parishes, but 125 is a fair estimate, with over 7,000 students before the end of Reconstruction. In Baton Rouge, for example, private schools reopened in 1865, and they bore the main burden of educating the town's white children during and after Reconstruction.[133]

Parochial schools played a large part in the system of nonpublic education. It was said in 1869 that every Catholic church above Canal Street in New Orleans had a school attached, as did most of those below. Thibodaux College and the Mt. Carmel Convent School at

132 King, *The Great South*, 97; *Legislative Documents, 1869–1877*; New Orleans *Daily Picayune*, June 25, 1870, May 5, September 29, 1872, November 22, 1874; Nordhoff, *The Cotton States*, 72; Marchand, *The Flight of a Century*, 168; Thomas H. Harris, *The Story of Public Education in Louisiana*, 42–44, 52; Bergerie, "Economic and Social History of Iberia Parish," 75; Porter, "Negro Education in Louisiana," 765–66; Brister, "History of Pineville," 57; Beasley, "Education in Louisiana During Reconstruction," viii, 152, 205.

133 Capers, *Occupied City*, 185–90; Beasley, "Education in Louisiana During Reconstruction," 59, 118–22, 152; Aertker, "A Social History of Baton Rouge," 76–77.

Thibodaux flourished during the 1870s, and "the brothers" school at
New Iberia was able to add a "commercial" department in 1872.
Parishioners of the Catholic Church of St. John in Iberville Parish
organized a stock company to finance a parochial school. The total
number of parochial schools in any year has not been determined,
but of secondary schools alone there were twenty-five in the state
during Reconstruction, nine of which were in New Orleans. Not all
parochial schools prospered. In north Louisiana, the survival of Catholic schools was doubtful, to say the least. The Daughters of the Cross
opened a school at Shreveport in 1860 and one at Monroe in 1866.
Before the end of the 1860s they were operating schools in Avoyelles
Parish, Rapides, and at Ile Brevelle, but the last two named closed in
the 1870s, as did a school in Natchitoches operated by the Order of
the Sacred Heart. The letters of Mother Hyacinth of the Daughters
of the Cross tell a fascinating story of the struggle for Catholic education in the Protestant regions of Louisiana.[134]

Protestant denominations sponsored a few schools for white children in Louisiana. It is difficult to say how many, because most were
short-lived and because it is impossible to determine whether or not
some of them were church-sponsored. Often a school was operated
by a Protestant pastor as a private venture on his part. A church-
sponsored school operated in Baton Rouge in 1866, and Episcopal-
sponsored schools for girls existed in Houma, Franklin, and New
Iberia in 1872. The Protestant German churches in New Orleans supported schools rather than have the children of their congregations
attend the unpopular "Radical" public schools. The Presbyterians
argued for church schools because of public school integration, because the books in use corrupted children by giving them a biased
yankee viewpoint of the Civil War, because children from Christian
homes were mixed with the disorderly and corrupt, because Presbyterians had an obligation to educate their own, and because the
public schools were "Godless." The Presbyterians did not act on these
principles to any great extent, however.[135]

134 *New Orleans Daily Picayune,* August 11, 1869, August 7, September 20, November 8, 28, 1872; Somers, *The Southern States Since the War,* 218; Mobley, "The
Academy Movement in Louisiana," 937–38; McCants (ed. and trans.), *They
Came to Louisiana,* 181, 211, *passim.*
135 New Iberia *Sugar Bowl,* quoted in New Orleans *Daily Picayune,* August 30, 1872;

Nonpublic schools for blacks also functioned. Three advertised for pupils in New Orleans as early as 1865. Most such schools were sponsored by freedmen's aid societies of various northern churches. Originally the sponsoring agencies planned for integrated schools, but in practice they attracted only black students. These schools were so closely identified with those of the Freedmen's Bureau that it is impossible to isolate them. Often, as noted, the aid society provided the teacher, and the bureau provided the building. The work of these organizations dropped off drastically after 1873 when the financial panic and loss of interest by northerners combined to reduce contributions. At the same time the freedmen's interest in education was declining. These church-sponsored schools for blacks were especially disliked by southern whites. One unregenerate rebel consigned all northern Methodist preachers to the gallows and then to hell. "There is no use of a H——l," he expostulated, "if such damned rascals are not sent to it."[136]

As stated earlier, it is well-nigh impossible to distinguish between secular private schools and those sponsored by Protestant churches. Mansfield Female College was Methodist at least part of the time, but if Keachi Female Academy had any church affiliation, it has not come to light. Two seemingly secular schools competed with Catholic institutions in Opelousas. The Germans of New Orleans had some secular schools as well as those affiliated with their churches, and there were a score or more additional unaffiliated schools in the city. The formation of secular private schools received impetus from the attempts to enforce racial integration in the public schools during the 1870s. A few "commercial" schools attempted to train boys for business work. In 1872 there were fourteen free elementary schools, almost all in north Louisiana or the Florida parishes, receiving Peabody Fund money. Though the total number of secular schools at all levels is impossible to determine, it is known that during the Reconstruction

---

Payne to Mrs. Sterrett, June 25, 1866, in Barnhart (ed.), "Reconstruction on the Lower Mississippi," 393; Nau, *The German People of New Orleans*, 86–87; *Southwestern Presbyterian*, September 7, 1871.

136 Morrow, "Northern Methodism in the South During Reconstruction," 216; see also New Orleans *Tribune*, September 17, 1865; Drake, "Freedmen's Aid Societies and Sectional Compromise," 178–82; Drake, "American Missionary Association and the Southern Negro," 158; Curry, *Education of Negroes Since 1860*, 23; Swint, *The Northern Teacher in the South*, 73.

years eighty-eight academies, twenty-five of them in New Orleans, operated under Protestant or secular auspices. Probably at least half of these were secular. If there were almost fifty secular secondary schools, there must have been two hundred or more such elementary schools.[137]

The role of the Peabody Fund has received considerable attention from students of Reconstruction education in Louisiana. This fund resulted from a trust formed in 1867 by philanthropist George Peabody. The national administrator of the fund during the 1870s was Dr. Barnas Sears, who was strongly opposed to integrated schools. The Louisiana agent of the fund was segregationist Robert M. Lusher, who had been state superintendent of education during presidential Reconstruction, and who would return to that position when Francis T. Nicholls was elected governor. Reasoning that integrated public schools were by the fact really schools for black children only, Sears and Lusher decided against any support for Louisiana public schools under Radical administrations. Grants in Louisiana went instead to private schools for white children and to normal schools for white teachers. This action by the managers of the Peabody Fund received much attention from Conservative newspapers at the time, and from defenders of racial discrimination afterward, but the role of the fund should not be overestimated. From 1868 through 1876 the Peabody Fund spent a total of only $74,545 in Louisiana, a very small fraction of the state's expenditure for public schools.[138]

Agitation over mixing of the races in the schools was almost constant in Reconstruction Louisiana, but the intensity of feeling on the

137 Opelousas *Sentinel*, January 25, 1866; New Orleans *Daily Picayune*, May 24–25, 1870, August 4, 14, October 29, 1872; Shreveport *Times*, June 12, 1872; King, *The Great South*, 97; R. T. Clark, Jr., "Reconstruction and the New Orleans German Colony," 511; Beasley, "Education in Louisiana During Reconstruction," 123; Mobley, "The Academy Movement in Louisiana," 738–936; Brister, "History of Pineville," 38–39; Highsmith, "Louisiana During Reconstruction," 366–67, 385–87.

138 *Southwestern Presbyterian*, August 5, 1869; New Orleans *Daily Picayune*, September 11, 1869, March 5, April 13, September 14, 1871, August 4, 1872; Stephens, "Education in Louisiana," 47; Curry, *George Peabody and the Peabody Fund*, 61, 147; Beasley, "Education in Louisiana During Reconstruction," 190; Frazier, *Black Bourgeoisie*, 65; Drake, "American Missionary Association and the Southern Negro," 203–204; Highsmith, "Louisiana During Reconstruction," 368–69; Earle H. West, "The Peabody Fund and Negro Education, 1867–1880," *History of Education Quarterly*, VI (Summer, 1966), 3, 11, 14–16.

subject waxed and waned. Seemingly there were a few white pupils in the early Freedmen's Bureau schools, but apparently there were none after 1867. In 1866 Franklin Institute opened in New Orleans with something over one hundred students about evenly divided between blacks and children of "French" or Italian parentage. The students fought racial battles daily, and this soon ended the experiment. During 1867 the editors of the *Tribune* argued for integration of the schools, and the other newspapers of the city fulminated against it. The *Picayune* was certain that "No honest black man can desire to thrust his child into white schools,"[139] but the *Tribune* maintained that mixed schools were necessary "so that we have in the future no superior and inferior classes, but only American citizens."[140] Probably it should be noted here that immediately following the war some of the old free Negro class, not desiring to be identified with the freedmen, also opposed mixed schools.[141]

As noted previously, the constitution of 1868 provided for integrated schools, and the Education Act of 1869 implemented this provision of the constitution by stating that any school official or teacher who should "refuse to receive into any school any child . . . who shall be lawfully entitled to admission" would be deemed guilty of a misdemeanor and subject to a fine of one hundred to five hundred dollars and up to six months imprisonment.[142] This law remained in effect throughout Louisiana Reconstruction, but its enforcement was another matter entirely.[143]

The evidence is curiously contradictory as to the existence and degree of race mixing in the public schools during the Warmoth administration. Outside of New Orleans mixing was rare if it existed at all. Warmoth himself certainly did nothing to promote integration, and Superintendent Conway was exceedingly cautious even in referring to the subject. However, in 1870, or not later than 1871, at least five elementary schools in the Second District of New Orleans

139 New Orleans *Daily Picayune*, September 22, 1867.
140 New Orleans *Tribune*, July 24, 1867.
141 White, *Freedmen's Bureau in Louisiana*, 186–87; Beasley, "Education in Louisiana During Reconstruction," 107.
142 *Acts of Louisiana*, 1869, 755.
143 New Orleans *Daily Picayune*, August 13, 1868; Cable, *The Negro Question*, 8–9; Thomas H. Harris, *The Story of Public Education in Louisiana*, 34; Vincent, "Negro Leadership in 1868," 344–45.

almost certainly had both white and black children in attendance. The Conservative *Picayune* fulminated against this state of affairs, but at the same time insisted that it was impossible. Since nothing is said about the resegregation of these schools before 1877, they presumably continued throughout Reconstruction to teach pupils of both races.[144]

Another rather tense period came in 1874 and 1875. A number of Negro boys attempting to enter the Central Boys' High School were ejected by the pupils. This led, with obvious adult encouragement, to the "policing" of the city schools by groups of boys from the Central High School. Twenty Negro girls were frightened away from the Lower Girls' High School, and other Negro children were driven from a number of elementary schools. According to the *Picayune*, "This work of purification was carried on entirely independent [*sic*] of the teachers and in the most peaceable manner."[145] The white boys, as might be expected, were soon out of control, and the same newspaper suggested that they return to their studies and leave administration of the schools to the authorities. The story often ends here, leaving the inference that integration was thus ended. Such was not the case. George Washington Cable, who was a reporter on the *Picayune* at the time, says that the girls driven from the high school in December, 1874, soon returned and that blacks continued to attend classes there until 1877. Additional agitation in the newspapers and on the streets took place when blacks were assigned to teach white children. An octoroon named Edmonds, Paris-educated and perhaps the best-qualified mathematics teacher in Louisiana, became the center of a storm of controversy when he was appointed to the Boys' Central High School. But he remained at his desk until 1877, as did those black women, "ladies in everything but society's credentials,"[146] who taught white children in the elementary schools.[147]

144 New Orleans *Daily Picayune*, February 9, 13, August 10, 20, 1870, February 16, 1871; *Southwestern Presbyterian*, September 7, 1871; Reports of the State Superintendent of Education, 1869–1871, in *Legislative Documents, 1869–1872*; White, *Freedmen's Bureau in Louisiana*, 187–88; Thomas H. Harris, *The Story of Public Education in Louisiana*, 37–38.
145 New Orleans *Daily Picayune*, December 18, 1874.
146 Cable, *The Negro Question*, 9.
147 *Ibid.*, 13, 28; Cable, *The Silent South*, 36–37; New Orleans *Daily Picayune*, December, 1874–January, 1875, February 19, September 12, 17–18, 24, 30, 1875;

The integration of schools existed outside of New Orleans only to a minimum degree. In Natchitoches, by one account, white boys drove Negro children from a public school and then drove the teacher away. According to Superintendent Brown's 1874 report, there were in the Second Division, which included Jefferson Parish west of the Mississippi, St. John, St. James, Lafourche, and Terrebonne parishes, 47 white children in mixed schools. Of 28,039 children in the Divison, 2,301 were attending private schools and 5,695 were attending public schools. Of those in public schools, only 805 were white. Obviously, most children attended no school at all. Obviously, also, so long as the public schools in the country parishes were open to both races, they would be mainly Negro schools.[148]

The fact that schools legally open to both races did in fact prevent white children's attendance in most of the state was the justification given by Governor Francis T. Nicholls in 1877 for separating the races. In June of that year the New Orleans School Board ruled that the city's schools should be segregated. A committee of Negroes called on Nicholls to protest this action, and one of them, a man whom Nicholls had appointed to public office, was quoted as saying that "the largest schools in our city . . . are mixed and there is never a complaint, the children get along harmoniously and the mixing of colors has had no evil effect."[149] Protests were of no avail, however, and a court suit was no more successful than reasoning with a redeemer government had been. Blacks were assured that they would have schools equal to those of the whites, and it is possible that Nicholls meant to keep this promise. Certainly his successors paid no attention to his pledge. In the 1880s there were only five public schools for the twenty thousand black children in New Orleans. The ten thousand or so who lived below Canal Street had no public schools

---

King, *The Great South,* 97; Highsmith, "Louisiana During Reconstruction," 362–64; Thomas H. Harris, *The Story of Public Education in Louisiana,* 38–39, 57; Porter, "Negro Education in Louisiana," 764; Schuler, "Women in Public Affairs During Reconstruction," 710; Louis R. Harlan, "Desegregation in New Orleans Public Schools During Reconstruction," *American Historical Review,* LXVII (April, 1962), 663–75.

148 Report of the Superintendent of Schools, 1874, in *Legislative Documents, 1874;* Thomas H. Harris, *The Story of Public Education in Louisiana,* 38; Lonn, *Reconstruction in Louisiana,* 357.

149 New Orleans *Daily Picayune,* June 27, 1877.

at all. If black schools in the country parishes were more nearly equal to the white schools, it was because the white schools were so terrible.[150]

8

Important developments in higher education took place during Reconstruction. The University of Louisiana, which was to become Tulane University, had existed before the Civil War and had closed during the conflict. The law school of this university reopened in 1865; the medical school reopened shortly thereafter. Each of the state constitutions, 1864, 1868, and 1879, provided for state support of the university, and the face value of this support was considerably more generous than in 1861. Even so, depreciation of state warrants was so great that it was not until 1883 that the school was actually able to realize the income provided by statute. The University of Louisiana did operate throughout the Reconstruction years, though it was often uncertain how much longer classes could continue. The university was very important, since it was almost the only source in the state of professionally trained men.[151]

The Louisiana State Seminary had been established at Alexandria before the Civil War, and, as is well known, future General William T. Sherman was its first superintendent. The coming of war brought classes to an end, but in 1865 the seminary reopened with four students. Although Carl Schurz complained that all the faculty positions were filled by former Confederate officers, the school made progress. Much of its success was owed to its postwar superintendent, Colonel David F. Boyd, who reached an understanding with Governor Warmoth that no Negroes would be forced into the school. Warmoth kept this agreement and also sponsored rather generous financial support.

On October 15, 1869, the facilities at Alexandria burned to the ground. Thereupon the seminary was moved to Baton Rouge, where it was installed in the buildings formerly used by the State School for

150 *Ibid.*, June 27, 29, July 11, September 27–29, October 15, 24, November 10, 1877; M. W. Warren, Jr., "A Study of Racial Attitudes in Louisiana," 81–82; McDaniel, "Nicholls and the End of Reconstruction," 476–77; Garnie W. McGinty, *Louisiana Redeemed: The Overthrow of Carpetbag Rule, 1876–1880* (New Orleans, 1941), 229.
151 Beasley, "Education in Louisiana During Reconstruction," 122–23; John P. Dyer, *Tulane: The Biography of a University, 1834–1965* (New York, 1966), 29–30.

the Deaf and Blind. Before the end of 1869 more than one hundred students were enrolled at the Baton Rouge campus. In 1870 Colonel Boyd recommended that the name of his school be changed to Louisiana State University, and the legislature agreed. At the same time the lawmakers provided that two students from each parish and twenty from New Orleans should attend the university each year at state expense. These students were to be selected by local officials. In July, 1872, the university was reported to have a faculty of nineteen people in seven departments.

Troubles began when a legislative committee, including two blacks, inspected the campus in 1871. Colonel Boyd was absent, and the commandant of cadets refused to shake hands with the Negro legislators. When Kellogg became governor all state funds were cut off except the fees of the students attending at state expense. All of those admitted were white. A rapid decline in student body and faculty resulted—the faculty at one time consisting of only three men—and the school barely managed to keep its doors open. Colonel Boyd proposed in 1875 that the university be integrated, probably as a response to the threat from the new Agricultural and Mechanical College. Nothing came of this suggestion, and after Nicholls seized the governorship and the university and the Agricultural and Mechanical College were united, the segregation policy continued.[152]

During the Civil War, Congress had passed the Morrill Act, giving federal land grants to the states for the purpose of establishing agricultural and mechanical colleges. After restoration, Louisiana became eligible for such a grant, and in 1869 the legislature acted to accept it. The school had to be established by 1874, or the grant would revert to the national government. When Kellogg came to power, the leading Radical politicians were determined that the new school should not be under Boyd's control, but they had a difficult time resolving disputes among themselves as to where it should be located. Temporarily it was established at Common and Baronne streets in New Orleans,

---

152 *Senate Executive Documents,* 39th Cong., 1st Sess., No. 2, p. 12; New Orleans *Daily Picayune,* October 19, November 11, 1869, April 12, 1870, July 4, 1872; *Acts of Louisiana, 1870,* 53–54; Highsmith, "Louisiana During Reconstruction," 320; M. W. Warren, Jr., "A Study of Racial Attitudes in Louisiana," 62–63; McDaniel, "Nicholls and the End of Reconstruction," 481–82; Coulter, *The South During Reconstruction,* 320.

but the permanent site was planned for the Chalmette battleground in St. Bernard Parish. Practical difficulties and political troubles prevented completion of the move to Chalmette, but some fields there were planted by the students. The Agricultural and Mechanical College was definitely a Radical institution, having boys of "all ages, condition and colors . . . in attendance,"[153] despite the fact that two directors were named by the Louisiana State Grange. Conservative opinion favored union with Louisiana State University from the beginning, and in 1877 the union was accomplished.[154]

A school at Jackson, Louisiana, had been established by the state in 1825 and received the name Centenary College when it was turned over to the southern Methodist church in 1845. Closed during the war, it reopened in October, 1865. Centenary survived Reconstruction, but it did not prosper. The 1872 session opened with only seventy-two students. Under state law, the college was obligated to accept twenty-two indigent students whose expenses were paid by the state, and the trustees lived in fear that one of these state scholarships might be granted to a Negro. When Warmoth's enemy, G. W. Carter, and equally Radical T. C. Anderson succeeded in getting the scholarships abolished, the trustees entered their gratitude in the minutes of their meeting.[155]

A normal school which had been established in New Orleans in 1857 had, like so many other educational institutions, closed as a result of the war. When it was proposed in 1864 that it be reopened, one senator averred that this teacher-training institution was a farce: "They want the scholars from the High School to attend, although the teachers in the Normal School are no more competent than those in

153 New Orleans *Daily Picayune*, January 29, 1875.
154 *Ibid.*, February 18, 1874, January 29, June 9, 1875, February 15, 1876; Shreveport *Times*, December 22, 1875, February 18, 1876; *Acts of Louisiana, 1869,* 62–63; *Acts of Louisiana, 1874,* 224–26; R. H. Ryland to Kellogg, February 11, 1876, in Kellogg Papers; Highsmith, "Louisiana During Reconstruction," 381–83; Gonzales, "William Pitt Kellogg," 482; Frederick W. Williamson, *Origin and Growth of Agricultural Extension in Louisiana, 1860–1948* (Baton Rouge, 1951), 11–17; Frederick W. Williamson, *Yesterday and Today in Louisiana Agriculture* (Baton Rouge, 1940), 48–49; McDaniel, "Nicholls and the End of Reconstruction," 480–83.
155 Broadside, Centenary College, August 22, 1866, in Centenary College Library; New Orleans *Daily Picayune*, June 27, 1867, October 16, 1872; Minutes of Trustees Meetings, Centenary College, July 13, 1871, in Centenary College Library.

the high schools."[156] Nonetheless, the normal school was reopened in 1868 in a house on Burgundy Street, from whence it moved to St. Charles Avenue. In 1870 it began getting some support from the Peabody Fund. Apparently only women attended. Basic subjects were arithmetic, grammar, United States history, and geography; there were also weekly lectures on methods of teaching. Enrollment averaged about eighty.[157]

In addition to this all-white school for training teachers, Union Normal for black teachers was established in 1869 on the corner of Camp and Race Streets. Apparently Straight University participated in this school in the beginning and then withdrew. Thanks to Peabody grants, short-term normal schools were established outside New Orleans at fifteen or more places. In 1871 some $11,200 was granted for teacher training at such places as Arcadia, Bastrop, Columbia, Minden, Shreveport, Amite, Baton Rouge, Thibodaux, Livonia, and elsewhere. So-called teaching institutes were also held at several locations. The most famous was in New Orleans, where Conservatives were outraged that white and black teachers had to sit together in the same room. A special normal school for Negroes was conducted in New Orleans in 1877, after "redemption."[158]

Three "universities" for blacks were set up by northern sponsors during Reconstruction. The Congregationalist American Missionary Association established Straight University in 1869, and the school received some help from the Freedmen's Bureau. Straight soon had over four hundred students, but only a handful of these were taking college-level courses; the remainder were, at best, at the secondary school level. The law school of Straight was attended by whites as well as blacks and qualified a considerable number of young men for the Louisiana bar. The legislation incorporating Straight provided for a normal school, which did function for a time, and for a medical school, which apparently did not.[159]

156 *Debates of the Senate of Louisiana, 1864*, 14.
157 New Orleans *Daily Picayune*, August 4, 1872; Beasley, "Education in Louisiana During Reconstruction," 174.
158 New Orleans *Daily Picayune*, April 13, June 2, 1871, June 4, August 4, 1872, June 4, 1876, November 16, 1877; Beasley, "Education in Louisiana During Reconstruction," 172, 174, 177–80.
159 *Acts of Louisiana, 1870*, 111–12; Drake, "American Missionary Association and the Southern Negro," 91–92, 171–72; Highsmith, "Louisiana During Reconstruc-

The northern Methodists founded Thompson University for blacks at Franklin, Louisiana, but this venture failed quickly. Support then was given to Union Normal School in New Orleans, which in 1873 received a legislative charter as New Orleans University. Like Straight, most of New Orleans University's students were at the elementary and secondary rather than the university level. Later New Orleans University and Straight University were to merge and become Dillard University.[160]

The American Baptist Home Missionary Society (Northern) established Leland University in New Orleans in 1871. Leland received several bequests from northern philanthropists and fairly generous support from the northern Baptist church. As a result, it had fewer financial problems during Reconstruction than other black colleges in Louisiana. It had an integrated faculty which continued to be mixed after Reconstruction was over. Eventually Leland was moved from New Orleans to the little town of Baker, north of Baton Rouge, where it continued to operate into the 1940s.[161]

After white Conservative rule had been restored to Louisiana, a constitutional convention was called to revise the constitution of 1868. P. B. S. Pinchback, T. T. Allain, and Henry Demas, all black Radicals, were delegates to this convention, and they succeeded in including in the new basic law an article calling for the establishment of a state-supported university for blacks. A bill establishing Southern University was introduced into the legislature and became law in April, 1880. The school was first located in New Orleans but later was moved to the present campus near Baton Rouge. It is notable that some black Radicals were opposed to the new school because they

tion," 384–85; Woodson, *The Negro Church*, 182; Bentley, *The Freedmen's Bureau*, 176.

160 *Acts of Louisiana, 1873*, 161–63; Rufus E. Clement, "The Historical Development of Higher Education for Negro Americans," *Journal of Negro Education*, XXXV (Fall, 1966), 247–48; Drake, "American Missionary Association and the Southern Negro," 31; Louisiana Conference Journals, 1865–1870 (Mississippi Mission Conference, 1865–68, divided to form the Louisiana and Mississippi Methodist Episcopal Conferences; microfilm of manuscripts in possession of Dillard University Library, Drew University Library, and Garrett Seminary Library, provided by Centenary College Library).

161 Beasley, "Education in Louisiana During Reconstruction," 173; Roussève, *The Negro in Louisiana*, 112–13; Highsmith, "Louisiana During Reconstruction," 384–85; Dethloff and Jones, "Race Relations in Louisiana," 312.

thought it an extension of the Jim Crow policies already in effect in the public schools. Early state appropriations, five to ten thousand dollars a year, were hardly generous, but Southern was probably the most important institution of higher education for Louisiana blacks from its founding through the first two thirds of the twentieth century.[162]

"The Reconstruction Party, even with all its taxing, stealing, and defrauding, and with the upper ranks of society at war as fiercely against its best principles as against its bad practices planted the whole of the South with public schools." Furthermore, "the master class [was] converted to a belief in their use and necessity."[163] In the long run, this was true, but in the short run, in Louisiana, the master class when restored to power almost destroyed the public school system. This was not primarily because of race prejudice; the Conservatives had a mandate for low taxes and economy, and this program hit the schools especially hard. The state appropriations for education, inadequate during Reconstruction, dropped almost 50 percent, and in 1880 the average teacher's salary was about thirty dollars a month. There seems to have been no improvement for the next ten years. Rather than Negroes' dominating the public schools, the reverse occurred. St. Landry Parish in 1877 had twenty-four schools for whites, eleven for blacks. There was even a wave of arson directed against schools sponsored by northern churches. Such a Negrophobe as T. H. Harris referred to Conservative school legislation as "fatal to progress" and a bar to improvement in education "for more than a quarter of a century."[164]

---

162 Roussève, *The Negro in Louisiana*, 141–42; Grosz, "Pinchback," 606; Porter, "Negro Education in Louisiana," 768–69; Memelo, "The Development of State Laws Concerning the Negro in Louisiana," 110; McDaniel, "Nicholls and the End of Recontruction," 483–84.
163 Cable, *The Negro Question*, 159.
164 Thomas H. Harris, *The Story of Public Education in Louisiana*, 71; see also p. 59; DuBois, *Black Reconstruction*, 637; New Orleans *Daily Picayune*, May 23, November 21, 1877, October 27, 1878; A. D. Mayo, "Southern Women in the Recent Educational Movement in the South," *Bureau of Education Circular of Information*, No. 1 (Washington, D.C., 1892), 80–81, quoted in Porter, "Negro Education in Louisiana," 746–47; M. B. Hillyard, *The New South* (Baltimore, 1887), 310; Carter, *The Angry Scar*, 189; Frazier, *The Negro in the United States*, 424; Drake, "American Missionary Association and the Southern Negro," 176.

XI   *"Redemption"*

S THE election year of 1876 dawned, Louisiana Republicans were far from united. Negroes maintained that Kellogg had given too many offices to whites, and white Republicans accused him of giving too many offices to Democrats. Pinchback, after his rejection by the United States Senate, felt that he had not had adequate backing from Louisiana Republican leaders. As late as May a factional quarrel broke out over the judgeship of the Superior District Court; Lieutenant-Governor Antoine supported John Lynch, who was strongly opposed by Kellogg. Much of the old animosity toward the Custom House Gang persisted. Warmoth returned to the party that spring, but as an opponent of the Kellogg administration. The *Picayune* ventured to hope that he would bring the Republicans the same fortune he had brought to the Fusionists four years earlier. Many onetime Republican whites had gone over to the Conservatives, and most remaining Scalawags were anything but enthusiastic. Jasper Blackburn of Homer asserted that the party was being run in the interest of Carpetbaggers and Negro "bummers," but warned that there were still enough honest Republicans in Louisiana to destroy the party if they could not purify it.[1]

1 New Orleans *Daily Picayune*, May 25, June 1, 18, August 15, September 10, 1876;

All was not sweetness and light within the Conservative, or Democratic, party. Old Whigs still found it distasteful to sleep in the same bed with Democrats. The rank and file of the White League was opposed to any compromise on the race question, but Conservative leaders knew that they had to have some black votes to win an election. The old hostility between city and country persisted. Party leaders had been divided by the Wheeler Compromise and its repudiation. Stronger than these divisive forces, however, was the desire to win control of Louisiana. The hatred of Radicalism was primarily racist, but the Bourbon planter-merchant class, which did not altogether share the Negrophobia of the mass of their party, had economic interests to protect. A convention of party leaders met in January, 1876; its purpose was not to draw up a program, but rather to achieve unity.

The *Picayune* asserted: "Questions of currency, of tariff and the like may occupy the attention of people who are secure in the enjoyment of the essential rights of freemen. Louisianians must remit those questions to a more fitting season."[2] The convention was successful to a remarkable degree in uniting opponents of Radicalism.[3]

The Republicans met in New Orleans on May 31, 1876, to select delegates to their party's national convention. This was a preliminary contest between Pinchback and Packard; Pinchback was named a delegate, but the Custom House faction was the obvious winner of this trial of strength. In the month which remained before the nominating convention for state offices met, Warmoth, again wearing his Republican coat, sought to drum up support for himself as a candidate for governor. He had some success, but not nearly enough.[4]

If the Republican nominating convention, which met first at Mechanics' Institute and then at the St. Charles Theater, was half as disorderly as Conservatives pictured it, it was a near-riot. It lasted for

---

J. R. G. Pitkin Letter, Department of Archives, Louisiana State University; Shreveport *Times*, June 15, July 22, 1876; McGinty, *Louisiana Redeemed*, 29; Coulter, *The South During Reconstruction*, 354–55, 359–60; Franklin, *Reconstruction After the Civil War*, 210–11.

2 New Orleans *Daily Picayune*, January 6, 1876.

3 *Ibid.*, April 23, August 31, 1876; Bone, "Louisiana in the Disputed Election of 1876," 432–34; Shugg, *Origins of Class Struggle in Louisiana*, 229–30.

4 Sypher to Warmoth, April 12, 1876, E. N. Robertson to Warmoth, June 13, 1876, Benjamin F. Butler to Warmoth, July 2, 1876, all in Warmoth Papers; New Orleans *Daily Picayune*, May 30–June 1, 1876; F. B. Harris, "Henry Clay Warmoth," 648.

a long, hot week, June 28 through July 5, and was characterized by shouting, fisticuffs, and one shooting. Pinchback was named temporary chairman, but this was the only victory achieved by the anti-Custom House forces. Kellogg, as expected, refused to accept renomination; Warmoth withdrew his name after the first ballot had shown his cause to be hopeless. On July 3, United States Marshal Stephen B. Packard was nominated for governor; C. C. Antoine was renominated for lieutenant-governor. William G. Brown was again made the candidate for superintendent of education, and Emile Honoré, George A. Johnson, and William H. Hunt were candidates for secretary of state, auditor, and attorney general. Antoine, Brown, and Honoré were Negroes.

Packard presumably was an able man; he had been the "brains" of the Custom House gang for years. His ticket was obviously designed to appeal to black voters, which was realistic, since no Republican could expect to attract significant white support in 1876. The real question was how firm black support would be. Pinchback was half-hearted, going so far at one time as to declare that he would work for Hayes's election, but not for Packard's. How much Warmoth's support was worth is problematical, but he rejected the nomination for Congress from the First District, and he obviously was not enthusiastic about the state ticket.[5]

On February 10, 1876, the Democratic State Central Committee had issued an address which said that the Democrats were resolved "to test the relative strength of intelligence and ignorance. They will use no violence, but all the means in their power will be employed to defeat the further rule of the vicious and ignorant in this state. . . . What remains to be done is the perfection of the Democratic-Conservative organization in all parishes."[6] The Conservative nominating convention met at Baton Rouge on July 24. Four major candidates contested for the gubernatorial nomination. McEnery and Louis Wiltz represented the hard-line last-ditch Democrats. D. B. Penn had the support of the old Whig merchants of New Orleans, and Francis T. Nicholls of Assumption Parish had the support of the old Whig plant-

---

5 New Orleans *Daily Picayune*, June 27–July 6, July 11, September 14, 19, 1876; Kendall, *History of New Orleans*, I, 294; Bone, "Louisiana in the Disputed Election of 1876," 431; Lonn, *Reconstruction in Louisiana*, 402–407.
6 Quoted in Lonn, *Reconstruction in Louisiana*, 400.

ers and of more than a few south Louisiana Democrats. Penn was out of contention by the time balloting began, and Wiltz led the voting on the first three ballots. After the third ballot, however, McEnery threw his support to Nicholls; this support, increased by the East Baton Rouge delegation, was enough to give Nicholls the nomination. Wiltz was nominated for lieutenant-governor. Other statewide candidates were White League leader H. N. Ogden for attorney general, William A. Strong for secretary of state, Allen Jumel for auditor, and Robert M. Lusher, once more, for superintendent of education.[7]

Nicholls was an ideal Conservative candidate. He was a much-wounded, one-armed former Confederate brigadier whose war record was worth thousands of votes. He had been little involved in politics during the early years of Reconstruction and thus had made few enemies. He was a patrician, and whites and blacks believed that his word was good. Finally, although he was certainly an unquestioning believer in white supremacy, he was not a victim of that furious Negrophobia which had come to possess so many Louisiana whites. Rather was his attitude paternalistic, and he could appeal for black votes with much more probable success than Wiltz or McEnery.[8]

The Republican platform expressed the usual claims of loyalty as contrasted with disloyalty, and it advocated federal aid to a southwestern railroad to the Pacific. The Democrats also favored a Pacific railroad, but they specified the Texas-Pacific line as set forth in a bill then before Congress. The Democrats made the usual charges of corruption and usurpation of power against the Republicans, then promised reform in government, reduction of the excessive powers of the governor, free and equal schools for all regardless of race, and maintenance of the financial "honor" of the state. The Democratic platform also explicitly recognized the binding effect of the Thirteenth, Fourteenth, and Fifteenth amendments to the United States Constitution, and the party pledged itself to protect every citizen, regardless of race, in the exercise of his rights. Every one of these pledges, except

7 New Orleans *Daily Picayune*, July 23–28, 1876; Bone, "Louisiana in the Disputed Election of 1876," 434; McDaniel, "Nicholls and the End of Reconstruction," 372; Lonn, *Reconstruction in Louisiana*, 408–10.

8 Barnes F. Lathrop (ed.), "An Autobiography of Francis T. Nicholls, 1835–1881," *Louisiana Historical Quarterly*, XVII (April, 1934), 246–54; Guion Griffis Johnson, "Southern Paternalism toward Negroes After Emancipation," *Journal of Southern History*, XXIII (November, 1957), 483–509.

possibly the acknowledgement of the Thirteenth Amendment, would be broken within a few years. Nicholls, in his acceptance speech, again reiterated support for constitutional rights for black citizens and the pledge to provide equal educational opportunities for all.[9]

The Republicans campaigned in the traditional manner. Money was raised from those who could expect to benefit from a Republican victory. Higher Custom House employees, for example, were expected to give $250. Parades and rallies were held throughout the state, except in a few areas where the danger of Democratic violence was too great. Warmoth and Pinchback may not have been overly enthusiastic in their support of the ticket, but they joined a list of speakers which included Packard, Kellogg, John Ray, J. R. G. Pitkin, who had replaced Packard as United States Marshal, Hugh J. Campbell, and Pierre Landry, Negro state senator from Ascension Parish. Nicholls ignored Packard's challenge to a series of debates. The organization of local Republican clubs among the blacks was continued, though "regulators" interfered in some areas.[10]

Control of the registration machinery was a great advantage in American elections in the nineteenth century, and elections in Louisiana were not exceptions. Even though the *Picayune* congratulated state registrar Michael Hahn for his impartiality, the Republicans made what they could of the fact that they controlled the registration machinery in most parishes. In New Orleans almost twenty-two thousand black voters had been registered up to October 14, despite the Conservative assertion that only about half that many blacks were qualified to vote in the city. During the same period, some thirty-three thousand white voters registered in New Orleans. In the rural parishes heavy pressure was put on Republican supervisors of registration; they were told that their status with the next administration would be determined by the extent to which they registered and got out the vote of the largest possible number of Republicans.[11]

9 New Orleans *Daily Picayune*, July 27, 1876; *Southwestern Presbyterian*, August 3, 1876; Bone, "Louisiana in the Disputed Election of 1876," 435–40; McDaniel, "Nicholls and the End of Reconstruction," 372–76.

10 New Orleans *Daily Picayune*, August–October, 1876; Shreveport *Times*, August–October, 1876; McGinty, *Louisiana Redeemed*, 43; Lonn, *Reconstruction in Louisiana*, 415–17, 432.

11 New Orleans *Daily Picayune*, August 30, October 17–19, November 3, 1876; Shaffer Papers, VII, September 12, 1876; Bone, "Louisiana in the Disputed Elec-

New Orleans, now under a Conservative city administration, had never been noted for simon-pure politics. Registration lists were padded with names of men long dead, moved away, or not yet born, and apparently every one of them was a Democrat. The Republicans found a means of dealing with this situation. Some twenty-nine thousand circulars advertising sewing machines were mailed to names and addresses of white voters on the registration lists. When circulars were returned undelivered, Metropolitan Police then checked to make sure that the addressees did not live at the address listed. When this was the case, warrants were sworn out against them for fraudulent registration and their names were stricken from the rolls. The number purged is uncertain, but it seems to have been nearly ten thousand. No doubt some of these were men who had moved since registering, but even Nicholls' campaign manager, the later infamous Major E. A. Burke, admitted that many fraudulent registrations were exposed. A curious fact about this event is that the Conservatives called it the "Sewing Machine Swindle," and it quickly was impressed on the public mind as a dishonest Republican trick![12]

The fact that federal troops were still on hand in Louisiana aided the Republican cause; their presence reduced preelection intimidation and helped to assure a peaceable election. But troops could not be everywhere; on election day, 1876, they were stationed at sixty-two places in the Department of the Gulf, but there were hundreds of polling places without troops. Some units, like those in West Feliciana, were under Democratic officers who did little to interfere with the intimidation of black voters. On the other hand, the troops at Monroe seemingly made a real effort to preserve the peace in Ouachita Parish. Certainly the statewide Republican vote would have been much smaller if the troops had not been on hand.[13]

The Democratic campaign objectives were really very simple. Nicholls was assured of almost the entire white vote. The few Carpetbag-

---

tion of 1876," 555–56; McDaniel, "Nicholls and the End of Reconstruction," 383–84; Lonn, *Reconstruction in Louisiana*, 427–28.

12 New Orleans *Daily Picayune*, October 13, 27–28, November 2, 1876; McDaniel, "Nicholls and the End of Reconstruction," 383–84; Lonn, *Reconstruction in Louisiana*, 428–29; McGinty, *Louisiana Redeemed*, 44–45.

13 Charles M. Barrow to Mrs. Hugh M. Bone, November 23, 1927, in Bone, "Louisiana in the Disputed Election of 1876," 101; New Orleans *Daily Picayune*, August 25, November 2–3, 1876; Sefton, *United States Army and Reconstruction*, 246–48.

gers and Scalawags who had resisted pressure to leave the Republican party were not likely to be won over at the last minute. Therefore the Democrats concentrated on keeping up the enthusiasm of white voters, winning over as many black voters as possible, and doing as much as they dared to prevent voting by blacks who remained loyal to the Republican party.

Conservative candidates fanned out through the state, declaiming against the corruption and extravagance of Radical government, extolling the virtues of Samuel J. Tilden, the Democratic candidate for president, urging that no effort be spared to get out the Conservative vote, and promising again and again to preserve for Negroes all the rights guaranteed to them by the Reconstruction amendments. White League racism was, at least publicly, forgotten. Negro speakers were called upon when they were available, and newspaper accounts of rallies took particular note of the number of blacks in attendance. How many Negroes were won over it is impossible to say. Not all of those who attended Conservative rallies voted Conservative. A black man in Baton Rouge, sporting a big red Tilden button, let it be known that he was as good a Radical as ever, but that the Tilden badge was his meal ticket.[14]

The degree to which black voters were intimidated in 1876 was hotly debated during and after the campaign and is still a matter of dispute. Intimidation was investigated by the Returning Board, by a committee from the Democratic national House of Representatives, and by another committee from the Republican United States Senate. As could be expected, the Returning Board's conclusions were almost wholly partisan, and the same can be said for the two congressional committees, which reached opposite conclusions. As one studies the testimony before these committees and the other evidence available, it is obvious that much violence and intimidation took place. The question then becomes whether the violence and intimidation, by

14 New Orleans *Daily Picayune*, July–November, 1876; Shreveport *Times*, July–November, 1876; New Orleans *Times*, July 28, 1876, quoted in McGinty, *Louisiana Redeemed*, 38; Howard T. Nicholls, "Francis T. Nicholls, Bourbon Democrat" (M.A. thesis, Louisiana State University, 1959), 43–44, 52–53; Kendall, *History of New Orleans*, I, 345; McDaniel, "Nicholls and the End of Reconstruction," 378; Lonn, *Reconstruction in Louisiana*, 422, 425; Windham, "White Supremacy in Louisiana," 114–25; Bone, "Louisiana in the Disputed Election of 1876," 558.

now called "bulldozing," were sufficient to have changed the outcome of the election.

Nothing is to be gained by going once more into specific examples of bulldozing. The records of the congressional committees abound with instances. The pattern was not unlike that of 1868. Economic pressure was used when it was effective. As one student of the period notes, the whites ardently courted Negroes who might vote for the Democratic ticket, but "they just as ardently pursued a program of violence toward those . . . who proved recalcitrant to their wooing."[15] The state central committee, in careful language, gave instructions that Conservatives should be careful to say nothing or do nothing which could be "construed into a threat of intimidation of any character. You cannot convince a Negro's reason, but you can impress him by positive statements continually repeated." Then the instructions went on to suggest that Conservative clubs be formed in different parts of each parish, that these clubs should meet frequently, and that occasionally the local clubs "shall form at their several places of meeting and proceed thence on horseback to the central rendezvous. . . . Proceedings of this character would impress the Negroes with a sense of your united strength."[16]

The way this strategy worked in practice was related years later by a man who took part. "We selected twelve men who could be depended upon . . . and I was selected the captain. . . . We held meetings every two weeks, at which speeches were made . . . to show the Negroes . . . their mistakes in going against us. . . . But the great influence used by the white Republican leaders . . . kept a great many aloof, and this element had to be worked on otherwise than through the clubs." The writer then went on to say that "nothing intimidates a Negro as much as mystery and seeing armed men riding around at night set them to thinking. . . . We seldom spent a whole night in our bed. Occasionally there were a few necks broken and straps used among the worst."[17]

"Bulldozing" was concentrated in five parishes, Morehouse, Ouachita, East Baton Rouge, East Feliciana, and West Feliciana, but

15 Windham, "White Supremacy in Louisiana," 125.
16 Quoted in McDaniel, "Nicholls and the End of Reconstruction," 379.
17 Barrow to Mrs. Bone, November 23, 1927, in Bone, "Louisiana in the Disputed Election of 1876," 100–101.

there were abundant instances of intimidation elsewhere. One newspaper, at least, had alerted Conservatives in April by pointing out that the Supreme Court's decision negating the Enforcement Acts was sure to have a great effect upon the political campaign in Louisiana.[18] Another paper, after giving the news of the destruction of Custer's command at the Little Big Horn, remarked: "If Sitting Bull can manage to keep the troops busy until after the November elections he will have the lasting gratitude of some of the Southern States."[19]

Intimidation by Conservatives, violent and otherwise, was not confined to blacks. White Republicans also were victims. Social pressure had greatly reduced the never-large numbers of native white Republicans, and many of the northerners who had settled in Louisiana had succumbed to the same pressure or had renounced Radicalism because of their dislike of the Kellogg regime. The white Republicans who remained were mainly Radical political leaders, and the Conservatives felt free to attack them directly. As previously noted Senator Marshall F. Twitchell lost both arms and George King was killed at Coushatta in May. Tax collector B. F. Dinkgrave of Ouachita Parish was shot dead in August as he rode to lunch. Other white Republicans were murdered in Red River, Caddo, Natchitoches, and East Baton Rouge parishes. In the last-named, the sheriff, the parish judge, and the tax collector were forced to resign by a mob which threatened their lives. In the Felicianas a number of stores owned by Republicans were burned; this was explained on the ground that the proprietors were buying stolen cotton, but it seems strange that action on such a matter was taken just before the election.

In fact, the evidence of widespread violence and intimidation is overwhelming. Bland Conservative denials before congressional committees were lies, no doubt regarded by the liars as in a good cause. Not all the violence was by Conservatives, however. There were instances, played up a great deal by Democratic papers, of Radical blacks breaking up meetings of black Democrats. But the five parishes named above were very definitely and very efficiently "bulldozed" by Conservative bands. In no other way could it be explained how East

18 New Orleans _Daily Picayune_, April 9, 1876.
19 Shreveport _Times_, July 7, 1876.

Feliciana, which normally cast a large Republican majority, did not report a single Republican vote.

To repeat, the question is not whether intimidation took place—that it did is a fact. The question to be considered is whether enough Negroes were persuaded, by whatever means, to vote Democratic so as to give a Democratic majority of the vote cast in the state. Certainly a great many were persuaded. The Democratic house investigating committee interviewed large numbers of blacks who freely testified that they had voted Conservative. Many of them were displeased with the Kellogg regime because of its failure to provide schools for their children. Others had suffered greatly in the depression and hoped that a change in government would bring improvement. Eight years of Radical rule had done very little for the average rural Negro, and if he believed the Conservative promises to protect his newly achieved constitutional rights, he might well have decided to vote for Nicholls and Tilden. Whether those who changed voluntarily outnumbered those who in one way or another were prevented from voting Radical will never be known.[20]

2

The election for both state and national office was held on November 7, 1876. Election day was quiet. "In New Orleans the places of business were all closed; the streets bore the appearance of Sunday."[21] In the country the polling places believed most likely to be the scene of

---

20 New Orleans *Daily Picayune*, May–December, 1876; Shreveport *Times*, May–November, 1876; Julius Emnemoses to C. C. Antoine, August 30, 1876, in Kellogg Papers; New Orleans *Republican*, August–November, 1876; Shaffer Papers, VII, November 5, 1876; *House Reports*, 44th Cong., 2nd Sess., No. 34, Part I, pp. 93–95, 100, 105, 111, 183, Part II, pp. 6, 37–38, *passim*; *Senate Executive Documents*, 44th Cong., 2nd Sess., No. 2, *passim*; *Senate Reports*, 44th Cong., 2nd Sess., No. 501, Vol. II, pp. 1,469, 1,478–80, Vol. III, p. 2,569, *passim*; John Sherman, *John Sherman's Recollections of Forty Years in the House, Senate and Cabinet* (New York, 1895), 458–60; Windham, "White Supremacy in Louisiana," 107–10, 125; McDaniel, "Nicholls and the End of Reconstruction," 397–81; Lonn, *Reconstruction in Louisiana*, 414–39; Highsmith, "Louisiana During Reconstruction," 326–27; McGinty, *Louisiana Redeemed*, 47–53; Bone, "Louisiana in the Disputed Election of 1876," *passim*; T. B. Tunnell, Jr., "The Negro, the Republican Party, and the Election of 1876 in Louisiana," *Louisiana History*, VII (Spring, 1966), 101–11.
21 *Southwestern Presbyterian*, November 9, 1876.

violence were supervised by troops. But the violence really took place, as in 1868, 1872, and 1874, before the day of the election. Preliminary reports of the vote for presidential electors showed eighty-four thousand for Tilden, about seventy-six thousand for Hayes. Indications were that the Nicholls ticket had outpolled the Packard ticket by about the same number. The Conservative press exulted: "Victory!" headlined the Shreveport *Times*. "Grand jubilee of Honest Men Throughout this Grand Universe. Packard and his brother carpetbaggers can begin to pack for their Hegira. The carnival of Thieves, State and National, is at an end."[22] On the same date the *Picayune* said, "We go to press with this issue entirely confident of the election of Tilden."[23]

The celebration was premature. Nationally, Tilden had 184 unchallenged electoral votes, and Hayes had only 165. Twenty votes were in dispute. One of these was in Oregon, and to this vote Hayes was obviously entitled. The remaining nineteen were in Florida, South Carolina, and Louisiana. If the Republicans could win all these disputed votes, then Hayes would become president by a majority of one. Tilden needed only one more electoral vote to win the White House. So far as the Louisiana state election was concerned, the vote would not be final until canvassed by the Returning Board. The interests of national and state Republicans coincided in having the Returning Board bring in a Republican majority. The excitement in Louisiana seems to have been less than in the country at large; the state had seen disputed elections regularly since Radical Reconstruction began and was not overly impressed with this one. Most collections of private papers contain no mention of the election. One prominent planter noted a great deal of political excitement on November 11, but his journal makes no other reference to politics for two weeks. The frenzy of the Conservative newspapers seems to have been intended to arouse public excitement rather than to have been in response to it.[24]

22 Shreveport *Times*, November 8, 1876.
23 New Orleans *Daily Picayune*, November 8, 1876.
24 Randall and Donald, *The Civil War and Reconstruction*, 692–93; Sherman, *John Sherman's Recollections*, 455; Shaffer Papers, VII, November 11, 27, 1876; Blaine, *Twenty Years of Congress*, 581; Lonn, *Reconstruction in Louisiana*, 437–

Louisiana law required that the Returning Board include representation from both parties. Originally one Oscar Arroyo had been a Conservative member, but he had resigned. The vacancy was never filled, and four Republicans, former governor James Madison Wells, T. C. Anderson of Opelousas, Louis M. Kenner, a freedman, and Gadane Cassanave, a prewar free man of color who had made a living as an undertaker, made up the Returning Board in late 1876. The report of the Democratic house of representatives committee which investigated the election referred to Wells as a "defaulter" against the state, said that Anderson was guilty of fraud, and that Kenner was a former whorehouse proprietor who had been indicted but not convicted for larceny. Cassanave, according to these gentlemen, was so ignorant that he was a willing accomplice to rascality. Senator Sherman, on the other hand, spoke highly of Wells and the other members of the board. The essential fact is that the Returning Board was wholly partisan. Under the law, originally designed to prevent Democratic election theft as practiced in 1868, it had the final voice in canvassing the vote. It could be expected to give every possible advantage to the Republicans.[25]

The Returning Board began its deliberations as soon as the returns had been reported. As one newspaper put it, "The problem upon which they are engaged is how to elect the Republican candidates with a Democratic majority. They have done it before and they will do it easily enough again."[26] In reality, it was not easy to do. National representatives of both parties were on hand for the hearings, so an appearance of equity had to be maintained. Also involved was a constitutional question as to whether or not the Returning Board had the power to canvass votes for presidential electors. Finally, simply throwing out the votes of the "bulldozed" parishes was not enough. This would elect the state Republican ticket, but it would leave two Hayes

---

38; Marguerite T. Leach, "The Aftermath of Reconstruction in Louisiana," *Louisiana Historical Quarterly*, XXXII (July, 1949), 637.

25 *House Reports*, 44th Cong., 2nd Sess., No. 156, p. 7; New Orleans *Daily Picayune*, November 17, 19, 1876; McDaniel, "Nicholls and the End of Reconstruction," 388–89; Gibson, *A Political Crime*, 155–56; McGinty, *Louisiana Redeemed*, 55–56; Lowrey, "James Madison Wells," 1,102; Lonn, *Reconstruction in Louisiana*, 443–44, 447–49.

26 New Orleans *Daily Picayune*, November 21, 1872.

electors with a minority. Hayes had to have every Louisiana electoral vote to win the presidency, and if Hayes did not win the presidency, no Republican regime could hope to survive in Louisiana.

The canvassing of votes from parishes where there was no dispute was complete on November 27. Then the board began to hear testimony concerning the fairness of the election in other parishes. More than three hundred witnesses were heard, many of them brought to New Orleans by U. S. Marshal Pitkin at federal expense. One could draw whatever conclusions he wished from the witnesses and affidavits heard by the Returning Board. Senator Sherman, as a Republican, thought the procedure eminently fair. The Democratic observers found it redolent with fraud. It appears evident today that the Returning Board did begin its deliberations with every intention of conducting a canvass which would give the state to Hayes and Packard. But this does not necessarily mean that its final decision was in error. Historian Ella Lonn, who definitely sympathized with the Conservatives, and who studied the testimony before the congressional committees which investigated the election, concluded that "in such a maze of assertions and denials, bribery and counter-bribery, and false testimony contradicted and retracted, the truth is well-nigh hopelessly buried."[27] This writer can only agree.[28]

An interesting sidelight on the Returning Board in 1876 was the alleged attempt of James Madison Wells to solicit a bribe for the board's decision. If the accusations were correct, Wells sent one Joseph Maddox to Washington to tell Republican party leaders that he needed $200,000 each for himself and Anderson, something less for the two black members, to count in Hayes. When the Republican leaders refused to consider this proposition, Maddox then approached the Democrats, according to his own testimony, and offered the presidency to Tilden for $1,000,000. There can be little doubt that Duncan F. Kenner approached Wells in New Orleans and offered him

27 Lonn, *Reconstruction in Louisiana*, 452.
28 *Ibid.*, 440–57, 561; Sherman, *John Sherman's Recollections*, 455–59; McGinty, *Louisiana Redeemed*, 58, 62–63; Lowrey, "James Madison Wells," 1,101–1,104; New Orleans *Daily Picayune*, November 10–December 15, 1876; McDaniel, "Nicholls and the End of Reconstruction," 289–90; New Orleans *Republican*, November 11–December 22, 1876.

money to count in the Democrats. According to Kenner, Wells demanded $200,000, which was more than Kenner could raise. Wells said that Kenner had offered him $200,000, but that he had refused the offer. The testimony is so conflicting that conclusions are difficult. One suspects, however, that the Democrats would have been happy to buy the presidency for $1,000,000 if they had had an opportunity.[29]

After concluding its public hearings, the Returning Board held two days of secret deliberations and then, on December 5, made its report. The returns from sixty-nine polling places in twenty-four parishes were thrown out. These boxes had cast 13,211 votes for Tilden electors, only 2,412 for Hayes electors. Thus was an apparent Democratic majority converted into a Republican majority. Packard, Antoine, and all other members of the statewide Republican ticket were declared elected. The Returning Board returned a state senate of nineteen Republicans and seventeen Democrats, a house of seventy-one Republicans, forty-three Democrats, and three independents. The Returning Board had certainly turned the results of the election around, but it should be emphasized that it had done nothing illegal. Its actions were fully within its legal powers.[30]

Obviously, Democrats were not willing to let matters rest at this point. The presidential electors of each party met and cast their votes for their candidates. When January came, the Packard legislature took its seat in the State House; the Nicholls legislature met first in St. Patrick's Hall, then in Odd Fellows' Hall. On January 8, both Nicholls and Packard were sworn in as governor of Louisiana. The people were not unduly excited. The existence of two governors and two legislatures was by now nothing new. The question was which governor and which legislature would survive. That would depend in part on events in Louisiana, but, more important, it would depend upon developments in Washington.[31]

29 Lowrey, "James Madison Wells," 1,105, 1,107; McDaniel, "Nicholls and the End of Reconstruction," 390–91; Lonn, *Reconstruction in Louisiana,* 457.
30 *House Reports,* 44th Cong., 2nd Sess., No. 100, *passim;* New Orleans *Daily Picayune,* December, 1876–January, 1877; New Orleans *Republican,* December, 1876; Lonn, *Reconstruction in Louisiana,* 459–61; McGinty, *Louisiana Redeemed,* 62–63; Bone, "Louisiana in the Disputed Election of 1876," 234–35.
31 New Orleans *Daily Picayune,* January, 1877.

3

Packard had only one real hope of holding power. That was by securing recognition and support from the federal government as Kellogg had done. If Hayes achieved the presidency, Packard had some right to expect support from Washington, because the returns which elected Hayes electors had also elected Packard. In Louisiana there was little the Republicans could do to assert their authority. Packard could only barricade himself and his legislature in the State House, guarded by Metropolitan Police, and keep his government in bare existence.

If Tilden became President, Nicholls' administration would certainly be recognized by Washington. A victory for Hayes, however, need not necessarily mean victory for Packard. Nicholls must, insofar as possible, demonstrate his control of Louisiana. At the same time he must avoid any action which would make federal intervention necessary. Last, but not least, he must do whatever he could to make his administration acceptable to Louisiana blacks and the few northern friends of the blacks who remained.

What Nicholls dreaded most was some rash act on the part of his followers. In statement after statement, before he was sworn in, in his inaugural address, and during the crucial three months which followed inauguration, he urged calm upon his supporters. He was surprisingly successful in keeping the passions of Louisiana Democrats in check. In January unusually cold weather came to his aid. The orange orchards in Plaquemines Parish were badly damaged; ice built up in the Mississippi at Vicksburg, and almost the whole state was covered with snow. Louisianians were not likely to move about much in cold weather for the simple reason that they did not have clothes suited to low temperatures. New Orleans was probably the place of greatest danger, but in February Mardi Gras afforded an opportunity for the people of the Crescent City to work off excess energy.

Nicholls missed no opportunity to assure Louisiana Negroes that he would fully protect their rights. He himself said later: "I set myself . . . to work to bring about good feeling and confidence between the races. . . . I was particularly anxious by kindness and strict justice and impartiality . . . to do away with the belief . . . that Democratic rule was inconsistent with their rights and their prosperity."[32] How sincere these professions were, one cannot say. Probably Nicholls himself was sincere, but his conception of protection of black rights was not likely to be the same as Pinchback's. One thing is certain. Nicholls, especially when he guaranteed protection of rights granted by the Fourteenth and Fifteenth amendments, did not speak for the vast majority of his followers.[33]

As 1877 dawned, President Grant had only two months to serve. He had refused to intervene in Mississippi in 1875 to save Radical claimants to office in that state. He had had enough of intervention in Louisiana, and he refused a request from Kellogg for federal troops to be used to install Packard's government. Grant did not remove the troops already stationed in Louisiana, but he concentrated them, plus a detachment of Marines, in New Orleans, where he thought that disturbances were most likely to break out. The commander, General Christopher C. Augur, was instructed at first simply to preserve the peace. Later he was told that if it was absolutely necessary to recognize one of the claimants to the governorship, it should be Packard, but this seems to have been intended as a warning to Nicholls and as a means of assuring the continued existence of the Packard legislature until after Hayes had been inaugurated as president.

Louisiana was abundantly represented in Washington in early 1877. The negotiations which led to the Compromise of 1877 were going on, but Randall Gibson, Major E. A. Burke, and E. John Ellis also had to help keep the Nicholls government in existence until a compromise was achieved. Gibson had been a college classmate of Secretary of War James D. Cameron, which gave him access to the inner councils of Grant's administration. E. John Ellis estimated that he talked with the president himself no less than fifty times during the crucial period from December, 1876, through February, 1877. Probably the arguments of these and other men were persuasive, but basically Grant did not act because, as his secretary wrote Packard, he felt that national public opinion would no longer tolerate the main-

32 Lathrop (ed.), "Autobiography of Nicholls," 257.
33 *Ibid.*, 257–58, 262–63; New Orleans *Daily Picayune*, January–April, 1877; Lonn, *Reconstruction in Louisiana*, 474, 478, 480–83, 492–93; McDaniel, "Nicholls and the End of Reconstruction," 402, 429–30; McGinty, *Louisiana Redeemed*, 91.

tenance of an unpopular state government in Louisiana by federal military force.

But Grant was not willing to completely abandon Packard. To preserve the *status quo* he forbade the appointment of state officials by either Packard or Nicholls unless both of them issued the commissions. Otherwise incumbents were to remain in office until the legitimacy of one government or the other was determined. In practice, Nicholls did appoint a few officials against Packard's will, but he was very careful not to push Grant too far. He did as much as he thought the president would stand, but no more.[34]

Nicholls wasted no time. He accepted Ogden's troops, the White League forces which had fought at Liberty Place, as the legal militia of the state, and the artillery in the state arsenal was taken over by the Washington Artillery, part of Ogden's command. Some of the new militiamen were sworn in as police, and they immediately took control of the New Orleans police stations. On the morning after his inauguration, Nicholls sent Ogden's forces against the Cabildo, the seat of the state supreme court. Kellogg and Packard had unwittingly encouraged such a coup, because they had not made appointments to replace the justices, all of whose terms had expired. Nicholls understood the use of force. He sent enough militia, artillery, and volunteers against the Cabildo to make resistance useless. His force consisted of about three thousand men, and there was no resistance. Federal troops in the city were under orders to prevent bloodshed, but since there was no bloodshed General Augur, who probably sympathized with Nicholls, had no reason to intervene. When the Metropolitan Police detailed to protect the court decided that discretion was the better part of valor, Chief Justice Ludeling concluded that the police were correct and abandoned the courtroom. Nicholls quickly appointed new justices to the Supreme Court and proceeded to take control of the lower courts.

Thus by sundown on January 9, Nicholls had been sworn in as governor, had achieved control of New Orleans police, and was master of

34 New Orleans *Daily Picayune*, January–March, 1877; McDaniel, "Nicholls and the End of Reconstruction," 405–407, 410–11, 419–20, 428–29; Sefton, *United States Army and Reconstruction*, 250; McGinty, *Louisiana Redeemed*, 99, 107–108.

the court system. Warmoth said later that Packard had lost his only chance of survival when he did not provoke an incident on January 9. This is probably true, but in view of President Grant's attitude, an incident might not have saved Packard. Nicholls' coup was carried out most skillfully. The threat of violence was in the air, but there was no violence. No attack was made on the Republican governor or legislature in the State House, but Nicholls had added control of New Orleans to the control he already exerted over nearly all rural areas. Packard was in the State House, but Francis T. Nicholls was *de facto* governor of Louisiana. Only direct federal intervention could oust him, and that possibility grew more unlikely as each day passed.[35]

Finance played an important part in the struggle between Nicholls and Packard. Republican tax collectors in Louisiana simply could not collect taxes. In many areas it was dangerous for them even to attempt collections. Therefore, the Packard legislature, barricaded in the State House, was unable to collect per diem or travel pay. The New Orleans *Republican* suspended publication as funds dried up. In time money was to prove decisive in enabling the Nicholls legislature, which could pay, to persuade more and more members of the Packard legislature to desert the State House.[36]

The sources of funds for the Nicholls government are not altogether clear. Citizens were asked to pay 5 percent of their 1877 taxes in advance, and mass meetings in many parishes endorsed this idea. Some secondary sources assert that the taxpayers were so enthusiastic that many paid 25 or 50 percent of their taxes in advance. This may have been true in a few instances, possibly even in many instances, but it is highly doubtful that a large number of Louisiana agriculturists had enough ready money on hand in late winter and early spring to voluntarily pay taxes in advance. Possibly merchants and bankers in New Orleans could do more, and those who held state bonds may have been encouraged to pay up by the fact that the price of state bonds rose as

35 New Orleans *Daily Picayune*, January 10–11, April 8, 1877; Prichard (ed.), "White League in New Orleans," 540–41; Lathrop (ed.), "Autobiography of Nicholls," 254–56, 260; Sefton, *United States Army and Reconstruction*, 249; McGinty, *Louisiana Redeemed*, 94.
36 Thibodaux *Sentinel*, January 30, 1877, quoted in New Orleans *Daily Picayune*, February 5, 1877; New Orleans *Daily Picayune*, February 2, 1877; McDaniel, "Nicholls and the End of Reconstruction," 397–98, 412, 434.

Nicholls gained political strength. Shortly before Grant went out of office, Nicholls felt strong enough to appoint a few tax collectors.[37]

The Louisiana Lottery played a large part, perhaps the largest part, in financing the Nicholls government. To what extent this support was voluntary and to what extent it was blackmail is difficult to say. A bill to abolish the lottery was introduced into the Nicholls legislature, a joint committee of the legislature called upon Howard, the head of the lottery, to ask his help, the bill to abolish the lottery was withdrawn, and Howard gave, according to one account, over $34,000 at this time. Later, seemingly, he gave more. The total contribution of the Louisiana Lottery may have amounted to $250,000, but one half of that would probably be more nearly correct. Obviously the lottery company was going over to the winning side, and its money contributed significantly to Nicholls' survival and eventual victory. Nicholls must have been aware of this support, but he insisted that he made no promises. Certainly he was an enemy of the lottery during both his terms as governor.[38]

The final rejection of Pinchback by the United States Senate in December, 1876, meant that Louisiana had two vacancies to fill in that body. The Packard legislature had no difficulty in choosing Kellogg for the full term, but there was a spirited contest between Pinchback, who sought vindication, and C. C. Antoine for the short term. Pinchback later made an unsuccessful claim to this seat. The Nicholls legislature avoided the senatorial question in January and February, but the calling of a special session to begin as soon as the regular session ended brought the election of United States senators to the fore. The contest was a spirited one, and for weeks no candidate was able to achieve a majority. Eventually, on April 24, Judge H. M. Spofford was elected to the full term. By this time Warmoth now a state representative, had come over to the Nicholls legislature, and his vote was cast for Spofford. Afterward, J. B. Eustis was elected to the short term. Kellogg, the Republican, was seated by the United States Senate

37 New Orleans *Daily Picayune*, January–February, 1877; McGinty, *Louisiana Redeemed*, 105; Lonn, *Reconstruction in Louisiana*, 493–94.

38 McDaniel, "Nicholls and the End of Reconstruction," 397, 410, 412; McGinty, *Louisiana Redeemed*, 185–86; Woodward, *Origins of the New South*, 11–12; Wiggins, "The Louisiana Press and the Lottery," 754; Kendall, *History of New Orleans*, I, 404.

and served a full six-year term. In time, however, Eustis, the Democrat, elected by a different legislature, was also seated. Obviously, expediency did not demand consistency.[39]

As will be noted, Rutherford B. Hayes became president of the United States after having agreed to permit the Democratic claimants to office in Louisiana, Florida, and South Carolina to take over the government of those states. This had to be done with a degree of finesse, however, because Hayes was president by virtue of the Republican electoral votes of those same states. His solution to the Louisiana problem was a "presidential commission." This commission had a Republican majority, but obviously it was instructed carefully as to what course to follow. It arrived in New Orleans on April 5, and conferred with Packard on April 6. Packard asked that the new president officially recognize his administration, put him in possession of the courts, and give him control of the state arsenals. If only this were done, he maintained, he could keep himself in power without further aid from the federal government. No doubt the commissioners listened to Packard politely, but they had not come to Louisiana to prop up his regime. Their task was to bring it down as quietly as possible; they set about doing just that, joining their efforts with Nicholls partisans to persuade members of the Packard legislature to go over to Nicholls. By mid-April only a handful of legislators recognized by both parties remained at the State House.[40]

4

Most Louisianians who thought about it probably believed that their political fate was being decided by events in Louisiana between November, 1876, and March, 1877. In reality, the way for every step taken in New Orleans was prepared by negotiations and tacit understandings between politicians at the national capital.

Whatever the Republican party may have been in 1856 or 1866, by 1876 it was a conservative party. Stevens and Sumner were dead, and the ideals of racial justice which had moved them were not easily

39 New Orleans *Daily Picayune*, November 19, 1876, April 8, 22, 25, 1877; Gonzales, "William Pitt Kellogg," 490–91; McDaniel, "Nicholls and the End of Reconstruction," 413; McGinty, *Louisiana Redeemed,* 112.
40 New Orleans *Daily Picayune*, April 6, 1877; Lonn, *Reconstruction in Louisiana,* 521–23; McDaniel, "Nicholls and the End of Reconstruction," 430–33.

found among the practical Republicans who now sat in the seats of power. Hayes, when he thought that he was defeated, said that he did not mind defeat, and that the country and the Republican party could stand it, "but I do care for the poor colored men of the South. . . . The result will be that the Southern people will practically treat the constitutional amendments as nullities, and then the colored man's fate will be worse than when he was in slavery."[41] Once he was president, Hayes did nothing to protect "the poor colored men of the South." Rather he devoted his efforts to attempting to bring white southerners into the Republican party.[42]

There were areas in which southern Conservatives and northern Republicans could reach agreement. In the first place, Republicans wanted the presidency. Mainly this was the normal thirst for office, but also there were issues, the tariff, banking, and others, which would be less susceptible to disadvantageous change if a Republican held the presidency. In addition, the Republicans were embarrassed by the disrepute of Carpetbag governments in national public opinion. The southern Democrats, it must be added, were in a beautiful bargaining position. If Tilden became president, it was certain that federal troops would be removed from the South and that Democratic regimes could take over in Florida, South Carolina, and Louisiana. But, by betraying Tilden, the South might get not only the restoration of white control of state and local government, but much more.

The South had had little part in the railroad boom of the 1860s and early 1870s, and the little largesse that had come South had gone largely into Republican pockets. The Bourbons who led the Conservatives wanted their share of the loaves and fishes which earlier had gone to northern economic and political leaders. This idea came to center upon the Texas-Pacific Railroad, and one of the conditions for southern support of Hayes—or, more accurately, southern nonsupport of Tilden—was an understanding that Hayes would lend his influence to obtaining federal subsidies for this project. Louisianians who had no hope of benefiting from a Texas-Pacific Railroad bill were none-

---

41 Quoted in C. Vann Woodward, *Reunion and Reaction: The Compromise of 1877 and the End of Reconstruction* (Rev. ed.; Garden City, N.Y., 1956), 25.
42 *Ibid.*, 36; Alexander, "Persistent Whiggery in the Confederate South," 305–29; Vincent P. DeSantis, "President Hayes' Southern Policy," *Journal of Southern History*, XXI (November, 1955), 476–79.

theless in favor of a program of federal internal improvements for their state. One particularly attractive idea was federal aid in restoring and maintaining the levee system. The years since the end of the war had demonstrated that this was more than riparian landowners or state governments could manage.[43]

As soon as the inconclusive results of the presidential election of 1876 were known, Republican leaders in Washington and Conservative leaders in the South sensed that the basis for a mutually advantageous compromise existed. The masses of southern white voters and the hardcore "Stalwarts" of the Republican party were opposed to compromise, but leaders were more pragmatic. The Hayes Republicans began discreetly sounding out former Whigs in the South, among them Colonel W. H. Roberts, editor of the New Orleans *Times* and former Confederate general Richard Taylor. Hayes's friends missed few opportunities to make friendly gestures toward the "Redeemers," and Hayes let it be known publicly that he favored internal improvements for the South. In the Democratic-controlled National House of Representatives an undeveloped plan to impeach Grant was quietly abandoned. Only four days before he left office, the president once more informed Louisiana Republicans that he did not believe that public opinion would "support the maintenance of state government in Louisiana by the use of the military," and that he agreed with public opinion.[44] C. Vann Woodward has given a superb account of the delicate feelers put forth, the indirect replies, the setbacks sustained, and the gradual progress toward agreement between leaders of the two sections in his *Reunion and Reaction,* which demonstrates the real complexity of a compromise hitherto greatly oversimplified.[45]

The agreement gradually worked out between Hayes Republicans and southern Democratic leaders during the months from the election of 1876 to Hayes's inauguration was basically simple. Southern members of Congress would not cooperate with northern Democrats to

43 New Orleans *Daily Picayune,* November 27, 1876, January 5, February 19, 22, March 8, 1877; Woodward, *Reunion and Reaction,* 11–13, 48, 55–57, 133–34, 142, 154, 156–57; DuBois, *Black Reconstruction,* 631; Tucker, "E. John Ellis," 688.
44 C. C. Sniffen and W. T. Sherman to S. B. Packard, March 1, 1887, in New Orleans *Daily Picayune,* March 3, 1877.
45 Woodward, *Reunion and Reaction,* 23–48, 158–59, 201–202, 204; Franklin, *Reconstruction After the Civil War,* 214–15; DeSantis, "Hayes' Southern Policy," 476–94.

prevent the official count of electoral votes and Hayes's inauguration. Secondly, southern Democrats would support Republican James A. Garfield for speaker of the House of Representatives, and Hayes would permit the Redeemers to take over the governments of Florida, South Carolina, and Louisiana. This concession by Hayes should not be given too much importance. Before the new president's inauguration, the Democrats in the House had succeeded in blocking the Army Appropriations Bill, which would have forced removal of the military anyway. Of much more consequence was Hayes's agreement to support the Texas-Pacific Railroad Bill and other internal improvements which would benefit the South. A conference held on February 26, 1877, in the hotel rooms of William M. Evarts, counsel for Andrew Johnson at his impeachment trial and soon to be Hayes's secretary of state, apparently completed or at least ratified the agreements already negotiated. E. A. Burke and E. John Ellis were Nicholls' chief representatives in Washington, and they did their work well.[46]

This compromise was not to last long, but it lasted long enough for Louisiana Conservative leaders. Nicholls was firmly established as governor of Louisiana, and Hayes was firmly ensconced as president of the United States. Probably the southern Conservatives could not have prevented the inauguration of Hayes, and probably Hayes would have had to abandon Packard without the agreement. Be this as it may, the compromise lasted only long enough to put the two men in office. Hayes was inaugurated on March 5, 1877, but when Congress was organized, Samuel Randall, the Democratic candidate for speaker, prevailed, even though a change of only nine votes would have elected Garfield. By the end of 1877 it had become clear to Hayes that he was not going to convert former southern Whigs to Republicanism, perhaps because they were succeeding so well in taking over the Democratic party in the South. Just before Christmas, Hayes denounced the Texas-Pacific Bill. The first steps in the compromise had been carried out, but the second stage was repudiated by both sides.[47]

46 New Orleans *Daily Picayune*, December 21, 1876, February 27, March 6, 1877; Blaine, *Twenty Years of Congress*, 595–96; Tucker, "E. John Ellis," 714; Woodward, *Reunion and Reaction*, 7–9, 208, 217–18, 220, 224, 251–52, 254–55; McDaniel, "Nicholls and the End of Reconstruction," 423–24; Dunning, *Reconstruction, Political and Economic*, 338–41.
47 Woodward, *Reunion and Reaction*, 190–91, 251–52; Blaine, *Twenty Years of*

5

As a result of the compromise, the demise of the Packard government in Louisiana was a foregone conclusion, but this was not so obvious in 1877 as it is today. Packard and his legislature, barricaded in the State House, protected directly by the Metropolitan Police and indirectly by federal troops under orders to prevent violence, held on in the hope of a change of heart in Washington or of some mistake on Nicholls' part. By the end of the second week in January, the Packard legislature had no quorum, largely because Pinchback, angry that he had not been elected again to the United States Senate, went over to the Nicholls legislature and took a number of his friends with him. Pinchback secured from Nicholls another public pledge to protect the equality of all men and to protect black people in the exercise of the rights granted them by the Reconstruction amendments. There were a few additional defections of Packard legislators during the winter, and in the country more and more unchallenged Republican office-holders were applying to Nicholls for their commissions. As the weeks passed, Nicholls grew stronger, Packard weaker.[48]

As indicated earlier, Nicholls' great worry was that some outbreak of violence on the part of his followers would force federal intervention. He must have been frightened on February 15, when a would-be assassin shot at and slightly wounded Packard. Packard knocked the man down, and a guard disarmed him. Some Democratic papers argued that the murder attempt was a sham, designed to arouse northern public opinion, but there is no real reason to believe this; on the other hand, the attack certainly was not approved by Democratic leaders. A martyred Packard would have been much more of a danger to Democratic hopes than the living Republican Carpetbagger.[49]

Hayes's inaugural address was no comfort to the men in the Louisiana State House. "The evils which afflict the Southern states can

Congress, 643–44; Alexander, "Persistent Whiggery in the Confederate South," 326–27; E. J. Ellis to T. C. W. Ellis, November 29, 1877, in Tucker, "E. John Ellis," 739; Patrick, *Reconstruction of the Nation,* 276.

48 New Orleans *Daily Picayune,* January–March, 1877; Grosz, "Pinchback," 604–605; McDaniel, "Nicholls and the End of Reconstruction," 395, 407–409; Lonn, *Reconstruction in Louisiana,* 477, 483, 489.

49 New Orleans *Daily Picayune,* February 16, March 3, 1877; McGinty, *Louisiana Redeemed,* 109.

only be removed . . . by the united and harmonious efforts of both races," he said, and "I am sincerely anxious to use every legitimate influence in favor of honest and efficient local self-government . . . for the promotion of the contentment and prosperity of their citizens."[50] At almost the same time the Nicholls House of Representatives put on pressure by adopting a resolution stating that members who did not take their seats by noon of March 8 should be expelled. Nicholls himself encouraged defections by giving patronage to those Republican senators and representatives who did join him, despite the objection of many Democrats. This brought a few more defections before Hayes's commission arrived, but some who had come over earlier, notably Senator Henry Demas, drifted back to the State House.[51]

It was the presidential commission which brought a final end to Packard's shadow government. Undoubtedly, some Republican legislators who had remained loyal to Packard through the winter were bought in the spring. The funds came in part from the lottery, in part from New Orleans businessmen, in part from other sources. Nicholls accepted the commission's proposal to seat Republicans from Plaquemines, Lafourche, St. Martin, Carroll, and Concordia parishes whose election was contested. By April 20, the Nicholls legislature had an undisputed quorum, even according to Returning Board count. The Democrat-dominated legislature, no doubt encouraged by the Hayes commission, voted to pay per diem and travel expenses to those members of the Packard legislature who had no seats under the new dispensation. Apparently the remnants of the Radical legislature met for the last time on April 21. Five days later all vestiges of the Packard government had vanished.[52]

Only when the problems of dual government had been solved did Hayes order federal troops to their barracks away from the vicinity of the State House. The date of their departure from Louisiana is uncertain, but April 24 marks the end of military intervention in Louisiana affairs. Two days later Governor Nicholls took possession of the

---

50 J. D. Richardson (ed.), *Messages and Papers of the Presidents*, VII, 443–44.
51 New Orleans *Daily Picayune*, March 5–April 3, 1877; McGinty, *Louisiana Redeemed*, 101.
52 New Orleans *Daily Picayune*, April, 1877; Shaffer Papers, VIII, April 19, 1877; Woodward, *Reunion and Reaction*, 239–40; Lonn, *Reconstruction in Louisiana*, 524–25.

State House. Symbolically, at least, Reconstruction had come to an end in Louisiana.[53] In faraway South Carolina Wade Hampton, whose situation closely resembled that of Nicholls, heard from a constituent: "Poor Louisiana, twin sister of S. C. in their late sufferings, have [*sic*] been graciously delivered from misrule . . . [events have] placed your hon self and Francis T. Nicholls . . . to govern the people."[54]

The end of Radical rule had come too gradually to be followed by a saturnalia or even dancing in the streets, but white Louisianians did rejoice. A joke first told in January, and perhaps based on fact, was enjoyed. William Chandler, chairman of the Republican National Committee, was said to have urged Packard to create a violent incident even if he had to die in the street. Packard supposedly wired back: "Your very polite invitation . . . 'to die in the street' is received. Owing to other pressing engagements I am constrained to decline, but would suggest the propriety of your coming to officiate in person."[55] In fact, no major white Republicans died in the streets or suffered violence of any kind after the fall of Packard. Members of the Returning Board were indicted, and Anderson was convicted, but he was pardoned and the others were never brought to trial. Packard, Pinchback, Wells, and others received federal jobs. Even armless Senator Twitchell became a consul in Canada. Warmoth remained in Louisiana and prospered financially and to some extent politically. Those who suffered were blacks from whom, despite Nicholls' promises, some of the inadequate protection they had enjoyed was removed.

53 New Orleans *Daily Picayune*, April 20–30, 1877.
54 W. G. Coleman to Wade Hampton, May 26, 1877, in Hampton Papers, South Carolina State Archives.
55 New Orleans *Daily Picayune*, January 16, 1877.

Epilogue

RECONSTRUCTION was at last over. Louisiana's white Unionists had become members of a Democratic party dominated by former Confederates. The political Carpetbaggers, with few exceptions, returned North to live out their years. The economic Carpetbaggers who had been successful remained; they tended to vote Republican in national elections, but they certainly were not Radicals. With a few exceptions, such as Pinchback and Henry Demas, black leaders disappeared from public view.

Black people still had the right to vote, but when they attempted to exercise it effectively, they were repressed as sternly as in 1868 or 1876. Indeed, there was almost as much intimidation in 1878 as two years earlier. Many blacks, in fact, did not vote; rather they were voted by dominant Democratic politicians until finally, in the Louisiana constitution of 1898, they were efficiently disfranchised. Politically, socially, and economically the status of the vast majority of Louisiana blacks declined for a half-century after 1877. There was to be little or no improvement in their condition for three quarters of a century.

What was true of blacks was true also of poor whites. The yeoman farmers and the increasing number of white tenant farmers were the most racist of Louisianians, but they suffered loss of status just as did the black farmers. The white agriculturists would rise in revolt in the 1890s, but the revolt would be suppressed. They would blame the black man for this defeat and support the disfranchising constitution of 1898, but tens of thousands of poor white farmers would likewise be disfranchised.

Politically, just as before the Civil War, Louisiana would be dominated by an alliance between great planters and New Orleans financial interests. These post-Reconstruction governments did not end corruption—far from it—but they did practice the economy they preached. They were so economical that public education and other state services to the people almost disappeared.

Slavery, of course, had been ended by presidential edict and then by constitutional amendment, but for the vast majority of rural blacks the serfdom or peonage of the sharecropping system must have been almost as galling as slavery. Black sharecroppers attempted to escape by migrating to the inhospitable plains of Kansas, but Kansas was no El Dorado. Sharecropping, as noted earlier, was probably the best solution available to the freedman just after the war, but it offered him almost no real chance for self-improvement, and it continued, with all its attendant evils, for almost a century.

The final question, then, is what, if anything, Reconstruction accomplished in Louisiana. The state did get a better constitution, but subsequent changes made the state's basic law a joke. Louisiana in 1900 was more like Louisiana in 1860 than it was like whatever dream Radical idealists had had. Like so many revolutions, Reconstruction in Louisiana brought only ephemeral changes, and when it was all over, things were much as they had been before. On the positive side there were the Reconstruction amendments, which would give to another generation an opportunity to accomplish what their ancestors had failed to achieve.

Bibliography

MANUSCRIPTS

Centenary College Library, Shreveport, La.

    Broadside, Centenary College, August 22, 1866

    Faculty Minutes, Centenary College of Louisiana, 1840–90. Typescript

    Henry Gerard Hall Diary, 1870–73. North Louisiana Historical Association Archives

    Louisiana Conference of the Methodist Episcopal Church, South. Conference Journals, 1865–70. Microfilm of manuscripts in Dillard University Library, Drew University Library, and Garrett Seminary Library, provided by Centenary College Library.

    ———. Manuscript Minutes, 1875–79

    Louisiana [Methodist] Conference Minutes, 1865–75

    New Orleans District Conference Minutes, Methodist Episcopal Church, 1869–80

    Recommendations for Ordination, Louisiana Conference, Methodist Episcopal Church, 1868

    Trustees' Meetings Minutes, Centenary College, 1840–1906

Dupre Library, Archives Department, University of Southwestern Louisiana, Lafayette

Paul Deballion Papers

De Clouet Family Papers

Louisiana State University, Department of Archives

André Family Papers

Barrow Family Papers

Albert A. Batchelor Papers

C. Bordis and Company Papers

Bringier Family Papers

Margaret Butler Correspondence, Butler Family Papers

S. H. Capell Papers

Clinton and Port Hudson Railroad Company Account Books, 1867–70

Hephzibah Church Books, Vol. II (1858–98), Merritt M. Shilg Memorial Collection

William P. Kellogg Papers

J. R. G. Pitkin Letter

Unification Movement Papers

Joseph Vidal Papers

Henry Clay Warmoth Papers

Presbyterian Historical Foundation, Montreat, N.C.

Louisiana Presbytery Minutes, 1856–82. Microfilm provided by Austin Presbyterian Theological Seminary, Austin, Tex.

New Orleans Presbytery Minutes, 1854–78. Microfilm provided by Austin Presbyterian Theological Seminary, Austin, Tex.

Pastoral Letter of the Southern [Presbyterian General] Assembly of 1865. Microfilm

Red River Presbytery Minutes, 1863–81. Microfilm provided by Austin Presbyterian Theological Seminary, Austin, Tex.

Russell Library, Northwestern State University, Natchitoches, La.

Egan Family Collection

South Carolina State Archives, Columbia, S.C.

Hampton Papers

Southern Historical Collection, University of North Carolina

Avery Family Papers

Bayne-Gayle Papers

Bayside Plantation Records

Caffery Papers

James Amédée Gaudet Papers
Gibson-Humphrey Papers
Eliza Guthrie Papers
Martha Holland Papers
Thomas Butler King Papers
Andrew McCollam Papers
William Porcher Miles Papers
Shaffer Papers
Slack Family Papers
Sarah L. Wadley Diary
Henry Clay Warmoth Papers
University of South Carolina Library, Manuscript Department
Williams-Chesnut-Manning Papers
University of Texas Archives, Austin
Boggy Bayou Baptist Church (Caddo Parish, Louisiana), Minute Book, 1860–65. Notes supplied by the late Tom Henderson Wells.

OFFICIAL DOCUMENTS AND PUBLICATIONS

Acts of Louisiana, 1864–1877.
Acts Passed by the Twenty-Seventh Legislature of the State of Louisiana [Confederate] *in Extra Session at Opelousas in January, 1863.* Natchitoches, La., 1864.
Ascension Parish Tax Assessment Rolls, 1870, 1880. Microfilm in office of comptroller, state of Louisiana.
Claiborne Parish Tax Assessment Rolls, 1871, 1876. Microfilm in office of comptroller, state of Louisiana.
Debates in the Convention for the Revision and Amendment of the Constitution of the State of Louisiana (1864). New Orleans, 1864.
Debates in the House of Representatives of the State of Louisiana, Sessions of 1864–65. New Orleans, 1865.
Debates in the House of Representatives of the State of Louisiana, Session of 1869. New Orleans, 1869.
Debates in the Senate of the State of Louisiana, Session of 1864–[1865]. New Orleans, 1865.
East Feliciana Parish Tax Assessment Rolls, 1871, 1880. Microfilm in office of comptroller, state of Louisiana.
E. W. Hilgard. "Report on the Cotton Production of the State of Louisiana,

with a General Discussion of the General Agricultural Features of the State." *U.S. Census, 1880, Report on Cotton Production.* Washington, D.C., 1883.

Journal of the Convention for the Revision and Amendment of the Constitution of Louisiana. New Orleans, 1864.

Louisiana Legislative Documents, 1864–1877. Louisiana Room, Louisiana State University Library.

Moore, Thomas O. *Annual Message of Governor Thomas O. Moore to the Twenty-Eighth General Assembly of the State of Louisiana, January, 1864.* Shreveport, La., 1864.

Official Journal of the Proceedings of the Convention for Framing a Constitution for the State of Louisiana, 1867–1868. New Orleans, 1868.

Official Journal of the Proceedings of the House of Representatives of the State of Louisiana at the Session Begun and Held in New Orleans, January 3, 1870. New Orleans, 1870.

Population of the United States in 1860: Compiled from the Original Returns of the Eighth Census under the Direction of the Secretary of the Interior. Washington, D.C., 1864.

Rapides Parish Tax Assessment Rolls, 1871, 1880. Microfilm in the office of the comptroller, state of Louisiana.

St. Mary Parish Tax Assessment Rolls, 1877. Microfilm in the office of the comptroller, state of Louisiana.

The Statistics of the Population of the United States . . . Ninth Census. Vol. I. Washington, D.C., 1872.

"Statistics on Cotton and Related Data." United States Bureau of Agricultural Economics, *Statistical Bulletin* 99. Washington, D.C., 1951.

Tensas Parish Tax Assessment Rolls, 1870, 1880. Microfilm in office of the comptroller, state of Louisiana.

U.S. *House Executive Documents.* 41st Cong., 2nd Sess., No. 142; 42nd Cong., 2nd Sess., No. 209; 42nd Cong., 3rd Sess., No. 91.

U.S. *House Miscellaneous Documents.* 41st Cong., 2nd Sess., Nos. 152, 154; 42nd Cong., 2nd Sess., Nos. 104, 211; 44th Cong., 2nd Sess., No. 34, Vol. IV; 45th Cong., 2nd Sess., No. 52.

U.S. *House Reports.* 39th Cong., 1st Sess., No. 30; 39th Cong., 2nd Sess., No. 16; 42nd Cong., 2nd Sess., No. 92; 43rd Cong., 1st Sess., Nos. 597, 732; 44th Cong., 1st Sess., No. 442; 44th Cong., 2nd Sess., Nos. 44, Vol. IV, 100, 156.

U.S. *Senate Executive Documents.* 39th Cong., 1st Sess., No. 2; 39th Cong., 2nd Sess., No. 6; 40th Cong., 1st Sess., No. 14; 40th Cong., 2nd Sess.,

No. 53; 42nd Cong., 3rd Sess., No. 47; 43rd Cong., 2nd Sess., Nos. 13, 17; 44th Cong., 2nd Sess., No. 2.

U.S. *Senate Reports.* 42nd Cong., 2nd Sess., No. 41; 42nd Cong., 3rd Sess., No. 457; 44th Cong., 2nd Sess., No. 501, 3 vols.

Winn Parish Tax Assessment Rolls, 1873, 1880. Microfilm in office of the comptroller, state of Louisiana.

PRINTED TRAVEL ACCOUNTS, DIARIES, LETTERS, MEMOIRS,
REMINISCENCES, AND OTHER CONTEMPORARY SOURCES

Abbott, Martin, ed. "Reconstruction in Louisiana: Three Letters." *Louisiana History,* I (Spring, 1960), 153–57.

Adamoli, Giulio. "Letter from America, 1867." *Louisiana Historical Quarterly,* VI (April, 1923), 271–79.

Ashcraft, Allan C. "A Reconstruction Description of Southern Louisiana." *Louisiana History,* IV (Winter, 1963), 85–88.

Avary, Myrta Lockett. *Dixie After the War: An Exposition of Social Conditions Existing in the South During the Twelve Years Succeeding the Fall of Richmond.* New York, 1906.

Baird, Samuel J. *The Discussion on Reunion: A Review.* Richmond, Va., 1888.

Banks, Nathaniel Prentiss. *Emancipated Labor in Louisiana.* N.p., 1864[?].

————. *The Reconstruction of States: Letter of Major General Banks to Senator Lane.* New York, 1865.

Barnhart, John D., ed. "Reconstruction on the Lower Mississippi." *Mississippi Valley Historical Review,* XXI (December, 1934), 387–96.

Biddle, Ellen McGowan. *Reminiscences of a Soldier's Wife.* Philadelphia, 1907.

Bigelow, Martha M., ed. "Plantation Lessee Problems in 1864." *Journal of Southern History,* XXVII (August, 1961), 328–60.

Blaine, James G. *Twenty Years of Congress: From Lincoln to Garfield, with a Review of the Events That Led to the Political Revolution of 1860.* 2 Vols. Norwich, Conn., 1893.

Cable, George W. *The Negro Question: A Selection of Writings on Civil Rights in the South.* Edited by Arlin Turner. Garden City, N.Y., 1958.

————. *The Silent South: Together with the Freedman's Case in Equity and the Convict Lease System.* New York, 1907.

Campbell, George. *White and Black: The Outcome of a Visit to the United States.* London, 1879.

Clemenceau, Georges. *American Reconstruction, 1865–1870, and the Impeachment of President Johnson.* New York, 1928.

Deedes, Henry. *Sketches of the South and West or Ten Months' Residence in the United States.* Edinburgh, 1869.

DeForest, John William. *A Union Officer in the Reconstruction.* Edited with an introduction and notes by James H. Croushore and David Morris Potter. New Haven, 1948.

Dennett, Daniel. *Louisiana As It Is: Its Topography and Material Resources . . . Reliable Information for . . . Any Who May Desire to Settle or Purchase Lands in the Gulf States.* New Orleans, 1876.

The Distinctive Principles of the Presbyterian Church in the United States, Commonly Called the Southern Presbyterian Church, as Set Forth in Formal Declarations, and Illustrated by Extracts from Proceedings of the General Assembly, from 1861–70. To Which Is Added Extracts from the Proceedings of the O. S. General Assembly from 1861–67; and of the N.S. Assembly from 1861–66. 2nd ed. Richmond, n.d.

Dixon, William Hepworth. *White Conquest.* 2 vols. London, 1876.

Eaton, John. *Grant, Lincoln and the Freedmen: Reminiscences of the Civil War with Special Reference to the Work for the Contrabands and Freedmen of the Mississippi Valley.* New York, 1907.

Erickson, Edgar L., ed. "Hunting for Cotton in Dixie: From the Civil War Diary of Captain Charles E. Wilcox." *Journal of Southern History,* IV (November, 1938), 473–513.

Fleming, Walter L., ed. *Documentary History of Reconstruction, Political, Social, Religious, Educational and Industrial, 1865 to the Present Time.* 2 vols. Reprint. Gloucester, Mass., 1960.

———. "A Ku Klux Document." *Mississippi Valley Historical Review,* I (March, 1915), 575–78.

Gaillardit, Frédéric. *L'Aristocratie en Amerique.* Paris, 1883.

Gardner's New Orleans Directory for the Year 1859. New Orleans, 1858.

Gardner's New Orleans Directory for the Year 1860. New Orleans, 1859.

Gatell, Frank Otto, ed. "The Slaveholder and the Abolitionist: Binding Up a Family's Wounds." *Journal of Southern History,* XXVII (August, 1961), 368–91.

Goddard, Frederick B. *Where to Emigrate and Why: Homes and Fortunes in the Boundless West and the Sunny South: Their Climate, Scenery, Soil, Productions, Railroads, Mining Interests, and General Resources; the Cost of Farm Lands, How to Obtain Titles, the Homestead and Other Land Laws, the Rates of Wages, &c. &c. with a Complete History and Description of the Pacific Railroad.* Philadelphia, 1869.

Greeley, Horace. *Mr. Greeley's Letters from Texas and the Lower Missis-sippi: To Which Are Added His Address to the Farmers of Texas and His Speech on His Return to New York, June 19, 1871.* New York, 1871.

Harris, T. H. *The Memoirs of T. H. Harris, State Superintendent of Public Education in Louisiana, 1908–1940.* Baton Rouge, 1963.

Hillyard, M. B. *The New South.* Baltimore, 1887.

Ives, C. A. *As I Remember.* Baton Rouge, 1964.

King, Edward. *The Great South: A Record of Journeys in Louisiana, Texas, the Indian Territory, Missouri, Arkansas, Mississippi, Alabama, Georgia, Florida, South Carolina, North Carolina, Kentucky, Tennessee, Virginia, West Virginia, and Maryland.* Hartford, Conn., 1875. Facsimile reprint, edited and with an introduction by W. Magruder Drake and Robert R. Jones. Baton Rouge, 1972.

Latham, Henry. *Black and White: A Journal of a Three Months Tour in the United States.* London, 1867.

Lathrop, Barnes F., ed. "An Autobiography of Francis T. Nicholls, 1835–1881." *Louisiana Historical Quarterly*, XVII (April, 1934), 246–67.

Lockett, Samuel H. *Louisiana As It Is: A Geographical and Topographical Description of the State.* Baton Rouge, 1970.

Loring, Francis William, and C. F. Atkinson. *Cotton Culture and the South Considered with Reference to Immigration.* Boston, 1869.

McCants, Sister Dorothea Olga, ed. and trans. *They Came to Louisiana: Letters of a Catholic Mission, 1854–1882.* Baton Rouge, 1970.

McRae, David. *The Americans at Home.* New York, 1952.

Marquette, C. C., ed. "Letters of a Yankee Sugar Planter." *Journal of Southern History*, VI (November, 1940), 521–46.

Minutes of the Meetings of the Synod of Mississippi, 1861–1880. Published annually at the place of meeting.

Mordell, Albert, comp. *Selected Essays by Gideon Welles: Lincoln's Administration.* New York, 1960.

Nicolay, John G., and John Hay, eds. *Complete Works of Abraham Lincoln.* 11 vols. New York, 1894.

Nordhoff, Charles. *The Cotton States in the Spring and Summer of 1865.* New York, 1876.

Prichard, Walter, ed. "A Forgotten Engineer: G. W. R. Bayley and His 'History of the Railroads of Louisiana'." *Louisiana Historical Quarterly*, XXX (October, 1947), 1,065–1,325.

———. "The Origin and Activities of the 'White League' in New Orleans (Reminiscences of a Participant in the Movement)." *Louisiana Historical Quarterly*, XXIII (April, 1940), 525–43.

————. "A Tourist's Description of Louisiana in 1860." *Louisiana Historical Quarterly,* XXI (October, 1938), 65–79.

Reid, Whitelaw. *After the War: A Southern Tour.* Cincinnati, 1866.

Rev. Dr. Bullock's Address to His Congregation at the Franklin Street Presbyterian Church, Baltimore, Giving His Reasons for Dissolving His Connection with the Old School General Assembly of the Presbyterian Church, June 12, 1866. Baltimore, 1866.

Richardson, Frank L. "My Recollections of the Battle of the Fourteenth of September, 1874, in New Orleans, La." *Louisiana Historical Quarterly,* III (October, 1920), 498–501.

Richardson, James D., ed. *A Compilation of the Messages and Papers of the Presidents.* 10 vols. Washington, D.C., 1903.

Schurz, Carl. *The Reminiscences of Carl Schurz, Volume III, 1863–1869. With a Sketch of His Life and Public Services from 1869 to 1906 by Frederic Bancroft and William A. Dunning.* New York, 1909.

Sherman, John. *John Sherman's Recollections of Forty Years in the House, Senate and Cabinet.* New York, 1895.

Shrewmaker, Kenneth E., and Andrew K. Prinz, eds. "A Yankee in Louisiana: Selections from the Diary and Correspondence of Henry R. Gardner, 1862–1866." *Louisiana History,* V (Summer, 1964), 271–95.

Skinner, J. E. Hilary. *After the Storm: Or Jonathan and His Neighbors in 1865–6.* 2 vols. London, 1866.

Somers, Robert. *The Southern States Since the War, 1870–71.* Rev. ed. University, Ala., 1965.

Taylor, Richard. *Destruction and Reconstruction: Personal Experiences of the Late War.* Edited by Charles P. Roland. Waltham, Mass., 1968.

Thorpe, Francis Newton, ed. *The Federal and State Constitutions: Colonial Charters and Other Organic Laws of the States, Territories, and Colonies Now or Heretofore Forming the United States of America.* 3 vols. Washington, D.C., 1909.

Trowbridge, John T. *A Picture of the Desolated States and the Work of Restoration, 1865–1868.* Hartford, Conn., 1868.

Warmoth, Henry Clay. *Letter of H. C. Warmoth, Claimant of a Seat in the House of Representatives as Delegate from the Territory of Louisiana, Addressed to Senator Williams, Chairman of the Sub-Committee on Reconstruction for Louisiana.* Washington, D.C., 1866.

————. *War, Politics and Reconstruction: Stormy Days in Louisiana.* New York, 1963.

NEWSPAPERS

Baton Rouge *Weekly Advocate*

Breaux Bridge *Attakapas Sentinel*

Marksville *Villager*

New Orleans *Daily Picayune*

New Orleans *Republican*

New Orleans *Southwestern Presbyterian* (microfilm provided by Austin Presbyterian Theological Seminary, Austin, Tex.)

New Orleans *Tribune*

Opelousas *Sentinel*

Placquemine *Iberville South*

St. Martinville *Courier of the Teche*

St. Martinville *St. Martin Democrat*

CONTEMPORARY PERIODICALS

De Bow's Review, Devoted to the Restoration of the Southern States and the Development of the Wealth and Resources of the Country. Journal of Literature, Education, Agriculture, Commerce, Internal Improvements, Manufactures, Mining and Statistics. After the War Series, 1866–70

Harper's Weekly, XI (January 12, 1867)

The Nation: A Weekly Journal Devoted to Politics, Literature, Science and Art, 1865–77

SECONDARY SOURCES

Books

Allen, James S. *Reconstruction: The Battle for Democracy (1865–1876).* New York, 1937.

Baudier, Roger. *The Catholic Church in Louisiana.* New Orleans, 1939; reprinted by Louisiana Library Association, Public Library Section, 1972.

Baughman, James P. *Charles Morgan and the Development of Southern Transportation.* Nashville, 1968.

Beale, Howard K. *The Critical Year: A Study of Andrew Johnson and Reconstruction.* New York, 1930.

Bell, B. Charles. *Presbyterianism in North Louisiana to 1929.* Published by Red River Presbytery, 1930.

Bentley, George R. *A History of the Freedmen's Bureau.* Philadelphia, 1955.

Blassingame, John W. *Black New Orleans, 1860–1880.* Chicago, 1973.

Bond, Horace Mann. *The Education of the Negro in the American Social Order.* New York, 1934.

Bowers, Claude G. *The Tragic Era: The Revolution After Lincoln.* Cambridge, Mass., 1929.

Brock, W. R. *An American Crisis: Congress and Reconstruction, 1865–1867.* London, 1963.

Brodie, Fawn M. *Thaddeus Stevens: Scourge of the South.* New York, 1959.

Bruce, Philip A. *The Plantation Negro as a Freeman: Observations on His Character, Condition, and Prospects in Virginia.* New York, 1889.

Burger, Nash K., and John K. Bettersworth. *South of Appomattox.* New York, 1959.

Burgess, John W. *Reconstruction and the Constitution.* New York, 1902.

Caldwell, Stephen A. *A Banking History of Louisiana.* Baton Rouge, 1935.

Capers, Gerald M. *Occupied City: New Orleans Under the Federals, 1862–1865.* Lexington, Ky., 1965.

Carter, Hodding. *The Angry Scar: The Story of Reconstruction.* Garden City, N.Y., 1959.

Carter, Hodding, and Betty Werlein Carter. *So Great a Good: A History of the Episcopal Church in Louisiana and of Christ Church Cathedral, 1805–1955.* Sewanee, Tenn., 1955.

Caskey, Willie M. *Secession and Restoration of Louisiana.* Baton Rouge, 1938.

Cassidy, Vincent H., and Amos E. Simpson. *Henry Watkins Allen of Louisiana.* Baton Rouge, 1964.

Coleman, Charles H. *The Election of 1868: The Democratic Effort to Regain Control.* New York, 1933.

Conway, Alan. *The Reconstruction of Georgia.* Minneapolis, 1966.

Coulter, E. Merton. *The South During Reconstruction, 1865–1877.* Baton Rouge, 1947. Vol. VIII of Wendell Holmes Stephenson and E. Merton Coulter (eds.), *A History of the South.* Baton Rouge, 1947–.

Cox, Lawanda, and John H. Cox. *Politics, Principle and Prejudice, 1865–1866.* New York, 1963.

Cox, Samuel S. *Three Decades of Federal Legislation, 1855–1885.* Providence, R.I., 1888.

Craven, Avery. *Reconstruction: The Ending of the Civil War.* New York, 1969.

Cross, Robert Alan. *The History of Southern Methodism in New Orleans.* New Orleans, 1931.

Crowe, Charles, ed. *The Age of the Civil War and Reconstruction, 1830–1900.* Homewood, Ill., 1966.

Cupit, John T. *A Brief History of Vernon Parish, Louisiana.* Rosepine, La., 1963.

Current, Richard Nelson. *Old Thad Stevens: A Story of Ambition.* Madison, Wis., 1942.

———. *Three Carpetbag Governors.* Baton Rouge, 1967.

Curry, J. L. M. *A Brief Sketch of George Peabody and a History of the Peabody Education Fund through Thirty Years.* Cambridge, Mass., 1898.

———. *Education of the Negroes Since 1860.* Baltimore, 1894.

Davis, Edwin Adams. *The Story of Louisiana.* 4 vols. New Orleans, 1960.

Davis, Susan Lawrence. *Authentic History of the Ku Klux Klan, 1865–1877.* New York, 1924.

Davis, William Watson. *The Civil War and Reconstruction in Florida.* Facsimile reproduction of 1913 edition. Gainesville, Fla., 1964.

Degler, Carl N. *Out of Our Past: The Forces That Shaped Modern America.* New York, 1959.

Donald, David. *Charles Sumner and the Rights of Man.* New York, 1970.

———. *Lincoln Reconsidered.* New York, 1956.

———. *The Politics of Reconstruction, 1863–1867.* Baton Rouge, 1965.

Donald, Henderson Hamilton. *The Negro Freedman: Life Conditions of the American Negro in the Early Years After Emancipation.* New York, 1952.

Dorris, Jonathan Truman. *Pardon and Amnesty Under Lincoln and Johnson: The Restoration of the Confederates to Their Rights and Privileges, 1861–1898.* Chapel Hill, 1953.

DuBois, W. E. Burghardt. *Black Reconstruction in America.* New York, 1962.

———. *The Negro Church.* Atlanta, 1903.

Duffy, John, ed. *The Rudolph Matas History of Medicine in Louisiana.* 2 vols. Baton Rouge, 1962.

Dufour, Charles L. *The Night the War Was Lost.* Garden City, N.Y., 1960.

Dunning, William Archibald. *Essays on the Civil War and Reconstruction and Related Topics.* New York, 1904.

————. *Reconstruction, Political and Economic, 1865–1877.* New York, 1962.

Dyer, John P. *Tulane: The Biography of a University, 1834–1965.* New York, 1966.

Eyraud, Jean M., and Donald J. Millet. *A History of St. John the Baptist Parish.* Marrero, La., 1939.

Ficklen, John Rose. *History of Reconstruction in Louisiana (Through 1868).* Reprint. Gloucester, Mass., 1966.

Fleming, Walter L. *Civil War and Reconstruction in Alabama.* New York, 1949.

————. *The Freedmen's Savings Bank: A Chapter in the Economic History of the Negro Race.* Chapel Hill, 1927.

Folmsbee, Stanley J., Robert E. Corlew, and Enoch L. Mitchell. *Tennessee: A Short History.* Knoxville, Tenn., 1969.

Foster, William Z. *The Negro People in American History.* New York, 1970.

Franklin, John Hope. *From Slavery to Freedom: A History of Negro Americans.* 3rd ed. New York, 1969.

————. *Reconstruction After the Civil War.* Chicago, 1961.

Frazier, E. Franklin. *Black Bourgeoisie.* Glencoe, Ill., 1957.

————. *The Negro Family in the United States.* Chicago, 1939.

————. *The Negro in the United States.* New York, 1957.

Garner, James Wilford. *Reconstruction in Mississippi.* New York, 1901.

————, ed. *Studies in Southern History and Politics Inscribed to William A. Dunning . . . by His Former Pupils, the Authors.* Port Washington, N.Y., 1914.

Gibson, A. M. *A Political Crime: The History of the Great Fraud.* New York, 1885.

Gillard, John T. *The Catholic Church and the American Negro.* Baltimore, 1929.

Gillette, William. *The Right to Vote: Politics and the Passage of the Fifteenth Amendment.* Baltimore, 1965.

Grace, Albert L. *The Heart of the Sugar Bowl: The Story of Iberville.* Plaquemine, La., 1946.

Harper, Robert Henry. *Louisiana Methodism.* Washington, 1949.

Harrington, Fred Harvey. *Fighting Politician: Major General N. P. Banks.* Philadelphia, 1948.

Harris, D. W., and B. M. Hulse. *The History of Claiborne Parish, Louisiana.* New Orleans, 1886.

Harris, Thomas H. *The Story of Public Education in Louisiana.* New Orleans, 1924.

Haworth, Paul L. *The Hayes-Tilden Disputed Election of 1876.* Cleveland, 1906.

Henry, Robert S. *The Story of Reconstruction.* Reprint. Gloucester, Mass., 1963.

Hesseltine, William B. *Lincoln's Plan of Reconstruction.* Reprint. Gloucester, Mass., 1960.

———. *Ulysses S. Grant, Politician.* New York, 1935.

———. *The Tragic Conflict.* New York, 1962.

Holzman, Robert S. *Stormy Ben Butler.* New York, 1954.

Horn, Stanley F. *Invisible Empire: The Story of the Ku Klux Klan, 1866–1871.* Reprint. New York, 1968.

Howard, Perry H. *Political Tendencies in Louisiana.* Rev. ed. Baton Rouge, 1970.

Hyman, Harold M. *Era of the Oath.* New York, 1954.

———, ed. *New Frontiers of the American Reconstruction.* Urbana, Ill., 1966.

———. *The Radical Republicans and Reconstruction, 1861–1870.* Indianapolis, 1967.

Jackson, Joy. *New Orleans in the Gilded Age: Politics and Urban Progress, 1880–1896.* Baton Rouge, 1969.

Johnston, Ruby F. *The Development of Negro Religion.* New York, 1954.

Kendall, John S. *The Golden Age of the New Orleans Theater.* Baton Rouge, 1952.

———. *History of New Orleans.* 3 vols. Chicago, 1922.

Knoles, George H., ed. *Sources in American History.* New York, 1970.

Landry, Stuart Omer. *The Battle of Liberty Place: The Overthrow of Carpetbag Rule in New Orleans—September 14, 1874.* New Orleans, 1955.

Leopold, Richard W., and Arthur S. Link, eds. *Problems in American History.* 2nd ed. Englewood Cliffs, N.J., 1957.

Lewinson, Paul. *Race, Class, and Party: A History of Negro Suffrage and White Politics in the South.* New York, 1963.

Logan, Rayford W. *The Betrayal of the Negro from Rutherford B. Hayes to Woodrow Wilson.* New York, 1965.

Lonn, Ella. *Reconstruction in Louisiana After 1868.* New York, 1918.

Lynd, Staughton, ed. *Reconstruction.* New York, 1967.

McConnell, Roland C. *Negro Troops of Antebellum Louisiana: A History of the Batalion of Free Men of Color*. Baton Rouge, 1968.

McGinty, Garnie W. *Louisiana Redeemed: The Overthrow of Carpetbag Rule, 1876–1880*. New Orleans, 1941.

McKitrick, Eric L. *Andrew Johnson and Reconstruction*. Chicago, 1960.

Marchand, Sidney A. *The Flight of a Century (1800–1900) in Ascension Parish, Louisiana*. Donaldsonville, La., 1936.

———. *The Story of Ascension Parish*. Donaldsonville, La., 1931.

Menn, Joseph Karl. *The Large Slaveholders of Louisiana, 1860*. New Orleans, 1964.

Milton, George Fort. *The Age of Hate: Andrew Johnson and the Radicals*. New York, 1930.

Murray, Andrew E. *Presbyterians and the Negro—a History*. Philadelphia, 1966.

Nau, John Frederick. *The German People of New Orleans, 1850–1900*. Leyden, Netherlands, 1958.

Nevins, Allan. *The War for the Union: The Improvised War, 1861–1862*. New York, 1959.

Nugent, Walter T. K. *Money and American Society, 1865–1880*. New York, 1968.

———. *The Money Question During Reconstruction*. New York, 1967.

Parton, James. *General Butler in New Orleans*. New York, 1864.

Patrick, Rembert W. *The Reconstruction of the Nation*. New York, 1967.

Randall, J. G. *The Civil War and Reconstruction*. New York, 1937.

Randall, J. G., and David Donald. *The Civil War and Reconstruction*. 2nd ed. New York, 1967.

Reed, Merl E. *New Orleans and the Railroads*. Baton Rouge, 1966.

Richardson, Harry V. *Dark Glory: A Picture of the Church among Negroes in the Rural South*. New York, 1947.

Roland, Charles P. *Louisiana Sugar Planters During the American Civil War*. Leyden, Netherlands, 1957.

Roussève, Charles Barthelmy. *The Negro in Louisiana: Aspects of His History and His Literature*. New Orleans, 1937.

St. Amant, Penrose. *A History of the Presbyterian Church in Louisiana*. New Orleans, 1961.

———. *A Short History of Louisiana Baptists*. Nashville, 1948.

Sandburg, Carl. *Abraham Lincoln: The War Years*. 4 vols. New York, 1939.

Sefton, James E. *The United States Army and Reconstruction, 1865–1877.* Baton Rouge, 1967.

Shannon, Fred A. *The Farmer's Last Frontier: Agriculture, 1860–1897.* New York, 1945. Vol. V of *The Economic History of the United States.*

Sharkey, Robert P. *Money, Class and Party: An Economic History of Civil War and Reconstruction.* Baltimore, 1959.

Shugg, Roger W. *Origins of Class Struggle in Louisiana: A Social History of White Farmers and Laborers During Slavery and After, 1840–1875.* Baton Rouge, 1939.

Singletary, Otis A. *Negro Militia and Reconstruction.* Austin, Texas, 1957.

Sitterson, J. Carlyle. *Sugar Country: The Cane Sugar Industry in the South, 1753–1950.* Lexington, Ky., 1953.

Skipworth, Henry. *East Feliciana, Louisiana, Past and Present.* New Orleans, 1892.

Smith, Samuel Denny. *The Negro in Congress, 1870–1901.* Chapel Hill, N.C., 1940.

Spero, Sterling D., and Abram L. Harris. *The Black Worker: The Negro and the Labor Movement.* Port Washington, N.Y., 1966.

Stampp, Kenneth M. *The Era of Reconstruction, 1865–1877.* New York, 1967.

Stone, Kate. *Brokenburn: The Journal of Kate Stone, 1861–1868.* Ed. John Q. Anderson. Rev. ed. Baton Rouge, 1972.

Stryker, Lloyd P. *Andrew Johnson: A Study in Courage.* New York, 1929.

Swint, Henry Lee. *The Northern Teacher in the South, 1862–1870.* New York, 1967.

Taylor, Joe Gray. *Negro Slavery in Louisiana.* Baton Rouge, 1963.

Thompson, Ernest Trice. *Presbyterian Missions in the Southern United States.* Richmond, Va., 1934.

Trefousse, Hans L. *Ben Butler: The South Called Him Beast.* New York, 1957.

Trelease, Allen W. *White Terror: The Ku Klux Klan Conspiracy and Southern Reconstruction.* New York, 1971.

Unger, Irwin. *The Greenback Era: A Social and Political History of American Finance, 1865–1879.* Princeton, 1964.

Warren, Charles. *The Supreme Court in United States History.* Rev. ed. New York, 1926.

Wesley, Charles H. *Negro Labor in the United States, 1850–1925: A Study in American Economic History.* New York, 1926.

Wharton, Vernon Lane. *The Negro in Mississippi, 1865–1890.* New York, 1965.

White, Howard Ashley. *The Freedmen's Bureau in Louisiana.* Baton Rouge, 1970.

Williams, T. Harry. *Lincoln and the Radicals.* Madison, Wis., 1941.

———. *P. G. T. Beauregard: Napoleon in Gray.* Baton Rouge, 1955.

———. *Romance and Realism in Southern Politics.* Baton Rouge, 1966.

Williamson, Frederick W. *Origin and Growth of Agricultural Extension in Louisiana, 1860–1948.* Baton Rouge, 1951.

———. *Yesterday and Today in Louisiana Agriculture.* Baton Rouge, 1940.

Wilson, Theodore Brantner. *The Black Codes of the South.* University, Ala., 1965.

Winston, Robert W. *Andrew Johnson: Plebian and Patriot.* New York, 1928.

Winther, Oscar Osburn. *The Transportation Frontier: Trans-Mississippi West, 1865–1890.* New York, 1964.

Woodman, Harold D. *King Cotton and His Retainers: Financing and Marketing the Cotton Crop of the South, 1800–1925.* Lexington, Ky., 1968.

Woodson, Carter G. *The History of the Negro Church.* Washington, 1921.

Woodward, C. Vann. *Origins of the New South, 1877–1913.* Rev. ed. Baton Rouge, 1971. Vol. IX of Wendell Holmes Stephenson and E. Merton Coulter, eds., *A History of the South.* Baton Rouge, 1947–.

———. *Reunion and Reaction: The Compromise of 1877 and the End of Reconstruction.* Rev. ed. Garden City, N.Y., 1956.

Woolfolk, George Ruble. *The Cotton Regency: The Northern Merchants and Reconstruction, 1865–1880.* New York, 1958.

Wynes, Charles E., ed. *The Negro in the South Since 1865: Selected Essays in American Negro History.* University, Ala., 1965.

Articles

Abbott, Martin. "Free Land, Free Labor, and the Freedmen's Bureau." *Agricultural History,* XXX (October, 1956), 151–56.

Alexander, Thomas B. "Persistent Whiggery in Mississippi: The Hinds County *Gazette.*" *Journal of Mississippi History,* XXIII (April, 1961), 71–93.

———. "Persistent Whiggery in the Confederate South, 1860–1877." *Journal of Southern History,* XXVII (August, 1961), 305–29.

————. "Whiggery and Reconstruction in Tennessee." *Journal of Southern History*, XVI (August, 1950), 291–305.

Alwes, Berthold C. "The History of the Louisiana State Lottery Company." *Louisiana Historical Quarterly*, XXVII (October, 1944), 964–1,118.

Amundson, Richard J. "Oakley Plantation: A Post–Civil War Venture in Louisiana." *Louisiana History*, IX (Winter, 1968), 21–42.

Anderson, George L. "The South and Problems of Post–Civil War Finance." *Journal of Southern History*, IX (May, 1943), 181–95.

Bailey, Kenneth K. "Southern White Protestantism at the Turn of the Century." *American Historical Review*, LXVIII (April, 1963), 618–35.

Beale, Howard K. "On Rewriting Reconstruction History." *American Historical Review*, XLV (July, 1940), 807–27.

Berthoff, Rowland T. "Southern Attitudes toward Immigration, 1865–1914." *Journal of Southern History*, XVII (August, 1951), 328–60.

Bone, Fanny Z. Lovell, "Louisiana in the Disputed Election of 1876." *Louisiana Historical Quarterly*, XIV (July, 1931), 408–40, (October, 1931), 549–66; XV (January, 1932), 93–116, (April, 1932), 234–267.

Boyd, Willis Dolmond, "Negro Colonization in the Reconstruction Era, 1865–1870." *Georgia Historical Quarterly*, XL (December, 1957), 360–82.

Brooks, Walter H. "The Evolution of the Negro Baptist Church." *Journal of Negro History*, VII (January, 1922), 11–22.

Brown, Ira V. "Lyman Abbott and Freedmen's Aid, 1865–1869." *Journal of Southern History*, XV (February, 1949), 22–38.

Bull, Jacqueline P. "The General Merchant in the Economic History of the New South." *Journal of Southern History*, XVIII (February, 1952), 37–59.

Burns, Francis P. "White Supremacy in the South: The Battle for Constitutional Government in New Orleans, July 30, 1866." *Louisiana Historical Quarterly*, XVIII (July, 1935), 581–616.

Calhoun, Robert Dabney. "A History of Concordia Parish, Louisiana." *Louisiana Historical Quarterly*, XV (January, 1932), 44–67; (April, 1932), 214–33; (July, 1932), 428–52; (October, 1932), 618–45; XVI (January, 1933), 92–124; (April, 1933), 307–29; (July, 1933), 454–78; (October, 1933), 598–607; XVII (January, 1934), 96–111.

Capers, Gerald M., Jr. "Confederates and Yankees in Occupied New Orleans, 1862–1865." *Journal of Southern History*, XXX (November, 1964), 405–26.

Carleton, Mark T. "The Politics of the Convict Lease System in Louisiana, 1868–1901." *Louisiana History*, VIII (Winter, 1967), 5–25.

Carpenter, John A. "Atrocities in the Reconstruction Period." *Journal of Negro History*, XLVII (October, 1962), 234–47.

Castel, Albert. "Andrew Johnson: His Historiographical Rise and Fall." *Mid-America*, XLV (July, 1963), 175–84.

Chenault, William W., and Robert C. Reinders. "The Northern-Born Community of New Orleans in the 1850's." *Journal of American History*, LI (September, 1964), 232–47.

Clark, Ira G. "State Legislation and Railroads of the Gulf Southwest." *Southwestern Social Science Quarterly*, XLI (Supplement, 1960), 268–82.

Clark, John G. "Radicals and Moderates on the Joint Committee on Reconstruction." *Mid-America*, XLV (April, 1963), 79–98.

Clark, Robert T., Jr. "The New Orleans German Colony in the Civil War." *Louisiana Historical Quarterly*, XX (October, 1937), 990–1,015.

———. "Reconstruction and the New Orleans German Colony." *Louisiana Historical Quarterly*, XXIII (April, 1940), 501–24.

Clark, Thomas D. "The Furnishing and Supply System in Southern Agriculture Since 1865." *Journal of Southern History*, XII (March, 1946), 24–44.

Claude, Richard. "Constitutional Voting Rights and Early U. S. Supreme Court Doctrine." *Journal of Negro History*, LI (April, 1966), 114–24.

Clement, Rufus E. "The Historical Development of Higher Education for Negro Americans." *Journal of Negro Education*, XXXV (Fall, 1966), 299–305.

Coben, Stanley. "Northeastern Business and Radical Reconstruction: A Reexamination." *Mississippi Valley Historical Review*, XLVI (June, 1959), 67–90.

Copeland, Fayette. "The New Orleans Press and Reconstruction." *Louisiana Historical Quarterly*, XXX (January, 1947), 149–337.

Cox, John, and Lawanda Cox. "General O. O. Howard and the Misrepresented Bureau." *Journal of Southern History*, XIX (November, 1953), 427–56.

Cox, Lawanda. "The Promise of Land for the Freedmen." *Mississippi Valley Historical Review*, XLV (December, 1958), 413–40.

Cox, Lawanda, and John H. Cox. "Negro Suffrage and Republican Politics: The Problem of Motivation in Reconstruction Historiography." *Journal of Southern History*, XXXIII (August, 1967), 303–30.

Dabney, Thomas Ewing. "The Butler Regime in Louisiana." *Louisiana Historical Quarterly*, XXVII (April, 1944), 487–526.

Davis, Donald W. "Ratification of the Constitution of 1868—Record of Votes." *Louisiana History*, VI (Summer, 1965), 301–305.

Davis, Jackson Beauregard. "The Life of Richard Taylor." *Louisiana Historical Quarterly*, XXIV (January, 1941), 49–126.

DeSantis, Vincent P. "President Hayes' Southern Policy." *Journal of Southern History*, XXI (November, 1955), 476–94.

———. "The Republican Party and the Southern Negro, 1877–1897." *Journal of Negro History*, XLV (April, 1960), 71–87.

Dethloff, Henry C. "The Alliance and the Lottery: Farmers Try for the Sweepstakes." *Louisiana History*, VI (Spring, 1965), 141–59.

Dethloff, Henry C., and Robert R. Jones. "Race Relations in Louisiana, 1877–1898." *Louisiana History*, IX (Fall, 1968), 301–23.

Dew, Charles B. "The Long Lost Returns: The Candidates and Their Totals in Louisiana's Secession Election." *Louisiana History*, X (Fall, 1969), 353–69.

Donald, David H. "The Scalawag in Mississippi Reconstruction." *Journal of Southern History*, X (November, 1944), 447–60.

Dorris, J. T. "Pardoning the Leaders of the Confederacy." *Mississippi Valley Historical Review*, XV (June, 1928), 3–21.

Downey, Matthew T. "Horace Greeley and the Politicians: The Liberal Republican Convention in 1872." *Journal of Southern History*, XXXIII (March, 1967), 727–50.

Doyle, Elizabeth Joan. "Nurseries of Treason: Schools in Occupied New Orleans." *Journal of Southern History*, XXVI (May, 1960), 161–79.

Drake, Richard B. "Freedmen's Aid Societies and Sectional Compromise." *Journal of Southern History*, XXXIX (May, 1963), 175–86.

DuBois, W. E. Burghardt. "Reconstruction and Its Benefits." *American Historical Review*, XV (July, 1910), 781–99.

Dufour, Charles L. "The Age of Warmoth." *Louisiana History*, VI (Fall, 1965), 335–64.

Ellis, David Maldwyn. "The Forfeiture of Railroad Land Grants, 1867–1894." *Mississippi Valley Historical Review*, XXXIII (June, 1946), 27–60.

Engelsmen, John Cornelius. "The Freedmen's Bureau in Louisiana." *Louisiana Historical Quarterly*, XXXII (January, 1949), 145–224.

Estaville, Lawrence E. "A Strategic Railroad: The New Orleans, Jackson and Great Northern in the Civil War." *Louisiana History*, XIV (Spring, 1972), 117–37.

Evans, Harry Howard. "James Robb, Banker and Pioneer Railroad Builder of Antebellum Louisiana." *Louisiana Historical Quarterly*, XXIII (January, 1945), 170–258.

Everett, Donald E. "Demands of the New Orleans Free Colored Population for Political Equality, 1862–1865." *Louisiana Historical Quarterly*, XXVII (January, 1944), 43–64.

Ewing, Cortez A. M. "Five Early Louisiana Impeachments." *Louisiana Historical Quarterly*, XXXI (July, 1948), 567–97.

Fels, Rendigs. "American Business Cycles, 1865–1879." *American Economic Review*, XLI (June, 1951), 325–49.

Fishel, Leslie H. "The Negro in Northern Politics, 1870–1900." *Mississippi Valley Historical Review*, XLII (December, 1955), 466–89.

————. "Northern Prejudice and Negro Suffrage, 1865–1870." *Journal of Negro History*, XXXIX (January, 1954), 8–26.

Forbes, Gerald. "A History of Caddo Oil and Gas Field." *Louisiana Historical Quarterly*, XXIX (January, 1946), 59–72.

Franklin, John Hope. "Whither Reconstruction Historiography?" *Journal of Negro Education*, XVII (Fall, 1948), 446–61.

Gates, Paul W. "Federal Land Policy in the South, 1866–1888." *Journal of Southern History*, VI (August, 1940), 304–30.

Gonzales, John Edmond. "William Pitt Kellogg: Reconstruction Governor of Louisiana, 1873–1877." *Louisiana Historical Quarterly*, XXIX 1946), 394–495.

Goodrich, Carter. "Public Aid to Railroads in the Reconstruction South." *Political Science Quarterly*, LXXI (September, 1956), 407–42.

Griffin, Richard W. "Problems of Southern Cotton Planters After the Civil War." *Georgia Historical Quarterly*, XXXIX (June, 1955), 103–17.

Grosz, Agnes Smith. "The Political Career of Pinckney Benton Stewart Pinchback." *Louisiana Historical Quarterly*, XXVII (April, 1944), 527–612.

Hair, Velma Lee. "The History of Crowley, Louisiana." *Louisiana Historical Quarterly*, XXVII (October, 1944), 1,119–1,225.

Harlan, Louis R. "Desegregation in New Orleans Public Schools During Reconstruction." *American Historical Review*, LXVII (April, 1962), 663–75.

Harris, Francis Byers. "Henry Clay Warmoth, Reconstruction Governor of Louisiana." *Louisiana Historical Quarterly*, XXX (April, 1947), 523–653.

Hart, W. O. "The New Orleans *Times* and the New Orleans *Democrat*." *Louisiana Historical Quarterly*, VIII (October, 1925), 574–84.

Hartzell, J. C. "Methodism and the Negro in the United States." *Journal of Negro History*, VIII (July, 1923), 301–15.

Hays, Willard. "Andrew Johnson's Reputation." *The East Tennessee Historical Society's Publication*, No. 31 (1959), 1–31; No. 32 (1960), 18–50.

Hesseltine, William B. "Economic Factors in the Abandonment of Reconstruction." *Mississippi Valley Historical Review*, XXII (September, 1935), 191–210.

Hickman, Nollie W. "The Yellow Pine Industries in St. Tammany, Tangipahoa, and Washington Parishes, 1840–1915." *Louisiana Studies*, V (Summer, 1966), 75–88.

Highsmith, William E. "Some Aspects of Reconstruction in the Heart of Louisiana." *Journal of Southern History*, XIII (November, 1947), 460–91.

Hyman, Harold M. "Johnson, Stanton, and Grant: A Reconsideration of the Army's Role in the Events Leading to Impeachment." *American Historical Review*, LXVI (October, 1960), 85–100.

James, Joseph B. "Southern Reaction to the Proposal of the Fourteenth Amendment." *Journal of Southern History*, XXII (November, 1956), 477–97.

Jenks, Leland L. "Railroads as an Economic Force in American Development." *Journal of Economic History*, IV (May, 1944), 1–20.

Johnson, Guion Griffis. "Southern Paternalism toward Negroes After Emancipation." *Journal of Southern History*, XXIII (November, 1957), 483–509.

Johnson, Howard Palmer. "New Orleans Under General Butler." *Louisiana Historical Quarterly*, XXIV (April, 1941), 434–536.

Johnson, Manie White. "The Colfax Riot of April, 1873." *Louisiana Historical Quarterly*, XIII (July, 1930), 391–427.

Kelly, Alfred H. "The Congressional Controversy over School Segregation, 1867–1875." *American Historical Review*, LXIV (April, 1959), 537–63.

Kerr, Homer H. "Migration into Texas, 1860–1880." *Southwestern Historical Quarterly*, LXX (October, 1966), 184–216.

Kolchin, Peter. "The Business Press and Reconstruction, 1865–1868." *Journal of Southern History*, XXXIII (May, 1967), 183–96.

Lair, William E., and James E. Rinehart. "Post–Civil War South and the Great Depression: A Suggested Parallel." *Mid-America*, XLVI (July, 1966), 206–10.

Landry, Thomas R. "The Political Career of Robert Charles Wickliffe, Governor of Louisiana, 1856–1860." *Louisiana Historical Quarterly*, XXV (July, 1942), 670–727.

Bibliography

Leach, Marguerite T. "The Aftermath of Reconstruction in Louisiana." *Louisiana Historical Quarterly*, XXXII (July, 1949), 631–716.

Lerner, Eugene M. "Southern Output and Agricultural Income." *Agricultural History*, XXXIII (July, 1959), 116–25.

Lestage, H. Oscar. "The White League in Louisiana and Its Participation in Reconstruction Riots." *Louisiana Historical Quarterly*, XVIII (July, 1935), 615–95.

Lewis, Elsie M. "The Political Mind of the Negro, 1865–1900." *Journal of Southern History*, XXI (May, 1955), 189–99.

Linden, Glenn M. "Radical Political and Economic Policies: The Senate, 1873–1877." *Civil War History*, XIV (September, 1968), 240–49.

———. "Radicals and Economic Policies: The Senate, 1861–1873." *Journal of Southern History*, XXXII (May, 1966), 189–99.

Lofton, Williston H. "Northern Labor and the Negro During the Civil War." *Journal of Negro History*, XXXIV (July, 1949), 251–73.

Lowrey, Walter M. "The Engineers and the Mississippi." *Louisiana History*, V (Summer, 1964), 233–55.

———. "The Political Career of James Madison Wells." *Louisiana Historical Quarterly*, XXXI (October, 1948), 995–1,123.

McDaniel, Hilda Mulvey. "Francis Tillou Nicholls and the End of Reconstruction." *Louisiana Historical Quarterly*, XXXII (April, 1949), 357–513.

McPherson, James M. "Abolitionists and the Civil Rights Act of 1875." *Journal of American History*, LII (December, 1965), 493–510.

———. "Abolitionists, Woman Suffrage, and the Negro, 1865–1869." *Mid-America*, XLVII (January, 1965), 40–47.

McWhiney, H. Grady, and Francis B. Simkins. "The Ghostly Legend of the Ku Klux Klan." *Negro History Bulletin*, XIV (February, 1951), 109–12.

May, J. Thomas. "The Freedmen's Bureau at the Local Level: A Study of a Louisiana Agent." *Louisiana History*, IX (Winter, 1968), 5–19.

Merrill, Louis Taylor. "General Benjamin F. Butler and the Widow Mumford." *Louisiana Historical Quarterly*, XXIX (April, 1946), 341–54.

Millet, Donald J. "The Lumber Industry of 'Imperial' Calcasieu, 1865–1900." *Louisiana History*, VII (Winter, 1966), 51–59.

Mims, Sam. "Louisiana's Administration of Swamp Land Funds." *Louisiana Historical Quarterly*, XXVIII (January, 1945), 277–325.

Mobley, James William. "The Academy Movement in Louisiana." *Louisiana Historical Quarterly*, XXX (July, 1947), 738–978.

Morrow, Ralph E. "Northern Methodism in the South During Reconstruction." *Mississippi Valley Historical Review*, XLI (September, 1954), 197–218.

Norgress, Rachel Edna. "The History of the Cypress Lumber Industry in Louisiana." *Louisiana Historical Quarterly*, XXX (July, 1947), 979–1,059.

O'Connor, Stella. "The Charity Hospital at New Orleans: An Administrative and Financial History, 1736–1941." *Louisiana Historical Quarterly*, XXXI (January, 1948), 1–109.

Odom, E. Dale. "The Vicksburg, Shreveport and Texas: The Fortunes of a Scalawag Railroad." *Southwestern Social Science Quarterly*, XLIV (December, 1963), 277–85.

Olsen, Otto H. "Reconsidering the Scalawags." *Civil War History*, XII (December, 1966), 304–20.

Otten, James T. "The Wheeler Adjustment in Louisiana: National Republicans Begin to Reappraise Their Reconstruction Policy." *Louisiana History*, XII (Fall, 1972), 349–67.

Patton, James W. "Tennessee's Attitude toward the Impeachment and Trial of Andrew Johnson." *East Tennessee Historical Society Publications*, No. 9 (1937), 65–76.

Perkins, A. E. "James Henri Burch and Oscar James Dunn in Louisiana." *Journal of Negro History*, XXII (July, 1937), 321–34.

Phillips, Ulrich B. "The Central Theme of Southern History." *American Historical Review*, XXXIV (October, 1928), 30–43.

———. "Plantations with Slave Labor and Free." *Agricultural History*, XII (January, 1938), 77–95.

Pitre, Althea D. "The Collapse of the Warmoth Regime, 1870–72." *Louisiana History*, VI (Spring, 1965), 161–87.

Porter, Betty. "The History of Negro Education in Louisiana." *Louisiana Historical Quarterly*, XXV (July, 1942), 728–821.

Pressly, Thomas J. "Radical Attitudes, Scholarship, and Reconstruction: A Review Essay." *Journal of Southern History*, XXXII (February, 1966), 88–93.

Randall, James G. "Captured and Abandoned Property During the Civil War." *American Historical Review*, XIX (October, 1913), 65–79.

———. "John Sherman and Reconstruction." *Mississippi Valley Historical Review*, XIX (December, 1932), 382–93.

Rawley, James A. "The General Amnesty Act of 1872: A Note." *Mississippi Valley Historical Review*, XLVII (December, 1960), 480–84.

Reed, Germaine A. "Race Legislation in Louisiana, 1877–1898." *Louisiana History*, VII (Fall, 1965), 379–92.

Reynolds, Donald E. "The New Orleans Riot of 1866, Reconsidered." *Louisiana History*, V (Winter, 1964), 5–27.

Richter, William L. "James Longstreet: From Rebel to Scalawag." *Louisiana History*, XI (Summer, 1970), 215–30.

Riddleberger, Patrick W. "The Radicals' Abandonment of the Negro During Reconstruction." *Journal of Negro History*, XLV (April, 1960), 88–102.

Romero, Sidney James. "The Political Career of Murphy James Foster, Governor of Louisiana, 1892–1900." *Louisiana Historical Quarterly*, XXVIII (October, 1945), 1,129–1,243.

Russ, William A., Jr. "Disfranchisement in Louisiana (1862–1870)." *Louisiana Historical Quarterly*, XVIII (July, 1935), 555–80.

———. "The Negro and White Disfranchisement During Radical Reconstruction." *Journal of Negro History*, XIX (April, 1934), 171–92.

———. "Registration and Disfranchisement Under Radical Reconstruction." *Mississippi Valley Historical Review*, XXI (September, 1934), 163–79.

———. "Was There Danger of a Second Civil War During Reconstruction?" *Mississippi Valley Historical Review*, XXV (June, 1938), 39–58.

Saloutes, Theodore, "The Grange in the South, 1870–1877." *Journal of Southern History*, XIX (November, 1953), 473–87.

———. "Southern Agriculture and the Problems of Readjustment, 1865–1877." *Agricultural History*, XXX (April, 1956), 58–76.

Schell, Herbert S. "Hugh McCulloch and the Treasury Department, 1865–1869." *Mississippi Valley Historical Review*, XVII (December, 1930), 403–21.

Schuler, Kathryn Reinhart. "Women in Public Affairs in Louisiana During Reconstruction." *Louisiana Historical Quarterly*, XIX (July, 1936), 668–750.

Scroggs, Jack B. "Southern Reconstruction: A Radical View." *Journal of Southern History*, XXIV (November, 1958), 407–29.

Sears, Alfred B. "Slavery and Retribution." *Southwestern Social Science Quarterly*, XLI (June, 1960), 3–13.

Shugg, Roger Wallace. "Suffrage and Representation in Ante-Bellum Louisiana." *Louisiana Historical Quarterly*, XIX (April, 1936), 390–406.

———. "Survival of the Plantation System in Louisiana." *Journal of Southern History*, III (May, 1937), 311–25.

Sigler, Jay A. "The Rise and Fall of the Three-Fifths Clause." *Mid-America,* XLVI (October, 1966), 271–77.

Simkins, Francis B. "New Viewpoints of Southern Reconstruction." *Journal of Southern History,* V (February, 1939), 48–61.

Sitterson, J. Carlyle. "The McCollams: A Planter Family of the Old and New South." *Journal of Southern History,* VI (August, 1940), 347–67.

————. "The Transition from Slave to Free Economy on the William J. Minor Plantation." *Agricultural History,* XVII (October, 1943), 216–24.

"Some Letters of Charles Etienne Gayarre on Literature and Politics, 1854–1885." *Louisiana Historical Quarterly,* XXXIII (April, 1950), 223–54.

Southall, Eugene Portlette. "The Attitude of the Methodist Episcopal Church, South, toward the Negro from 1844 to 1870." *Journal of Negro History,* XVI (October, 1931), 359–70.

Sproat, John G. "Blueprint for Radical Reconstruction." *Journal of Southern History,* XXIII (February, 1957), 25–44.

Stephens, Edwin Lewis. "Education in Louisiana in the Closing Decades of the Nineteenth Century." *Louisiana Historical Quarterly,* XVI (January, 1933), 38–56.

Stover, John F. "Northern Financial Interests in Southern Railroads, 1865–1900." *Georgia Historical Quarterly,* XXXIX (September, 1955), 205–20.

Suarez, Raleigh A. "Bargains, Bills, and Bankruptcies: Business Activity in Rural Antebellum Louisiana." *Louisiana History,* VII (Summer, 1966), 189–206.

————. "Chronicle of a Failure: Public Education in Antebellum Louisiana." *Louisiana History,* XII (Spring, 1971), 109–22.

Sweet, William W. "Methodist Church Influence in Southern Politics." *Mississippi Valley Historical Review,* I (March, 1915), 546–60.

Swinney, Everette. "Enforcing the Fifteenth Amendment, 1870–1877." *Journal of Southern History,* XXVIII (May, 1962), 202–18.

Taylor, Alrutheus A. "Historians of the Reconstruction." *Journal of Negro History,* XXIII (January, 1938), 16–34.

————. "Negro Congressmen a Generation After." *Journal of Negro History,* VII (April, 1922), 127–71.

Taylor, Ethel. "Discontent in Confederate Louisiana." *Louisiana History,* II (Fall, 1961), 410–28.

Taylor, Joe Gray. "The Food of the New South (1875–1940)." *Georgia Review,* XX (Spring, 1966), 9–28.

————. "New Orleans and Reconstruction." *Louisiana History*, IX (Summer, 1968), 189–208.

————. "Slavery in Louisiana During the Civil War." *Louisiana History*, VIII (Winter, 1967), 27–34.

Taylor, Rosser. "Fertilizers and Farming in the Southeast, 1840–1950." *North Carolina Historical Review*, XXX (July, 1953), 305–28.

Tebeau, C. W. "Some Aspects of Planter-Freedman Relations, 1865–1880." *Journal of Negro History*, XXI (April, 1936), 130–50.

Touchstone, Blake. "Voodoo in New Orleans." *Louisiana History*, XIII (Fall, 1972), 371–86.

Trefousse, Hans. "Ben Wade and the Negro." *Ohio Historical Quarterly*, LXVIII (April, 1959), 161–76.

Tucker, Robert Cinnamunde. "The Life and Public Service of E. John Ellis." *Louisiana Historical Quarterly*, XXIX (July, 1946), 679–770.

Tunnell, T. B., Jr. "The Negro, the Republican Party, and the Election of 1876 in Louisiana." *Louisiana History*, VII (Spring, 1966), 101–16.

Ulmer, Grace. "Economic and Social Development of Calcasieu Parish, Louisiana, 1840–1912." *Louisiana Historical Quarterly*, XXXII (July, 1949), 521–630.

Uzee, Philip D. "The Beginnings of the Louisiana Republican Party." *Louisiana History*, XII (Summer, 1971), 197–211.

————. "The Republican Party in the Louisiana Election of 1896." *Louisiana History*, II (Summer, 1961), 332–44.

Vaughn, William P. "Partners in Segregation: Barnas Sears and the Peabody Fund." *Civil War History*, X (1964), 260–74.

Vincent, Charles. "Negro Leadership in Programs in the Louisiana Constitutional Convention of 1868." *Louisiana History*, X (Fall, 1969), 339–51.

Violette, E. M. "Donelson Caffery—a Louisiana Democrat Out of Line." *Louisiana Historical Quarterly*, XIV (October, 1931), 521–32.

Weisberger, Bernard. "The Dark and Bloody Ground of Reconstruction Historiography." *Journal of Southern History*, XXV (November, 1959), 427–47.

West, Earle H. "The Peabody Education Fund and Negro Education, 1867–1880." *History of Education Quarterly*, VI (Summer, 1966), 3–21.

Wiggins, Richard H. "The Louisiana Press and the Lottery." *Louisiana Historical Quarterly*, XXXI (July, 1948), 716–844.

Wiley, Bell I. "Vicissitudes of Early Reconstruction Farming in the Lower

Mississippi Valley." *Journal of Southern History*, III (November, 1937), 441–52.

Williams, T. Harry. "An Analysis of Some Reconstruction Attitudes." *Journal of Southern History*, XII (November, 1946), 469–86.

————. "The Louisiana Unification Movement of 1873." *Journal of Southern History*, XI (August, 1945), 349–69.

Wood, Forrest G. "On Revising Reconstruction History: Negro Suffrage, White Disfranchisement, and Common Sense." *Journal of Negro History*, LI (April, 1966), 98–113.

Woodward, C. Vann. "The Anti-Slavery Myth." *American Scholar*, XXXI (Spring, 1962), 312–28.

————. "Equality: America's Deferred Commitment." *American Scholar*, XXVII (Autumn, 1958), 459–72.

————. "The North and the South of It." *American Scholar*, XXXV (Autumn, 1966), 647–58.

————. "Seeds of Failure in Radical Race Policy." *Proceedings of the American Philosophical Society*, CX (February, 1966), 1–9.

Woody, Robert H. "The Labor and Emigration Problem of South Carolina During Reconstruction." *Mississippi Valley Historical Review*, XVIII (September, 1931), 195–212.

Zeichner, Oscar. "The Transition from Slave to Free Agricultural Labor in the Southern States." *Agricultural History*, XIII (January, 1939), 22–32.

Unpublished Theses and Dissertations

Aertker, Robert Joseph. "A Social History of Baton Rouge During the Civil War and Early Reconstruction." M.A. thesis, Louisiana State University, 1947.

Beasley, Leon Odom. "A History of Education in Louisiana During the Reconstruction Period, 1862–1877." Ph.D. dissertation, Louisiana State University, 1957.

Bergerie, Maurine. "Economic and Social History of Iberia Parish, 1868–1900." M.A. thesis, Louisiana State University, 1956.

Binning, Francis Wayne. "Henry Clay Warmoth and Louisiana Reconstruction." Ph.D. dissertation, University of North Carolina, 1969.

Brister, Elaine Holmes. "A History of Pineville, Louisiana." M.A. thesis, Louisiana State University, 1948.

Clay, Floyd M. "Economic Survival of the Plantation System within the Feliciana Parishes, 1865–1880." M.A. thesis, Louisiana State University, 1962.

Constantin, Roland Paul. "The Louisiana 'Black Code' Legislation of 1865." M.A. thesis, Louisiana State University, 1956.

Daspit, Alice Douglas. "The Governors' Messages of Louisiana, 1860–1900." M.A. thesis, Louisiana State University, 1932.

DeLatte, Carolyn Elizabeth. "Reconstruction in St. Landry through 1868." M.A. thesis, McNeese State University, 1972.

Drake, Richard Bryant. "The American Missionary Association and the Southern Negro, 1861–1868." Ph.D. dissertation, Emory University, 1957.

Ellis, Dorothy Lois. "The Transition from Slave Labor to Free Labor with Special Reference to Louisiana." M.A. thesis, Louisiana State University, 1932.

Estaville, Lawrence E., Jr. "Louisiana Railroads During the Civil War." M.A. thesis, McNeese State University, Lake Charles, La., 1970.

Gahn, Robert. "History of Evangeline Parish." M.A. thesis, Louisiana State University, 1941.

Highsmith, William E. "Louisiana During Reconstruction," Ph.D. dissertation, Louisiana State University, 1953.

————. "Social and Economic Conditions in Rapides Parish During Reconstruction." M.A. thesis, Louisiana State University, 1947.

Langridge, Leland A., Jr. "Asiatic Cholera in Louisiana 1832–1873." M.A. thesis, Louisiana State University, 1955.

Leavens, Finnian Patrick. *"L'Union* and the *New Orleans Tribune* and Louisiana Reconstruction." M.A. thesis, Louisiana State University, 1966.

Marsala, Vincent J. G. "The Louisiana Unification Movement of 1873." M.A. thesis, Louisiana State University, 1962.

May, Jude Thomas. "The Medical Care of Blacks in Louisiana During Occupation and Reconstruction, 1862–1868: Its Social and Political Background." Ph.D. dissertation, Tulane University, 1971.

Memelo, Germaine A. "The Development of State Laws Concerning the Negro in Louisiana (1864–1900)." M.A. thesis, Louisiana State University, 1956.

Mills, Wynona Gillmore. "James Govan Taliaferro (1798–1876): Louisiana Unionist and Scalawag." M.A. thesis, Louisiana State University, 1968.

Nicholls, Howard T. "Francis T. Nicholls, Bourbon Democrat." M.A. thesis, Louisiana State University, 1959.

Pope, Ida Waller. "The Coushatta Massacre." M.A. thesis, McNeese State University, 1968.

Ratliffe, Theodore John. "The Life and Service to Public Education of John McNeese." M.A. thesis, Louisiana State University, 1933.

Shoalmire, Jimmie G. "Carpetbagger Extraordinary: Marshall Harvey Twitchell, 1840–1905." Ph.D. dissertation, Mississippi State University, 1969.

Singletary, Otis Arnold. "The Reassertion of White Supremacy in Louisiana." M.A. thesis, Louisiana State University, 1949.

Uzee, Philip D. "Republican Politics in Louisiana, 1877–1900." Ph.D. dissertation, Louisiana State University, 1950.

Vincent, Charles. "Negro Leadership in Louisiana, 1862–1870." M.A. thesis, Louisiana State University, 1966.

Warren, Millard Whitfield, Jr. "A Study of Racial Views, Attitudes and Relations in Louisiana, 1877–1902." M.A. thesis, Louisiana State University, 1965.

White, Howard Ashley. "The Freedmen's Bureau in Louisiana." Ph.D. dissertation, Tulane University, 1956.

White, John A. "The Port of New Orleans since 1850." M.A. thesis, Tulane University, 1924.

Windham, Allie Bayne. "Methods and Mechanisms Used to Restore White Supremacy in Louisiana, 1872–1876." M.A. thesis, Louisiana State University, 1948.

Index

Abbott, R. R., 45
Abell, Edmund, 44, 46–48, 53, 105
Abney, T. W., 285, 287–89
Acadia Parish, 389
African Missionary Baptist Convention, 445
Agricultural and Mechanical College, 475–76
Agriculture, 346, 351, 382, 408
Alexandria, La., 166, 297, 338, 344, 398–99, 474
Algiers, La., 92, 190, 318, 387, 419
Allain, T. T., 240, 258, 278, 301, 478
Allen, Henry Watkins, 10, 64, 72
Allen, Levi, 268–71
American Baptist Home Missionary Society, 478
American Colonization Society, 434
American Missionary Association, 458, 477
Amite, La., 398, 477
Anderson, T. C., 181, 226, 241, 466, 476, 491–92, 505
Angell, John B., 291–93, 296
Anti-Semitism, 402
Antoine, C. C., 201, 221, 233, 235, 266, 277, 480, 482, 493, 498
Appropriations, 84–85, 150, 178, 262, 266
Arkansas, 168, 291, 306
Armistead, Samuel, 236

Arroyo, Oscar, 491
Ascension Parish, 186, 316, 366, 432, 466, 484
Assumption Parish, 78, 229, 309, 333, 345, 391, 482
Atrocities, 64, 93–94, 96, 122, 134
Attainder of treason, 335
Attakapas region, 275, 437
Augur, Christopher C., 495–96
Avery, D. C., 370
Avery Island, 86, 344, 356
Avoyelles Parish, 44, 159, 264, 286, 324, 468

Badger, A. S., 227, 274–75, 294, 387
Baird, Absalom, 106–107, 109–110, 336, 426, 457
Baker, La., 478
Banks, 7–8, 77, 347, 348, 350, 354, 358, 359, 362, 366, 401
Banks, Nathaniel P.: and Constitution of 1864, p. 52; and Louisiana state government, 24–31, 42–43; and Negroes, 11, 20, 32–33, 38, 47; and public education, 48; and Red River campaign, 31–32, 41, 43–44, 46; succeeds Butler, 18–19; mentioned, 58–59, 71, 76, 251, 322, 329, 455
Barrow, C. J., 64